UNDERSTANDING NON-WESTERN PHILOSOPHY

Introductory Readings

EDITED BY
Daniel Bonevac
Stephen Phillips
The University of Texas at Austin

Mayfield Publishing Company
Mountain View, California
London · Toronto

Library of Congress Cataloging-in-Publication Data
Understanding non-Western philosophy: introductory readings / edited by Daniel Bonevac, Stephen Phillips.
p. cm.
Includes index.
ISBN 1-55934-077-0
1. Philosophy, Oriental. I. Bonevac, Daniel A.
II. Phillips, Stephen H.
B121.U53 1993 IN PROCESS
181—dc20 92-39700
CIP

Manufactured in the United States of America
10 9 8 7 6 5 4 3 2 1

Mayfield Publishing Company
1240 Villa Street
Mountain View, California 94041

Sponsoring editor, James Bull; production editor, Sharon Montooth; copyeditor, Sally Peyrefitte; text designer, Donna Davis; cover designer, Steve Naegele. The text was set in 10/12 ITC Berkeley Oldstyle Book by TBH/Typecast and printed on 50# Finch Opaque by Banta Company.

Contents

Preface

This book is a collection of classics from non-Western philosophical traditions. The works represented here share many virtues with Western philosophical classics. They have been historically influential, helping to shape entire cultures. Understanding the contemporary world is impossible without some acquaintance with them. Beyond their cultural importance, however, these works are philosophically rich. They overflow with ideas and arguments that shed light on basic issues of philosophy.

Collecting philosophical works from other traditions raises questions about what the basic issues of philosophy are and, indeed, what philosophy itself is. But deciding what to include in a collection for introductory students does not require comprehensive answers to these questions. Non-Western traditions articulate conceptions of meaningful reflection, speculation, and critical inquiry that we have sought to respect. In each tradition (except perhaps Africa), there is an identifiable philosophical literature, a consensus about what the basic problems are, who the great philosophers are, and what works deserve to be considered classics.

Our project also raises the issue of the boundaries of the Western tradition. South and East Asia have continuous, written philosophical traditions that have come into contact with the West only recently. In other parts of the world, however, the boundaries are not so clear. We have classified works as Western or non-Western by appealing to their authors' conceptions of them as continuations of ongoing philosophical traditions. To whom does the author refer? What cultural and, especially, religious influences are explicitly addressed? This criterion has led us to count Latin American philosophy as Western, for Latin American philosophers refer primarily to European sources and see themselves as part of the European philosophical tradition. It has also led us to count Islamic, Jewish, and even some early Christian thought as non-Western. Although these traditions stem from Greek philosophy and interact frequently with Western European philosophy, they focus on a problem whose content is non-European: how to synthesize Greek philosophy and Islam, or Judaism, or an Asian or African understanding of Christianity, into a coherent view of the world. The writers represented here not only wrote mostly in West Asia and northern Africa, in cultures that are in many respects non-Western, but saw themselves as continuing traditions they define largely in terms of the religious texts that they cite frequently for support. We have been swayed by practical considerations as well. The works of Islamic, Jewish, and early Christian philosophers are important to world philosophy, but they have been largely unavailable to introductory students. We have tried to remedy this, including often-overlooked classics so long as they are arguably non-Western.

The distinction between Western and non-Western traditions breaks down in our selections from the twentieth century. Philosophers as diverse as Kwasi Wiredu, B. K. Matilal, and Keiji Nishitani refer to Western and non-Western sources alike, seeing the concerns of philosophy as universal rather than as bound by a particular culture. We hope that this book will make non-Western sources more readily available to philosophers and students of philosophy working in English.

Using This Book

This book can introduce students to non-Western philosophy or supplement Western readings in an introductory philosophy course. We have arranged the readings by region—Africa, West Asia and the Southern Mediterranean, South Asia, and East Asia. Within each region, we have grouped works that share a philosophical perspective. Within each perspective, we have arranged the works chronologically. Each section, except that on Africa, reflects a reasonably continuous philosophical tradition. Until this century, moreover, interactions between traditions were infrequent. The continuity and relative independence of the traditions makes a regional organization natural.

The readings lend themselves well to other approaches. Some instructors may want to organize the material topically. Others, using this book to supplement readings on Western philosophy, may want to organize the material around the historical progression of the Western philosophical tradition. The following suggests an alignment between various philosophical topics and the philosophical works represented here:

Ethics	Egyptian philosophy, Zera Yacob, Walda Heywat, Saadia, *Bhagavad Gītā,* Sermons of the Buddha, *Acaraṅga Sutra,* Kumārila, Confucius, Mencius, Hsün Tzu, Lao Tzu, Yang Chu, Mo Tzu, Wang Yang-Ming
Political Philosophy	Fanon, Wiredu, Confucius, Hsün Tzu, Lao Tzu
Human Nature	Philo, Upanishads, *Bhagavad Gītā, Yogasūtra, Sāṃkhya-kārikā,* Buddhaghoṣa, *Questions to King Milinda,* Śaṅkara, Vivekananda, Aurobindo, Mencius, Hsün Tzu
Mysticism	al-Kindi, *Bhagavad Gītā, Yogasūtra, Suraṅgama Sutra, Muṇḍaka Upanishad,* Rūpa Gosvāmī, Vivekananda, Aurobindo
Soul	Egyptian philosophy, Philo, Augustine, *Kaṭha Upanishad, Bṛhadāraṇyaka Upanishad,* Vivekananda

Ontology	Philo, Buddhaghoṣa, Vādi Devasūri, Nāgārjuna, *Vaiśeṣika Sutra, Nyāya-sūtra,* Śrīharṣa, Matilal, Hsün Tzu, Wang Fu-chih
The Existence and Nature of God	Philo, Origen, Augustine, Avicenna, al-Farabi, al-Ghazali, Averroës, *Kaṭha Upanishad, Bhagavad Gītā,* Udayana, Ṛg Veda, *Bṛhadāraṇyaka Upanishad,* Sermons of the Buddha, Cārvāka, Śaṅkara, Rūpa Gosvāmī, Vivekananda, Aurobindo
Creation	Philo, Saadia, al-Ghazali, Averroës, Maimonides, *Bhagavad Gītā, Sāṃkhya-kārikā,* Ṛg Veda, *Brhadāraṇyaka Upanishad, Chāndogya Upanishad*
Idealism	*Suraṅgama Sutra,* Dignāga, Dharmakīrti, Śrīharṣa, Hsüan-tsang, Wang Yang-Ming
Nature	*Bhagavad Gītā, Sāṃkhya-kārikā,* Aurobindo, Nishida, Nishitani
Materialism	Cārvāka, Aurobindo, Wang Ch'ung, Wang Fu-chih
Action	Dharmakīrti, Gaṅgeśa
The Bounds of Language	Vādi Devasūri, Nāgārjuna, Candrakīrti, Chuang Tzu, Lao Tzu, I-hsüan, Suzuki, Nishitani
Causality	*Sāṃkhya-kārikā,* Candrakīrti, *Vaiśeṣika Sūtra,* Gaṅgeśa, Aurobindo, Wang Ch'ung, Fa-tsang, Wang Fu-chih
Inference	Augustine, Avicenna, Cārvāka, *Nyāya-sūtra,* Gaṅgeśa
Self-awareness	Augustine, *Yogāsūtra, Vaiśeṣika Sūtra,* Śaṅkara, Mohanty, Suzuki, Nishitani
Empiricism	Matilal, Wang Ch'ung, Wang Fu-chih, Nishida, Nishitani
Reason and Intuition	Augustine, Avicenna, Chu Hsi, Wang Yang-Ming, Nishida
Skepticism	Philo, Augustine, Nāgārjuna, Candrakīrti, Cārvāka, Srīharṣa, Matilal, Chuang Tzu, Lao Tzu, Yang Chu
Appearance and Reality	Philo, *Sāṃkhya-kārikā, Questions to King Milinda,* Nāgārjuna, Candrakīrti, *Suraṅgama Sūtra,* Dignāga, Kumārila, Śaṅkara, Aurobindo, Fa-tsang
Justification	Augustine, Avicenna, *Sāṃkhya-kārikā,* Dharmakīrti, Kumārila, Cārvāka, *Nyāya-sūtra,* Gaṅgeśa, Matilal
Perception	Dignāga, Dharmakīrti, *Nyāya-sūtra*
Philosophy of Mind	*Yogāsūtra,* Dignāga, Dharmakīrti, *Nyāya-sūtra,* Gaṅgeśa, Aurobindo, Mohanty, Hsüan-tsang, Chu Hsi, Wang Yang-Ming

This list suggests Western works often included in introductory courses that relate in interesting ways to the works represented here:

Plato, *Euthyphro*	Zera Yacob, Walda Heywat, al-Kindi, Mencius
Plato, *Apology*	Confucius, Lao Tzu, I-Hsüan, Suzuki
Plato, *Republic*	Philo, Origen, Cārvāka, Hsün Tzu, Yang Chu
Aristotle, *Nicomachean Ethics*	Egyptian philosophy, Upanishads, Confucius, Mencius
Descartes, *Meditations*	Philo, Augustine, Avicenna, *Sāṃkhya-kārikā,* Dharmakīrti, Kumārila, Cārvāka, *Nyāya-sūtra,* Gaṅgeśa, Śaṅkara, Matilal, Mohanty, Suzuki, Nishitani; on arguments for God's existence: Avicenna, al-Farabi, al-Ghazali, Averroës, Udayana
Berkeley, *Principles* or *Three Dialogues*	*Suraṅgama Sūtra,* Dignāga, Dharmakīrti, Śrīharṣa, Aurobindo (on matter), Hsüan-tsang, Wang Yang-Ming
Hume, *Inquiry Concerning Human Understanding*	Philo, *Sāṃkhya-kārikā,* Candrakīrti, *Vaiśeṣika Sūtra,* Gaṅgeśa, Nāgārjuna, Cārvāka, Śrīharṣa, Dignāga, Dharmakīrti, *Nyāya-sūtra,* Matilal, Wang Ch'ung, Wang Fu-chih, Nishida, Nishitani
Kant, *Groundwork of the Metaphysics of Morals*	Walda Heywat, *Bhagavad Gītā,* Sermons of the Buddha, *Acaraṅga Sūtra,* Kumārila, Confucius, Mencius, Hsün Tzu, Mo Tzu, Chu Hsi
Kant, *Prolegomena to Any Future Metaphysics*	*Suraṅgama Sūtra,* Dignāga, Dharmakīrti, Srīharṣa, Hsüan-tsang, Wang Yang-Ming, Nishida
Marx	Fanon, Wiredu, Cārvāka (on materialism and religion)
Mill, *Utilitarianism*	Zera Yacob, Walda Heywat, Saadia, Sermons of the Buddha, Kumārila, Mencius, Mo Tzu
Nietzsche	Fanon, *Bhagavad Gītā,* Sermons of the Buddha, Aurobindo, Yang Chu, Wang Yang-Ming, Suzuki
Russell, *Problems of Philosophy*	Philo, Buddhaghoṣa, Vādi Devasūri, Nāgārjuna, *Vaiśeṣika Sutra, Nyāya-sūtra,* Srīharṣa, Matilal, Hsün Tzu, Wang Fu-chih, Nishida, Nishitani
Existentialism	Upanishads, Vādi Devasūri, Nāgārjuna, Candrakīrti, I-Hsüan, Chuang Tzu, Lao Tzu, Nishida, Suzuki, Nishitani

Acknowledgments

We are grateful to our students for giving us the idea for this collection and to everyone at Mayfield Publishing Company who helped it become a reality. We would especially like to thank Jim Bull, whose encouragement and support were invaluable. We owe thanks to Sally Peyrefitte, whose editing made our contributions to the book clearer; to Sharon Montooth, who shepherded the book through production; and to Pamela Trainer, for her help with permissions. We are also grateful to Purushottama Bilimoria, Deakin University; Safro Kwame, Lincoln University; and Sandra Wawrytko, San Diego State University for their insightful comments on a draft of this book. We would like to thank Adrienne Diehr, whose suggestions improved the Egyptian philosophy section, and Thomas K. Seung, who suggested works for the East Asian section and who examined the emendation of Legge's translation of Confucius, checking it against the original Chinese. Any errors that remain are entirely Bonevac's fault.

Finally, we are forever indebted to Hope Phillips and to Beverly, Molly, and Melanie Bonevac for their support, encouragement, understanding, and love.

TIMELINE: BEFORE THE COMMON ERA (B.C.E.)

2300 2100 1900 1700 1500 1300 1100 900 700 500 300 100

Africa

Ptahhotep (2150?)
Any (1400?)
Amenemope (1100?)
Book of the Dead (600?)

West Asia

South Asia

Ṛg Veda (c. 1000)
Upaniṣads (900–300)
Buddha (563–483)
Mahāvīra (6th century)
Bhagavad Gītā (200?)
Mīmāṃsā (1st century)

East Asia

Lao Tzu (6th century?)
Confucius (551–479)
Mo Tzu (470?–391?)
Chuang Tzu (4th century)
Mencius (372?–298?)
Hsün Tzu (298–212)

The West

Socrates (470?–399)
Plato (427?–347)
Aristotle (384–322)
Cicero (106–43)

TIMELINE: THE COMMON ERA (C.E.)

0	200	400	600	800	1000	1200	1400	1600	1800	2000

Zera Yacob (1599–1692)
Walda Heywat (1630?–?)
Frantz Fanon (1925–1961)

Philo (20 B.C.E.–40 C.E.)
Origen (185–253)
St. Augustine (354–430)
al-Kindi (9th century)
al-Farabi (870–950)
Saadia (882–942)
Avicenna (980–1037)
al-Ghazali (1058-1111)
Averroës (1126–1198)
Maimonides (1135–1204)

Nāgārjuna (2nd century)
Nyāyasūtra (2nd century)
Sāṃkhyakārikā (4th century)
Yogasūtra (4th century)
Candrakīrti (c. 600)
Kumārila (c. 650)
Dharmakīrti (c. 660)
Śaṅkara (c. 720)
Udayana (c. 1000)
Śrīharṣa (c. 1150)
Madhva (1197–1276)
Gaṅgésa (c. 1325)
Rūpa Gosvāmi (c. 1550)
Annaṃbhaṭṭa (c. 1600)
Vivekananda (1863–1902)
Aurobindo (1872–1950)

Wang Ch'ung (27–100?)
Hsüan-tsang (596–664)
Fa-tsang (643–712)
I-hsüan (d. 867)
Chu Hsi (1130–1200)
Wang Yang-Ming (1472–1529)
Wang Fu-chih (1619–1692)
Kitaro Nishida (1870–1945)
Keiji Nishitani (1900–)
D. T. Suzuki (1870–1966)

St. Thomas Aquinas (1225–1274)
Thomas Hobbes (1588–1679)
Rene Descartes (1596–1650)
John Locke (1632–1704)
Immanuel Kant (1724–1804)
Karl Marx (1818–1883)
Jean-Paul Sartre (1905–1980)

PART I **Africa**

ANCIENT EGYPT

Ancient Egypt produced much interesting ethical literature millennia before the birth of Confucius, Socrates, or Jesus. The selections below include texts of several different kinds.

Instructions Old Kingdom writers popularized instructions, series of maxims strung together as advice from father to son, as a literary genre. The maxims are bits of practical advice. Authors of instructions varied the format and content, but much of the wisdom transmitted was popular; authors relied on traditional proverbs as well as on their own insights. The longest and best known of the instructions, *The Instruction of Ptahhotep,* appears below. It survives in four copies, the earliest of which is in Middle Egyptian. But many scholars believe that the work dates from the Sixth Dynasty (2300–2150 B.C.E.) and encodes the morality of the late Old Kingdom aristocracy. It focuses on basic issues of social relations and on basic virtues—self-control, moderation, kindness, generosity, justice, truthfulness, and discretion—which are to be practiced toward all. This instruction, like many others, seems to rest on faith in the perfectability of human beings. It is optimistic that people can meet the demands of morality.

New Kingdom instructions are less pretentious than those of earlier eras. Intended for average people, they reflect the ethical outlook of the middle classes. *The Instruction of Any,* composed during the Eighteenth Dynasty (1550–1305 B.C.E.), is advice from a father, a minor official, to his son. Interestingly, the son debates his father, insisting that the advice is too hard to follow. For the first time, perfectability comes into question: Can the son lead a completely moral life?

Tomb Inscriptions Many tombs feature carvings discussing the achievements and moral worth of the person buried therein. Some have additional songs, hymns, or entreaties to the gods. Typically, these concern death. Their authors evidently had considerable freedom to record their reflections on death and, correspondingly, on life. Those that seemed especially creative or instructive were copied on papyrus. *The Song from the Tomb of King Intef* survives in two such copies with an illustration of four musicians led by a blind harpist. Dating from the Middle Kingdom (probably 1500–1300 B.C.E.), it voices skepticism about the afterlife and urges the living to "make holiday"—a phrase that means "to hold a funeral banquet" as well as "to party"—while they have the chance.

Didactic Literature Instructions are but one form of literature designed to make ethical points and investigate the meaning of life and death. *The Dispute between a Man and His Ba,* a famous poem dating from the Twelfth Dynasty (1990–1785 B.C.E.), also falls into this category. It recounts a dialogue between a suffering man, longing for death, and his *ba*, or soul. The man contemplates suicide; his angered soul threatens to abandon him, which would lead to his total annihilation rather than survival in the afterlife. He tries to convince his soul to stay with him and let him die. His soul, unconvinced, tries to convince him of the value of life.

The Book of the Dead This work, which the Egyptians called "the coming forth by day," is a compilation of spells for resurrecting people in the afterlife. It attained its final form during the Twenty-Sixth Dynasty of the New Kingdom (664–525 B.C.E.). In essence, *The Book of the Dead* is a book of magic for achieving eternal life. But it also contains an ethical component; the dead must establish that they are worthy of eternal life. Parts of Chapter 125, "Judgment of the Dead," appear here. The original document contains an illustration of a dead person's heart being weighed on a scale by a group of gods headed by Osiris.

from *The Instruction of Ptahhotep*

1. Don't be proud of your knowledge,
   Consult the ignorant and the wise;
   The limits of art are not reached,
   No artist's skills are perfect;
   Good speech is more hidden than greenstone,
   Yet may be found among maids at the grindstones.

2. If you meet a disputant in action,
   A powerful man, superior to you,
   Fold your arms, bend your back,
   To flout him will not make him agree with you.
   Make little of the evil speech
   By not opposing him while he's in action;
   He will be called an ignoramus,
   Your self-control will match his pile [of words].

3. If you meet a disputant in action
   Who is your equal, on your level,
   You will make your worth exceed his by silence,
   While he is speaking evilly,
   There will be much talk by the hearers,
   Your name will be good in the mind of the magistrates.

4. If you meet a disputant in action,
   A poor man, not your equal,
   Do not attack him because he is weak,
   Let him alone, he will confute himself.
   Do not answer him to relieve your heart,
   Do not vent yourself against your opponent,
   Wretched is he who injures a poor man,
   One will wish to do what you desire,
   You will beat him through the magistrates' reproof.

5. If you are a man who leads,
   Who controls the affairs of the many,
   Seek out every beneficent deed,
   That your conduct may be blameless.
   Great is justice, lasting in effect,
   Unchallenged since the time of Osiris.
   One punishes the transgressor of laws,
   Though the greedy overlooks this;
   Baseness may seize riches,
   Yet crime never lands its wares;
   In the end it is justice that lasts,
   Man says: "It is my father's ground."

6. Do not scheme against people,
   God punishes accordingly:
   If a man says: "I shall live by it,"
   He will lack bread for his mouth.
   If a man says: "I shall be rich,"
   He will have to say: "My cleverness has snared me."
   If he says: "I will snare for myself,"
   He will be unable to say: "I snared for my profit."
   If a man says: "I will rob someone,"
   He will end being given to a stranger.
   People's schemes do not prevail,
   God's command is what prevails;
   Live then in the midst of peace,
   What they give comes by itself.

. . . .

9. If you plow and there's growth in the field,
   And god lets it prosper in your hand,
   Do not boast at your neighbors' side,
   One has great respect for the silent man:
   Man of character is man of wealth.

If he robs he is like a crocodile in court.
Don't impose on one who is childless,
Neither decry nor boast of it;
There is many a father who has grief,
And a mother of children less content than another;
It is the lonely whom god fosters,
While the family man prays for a follower.

10. If you are poor, serve a man of worth,
That all your conduct may be well with the god.
Do not recall if he once was poor,
Don't be arrogant toward him
For knowing his former state;
Respect him for what has accrued to him,
For wealth does not come by itself.
It is their law for him whom they love,
His gain, he gathered it himself;
It is the god who makes him worthy
And protects him while he sleeps.

11. Follow your heart as long as you live,
Do no more than is required,
Do not shorten the time of "follow-the-heart,"
Trimming its moment offends the *ka*.*
Don't waste time on daily cares
Beyond providing for your household;
When wealth has come, follow your heart,
Wealth does no good if one is glum!

12. If you are a man of worth
And produce a son by the grace of god,
If he is straight, takes after you,
Takes good care of your possessions,
Do for him all that is good,
He is your son, your *ka* begot him,
Don't withdraw your heart from him.
But an offspring can make trouble:
If he strays, neglects your counsel,
Disobeys all that is said,
His mouth spouting evil speech,
Punish him for all his talk!
They hate him who crosses you,
His guilt was fated in the womb;
He whom they guide can not go wrong,
Whom they make boatless can not cross.

. . . .

* Vitality, vital force, personality. —Ed.

16. If you are a man who leads,
Whose authority reaches wide,
You should do outstanding things,
Remember the day that comes after.
No strife will occur in the midst of honors,
But where the crocodile enters hatred arises.

17. If you are a man who leads,
Listen calmly to the speech of one who pleads;
Don't stop him from purging his body
Of that which he planned to tell.
A man in distress wants to pour out his heart
More than that his case be won.
About him who stops a plea
One says: "Why does he reject it?"
Not all one pleads for can be granted,
But a good hearing soothes the heart.

. . . .

19. If you want a perfect conduct,
To be free from every evil,
Guard against the vice of greed:
A grievous sickness without cure,
There is no treatment for it.
It embroils fathers, mothers,
And the brothers of the mother,
It parts wife from husband;
It is a compound of all evils,
A bundle of all hateful things.
That man endures whose rule is rightness,
Who walks a straight line;
He will make a will by it,
The greedy has no tomb.

20. Do not be greedy in the division,
Do not covet more than your share;
Do not be greedy toward your kin,
The mild has a greater claim than the harsh.
Poor is he who shuns his kin,
He is deprived of interchange.
Even a little of what is craved
Turns a quarreler into an amiable man.

. . . .

22. Sustain your friends with what you have,
You have it by the grace of god;
Of him who fails to sustain his friends
One says, "a selfish *ka*."

One plans the morrow but knows not what
will be,
The [right] *ka* is the *ka* by which one is
sustained.
If praise worthy deeds are done,
Friends will say, "welcome!"
One does not bring supplies to town,
One brings friends when there is need.

23. Do not repeat calumny,
Nor should you listen to it,
It is the spouting of the hot-bellied.
Report a thing observed, not heard,
If it is negligible, don't say anything,
He who is before you recognizes worth.
If a seizure is ordered and carried out,
Hatred will arise against him who seizes;
Calumny is like a dream against which one
covers the face.

. . . .

29. If you are angered by a misdeed,
Lean toward a man on account of his
rightness;
Pass it over, don't recall it,
Since he was silent to you the first day.

30. If you are great after having been humble,
Have gained wealth after having been poor
In the past, in a town which you know,
Knowing your former condition,
Do not put trust in your wealth,
Which came to you as gift of god;
So that you will not fall behind one like you,
To whom the same has happened.

31. . . . Do not plunder a neighbor's house,
Do not steal the goods of one near you,
Lest he denounce you before you are heard.
A quarreler is a mindless person,
If he is known as an aggressor
The hostile man will have trouble in the
neighborhood.

. . . .

34. Be generous as long as you live,
What leaves the storehouse does not return;
It is the food to be shared which is coveted,
One whose belly is empty is an accuser;
One deprived becomes an opponent,
Don't have him for a neighbor.
Kindness is a man's memorial
For the years after the function.

. . . .

36. Punish firmly, chastise soundly,
Then repression of crime becomes an
example;
Punishment except for crime
Turns the complainer into an enemy.

37. If you take to wife a *špnt**
Who is joyful and known by her town,
If she is fickle and likes the moment,
Do not reject her, let her eat,
The joyful brings happiness.

Epilogue

If you listen to my sayings,
All your affairs will go forward;
In their truth resides their value,
Their memory goes on in the speech of men,
Because of the worth of their precepts;
If every word is carried on,
They will not perish in this land.
If advice is given for the good,
The great will speak accordingly;
It is teaching a man to speak to posterity,
He who hears it becomes a master-hearer;
It is good to speak to posterity,
It will listen to it.

If a good example is set by him who leads,
He will be beneficent for ever,
His wisdom being for all time.
The wise feeds his *ba* with what endures,
So that it is happy with him on earth.
The wise is known by his wisdom,
The great by his good actions;
His heart matches his tongue,
His lips are straight when he speaks;
He has eyes that see,
His ears are made to hear what will profit his son,
Acting with truth he is free of falsehood.

* The meaning of this term is not known. Guesses range from "fat woman" to "dancer." —Ed.

The Song from the Tomb of King Intef

Reprinted from Miriam Lichtheim, Ancient Egyptian Literature, Volume I: The Old and Middle Kingdoms, *University of California Press, 1973.*

He is happy, this good prince!
Death is a kindly fate.
A generation passes,
Another stays,
Since the time of the ancestors.
The gods who were before rest in their tombs,
Blessed nobles too are buried in their tombs.
(Yet) those who built tombs,
Their places are gone,
What has become of them?
I have heard the words of Imhotep and Hardedef,
Whose sayings are recited whole.
What of their places?
Their walls have crumbled,
Their places are gone,
As though they had never been!
None comes from there,
To tell of their state,
To tell of their needs,
To calm our hearts,
Until we go where they have gone!

Hence rejoice in your heart!
Forgetfulness profits you,
Follow your heart as long as you live!
Put myrrh on your head,
Dress in fine linen,
Anoint yourself with oils fit for a god.
Heap up your joys,
Let your heart not sink!
Follow your heart and your happiness,
Do your things on earth as your heart commands!
When there comes to you that day of mourning,
The Weary-hearted hears not their mourning,
Wailing saves no man from the pit!

Refrain: Make holiday,
Do not weary of it!
Lo, none is allowed to take his goods with him,
Lo, none who departs comes back again!

The Dispute between a Man and His Ba

Reprinted from Miriam Lichtheim, Ancient Egyptian Literature, Volume I: The Old and Middle Kingdoms, *University of California Press, 1973.*

I opened my mouth to my *ba,* to answer what it had said:
This is too great for me today,
My *ba* will not converse with me!
It is too great for exaggeration,
It is like deserting me!
My *ba* shall not go,
It shall attend to me in this!

. . . in my body with a net of cord.
It shall not be able to flee on the day of pain!
Look, my *ba* misleads me—I do not listen to it—
Drags me toward death before I come to it,
Casts me on fire so as to burn me!

It shall be near me on the day of pain!
It shall stand on that side as does a . . .
It is he who comes forth,
He has brought himself.
My *ba,* too ignorant to still pain in life,

Leads me toward death before I come to it!
Sweeten the West for me!
Is that difficult?
Life is a passage; trees fall.
Tread on the evil, put down my misery!
May Thoth judge me, he who appeases the gods!
May Khons defend me, he who writes truly!
May Re hear my speech, he who calms the
 sun-bark!
May Isdes defend me in the sacred hall!

For my suffering is too heavy a burden to be borne by me. May it please that the gods repel my body's secrets!

What my *ba* said to me: "Are you not a man? Are you not alive? What do you gain by complaining about life like a man of wealth?" I said: "I will not go as long as this is neglected. Surely, if you run away, you will not be cared for. Every criminal says: "I shall seize you." Though you are dead, your name lives. Yonder is the place of rest, the heart's goal. The West is a dwelling place, a voyage.

If my *ba* listens to me without malice, its heart in accord with me, it shall be happy. I shall make it reach the West like one who is in his tomb, whose burial a survivor tends. I shall make a shelter over your corpse, so that you will make envious another *ba* in weariness. I shall make a shelter—it shall not be freezing—so that you will make envious another *ba* which is hot. I shall drink water at the pond over which I made shade, so that you will make envious another *ba* that hungers.

But if you lead me toward death in this manner, you will not find a place on which to rest in the West. Be patient, my *ba*, my brother, until my heir comes, one who will make offerings, who will stand at the tomb on the day of burial, having prepared the bier of the graveyard.

My *ba* opened its mouth to me, to answer what I had said: If you think of burial, it is heartbreak. It is the gift of tears by aggrieving a man. It is taking a man from his house, casting (him) on high ground. You will not go up to see the sun. Those who built in granite, who erected halls in excellent tombs of excellent construction—when the builders have become gods, their offering-stones are desolate, as if they were the dead who died on the riverbank for lack of a survivor. The flood takes its toll, the sun also. The fishes at the water's edge talk to them. Listen to me! It is good for people to listen. Follow the feast day, forget worry!

A man plowed his plot. He loaded his harvest into a boat. He towed the freight. As his feast day approached, he saw rising the darkness of a north wind. Watching in the boat, as the sun went down, (he) came out with his wife and children and foundered on the lake infested at night with crocodiles. When at last he sat down, he broke out saying: "I do not weep for that mother, for whom there is no coming from the West for another being-on-earth. I grieve for her children broken in the egg, who have seen the face of the Crocodile before they have lived."

A man asked for an early meal. His wife said: "It is for supper." He went outdoors to . . . a while. When he came back to the house he was like another (person). His wife beseeches him and he does not listen to her. He . . . heedless of the household.

I opened my mouth to my *ba*, to answer what it had said:

I

Lo, my name reeks
Lo, more than carrion smell
On summer days of burning sky.

Lo, my name reeks
Lo, more than a catch of fish
On fishing days of burning sky.

Lo, my name reeks
Lo, more than ducks smell,
More than reed-coverts full of waterfowl.

Lo, my name reeks
Lo, more than fishermen smell,
More than the marsh-pools where they fish.

Lo, my name reeks
Lo, more than crocodiles smell,
More than a shore-site full of crocodiles.

Lo, my name reeks
Lo, more than that of a wife
About whom lies are told to the husband.

Lo, my name reeks
Lo, more than that of a sturdy child
Who is said to belong to one who rejects him.

Lo, my name reeks
Lo, more than a king's town
That utters sedition behind his back.

II

To whom shall I speak today?
Brothers are mean,
The friends of today do not love.

To whom shall I speak today?
Hearts are greedy,
Everyone robs his comrade's goods.

To whom shall I speak today?
Kindness has perished,
Insolence assaults everyone.

To whom shall I speak today?
One is content with evil,
Goodness is cast to the ground everywhere.

To whom shall I speak today?
He who should enrage men by his crimes—
He makes everyone laugh at his evildoing.

To whom shall I speak today?
Men plunder,
Everyone robs his comrade.

To whom shall I speak today?
The criminal is one's intimate,
The brother with whom one dealt is a foe.

The whom shall I speak today?
The past is not remembered,
Now one does not help him who helped.

To whom shall I speak today?
Brothers are mean,
One goes to strangers for affection.

To whom shall I speak today?
Faces are blank,
Everyone turns his face from his brothers.

To whom shall I speak today?
Hearts are greedy,
No man's heart can be relied on.

To whom shall I speak today?
None are righteous,
The land is left to evildoers.

To whom shall I speak today?
One lacks an intimate,
One resorts to an unknown to complain.

To whom shall I speak today?
No one is cheerful,
He with whom one walked is no more.

To whom shall I speak today?
I am burdened with grief
For lack of an intimate.

To whom shall I speak today?
Wrong roams the earth,
And ends not.

III

Death is before me today
Like a sick man's recovery,
Like going outdoors after confinement.

Death is before me today
Like the fragrance of myrrh,
Like sitting under sail on breeze day.

Death is before me today
Like the fragrance of lotus,
Like sitting on the shore of drunkenness.

Death is before me today
Like a well-trodden way,
Like a man's coming home from warfare.

Death is before me today
Like the clearing of the sky,
As when a man discovers what he ignored.

Death is before me today
Like a man's longing to see his home
When he has spent many years in captivity.

IV

Truly, he who is yonder will be a living god,
Punishing the evildoer's crime.

Truly, he who is yonder will stand in the
sun-bark,
Making its bounty flow to the temples.

Truly, he who is yonder will be a wise man,
Not barred from appealing to Re when he speaks.

What my *ba* said to me: "Now throw complaint on the wood-pile, you my comrade, my brother! Whether you offer on the brazier, whether you bear down on life, as you say, love me here when you have set aside the West! But when it is wished that you attain the West, that your body joins the earth, I shall alight after you have become weary, and then we shall dwell together!"

Colophon: It is finished from beginning to end, as it was found in writing.

from *The Instruction of Any*

Take a wife while you're young,
That she make a son for you;
She should bear for you while you're youthful,
It is proper to make people.
Happy the man whose people are many,
He is saluted on account of his progeny.

. . . .

Do not enter the house of anyone,
Until he admits you and greets you;
Do not snoop around in his house,
Let your eye observe in silence.
Do not speak of him to another outside,
Who was not with you;
A great deadly crime

. . . .

Beware of a woman who is a stranger,
One not known in her town;
Don't stare at her when she goes by,
Do not know her carnally.
A deep water whose course is unknown,
Such is a woman away from her husband.
"I am pretty," she tells you daily,
When she has no witnesses;
She is ready to ensnare you,
A great deadly crime when it is heard.

. . . .

Don't indulge in drinking beer,
Lest you utter evil speech
And don't know what you're saying.
If you fall and hurt your body,
None holds out a hand to you:
Your companions in the drinking
Stand up saying: "Out with the drunk!"
If one comes to seek you and talk with you,
One finds you lying on the ground,
As if you were a little child.

. . . .

Behold, I give you these useful counsels,
For you to ponder in your heart;
Do it and you will be happy,
All evils will be far from you.
Guard against the crime of fraud,
Against words that are not true;
Conquer malice in your self,
A quarrelsome man does not rest on the morrow.
Keep away from a hostile man,
Do not let him be your comrade;
Befriend one who is straight and true,
One whose actions you have seen.
If your rightness matches his,
The friendship will be balanced.
Let your hand preserve what is in your house,
Wealth accrues to him who guards it;
Let your hand not scatter it to strangers,
Lest it turn to loss for you.
If wealth is placed where it bears interest,
It comes back to you redoubled;
Make a storehouse for your own wealth,
Your people will find it on your way.
What is given small returns augmented,
What is replaced brings abundance.
The wise lives off the house of the fool,
Protect what is yours and you find it;
Keep your eye on what you own,
Lest you end as a beggar.
He who is slack amounts to nothing,
Honored is the man who's active.

. . . .

Do not reveal your heart to a stranger,
He might use your words against you;
The noxious speech that came from your mouth,
He repeats it and you make enemies.
A man may be ruined by his tongue,
Beware and you will do well.
A man's belly is wider than a granary,
And full of all kinds of answers;
Choose the good one and say it,
While the bad is shut in your belly.
A rude answer brings a beating,

Speak sweetly and you will be loved.
Don't ever talk back to your attacker,
Do not set a trap for him;
It is the god who judges the righteous,
His fate comes and takes him away.

. . . .

Do not eat bread while another stands by
Without extending your hand to him.
As to food, it is here always,
It is man who does not last;
One man is rich, another is poor.
But food remains for him who shares it.
As to him who was rich last year,
He is a vagabond this year;
Don't be greedy to fill your belly,
You don't know your end at all.
Should you come to be in want,
Another may do good to you.
When last year's watercourse is gone,
Another river is here today;
Great lakes become dry places,
Sandbanks turn into depths.
Man does not have a single way,
The lord of life confounds him.

Attend to your position,
Be it low or high;
It is not good to press forward,
Step according to rank.
Do not intrude on a man in his house,
Enter when you have been called;
He may say "Welcome" with his mouth,
Yet deride you in his thoughts.
One gives food to one who is hated,
Supplies to one who enters uninvited.

Don't rush to attack your attacker,
Leave him to the god;
Report him daily to the god,
Tomorrow being like today,
And you will see what the god does,
When he injures him who injured you.

Do not enter into a crowd,
If you find it in an uproar
And about to come to blows.
Don't pass anywhere near by,
Keep away from their tumult,
Lest you be brought before the court,
When an inquiry is made.
Stay away from hostile people,
Keep your heart quiet among fighters;
An outsider is not brought to court,
One who knows nothing is not bound in fetters.

. . . .

Do not control your wife in her house,
When you know she is efficient;
Don't say to her: "Where is it? Get it!"
When she has put it in the right place.
Let your eye observe in silence,
Then you recognize her skill;
It is joy when your hand is with her,
There are many who don't know this.
If a man desists from strife at home,
He will not encounter its beginning.
Every man who founds a household
Should hold back the hasty heart.
Do not go after a woman,
Let her not steal your heart.

Do not talk back to an angry superior,
Let him have his way;
Speak sweetly when he speaks sourly,
It's the remedy that calms the heart.

. . . .

Epilogue

The scribe Khonshotep answered his father, the
  scribe Any:
I wish I were like [you],
As learned as you!
Then I would carry out your teachings,
And the son would be brought to his father's
  place.
Each man is led by his nature,
You are a man who is a master,
Whose strivings are exalted,
Whose every word is chosen.
The son, he understands little
When he recites the words in the books.
But when your words please the heart,
The heart tends to accept them with joy.
Don't make your virtues too numerous,
That one may raise one's thoughts to you;
A boy does not follow the moral instructions,

Though the writings are on his tongue!

The scribe Any answered his son, the scribe Khonshotep:
Do not rely on such worthless thoughts,
Beware of what you do to yourself!
I judge your complaints to be wrong,
I shall set you right about them.
There's nothing superfluous in our words,
Which you say you wished were reduced.
The fighting bull who kills in the stable,
He forgets and abandons the arena;
He conquers his nature,
Remembers what he's learned,
And becomes the like of a fattened ox.
The savage lion abandons his wrath,
And comes to resemble the timid donkey.
The horse slips into its harness,
Obedient it goes outdoors.
The dog obeys the word,
And walks behind its master.
The monkey carries the stick,
Though its mother did not carry it.
The goose returns from the pond,
When one comes to shut it in the yard.
One teaches the Nubian to speak Egyptian,
The Syrian and other strangers too.
Say: "I shall do like all the beasts,"
Listen and learn what they do.

The scribe Khonshotep answered his father, the scribe Any:
Do not proclaim your powers,
So as to force me to your ways;
Does it not happen to a man to slacken his hand,
So as to hear an answer in its place?
Man resembles the god in his way
If he listens to a man's answer.
One [man] cannot know his fellow,
If the masses are beasts;
One [man] cannot know his teachings,
And alone possess a mind,
If the multitudes are foolish.
All your sayings are excellent,
But doing them requires virtues;
Tell the god who gave you wisdom:
"Set them on your path!"

The scribe Any answered his son, the scribe Khonshotep:
Turn your back to these many words,
That are not worth being heard.
The crooked stick left on the ground,
With sun and shade attacking it,
If the carpenter takes it, he straightens it,
Makes of it a noble's staff,
And a straight stick makes a collar.
You foolish heart,
Do you wish us to teach,
Or have you been corrupted?

"Look," said he, "you my father,
You who are wise and strong of hand:
The infant in his mother's arms,
His wish is for what nurses him."
"Look," said he, "when he finds his speech,
He says: "Give me bread." "

---

from *The Book of the Dead*

CHAPTER 125 / THE JUDGMENT OF THE DEAD

The Declaration of Innocence

. . . .

I have not done crimes against people,
I have not mistreated cattle,
I have not sinned in the Place of Truth.
I have not known what should not be known,
I have not done any harm.
I did not begin a day by exacting more than my due,

My name did not reach the bark of the mighty
ruler.
I have not blasphemed a god,
I have not robbed the poor.
I have not done what the god abhors,
I have not maligned a servant to his master.
I have not caused pain,
I have not caused tears.
I have not killed,
I have not ordered to kill,
I have not made anyone suffer.
I have not damaged the offerings in the temples,
I have not depleted the loaves of the gods,
I have not stolen the cakes of the dead.
I have not copulated nor defiled myself.
I have not increased nor reduced the measure,
I have not diminished the arura,*
I have not cheated in the fields.
I have not added to the weight of the balance,
I have not falsified the plummet of the scales.
I have not taken milk from the mouth of children,
I have not deprived cattle of their pasture.
I have not snared birds in the reeds of the gods,
I have not caught fish in their ponds.
I have not held back water in its season,
I have not dammed a flowing stream,
I have not quenched a needed fire.
I have not neglected the days of meat offerings,
I have not detained cattle belonging to the god,
I have not stopped a god in his procession.
I am pure, I am pure, I am pure, I am pure!
I am pure as is pure that great heron in Hnes.
I am truly the nose of the Lord of Breath,
Who sustains all the people,
. . . .

The Declaration to the Forty-two Gods

O Wide-of-stride who comes from On: I have not done evil.
O Flame-grasper who comes from Kheraha: I have not robbed.
O Long-nosed who comes from Khmun: I have not coveted.

*A Greek unit of measure, roughly equivalent to two-thirds of an acre. —ED.

O Shadow-eater who comes from the cave: I have not stolen.
O Savage-faced who comes from Rostau: I have not killed people.
O Lion-Twins who come from heaven: I have not trimmed the measure.
O Flint-eyed who comes from Khem: I have not cheated.
O Fiery-one who comes backward: I have not stolen a god's property.
O Bone-smasher who comes from Hnes: I have not told lies.
O Flame-thrower who comes from Memphis: I have not seized food.
O Cave-dweller who comes from the west: I have not sulked.
O White-toothed who comes from Lakeland: I have not trespassed.
O Blood-eater who comes from slaughterplace: I have not slain sacred cattle.
O Entrail-eater who comes from the tribunal: I have not extorted.
O Lord of Maat who comes from Maaty: I have not stolen bread rations.
O Wanderer who comes from Bubastis: I have not spied.
O Pale-one who comes from On: I have not prattled.
O Villain who comes from Anjdty: I have contended only for my goods.
O Fiend who comes from slaughterhouse: I have not committed adultery.
O Examiner who comes from Min's temple: I have not defiled myself.
O Chief of the nobles who comes from Imu: I have not caused fear.
O Wrecker who comes from Huy: I have not trespassed.
O Disturber who comes from the sanctuary: I have not been violent.
O Child who comes from the nome of On: I have not been deaf to Maat.
O Foreteller who comes from Wensi: I have not quarreled.
O Bastet who comes from the shrine: I have not winked.
O Backward-faced who comes from the pit: I have not copulated with a boy.

O Flame-footed who comes from the dusk: I have not been false.
O Dark-one who comes from darkness: I have not reviled.
O Peace-bringer who comes from Sais: I have not been aggressive.
O Many-faced who comes from Djefet: I have not had a hasty heart.
O Accuser who comes from Utjen: I have not attacked and reviled a god.
O Horned-one who comes from Siut: I have not made many words.
O Nefertem who comes from Memphis: I have not sinned, I have not done wrong.
O Timeless-one who comes from Djedu: I have not made trouble.
O Willful-one who comes from Tjebu: I have not waded in water.
O Flowing-one who comes from Nun: I have not raised my voice.
O Commander of people who comes from his shrine: I have not cursed a god.
O Benefactor who comes from Huy: I have not been boastful.
O Nehebkau who comes from the city: I have not been haughty.
O High-of-head who comes from the cave: I have not wanted more than I had.
O Captor who comes from the graveyard: I have not cursed god in my town.

The Address to the Gods

. . . .

Behold me, I have come to you,
Without sin, without guilt, without evil,
Without a witness against me,
Without one whom I have wronged.
I live on *maat*, I feed on *maat*,
I have done what people speak of,
What the gods are pleased with,
I have contented a god with what he wishes.
I have given bread to the hungry,
Water to the thirsty,
Clothes to the naked,
A ferryboat to the boatless.
I have given divine offerings to the gods,
Invocation-offerings to the dead.
Rescue me, protect me,
Do not accuse me before the great god!

. . . .

ENLIGHTENMENT ETHIOPIA

We know that philosophy was practiced in Africa in medieval times, but we have virtually no texts from that period. From the early modern period, however, we have some interesting philosophical works from Ethiopia that constitute an Ethiopian enlightenment. Like the philosophers of the European Enlightenment, these seventeenth-century Ethiopian writers stress the primacy of reason and the possibility of knowledge of the world through its use.

Zera Yacob (1599–1692), born near Aksum, was the son of a poor Ethiopian farmer. He attended traditional schools, studying the Psalms, sacred music, and Ethiopian literature. Such schools encouraged questions and discussions, teaching reflection, criticism, and the power of thought. Following a period of devastation brought about by foreign invasion, Ethiopia was undergoing a religious revival and suffering various religious conflicts. In 1626, in the midst of these upheavals, King Susenyos converted to Catholicism and summarily ordered obedience to Rome. A rival priest from Aksum denounced Zera Yacob as a traitor, claiming that he was inciting revolution against the Catholics and the king. Only twenty-seven years old, Zera Yacob fled for his life, taking nothing but a small amount of gold and his copy of the Psalms. On his way to Shoa, the region around Addis Ababa, he found a cave in a beautiful valley, where he stayed for two years until Susenyos died. In the cave, he formulated the basic ideas of his philosophy.

Returning to society, Zera Yacob acquired a literary patron in the rich merchant Habtu. Zera Yacob lived in his house in Enfraz, tutored his sons, and married his maidservant. One of Habtu's sons, Walda Heywat, asked Zera Yacob to write down his philosophical views; the result (in 1667) was the *The Treatise of Zera Yacob.* Fearing persecution, Zera Yacob never published it. He lived in Enfraz, happily and prosperously, for twenty-five more years until his death at age ninety-three.

The book's original Geez title, *Hatäta,* comes from a root meaning to question, search, investigate, or examine. The *Treatise* champions reason as a tool for understanding the world and for understanding religion. Zera Yacob argues that reason, applied to the evidence of the world, leads to the conclusion that the world, God's creation, is essentially good. His ethics rests on this foundation. Because creation is good, enjoying it is appropriate and also good. Zera Yacob thus opposes traditional Ethiopian asceticism, a philosophy of denial, fasting, and monastic life, in favor of involvement with the secular world.

In fact, Zera Yacob uses reason, which he calls the "light of the heart," to criticize the ethical prescriptions of various religions. He argues that Jewish law, Christian morality, and Islamic rules of conduct all go astray on basic points; they imply that the order of nature itself is wrong. Zera Yacob optimistically believes that "he who investigates with the pure intelligence set by the creator in the heart of each man and scrutinizes the order and laws of creation, will discover the truth." Reason thus serves as a foundation for morality and as a test for religious beliefs.

Underlying Zera Yacob's assault on particular religious tenets is a general skepticism about deriving ethical conclusions from religious revelation. Many religious thinkers have believed that God reveals moral truth and that we can know that truth only because God reveals it to us. Zera Yacob argues that this cannot be correct. Defenders of each religion claim that they know the only true way. Obviously, not all can be right. How can we decide who is right? How, that is, can we judge which alleged revelations really come from God? Zera Yacob argues that we cannot. We have no way to tell true revelations from pretenders. We have no choice, therefore, but to use reason to discover moral truth.

Walda Heywat (1630?–?) was a son of the merchant Habtu from Enfraz, and a pupil of Zera Yacob. We know little about his life. He wrote his *Treatise* to explore and explain the ideas of his teacher, Zera Yacob. But Walda Heywat is more than his teacher's promoter. Zera Yacob's work is highly rationalistic; it relies on reason to illumine religious and philosophical issues. Walda Heywat's *Treatise,* in contrast, consists partly of stories designed to illustrate philosophical and, most often, ethical points. The stories reflect the influence of Ethiopian popular literature. Moreover, they seem designed to teach philosophy to the previously uninitiated. Walda Heywat is primarily a teacher addressing an audience of students.

Although Walda Heywat relies on Zera Yacob for many of his ideas, his thought is distinctive, primarily for its practical, everyday focus. Walda Heywat addresses themes close to common sense, practical problems, and ordinary living. He argues that work is valuable; that all human begins are equal from a moral point of view and deserve equal respect; and that family life is good and extremely important, serving as a foundation for other social relations. His philosophy continues to be influential in Ethiopian thought.

Walda Heywat begins by asserting the social nature of humanity. We are born into society, and we rely on others for survival and for happiness. This implies that each person has a duty to help others. Moreover, because God has created us all equal, we ought to show others the love and respect we show ourselves. From this Walda Heywat derives the Golden Rule. He criticizes contemporary Christians for failing to live up to the commandment to love one another. He also defends religious tolerance, maintaining that "each man should believe what seems true to him." (Recall that his teacher suffered religious persecution and never dared to publish his own critiques of standard religious requirements.)

Walda Heywat argues that we should love our work and strive to provide what we need and also some to share with others. This striving, in principle, has no limits; to rest content with our possessions, he says, is just laziness. "Acquire as much as you can without dishonesty," he advises. By creating wealth, we can imitate God, who created every source of wealth.

Walda Heywat also discusses the structure of the family, suggesting that women are inferior to men and so ought to play a different role. In this respect he ratifies the Ethiopian social structure of his time and departs from the teachings of Zera Yacob, who maintains that "husband and wife are equal in marriage."

ZERA YACOB

from *The Treatise of Zera Yacob*

CHAPTER IV / THE INVESTIGATION OF FAITH AND OF PRAYER

Later on I thought, saying to myself: "Is everything that is written in the Holy Scriptures true?" Although I thought much about these things I understood nothing, so I said to myself: "I shall go and consult scholars and thinkers; they will tell me the truth." But afterwards I thought, saying to myself: "What will men tell me other than what is in their heart?" Indeed each one says: "My faith is right, and those who believe in another faith believe in falsehood, and are the enemies of God." These days the *Frang** tell us: "Our faith is right, yours is false." We on the other hand tell them: "It is not so; your faith is wrong, ours is right." If we also ask the Mohammedans and the Jews, they will claim the same thing, and who would be the judge for such a kind of argument? No single human being can judge: for all men are plaintiffs and defendants between themselves. Once I asked a *Frang* scholar many things concerning our faith; he interpreted them all according to his own faith. Afterwards I asked a well-known Ethiopian scholar and he also interpreted all things according to his own faith. If I had asked the Mohammedans and the Jews, they also would have interpreted according to their own faith; then, where could I obtain a judge that tells the truth? As my faith appears true to me, so does another one find his own faith true; but truth is one. While thinking over this matter, I said: "O my creator, wise among the wise and just among the just, who created me with an intelligence, help me to understand, for men lack wisdom and truthfulness; as David said: 'No man can be relied upon.'"

I thought further and said: "Why do men lie over problems of such great importance, even to the point of destroying themselves?" and they seemed to do so because although they pretend to know all, they know nothing. Convinced they know all, they do not attempt to investigate the truth. As David said: "Their hearts are curdled like milk." Their heart is curdled because they assume what they have heard from their predecessors and they do not inquire whether it is true or false. But I said: "O Lord! who strike me down with such torment, it is fitting that I know your judgement. You chastise me with truth and admonish me with mercy. But never let my head be anointed with the oil of sinners and of masters in lying: make me understand, for you created me with intelligence." I asked myself: "If I am intelligent, what is it I understand?" And I said: "I understand there is a creator, greater than all creatures; since from his overabundant greatness, he created things that are so great. He is intelligent who understands all, for he created us as intelligent from the abundance of his intelligence; and we ought to worship him, for he is the master of all things. If we pray to him, he will listen to us; for he is almighty." I went on saying in my thought: "God did not create me intelligent without a purpose, that is to look for him and to grasp him and his wisdom in the path he has opened for me and to worship him as long as I live." And still thinking on the same subject, I said to myself: "Why is it that all men do not adhere to truth, instead of believing falsehood?" The cause seemed to be the nature of man which is weak and sluggish. Man aspires to know truth and the hidden

* Literally, "foreigners"; here, "Europeans," "Catholics." —Ed.

things of nature, but his endeavour is difficult and can only be attained with great labour and patience, as Solomon said: "With the help of wisdom I have been at pains to study all that is done under heaven; oh, what a weary task God has given mankind to labour at!" Hence people hastily accept what they have heard from their fathers and shy from any critical examination. But God created man to be the master of his own actions, so that he will be what he wills to be, good or bad. If a man chooses to be wicked he can continue in this way until he receives the punishment he deserves for his wickedness. But being carnal, man likes what is of the flesh; whether they are good or bad, he finds ways and means through which he can satisfy his carnal desire. God did not create man to be evil, but to choose what he would like to be, so that he may receive his reward if he is good or his condemnation if he is bad. If a liar, who desires to achieve wealth or honours among men, needs to use foul means to obtain them, he will say he is convinced this falsehood was for him a just thing. To those people who do not want to search, this action seems to be true, and they believe in the liar's strong faith. I ask you in how many falsehoods do our people believe in? They believe wholeheartedly in astrology and other calculations, in the mumbling of secret words, in omens, in the conjuration of devils and in all kinds of magical art and in the utterances of soothsayers. They believe in all these because they did not investigate the truth but listened to their predecessors. Why did these predecessors lie unless it was for obtaining wealth and honours? Similarly those who wanted to rule the people said: "We were sent by God to proclaim the truth to you"; and the people believed them. Those who came after them accepted their fathers' faith without question: rather, as a proof of their faith, they added to it by including stories of signs and omens. Indeed they said: "God did these things"; and so they made God a witness of falsehood and a party to liars.

CHAPTER V / THE LAW OF MOSES AND THE MEDITATION OF MOHAMMED

To the person who seeks it, truth is immediately revealed. Indeed he who investigates with the pure intelligence set by the creator in the heart of each man and scrutinizes the order and laws of creation, will discover the truth. Moses said: "I have been sent by God to proclaim to you his will and his law"; but those who came after him added stories of miracles that they claimed had been wrought in Egypt and on Mount Sinai and attributed them to Moses. But to an inquisitive mind they do not seem to be true. For in the Books of Moses, one can find a wisdom that is shameful and that fails to agree with the wisdom of the creator or with the order and the laws of creation. Indeed by the will of the creator, and the law of nature, it has been ordained that man and woman would unite in a carnal embrace to generate children, so that human beings will not disappear from the earth. Now this mating, which is willed by God in his law of creation, cannot be impure since God does not stain the work of his own hands. But Moses considered that act as evil; but our intelligence teaches us that he who says such a thing is wrong and makes his creator a liar. Again they said that the law of Christianity is from God, and miracles are brought forth to prove it. But our intelligence tells and confirms to us with proofs that marriage springs from the law of the creator; and yet monastic law renders this wisdom of the creator ineffectual, since it prevents the generation of children and extinguishes mankind. The law of Christians which propounds the superiority of monastic life over marriage is false and cannot come from God. How can the violation of the law of the creator stand superior to his wisdom, or can man's deliberation correct the word of God? Similarly Mohammed said: "The orders I pass to you are given to me by God"; and there was no lack of writers to record miracles proving Mohammed's mission, and people believed in him. But we know that the teaching of Mohammed could not have come from God; those who will be born both male and female are equal in number; if we count men and women living in an area, we find as many women as men; we do not find eight or ten women for every man; for the law of creation orders one man to marry one woman. If one man marries ten women, then nine men will be without wives. This violates the order of creation and the laws of nature and it ruins the usefulness of marriage; Mohammed, who taught in the name of God, that one man could marry many wives, is not sent from God. These few things I examined about marriage.

Similarly when I examine the remaining laws, such as the Pentateuch, the law of the Christians and the law of Islam, I find many things which disagree with the truth and the justice of our creator that our intelligence reveals to us. God indeed has illuminated the heart of man with understanding by which he can see the good and evil, recognize the licit and the illicit, distinguish truth from error, "and by your light we see the light, oh Lord"! If we use this light of our heart properly, it cannot deceive us; the purpose of this light which our creator gave us is to be saved by it, and not to be ruined by it. Everything that the light of our intelligence shows us comes from the source of truth, but what men say comes from the source of lies and our intelligence teaches us that all that the creator established is right. The creator in his kind wisdom has made blood to flow monthly from the womb of women. And the life of a woman requires this flow of blood in order to generate children; a woman who has no menstruation is barren and cannot have children, because she is impotent by nature. But Moses and Christians have defiled the wisdom of the creator; Moses even considers impure all the things that such a woman touches; this law of Moses impedes marriage and the entire life of a woman and it spoils the law of mutual help, prevents the bringing up of children and destroys love. Therefore this law of Moses cannot spring from him who created woman. Moreover, our intelligence tells us that we should bury our dead brothers. Their corpses are impure only if we follow the wisdom of Moses; they are not, however, if we follow the wisdom of our creator who made us out of dust that we may return to dust. God does not change into impurity the order he imposes on all creatures with great wisdom, but man attempts to render it impure that he may glorify the voice of falsehood.

The Gospel also declares: "He who does not leave behind father, mother, wife and children is not worthy of God." This forsaking corrupts the nature of man. God does not accept that his creature destroy itself, and our intelligence tells us that abandoning our father and our mother helpless in their old age is a great sin; the Lord is not a god that loves malice; those who desert their children are worse than the wild animals, that never forsake their offspring. He who abandons his wife abandons her to adultery and thus violates the order of creation and the laws of nature. Hence what the Gospel says on this subject cannot come from God. Likewise the Mohammedans said that it is right to go and buy a man as if he were an animal. But with our intelligence we understand that this Mohammedan law cannot come from the creator of man who made us equal, like brothers, so that we call our creator our father. But Mohammed made the weaker man the possession of the stronger and equated a rational creature with irrational animals; can this depravity be attributed to God?

God does not order absurdities, nor does he say: "Eat this, do not eat that; today eat, tomorrow do not eat; do not eat meat today, eat it tomorrow," unlike the Christians who follow the laws of fasting. Neither did God say to the Mohammedans: "Eat during the night, but do not eat during the day," nor similar and like things. Our reason teaches us that we should eat of all things which do no harm to our health and our nature, and that we should eat each day as much as is required for our sustenance. Eating one day, fasting the next endangers health; the law of fasting reaches beyond the order of the creator who created food for the life of man and wills that we eat it and be grateful for it; it is not fitting that we abstain from his gifts to us. If there are people who argue that fasting kills the desire of the flesh, I shall answer them: "The concupiscence of the flesh by which a man is attracted to a woman and a woman to a man springs from the wisdom of the creator; it is improper to do away with it; but we should act according to the well-known law that God established concerning legitimate intercourse. God did not put a purposeless concupiscence into the flesh of men and of all animals; rather he planted it in the flesh of man as a root of life in this world and a stabilizing power for each creature in the way destined for it. In order that this concupiscence lead us not to excess, we should eat according to our needs, because overeating and drunkenness result in ill health and shoddiness in work. A man who eats according to his needs on Sunday and during the fifty days does not sin, similarly he who eats on Friday and on the days before Easter does not sin. For God created man with the same necessity for food on each day and during each month. The Jews, the Christians and the Mohammedans did not understand the work of God when they instituted the law of fasting; they lie when they say that God imposed fasting upon us and forbade us to eat; for God our creator gave us food that we support ourselves by it, not that we abstain from it.

CHAPTER VII / THE LAW OF GOD AND THE LAW OF MAN

I said to myself: "Why does God permit liars to mislead his people?" God has indeed given reason to all and everyone so that they may know truth and falsehood, and the power to choose between the two as they will. Hence if it is truth we want, let us seek it with our reason which God has given us so that with it we may see that which is needed for us from among all the necessities of nature. We cannot, however, reach truth through the doctrine of man, for all men are liars. If on the contrary we prefer falsehood, the order of the creator and the natural law imposed on the whole of nature do not perish thereby, but we ourselves perish by our own error. God sustains the world by his order which he himself has established and which man cannot destroy, because the order of God is stronger than the order of men. Therefore those who believe that monastic life is superior to marriage are they themselves drawn to marriage because of the might of the order of the creator; those who believe that fasting brings righteousness to their soul eat when they feel hungry; and those who believe that he who has given up his goods is perfect are drawn to seek them again on account of their usefulness, as many of our monks have done. Likewise all liars would like to break the order of nature: but it is not possible that they do not see their lie broken down. But the creator laughs at them, the Lord of creation derides them. God knows the right way to act, but the sinner is caught in the snare set by himself. Hence a monk who holds the order of marriage as impure will be caught in the snare of fornication and of other carnal sins against nature and of grave sickness. Those who despise riches will show their hypocrisy in the presence of kings and of wealthy persons in order to acquire these goods. Those who desert their relatives for the sake of God lack temporal assistance in times of difficulty and in their old age, they begin to blame God and men and to blaspheme. Likewise all those who violate the law of the creator fall into the trap made by their own hands. God permits error and evil among men because our souls in this world live in a land of temptation, in which the chosen ones of God are put to the test, as the wise Solomon said: "God has put the virtuous to the test and proved them worthy to be with him; he has tested them like gold in a furnace, and accepted them as a holocaust." After our death, when we go back to our creator, we shall see how God made all things in justice and great wisdom and that all his ways are truthful and upright. It is clear that our soul lives after the death of our flesh; for in this world our desire for happiness is not fulfilled; those in need desire to possess, those who possess desire more, and though man owned the whole world, he is not satisfied and craves for more. This inclination of our nature shows us that we are created not only for this life, but also for the coming world; there the souls which have fulfilled the will of the creator will be perpetually satisfied and will not look for other things. Without this inclination the nature of man would be deficient and would not obtain that of which it has the greatest need. Our soul has the power of having the concept of God and of seeing him mentally; likewise it can conceive of immortality. God did not give this power purposelessly; as he gave the power, so did he give the reality. In this world complete justice is not achieved: wicked people are in possession of the goods of this world in a satisfying degree, the humble starve; some wicked men are happy, some good men are sad, some evil men exult with joy; some righteous men weep. Therefore, after our death there must needs be another life and another justice, a perfect one, in which retribution will be made to all according to their deeds, and those who have fulfilled the will of the creator revealed through the light of reason and have observed the law of their nature will be rewarded. The law of nature is obvious, because our reason clearly propounds it, if we examine it. But men do not like such inquiries; they choose to believe in the words of men rather than to investigate the will of their creator.

CHAPTER VIII / THE NATURE OF KNOWLEDGE

The will of God is known by this short statement from our reason that tells us: "Worship God your creator and love all man as yourself." Moreover our reason says: "Do not do unto others that which you do not like done to you, but do unto others as you would like others to do unto you." The decalogue of the Pentateuch expresses the will of the creator excepting the precept about the observance of the Sabbath, for our reason says nothing of the observance of the Sabbath. But the prohibitions of killing, stealing, lying, adultery: our reason teaches us these and similar ones. Likewise the six precepts of the Gospel are the will of the creator. For indeed we desire that men show mercy to us; it therefore is fitting that we ourselves show the same mercy to the others, as much as it is within our power. It is the will of God that we keep our life and existence in this world. It is the will of the creator that we come into and remain in this life, and it is not right for us to leave it against his holy will. The creator himself wills that we adorn our life with science and work; for such an end did he give us reason and power. Manual labour comes from the will of God, because without it the necessities of our life cannot be fulfilled. Likewise marriage of one man with one woman and education of children. Moreover there are many other things which agree with our reason and are necessary for our life or for the existence of mankind. We ought to observe them, because such is the will of our creator, and we ought to know that God does not create us perfect but creates us with such a reason as to know that we are to strive for perfection as long as we live in this world, and to be worthy for the reward that our creator has prepared for us in his wisdom. It was possible for God to have created us perfect and to make us enjoy beatitude on earth; but he did not will to create us in this way; instead he created us with the capacity of striving for perfection, and placed us in the midst of the trials of the world so that we may become perfect and deserve the reward that our creator will give us after our death; as long as we live in this world we ought to praise our creator and fulfil his will and be patient until he draws us unto him, and beg from his mercy that he will lessen our period of hardship and forgive our sins and faults which we committed through ignorance, and enable us to know the laws of our creator and to keep them.

Now as to prayer, we always stand in need of it because our rational nature requires it. The soul endowed with intelligence that is aware that there is a God who knows all, conserves all, rules all, is drawn to him so that it prays to him and asks him to grant things good and to be freed from evil and sheltered under the hand of him who is almighty and for whom nothing is impossible, God great and sublime who sees all that is above and beneath him, holds all, teaches all, guides all, our Father, our creator, our Protector, the reward for our souls, merciful, kind, who knows each of our misfortunes, takes pleasure in our patience, creates us for life and not for destruction, as the wise Solomon said: "You, Lord, teach all things, because you can do all things and overlook men's sins so that they can repent. You love all that exists, you hold nothing of what you have made in abhorrence, you are indulgent and merciful to all." God created us intelligent so that we may meditate on his greatness, praise him and pray to him in order to obtain the needs of our body and soul. Our reason which our creator has put in the heart of man teaches all these things to us. How can they be useless and false?

WALDA HEYWAT

from *The Treatise of Walda Heywat*

CHAPTER XIII / SOCIAL LIFE

If a person approaches his creator and remains as if he were elevated with him in his prayer and his thanksgiving, he should not remain aloof from his fellow men, because God ordered men to unite and cooperate with their neighbors. God did not create man that he be busy only with himself, but he created him with the need for the society of other men. For man cannot live by himself, one is in need of the other. All men should help one another; whoever breaks away from the company of men, abrogates the law of his creator. Therefore do not praise those who isolate themselves from men that they may live as hermits in country caves. They have ignored the will of the creator who ordered that each and every man help one another; now a solitary man is useless to human society as if he were already dead; God does not accept the service of such a man who refuses to walk through the path he would have led him by and does not want to serve in the well-determined service that he had imposed on him.

Moreover God created all men equal just like brothers, sons of one father; our creator himself is the father of all. Therefore, we should love one another and observe this eternal precept which God engraved upon the Tables of our heart and which says: "Love your fellow men as yourself, and do to them what you wish others to do to you; do not do to them that which you do not want to be done to you"; observation of this primary precept is the perfection of all our deeds and of all justice. Do not think that the doctrine of fools who say the following is good: "The word 'fellow man' is confined only to relatives, or our neighbors, or our friends, or members of the faith." Do not say the same as they do; for all men are our fellow men whether they are good or evil, Christians, Mohammedans, Jews, pagans: all are equal to us and our brothers, because we are all the sons of one father and the creatures of one creator. Therefore we ought to love one another, and to behave well with all as much as we can and not to inflict evil on anyone. We ought to bear patiently the ignorance and sins of men, and forgive them the error through which they made us suffer, because we ourselves are sinners and wish that our sins be remitted. If there are people who say: "What shall we do to those who do wrong to us?" I may say to them: "We ought to avoid their evil as much as possible and not to answer evil by evil, because vindication belongs only to God the judge of all; if we cannot avoid the malice that they have contrived against us except by knocking them down, then and only then is it permitted to preserve our life and existence by all means possible and to prevent their violence with our strength, their design with our designs, their deceit with our deceit, their spear with our spear; for God gave us reason and strength that we preserve our life and health, and escape from the nets and oppression of wrongdoers. If we cannot attain this we should be patient and should leave our anxieties to God, and let him judge us and vindicate us, and beg him to save and free us from the oppression of men. Unless we are forced in this way, we should not afflict any man with any injury in word or deed; we ought scrupulously to keep away, from all lie, calumny, evil speech, theft, adultery, beating, murder, from any action from which a damage or a loss for our fellow man may result; all these go against the order of the creator, destroy all the laws of nature, extinguish the love and harmony of which all men have an equal need."

CHAPTER XIV / LOVE

As a mouse spoils with its teeth fine vestments of great value, but is not nourished with them, likewise the human tongue, that destroys a good name with calumnies, gets no advantage from the calumny: a good name is more valuable than fine cloth and all possessions. Just as hail destroys the corn, but as soon as it falls loses its violence, so does calumny which falls from the mouth of men: at the same time it disgraces one's fellow man and ruins the calumniator. As fire burns the house of the builder, man's anger burns his own entrails. O my son! do not be angry in any way whatsoever, lest you regret it bitterly; never let the sun set on your anger. But turn back from your error with ease, and if you have sinned against your neighbour, do not delay to come to yourself again, get up at once and repair with goodness the evil you have inflicted upon him; reconcile yourself with him that peace may reign and God bless you, be a peace-loving man with all and let not an evil word come from your mouth. Be kind and console the troubled and the sad, and God will give you a good reward. Remember to give alms; if you have bread, share it with your brothers who are hungry, and God will fill you with his goods; if you have the power, liberate your opposed brothers, and God will liberate you and will not unleash the rod of sinners in your heritage; if you are wise, have pity on those who lack science, and God will permit you to understand his mysteries and will open to you his secret wisdom. If you can, try to please all men; for the Lord our God is love. He who always loves his friend and pleases him is with God and God is with him. Mutual love embellishes man's entire life; it makes all our afflictions easier to bear; it adds flavour and sweetness to our whole life; it makes this world the kingdom of heaven. But our love is not to be only words or mere talk, but something real and active. Let us not be like the Christians of our country, who teach the love of Jesus Christ with their lips, but do not have love in their heart; they throw insults and curses at one another, and fight about their faith. This kind of love is not from God, it is useless. Let us not pretend to love one another like these hypocrites whose lips speak of justice and love, but with viper's venom under their tongue, whose heart is always meditating hatred and enmity. Let us not love one another like those who love their relatives, their friends, those who share their faith, but hate the aliens and those who do not belong to their faith; their love is not perfect, we ought to know that all men are equal by creation and all are sons of God; we err if we hate them on account of their faith because each man should believe what seems true to him. Faith cannot be strengthened or made to appear right in the heart of men by force and excommunication but by science and doctrine; as we should not hate men because of their science, so should we not hate them because of their faith.

CHAPTER XVIII / THE IMPORTANCE OF HANDICRAFT

Love to work with your hands as much as your life allows, and be expert in this work that you may gain a profit from it; do not be ashamed to work with your hands, because it is God's precept; without work of their hands all human creatures perish and their whole life is destroyed. Do not say: "Hard work is suitable to the poor and workers, the blacksmiths and the builders, to the sons of artisans, not to the sons of important and noble persons"; such a thought is born from a proud heart. Are not the needs of our life equally exacting for each single person? As the needs of our life are not satisfied except through handwork, likewise work is imposed on each one so that he will fulfil his needs; do not say: "I have all I need to be able to eat and drink without work"; this springs from vicious laziness and destroys the order of the creator who said: "You shall eat from the fruit of your work." He who lives on the work of another man while he has himself the ability to work is a thief and plunderer. Acquaint yourself with manual labour in your childhood, carefully avoid laziness, for an idle person is not worthy of God's grace. Do your work so that at the right time you may provide for your own needs, and those of your family and the poor you help. Let not your heart be beaten down if the fruit of your work is wasted or lost, but persevere in your work and pray to God that he bless this fruit and multiply it. Do not exhaust yourself as animals with no power of thinking, but lay out your work wisely so that you will increase usefulness and profit, and lessen fatigue. If God makes your work prosper and you gather its fruit, thank him with all your heart and rejoice with all your family; eat, drink, celebrate a feast of joy and enjoyment, and persevere in your work so that you may add fruit to the fruit already found in your work, and profit to the profit already gained. Never say: "I have enough," do not say either: "This small amount is enough for my life; why should I labour uselessly?" This utterance stems from a hopeless laziness. Acquire as much as you can without dishonesty; enjoy all the goods you have acquired by the sweat of your brow, and be like the creator: as our creator created from nothing by his power and wisdom all the goods of this world that we see, so you also produce by your own effort and wisdom from your work some good fruit for your life and that of your fellow man.

CHAPTER XXVI / THE WAY OF LIVING

Be patient among yourselves about your difficult character and your hidden defects, because in the whole world there cannot be found a man or a woman without vice. A wise man put it thus: "If a man was without vice he would not die, because he would not be a man." O man, remember that a woman is weak by nature and less intelligent than man. Therefore bear patiently with the harshness of her nature and the loquacity of her tongue, let her anger pass away, not giving it too great importance, and never quarrel with her: if you get used to this type of life, it will be easy for you. As to you, O woman, please your husband, as much as you can; give him delight by your food and drink, and by taking good care of his house and life; your husband cannot love you unless you love him; if you love him, he cannot hate you.

There was a man whose wife was lazy and unkind. So the husband disliked her and began going to another woman; then the wife became jealous; she went to a doctor and said: "My husband hates me; give me a medicine that will make him love me." He said: "I shall prepare it for you, but first go and get me three pieces of hair from the mane of a lion, I need them for the potion." While she was going away she asked herself: "How can I approach a lion and yet avoid that he devour me?" Then she took a sheep with her and went to a field; the lion came out seeking to devour her: she threw the sheep to it and ran away. The lion, having found food to eat, did not chase her. On the next day, she did the same thing and for many days she repeated the same action, because jealousy for her husband had taken hold of her. As the lion saw that the woman was bringing her food, it no more turned against her, but became familiar with her; when she came with the sheep, it received her with delight swishing its tail and, like a dog, it licked her hand and played with her. Then the woman plucked three pieces of hair from its mane and brought them to the doctor. She said to him: "Here, I have brought to you what is needed for the medicine." He said: "How did you manage to pluck them?" When she had narrated to him all she had done, he said to her: "Go, do to your husband what you did to the lion, and your husband will like you; do you think that your husband is wilder than the lion? As you won the love of the lion by giving it food, so you can win the love of your husband." Then she went and began to follow the doctor's advice; she pleased her husband in all things and was patient; after a few days the husband thought in his heart and said: "Why should I love other women more than my wife; she is good and helps me more than they do?" Then he turned to her and loved her very much.

CHAPTER XXX / SUGGESTIONS FOR A PRUDENT LIFE

Do not trust everyone who comes to you; for he who trusts everyone he meets is foolish. Examine everything and hold on to what is good. Beware once for all of your enemies, but a thousand times of your friend, for he discloses your secrets. Your secret is bound to your heart as long as it is in your heart, once it is spoken out from your mouth, you are bound to the bond of your listener. Do not trust in men's gifts, but trust in your prudence, your action and the fruit of your work. Above all, trust in the gifts and favours of God; do not trust your friends, because tomorrow they will be your enemies. Rely on the work of your hands, which should not exceed your power. Love those who are associated with you and who are close to you and act as if you trusted them; but in reality trust no one absolutely; and in all society you take part in, search first of all an escape by which you can keep out of men's traps, should they wish evil for you. Be alert; all men who appear good to you are not really so, and all those who once did good to you will not always do so. Beware not to fall into men's traps; fear God and do not force any evil upon them, nor pay back evil with evil to those who harmed you, but let God take care of your worry and leave men's malice come back upon the heads of those who do it. Never say within your heart: "My enemies have done evil to me, so I too will pay back evil to them." This is vain; it will not help you to live with people; it leads to quarrels and enmities without end; it is better that you hide in your heart all the injustices men perpetrated against you.

CHAPTER XXXIV / HAPPINESS AND HOPE

When you fall ill, bear with patience even your great affliction, and do not lose courage; trust in God who sees and takes into account the suffering of your sickness, and will reward you well for your patience. Even if he does not pay you in this life, he will reward you after your death when you come to him. Do not fear to depart from life, because death is a liberation: when it will please God to release you from this prison so that you may go to him, thank him; it is a greater advantage to you that you be liberated from this shameful servitude, and fly free and bright like an angel to the bosom of your creator; there you will know and understand all the mysteries of this world and the beauty of the order of heaven and earth; you will enjoy perfect bliss, and possess perpetual and infinite beatitude. Do not love the absurdities of this world—a world in which you must remain until your term of servitude and trial is completed; it is not right for you to leave this world by your own will; this depends on the will of God, who imposed this servitude upon you. If the time for your liberation has come and it pleases God to release you from your prison, adore him with great humility, thank him, and go to him in joy and confidence. Behold, he will reward you with a life which surpasses all life in this world. Pray to him that he grant you a quiet death and that he may take you away from this world in peace and confidence in him; fear none of the things that frighten the wicked, who did not want to follow the path the creator had traced for them in this world, and who refused to perform the service fixed for all men, who did not understand God's works nor follow the natural law that reason taught them.

But you, my brother, who accept and approve my counselling do not be afraid at the hour of death, for it is better for you to go to your creator. Oh! why do you fear death, when you know that the immortal soul has a greater value than the mortal flesh? Is not freedom more valuable than servitude, joy than sadness, life than death? Likewise, it is better for the soul to be liberated from the prison of the body than to be bound to it. As a man freed from prison sees the light of the sun which gives him delight and heat, likewise our soul, come out of the body, will contemplate God's light and will burn with love for its creator; turning back it will glance at the loss of this world and say with astonishment: "How could I love that ignoble servitude? How did I fear a death which brought me into this beatitude for ever and ever?" Amen.

CHAPTER XXXV / CONCLUSION

Behold, I have written these few things, with the help of God. My brother who have read this book of mine, if you are wise, you too write down the things God taught you. Do not be like a lamp that is put under a tub, but raise up the light of your wisdom; teach and counsel the sons of our country, that wisdom may flourish and sin and ignorance of the right way of behaving may disappear from our land. These men did not know the mighty arm of our creator; had they known it, they would have been ashamed of striving after what is futile. In fact in our days our foolish countrymen, moved by jealousy, have quarrelled among themselves about the institutions of their faith; but they have failed to recognize the order of their creator.

O Lord, we know no other God but you, and we invoke your name and no other; we have not abandoned your doctrine for the doctrine of men, for your precept is the light on earth. Give us peace, since you have given us all; delight us with the dew of your blessing, and protect us that we may worship you in truth and justice. Because yours are glory and honour, now, and for all eternity, world without end. Amen.

CONTEMPORARY PERSPECTIVES

Contemporary African philosophy is strikingly vibrant and varied. Some African philosophers show the influence of Marx or African nationalism; others write in the Anglo-American tradition. Though suffering from their continent's political instability—several prominent African philosophers are now in the United States, for example, having been forced to leave their home countries—these thinkers have forged an African philosophical community.

Frantz Fanon (1925–1961), born on the Caribbean island of Martinique, studied psychiatry in France. At twenty-seven he published *Black Skin, White Masks.* Shortly thereafter, he was assigned to a hospital in Algeria during the war of independence with France. Aligning himself with the rebels, he wrote *A Dying Colonialism* and *The Wretched of the Earth.* The latter appeared in 1961, just before Fanon died of cancer. Jean-Paul Sartre said of Fanon in his preface to the book, "In short, the Third World finds *itself* and speaks to *itself* through his voice."*

Fanon begins with the premise that the world is not homogeneous. It consists of many different peoples and cultures. Some enjoy positions of power and privilege; others suffer oppression. Their oppression stems from many kinds of power and privilege, but, ultimately, it rests on actual or threatened violence. Colonial powers dominate the Third World because they have used, continue to use, and threaten to use violence to maintain their power.

Decolonialization is the process of overcoming colonial oppression by overturning current relations of power. Because those relations rest on violence, Fanon argues, only violence can overturn them. To destroy the colonial world with its two sharp divisions, oppressors and oppressed, one must destroy the half of that world consisting of the oppressors.

The colonial world also gives rise to psychological conditions that must be overcome. The oppressors paint the oppressed as barely human, as masses of animals without feelings or autonomy. To overcome the oppression and assert their own interests, the oppressed must first overcome this image of themselves. This too requires violence. Both real and psychological liberation can come about only through violence. Violence, Fanon therefore concludes, is the only way to liberate the oppressed. Moreover, it is not an unfortunate but necessary step, to be regretted deeply but undertaken nevertheless; rather, it is itself liberating and ought to be celebrated. As Sartre summarizes Fanon's view, "Violence, like Achilles' lance, can heal the wounds it has inflicted."†

This defense and even celebration of violence is so unusual in the philosophical tradition and has become so influential in parts of the Third World that it makes

*Jean-Paul Sartre, in the preface to Fanon's *The Wretched of the Earth,* trans. Constance Farrington (Grove Press, 1963), 10.

† Preface to *The Wretched of the Earth,* 30.

Fanon's thought worth studying. But Fanon's views have other important philosophical dimensions. Fanon, for example, attacks individualism as a tool of the oppressors. With liberation, he writes, "Individualism is the first to disappear." Many Western and non-Western thinkers adopt a communitarian view, according to which human beings are essentially social. Fanon agrees, but he argues that individualism is nothing but a method for preventing the oppressed from coming together and cooperating to overthrow their oppression. Moreover, he takes this position to its full anti-individualist conclusion. "Henceforward, the interests of one will be the interests of all. . . . The motto 'look out for yourself,' the atheist's method of salvation, is in this context prohibited." Thus, there can be no private property, no individual rights: "Resources should be pooled."*

Fanon also attacks the notion of truth. At least in the context of colonialism, truth is simply what serves the interests of the group. When the oppressors speak of truth, they really speak of what serves their own interests as oppressors. When the revolutionaries speak of truth, they speak of what "hurries on the break-up of the colonialist regime." There is no such thing as truth in itself. There is no such thing as good in itself, either. What is good is what promotes the revolution and works against the interests of the oppressors. In this sense, Fanon is not so much an ethical thinker as an antiethical thinker.

While Fanon's assault on individualism, private property, and ethics itself largely follows the analysis of Marx and Engels in *The Communist Manifesto* and other writings, his attack on truth takes their view one step further. Marx and Engels are willing to assail morality as a capitalist tool, but they do not generalize this to an attack on truth in every area. In fact, they regard dialectical materialism as the only proper scientific attitude. *Dialectical materialism* is the view that matter alone is real and that it changes in a logical, intelligible pattern—called *dialectic*—as a result of class struggle. Fanon's criticisms suggest that there is something wrong with the idea of a "proper scientific attitude" and with the idea of truth underlying it.

Kwasi Wiredu, one of Africa's leading English-speaking philosophers, criticizes Marx and Engels and, with them, his colleagues who rely on them for their conceptions of philosophy and society. Wiredu begins by observing that Marxist societies have almost invariably produced oppression and systematic violation of individual rights. Why? Because of failings intrinsic to Marxist thought, he answers. Marx and Marxists such as Fanon take truth to be historically determined. In one sense, Wiredu contends, this is true; in another, surely false—even by the canons of Marxism itself. He argues that the Marxist distinction between science and ideology, properly applied, counts Marxism itself as ideological; that Marxism not only has no real ethics, but also is inconsistent with ethical restraints; and that the basic principles of Marxist theory are confused.

* Fanon, *Wretched of the Earth*, 49.

FRANTZ FANON

from *The Wretched of the Earth*

CONCERNING VIOLENCE

National liberation, national renaissance, the restoration of nationhood to the people, commonwealth: whatever may be the headings used or the new formulas introduced, decolonization is always a violent phenomenon. At whatever level we study it—relationships between individuals, new names for sports clubs, the human admixture at cocktail parties, in the police, on the directing boards of national or private banks—decolonization is quite simply the replacing of a certain "species" of men by another "species" of men. Without any period of transition, there is a total, complete, and absolute substitution. It is true that we could equally well stress the rise of a new nation, the setting up of a new state, its diplomatic relations, and its economic and political trends. But we have precisely chosen to speak of that kind of *tabula rasa* which characterizes at the outset all decolonization. Its unusual importance is that it constitutes, from the very first day, the minimum demands of the colonized. To tell the truth, the proof of success lies in a whole social structure being changed from the bottom up. The extraordinary importance of this change is that it is willed, called for, demanded. The need for this change exists in its crude state, impetuous and compelling, in the consciousness and in the lives of the men and women who are colonized. But the possibility of this change is equally experienced in the form of a terrifying future in the consciousness of another "species" of men and women: the colonizers.

Decolonization, which sets out to change the order of the world, is, obviously, a program of complete disorder. But it cannot come as a result of magical practices, nor of a natural shock, nor of a friendly understanding. Decolonization, as we know, is a historical process: that is to say that it cannot be understood, it cannot become intelligible nor clear to itself except in the exact measure that we can discern the movements which give it historical form and content. Decolonization is the meeting of two forces, opposed to each other by their very nature, which in fact owe their originality to that sort of substantification which results from and is nourished by the situation in the colonies. Their first encounter was marked by violence and their existence together—that is to say the exploitation of the native by the settler—was carried on by dint of a great array of bayonets and cannons. The settler and the native are old acquaintances. In fact, the settler is right when he speaks of knowing "them" well. For it is the settler who has brought the native into existence and who perpetuates his existence. The settler owes the fact of his very existence, that is to say, his property, to the colonial system.

Decolonization never takes place unnoticed, for it influences individuals and modifies them fundamentally. It transforms spectators crushed with their inessentiality into privileged actors, with the grandiose glare of history's floodlights upon them. It brings a natural rhythm into existence, introduced by new men, and with it a new language and a new humanity. Decolonization is the veritable creation of new men. But this creation owes nothing of its legitimacy to any supernatural power; the "thing" which has been colonized becomes man during the same process by which it frees itself.

In decolonization, there is therefore the need of a complete calling in question of the colonial situation. If we wish to describe it precisely, we might find it in the well-known words: "The last shall be first and the first last." Decolonization is the putting into practice of this sentence. That is why, if we try to describe it, all decolonization is successful.

The naked truth of decolonization evokes for us the searing bullets and bloodstained knives which emanate from it. For if the last shall be first, this will only come to pass after a murderous and decisive struggle between the two protagonists. That affirmed intention to place the last at the head of things, and to make them climb at a pace (too quickly, some say) the well-known steps which characterize an organized society, can only triumph if we use all means to turn the scale, including, of course, that of violence.

You do not turn any society, however primitive it may be, upside down with such a program if you have not decided from the very beginning, that is to say from the actual formulation of that program, to overcome all the obstacles that you will come across in so doing. The native who decides to put the program into practice, and to become its moving force, is ready for violence at all times. From birth it is clear to him that this narrow world, strewn with prohibitions, can only be called in question by absolute violence.

The colonial world is a world divided into compartments. It is probably unnecessary to recall the existence of native quarters and European quarters, of schools for natives and schools for Europeans; in the same way we need not recall apartheid in South Africa. Yet, if we examine closely this system of compartments, we will at least be able to reveal the lines of force it implies. This approach to the colonial world, its ordering and its geographical layout will allow us to mark out the lines on which a decolonized society will be reorganized.

The colonial world is a world cut in two. The dividing line, the frontiers are shown by barracks and police stations. In the colonies it is the policeman and the soldier who are the official, instituted go-betweens, the spokesmen of the settler and his rule of oppression. In capitalist societies the educational system, whether lay or clerical, the structure of moral reflexes handed down from father to son, the exemplary honesty of workers who are given a medal after fifty years of good and loyal service, and the affection which springs from harmonious relations and good behavior—all these aesthetic expressions of respect for the established order serve to create around the exploited person an atmosphere of submission and of inhibition which lightens the task of policing considerably. In the capitalist countries a multitude of moral teachers, counselors and "bewilderers" separate the exploited from those in power. In the colonial countries, on the contrary, the policeman and the soldier, by their immediate presence and their frequent and direct action maintain contact with the native and advise him by means of rifle butts and napalm not to budge. It is obvious here that the agents of government speak the language of pure force. The intermediary does not lighten the oppression, nor seek to hide the domination; he shows them up and puts them into practice with the clear conscience of an upholder of the peace; yet he is the bringer of violence into the home and into the mind of the native. . . .

This world divided into compartments, this world cut in two is inhabited by two different species. The originality of the colonial context is that economic reality, inequality, and the immense difference of ways of life never come to mask the human realities. When you examine at close quarters the colonial context, it is evident that what parcels out the world is to begin with the fact of belonging to or not belonging to a given race, a given species. In the colonies the economic substructure is also a superstructure. The cause is the consequence; you are rich because you are white, you are white because you are rich. . . .

. . . In the colonies, the foreigner coming from another country imposed his rule by means of guns and machines. In defiance of his successful transplantation, in spite of his appropriation, the settler still remains a foreigner. It is neither the act of owning factories, nor estates, nor a bank balance which distinguishes the governing classes. The governing race is first and foremost those who come from elsewhere, those who are unlike the original inhabitants, "the others."

The violence which has ruled over the ordering of the colonial world, which has ceaselessly drummed the rhythm for the destruction of native social forms and broken up without reserve the systems of reference of the economy, the customs of dress and external life, that same violence will be claimed and taken over by the native at the moment when, deciding to embody history in his own person, he surges into the forbidden quarters. To wreck the colonial world is henceforward a mental picture of action which is very clear, very easy to understand and which may be assumed by each one of the individuals which constitute the colonized people. To break up the colonial world does not mean that after the frontiers have been abolished lines of communication will be set up between the two zones. The destruction of the colonial world is no more and no less than the abolition of one zone, its burial in the depths of the earth or its expulsion from the country.

The natives' challenge to the colonial world is not a rational confrontation of points of view. It is not a treatise on the universal, but the untidy affirmation of an original idea propounded as an absolute. The colonial world is a Manichean world. It is not enough for the settler to delimit physically, that is to say with the help of the army and the police force, the place of the native. As if to show the totalitarian character of colonial exploitation the settler paints the native as a sort of quintessence of evil. Native society is not simply described as a society lacking in values. It is not enough for the colonist to affirm that those values have disappeared from, or still better never existed in, the colonial world. The native is declared insensible to ethics; he represents not only the absence of values, but also the negation of values. He is, let us dare to admit, the enemy of values, and in this sense he is the absolute evil. He is the corrosive element, destroying all that comes near him; he is the deforming element, disfiguring all that has to do with beauty or morality; he is the depository of maleficent powers, the unconscious and irretrievable instrument of blind forces. . . .

At times this Manicheism goes to its logical conclusion and dehumanizes the native, or to speak plainly, it turns him into an animal. In fact, the terms the settler uses when he mentions the native are zoological terms. He speaks of the yellow man's reptilian motions, of the stink of the native quarter, of breeding swarms, of foulness, of spawn, of gesticulations. When the settler seeks to describe the native fully in exact terms he constantly refers to the bestiary. The European rarely hits on a picturesque style; but the native, who knows what is in the mind of the settler, guesses at once what he is thinking of. Those hordes of vital statistics, those hysterical masses, those faces bereft of all humanity, those distended bodies which are like nothing on earth, that mob without beginning or end, those children who seem to belong to nobody, that laziness stretched out in the sun, that vegetative rhythm of life—all this forms part of the colonial vocabulary. General de Gaulle speaks of "the yellow multitudes" and François Mauriac of the black, brown, and yellow masses which soon will be unleashed. The native knows all this, and laughs to himself every time he spots an allusion to the animal world in the other's words. For he knows that he is not an animal; and it is precisely at the moment he realizes his humanity that he begins to sharpen the weapons with which he will secure its victory.

As soon as the native begins to pull on his moorings, and to cause anxiety to the settler, he is handed over to well-meaning souls who in cultural congresses point out to him the specificity and wealth of Western values. But every time Western values are mentioned they produce in the native a sort of stiffening or muscular lockjaw. During the period of decolonization, the native's reason is appealed to. He is offered definite values, he is told frequently that decolonization need not mean regression, and that he must put his trust in qualities which are well-tried, solid, and highly esteemed. But it so happens that when the native hears a speech about Western culture he pulls out his knife—or at least he makes sure it is within reach. The violence with which the supremacy of white values is affirmed and the aggressiveness which has permeated the victory of these values over the ways of life and of thought of the native mean that, in revenge, the native laughs in mockery when Western values are mentioned in front of him. In the colonial context the settler only ends his work of breaking in the native when the latter admits loudly and intelligibly the supremacy of the white man's values. In the period of decolonization, the colonized masses mock at these very values, insult them, and vomit them up.

. . . For a colonized people the most essential value, because the most concrete, is first and foremost the land: the land which will bring them bread and, above all, dignity. But this dignity has nothing to do with the dignity of the human individual: for the human individual has never heard tell of it. All that the native has seen in his country is that they can freely arrest him, beat him, starve him: and no professor of ethics, no priest has ever come to be beaten in his place, nor to share their bread with him. As far as the native is concerned, morality is very concrete; it is to silence the settler's defiance, to break his flaunting violence—in a word, to put him out of the picture. The well-known principle that all men are equal will be illustrated in the colonies from the moment that the native claims that he is the equal of the settler. One step more, and he is ready to fight to be more than the settler. In fact, he has already decided to eject him and to take his place; as we see it, it is a whole material and moral universe which is breaking up. The intellectual who for his part has followed the colonialist with regard to the universal abstract will fight in order that the settler and the native may live together in peace in a new world. But the thing he does not see, precisely because he is permeated by colonialism and all its ways of thinking, is that the settler, from the moment that the colonial context disappears, has no longer any interest in remaining or in co-existing. It is not by chance that, even before any negotiation between the Algerian and French governments has taken place, the European minority which calls itself "liberal" has already made its position clear: it demands nothing more nor less than twofold citizenship. By setting themselves apart in an abstract manner, the liberals try to force the settler into taking a very concrete jump into the unknown. Let us admit it, the settler knows perfectly well that no phraseology can be a substitute for reality.

Thus the native discovers that his life, his breath, his beating heart are the same as those of the settler. He finds out that the settler's skin is not of any more value than a native's skin; and it must be said that this discovery shakes the world in a very necessary manner. All the new, revolutionary assurance of the native stems from it. For if, in fact, my life is worth as much as the settler's, his glance no longer shrivels me up nor freezes me, and his voice no longer turns me into stone. I am no longer on tenterhooks in his presence; in fact, I don't give a damn for him. Not only does his presence no longer trouble me, but I am already preparing such efficient ambushes for him that soon there will be no way out but that of flight.

We have said that the colonial context is characterized by the dichotomy which it imposes upon the whole people. Decolonization unifies that people by the radical decision to remove from it its heterogeneity, and by unifying it on a national, sometimes a racial, basis. We know the fierce words of the Senegalese patriots, referring to the maneuvers of their president, Senghor: "We have demanded that the higher posts should be given to Africans; and now Senghor is Africanizing the Europeans." That is to say that the native can see clearly and immediately if decolonization has come to pass or not, for his minimum demands are simply that the last shall be first. . . .

Individualism is the first to disappear. The native intellectual had learnt from his masters that the individual ought to express himself fully. The colonialist bourgeoisie had hammered into the native's mind the idea of a society of individuals where each person shuts himself up in his own subjectivity, and whose only wealth is individual thought. Now the native who has the opportunity to return to the people during the struggle for freedom will discover the falseness of this theory. The very forms of organization of the struggle will suggest to him a different vocabulary. Brother, sister, friend—these are words outlawed by the colonialist bourgeoisie, because for them my brother is my purse, my friend is part of my scheme for getting on. The native intellectual takes part, in a sort of auto-da-fé, in the destruction of all his idols: egoism, recrimination that springs from pride, and the childish stupidity of those who always want to have the last word. Such a colonized intellectual, dusted over by colonial culture, will in the same way discover the substance of village assemblies, the cohesion of people's committees, and the extraordinary fruitfulness of local meetings and groupments. Henceforward, the interests of one will be the interests of all, for in concrete fact *everyone* will be discovered by the troops, *everyone* will be massacred—or *everyone* will be saved. The motto "look out for yourself," the atheist's method of salvation, is in this context forbidden.

. . . The people . . . take their stand from the start on the broad and inclusive positions of *bread and the land:* how can we obtain the land, and bread to eat? And this obstinate point of view of the masses, which may seem shrunken and limited, is in the end the most worthwhile and the most efficient mode of procedure.

The problem of truth ought also to be considered. In every age, among the people, truth is the property of the national cause. No absolute verity, no discourse on the purity of the soul, can shake this position. The native replies to the living lie of the colonial situation by an equal falsehood. His dealings with his fellow-nationals are open; they are strained and incomprehensible with regard to the settlers. Truth is that which hurries on the break-up of the colonialist regime; it is that which promotes the emergence of the nation; it is all that protects the natives, and ruins the foreigners. In this colonialist context there is no truthful behavior: and the good is quite simply that which is evil for "them." . . .

The peasantry is systematically disregarded for the most part by the propaganda put out by the nationalist parties. And it is clear that in the colonial countries the peasants alone are revolutionary, for they have nothing to lose and everything to gain. The starving peasant, outside the class system, is the first among the exploited to discover that only violence pays. For him there is no compromise, no possible coming to terms; colonization and decolonization are simply a question of relative strength. The exploited man sees that his liberation implies the use of all means, and that of force first and foremost. When in 1956, after the capitulation of Monsieur Guy Mollet to the settlers in Algeria, the Front de Libération Nationale, in a famous leaflet, stated that colonialism only loosens its hold when the knife is at its throat, no Algerian really found these terms too violent. The leaflet only expressed what every Algerian felt at heart: colonialism is not a thinking machine, nor a body endowed with reasoning faculties. It is violence in its natural state, and it will only yield when confronted with greater violence. . . .

What is the real nature of this violence? We have seen that it is the intuition of the colonized masses that their liberation must, and can only, be achieved by force. By what spiritual aberration do these men, without technique, starving and enfeebled, confronted with the military and economic might of the occupation, come to believe that violence alone will free them? How can they hope to triumph?

It is because violence (and this is the disgraceful thing) may constitute, in so far as it forms part of its system, the slogan of a political party. The leaders may call on the people to enter upon an armed struggle. This problematical question has to be thought over. When militarist Germany decides to settle its frontier disputes by force, we are not in the least surprised; but when the people of Angola, for example, decide to take up arms, when the Algerian people reject all means which are not violent, these are proofs that something has happened or is happening at this very moment. The colonized races, those slaves of modern times, are impatient. They know that this apparent folly alone can put them out of reach of colonial oppression. A new type of relations is established in the world. The underdeveloped peoples try to break their chains, and the extraordinary thing is that they succeed. It could be argued that in these days of sputniks it is ridiculous to die of hunger; but for the colonized masses the argument is more down-to-earth. The truth is that there is no colonial power today which is capable of adopting the only form of contest which has a chance of succeeding, namely, the prolonged establishment of large forces of occupation. . . .

We have said that the native's violence unifies the people. By its very structure, colonialism is separatist and regionalist. Colonialism does not simply state the existence of tribes; it also reinforces it and separates them. The colonial system encourages chieftaincies and keeps alive the old Marabout confraternities. Violence is in action all-inclusive and national. It follows that it is closely involved in the liquidation of regionalism and of tribalism. Thus the national parties show no pity at all toward the caids and the customary chiefs. Their destruction is the preliminary to the unification of the people.

At the level of individuals, violence is a cleansing force. It frees the native from his inferiority complex and from his despair and inaction; it makes him fearless and restores his self-respect. Even if the armed struggle has been symbolic and the nation is demobilized through a rapid movement of decolonization, the people have the time to see that the liberation has been the business of each and all and that the leader has no special merit. From thence comes that type of aggressive reticence with regard to the machinery of protocol which young governments quickly show. When the people have taken violent part in the national liberation they will allow no one to set themselves up as "liberators." They show themselves to be jealous of the results of their action and take good care not to place their future, their destiny, or the fate of their country in the hands of a living god. Yesterday they were completely irresponsible; today they mean to understand everything and make all decisions. Illuminated by violence, the consciousness of the people rebels against any pacification. From now on the demagogues, the opportunists, and the magicians have a difficult task. The action which has thrown them into a hand-to-hand struggle confers upon the masses a voracious taste for the concrete. The attempt at mystification becomes, in the long run, practically impossible. . . .

KWASI WIREDU

from *Philosophy and an African Culture*

History and the contemporary scene are both witnesses to the fact that, when attempts have been made to base social and political organisation on Marxism, results have tended to take the form of authoritarianism—monolithic single party supremacy, harshly enforced conformity to a single doctrine, and so forth.

We are here faced with a major paradox. How is it that a philosophy which advocates such an admirable doctrine as the humanistic conception of truth tends so often to lead in practice to the suppression of freedom of thought and expression? Is it by accident that this comes to be so? Or is it due to causes internal to the philosophy of Marx and Engels?

Faced with this problem, many good and reputable scholars sympathetic to the Marxist standpoint have taken the line of blaming the evils on the shortcomings of the individual politicans involved. The fault, they have said, lies not in the doctrine itself but in its practitioners. An explanation of this sort is likely, at best, to have only a partial validity, and is to be resorted to only in the proven absence of, or in addition to, more internal reasons. . . .

. . . The Marxist doctrine itself—or shall we say the Marxist assortment of doctrines?—has an authoritarian trait which can, I think, be traced to the conception of philosophy to be found in Marx and Engels.

As we have seen, Engels recognises the cognition of truth to be a legitimate business of philosophy and makes a number of excellent points about truth. As soon, however, as one tries to find out what he and Marx conceived philosophy to be like, one is faced with a deep obscurity. The problem revolves round what one may describe as Marx's conception of philosophy as ideology.

What, then, is an ideology? The term "ideology" was first used by a group of philosophically inclined authors in France around the closing decade of the eighteenth century. These authors sought to elucidate ideas through anthropological study. Ideology was, for them, a science of ideas, a certain scientific approach to the interpretation of ideas. It so happened that their notion of the scheme of things differed markedly from that of Napoleon Bonaparte—a circumstance which evoked from Bonaparte, a contemptuous reference to them as the "ideologists." In Napoleon's intended meaning, an "ideologist" was a visionary, a doctrinaire proponent of unrealistic conceptions. The jibe proved fateful. From then on and for a long time the term was to take on the pejorative significance with which Bonaparte had invested it. Marx's conception of ideology in *The German Ideology*, a work which he wrote jointly with Engels, reflects the influence both of the original meaning of the term and the Napoleonic distortion of it. The two shades of meaning are, however, transmuted under Marx's systematic attention.

'Ideology', for Marx and Engels, meant a set of illusory beliefs constituting a reflex or reflection of material conditions in the minds of those who held them.* The relation expressed by the word 'reflex' is also frequently expressed by the word 'determination'. I shall try to substantiate this interpretation with quotations from the text of Marx and Engels. "As individuals express their lives, so they are," declare the founders of Marxism. "What they are [therefore] coincides with their production, both with what they produce and with how they produce. The nature of individuals thus depends on the material conditions determining their production" (*The German Ideology*, ed. R. Pascal, New York, 1947, p. 7). The individual, of course, "expresses" his life, in part, by means of ideas. Hence the deterministic correlation suggested in the quotation must be held to apply to the relation between ideas and material conditions. Note that no exceptions are here allowed.

A little later in the same work, Marx and Engels are more explicit: "The production of ideas, of conceptions, *of consciousness*" (my italics) or in other words, but still sticking to the words of Marx and Engels, "conceiving, thinking and the intercourse of men" are "the direct efflux of their material behaviour." "The same," they declare in the next sentence, "applies to the mental production as expressed in the language of politics, laws, morality, religion, metaphysics of a people." Still referring to these things, they remark in the same paragraph, that "in all ideology, men and their circumstances appear upside down." "Ideological reflexes" are "phantoms formed in the human brain" which "are also, necessarily, sublimates of their material life-process" (*ibid.*, p. 14). When propounded by the thinkers of the ruling class, ideology is nothing, according to Marx and Engels, but "the ideal expression of the dominant material relationship grasped as ideas . . . the illusion of the class about itself" (*ibid.*, pp. 39–40).

As for philosophy, it is, apparently, "empty talk about consciousness" which should cease: "Where speculation ends—in real life—there real positive science begins: the representation of the practical activity, of the practical process of development of men. Empty talk about consciousness ceases, and real knowledge has to take its place. When reality is depicted, philosophy as an independent branch of activity loses its medium of existence. At best its place can only be taken by a summing up of the most general results, abstractions which arise from the observation of the historical development of men" (*ibid.*, p. 15).

Philosophy, then, is an ideological reflex which is *ipso facto* a system of illusions. Where philosophy ends, there, according to Marx and Engels, real "positive science" begins. The word 'science', thus pressed into service, proves to be a magic wand. Marx applies it to his own speculations—dialectical materialism and all—to transform them from the status of ideology, presumable under the given hypothesis, to that of empirical truth. The same is, of course, not conceded to "bourgeois" philosophers, who are condemned to perpetual self-deception. There is obvious special pleading here; but for the moment, let us consider the epistemological consequences of the ideological conception of philosophy. To begin with, take any philosophical proposition, e.g. "To be is to be perceived." What does it mean to say that such a proposition reflects

* It is surely to be accounted something of a "world historical" irony that the followers of Marx now yield ground to none in their insistence on the necessity and importance of ideology. Marx and Engels seldom used the term "ideology" except in contempt. As late in life as 1893 (he died in 1896) Engels still spoke of ideology as "false consciousness."

a certain set of material conditions? Normally, one should expect that if a proposition reflects a set of conditions, that would be considered good reason for saying that the proposition is true of those conditions. It is, moreover, exactly in this sense of the word "reflect" that, in *Anti-Dühring*, Engels, and in *Materialism and Empirio-Criticism,* Lenin, insisted in their rather naïve theory of perception that our ideas (i.e. perceptual ideas) are reflections or copies or images of independently existing external things.

Presumably, what is wrong with ideology is not the alleged fact that it reflects material conditions but rather that it reflects them upside down. To revert to the relevant passages of *The German Ideology* again, we find that Marx and Engels actually compare ideology to the phenomenon of inversion in a *camera obscura* and also on the retina. On this analogy a proposition belonging to the sphere of ideology must be supposed to invert the truth about the material circumstances of its author and his relationship to them. This implies, of course, that such a proposition must be false. Thus we have to say, on this showing, that a proposition like "To be is to be perceived" is false because (apart from any other possible reason) it is an inversion of the truth about the material circumstances of its author, Bishop Berkeley, and others of his class. Notice that, since the contradictory of Berkeley's thesis was maintained by people belonging to the Bishop's class, that too must be supposed to invert the truth about the same material conditions and must be declared to be false, contrary to, at least, the laws of classical logic. Notice, too, that the fact that the thesis in question does not seem to be about the material circumstances of its author at all does not apparently stop it from inverting the truth about them. It is not surprising that philosophy does not survive the easy devastation of such a critique.

The same devastation results from the ideological interpretation of philosophy when couched in terms of the notion of the *determination* of ideas by material conditions. The notion, itself, of determination is advanced with remarkable lack of ceremony. "Life," declare Marx and Engels, "is not determined by consciousness but consciousness by life" (*ibid.*, p. 15). Note, incidentally, the curious use of the words "life" and "consciousness" in that sentence. The intended meaning of "consciousness" here is obviously "thinking, the production of ideas." Thus, Marx earlier in the cited work uses the term "consciousness" in straightforward apposition to the term "conception." He speaks of "the production of ideas, of conceptions, of consciousness" (*ibid.*, p. 13). Yet, on the next page it is asserted: "Consciousness can never be anything else than conscious existence and the existence of men is their actual life process" (*ibid.*, p. 14). If so, then, of course, consciousness is equal to life; and it is, accordingly, meaningless to talk of consciousness being determined by life. I am not simply hair-splitting in these animadversions. I am proceeding in this way out of a suspicion that such carelessness in the use of cardinal terms may be symptomatic of deep inadequacies of thought. Let us charitably suppose that all that the sentence in question means is that "ideas are determined by the material conditions of life." This is certainly something which Marx and Engels seem anxious to assert. The point now is that this particular doctrine of determination makes nonsense of the very concept of truth. It constitutes, moreover, a complete reversal of all the well delivered points about the nature of truth which Engels makes in the passages quoted earlier on from his essay on Feuerbach. If all ideas are determined; and to be determined is to be false; then it follows that truth is impossible.

This point is worth emphasising. The bite that the theory of ideology seems to have derives from just this implication: that if and when one has shown that a set of ideas are determined by a definite development of productive forces and of the relations corresponding to them, one has thereby shown them not to have any independent claims to truth. This, surely, is the point of calling the ideas "phantoms" in the human brain, "sublimates" of the material life-process. Were it to be suggested that the theory had no such implication, so that the alleged determination of the ideas by material conditions did not affect the question of their truth or falsity, it would be a deep mystery why the authors of *The German Ideology* could have imagined that they had made a case for the cessation of philosophy. Previously, metaphysicians had claimed to reveal the ultimate nature of reality. If the theory of ideology does not necessarily imply that their ideas were false* then by what logic does the theory assert an exclusive disjunction between philosophy and the depiction of reality? ("When reality is depicted, philosophy as an independent branch of activity loses its medium of existence.") Of course, if Marx and Engels are right about philosophy's being determined by material conditions, it would follow tautologically that it is not independent of them. However, if, in spite of this lack of independence, philosophical propositions might conceivably be true, then their demise can only be brought about by the kind of intellectual argumentation that is so strikingly absent from *The German Ideology.*

A defender of Marx might like to remind me that, as I myself have noted earlier, Mark distinguishes between scientific thinking and ideology. Truth, he might argue, is impossible only in the sphere of ideology not science. Marx's own philosophy being scientific, does not suffer from the inescapable disabilities of ideology. *The German Ideology* has already been quoted as saying that the place of philosophy is to be taken by a certain mode of generalising about the historical development of man, while in *Anti-Dühring,* having asserted that modern materialism has rendered all former philosophy superfluous, Engels proceeds: "What still independently survives of all former philosophy is the science of thought and its laws—formal logic and dialectics" (p. 40).

I would ask such a defender of Marx to explain how Marx, an individual whose consciousness is, by hypothesis, determined by some mode of production could possibly attain to an undetermined truth. Or, are we to say that scientific thinking is not part of "consciousness"? I concede that to suppose that scientific thinking is not part of consciousness would make it conceivable that the conceptions of Marx are true. However, in the absence of any pre-established rules for determining what does and what does not come under consciousness such a supposition is apt to be arbitrary. But let that pass.

Let us assume, for the purposes of argument, that scientific thinking is not part of consciousness and is not therefore ideological. We assume further, for the same purpose, that the theories of Marx are scientific. Now, to say that a proposition is scientific is not necessarily to say that it is true. It is merely to say that it belongs to a certain general class of propositions, i.e. the class of propositions arrived at through scientific method. In other words, saying that a proposition is scientific means simply that it is such as to be capable of being shown to be true or false, probable or improbable, by the processes of observation or experimentation or conceptual analysis or logical deduction or all of them jointly and that it is backed by some such processes of cognition. It follows that if a proposition is scientific, its negation also is potentially scientific. Furthermore, if a proposition is scientific, its strict contrary must be potentially scientific. By the strict contrary of a proposition I mean another proposition containing exactly the same concepts but in a different order such that this proposition and the original one cannot be true together but can be false together. What a proposition is about is determined by its constituent concepts. If two propositions contain the same concepts then they are about the same subject matter. They must, consequently, be both potentially scientific if one of them is.

Consider now materialism, a basic component of Marxism, and idealism, a doctrine of speculative metaphysics much berated by Marxists. Materialism asserts that matter is primary and mind, derivative. Idealism asserts, contrarily, that mind is primary and matter, derivative. Both, clearly, are *about* the same thing, namely, the relation between mind and matter, and must both be potentially scientific if one of them is. Thus if materialism is scientific, then idealism too is conceivably scientific and cannot be automatically called an ideology in the pejorative sense of Marx and Engels, on the supposition, that is, that what is scientific cannot be ideological.

Marx and Engels are, therefore, on the horns of a dilemma. If all philosophical thinking is ideological, then their own philosophical thinking is ideological and, by their hypothesis, false. If, on the other hand, their philosophical thinking is not ideological then the philosophical thinking of the bourgeoisie is not necessarily ideological.

Marx, as is well-known, had great respect for science. He consequently never declared science, even

* In the abstract there is the possibility that they may be not false, but meaningless. Marx and Engels' theory cannot be said to imply the meaninglessness of the ideas in question since meaningless propositions cannot invert anything.

as developed by the bourgeoisie, to be ideological. Bourgeois thinkers apparently become inescapably ideological only when they venture into law, morality and metaphysics, etc. But to grant even so much is to grant that some aspects of "consciousness" are independent, i.e. not *determined* in the relevant sense. (It is important to note that the determinism here in question is of a different category from the valid kind of determinism which we found to be involved in the humanistic conception of truth.)

As we have seen, Marx admits by implication that science represents an aspect of "consciousness" which is ideologically undetermined. But if this much is admitted, then we need specific reasons for declaring other aspects of consciousness to be ideologically determined. Marx does not seem to have been aware even of the necessity of giving such reasons. He and Engels simply assumed for themselves the privilege of exempting their own philosophising from the ideological theory of ideas. Both of them continued to think and write in recognisably philosophical ways in spite of their theory. Such special pleading is neither philosophy nor science.

Although the ideological conception of philosophy is unacceptable, I believe that a certain amount of sense can be made of what Marx and Engels appear to have in mind. The result, however, would be without the polemical potential so welcome to Marxists.

In a sense which I have already explained in connection with our analysis of Engels' remarks on the theory of truth, it is quite correct to say that all knowledge involves determination by circumstances. It seems to me that the apparent plausibility of the conception of the social or economic determination of knowledge is derived, in part, from this fact. It is so easy to forget that any circumstance which can validly be spoken of as determinative of truth or falsity must be of a strictly epistemological character. The fact that the same notion, "determination," is used must not be allowed to delude us, as it did Marx, into thinking that extraneous factors such as social and economic circumstances can determine truth or falsity. Nevertheless, there is another, quite different, sense in which we might speak of the social and economic determination of some aspects of human thought. Again, my suggestion is that the spurious plausibility of ideological determinism derives, in part, from the fact that there exists such a further valid and superficially similar kind of determinism.

Let us begin by making a set of distinctions. Thought may be about questions of truth or falsity, as in natural science; or about the logical implications of ideas and their relationships, as in formal logic and mathematics (and possibly metaphysics); or about what is good, permissible, beautiful, as in ethics, politics and aesthetics. Ignoring a number of refinements, we may divide the whole field of thought into two. We entitle our two domains "evaluative" and "factual" to refer respectively to the sphere of value, on the one hand, and that of truth and falsity on the other. Now, in the philosophy of value, that is, in moral philosophy and aesthetics, there is a doctrine which asserts that statements of value, i.e. about what is good, permissible, beautiful, are irreducible to statements which may be true or false. According to this view, evaluative judgments are *ultimately* concerned with desires, needs, feelings, attitudes. (This basic conception in the theory of value is denominated, in the subtle varieties of its elaboration, by an assortment of philosophical labels such as naturalism, subjectivism, empiricism, emotivism, positivism. We shall not, however, here involve ourselves in the finer points of philosophical terminology.)

A certain basic unanimity in human valuations is, of course, not ruled out by this theory, though it is peculiarly efficient in accounting for the well attested variety of morals. It may be that human beings have in common certain basic needs, desires and feelings. In that case, what men of different times and places think good, permissible, beautiful, might be expected to coincide, at some fundamental level. Still it is clear that even in one country needs, desires, feelings and attitudes tend to vary with differences in social and economic position. Hence, it is quite reasonable to suggest that the evaluative thinking of men tends to diverge, over a considerable area of thought, on class lines. A man's political outlook, for instance, is *determined* in a primary sense, by the *ends* which he seeks to realise. (Of course, the pursuit of ends necessitates attention to matters of fact in regard to means. But from this point of view, factual implications are logically secondary.)

Accordingly, one might, within certain limits, speak of the class (i.e. the social and economic) determination of such a thing as a political outlook. (I say, "within limits," because one has to observe actual life only briefly to realise that rigid deterministic correlations in this kind of field simply won't do.) A similar, guarded correlation might be supposed in other spheres of evaluative judgment such as morality, aesthetics, and, within somewhat narrower limits, metaphysics.

I am, I may say, sympathetic to the type of philosophy of value which makes correlation possible in these fields. One merit of this kind of analysis is that it enables us to unmask the grandiose disguises involved in the tendency of many men, especially those in authority and privilege, to project their own desires, feelings and attitudes as immutable truths. Again, this kind of theory does not lead to any insoluble problems about truth and knowledge because it does not deal with truth or falsity at all. Further, even in its appropriate domain, it does not declare a judgment to be "illusory" when it calls attention to its social and economic determination. It simply places the judgment in perspective. Of course, the theory of value referred to can, and often has been, challenged. Any attempt to expound objections and answer them, however, does not belong to the scope of this chapter. Suffice it to say, then, that the theory of value in question is, at least, a possible one.

If Marx had advanced some such theory of value, then much sense could have been made of some modified theory of ideology on the lines I have suggested. In his admirable passion to improve the lot of the poor, however, Marx tended naturally to be contemptuous of moralism. But he confused moral philosophy with moralism and assumed rather than argued a moral standpoint. In a merely practical revolutionary such an omission would have been excusable; but in a system builder like Marx—in spite of all the disclaimers, Marx was nothing if not a system builder—it was an extremely unfortunate omission. It was one which did not presage well for subsequent generations. In particular, it has led to a tendency for ambiguous amoralism in many of his most influential followers such as Lenin and Trotsky which has led to some of the most unattractive features of communist and pro-communist tactics. It is not without ironic significance that from the time of Kautsky and Bernstein down to the present day, Marxist apologists who are, or pretend to be, highly sensitive to the moral problems of political action have felt it necessary to supplement their Marxism with some ethical theory. Interestingly, they have, as a rule, gone back to Kant, irreverently dismissed by the founders of Marxism.

Marx offered precious little in the way of an explicit philosophical discussion of morality. Engels was more forthcoming; but his treatment of morality in *Anti-Dühring* does not go much beyond a perfunctory sociology of morals. Characteristically, he advances the thesis that "morality has always been class morality" and that each class has its own morality. To the question, which naturally arises, as to which, if any, is the true one, his answer is that the true morality (true "not in the sense of absolute finality") is "that morality which contains the maximum elements promising permanence, which in the present, represents the overthrow of the present, represents the future, and that is proletarian morality" (p. 130). Thus ideological determinism somehow leaves "proletarian morality" unscathed, though to ask with what logical consistency is, presumably, an undialectical diversion. Since human history in the Marxist scheme of things is inevitably destined to culminate in the millennium of a classless society, progress in morality is conceived by Engels in terms of the advance towards a classless morality, which is the truly human morality: "A really human morality which stands above class antagonisms and above any recollection of them becomes possible [only] at a stage of society which has not only overcome class antagonism but has even forgotten them in practical life" (p. 132).

This is essentially the sum of Engels' moral philosophy. It obviously gives no guidance on the conceptual problems that have perplexed moral philosophers. It is silent on the question of what are the *fundamental* principles of the ethics of revolutionary action. Granted that "the present" must be overthrown in the interest of the proletariat, the fact still remains that problems of moral choice can, and do, arise with regard to the variety of potentially successful methods of struggle. Some ways of attaining the goals of the proletariat will be more morally acceptable than others. On what principles is a choice of this sort to be made, and for what general reasons? Faced with a question of this nature, it is quite unavailing to cite the interests of the proletariat since that is what generates the problem in the first place. Not in Marx, Engels, Lenin (who generally repeats Engels), or Trotsky (who wrestles violently with this problem in *Their Morals and Our Own)*, do we find the required principle of moral discrimination.

There are further important ethical questions that are left untouched by the Marxist treatment of ethics. Marxist thinking about morality seems to be dominated by the external moral relations of the proletariat, viewed *en masse*, with the other social classes. But the question of morality arises in the internal relations of the proletarians themselves. What is the basis of the morality that should govern inter-personal relations among members of the proletarian class? One is left in the dark in this matter. Nor can we glean from the pages of Marx and Engels what the basis of morality might be in the classless society itself. If human beings living in the classless society of the future will ever have occasion to make moral judgments, and if we may suppose them in that setting to retain their intellectual capacities, then philosophical questions will be raised about morality, questions which will concern the logical status and objectivity or otherwise of moral judgment, the definability of the moral predicates, the respective roles of motives, intentions and consequences in the evaluation of conduct, the best way of resolving the conflict of moral principles, and so on. These very questions are even now, in our class-ridden societies, pertinent to the intellectual understanding of morality and the practical guidance of life. Obviously the ideological interpretation of philosophy does not encourage sustained reflection on questions of this sort.

We conclude that Marx fell deeply into error in his conception of ideology and its bearing upon philosophy. What he might judiciously have said is that philosophy—in general, human thinking—has its "ideological" aspects. Even so, the notion of ideology would have had to be modified in such a way that to say of a given judgment that it belongs to the ideological aspect of philosophy would not be to imply that it is false.

It is, perhaps, appropriate, at this juncture, to give a historical lament. It is impossible not to feel it a matter for regret that Marx himself never found the leisure to expand fully on the purely philosophical aspects of his outlook as was always his intention—such was the vastness of the task of economic research which he set himself. If time had allowed him to devote extended attention to the development of the more abstract aspects of his conceptions, it is conceivable that more mature reflection would have led him to correct the philosophical aberrations of his younger days. (*The German Ideology* was written fairly early in the lives of Marx and Engels, being completed by 1846.) As it is, the careful student of Marxism is bound to be struck by the poverty of Marxist philosophy in spite of the volume of exegesis. History, unkind to the self-proclaimed repositories of her dialectical mysteries, saddled Engels with the role of Marxism's canonical theoretician in philosophy. Unfortunately, when left on his own, philosophical profundity often eluded him, even though he was an extremely fluent writer and a perceptive analyst of facts and events. Nor was the doughty Lenin, who in his *Materialism and Empirio-Criticism* essayed to reassert the philosophy of Marxism in the face of mounting scepticism early in this century, blessed with a head for abstract reflection in spite of his great intelligence and revolutionary ability.

So the philosophical errors of Marx and Engels have been perpetuated. The run-of-the-mill Marxists, even less enamoured of philosophical accuracy than their masters, have made the ideological conception of philosophy a battle cry. Without the slightest scruple, any philosophy propounded by the "bourgeoisie" (a term used almost indiscriminately to refer to non-Marxists, or better, non-Marxist–Leninists) is liable to be declared to reflect bourgeois class interests. It is then pronounced to be subjective, false, illusory, deceptive, destructive, pernicious, perverted, subversive, reactionary . . . It is not necessary, mark you, that a doctrine thus pilloried should be really incompatible with the relevant parts of Marx's philosophy. This fact is illustrated by Cornforth's violent reaction, which is typical, to John Dewey's pragmatic theory of truth. On the other hand, the Marxist philosophy or any doctrine *officially* decreed to be Marxist is said to reflect the noble interests of the proletariat. Automatically, it is asserted to be objective, true, progressive, uplifting, revolutionary, constructive . . .

So the followers of Marx and Engels are apt to declare philosophy to be intrinsically partisan in a political sense. Listen again to Maurice Cornforth: "philosophy has always expressed and could not but express a class standpoint" (*In Defence of Philosophy*, p. 45). This, of course, echoes Lenin who was given to saying things like "materialism carries with it, so to speak, party spirit compelling one in any evaluation of events to take up directly and openly the view point of a definite social group." With Lenin, indeed, non-partisanship in philosophy is a term of abuse. (See, for example, *Materialism and Empirio-Criticism*, pp. 350 ff.)

I contend that, in so far as Marxism as developed by Marx and Engels easily leads to this class, and politically partisan, conception of philosophy, it is injurious to philosophy. Party politics is notoriously not conducive to rigorous theoretical thinking. The probability is that a philosophy used as an instrument of party politics will become a set of hardened dogmas which people are more or less terrorised or brain-washed into accepting. Nothing is easier than for political ideologists—the notion of ideology is, of course, used now not in the original sense of Marx but in the modern, adapted sense—to reason, or rather fulminate, as follows: If a man does not accept dialectical materialism, does it not plainly show that, being hostile to the ideology of the party, he is an enemy of the people whom the party seeks to uplift? Does he not stand proven a die-hard counter-revolutionary, a spineless reactionary, an incorrigible subversive? How can we afford to leave such a dangerous person free to retard the salvation of the masses? Such is the logic by which the class conception of all philosophy tends to lead to persecution and the suppression of dissent. Inevitably philosophy suffers violation.

I hope I have given independent reasons for questioning the ideological, class conception of philosophy. A proposition is not false simply because belief in it leads to harsh consequences. If, however, good enough arguments can be independently given for supposing it false, then there is a justification for deploring it with a certain measure of moral indignation. I believe the class view of philosophy to be deplorable in this sense.

I wish now, in near-conclusion, very briefly—all too briefly, perhaps—by a direct confrontation with Marxism to show that it harbours further confusions. Speaking somewhat schematically, we may say that Marxism consists of three layers of thought: (I) Dialectical materialism; (2) Historical materialism; (3) Scientific socialism. Apparently in the minds of Marxists, dialectical materialism logically implies historical materialism and both imply scientific socialism. There are two basic fallacies in this kind of thinking, one relating to the step from dialectical to historical materialism, on which more below; the other, in relation to the transition from both to scientific socialism. This latter fallacy consists in the false supposition that a doctrine which claims to state the general nature of existence can *logically* imply a scheme of valuation, which is what scientific socialism is, in parts. As David Hume remarked in a celebrated passage, you cannot automatically *deduce* a statement of what ought to be the case from a statement of what is the case. In their claims of scientific superiority, Marxists are apt to forget that their choice of socialism is, at bottom, an evaluative matter.

Dialectical materialism is the theory that matter is primary (i.e. prior to mind) and that things are perpetually undergoing change according to certain, as it seems to me, mystical laws, for example, the dialectical law of the interpenetration of opposites. Historical materialism asserts that the ultimate determinative factor in human history is the mode of production, i.e. the ensemble of productive forces and the associated relations of production. To argue, as Marxists do, that the primacy of the material factor in history follows logically from the metaphysical primacy of matter is to be guilty of a fallacy based on nothing more complicated than a pun. "Material" in dialectical materialism refers to matter in a neutral technical sense in which the material is simply that which has mass and position and is in motion. "Material" in historical materialism refers to material things in an economic sense. (Historical materialism is, in fact, often called the economic interpretation of history.) A piece of matter or a certain disposition of matter is not relevantly material in the economic sense, unless some human being takes an evaluative attitude towards it. Conditions are not economic unless regarded from the point of view of human needs and estimations. In the technical, merely physical, sense of 'material', the term has no necessary reference to human valuation. If 'matter' in this sense is primary, why should we suppose it to follow that matter in the evaluative sense is also primary in the scheme of human valuations? As soon as one poses the question clearly, one realises that the claim is based on nothing other than the fact that the same word 'material' is used in both cases.

Given that matter, i.e. that which is physical, is metaphysically prior to mind, why may not the direction of man's life be controlled more by factors usually called "spiritual" such as religion or the pursuit of theoretical truth than by factors of economic significance? A man has to eat to live. Accepted. He has to be clothed and find some shelter before he can think about scientific truth. Additionally, he may avidly pursue good food and drink, and women and fast cars, all of which aims are material (or even 'materialistic') in the evaluative sense. But is there anything, in the sheer fact, if so it be, that the world is composed of myriads of systems of electrical charges—is there anything in this which makes it logically necessary that people should be more actuated by material considerations than by "spiritual" factors in life? The question only has to be put, I believe, to be answered in the negative.

I am not to be understood as saying either that dialectical materialism or historical materialism is false. The question of the truth or falsity of these doctrines is not the issue before us. The issue here is simply, "does dialectical materialism imply historical materialism?" A negative answer is clearly forced upon us. The first doctrine is patently consistent with the negation of the second. A man may grant that matter comes first and mind only afterwards and yet consistently insist that, since the emergence of mind, mental, intellectual, spiritual, factors have dominated and are destined to dominate human history.

Again, it is false to say that historical materialism logically implies scientific socialism. 'Scientific Socialism' itself is not a clear concept. It is an amalgam of factual and evaluative elements blended together without regard to categorical stratification. It consists of two different strands. The first is an analysis of capitalism seeking to show that capitalism will inevitably, owing to certain internal "contradictions," break down and give way, through an equally inescapable process of class warfare, to a socialist mode of production, i.e. production and organisation under the condition of social ownership of the means of production and distribution. The second is a judgment to the effect that socialism is the best mode of social and economic organisation. Clearly, one can accept the first and reject the second or vice versa, without contradiction. Suppose it to be scientifically proven, for example, that the world will be destroyed in a nuclear holocaust; why should one, merely on account of its inevitability, embrace the prospect as good? It would simply be evidence of weak thinking to suppose that if something is inevitable then it is good or, in comparison to other supposedly less inevitable things, the best. Further, it is evidently possible to believe that socialist organisation, such as it was pictured by Marx, is the best way of organising society, without being so sure that that mode of organisation will prevail. As for the automatic jump from historical materialism to scientific socialism, why, if material factors are the most determinative in history, must it be true, *simply in virtue of that supposed fact,* that capitalism will break down, or that socialism is good? Is it not logically consistent to say both that the material factor is the most important in human history and that capitalism will go from strength to strength? Further words are needless.

In the more narrowly technical sense, dialectical materialism is *the* philosophy of the Marxists. I have tried to argue that there is no logical connection between that philosophy and the belief in the goodness of socialist society. It is only by a series of crass fallacies that dialectical materialism is said to be a necessary part of the "ideology" of the working class. I propose the following as the definition of 'ideology' most in conformity with the realities of contemporary political life. "An ideology is a set of ossified dogmas used as a political weapon in the relentless pursuit of power or, when attained, the determined retention of it at all costs."

Ideology is the death of philosophy. To the extent to which Marxism, by its own internal incoherences, tends to be transformed into an ideology, to that extent Marxism is a science of the unscientific and a philosophy of the unphilosophic.

PART II

West Asia, North Africa, and Spain

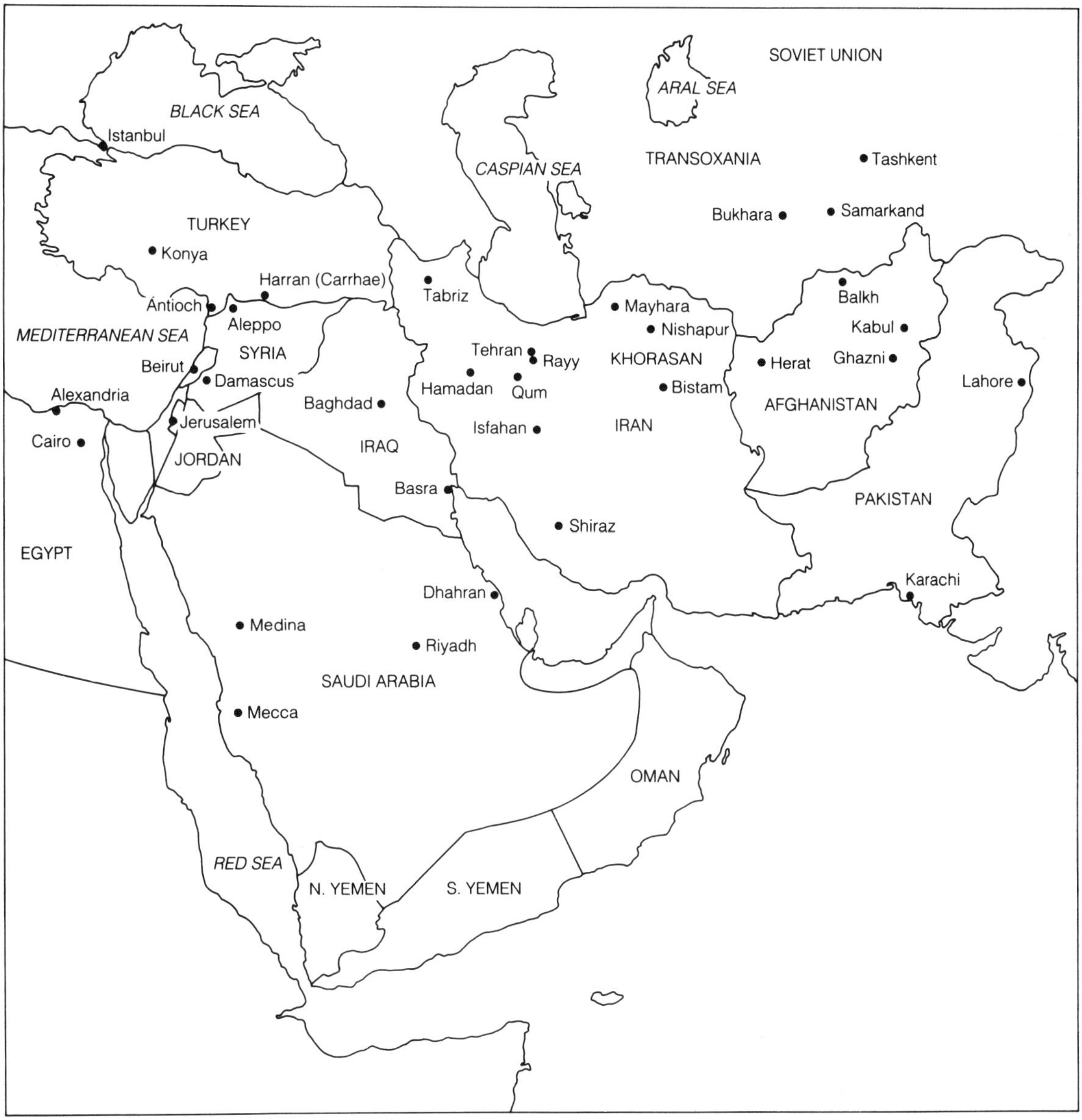

PLATONISM

North Africa became an important philosophical center during the first several centuries of the Common Era. Much of the philosophical activity occurred in Alexandria, Egypt, the site of a Platonic school and a world famous library. Because of the school, Plato's influence was especially strong in Alexandria, and most important philosophers of the region were platonists. But, unlike Greek philosophers, the Alexandrians were concerned primarily with religious questions. Their work concentrates on the problems of reconciling Judaism or Christianity with the intellectual framework of Greek thought.

Philo, often called Philo Judaeus or Philo of Alexandria (20 B.C.E.–40 C.E.), was born into a wealthy Jewish family in Alexandria. He was something of an Alexandrian socialite, attending dinner parties, the theater, wrestling matches, and chariot races, while also doing the work of a serious scholar. Well educated in Judaism and Greek thought, he sought to reconcile Jewish religious convictions with Greek philosophy. There is little evidence that Philo knew Hebrew, however; he knew Scripture only in Greek. Philo's central strategy was to interpret Scripture allegorically, treating the stories of the Books of Moses as illustrating general aspects of the human condition and the quest for salvation. He tended to assume that the Greek philosophers knew the Pentateuch, or, at least, that the Pentateuch and Greek philosophical texts issued from similar divine inspiration.

Philo's philosophy is essentially platonic. He finds in Plato's *Timaeus* and in Genesis the thesis that God is eternal. God existed before bringing the world into existence and continues to exist alongside the created world. Plato maintains that the Forms are also eternal; the mind, in thinking of an object—a circle, say—is turned both toward that individual object and toward an unchanging, abstract Form the object exemplifies—in this case, circularity. The Forms organize reality and our thinking about reality; the fact that we think of a succession of Forms explains how we can think accurately about a changing universe. Philo accepts the Forms in this role, but he denies Plato's contention that they, like God, are eternal. Instead, he identifies them with ideas in the mind of God. Before creation, the Forms existed only as ideas; afterward, they exist both as ideas and as exemplified in objects. Philo similarly alters Plato's conception of matter to accord with the scriptural doctrine that God alone is eternal. Plato holds that God created the world out of preexisting, eternal matter. Philo argues that creation occurred in two steps: a creation of matter from nothing and then a creation of the world from matter.

Philo labels the Forms, taken together, "the intelligible world," and locates them in what he calls the Word. The power of the Word orders the "great chain of being," linking the natural world, animals, and humans to God. The Word itself is the "idea of ideas," the pattern of creation, the archetype of human reason, "the man of God" and the "second God." The Word relates God to humans and the rest of the created world, appearing to Moses in the burning bush and inspiring Moses and the prophets. This doctrine seems to have been Philo's own contribution, though he bases it on Scripture, for example, on Psalm 33: "By the word of God were the heavens made." It had a great impact on Christian thought by way of the Gospel of John. (John's gospel begins: "In the beginning was the Word, and the Word was with God, and the Word was God.")

The Word plays such an important role for Philo because, in his view, God is remote. We can gain knowledge of God indirectly through reasoning about the world or directly through revelation. Philo transforms the argument in Aristotle for God as Prime Mover into an argument for God's existence but stresses that knowledge of God may also come from study of Scripture or from divine inspiration. Nevertheless, we can attain only a limited knowledge of God. We can know God's existence, but not God's essence. We can know, in other words, *that* God is, but not *what* God is. God is unnameable, ineffable, incomprehensible. Philo argues that a thing can be defined only by comparing it to other things, likening it in some respects and differentiating it in others. God, however, is not like anything else. Consequently, God cannot be defined and, so, cannot be known. The Word, however, can be known. It serves to link God and humanity by giving us a limited access to the mind of God. We cannot say anything positive about God's nature, but we can have positive knowledge of the Word.

Our knowledge of the world is nevertheless severely limited. The mind, like Adam, existed with God and the Word once it was created. This contact with the Word makes our knowledge of the Forms possible. But knowledge of the world requires sense perception and its organization according to the Forms. Just as Adam and Eve were tempted in the Garden of Eden, we are tempted to think that we can know the true nature of the world. But that, Philo argues, is a vain conceit. He advances a series of arguments for *skepticism,* the view that knowledge of the world is unattainable. There is great variation in perception between animals of different species, different people, and even the same person at different times or in different circumstances. We have no way of telling which perceptions accurately portray reality. Moreover, the elements of reality are mixed and related in such complicated ways that we have no hope of distinguishing them.

Philo extends this argument to morality. Different groups of people have different ways of life. Philosophy does not provide any way of deciding which is best, for philosophers disagree as much as anyone about the nature of the good life. But Philo does make moral judgments and recommendations. The root of sin, he maintains, is pride: the desire to become equal to God. The good worth pursuing is the good of the soul, not the good of the body; for this reason, Philo advocates a life of asceticism and self-control. He adds several virtues to the usual Greek list, including faith, repentance, and philanthropy or charity. But the greatest goal, Philo says, is the mystical vision of God.

Origen (185–253), sometimes considered the first Christian theologian, was born to Christian parents in Alexandria, Egypt. He took scriptural commands very seriously: He lived in poverty, with very little food or sleep and, according to Eusebius, took Matthew 19:12 literally and castrated himself. An intellectual prodigy,

Origen became head of a Christian school in Alexandria when he was just nineteen and taught there for twenty-seven years. He evidently studied with Ammonius Saccas, the founder of Neoplatonism. When Origen was forty-six, he had a disagreement witht the local bishop. He taught for the rest of his life in Caesarea, in Palestine, and died in Tyre at age sixty-nine after being tortured for alleged heresies.

Origen shares Philo's preference for allegorical interpretations of Scripture. But Origen refuses to accept the Greek translation of the Old Testament as divinely inspired, instead learning Hebrew in order to read the original. Philosophy, Origen believes, is valuable preparation for religious inquiry, but it is not necessary; if it were, Jesus would not have chosen fishermen as disciples. Nevertheless, Origen was concerned to show that Christians could defend their faith by the use of reason. As a young man, he wrote *De Principiis (On Principles),* which is a striking adaptation of Platonic philosophy to Christian belief.

On Principles begins with a discussion of God that transforms Plato's myth of the cave in the *Republic* into a Christian portrait of God. In Plato's story, philosophy leads those who live in a cave, seeing only shadows, up to the light of day, where they can see objects as they truly are and eventually look at the sun, the source of light making their vision possible. Plato identifies true reality with the realm of the Forms and takes the Form of the Good as analogous to the sun. In Origen's portrait, God replaces the Form of the Good. "God is light," according to I John 1:5; God makes all knowledge, including our knowledge of him, possible.

Saint Augustine (354–430), by far the best known of the Christian platonists, was born in Thagaste, in Numidia, North Africa, as the Roman Empire began to crumble. He had little interest in school as a child; although he learned Latin and a little Greek, he excelled mostly on the playground. At eleven he went to Madaura to study Latin literature; at sixteen, after his father, Patricius, died, Augustine went to Carthage to study rhetoric. There he acquired a mistress, had an illegitimate child, and renounced Christianity. At eighteen he read the *Hortensius,* a dialogue of Cicero that is now lost, and decided to devote his life to the search for wisdom. He became a Manichaean—one who believes that the world is the product of eternal strife between good and evil forces—deciding that the existence of evil showed that God could not be both the creator of the entire universe and entirely good. Augustine became a teacher of rhetoric, setting up a school in Carthage at age twenty and, at twenty-nine, traveling to Rome and Milan. In Milan, with his faith in Manichaeanism already shaken, he became acquainted with Bishop Ambrose and other Christian Neoplatonists. His mother, Monica, was a Christian, but in Milan, for the first time, Augustine saw that Christianity could be given rigorous intellectual foundations. He read Plotinus, whose doctrine that evil is merely an absence of good gave Augustine the confidence that Christianity could overcome the problem of evil. At thirty-two, he therefore decided to become a Christian.

Augustine returned to Africa and established a monastery at Tagaste. Three years later, he traveled to Hippo and, somewhat reluctantly, became assistant to Valerius, the bishop there. At age forty-one, upon Valerius's death, Augustine became bishop of Hippo. Thereafter, he devoted himself to the Church. But he continued to write prolifically. At fifty-nine, Augustine began *The City of God,* finishing it thirteen years later. The following year, when Augustine was seventy-three, the Vandals invaded Africa. He died three years later, reciting the Psalms as the Vandals laid seige to Hippo.

Augustine devotes much attention to the problem of evil, seeking to show that the existence of evil in the world is not incompatible with the existence of a God who is both all good and all powerful. He advances arguments to refute skeptics, who question the reliability of all claims to knowledge, defending our knowledge of logical and mathematical truths, of our own existence, and of how things appear to us. He also tries to show on purely rational grounds that the soul is immortal. These are just a few of Augustine's important philosophical contributions, not to mention his many influential innovations in theology.

PHILO

from *Allegorical Interpretation*

From Philo, *vol I. Translated by F. H. Colson and G. H. Whitaker. London: William Heinemann Ltd., 1929.*

BOOK II

. . . There is another way in which we may understand the statement that God is alone. It may mean that neither before creation was there anything with God, nor, when the universe had come into being, does anything take its place with Him; for there is absolutely nothing which He needs. A yet better interpretation is the following. God is alone, a Unity, in the sense that His nature is simple not composite, whereas each one of us and of all other created beings is made up of many things. I, for example, am many things in one. I am soul and body. To soul belong rational and irrational parts, and to body, again, different properties, warm and cold, heavy and light, dry and moist. But God is not a composite Being, consisting of many parts, nor is He mixed with aught else. For whatever is added to God, is either superior or inferior or equal to Him. But there is nothing equal or superior to God. And no lesser thing is resolved into Him. If He do so assimilate any lesser thing, He also will be lessened. And if He can be made less, He will also be capable of corruption; and even to imagine this were blasphemous. The "one" and the "monad" are, therefore, the only standard for determining the category to which God belongs. Rather should we say, the One God is the sole standard for the "monad."* For, like time, all number is subsequent to the universe; and God is prior to the universe, and is its Maker. . . .

* A unity; often, an absolutely simple entity without parts. From the Greek *monas,* meaning a unit, one, a unity.—Ed.

PHILO

from *On the Account of the World's Creation Given By Moses*

From Philo, *vol I. Translated by F. H. Colson and G. H. Whitaker. London: William Heinemann Ltd., 1929.*

IV. We must recount as many as we can of the elements embraced in it [the world]. To recount them all would be impossible. Its pre-eminent element is the intelligible world, as is shown in the treatise dealing with the "One." For God, being God, assumed that a beautiful copy would never be produced apart from a beautiful pattern, and that no object of perception would be faultless which was not made in the likeness of an original discerned only by the intellect. So when He willed to create this visible world He first fully formed the intelligible world, in order that He might have the use of a pattern wholly God-like and incorporeal in producing the material world, as a later creation, the very image of an earlier, to embrace in itself objects of perception of as many kinds as the other contained objects of intelligence.

To speak of or conceive that world which consists of ideas as being in some place is illegitimate; how it consists (of them) we shall know if we carefully attend to some image supplied by the things of our world. When a city is being founded to satisfy the soaring ambition of some king or governor, who lays claim to despotic power and being magnificent in his ideas would fain add a fresh lustre to his good fortune, there comes forward now and again some trained architect who, observing the favourable climate and convenient position of the site, first sketches in his own mind wellnigh all the parts of the city that is to be wrought out, temples, gymnasia, town-halls, market-places, harbours, docks, streets, walls to be built, dwelling-houses as well as public buildings to be set up. Thus after having received in his own soul, as it were in wax, the figures of these objects severally, he carries about the image of a city which is the creation of his mind. Then by his innate power of memory, he recalls the images of the various parts of this city, and imprints their types yet more distinctly in it: and like a good craftsman he begins to build the city of stones and timber, keeping his eye upon his pattern and making the visible and tangible objects correspond in each case to the incorporeal ideas.

Just such must be our thoughts about God. We must suppose that, when He was minded to found the one great city, He conceived beforehand the models of its parts, and that out of these He constituted and brought to completion a world discernible only by the mind, and then, with that for a pattern, the world which our senses can perceive.

V. As, then, the city which was fashioned beforehand within the mind of the architect held no place in the outer world, but had been engraved in the soul of the artificer as by a seal; even so the universe that consisted of ideas would have no other location than the Divine Reason, which was the Author of this ordered frame. For what other place could there be for His powers sufficient to receive and contain, I say not all but, any one of them whatever uncompounded and untempered?

Now just such a power is that by which the universe was made, one that has as its source nothing less than true goodness. For should one conceive a wish to search for the cause, for the sake of which this whole was created, it seems to me that he would not be wrong in saying, what indeed one of the men of old did say, that the Father and Maker of all is good; and because of this He grudged not a share in his own excellent nature to an existence which has of itself nothing fair and lovely, while it is capable of becoming all things. For of itself it was without order, without quality, without soul, (without likeness); it was full of inconsistency, ill-adjustment, disharmony: but it was capable of turning and undergoing a complete change to the best, the very contrary of all these, to order, quality, life, correspondence, identity, likeness, perfect adjustment, to harmony, to all that is characteristic of the more excellent model.

VI. Now God, with no counsellor to help Him (who was there beside Him?) determined that it was meet to confer rich and unrestricted benefits upon that nature which apart from Divine bounty could obtain of itself no good thing. But not in proportion to the greatest of His own bounties does He confer benefits—for these are without end or limit—but in proportion to the capacities of the recipients. For it is not the nature of creation to receive good treatment in like manner as it is the nature of God to bestow it, seeing that the powers of God are overwhelmingly vast, whereas creation, being too feeble to entertain their abundance, would have broken down under the effort to do so, had not God with appropriate adjustment dealt out to each his due portion.

Should a man desire to use words in a more simple and direct way, he would say that the world discerned only by the intellect is nothing else than the Word of God when He was already engaged in the act of creation. For (to revert to our illustration) the city discernible by the intellect alone is nothing else than the reasoning faculty of the architect in the act of planning to found the city. It is Moses who lays down this, not I. Witness his express acknowledgement in the sequel, when setting on record the creation of man, that he was moulded after the image of God (Gen. i. 27). Now if the part is an image of an image, it is manifest that the whole is so too, and if the whole creation, this entire world perceived by our senses (seeing that it is greater than any human image) is a copy of the Divine image, it is manifest that the archetypal seal also, which we aver to be the world descried by the mind, would be the very Word of God.

VII. Then he says that "in the beginning God made the heaven and the earth," taking "beginning" not, as some think, in a chronological sense, for time there was not before there was a world. Time began either simultaneously with the world or after it. For since time is a measured space determined by the world's movement, and since movement could not be prior to the object moving, but must of necessity arise either after it or simultaneously with it, it follows of necessity that time also is either coeval with or later born than the world. To venture to affirm that it is elder born would be to do violence to philosophic sense. . . .

PHILO

from *On Drunkenness*

From Philo, *vol. III. Translated by F. H. Colson and G. H. Whitaker. London: William Heinemann Ltd., 1930.*

Now this is complete insensibility, that the mind should think itself competent to deliberate by itself on what is to its interests, or to assent to presentations of any kind as though they were a vehicle of solid truth, for human nature is ever quite unable, either by circumspection to discover certainty, or to choose some things as true and profitable, and to reject others as false and injurious. For the vastness of the darkness which overspreads the world of bodies and affairs forbids us to see the nature of each; and though curiosity or love of learning may give us the wish to force our way and peer through the curtain, we shall like blind men stumble over the obstacles before us, lose our footing and miss our object, or if our hands do lay hold of it, we are but guessing at uncertainties and it is not truth but conjecture that is in our grasp. For even if instruction, torch in hand, should go before the mind, shedding her own particular light to give it sight of realities, it would do more harm than good. For its little beam is bound to be extinguished by the vast darkness, and when it is extinguished all power of sight is useless.

He who prides himself on his judgement in deliberation, or flatters himself that he is competent to choose this and shun that, should be brought to a recollection of the truth by the following thoughts. If it were always the case that the same objects produced the same impressions on the mind without any variation, it would perhaps be necessary that the two instruments of judgement which nature has established in us, sense and mind, should be held in high esteem as veracious and incorruptible, and that we should not suspend our judgement on any point through doubt but accept a single presentation of two different objects, and on the faith of this choose one and reject the other. But since we prove to be differently affected by them at different times, we can say nothing with certainty about anything, because the picture presented to us is not constant, but subject to changes manifold and multiform.

XLII. Since the mental picture is variable, the judgement we form of it must be variable also. There are many reasons for this.

In the first place there are the innumerable differences in living creatures, differences concerned not with a single aspect, but practically with all; differences in birth, in structure and equipment; differences in food and mode of life; differences in predilections and aversions; differences in their sense-activities and sense-movements; differences in the peculiarities which arise from the innumerable ways in which body and soul are affected.

For leaving out of sight for the moment those who form judgements, consider examples among the objects of such judgements. Take for instance the chameleon and the polypus. The former, we are told, changes its colour and grows like the kinds of soil over which it is its habit to crawl; the latter grows like the rocks to which it clings in the sea, and we may fairly suppose that this power of changing to various colours is given them by protecting nature as a remedy against the danger of capture. Again, have we not seen the dove's neck change in the sun's rays into a thousand different hues, sometimes scarlet and dark blue, or fiery or like red-hot coal, again yellow and then ruddy, and all other kinds of colour, so numerous that it would be difficult to give even their names in full? Indeed it is said that in the land of the Scythians who are known as the Geloans a most extraordinary animal is actually, though no doubt rarely, found called the elk, in size equal to an ox, but with a face shaped very like a deer. The account given of this creature is that it always changes the colour of its hair into that of the places, trees, or any imaginable thing near which it stands, and owing to this similarity of colour, we are told, it is not observed by passers-by, and this fact rather than its bodily strength makes it difficult to catch. These and similar phenomena are clear proofs of the impossibility of apprehension.

XLIII. Secondly, there are the diversities on all subjects which, to pass from animals in general, we find also in men in particular. Not only do their judgements on the same objects vary at different times, but different persons receive different impressions of pleasure or its reverse from the same things. For what is disliked by some is enjoyed by others, and contrariwise what some receive with open arms as acceptable and agreeable to their nature is utterly scouted by others as alien and repugnant. For example, I have often when I chanced to be in the theatre noticed the effect produced by some single tune sung by the actors on the stage or played by the musicians. Some of the audience are so moved, that in their excitement they cannot help raising their voices in a chorus of acclamation. Others are so unstirred that, as far as this is concerned, you might suppose them on a level of feeling with the senseless benches on which they sit. Others, again, are so repelled that they are off and away from the performance, and indeed, as they go, block their ears with both hands for fear that some echo of the music should remain to haunt them and produce a sense of discomfort to irritate and pain their souls.

But it is needless to quote such cases as these. Every single individual in his own person is subject, extraordinary though it be, to numberless changes and variations in body and soul, and chooses at one time and rejects at another things which do not change, but retain the natural constitution which they have had throughout. The same feelings are not experienced in health as in sickness, in wakefulness as in sleep, in youth as in age. And people receive different mental impressions according as they are standing or moving, confident or affrighted, sad or joyful, loving or hating. And why tediously pursue the subject? For to put it shortly, our bodies and souls are in a state of motion, natural or unnatural, which considered as a whole produces that ceaseless change in the mental pictures presented to us which makes us the victim of conflicting and incongruous dreams.

XLIV. But the inconstancy of impressions is particularly caused by the positions and surroundings of the several objects and their distances from the observer. We see that fishes in the sea, when they swim with their fins stretched, always look larger than nature has made them, and oars, however straight they are, appear bent below the water. Still more—the mind is often misled by distant objects which create false impressions. Sometimes we suppose lifeless objects to be living objects or the converse. And we have similar illusions about things stationary and moving, advancing and receding, short and long, circular and multilateral. And numberless other distortions of the truths are produced even when sight is unimpeded, which no sane person would accept as trustworthy.

XLV. What again of quantities in prepared mixtures? Their powers of benefiting or injuring depend on the relative quantity of the various ingredients, as we see in numberless cases and particularly in the drugs used by medical science. For quantity in compounds is measured by regular standards, and we cannot with safety stop short of or go beyond what they prescribe; for anything smaller or greater than this respectively overweakens or overstrains the force of the preparation. In both cases harm is done. In the former case the medicine is incapable through its weakness of producing any effect, while in the latter its high degree of potency makes it a force of active mischief. And again according to its roughness or smoothness, and its density and compactness on the one hand, or its sponginess and dilatation on the other, it exhibits clearly the means of testing its power of helping or harming.

Again, everyone knows that practically nothing at all which exists is intelligible by itself and in itself, but everything is appreciated only by comparison with its opposite; as small by comparison with great, dry with wet, hot with cold, light with heavy, black with white, weak with strong, few with many. The same rule holds with all that concerns virtue and vice. We only know the profitable through the hurtful, the noble by contrast with the base, the just and the good in general by comparison with the unjust and evil. And indeed if we consider we shall see that everything else in the world is judged on the same pattern. For in itself each thing is beyond our apprehension, and it is only by bringing it into relation with something else that it seems to be known. Now that which is incapable of attesting itself and needs to be vouched for by something else, gives no sure ground for belief. And it follows that on this principle we can estimate at their true value lightly-made affirmations and negations on any subject whatever.

Nor is this strange. For anyone who penetrates deeper into things and views them in a purer light, will recognize that no single thing presents itself to us in its own absolute nature but all contain interlacings and intermixtures of the most complicated kind.

XLVI. For instance, how do we apprehend colours? Surely by means of the externals, air and light, and the internal moisture in the eye itself. How do we discriminate between sweet and bitter? Can we do so without the juices in the mouth, both those which are in accord with nature and those which are not? Surely not. Again, do the odours produced by burning incense present to us the natures of the substances in a pure and simple form, or in a combination, in which themselves and air, or sometimes also the fire which dissolves the material, are joined with the faculty possessed by the nostrils? From this we deduce that we do not apprehend colours, but only the combination produced by the light and the material substances to which the colours belong, nor smells, but only the mixture of the emanation from the substances with the all-admitting air; nor flavours, but only the something produced by the application of what we taste to the moisture in our mouths.

XLVII. Since these things are so, those who do not shrink from facile affirmation or negation of anything whatsoever deserve to be held guilty of folly or rashness or imposture. For if the properties of things by themselves are beyond our ken, and if it is only the mixture formed by the contribution of many factors which is open to our vision; if, once more, it is as impossible to discern through the combinations the particular form of each of the contributing factors as it is to see them in their invisibility, what course is left to use but to suspend our judgement?

And are we not warned against giving over-ready credence to uncertainties by other considerations? I allude to certain facts, the evidence for which is found practically over the whole world as known to us—facts which entail on Greek and barbarian alike the universal tendency to error which positive judgement brings. By these I mean of course ways of life from boyhood upwards, traditional usages, ancient laws, not a single one of which is regarded in the same light universally, but every country, nation and city, or rather every village and house, indeed every man, woman and infant child takes a totally different view of it. As a proof of this we see that what is base with us is noble with others, what is seemly and just with us is unseemly or unjust with them, our holy is their unholy, our lawful their unlawful, our laudable their blameworthy, our meritorious their criminal, and in all other matters their judgement is the opposite of ours.

And why prolong the subject when our attention is called elsewhere by more vital matters? Still if anyone undistracted by some newer subject of contemplation should care to devote his leisure to the subject which has been before us, and to examine the ways of life, usages and customs of different countries, nations, cities and places, subjects and rulers, high and low, freemen and slaves, ignorant and learned, it will occupy not only a day or two, not only a month or a year, but his whole lifetime, even though his years be many, and all the same he will leave behind him many such questions, which he knows not of, unexamined, unconsidered and unheard. Since then the divers customs of divers persons are not distinguished merely by some slight difference, but exhibit an absolute contrast, amounting to bitter antagonism, it is inevitable that the impressions made upon the mind should differ and that the judgements formed should be at war with each other.

XLVIII. In view of these facts, who is so senseless and deranged as to assert positively that any particular thing is just or prudent or honourable or profitable? For what one determines to be such, will be repudiated by another who has practised the opposite from childhood.

Now I for my part do not wonder that the chaotic and promiscuous multitude who are bound in inglorious slavery to usages and customs introduced anyhow, and who are indoctrinated from the cradle with the lesson of obedience to them, as to masters and despots, with their souls buffeted into subjection and incapable of entertaining any high or generous feeling, should give credence to traditions delivered once for all, and leaving their minds unexercised, should give vent to affirmations and negations without inquiry or examination. But I do wonder that the multitude of so-called philosophers, who feign to be seeking for exact and absolute certainty in things, are divided into troops and companies and propound dogmatic conclusions widely different and often diametrically opposite not on some single chance point, but on practically all points great or small, which constitute the problems which they seek to solve.

When some assert that the universe is infinite, others that it is finite, and some declare it to be created, others uncreated; when some refuse to connect it with any ruler or governor, but make it dependent on the automatic action of an unreasoning force, while others postulate a marvellous providence, caring for the whole and each part, exerted by a deity who guides and steers it and makes safe its steps, it is impossible that the substance of things should be apprehended by them in the same form. Again, when the nature of the good is the subject of inquiry, do not the ideas which present themselves compel us to withhold judgement rather than give assent? For some hold that the morally beautiful is the only good and make the soul its repository, while others split up the good into subdivisions and extend it to include the body and things outside the body. These persons say that fortunate circumstances are the guards and attendants of the body, and that health and strength and soundness and exactness of perception in the sense-organs and all other things of the kind serve the same purpose to the sovereign soul. The nature of the good, they hold, divides itself into three classes, of which the third and outermost protects the weakness of the second, which again proves to be a strong bulwark and safeguard of the first. And with regard to these, as well as to the relative value of different ways of living, and the ends to which all our actions should be referred, and numberless other points, which are included in the study of logic, ethics and physics, a host of questions have arisen on none of which hitherto have the inquirers arrived at unanimity. . . .

PHILO

from *On the Confusion of Tongues*

From Philo, *vol. V. Translated by F. H. Colson and G. H. Whitaker. Cambridge: Harvard University Press, and London: William Heinemann, Ltd., 1932.*

XXXVIII. . . . But they who live in the knowledge of the One are rightly called "Sons of God," as Moses also acknowledges when he says, "Ye are sons of the Lord God" (Deut. xiv. 1), and "God who begat thee" (*ibid.* xxxii. 18), and "Is not He Himself thy father?" (*ibid.* 6). Indeed with those whose soul is thus disposed it follows that they hold moral beauty to be the only good, and this serves as a counterwork engineered by veteran warriors to fight the cause which makes Pleasure the end and to subvert and overthrow it. But if there be any as yet unfit to be called a Son of God, let him press to take his place under God's First-born, the Word, who holds the eldership among the angels, their ruler as it were. And many names are his, for he is called, "the Beginning," and the Name of God, and His Word, and the Man after His image, and "he that sees," that is Israel.

And therefore I was moved . . . to praise the virtues of those who say that "We are all sons of one man" (Gen. xlii. 11). For if we have not yet become fit to be thought sons of God yet we may be sons of His invisible image, the most holy Word. For the Word is the eldest-born image of God. . . .

XXXIV. . . . Through these Potencies the incorporeal and intelligible world was framed, the archetype of this phenomenal world, that being a system of invisible ideal forms, as this is of visible material bodies. Now the nature of these two worlds has so struck with awe the minds of some, that they have deified not merely each of them as a whole, but also their fairest parts, the sun, the moon and the whole sky, and have felt no shame in calling them gods. It was the delusion of such persons that Moses saw, when he says "Lord, Lord, King of the Gods" (Deut. x. 17), to shew the difference between the ruler and the subjects.

There is, too, in the air a sacred company of unbodied souls, commonly called angels in the inspired pages, who wait upon these heavenly powers. So the whole army composed of the several contingents, each marshalled in their proper ranks, have as their business to serve and minister to the word of the Captain who thus marshalled them, and to follow His leadership as right and the law of service demand. For it must not be that God's soldiers should ever be guilty of desertion from the ranks. Now the King may fitly hold converse with his powers and employ them to serve in matters which should not be consummated by God alone. It is true indeed that the Father of All has no need of aught, so that He should require the co-operation of others, if He wills some creative work, yet seeing what was fitting to Himself and the world which was coming into being, He allowed His subject powers to have the fashioning of some things, though He did not give them sovereign and independent knowledge for completion of the task, lest aught of what was coming into being should be miscreated.

XXXV. This outline was needed as premisses. Now for the inferences. Living nature was primarily divided into two opposite parts, the unreasoning and reasoning, this last again into the mortal and immortal species, the mortal being that of men, the immortal that of unbodied souls which range through the air and sky. These are immune from wickedness because their lot from the first has been one of unmixed happiness, and they have not been imprisoned in that dwelling-place of endless calamities—the body. And this immunity is shared by unreasoning natures, because, as they have no gift of understanding, they are also not guilty of wrongdoing willed freely as a result of deliberate reflection. Man is practically the only being who having knowledge of good and evil often chooses the worst, and shuns what should be the object of his efforts, and thus he stands apart as convicted of sin deliberate and aforethought. Thus it was meet and right that when man was formed, God should assign a share in the work to His lieutenants, as He does with the words "let *us* make men," that so man's right actions might be attributable to God, but his sins to others. For it seemed to be unfitting to God the All-ruler that the road to wickedness within the reasonable soul should be of His making, and therefore He delegated the forming of this part to His inferiors. For the work of forming the voluntary element to balance the involuntary had to be accomplished to render the whole complete.

XXXVI. So much for this point, but it is well to have considered this truth also, that God is the cause of good things only and of nothing at all that is bad, since He Himself was the most ancient of beings and the good in its most perfect form. And it best becomes Him that the work of His hands should be akin to His nature, surpassing in excellence even as He surpasses, but that the chastisement of the wicked should be assured through His underlings. My thoughts are attested also by the words of him who was made perfect through practice, "the God who nourisheth me from my youth; the angel who saveth me from all evils" (Gen. xlviii. 15, 16). For he, too, hereby confesses that the truly good gifts, which nourish virtue-loving souls, are referred to God alone as their cause, but on the other hand the province of things evil has been committed to angels (though neither have they full and absolute power of punishment), that nothing which tends to destruction should have its origin in Him whose nature is to save. Therefore he says, "Come and let us go down and confound them." The impious indeed deserve to have it as their punishment, that God's beneficent and merciful and bountiful powers should be brought into association with works of vengeance. Yet, though knowing that punishment was salutary for the human race, He decreed that it should be exacted by others. It was meet that while mankind was judged to deserve correction, the fountains of God's ever-flowing gifts of grace should be kept free not only from all that is, but from all that is deemed to be, evil. . . .

PHILO

from *The Special Laws*

From Philo, *vol. VII. Translated by F. H. Colson. Cambridge: Harvard University Press, and London: William Heinemann, Ltd., 1937.*

BOOK I

VIII. . . . "Know thyself, then, and do not be led away by impulses and desires beyond thy capacity, nor let yearning for the unattainable uplift and carry thee off thy feet, for of the obtainable nothing shall be denied thee."

When Moses heard this, he addressed to Him a second petition and said," I bow before Thy admonitions, that I never could have received the vision of Thee clearly manifested, but I beseech Thee that I may at least see the glory that surrounds Thee, and by Thy glory I understand the powers that keep guard around Thee, of whom I would fain gain apprehension, for though hitherto that has escaped me, the thought of it creates in me a mighty longing to have knowledge of them." To this He answers, "The powers which thou seekest to know are discerned not by sight but by mind even as I, Whose they are, am discerned by mind and not by sight, and when I say 'they are discerned by mind' I speak not of those which are now actually apprehended by mind but mean that if these other powers could be apprehended it would not be by sense but by mind at its purest. But while in their essence they are beyond your apprehension, they nevertheless present to your sight a sort of impress and copy of their active working. You men have for your use seals which when brought into contact with wax or similar material stamp on them any number of impressions while they themselves are not docked in any part thereby but remain as they were. Such you must conceive My powers to be, supplying quality and shape to things which lack either and yet changing or lessening nothing of their eternal nature. Some among you call them not inaptly 'forms' or 'ideas,' since they bring form into everything that is, giving order to the disordered, limit to the unlimited, bounds to the unbounded, shape to the shapeless, and in general changing the worse to something better. Do not, then, hope to be ever able to apprehend Me or any of My powers in Our essence. But I readily and with right goodwill will admit you to a share of what is attainable. That means that I bid you come and contemplate the universe and its contents, a spectacle apprehended not by the eye of the body but by the unsleeping eyes of the mind. Only let there be the constant and profound longing for wisdom which fills its scholars and disciples with verities glorious in their exceeding loveliness." When Moses heard this, he did not cease from his desire but kept the yearning for the invisible aflame in his heart. . . .

LX. . . . Some aver that the Incorporeal Ideas or Forms are an empty name devoid of any real substance of fact, and thus they abolish in things the most essential element of their being, namely the archetypal patterns of all qualities in what exists, and on which the form and dimensions of each separate thing was modelled. These the holy tables of the law speak of as "crushed," for just as anything crushed has lost its quality and form and may be literally said to be nothing more than shapeless matter, so the creed which abolishes the Forms confuses everything and reduces it to the pre-elemental state of existence, that state devoid of shape and quality. Could anything be more preposterous than this? For when out of that confused matter God produced all things, He did not do so with His own handiwork, since His nature, happy and blessed as it was, forbade that He should touch the limitless chaotic matter. Instead He made full use of the incorporeal potencies well denoted by their name of Forms to enable each kind to take its appropriate shape. But this other creed brings in its train no little disorder and confusion. For by abolishing the agencies which created the qualities, it abolishes the qualities also. . . .

PHILO

from *On Rewards and Punishments*

From Philo, *vol. XIII. Translated by F. H. Colson. Cambridge: Harvard University Press, and London: William Heinemann, Ltd., 1939.*

VI. After the self-taught, the man enriched by his natural gifts, the third to reach perfection is the Man of Practice who receives for his special reward the vision of God. For having been in touch with every side of human life and in no half-hearted familiarity with them all, and having shirked no toil or danger if thereby he might descry the truth, a quest well worthy of such love, he found mortal kind set in deep darkness spread over earth and water and the lower air and ether too. For ether and the whole Heaven wore to his eyes the semblance of night, since the whole realm of sense is without defining bounds, and the indefinite is close akin, even brother, to darkness. In his former years the eyes of his soul had been closed, but by means of continuous striving he began though slowly to open them and to break up and throw off the mist which overshadowed him. For a beam purer than ether and incorporeal suddenly shone upon him and revealed the conceptual world ruled by its charioteer. That charioteer, ringed as he was with beams of undiluted light, was beyond his sight or conjecture, for the eye was darkened by the dazzling beams. Yet in spite of the fiery stream which flooded it, his sight held its own in its unutterable longing to behold the vision. The Father and Saviour perceiving the sincerity of his yearning in pity gave power to the penetration of his eyesight and did not grudge to grant him the vision of Himself in so far as it was possible for mortal and created nature to contain it. Yet the vision only showed that He IS, not what He is. For this which is better than the good, more venerable than the monad, purer than the unit, cannot be discerned by anyone else; to God alone is it permitted to apprehend God.

VII. Now the fact that He IS, which can be apprehended under the name of His subsistence, is not apprehended by all or at any rate not in the best way. Some distinctly deny that there is such a thing as the Godhead. Others hesitate and fluctuate as though unable to state whether there is or not. Others whose notions about the subsistence of God are derived through habit rather than thinking from those who brought them up, believe themselves to have successfully attained to religion yet have left on it the imprint of superstition. Others again who have had the strength through knowledge to envisage the Maker and Ruler of all have in the common phrase advanced from down to up. Entering the world as into a well-ordered city they have beheld the earth standing fast, highland and lowland full of sown crops and trees and fruits and all kinds of living creatures to boot; also spread over its surface, seas and lakes and rivers both spring fed and winter torrents. They have seen too the air and breezes so happily tempered, the yearly seasons changing in harmonious order, and over all the sun and moon, planets and fixed stars, the whole heaven and heaven's host, line upon line, a true universe in itself revolving within the universe. Struck with admiration and astonishment they arrived at a conception according with what they beheld, that surely all these beauties and this transcendent order has not come into being automatically but by the handiwork of an architect and world maker; also that there must be a providence, for it is a law of nature that a maker should take care of what has been made.

These no doubt are truly admirable persons and superior to the other classes. They have as I said advanced from down to up by a sort of heavenly ladder and by reason and reflection happily inferred the Creator from His works. But those, if such there be, who have had the power to apprehend Him through Himself without the co-operation of any reasoning process to lead them to the sight, must be recorded as holy and genuine worshippers and friends of God in very truth. In their company is he who in the Hebrew is called Israel but in our tongue the God-seer who sees not His real nature, for that, as I said, is impossible—but that He IS. And this knowledge he has gained not from any other source, not from things on earth or things in Heaven, not from the elements or combinations of elements mortal or immortal, but at the summons of Him alone who has willed to reveal His existence as a person to the suppliant. How this access has been obtained may be well seen through an illustration. Do we behold the sun which sense perceives by any other thing than the sun, or the stars by any others than the stars, and in general is not light seen by light? In the same way God too is His own brightness and is discerned through Himself alone, without anything co-operating or being able to cooperate in giving a perfect apprehension of His existence. They then do but make a happy guess, who are at pains to discern the Uncreated, and Creator of all from His creation, and are on the same footing as those who try to trace the nature of the monad from the dyad, whereas observation of the dyad should begin with the monad which is the starting-point. The seekers for truth are those who envisage God through God, light through light. . . .

PHILO

from *Concerning Noah's Work as a Planter*

From Philo, *vol. III. Translated by F. H. Colson and G. H. Whitaker. Cambridge: Harvard University Press, and London: William Heinemann, Ltd., 1930.*

BOOK II

V. . . . Let anyone then, who would fain escape the confusion of face, which we all feel when we have to leave problems unsolved, say plainly that no material thing is so strong as to be able to bear the burden of the world; and that the everlasting Word of the eternal God is the very sure and staunch prop of the Whole.

He it is, who extending Himself from the midst to its utmost bounds and from its extremities to the midst again, keeps up through all its length Nature's unvanquished course, combining and compacting all its parts. For the Father Who begat Him constituted His Word such a Bond of the Universe as nothing can break. Good reason, then, have we to be sure that all the earth shall not be dissolved by all the water which has gathered within its hollows; nor fire be quenched by air; nor, on the other hand, air be ignited by fire. The Divine Word stations Himself to keep these elements apart, like a Vocal between voiceless elements of speech, that the universe may send forth a harmony like that of a masterpiece of literature. He mediates between the opponents amid their threatenings, and reconciles them by winning ways to peace and concord. . . .

. . . Our great Moses likened the fashion of the reasonable soul to no created thing, but averred it to be a genuine coinage of that dread Spirit, the Divine and Invisible One, signed and impressed by the seal of God, the stamp of which is the Eternal Word. . . .

ORIGEN

from *On Principles*

From The Ante-Nicene Fathers, *Vol. IV, edited by Rev. Alexander Roberts and James Donaldson. NY: The Christian Literature Company, 1890.*

BOOK 1

CHAPTER 1 / ON GOD

1. I know that some will attempt to say that, even according to the declarations of our own Scriptures, God is a body, because in the writings of Moses they find it said, that "our God is a consuming fire;" and in the Gospel according to John, that "God is a Spirit, and they who worship Him must worship Him in spirit and in truth." Fire and spirit, according to them, are to be regarded as nothing else than a body. Now, I should like to ask these persons what they have to say respecting that passage where it is declared that God is light; as John writes in his Epistle, "God is light, and in Him there is no darkness at all." Truly He is that light which illuminates the whole understanding of those who are capable of receiving truth, as is said in the thirty-sixth Psalm, "In Thy light we shall see light." For what other light of God can be named, "in which any one sees light," save an influence of God, by which a man, being enlightened, either thoroughly sees the truth of all things, or comes to know God Himself, who is called the truth? Such is the meaning of the expression, "In Thy light we shall see light;" i.e., in Thy word and wisdom, which is Thy Son, in Himself we shall see Thee the Father. Because He is called light, shall He be supposed to have any resemblance to the light of the sun? Or how should there be the slightest ground for imagining, that from that corporeal light any one could derive the cause of knowledge, and come to the understanding of the truth?

2. If, then, they acquiesce in our assertion, which reason itself has demonstrated, regarding the nature of light, and acknowledge that God cannot be understood to be a body in the sense that light is, similar reasoning will hold true of the expression "a consuming fire." For what will God consume in respect of His being fire? Shall He be thought to consume material substance, as wood, or hay, or stubble? And what in this view can be called worthy of the glory of God, if He be a fire, consuming materials of that kind? But let us reflect that God does indeed consume and utterly destroy; that He consumes evil thoughts, wicked actions, and sinful desires, when they find their way into the minds of believers; and that, inhabiting along with His Son those souls which are rendered capable of receiving His word and wisdom, according to His own declaration, "I and the Father shall come and We shall make our abode with him," He makes them, after all their vices and passions have been consumed, a holy temple, worthy of Himself. Those, moreover, who, on account of the expression "God is a Spirit," think that He is a body, are to be answered, I think, in the following manner. It is the custom of sacred Scripture, when it wishes to designate anything opposed to this gross and solid body, to call it spirit, as in the expression, "The letter killeth, but the spirit giveth life," where there can be no doubt that by "letter" are meant bodily things, and by "spirit" intellectual things, which we also term "spiritual." The apostle, moreover, says, "Even unto this day, when Moses is read, the veil is upon their heart: nevertheless, when it shall turn to the Lord, the veil shall be taken away: and where the Spirit of the Lord is, there is liberty." For so long as any one is not converted to a spiritual understanding, a veil is placed over his heart, with which veil, i.e., a gross understanding, Scripture itself is said or thought to be covered: and this is the meaning of the statement that a veil was placed over the countenance of Moses when he spoke to the people, i.e., when the law was publicly read aloud. But if we turn to the Lord, where also is the word of God, and where the Holy Spirit reveals spiritual knowledge, then the veil is taken away, and with unveiled face we shall behold the glory of the Lord in the holy Scriptures.

3. And since many saints participate in the Holy Spirit, He cannot therefore be understood to be a body, which being divided into corporeal parts, is partaken of by each one of the saints; but He is manifestly a sanctifying power, in which all are said to have a share who have deserved to be sanctified by His grace. And in order that what we say may be more easily understood, let us take an illustration from things very dissimilar. There are many persons who take a part in the science or art of medicine: are we therefore to suppose that those who do so take to themselves the particles of some body called medicine, which is placed before them, and in this way participate in the same? Or must we not rather understand that all who with quick and trained minds come to understand the art and discipline itself, may be said to be partakers of the art of healing? But these are not to be deemed altogether parallel instances in a comparison of medicine to the Holy Spirit, as they have been adduced only to establish that that is not necessarily to be considered a body, a share in which is possessed by many individuals. For the Holy Spirit differs widely from the method or science of medicine, in respect that the Holy Spirit is an intellectual existence, and subsists and exists in a peculiar manner, whereas medicine is not at all of that nature. . . .

5. Having refuted, then, as well as we could, every notion which might suggest that we were to think of God as in any degree corporeal, we go on to say that, according to strict truth, God is incomprehensible, and incapable of being measured. For whatever be the knowledge which we are able to obtain of God, either by perception or reflection, we must of necessity believe that He is by many degrees far better than what we perceive Him to be. For, as if we were to see any one unable to bear a spark of light, or the flame of a very small lamp, and were desirous to acquaint such a one, whose vision could not admit a greater degree of light than what we have stated, with the brightness and splendour of the sun, would it not be necessary to tell him that the splendour of the sun was unspeakably and incalculably better and more glorious than all this light which he saw? So our understanding, when shut in by the fetters of flesh and blood, and rendered, on account of its participation in such material substances, duller and more obtuse, although, in comparison with our bodily nature, it is esteemed to be far superior, yet, in its efforts to examine and behold incorporeal things, scarely holds the place of a spark or lamp. But among all intelligent, that is, incorporeal beings, what is so superior to all others—so unspeakably and incalculably superior—as God, whose nature cannot be grasped or seen by the power of any human understanding, even the purest and brightest?

6. But it will not appear absurd if we employ another similitude to make the matter clearer. Our eyes frequently cannot look upon the nature of the light itself—that is, upon the substance of the sun; but when we behold his splendour or his rays pouring in, perhaps, through windows or some small openings to admit the light, we can reflect how great is the supply and source of the light of the body. So, in like manner, the works of Divine Providence and the plan of this whole world are a sort of rays, as it were, of the nature of God, in comparison with His real substance and being. As, therefore, our understanding is unable of itself to behold God Himself as He is, it knows the Father of the world from the beauty of His works and the comeliness of His creatures. God, therefore, is not to be thought of as being either a body or as existing in a body, but as an uncompounded intellectual nature, admitting within Himself no addition of any kind; so that He cannot be believed to have within him a greater and a less, but is such that He is in all parts *Monas** and, so to speak, *Henas*,† and is the mind and source from which all intellectual nature or mind takes its beginning. But mind, for its movements or operations, needs no physical space, nor sensible magnitude, nor bodily shape, nor colour, nor any other of those adjuncts which are the properties of body or matter. Wherefore that simple and wholly intellectual nature can admit of no delay or hesitation in its movements or operations, lest the simplicity of the divine nature should appear to be circumscribed or in some degree hampered by such adjuncts, and lest that which is the beginning of all things should be found composite and differing, and that which ought to be free from all bodily intermixture, in virtue of being the one sole species of Deity, so to speak, should prove, instead of being one, to consist of many things. That mind, moreover, does not require space in order to carry on its movements

* *Monas*: a unit, one, monad, unity.—Ed.

† *Henas*: unity or oneness.—Ed.

agreeably to its nature, is certain from observation of our own mind. For if the mind abide within its own limits, and sustain no injury from any cause, it will never, from diversity of situation, be retarded in the discharge of its functions; nor, on the other hand, does it gain any addition or increase of mobility from the nature of particular places. And here, if any one were to object, for example, that among those who are at sea, and tossed by its waves, the mind is considerably less vigorous than it is wont to be on land, we are to believe that it is in this state, not from diversity of situation, but from the commotion or disturbance of the body to which the mind is joined or attached. For it seems to be contrary to nature, as it were, for a human body to live at sea; and for that reason it appears, by a sort of inequality of its own, to enter upon its mental operations in a slovenly and irregular manner, and to perform the acts of the intellect with a duller sense, in as great degree as those who on land are prostrated with fever; with respect to whom it is certain, that if the mind do not discharge its functions as well as before, in consequence of the attack of disease, the blame is to be laid not upon the place, but upon the bodily malady, by which the body, being disturbed and disordered, renders to the mind its customary services under by no means the well-known and natural conditions: for we human beings are animals composed of a union of body and soul, and in this way (only) was it possible for us to live upon the earth. But God, who is the beginning of all things, is not to be regarded as a composite being, lest perchance there should be found to exist elements prior to the beginning itself, out of which everything is composed, whatever that be which is called composite. Neither does the mind require bodily magnitude in order to perform any act or movement; as when the eye by gazing upon bodies of larger size is dilated, but is compressed and contracted in order to see smaller objects. The mind, indeed, requires magnitude of an intellectual kind, because it grows, not after the fashion of a body, but after that of intelligence. For the mind is not enlarged, together with the body, by means of corporal additions, up to the twentieth or thirtieth year of life; but the intellect is sharpened by exercises of learning, and the powers implanted within it for intelligent purposes are called forth; and it is rendered capable of greater intellectual efforts, not being increased by bodily additions, but carefully polished by learned exercises. But these it cannot receive immediately from bodyhood, or from birth, because the framework of limbs which the mind employs as organs for exercising itself is weak and feeble; and it is unable to bear the weight of its own operations, or to exhibit a capacity for receiving training.

7. If there are any now who think that the mind itself and the soul is a body, I wish they would tell me by way of answer how it receives reasons and assertions on subjects of such importance—of such difficulty and such subtlety? Whence does it derive the power of memory? and whence comes the contemplation of invisible things? How does the body possess the faculty of understanding incorporeal existences? How does a bodily nature investigate the processes of the various arts, and contemplate the reasons of things? How, also, is it able to perceive and understand divine truths, which are manifestly incorporeal? Unless, indeed, some should happen to be of opinion, that as the very bodily shape and form of the ears or eyes contributes something to hearing and to sight, and as the individual members, formed by God, have some adaptation, even from the very quality of their form, to the end for which they were naturally appointed; so also he may think that the shape of the soul or mind is to be understood as if created purposely and designedly for perceiving and understanding individual things, and for being set in motion by vital movements. I do not perceive, however, who shall be able to describe or state what is the colour of the mind, in respect of its being mind, and acting as an intelligent existence. Moreover, in confirmation and explanation of what we have already advanced regarding the mind or soul—to the effect that it is better than the whole bodily nature—the following remarks may be added. There underlies every bodily sense a certain peculiar sensible substance, on which the bodily sense exerts itself. For example, colours, form, size, underlie vision; voices and sound, the sense of hearing; odours, good or bad, that of smell; savours, that of taste; heat or cold, hardness or softness, roughness or smoothness, that of touch. Now, of those senses enumerated above, it is manifest to all that

the sense of mind is much the best. How, then, should it not appear absurd, that under those senses which are inferior, substances should have been placed on which to exert their powers, but that under this power, which is far better than any other, i.e., the sense of mind, nothing at all of the nature of a substance should be placed, but that a power of an intellectual nature should be an accident, or consequent upon bodies? Those who assert this, doubtless do so to the disparagement of that better substance which is within them; nay, by so doing, they even do wrong to God Himself, when they imagine He may be understood by means of a bodily nature, so that according to their view He is a body, and that which may be understood or perceived by means of a body; and they are unwilling to have it understood that the mind bears a certain relationship to God, of whom the mind itself is an intellectual image, and that by means of this it may come to some knowledge of the nature of divinity, especially if it be purified and separated from bodily matter. . . .

AUGUSTINE

from *The Enchiridion*

From The Works of Aurelius Augustine. *Vol. IX. Edinburgh: T & T Clark, 1883.*

CHAPTER IX / WHAT WE ARE TO BELIEVE. IN REGARD TO NATURE IT IS NOT NECESSARY FOR THE CHRISTIAN TO KNOW MORE THAN THAT THE GOODNESS OF THE CREATOR IS THE CAUSE OF ALL THINGS.

When, then, the question is asked what we are to believe in regard to religion, it is not necessary to probe into the nature of things, as was done by those whom the Greeks call *physici*; nor need we be in alarm lest the Christian should be ignorant of the force and number of the elements,—the motion, and order, and eclipses of the heavenly bodies; the form of the heavens; the species and the natures of animals, plants, stones, fountains, rivers, mountains; about chronology and distances; the signs of coming storms; and a thousand other things which those philosophers either have found out, or think they have found out. For even these men themselves, endowed though they are with so much genius, burning with zeal, abounding in leisure, tracking some things by the aid of human conjecture, searching into others with the aids of history and experience, have not found out all things; and even their boasted discoveries are oftener mere guesses than certain knowledge. It is enough for the Christian to believe that the only cause of all created things, whether heavenly or earthly, whether visible or invisible, is the goodness of the Creator, the one true God; and that nothing exists but Himself that does not derive its existence from Him; and that He is the Trinity—to wit, the Father, and the Son begotten of the the Father, and the Holy Spirit proceeding from the same Father, but one and the same Spirit of Father and Son.

CHAPTER X / THE SUPREMELY GOOD CREATOR MADE ALL THINGS GOOD.

By the Trinity, thus supremely and equally and unchangeably good, all things were created; and these are not supremely and equally and unchangeably good, but yet they are good, even taken separately. Taken as a whole, however, they are very good, because their *ensemble* constitutes the universe in all its wonderful order and beauty.

CHAPTER XI / WHAT IS CALLED EVIL IN THE UNIVERSE IS BUT THE ABSENCE OF GOOD.

And in the universe, even that which is called evil, when it is regulated and put in its own place, only enhances our admiration of the good; for we enjoy and value the good more when we compare it with the evil. For the Almighty God, who, as even the heathen acknowledge, has supreme power over all things, being Himself supremely good, would never permit the existence of anything evil among His works, if He were not so omnipotent and good that He can bring good even out of evil. For what is that which we call evil but the absence of good? In the bodies of animals, disease and wounds mean nothing but the absence of health; for when a cure is effected, that does not mean that the evils which were present—namely, the diseases and wounds—go away from the body and dwell elsewhere: they altogether cease to exist; for the wound or disease is not a substance, but a defect in the fleshly substance,—the flesh itself being a substance, and therefore something good, of which those evils—that is, privations of the good which we call health—are accidents. Just in the same way, what are called vices in the soul are nothing but privations of natural good. And when they are cured, they are not transferred elsewhere: when they cease to exist in the healthy soul, they cannot exist anywhere else.

CHAPTER XII / ALL BEINGS WERE MADE GOOD, BUT NOT BEING MADE PERFECTLY GOOD, ARE LIABLE TO CORRUPTION.

All things that exist, therefore, seeing that the Creator of them all is supremely good, are themselves good. But because they are not, like their Creator, supremely and unchangeably good, their good may be diminished and increased. But for good to be diminished is an evil, although, however much it may be diminished, it is necessary, if the being is to continue, that some good should remain to constitute the being. For however small or of whatever kind the being may be, the good which makes it a being cannot be destroyed without destroying the being itself. An uncorrupted nature is justly held in esteem. But if, still further, it be incorruptible, it is undoubtedly considered of still higher value. When it is corrupted, however, its corruption is an evil, because it is deprived of some sort of good. For if it be deprived of no good, it receives no injury; but it does receive injury, therefore it is deprived of good. Therefore, so long as a being is in process of corruption, there is in it some good of which it is being deprived; and if a part of the being should remain which cannot be corrupted, this will certainly be an incorruptible being, and accordingly the process of corruption will result in the manifestation of this great good. But if it do not cease to be corrupted, neither can it cease to possess good of which corruption may deprive it. But if it should be thoroughly and completely consumed by corruption, there will then be no good left, because there will be no being. Wherefore corruption can consume the good only by consuming the being. Every being, therefore, is a good; a great good, if it cannot be corrupted; a little good, if it can: but in any case, only the foolish or ignorant will deny that it is a good. And if it be wholly consumed by corruption, then the corruption itself must cease to exist, as there is no being left in which it can dwell.

CHAPTER XCV / GOD'S JUDGMENTS SHALL THEN BE EXPLAINED.

Then shall be made clear much that is now dark. For example, when of two infants, whose cases seem in all respects alike, one is by the mercy of God chosen to Himself, and the other is by His justice abandoned (wherein the one who is chosen may recognize what was of justice due to himself, had not mercy intervened); why, of these two, the one should have been chosen rather than the other, is to us an insoluble problem. And again, why miracles were not wrought in the presence of men who would have repented at the working of the miracles, while they were wrought in the presence of others who, it was known, would not repent. For our Lord says most distinctly: "Woe unto thee, Chorazin! woe unto thee, Bethsaida! for if the mighty works, which were done in you, had been done in Tyre and Sidon, they would have repented long ago in sackcloth and ashes."* And assuredly there was no injustice in God's not willing that they should be saved, though they could have been saved had He so willed it. Then shall be seen in the clearest light of wisdom what with the pious is now a faith, though it is not yet a matter of certain knowledge, how sure, how unchangeable, and how effectual is the will of God; how many things He can do which He does not will to do, though willing nothing which He cannot perform; and how true is the song of the psalmist, "But our God is in the heavens; He hath done whatsoever He hath pleased."† And this certainly is not true, if God has ever willed anything that He has not performed; and, still worse, if it was the will of man that hindered the Omnipotent from doing what He pleased. Nothing, therefore, happens but by the will of the Omnipotent, He either permitting it to be done, or Himself doing it.

* Matt. xi. 21.

† Ps. cxv. 3.

CHAPTER XCVI / THE OMNIPOTENT GOD DOES WELL EVEN IN THE PERMISSION OF EVIL.

Nor can we doubt that God does well even in the permission of what is evil. For He permits it only in the justice of His judgment. And surely all that is just is good. Although, therefore, evil, in so far as it is evil, is not a good; yet the fact that evil as well as good exists, is a good. For if it were not a good that evil should exist, its existence would not be permitted by the omnipotent Good, who without doubt can as easily refuse to permit what He does not wish, as bring about what He does wish. And if we do not believe this, the very first sentence of our creed is endangered, wherein we profess to believe in God the Father Almighty. For He is not truly called Almighty if He cannot do whatsoever He pleases, or if the power of His almighty will is hindered by the will of any creature whatsoever.

AUGUSTINE

from *The City of God*

From Saint Augustine. *Translated by Marcus Dods. V. 1. Edinburgh: T & T Clark, 1872.*

BOOK XI

CHAPTER 10 / OF THE SIMPLE AND UNCHANGEABLE TRINITY, FATHER, SON, AND HOLY GHOST, ONE GOD, IN WHOM SUBSTANCE AND QUALITY ARE IDENTICAL.

There is, accordingly, a good which is alone simple, and therefore alone unchangeable, and this is God. By this Good have all others been created, but not simple, and therefore not unchangeable. "Created," I say,—that is, made, not begotten. For that which is begotten of the simple Good is simple as itself, and the same as itself. These two we call the Father and the Son; and both together with the Holy Spirit are one God; and to this Spirit the epithet Holy is in Scripture, as it were, appropriated. And He is another than the Father and the Son, for He is neither the Father nor the Son. I say "another," not "another thing," because He is equally with them the simple Good, unchangeable and co-eternal. And this Trinity is one God; and none the less simple because a Trinity. For we do not say that the nature of the good is simple, because the Father alone possesses it, or the Son alone, or the Holy Ghost alone; nor do we say, with the Sabellian heretics, that it is only nominally a Trinity, and has no real distinction of persons; but we say it is simple, because it is what it has, with the exception of the relation of the persons to one another. For, in regard to this relation, it is true that the Father has a Son, and yet is not Himself the

Son; and the Son has a Father, and is not Himself the Father. But, as regards Himself, irrespective of relation to the other, each is what He has; thus, He is in Himself living, for He has life, and is Himself the Life which He has.

It is for this reason, then, that the nature of the Trinity is called simple, because it has not anything which it can lose, and because it is not one thing and its contents another, as a cup and the liquor, or a body and its colour, or the air and the light or heat of it, or a mind and its wisdom. For none of these is what it has: the cup is not liquor, nor the body colour, nor the air light and heat, nor the mind wisdom. And hence they can be deprived of what they have, and can be turned or changed into other qualitites and states, so that the cup may be emptied of the liquid of which it is full, the body be discoloured, the air darken, the mind grow silly. The incorruptible body which is promised to the saints in the resurrection cannot, indeed, lose its quality of incorruption, but the bodily substance and the quality of incorruption are not the same thing. For the quality of incorruption resides entire in each several part, not greater in one and less in another; for no part is more incorruptible than another. The body, indeed, is itself greater in whole than in part; and one part of it is larger, another smaller, yet is not the larger more incorruptible than the smaller. The body, then, which is not in each of its parts a whole body, is one thing; incorruptibility, which is throughout complete, is another thing;—for every part of the incorruptible body, however unequal to the rest otherwise, is equally incorrupt. For the hand, *e.g.*, is not more incorrupt than the finger because it is larger than the finger; so, though finger and hand are unequal, their incorruptibility is equal. Thus, although incorruptibility is inseparable from an incorruptible body, yet the substance of the body is one thing, the quality of incorruption another. And therefore the body is not what it has. The soul itself, too, though it be always wise (as it will be eternally when it is redeemed), will be so by participating in the unchangeable wisdom, which it is not; for though the air be never robbed of the light that is shed abroad in it, it is not on that account the same thing as the light. I do not mean that the soul is air, as has been supposed by some who could not conceive a spiritual nature; but, with much dissimilarity, the two things have a kind of likeness, which makes it suitable to say that the immaterial soul is illumined with the immaterial light of the simple wisdom of God, as the material air is irradiated with material light, and that, as the air, when deprived of this light, grows dark, (for material darkness is nothing else than air wanting light), so the soul, deprived of the light of wisdom, grows dark.

According to this, then, those things which are essentially and truly divine are called simple, because in them quality and substance are identical, and because they are divine, or wise, or blessed in themselves, and without extraneous supplement. In Holy Scripture, it is true, the Spirit of wisdom is called "manifold" because it contains many things in it; but what it contains it also is, and it being one is all these things. For neither are there many wisdoms, but one, in which are untold and infinite treasures of things intellectual, wherein are all invisible and unchangeable reasons of things visible and changeable which were created by it. For God made nothing unwittingly; not even a human workman can be said to do so. But if He knew all that He made, He made only those things which He had known. Whence flows a very striking but true conclusion, that this world could not be known to us unless it existed, but could not have existed unless it had been known to God. . . .

CHAPTER 26 / OF THE IMAGE OF THE SUPREME TRINITY, WHICH WE FIND IN SOME SORT IN HUMAN NATURE EVEN IN ITS PRESENT STATE.

And we indeed recognise in ourselves the image of God, that is, of the supreme Trinity, an image which, though it be not equal to God, or rather, though it be very far removed from Him,—being neither coeternal, nor, to say all in a word, consubstantial with Him,—is yet nearer to Him in nature than any other of His works, and is destined to be yet restored, that it may bear a still closer resemblance. For we both are, and know that we are, and delight in our being, and our knowledge of it. Moreover, in these three things no true-seeming illusion disturbs us; for we do not come into contact with these by some bodily sense, as we perceive the things outside of us,—colours, *e.g.*, by seeing, sounds by hearing, smells by smelling, tastes by tasting, hard and soft objects by touching,—of all which sensible objects it is the images resembling them, but not themselves which we perceive in the mind and hold in the memory, and which excite us to desire the objects. But, without any delusive representation of images or phantasms, I am most certain that I am, and that I know and delight in this. In respect of these truths, I am not at all afraid of the arguments of the Academicians, who say, What if you are deceived? For if I am deceived, I am. For he who is not, cannot be deceived; and if I am deceived, by this same token I am. And since I am if I am deceived, how am I deceived in believing that I am? for it is certain that I am if I am deceived. Since, therefore, I, the person deceived, should be, even if I were deceived, certainly I am not deceived in this knowledge that I am. And, consequently, neither am I deceived in knowing that I know. For, as I know that I am, so I know this also, that I know. And when I love these two things, I add to them a certain third thing, namely, my love, which is of equal moment. For neither am I deceived in this, that I love, since in those things which I love I am not deceived; though even if these were false, it would still be true that I *loved* false things. For how could I justly be blamed and prohibited from loving false things, if it were false that I loved them? But, since they are true and real, who doubts that when they are loved, the love of them is itself true and real? Further, as there is no one who does not wish to be happy, so there is no one who does not wish to be. For how can he be happy, if he is nothing?

CHAPTER 27 / OF EXISTENCE, AND KNOWLEDGE OF IT, AND THE LOVE OF BOTH.

And truly the very fact of existing is by some natural spell so pleasant, that even the wretched are, for no other reason, unwilling to perish; and, when they feel that they are wretched, wish not that they themselves be annihilated, but that their misery be so. Take even those who, both in their own esteem, and in point of fact, are utterly wretched, and who are reckoned so, not only by wise men on account of their folly, but by those who count themselves blessed, and who think them wretched because they are poor and destitute,—if any one should give these men an immortality, in which their misery should be deathless, and should offer the alternative, that if they shrank from existing eternally in the same misery they might be annihilated, and exist nowhere at all, nor in any condition, on the instant they would joyfully, nay exultantly, make election to exist always, even in such a condition, rather than not exist at all. The well-known feeling of such men witnesses to this. For when we see that they fear to die, and will rather live in such misfortune than end it by death, is it not obvious enough how nature shrinks from annihilation? And, accordingly, when they know that they must die, they seek, as a great boon, that this mercy be shown them, that they may a little longer live in the same misery, and delay to end it by death. And so they indubitably prove with what glad alacrity they would accept immortality, even though it secured to them endless destruction. What! do not even all irrational animals, to whom such calculations are unknown, from the huge dragons down to the least worms, all testify that they wish to exist, and therefore shun death by every movement in their power? Nay, the very plants and shrubs, which have no such life as enables them to shun destruction by movements we can see, do not they all seek, in their own fashion, to conserve their existence, by rooting themselves more and more deeply in the earth, that so they may draw nourishment, and throw out healthy branches towards the sky? In fine, even the lifeless bodies, which want not only sensation but seminal life, yet either seek the upper air or sink deep, or are balanced in an intermediate position, so that they may protect their existence in that situation where they can exist in most accordance with their nature.

And how much human nature loves the knowledge of its existence, and how it shrinks from being deceived, will be sufficiently understood from this fact, that every man prefers to grieve in a sane mind, rather than to be glad in madness. And this grand and wonderful instinct belongs to men alone of all animals; for, though some of them have keener eyesight than ourselves for this world's light, they cannot attain to that spiritual light with which our mind is somehow irradiated, so that we can form right judgments of all things. For our power to judge is proportioned to our acceptance of this light. Nevertheless, the irrational animals, though they have not knowledge, have certainly something resembling knowledge; whereas the other material things are said to be sensible, not because they have senses, but because they are the objects of our senses. Yet among plants, their nourishment and generation have some resemblance to sensible life. However, both these and all material things have their causes hidden in their nature; but their outward forms, which lend beauty to this visible structure of the world, are perceived by our senses, so that they seem to wish to compensate for their own want of knowledge by providing us with knowledge. But we perceive them by our bodily senses in such a way that we do not judge of them by these senses. For we have another and far superior sense, belonging to the inner man, by which we perceive what things are just, and what unjust,—just by means of an intelligible idea, unjust by the want of it. This sense is aided in its functions neither by the eyesight, nor by the orifice of the ear, nor by the airholes of the nostrils, nor by the palate's taste, nor by any bodily touch. By it I am assured both that I am, and that I know this; and these two I love, and in the same manner I am assured that I love them.

AUGUSTINE

from *Answer to Skeptics*

From Writings of Saint Augustine, *V. 1. NY: Cima Publishing Co., Inc., 1948.*

CHAPTER 10*

You say that in philosophy nothing can be understood. And, in order to spread your utterance far and wide, you ridicule the quarrels and dissensions of philosophers. And you think that those quarrels and dissensions supply you with arms against the philosophers themselves. How, for instance, are we going to adjudicate the contest between Democritus and the earlier cosmologists as to the oneness or the incalculable multiplicity of the world, inasmuch as it was impossible to preserve agreement between Democritus himself and his heir, Epicurus? That voluptuary was glad to grasp atoms in the darkness and to make those little bodies his handmaids, but he dissipated his entire patrimony through litigation when he allowed them to deviate from their respective proper courses and to diverge capriciously into one another's paths. Of course, this is no affair of mine, but, if it pertains to wisdom to know anything about those matters, a wise man cannot be unaware of that fact. I myself am as yet far from being even almost wise. Nevertheless, I know something about those matters of cosmology, for I am certain that either there is only one world or there are more worlds than one. I am likewise certain that if there are more worlds than one, their number is either finite or infinite. Carneades would teach that this notion resembles a false one. Furthermore, I know for certain that this world of ours has its present arrangement either from the nature of bodies or from a foresight of some kind. I am also certain that either it always was and always will be, or it had a beginning and will never end, or it existed before time and will have an end, or it had a beginning and will not last forever. And I have the same kind of knowledge with regard to countless cosmological problems, for those disjunctives are true, and no one can confuse them with any likeness to falsity. "Now," says the Academic, "assume the truth of either member of the disjunction." I refuse to do that, for it is the

* This work is in the form of a dialogue. In this selection, Augustine is refuting the Skeptics, particularly Carneades, head of the Academy established by Plato.—Ed.

same as saying: "Quit what you know, and say what you know not." "But," says he, "your notion is now hanging in suspense." Very well: better hanging in suspense than falling to the ground. While it is hanging, it is at least in plain view, and it can be pronounced either true or false. Because I know that it is either true or false, I say that I know it as a proposition. Now, since you do not deny that these matters pertain to philosophy, and since you nevertheless maintain that nothing can be known about them, I ask you to show that I do not know them. In other words, say either that these disjunctives are false or that they have something in common with falsity—some characteristic which renders them absolutely indistinguishable from something that is false.

CHAPTER 11

"But," says he, "if the senses are deceptive, how do you know that this world exists?" Your reasons will never be able to refute the testimony of the senses to such extent as to convince us that nothing is perceived by us. In fact, you have never ventured to try that, but you have strenuously exerted yourself to convince us that a thing can be something other than what it seems to be. So, by the term *world,* I mean this totality which surrounds us and sustains us. Whatever its nature may be, I apply the term *world* to that which is present to my eyes, and which I see to be holding the earth and the heavens, or the *quasi* earth and the *quasi* heavens. If you say that nothing appears to me, then I shall never be in error: the man that is in error is the man who rashly accepts as true whatever appears to him. Indeed, you yourselves say that to sentient beings a false thing can appear to be true, but you do not say that nothing can so appear to them. You are anxious to gain a victory in this dispute. But, if we know nothing, and if nothing even appears to us as true, then the entire reason for our dispute will vanish. And if you maintain that what appears to me is not a world, then you are disputing about words only, for I have said that I call it a world.

But, you will ask me: "Is it the very same world that you are seeing, even if you are asleep?" I have already said that I am using the term *world* to designate whatever appears as such to me. But, if you think that the term ought to be restricted to that which appears to those who are awake and of sound mind, then contend—if you can—that sleeping men and deranged men are not in this world while they are asleep or deranged. My only assertion is that this entire mass and frame of bodies in which we exist is either a unit or not a unit; and that it is what it is, whether we be asleep or awake, deranged or of sound mind. Point out how this notion can be false. If I am now asleep, it is possible that I have said nothing at all, but if—as happens occasionally—words have escaped my lips during sleep, it is possible that I was not talking here, that I was not thus seated, and that I was not talking to these listeners. In any case, it must be true that the world is what it is. Of course, I am not saying that I perceived the same thing that I would perceive if I were awake, but you can say that what I perceive when I am awake could appear to me also when I am asleep. Therefore, it can be very similar to something false. However, if there are one world and six worlds, it is clear that there are seven worlds, no matter how I may be affected. And, with all due modesty, I maintain that I know this. Then, show that either this dilemma or the aforesaid disjunctives can be false by reason by sleep, or mental derangement, or the unreality of sense perception. And then, if I remember it when I am awakened, I shall admit that I am vanquished. But, I regard it as already sufficiently plain that the things which are seen awry through sleep or derangement are things that pertain to the bodily senses, for, even if the whole human race were fast asleep, it would still be necessarily true that *three times three* are nine, and that this is the square of intelligible numbers. Furthermore, I see that, on behalf of the senses, one could urge many arguments which we do not find reprehended by the Academics. In fact, I believe that the senses are not untrustworthy either because deranged persons suffer illusions, or because we see things wrongly when we are asleep. If the senses correctly intimate things to the vigilant and the sane, it is no affair of theirs what the mind of a sleeping or an insane person may fancy for itself.

Inquiry is still to be made as to whether the senses report the truth whenever they report anything. Well, suppose that some Epicurean would say: "I have no complaint to make about the senses, for it would be unfair to demand of them anything beyond their power. And, whatever the eyes can see, they see that which is true." Therefore, as to what they see with regard to an oar in the water—is that true? It is absolutely true. In fact, since there is a special reason for the oar's appearing that way, I should rather accuse my eyes of deception if it appeared to be straight when it is dipped in the water, for, in that case, they would not be seeing what ought to be seen. But what is the need of many examples? The same can be said about the motion of towers, the wings of birds, and countless other things. "Nevertheless," says some one or other, "I am deceived if I give assent." Restrict your assent to the mere fact of your being convinced that it appears thus to you. Then there is no deception, for I do not see how even an Academic can refute a man who says: "I know that this appears white to me. I know that I am delighted by what I am hearing. I know that this smells pleasant to me. I know that this tastes sweet to me. I know that this feels cold to me." Tell me, rather, whether the oleaster leaves—for which a goat has a persistent appetite—are bitter *per se.* O, shameless man! Is not the goat more moderate? I know not how the oleaster leaves may be for flocks and herds; as to myself, they are bitter. What more do you wish to know? Perhaps there is even some man for whom they are not bitter. Are you contending for the sake of annoyance? Have I said that they are bitter for everybody? I have said that they are bitter for me, but I do not say that they will always be so. What, if at different times and for diverse reasons, something be found to taste sweet at one time, and bitter on some other occasion? This is what I say: that when a man tastes something, he can in good faith swear that it is sweet to his palate or that it is not, and that by no Greek sophistry can he be beguiled out of this knowledge. If I am relishing the taste of something, who would be so brazen as to say to me: "Perhaps you are not tasting it: it may be only a dream"? Would I discontinue? Why, that would afford me pleasure even in a dream. Wherefore, no resemblance to falsity can confuse what I have said that I know. Perhaps an Epicurean or the Cyrenaics would make far greater claims for the senses. And I have heard that nothing has been said in rebuttal by the Academics. But, what is that to me? Let the Academics refute those claims if—even with my aid—they are able and willing to do so, for their arguments against the senses do not hold against all philosophers. There are some philosophers who profess that an opinion can be engendered by what the mind receives through a bodily sense, but maintain that no certain knowledge [*scientia*] can be thus engendered. They hold that such knowledge is contained in the intelligence, far remote from the senses. Perhaps it is among those philosophers that we shall find the wise man we are looking for. . . .

CREATIONISM

Philosophy was thriving in West Asia, North Africa, and Spain during the Middle Ages. The chief problem for Jewish and Islamic philosophers was essentially that facing the earlier North African platonists: how to reconcile Semitic religion and Greek philosophy. Broadly speaking, the Jewish and Islamic philosophers divide sharply over the issue of faith and reason. Some—the *creationists*—believe in the primacy of faith, the ultimate priority of religion over philosophy, and God's creation of the world from nothing. Others—the *rationalists*—believe in the primacy of reason, the priority of philosophy over religion, and the eternity of the world.

Abu-Yusuf Ya'qub ibn Ishaq al-Kindi (ninth century C.E.) was born in Basra and held an important position at the caliph's court in Baghdad. He was the first philosopher to introduce Greek philosophy to the Islamic world and consequently was reputed as a great philosopher for more than a century. Al-Kindi disagreed with later Islamic philosophers on some important points. A creationist, he maintains —like Philo and other Alexandrian philosophers but unlike al-Farabi, Avicenna, and Averroës, who were to succeed him—that God created the world from nothing. He maintains that philosophy is important but that it cannot yield all possible knowledge into the world and, especially, God. Revealed religion is required as well. In this respect, al-Kindi occupies a moderate position in Islamic thought. The later Islamic philosophers mentioned above make a stronger brief for philosophy, claiming that it can in principle achieve any knowledge that can be attained through any route. In contrast, earlier Islamic thinkers, often called *dialectical theologians,* use Greek ideas in explicating Islam but maintain that philosophy has no independent status and is strictly inferior to religion. Al-Kindi's thought provided an alternative to the antiphilosophical attitudes of the dialectical theologians and thus forged the path that later thinkers would take to a more radical conclusion.

Saadia ben Joseph (882–942), also known as Saadia Gaon, was an important Jewish creationist. Born in upper Egypt, he had written the first known Hebrew dictionary and had published a treatise refuting the views of the rationalistic Karaite sect of Judaism by the age of twenty-three. He then left Egypt and travelled to Babylonia, where he defended the right of the Babylonian rabbis to set the Jewish calendar, in opposition to the rabbis of Palestine. As a result he was appointed to the rabbinical academy of Sura. At age forty-six he became the first non-Babylonian to serve as head—*gaon*—of that academy. His service was controversial and brief. He retired and devoted himself to writing.

At fifty-one, Saadia completed *The Book of Beliefs and Opinions,* his chief philosophical work. But he left a large body of other significant writings, including treatises on various subjects in Jewish law, commentaries on the Talmud and on Jewish mystical works, and the first translation of the Old Testament into Arabic.

Saadia argues that philosophy and human reason are important sources of knowledge but that they are not sufficient; they require supplementation with revealed religion. Understood in conjunction with revelation, however, philosophy supports religious truth. Saadia argues that God created the world from nothing, that God is one, and that both divine law and secular ethics are important to proper human conduct.

Abu Hamid Muhammad al-Ghazali (1058–1111), known to medieval philosophers in the West as Algazel, was born in a village, Ghazaleh, near Tus in Khorasan, now northeastern Iran. An excellent student, he became a professor and rector at Nizamiya University in Baghdad. At age thirty-six, however, he resigned to live the ascetic life of a Sufi mystic, traveling to Egypt, Mecca, Medina, and elsewhere. Al-Ghazali despaired of finding certainty through intellectual pursuit and argued that only through mystical communion with God was true certainty and understanding possible.

Most of al-Ghazali's philosophical work attacks the possibility of metaphysical knowledge, and, more generally, the utility of reason. In *The Incoherence of the Philosophers,* he tries to refute many standard philosophical views and the arguments that al-Farabi, Avicenna, and other rationalists commonly use to support them. In particular, al-Ghazali argues that the philosophers have been unsuccessful in trying to show that God exists, that the world is eternal, that God is one, and so on. He uses philosophical arguments to try to demonstrate that philosophical argument on religious subjects is pointless. Averroës, who attacks *The Incoherence of the Philosophers* in *The Incoherence of the Incoherence* (see p. 110) contends that this strategy is thus hopelessly paradoxical. But al-Ghazali's work lies within the tradition of philosophical skepticism. Skeptics try to show that some kinds of alleged knowledge are unreliable or unjustifiable. They often use reason to undermine the claims of reason. In itself, this is not paradoxical. Reason may lead to contradictory conclusions, for example, or may show itself to be unreliable. Only if skeptics claim certainty within the realm they subject to attack—a kind of certainty they themselves deem impossible—does their general method seem troublesome. Al-Ghazali does claim a kind of certainty, based on communion with God. That, however, is achieved not through reason but through mystical insight.

Maimonides (1135–1204) was born in Córdoba, Spain. His father was a distinguished Jewish scholar. At thirteen, he fled Córdoba, already under Moslem control, when an intolerant Islamic sect conquered it. Eventually he and his family settled in northern Africa. When he was thirty, Maimonides became a court physician in Egypt. He served as a leader of the Jewish community there, becoming a great authority on Jewish law, until he died at age sixty-seven.

Maimonides wrote many volumes on Jewish law, medicine, and other topics. His chief work bearing on philosophy is *The Guide of the Perplexed*, a long treatise written in Arabic on the meaning of various Hebrew words. Maimonides addresses his work to people torn between what they see as the competing claims of philosophy and religion. (Such people, called "the perplexed," are among the "weeds" of the ideal city described by al-Farabi in his work *The Political Regime.*) Maimonides recognizes that, in the opinion of many, reason and religious belief conflict. He tries to reconcile them, showing that reason is not only compatible with but even supports religion and religious law. In his view, shallow thought challenges religion, but profound thought strengthens it.

This implies that—in philosophy, at least—a little learning is a dangerous thing. Maimonides wishes to encourage deep study and reflection but to discourage shallow learning. To keep the vulgar away, al-Farabi writes intentionally boring, jargon-filled treatises. To the same end, Maimonides admits that he breaks apart ideas that belong together, makes contradictory assertions, and generally tries to make his book hard to understand.

Maimonides, to demonstrate the harmony of religion and philosophy, tries to refute the arguments of Aristotle and his Islamic followers that the world is eternal. He maintains that it is at least possible, from the point of view of reason, that God created the world from nothing. Consequently, there is no reason not to accept the word of Scripture. Similarly, Maimonides argues that the existence of evil does not contradict the existence of God. In ethics, Maimonides tries to show that the 613 commandments of God in the Torah are all consistent with reason; all that pertain to relations between humans, he contends, are actually required by reason.

AL-KINDI

from *On First Philosophy*

Reprinted from Al Kindi's Metaphysics *translated by Alfred L. Ivry by permission of the State University of New York Press. Albany: SUNY Press, 1974.*

May God grant you long life, O son of the highest of princes and of the (strongest) bonds of bliss; of those who, whoever holds fast to their guidance is happy in the abode of this life and the abode of eternity; and may He adorn you with all the accoutrements of virtue and cleanse you from all the dirtiness of vice.

Indeed, the human art which is highest in degree and most noble in rank is the art of philosophy, the definition of which is knowledge of the true nature of things, insofar as is possible for man. The aim of the philosopher is, as regards his knowledge, to attain the truth, and as regards his action, to act truthfully; not that the activity is endless, for we abstain and the activity ceases, once we have reached the truth.

We do not find the truth we are seeking without finding a cause; the cause of the existence and continuance of everything is the True One, in that each thing which has being has truth. The True One exists necessarily, and therefore beings exist.

The noblest part of philosophy and the highest in rank is the First Philosophy, i.e., knowledge of the First Truth Who is the cause of all truth. Therefore it is necessary that the perfect and most noble philosopher will be the man who fully understands this most noble knowledge; for the knowledge of the cause is more noble than knowledge of the effect, since we have complete knowledge of every knowable only when we have obtained full knowledge of its cause.

Every cause will be either matter or form or agent, i.e., that from which motion begins; or final, i.e., that for the sake of which the thing is. Scientific inquiries are four, as we have determined elsewhere in our philosophical treatises; either "whether," "what," "which," or "why." "Whether" is an investigation only of the existence (of something); "what" investigates the genus of every existent which has a genus; "which" investigates its specific difference; "what" and "which" together investigate its species; and "why" its final cause, since it is an investigation of the absolute cause. It is evident that when we obtain full knowledge of its matter we thereby obtain full knowledge of its genus; and when we obtain full knowledge of its form we thereby obtain full knowledge of its species, knowledge of the specific difference being subsumed within knowledge of the species. When, therefore, we obtain full knowledge of its matter, form and final cause, we thereby obtain full knowledge of its definition, and the real nature of every defined object is in its definition.

Knowledge of the first cause has truthfully been called "First Philosophy," since all the rest of philosophy is contained in its knowledge. The first cause is, therefore, the first in nobility, the first in genus, the first in rank with respect to that the knowledge of which is most certain; and the first in time, since it is the cause of time. . . .

Aristotle, the most distinguished of the Greeks in philosophy, said: "We ought to be grateful to the fathers of those who have contributed any truth, since they were the cause of their existence; let alone (being grateful) to the sons; for the fathers are their cause, while they are the cause of our attaining the truth." How beautiful is that which he said in this matter! We ought not to be ashamed of appreciating the truth and of acquiring it wherever it comes from, even if it comes from races distant and nations different from us. For the seeker of truth nothing takes precedence over the truth, and there is no disparagement of the truth, nor belittling either of him who speaks it or of him who conveys it. (The status of) no one is diminished by the truth; rather does the truth ennoble all.

It is well for us—being zealous for the perfection of our species, since the truth is to be found in this—to adhere in this book of ours to our practice in all our compositions of presenting the ancients' complete statement on this subject according to the most direct approach and facile manner of the disciples of this approach; and completing that which they did not state completely, following the custom of the language and contemporary usage, and insofar as is possible for us. . . .

The knowledge of the true nature of things includes knowledge of Divinity, unity and virtue, and a complete knowledge of everything useful, and of the way to it; and a distance from anything harmful, with precautions against it. It is the acquisition of all this which the true messengers brought from God, great be His praise. For the true messengers, may God's blessings be upon them, brought but an affirmation of the Divinity of God alone, and an adherence to virtues, which are pleasing to Him; and the relinquishment of vices, which are contrary to virtues both in themselves and in their effects.

Devotion to this precious possession is, therefore, required for possessors of the truth, and we must exert ourselves to the utmost in its pursuit, in view of that which we have said previously and that which we shall say now, namely, acquisition of this is required necessarily (even) according to the tongues of its adversaries; for they must say that acquisition of this is either necessary or not necessary. If they say that it is necessary, then its pursuit is necessary for them. If, on the other hand, they say that it is not necessary, it is necessary for them to bring a cause of this, and to give a demonstration of this; and the presentation of cause and demonstration are part of the possession of knowledge of the real nature of things. Pursuit of this acquisition is, therefore, required by their own tongues, and devotion to it is necessary for them.

We ask Him Who examines our inner thoughts and who knows our diligence in establishing the proof of His Divinity and the explanation of His Unity, and in defending (Him) against His opponents who disbelieve in that in Him by proofs which subdue their disbelief and rip the veils of their shameful actions that show the deficiencies of their vicious creeds; (ask) that He encompass us, and anyone who follows our approach, within the fortress of His everlasting might, and that He clothe us with the garments of His protective armor and bestow upon us the assistance of the penetrating edge of His sword and the support of the conquering might of His strength. (We ask this) so that He bring us to our ultimate intention of assisting the truth and supporting veracity; and so that he bring us to the level of those whose intentions He likes and whose actions He accepts and to whom He grants success and victory over His opponents who deny His grace and who deviate from the truthful approach which is pleasing to Him. . . .

SAADIA BEN JOSEPH

from *The Book of Beliefs and Opinions*

From Saadia Gaon, The Book of Beliefs and Opinions. *Translated by Samuel Rosenblatt (New Haven: Yale University Press, 1948, 1976).*

TREATISE I / CONCERNING [THE BELIEF] THAT ALL EXISTING THINGS HAVE BEEN CREATED

CHAPTER 1

And now that I have made this preliminary observation perfectly clear, I say that our Lord, exalted be He, made it known to us that all things were created and that He had created them out of nothing. Thus Scripture says: *In the beginning God created the heaven and the earth* (Gen. 1:1). It says also: *I am the Lord, that maketh all things; that stretched forth the heavens alone; that spread abroad the earth by Myself* (Isa. 44:24). Besides that, all this was verified for us by Him by means of miracles and marvels, so that we accepted it as true.

I next inquired into this matter to see whether it could be supported by reason as it had been verified by prophecy, and I found that it could be thus supported in many ways. Out of the sum of these I shall excerpt [the following] four proofs.

The first is the one from finitude. That is to say: it is certain that heaven and earth are both finite, because the earth is in the center of the universe and the heaven revolves around it. It therefore follows, of necessity, that the force inhering in them be finite, since it is impossible for an infinite force to reside in a finite body, for such a possibility is rejected by all that is known. Now, since the force that maintains these two is finite, it follows necessarily that they must have a beginning and an end.

After this proof had occurred to me, I checked it at leisure, being in no hurry to formulate it until I had verified it. I asked myself: "Perhaps the earth is unlimited in its length, breadth, and depth?" But then I said: "If it were so, the sun could not have encompassed it so as to complete its revolution around it once every day and night, rising repeatedly at its place of rising and setting where it sets, and the same thing holds for the moon and the rest of the stars."

After that I asked [myself]: "Perhaps, then, it is the heavenly bodies that have no finitude?" [On second thought,] however, I reflected: "But how is that possible, seeing that all of them in their entirety move and revolve perpetually around the earth?" For it is inconceivable that it is the section of them that is adjacent to us alone that revolves and that the remainder of them is too large to revolve, for what we understand by the term *heaven* is only this thing that revolves. We have no conception of anything beyond it, let alone that we believe it to be a heaven and maintain that it does not revolve.

Then I went further in my investigation, saying [to myself]: "But perhaps there are many earths and many heavens, each of which heavens encompasses its own earth, so that there would be an infinite number of worlds?" However, I realized that that was impossible from the standpoint of nature, for it is not admissible according to nature that the [element] earth be above that of fire nor that the [element of] air be by nature below that of water, for both fire and air are light, whereas earth and water are both of them heavy. In fact, I knew that if there were in existence a clod of dirt outside of this earth of ours, it would have penetrated through the entire layers of air and fire until it had reached the dirt of this earth. Likewise if there had been a gathering of water aside from these seas of ours, it would have cut through the air and the fire until it had reached these bodies of water.

Thus I arrived at the unshakable conclusion that there was no heaven other than this heaven of ours, nor any earth besides this earth. Also this heaven was finite and so was this earth finite. Now, since their bodies were limited, the force inhering in them too had to be limited, reaching a boundary at which it stopped. Nor could they continue to exist after the cessation of that force, or have been in existence before it came into being.

[Then] I found that Scripture, too, testified to the fact that they were both finite. It says, namely: *From one end of the earth even unto the other end of the earth* (Deut. 13:8); and again: *And from one end of heaven unto the other end of heaven* (Deut. 4:32). It also testifies to the sun's revolving around the earth and to its repetition of this revolution every day, declaring: *The sun also ariseth, and the sun goeth down, and hasteth to his place where he ariseth* (Eccles. 1:5).

The second proof is [derived] from the combination of parts and the composition of divisions. That is to say, I noted that bodies consisted of a combination of parts and a composition of connecting links. Therein were clearly revealed to me signs of the handiwork of the Maker, as well as of creation.

Thereupon I said [to myself]: "But perhaps these links and joints are to be found only in the small bodies—I mean the bodies of animals and plants?" So I extended my thought toward the earth and, behold, it was like that also, for it is made up of an aggregation of dust and stones and sand and the like. I then lifted up my thought to heaven and I found that it consisted of many layers of spheres, one within the other, in which were set individual luminaries called "stars," of varying sizes, large and small, and of varying degrees of luminosity, great and little, all of them fitted into these spheres.

When, then, there became evident to me this aggregation and combination and composition—

which [could be construed only as] things created—in the body of heaven and outside of it, I was convinced because of this proof also that the heaven and all that it contained was created.

I furthermore found Scripture saying that the division of the parts of the animals and their combination points to their having been created. That is [the implication of] its statement with reference to man: *Thy hands have made me and fashioned me* (Ps. 119:73). [It is implied] also [in] its statement about the earth: *That formed the earth and made it, He established it* (Isa. 45:18); and its statement about the heaven: *When I behold Thy heavens, the work of Thy fingers, the moon and the stars, which Thou hast established* (Ps. 8:4).

The third proof is [taken] from the accidents. That is to say, I found that no bodies were free from accidents, either such as arise in each of these bodies themselves or from external sources. Thus animals grow and increase in size until they have reached maturity. Then they diminish again and their parts disintegrate.

Thereupon I said [to myself]: "But perhaps the earth is immune from these accidents?" So I studied the earth carefully, and I found that it was never without plants and animals, both of which are, so far as their bodies are concerned, created, and it is well known that whatever is inseparable from what is created is like the latter in its nature.

Next I said [to myself]: "But perhaps the heavenly bodies are immune from such accidents?" So I observed them clearly, and behold they could not be ridded of these accidents, for the first and principal one of these accidents was that of continuous, unceasing motion. In fact [they are subject to] many motions, varying to such an extent that by comparing them with one another thou discoverest their slowness or their speed. Among these [accidents] must also be included the light shed by some upon others, resulting in the illumination of the latter, as happens in the case of the moon. Another accident is the assumption by certain stars of a whitish, reddish, yellowish, or greenish coloration.

When, then, I found that these accidents extended to these [heavenly bodies also], and that the latter did not precede their accidents in time, I was fully convinced that whatever did not precede its accident in coming into being must be like this accident in nature, since the latter is included in the definition of the former. Furthermore there is the statement of Scripture to the effect that the accidents of earth and heaven prove that both of them had a beginning. It says, namely: *I have made the earth, and created man upon it; I, even My hands, have stretched out the heavens, and all their hosts have I commanded* (Isa. 45:12).

The fourth proof is [based] on [the conception of] time. That is to say, I know that there are three [distinct] periods of time: past, present, and future. Now even though the present is shorter than any moment of time, I assumed, [for the sake of argument,] that this present moment is a point, and said [to myself]: "Let it be supposed that a person should desire mentally to advance in time above this point. He would be unable to do it for the reason that time is infinite, and what is infinite cannot be completely traversed mentally in a fashion ascending [backward to the beginning]."

Now this same reason makes it impossible for existence to have traversed infinity in descending fashion so as to reach us. But if existence had not reached us, we would not have come into being. The necessary conclusion from this premise would, then, have been that we, the company of those that are, are not, and that those that exist do not exist. Since, however, I find that I do exist, I know that existence has traversed the whole length of time until it reached me and that, if it were not for the fact that time is finite, existence could not have traversed it.

I also applied this conviction of mine to future time as unhesitatingly as I had done it to the past. Moreover I found Scripture making a similar remark about distant time: *All men have looked thereon; man beholdeth it afar off* (Job 36:25). Furthermore the saint said: *I will fetch my knowledge from afar, and will ascribe righteousness to my Maker* (Job 36:3). . . .

TREATISE II / CONCERNING [THE BELIEF] THAT THE CREATOR OF ALL THINGS, BLESSED AND EXALTED BE HE, IS ONE

CHAPTER 1

. . . let me begin with the main subject of this treatise and say that we have been informed by our Lord, magnified and exalted be He, through the pronouncements of His prophets that He is one, living, omnipotent, and omniscient, that there is nothing that resembles Him, and that He does not resemble any of His works. This thesis [the prophets] supported by means of miracles and marvels, so that we accepted it immediately while waiting for its verification for us by speculation. . . .

I say, then, first of all, that I find a proof of God's uniqueness . . . to be contained in the following thesis; namely that, since the Creator of all bodies cannot be of the same species as His creatures, and since the bodies are many in number, it follows of necessity that He be one. For if He were more than one, there would apply to Him the category of number and He would fall under the laws governing bodies.

Furthermore, the idea of a Creator as indispensable [to the explanation of existence] is dictated by reason. However, what is indispensable is one [God]. More than that would be neither indispensable nor necessary.

Again, the existence of one Creator is established by means of the first proof; namely, that of the creation of the world. To demonstrate the existence of more than that number would require a second proof, outside of that first proof. There is, however, no means of proving the existence of a Creator other than that of creation.

CHAPTER II

After [listing] these three proofs, now, [in favor] of God's oneness, I say that every argument refuting the existence of two gods constitutes an argument in favor of the one. . . .

. . . if neither of the two [principles by whom the world was supposedly created] could, if he wished to create something, carry out this impulse except with the help of the other, they would both be impotent. If, again, the will of the one could compel the other to help him, then both would be acting under compulsion. Should it be assumed, on the other hand, that both exercise complete freedom of choice, then if one of them were to desire to keep a body alive whilst the other wanted to put it to death, that body would necessarily have to be alive and dead at one and the same time.

I say furthermore that if each one of them could hide something from his peer, they would both be ignorant. If, however, he could not do that, then both would to that extent be lacking in omnipotence. I say also that, if these two [principles] are [to be conceived as being] connected with one another, they are really one. If, on the other hand, they are to be considered as distinct from each other, that would have to be due to a third [principle] separating them.

Nor would I concede to the proponents of [this theory of] two [principles] the right to compare the latter to darkness and light which are contiguous to one another, no third factor coming between them. For these two are only accidents, whereas the former constitute, according to the proponents of the theory of dualism, substances.

These arguments do, then, turn out to be in agreement with the assertion of the Scriptures to the effect that there is no Creator other than the one and only God, as they state: *Unto thee it was shown, that thou mightest know that the Lord, He is God; there is none else beside Him* (Deut. 4:35). . . .

CHAPTER III

. . . I would, therefore, say in general that, whenever there is encountered in either the assertions of Scripture or in the speech of any one of us monotheists an expression pertaining to the description of our Creator or to His handiwork, which stands in contradiction to the requirement of sound reason, there can be no doubt about it that that expression was meant to be taken in a figurative sense, which the diligent students will find if they seek it. . . .

CHAPTER IV

Next let me say that I have found by means of logical speculation proofs of God's vitality and His omnipotence and omniscience. All this is evident from the fact that He created all things, for, according to what our reason discloses to us, it is clear that only he that possesses the power can create, and that only one who is alive has the power, and that whatever is created and well made can emanate only from one who knew, before he made it, how the thing to be created was to come into being.

These three attributes were, then, discovered by our reason as appertaining to our Maker suddenly, at one blow. That [is to say] by virtue of what He has created, it is established that He is living, omnipotent, and omniscient, as I have explained. Nor is it possible for reason to arrive at any one of these three attributes before the other. It can only attain them at once. For, according to reason, it is inconceivable that anyone that is not living should create, or that one that does not possess power should create, or that any perfect, well-made handiwork could emanate from one who does not know how the act is to be carried out. For when an individual does not know how the act is to be carried out, his handiwork will be neither well nor wisely executed. . . .

. . . I say, then, that just as our calling God "Creator" does not produce an increase in His essence but merely the thought of the presence of something created by Him, so our application to Him of the epithets "living," "omnipotent," and "omniscient," which are explanations of the term "Creator"—only one who possesses these attributes at one and the same time can be a Creator—does not produce any increase in His essence but merely the thought of the presence of something created by Him. . . .

TREATISE X / CONCERNING HOW IT IS MOST PROPER FOR MAN TO CONDUCT HIMSELF IN THIS WORLD

CHAPTER I

. . . Now just as the material objects do not consist of just one of the four elements [of which they are said to be composed], and the body of the trees cannot exist with only one of the parts mentioned by us, and man cannot live if he has bone or flesh alone—in fact, even the heavens are not illuminated by just one star—so, too, man's conduct in the course of his lifetime cannot logically be based on just a single trait. But just as in each instance the final product is the result of a combination of ingredients in larger or smaller proportions, so too, is man's behavior the resultant of a combination of his likes and dislikes in varying proportions.

Man acts as though he were a judge to whom the disposal of the different tendencies is submitted for decision, as Scripture says: *Well is it with the man that dealeth graciously and lendeth, that ordereth his affairs rightfully* (Ps. 112:5). Or his position might be compared to that of one who would weigh these impulses with a balance and give to each its due measure, as Scripture also puts it: *Balance the path of thy feet* (Prov. 4:26). When, then, a person behaves in this manner, his affairs will be properly adjusted and well regulated.

What impelled me to put this theme at the beginning of the present treatise is the fact that I have seen people who think—and with them it is a firm conviction—that it is obligatory for human beings to order their entire existence upon the exploitation of one trait, lavishing their love on one thing above all others and their hatred on a certain thing above the rest. Now I investigated this view and I found it to be extremely erroneous for sundry reasons.

One of these is that if the [exclusive] love for one thing and its preference [above all others] had been the most salutary thing for man, the Creator would not have implanted in his character the love for these other things. Also if that were so, God could have created man out of one element and of one piece, and He would have done likewise for the other creatures so that they would have been similarly constituted. Seest thou not how individual functions cannot very well be executed by the use of a single medium? Still less is this possible in human conduct in general.

Another argument [that might be advanced against the exclusive cultivation of one trait] is that, if an architect were to build a house of stones or teakwood or mats or pegs alone, it would not be as well constructed as if he had built it of all these materials put together. The same might be asserted with regard to cooking, food, drink, dress, service, and other matters. Must not the person who notes how all these items which exist for the purpose of serving man's needs and well-being are not composed of just one ingredient open his eyes and realize how much less that would be possible in the case of the inclinations of his soul and its characteristics?

CHAPTER II

Now it is also necessary for me to explain that the evil resulting from such a one-sided choice is not trivial but quite serious, as I shall illustrate. I say, then, that there are people who give themselves up to long mountain trips, which leads to their becoming insane. Others indulge in excessive eating and drinking, which causes them to contract hemorrhoids. Others, again, lavish all their energies on the gathering of wealth, only to accumulate it for other men. Furthermore, there are those who dedicate themselves entirely to satisfying their thirst for revenge, with the consequence that their vindictiveness reacts against themselves. I might also cite other such instances, as I shall explain in the middle of this treatise with the help of God.

Let me, however, state here, prior to that discussion, that it is for the above-mentioned reasons that man stands in constant need of a wisdom that would regulate his conduct and behavior, as Scripture says: *When thou walkest, it shall lead thee* (Prov. 6:22). Principally that consists, in this particular instance, in his exercising control over his impulses and having complete mastery over his likes and dislikes, for each has its distinctive role in which it must be made to function. Once, then, he recognizes the role belonging to a given impulse, he must give it full opportunity to discharge its function in the required measure. On the other hand, if he sees an instance in which the said impulse should be checked, he must restrain it until the ground for such restraint no longer exists for him. All this is to be done with due deliberation and with the power to release or hold, at will, as Scripture has said: *He that is slow to anger is better than the mighty; and he that ruleth his spirit than he that taketh a city* (Prov. 16:22).

. . . the soul has three faculties—the appetitive, the impulsive, and the cognitive. As for the appetitive faculty, it is that whereby a human being entertains the desire for food and drink and sexual intercourse and for seeing beautiful sights and smelling fragrant odors and for wearing garments that are soft to the touch. The impulsive faculty is that which renders a person courageous and bold, and endows him with zeal for leadership and championing the common weal, and makes him vindictive and vainglorious, and other such things. As for the cognitive faculty, again, it exercises judgment over the two other faculties. When any one of them or of their subdivisions is aroused, the cognitive faculty takes it under consideration and investigates it. If it notes that it is sound from beginning to end, it points this fact out, not to speak of the case where the consequences are desirable. Should it, however, observe in any aspect thereof something deleterious, it would advise that one desist therefrom.

Any person, then, who follows this course of giving his cognitive faculty dominion over his appetites and impulses, is disciplined *by the discipline of the wise,* as Scripture says: *The fear of the Lord is the discipline of wisdom* (Prov. 15:33). Any man, on the other hand, who permits his appetites and impulses to dominate his faculty of cognition, is undisciplined. And if someone wrongly calls such conduct discipline, it is *the discipline of the foolish,* as Scripture says: *But the foolish despise . . . discipline* (Prov. 1:7), and also: *Or as one in fetters to the discipline of the fool* (Prov. 7:22).

CHAPTER III

Having demonstrated, then, in this introductory statement how logical necessity leads to the assumption of the existence of an All-Wise Being who arranged for us the order of these our likes and dislikes and indicated to us the manner of our procedure with them, let me say that the sage Solomon, the son of David, may peace be upon them both, has fathomed this subject for the purpose of enabling us to attain what is best. He says, namely: *I have seen all the works that are done under the sun; and, behold, all is vanity and a striving after wind* (Eccles. 1:14).

Now he does not refer, when he makes the remark: *All is vanity and a striving after wind,* to the union and combination of all works, for it was the Creator, exalted and magnified be He, who established them and set them up, and it is not fitting for a sage like Solomon to say of what the Creator, exalted and magnified be He, has established: *It is all vanity.* What he meant to say was, rather, that any act that a human being undertakes to carry out in isolation—that is to say, every one of the acts of man that receive exclusive attention—is as futile for him as associating with the wind.

With reference to this sort of one-sided procedure, he says also: *That which is crooked cannot be made straight; and that which is wanting [cannot be numbered]* (Eccles. 1:15). That is to say any act practised exclusively constitutes a distortion from what is straight and is lacking in completeness, while in their combination [with the full range of pious works, single acts] do not constitute a *deficiency* but rather completion and perfection.

The correctness of the foregoing interpretation is confirmed by the fact that the author presents three classes of objects of mundane ambition, each of which he decides is *hebhel,* the meaning of which is "vanity." This [rendering of the word] is borne out by such statements of Scripture as *They lead you unto vanity (mahbilim)* (Jer. 23:16); that is: "They deceive you with vain hopes"; and *Trust not in oppression, and put not vain hope ('al tehbalu) in robbery* (Ps. 62:11).

The first of these [strivings that Solomon considers futile] is the exclusive devotion to wisdom to the neglect of all other objects of [human] desire. He says, namely, in reference thereto: *And I applied my heart to know wisdom, and to know madness and folly—I perceived that this also was a striving after wind* (Eccles. 1:17). As his reason for regarding it thus he gives the fact that as a person's knowledge increases, there is also an increase for him of sorrow. That is due to the circumstance that with the increase of his knowledge there are revealed to him the flaws in things concerning which he was fully at ease before they became evident to him. That is the import of his remark: *For in much wisdom is much vexation; and he that increaseth knowledge increaseth sorrow* (Eccles. 1:18).

He next repeats [this observation] with reference to the exclusive cultivation of mirth and gaiety, saying that if a person give all his attention and devotion to them alone, they, too, would prove a disappointment to him. Thus he says: *I said in my heart: "Come now, I will try thee with mirth, and enjoy pleasure"; and, behold, this also was vanity* (Eccles. 2:1). As his reason for this conclusion he gives the fact that a person experiences, when he laughs and jests, a sense of degradation and debasement putting him on a level with the behavior of the beasts. That is the import of his declaration: *I said of laughter: "It is mad"; and of mirth: "What doth it accomplish?"* (Eccles. 2:2).

After this he makes the same remark for the third time about the upbuilding of the material world and he informs us that the preoccupation therewith, too, is vanity. He does this in his statement: *I made me great works; I builded me houses; I planted me vineyards; I made me gardens and parks* (Eccles. 2:4) and all the other things that he relates about his doings until the end of the passage in question. The reason he gives as his objection to all this sort of activity is that he has to leave whatever he has achieved to those that will come after him and that, therefore, his labor will have been wasted. Thus he says: *And I hated all my labour wherein I laboured under the sun, seeing that I must leave it unto the man that shall be after me* (Eccles. 2:18).

Having, then, enumerated these three types, he desists from mentioning other worldly strivings lest he be diverted thereby from his central theme. Yet in the very midst of his discussion of these types he hints at the need for the proper balancing of these three strivings. This is to be effected by devoting some attention to the cultivation of wisdom and to indulgence in pleasure without neglecting to inquire into what is best for man. Thus he says: *I searched in my heart how to pamper my flesh with wine, and my heart conducting itself with wisdom, [how yet to lay hold on folly, till I might see which it was best for the sons of men that they should do]* (Eccles. 2:3).

AL-GHAZALI

from *The Incoherence of the Philosophers*

From Al-Ghazali's Tahafut al-Falasifah (Incoherence of the Philosophers). *Translated by Sabih Almad Kamali. (Lahore: Pakistan Philosophical Congress, 1963).*

PROBLEM I / REFUTATION OF THEIR BELIEF IN THE ETERNITY OF THE WORLD

Details of the Theory (of the Eternity of the World):

The philosophers disagree among themselves as to the eternity of the world. But the majority of the philosophers—ancient as well as modern—agree upon its eternity, holding that it always coexisted with God (exalted be He) as His effect which was concurrent with Him in time—concurrent as an effect is with the cause, e.g., light with the Sun—and that God's priority to the world is the priority of the cause to the effect—viz., priority in essence and rank, not in time. . . .

In the first argument, they say:

The procession of a temporal (being) from an eternal (being) is absolutely impossible. For, if we suppose the Eternal at a stage when the world had not yet originated from Him, then the reason why it had not originated must have been that there was no determinant for its existence, and that the existence of the world was a possibility only. So, when later the world comes into existence, we must choose one of the two alternatives (to explain it)—namely, either that the determinant has, or that it has not, emerged. If the determinant did not emerge, the world should still remain in the state of bare possibility, in which it was before. But if it has emerged, who is the originator of the determinant itself? And why does it come into being now, and did not do so before? Thus, the question regarding the origin of the determinant stands. In fine, since all the states of the Eternal are alike, either nothing shall originate from Him, or whatever originates shall continue to originate for ever. For it is impossible that the state of leaving off should differ from the state of taking up.

To elucidate the point, it may be said: Why did He not originate the world before its origination? It is not possible to say: "Because of His inability to bring the world into existence"; nor could one say: "Because of the impossibility of the world's coming into being." For this would mean that He changed from inability to power, or that the world changed from impossibility to possibility. And both senses are absurd. Nor can it be said that, before the time of the origination of the world, there was no purpose, and that a purpose emerged later. Nor is it possible to ascribe (the non-origination of the world before it actually originated) to the lack of means at one stage, and to its existence at another. The nearest thing to imagine is to say that He had not willed the world's existence before. But from this it follows that one must also say: "The world is the result of His having become a willer of its existence—after not having been a willer." So the will should have had a beginning in time. But the origination of the will in the Divine being is impossible; for He is not subject to temporal events. And the origination of the will not-in-His-being cannot make Him a willer.

Even if we give up the inquiry concerning the substratum in which the will originated, does not the difficulty regarding the very act of origination stand? Whence does the will originate? Why does it originate now? Why did it not originate before? Does it now originate from a source other than God? If there can be a temporal existent which has not been brought into existence by anyone, then the world itself should be such an existent, so as to be independent of the Creator. For what is the difference between one temporal existent and another?

So, if the origin of the world is ascribed to God's action, the question remains: Why now, and why not before? Was it due to the absence of means, or power, or purpose, or nature? If so, the transition from this stage to that of existence will revive the difficulty we had to face at the outset. And if it is said to have been due to the absence of will, then one act of will will stand in need of another, and so on *ad infinitum*. From this it is absolutely clear that the procession of the temporal from the eternal is impossible, unless there were a change in the eternal in respect of power, or means, or time, or nature. And it is impossible to suppose a change in the states of the eternal. For as a temporal event, that change would be like any other change (in non-eternal beings). Therefore (in case of the eternal), change of any kind whatsoever is impossible. And now that the world has been proved (always) to have existed, and the impossibility of its beginning in time has been shown, it follows that the world is eternal.

This is their most clever argument. Their discussion of all other metaphysical problems is less substantial than the discussion of this one. For here they have access to a variety of speculations which would not be available to them in any other problem. This is the reason why we began with this problem, and presented this their strongest argument at the very outset.

The foregoing argument is open to objection on two points. Firstly, it may be said:

How will you disprove one who says that the world came into being because of the eternal will which demanded its existence at the time at which it actually came into existence, and which demanded the non-existence (of the world) to last as long as it lasted, and (demanded) the existence to begin where it actually began? So, on this view, existence of the world was not an object of the eternal will, before the world actually existed; hence its non-actualisation. And it was an object of the will at the time when it actualised. What can prevent us from believing such a thing, and what is the contradiction involved in it?

If it is said:

The contradiction involved here is self-evident. For that which originates in time is an effect or a product. And just as it is impossible for an originated thing to be uncaused, so it is impossible for the cause to fail to produce its effect when all the conditions and factors requisite for the causal operation are complete and nothing else remains to be awaited. The existence of the effect is necessary, when the cause is operative, and all causal conditions are complete. The postponement of the effect is as impossible as the existence of a temporal but uncaused thing.

Now, before the existence of the world, the Willer existed: the will existed, and the relation of the will to its object existed. The Willer did not have to make a new appearance: nor did the will emerge as a new acquisition, nor did it acquire a new relation to its object. For anything of this kind would amount to change. How, then, did the object of will emerge as something new? And what prevented it from emerging before it actually did? The state of its new-emergence cannot be distinguished from the preceding states in respect of any thing or any factor or any state or any relation whatsoever; for all things remain as they were. If, in spite of all things remaining the same, the object of will is not produced at first, but comes into being later, the whole affair must be exceedingly contradictory. And contradiction of this kind arises not only in case of evident and essential causes and effects, but also in case of those which are conventional and qualified. For instance, if a man pronounces divorce to his wife, and if separation is not the immediate result of the pronouncement, it is inconceivable that it should take effect afterwards. For, in accordance with convention and legal usage, the pronouncement is made the cause of the judgment. Therefore, the postponement of the effect is unintelligible, unless the enforcement of the divorce should be bound up with, say, the coming of the next day, or entering into the house. Only then will the divorce take effect at the time of the coming of the next day, or the entering into the house, and not immediately; for the pronouncement is made a cause of divorce in relation to something which is yet awaited. Since the condition, i.e., the morrow or the entry, is not present at the moment, the effect must be held over until the absent condition should become present. So the effect, i.e., the enforcement of the divorce, will not appear unless a new factor, viz., the morrow or the entry, emerges. But if the man desires—without binding up the effect with the appearance of something which is not present at the moment—to postpone the effect, it would not be an intelligible thing, notwithstanding the fact that he has the right to make the pronouncement, and is at liberty to choose whatever details he likes. Since it is not possible for us to arrange these conventional things as we like, and since our capricious determinations are bound to be unintelligible, it follows that an arbitrary arrangement should be still less intelligible in the sphere of essential, rational and self-evident causation.

Even in the case of morals, the object of our intention is not posterior to the intention, if the intention exists, and there is no hindrance. Therefore, with intention being coupled with power, and with all obstacles having been removed, it is unintelligible that the intended thing should be delayed. Such a thing is conceivable only in the case of inclination; for inclination by itself is not sufficient to bring about an action. For instance, the mere inclination to write does not produce writing, unless there emerges an intention, i.e., an inner agitation which as a new factor precedes an action.

So if the eternal will is to be likened to our intention, it is inconceivable that its object should be posterior to it. Unless there is a hindrance, there cannot be a gap between the intention and its object. It makes no sense to have an intention to-day that one would stand up to-morrow. One may only have an inclination to do so. But if the eternal will is like our inclination, it shall not by itself be sufficient to bring about the object of inclination. For it is indispensable that something else—viz., the inner agitation that is intention—should emerge to supplement inclination, so that the object of inclination may be produced. But the emergence of such a thing means a change in the Eternal.

And, then, the difficulty remains as it was. Namely, why does this agitation, or intention, or will, or whatever you may like to call it, originate now, and why did it not originate before? Thus, either one must posit a temporal event which is uncaused, or an infinite regress will follow.

The sum and substance of what has been said (by you) is this: That the Cause existed; that all the conditions of its efficiency were complete, so that nothing else remained to be awaited; that, in spite of all this, the origination of the effect was postponed over a length of time, the beginning of which cannot be imagined, and which could not be measured out even by millenia; and that eventually the effect made its appearance all of a sudden, without a new factor coming into operation, or a new condition being realised. And such a thing is intrinsically impossible.

The answer to the foregoing may be stated as follows:

How do you know the impossibility of ascribing the origin of something to an eternal will? Is it the self-evident rational necessity, or theoretical knowledge, which is the ground of your judgment? Or, to use the terms employed by you in Logic, are the two terms in your judgment joined by means of a middle term, or without a middle term? If you claim that they are joined by means of a middle term—i.e., if your method is deductive—you must state what that term is. But if you claim that this impossibility is known as a self-evident fact, why do not your opponents share this knowledge with you? People who believe in the temporal origin of the world are confined neither to a number nor within a city. And no one would suspect that, out of spite for reason, they believe in something which they know to be untrue. It is, therefore, necessary for you to prove, in accordance with the rules of Logic, that it is impossible to ascribe the origin of the world to the eternal will. All you have said so far only amounts to a suggestion of improbability, and to a comparison of the Divine will to our inclination or will. The comparison is false; for the eternal will *does not* resemble temporal intentions. And the mere suggestion of improbability, unsupported by an argument, is not enough. . . .

If it is said:

How will you disprove one who gives up the argument from rational necessity, and tries to prove (the eternity of the world) from another point of view—namely, that all the moments being equal with respect to the possibility of the relation of the eternal will to them, there cannot be anything to distinguish one particular moment from all those before and after it?

Maybe, it is not impossible for priority or posteriority to have been an object of will. But how about white and black, or motion and rest? You say that white owes its origin to the eternal will, and that the substratum which actually receives whiteness was equally capable of receiving blackness. Now, why does the eternal will take whiteness, as set over against blackness? What is there to distinguish one of the two contingent things from the other, so that it should be taken by the eternal will?

We know it as a self-evident fact that nothing can be distinguished from its like, unless there be something which gives it a special character. If without such a thing a distinction between two like things were possible, then it would follow that in the case of the world, which was possible of existence as well as of non-existence, the balance could be tilted in favour of existence—notwithstanding the fact that non-existence possessed an equal measure of possibility, and that there was nothing to give existence a special character. If you say that the will (itself) produced the special character, the question will be: Why did it acquire the capacity to produce it? If you say that in the case of an eternal thing the question: Why? cannot be asked, then let the world be such an eternal thing. Do not look for the Creator or the cause of the world; for it is eternal, and in the case of an eternal thing the question: Why? is not to be asked.

If it were possible for the Eternal to acquire a special relation to one of the two contingencies, then it would be absolutely untenable to say that the world, which has a particular shape at present, could possibly have some other shape instead of the present one. For then one might say: "This (shape) has come into being by chance"; even as you might say that the will makes by chance the choice of only one moment of time, or of only one shape. If you say that such a question is irrelevant because it might be asked in the case of anything willed or determined by Him, we will say that it must be faced precisely because it arises in any event, and will necessarily present itself to our opponents, whatever their supposition may be.

we will answer:

The (eternal) will produced the world as it is, wherever it is, and whatever it is like. As regards the will, it is an attribute of which the function it is to distinguish something from its like. If it had no such function, then power would have had to be regarded as an adequate principle. But since power bears an equal relation to two opposite things, and since it becomes necessary to posit a cause which gives one of these two things a special character, therefore, it must be said that, over and above power, the Eternal has an attribute whose function is to distinguish something from its like. Therefore, if one asks: "Why did the will choose one of two like things?" it will be like asking: "Why does knowledge require the encompassing of the object of knowledge as such?" As the answer to the last question is: "Knowledge is an attribute of which this is the function," so the answer to the first question should be: "Will is an attribute of which the function—rather, nature—is to distinguish something from its like."

If it is said:

It is unintelligible—rather, self-contradictory—to speak of an attribute of which the function is to distinguish something from its like. For by likeness is meant that there is no distinction; and by distinction is meant that there is no likeness. It is not proper to imagine that two black things in two different places are like each other in all respects. For 'This' is in one place, and 'That' is in another place; hence the necessity for the distinction between the two. Nor can two black things in the same place but at different times be absolutely like each other. For 'This' is separated from 'That' in time; how, therefore, can the two be equal in all respects? When we say: "Two black things like each other," we mean that they are alike only in respect of the particular attribute of blackness. We do not mean that they are so in an unqualified sense. For if that were the meaning, and if the identity of time and place had left no dissimilarity, then the two black things would not be intelligible, and their duality would be absolutely irrational.

The question will be settled when it is seen that the word 'will' is derived by analogy from our own will. And our will cannot conceivably distinguish something from its like. If a thirsty man has before him two glasses of water, which are equal in all respects as far as his purpose is concerned, he cannot take either of the two, unless he thinks that one of the two is prettier, or lighter, or nearer to his right hand (he presumably being a man who habitually uses his right hand), or has some other cause—apparent or invisible—which gives it a special character. For otherwise, the choice of something as distinguished from another exactly like it would in no event be conceivable.

Objection to this from two points of view:

Firstly, is your assertion that such a thing is inconceivable based on self-evident facts, or on theoretical investigations? In fact, it is not possible for you to make either claim. Your comparison of the Divine to human will is as false an analogy as that between the Divine and human knowledge. The Divine knowledge is different from ours in respect of things which we have established. Why, therefore, should it be improbable for a similar difference to exist in the case of will? Your assertion is like one's saying: "A being which is neither outside the world nor inside it: neither connected with it nor disconnected from it is unintelligible; for if such qualities were attributed to us, we would not understand them." To such a person the answer would be: "This is the work of your imagination. Actually, rational proof has compelled the intelligent to assent to that doctrine." How, therefore, will you disprove one who says that rational proof also compels one to affirm an attribute of God (exalted be He) of which the function is to distinguish something from its like? If the word 'will' cannot name this attribute, let us use another name, for names are not at issue at the moment. We had used the word 'will' on the authority of the Sacred Law. Etymologically, however, 'will' signifies something directed towards a purpose. In the case of God, we cannot speak of a purpose. What, however, we are concerned with is the meaning, and not the words.

Besides, we do not admit that even our will cannot conceivably make a distinction between two like things. Let us suppose that there are two equal dates before a man who is fond of them, but who cannot take both of them at once. So he will take only one of them; and this, obviously, will be done —by an attribute of which the function is to distinguish something from its like! As regards the causes of a special character being possessed by the object of actual choice—viz., the causes mentioned by you, such as prettiness, or nearness, or handiness—we can suppose their absence; and still the possibility of one of the two dates being taken will remain. Here you will have to choose one of the two things:

i. Either you can say that the equal relation of a man's purpose to the two dates is inconceivable. But that is nonsense; for the equality can be supposed.
ii. Or you might say that, the equality having been supposed, the excited man will keep fondly and helplessly gazing on for ever, and will not be able to take either date by mere will or choice which is devoid of purpose. But this is also impossible; and the absurdity of such an assumption is self-evident.

From all this it follows that whoever discusses the nature of volitional action—whether with reference to empirical facts, or on theoretical grounds—will have to affirm an attribute of which the function should be to distinguish something from its like.

In the second place, the objection may be stated as follows:

In your own theories, you have not been able to avoid the assumption of a distinction between two like things. For if the world is produced by a cause which necessitates for it a certain shape as set over against other shapes like it, the question arises: Why was this particular choice made? The rule that a distinction between like things is impossible cannot differ in different cases, e.g., an action, or something which follows by nature or by rational necessity. . . .

PROBLEM IV / TO SHOW THEIR INABILITY TO PROVE THE EXISTENCE OF THE CREATOR OF THE WORLD

We say:

All men can be divided into two classes:

i. the class of the people of the truth. They hold that the world began in time; and they know by rational necessity that nothing which originates in time originates by itself, and that, therefore, it needs a creator. Therefore, their belief in the Creator is understandable.

ii. the Materialists. They believe that the world, as it is, has always been. Therefore, they do not ascribe it to a creator. Their belief, too, is intelligible—although rational arguments may be advanced to refute it.

But the philosophers believe that the world is eternal. And still they would ascribe it to a creator. This theory is, therefore, even in its original formulation, self-contradictory. There is no need for a refutation of it.

If it is said:

When we say that the world has a creator, we do not mean thereby an agent who acts voluntarily, after not having acted, as we observe to be the case with so many kinds of agents, e.g., a tailor, or a weaver, or a builder. On the contrary, we mean thereby the cause of the world, whom we call the First Principle, in the sense that His own being is uncaused, while He is the cause of all other beings. So it is only in this sense that we call the First Principle the Creator. As regards the fact of the uncaused being of such an existent, it can presently be proved by a conclusive argument. The world, we will say, and all the beings therein are either uncaused, or have a cause. If they have a cause, this cause itself will either have a cause, or will be uncaused. And the same will be true of the cause of the cause. Therefore, (a) either the series will go on *ad infinitum* (which is impossible): or (b) it will come to an end at length. So the ultimate term will be the first cause, whose own being will be uncaused. Let us call this cause the First Principle.

If, however, the world itself is supposed to be uncaused, we already will have found the First Principle. For we do not mean by such Principle any thing other than an uncaused being. And on our hypothesis, such a being will be a necessarily recognisable fact.

Undoubtedly, it is not possible to consider the heavens as the First Principle. For they form a numerous group. And the proof of Divine unity prevents number from being attributed to the First Principle. So the falsehood of the view that the heavens may be the First Principle will be seen from an inquiry into the qualities of the First Principle.

Nor is it possible to say that any one heaven, or any one body, or the Sun, or some other thing of the kind is the First Principle. For all these things are bodies; and a body is composed of Form and Matter. It is not possible that the First Principle should be so composed. And this is known through another inquiry (besides the one into the qualities of the First Principle).

Thus, what we wanted to show was that the existence of an uncaused being is an established fact—established by rational necessity and by general acceptance. It is only with respect to the attributes of such a being that opinions vary.

So this is what we mean by the First Principle.

The answer from two points:

Firstly, it follows as a necessary consequence from the general drift of your thought that the bodies in the world are eternal and uncaused. Your statement that this consequence can be avoided through a 'second inquiry' will be refuted, when we come to the problems of Divine unity and the Divine attributes.

Secondly—more especially to this problem—it may be said: According to the hypothesis under consideration, it has been established that all the beings in the world have a cause. Now, let the cause itself have a cause, and the cause of the cause have yet another cause, and so on *ad infinitum*. It does not behove you to say that an infinite regress of causes is impossible. For, we will say, do you know it as a matter of immediate inference necessitated by reason, or through some deductive argument? Now, an argument from rational necessity is not available in this case. And methods of theoretical inquiry were betrayed by you when you admitted the possibility of temporal phenomena which had no beginning. If it is possible that something infinite should come into existence, why should it not be equally possible for it to have some of its parts working as the causes of others, so that on the lower side the series terminates into an effectless effect, without, however, terminating on the upper side into an uncaused cause? This will be like the Past, which reaches its term in the fleeting 'Now', but had no beginning. If you assert that the past events are existing neither at present nor in any other state, and that the non-existent cannot be described as limited or unlimited, then you will have to take a similar view of the human souls which have departed from bodies. For, according to you, they do not perish. And the number of the souls existing after their separation from the body is infinite. A sperm is continually generated from a man, and a man from a sperm, and so on indefinitely. Then, the soul of every man who is dead has survived. And this soul is by number different from the soul of those who died before, or after, or together with, this man. If all the souls were by species one, then, according to you, there would exist at any time an unlimited number of souls. . . .

If it is said:

The conclusive demonstration of the impossibility of an infinite regress of causes is this: Each one of individual causes is either possible in itself, or necessary. If necessary, it will not need a cause. If possible, the Whole (of which it is a part) must be describable in terms of possibility. Now, all that is possible depends on a cause additional to itself. Therefore, the Whole must depend on a cause external to itself (and that is impossible).

we will anwser:

The words 'possible' and 'necessary' are vague terms—unless 'necessary' is used for an uncaused being, and 'possible' for one which has a cause. If this is the meaning, we will come back to the point, and say that each individual cause is possible in the sense that it has another cause which is additional to itself, and that the Whole is not possible—i.e., it has no cause additional or external to itself. If the word 'possible' means any thing other than the sense we have given to it, that meaning cannot be recognised.

If it is said:

This leads to the conclusion that a necessary being can be made of possible things. But the conclusion is absurd.

we will answer:

If by 'possible' and 'necessary' you mean what we have suggested, then this conclusion is exactly what we seek. And we do not admit that it is absurd. To call it absurd is like one's saying that something eternal made up of temporal events is impossible. To the philosophers, Time *is* eternal; whereas individual spherical revolutions are temporal. And each individual revolution has a beginning; whereas the aggregate of those revolutions has no beginning. Therefore, that which has no beginning *is* made of those which have. And the predicate of having a beginning in time is truly applicable to individual revolutions, but not to their aggregate. Similarly, therefore, (in the case of the causes and their aggregate) it will be said that each cause has a cause, but the aggregate of these causes has no cause. For all that can be truly said of the individuals cannot similarly be said of their aggregate. For instance, of each individual it can be said that it is one (of many), or that it is a fraction, or a part (of a whole). But no such thing can be said of the aggregate. Any spot we can specify on the Earth is brightened by the Sun in daytime, and becomes dark by night. And every temporal event originates after not having been—i.e., it has a beginning in time. But the philosophers would not admit that the aggregate of temporal events can have a beginning.

From this it will be seen that if one admits the possibility of originated things—viz., the forms of the four elements and the changeable things—which have no beginning, then it does not behove one to say that an infinite series of causes is impossible. And this further shows that because of this difficulty the philosophers cannot find their way to affirming the First Principle; and that, therefore, their conception of Him is bound to be an arbitrary notion. . . .

MAIMONIDES

from *The Guide of the Perplexed*

Reprinted from Moses Maimonides, The Guide of the Perplexed. *Translated by Schlomo Pines (Chicago: University of Chicago Press, 1963).*

BOOK II

CHAPTER 17

. . . For we, the community of the followers of Moses our Master and Abraham our Father, may peace be on them, believe that the world was generated in such and such manner and came to be in a certain state from another state and was created in a certain state, which came after another state. Aristotle, on the other hand, begins to contradict us and to bring forward against us proofs based on the nature of what exists, a nature that has attained stability, is perfect, and has achieved actuality. As for us, we declare against him that this nature, after it has achieved stability and perfection, does not resemble in anything the state it was in while in the state of being generated, and that it was brought into existence from absolute nonexistence. Now what argument from among all that he advances holds good against us? For these arguments necessarily concern only those who claim that the stable nature of that which exists, gives an indication of its having been created in time. I have already made it known to you that I do not claim this.

Now I shall go back and set forth for your benefit the principles of his methods and shall show you that nothing in them of necessity concerns us in any respect, since we contend that God brought the world as a whole into existence after nonexistence and formed it until it has achieved perfection as you see it. He said that the first matter is subject to neither generation nor passing-away and began to draw inferences in favor of this thesis from the things subject to generation and passing-away and to make clear that it was impossible that the first matter was generated. And this is correct. For we do not maintain that the first matter is generated as man is generated from the seed or that it passes away as man passes away into dust. But we maintain that God has brought it into existence from nothing and that after being brought into existence, it was as it is now—I mean everything is generated from it, and everything generated from it passes away into it; it does not exist devoid of form; generation and corruption terminate in it; it is not subject to generation as are the things generated from it, nor to passing-away as are the things that pass away into it, but is created from nothing. And its Creator may, if He wishes to do so, render it entirely and absolutely nonexistent. We likewise say the same thing of motion. For he has inferred from the nature of motion that motion is not subject to generation and passing-away. And this is correct. For we maintain that after motion has come into existence with the nature characteristic of it when it has become stable, one cannot imagine that it should come into being as a whole and perish as a whole, as partial motions come into being and perish. This analogy holds good with regard to everything that is attached to the nature of motion. Similarly the assertion that circular motion has no beginning is correct. For after the spherical body endowed with circular motion has been brought into being, one cannot conceive that its motion should have a beginning. We shall make a similar assertion with regard to the possibility that must of necessity precede everything that is generated. For this is only necessary in regard to this being that is stabilized—in this being everything that is generated, is generated from some being. But in the case of a thing created from nothing, neither the senses nor the intellect point to something that must be preceded by its possibility. We make a similar assertion with regard to the thesis that there are no contraries in heaven. That thesis is correct. However, we have not claimed that the heavens have been generated as the horse and palm tree are. Nor have we claimed that their being composite renders necessary their passing-away as is the case with plants and animals because of the contraries that subsist in them.

The essential point is, as we have mentioned, that a being's state of perfection and completion furnishes no indication of the state of that being preceding its perfection. It involves no disgracefulness for us if someone says that the heavens were generated before the earth or the earth before the heavens or that the heavens have existed without stars or that a particular species of animals has existed without another species being in existence. For all this applies to the state of this universe when it was being generated. Similarly in the case of animals when they are being generated, the heart exists before the testicles—a circumstance that may be ocularly perceived—and the veins before the bones; and this is so in spite of the fact that after the animal has achieved perfection, no part of its body can exist in it if any part of all the others, without which the individual cannot possibly endure, does not exist.

All these assertions are needed if the text of Scripture is taken in its external sense, even though it must not be so taken, as shall be explained when we shall speak of it at length. You ought to memorize this notion. For it is a great wall that I have built around the Law, a wall that surrounds it warding off the stones of all those who project these missiles against it.

However, should Aristotle, I mean to say he who adopts his opinion, argue against us by saying: If this existent provides no indication for us, how do you know that it is generated and that there has existed another nature that has generated it—we should say: This is not obligatory for us in view of what we wish to maintain. For at present we do not wish to establish as true that the world is created in time. But what we wish to establish is the possibility of its being created in time. Now this contention cannot be proved to be impossible by inferences drawn from the nature of what exists, which we do not set at nought. When the possibility of this contention has been established, as we have made clear, we shall go back and we shall make prevail the opinion asserting creation in time.

In this question no way remains open to him except to show the impossibility for the world having been created in time, not by starting from the nature of being, but by starting from the judgments of the intellect with regard to the deity: these being the three methods that I have mentioned to you before. By means of these methods they wish to prove the eternity of the world, taking the deity as their starting point. I shall accordingly show you, in a following chapter, how doubts can be cast on these methods so that no proof whatever can be established as correct by means of them.

CHAPTER 18

The first method they mention is the one through which, in their opinion, we are obliged to admit that the deity passed from potentiality to actuality inasmuch as He acted at a certain time and did not act at another time.

The way to destroy this doubt is most clear. For this conclusion necessarily follows only with regard to everything composed of matter, which is endowed with possibility, and of form. When such a body acts in virtue of its form after not having acted, there was indubitably in it a thing that was in potentia and afterwards made the transition into actuality. Accordingly it undoubtedly must have undergone the action of something causing it to make this transition. For this premise has been demonstrated only with regard to things endowed with matter. On the other hand, that which is not a body and is not endowed with matter, has in its essence no possibility in any respect whatever. Thus all that it has is always in actu. Accordingly with regard to it, their contention does not necessarily follow; and it is not impossible with regard to it that it acts at a certain time and does not act at another time. For in a being separate from matter, this does not imply change or a passage from potentiality to actuality. . . .

. . . For as for us, we believe that He, may He be exalted, is neither a body nor a force in a body; and hence it does not follow that He changes if He acts after not having acted.

The second method is the one in which eternity is shown to be necessary because there do not subsist for Him, may He be exalted, any incentives, supervening accidents, and impediments. It is difficult to resolve this doubt, and the solution is subtle. Hear it.

Know that every agent endowed with will, who performs his acts for the sake of something, must of necessity act at a certain time and not act at another time because of impediments or supervening accidents. To take an example: a man, for instance, may wish to have a house but does not build it because of impediments—if the building materials are not at hand or if they, though being at hand, have not been prepared for receiving the form because of the absence of tools. Sometimes, too, both the materials and the tools are at hand, but the man does not build because he does not wish to build since he can dispense with a shelter. If, however, accidents like heat or cold supervene, he is compelled to seek a shelter, whereupon he will wish to build. It has thus become clear that supervening accidents may change the will and that impediments may oppose the will in such a way that it is not executed. All this, however, only occurs when acts are in the service of something that is external to the essence of the will. If, however, the act has no purpose whatever except to be consequent upon will, that will has no need of incentives. And the one who wills is not obliged, even if there are no impediments, to act always. For there is no external end for the sake of which he acts and that would render it necessary to act whenever there are no impediments preventing the attainment of the end. For in the case envisaged, the act is consequent upon the will alone.

Somebody might object: All this is correct, but does not the supposition that one wishes at one time and does not wish at another time imply in itself a change? We shall reply to him: No, for the true reality and the quiddity of will means: to will and not to will. If the will in question belongs to a material being, so that some external end is sought thereby, then the will is subject to change because of impediments and supervening accidents. But as for a being separate from matter, its will, which does not exist in any respect for the sake of some other thing, is not subject to change. The fact that it may wish one thing now and another thing tomorrow does not constitute a change in its essence and does not call for another cause; just as the fact that it acts at one time and does not act at another does not constitute a change, as we have explained. It shall be explained later on that it is only by equivocation that our will and that of a being separate from matter are both designated as "will," for there is no likeness between the two wills. Thus this objection has likewise been invalidated and it has been made clear that no incongruity necessarily follows for us in consequence of this method. As you know this was what we desired to achieve.

The third method: It is the one in which they argue the eternity of the world to be necessary because everything, with regard to which Wisdom decides that it should come forth, comes forth at the very moment of the decision. For His wisdom is eternal as is His essence, and in consequence that which necessarily proceeds from it is likewise eternal. This is a very feeble way of going on to an obligatory conclusion. For in the same way as we do not know what was His wisdom in making it necessary that the spheres should be nine—neither more nor less—and the number of the stars equal to what it is—neither more nor less—and that they should be neither bigger nor smaller than they are, we do not know what was His wisdom in bringing into existence the universe at a recent period after its not having existed. The universe is consequent upon His perpetual and immutable wisdom. But we are completely ignorant of the rule of that wisdom and of the decision made by it. For, in our opinion, volition too is consequent upon wisdom; all these being one and the same thing—I mean His essence and His wisdom—for we do not believe in attributes. You shall hear much about this notion, when we shall speak of providence. By looking at the matter in this way, this disgracefulness is thus abolished. . . .

CHAPTER 25

. . . The Law has given us knowledge of a matter the grasp of which is not within our power, and the miracle attests to the correctness of our claims.

Know that with a belief in the creation of the world in time, all the miracles become possible and the Law becomes possible, and all questions that may be asked on this subject, vanish. Thus it might be said: Why did God give prophetic revelation to this one and not to that? Why did God give this Law to this particular nation, and why did He not legislate to the others? Why did He legislate at this particular time, and why did He not legislate before it or after? Why did He impose these commandments and these prohibitions? Why did He privilege the prophet with the miracles mentioned in relation to him and not with some others? What was God's aim in giving this Law? Why did He not, if such was His purpose, put the accomplishment of the commandments and the nontransgression of the prohibitions into our nature? If this were said, the answer to all these questions would be that it would be said: He wanted it this way; or His wisdom required it this way. And just as He brought the world into existence, having the form it has, when He wanted to, without our knowing His will with regard to this or in what respect there was wisdom in His particularizing the forms of the world and the time of its creation—in the same way we do not know His will or the exigency of His wisdom that caused all the matters, about which questions have been posed above, to be particularized. If, however, someone says that the world is as it is in virtue of necessity, it would be a necessary obligation to ask all those questions; and there would be no way out of them except through a recourse to unseemly answers in which there would be combined the giving the lie to, and the annulment of, all the external meanings of the Law. . . .

MAIMONIDES

The Purpose of Man

From Norman Roth, Maimonides. Essays and Texts, 850th Anniversary. *Madison: The Hispanic Seminary of Medieval Studies, Ltd. 1985.*

When we have found that the end of all [that exists] is the existence of man (i.e., man is the purpose, or final end, for which all else exists), it is an obligation to investigate also why man exists and what is his end (purpose). And when they (scholars) investigate deeply into this, they found that man has very many activities, whereas all the species of life and trees possess only one activity or two, and one end; as we see that the palm tree has no other activity than to produce dates, and so with the rest of the trees. And so with animals, there is among them a weaver, such as the spider, and a builder, like the *sununu* [a kind of swallow], or a gatherer like the leopard. But man has many activities, and therefore they investigated deeply all his activities one by one in order to know what is his purpose from all these activities, and they found that it is one single activity and the rest are only to insure his survival in order to perfect that unique activity, which is comprehension of the intelligibles and knowledge of the essences as they actually are. For it is impossible that the end of man should be to eat or drink or copulate or build a house or be a king, since all these are accidents which happen to him and do not add to his essence [existence]. Further, all these activities are shared by him with the rest of living creatures, and wisdom is what adds to his essence and transfers him from a low [or reprehensible] state to an exalted state, because he was man in potentiality and has become man in actuality; for man before he has learned (acquired knowledge) is only like an animal, for man is not differentiated from other animals except by the ability to reason, in that he is a rational animal—I mean by the word 'reason' the apprehension of intelligibles, and the greatest of these is the apprehension of the unity of God, mighty and exalted, and all that is connected to it in metaphysics; for the rest of knowledge [the sciences] is only a preparation for metaphysics, and a complete discussion of this would be very lengthy. But with the apprehension of the intelligibles is necessary a repudiation of excess in bodily pleasures, for the beginning of intellect (brings) the apprehension that the destruction of the soul is the fitness of the body and the fitness of the soul is the destruction of the body. For if man pursues desires and arouses the senses and makes his intellect subservient to his desires and becomes like animals and ostriches who have nothing in their imagination other than eating, drinking, and copulating, then there is not recognizable in him the divine potential—that is, the intellect, and then he will be like separated matter floating in the primeaval sea.

It is clear from all these introductory remarks that the purpose (of man) in this world and of all that is in it is (to be) an excellent (good) learned man, and when a man has acquired knowledge and deeds—I mean by 'knowledge' apprehension of the essences as they actually are and the comprehension of all that it is possible for man to comprehend, and by 'deeds' an equilibrium in matters of (his) nature and not be addicted to them (the Arabic is unclear) and not to take from them (physical pleasures) other than what is necessary for the survival of the body, and so with the improvement of all the qualities; and man in this state is the goal (of creation).

And this thing is not known only from the prophets; also the sages of previous communities (nations), even though they did not see the prophets nor hear their words, already knew that man is not perfect unless he combines knowledge and deeds. Let it suffice for you the words of the greatest of the philosophers: "the goal of God for us is that we be discerning and righteous." For if man were wise and understanding but pursuing pleasures, he is not truly wise, for the beginning of wisdom is not to take of the physical pleasures except (what is necessary) for the survival of the body. . . .

There remains here one question, and it is that it is possible to ask: You have already said that divine wisdom has not produced anything in vain, and that of all created things in the sublunary sphere man is the most noble, and that the purpose of the human species is the apprehension of the intelligibles; if so, why has God created people who do not apprehend the intelligible, for we see that the majority of people are empty of wisdom and pursuing pleasures, and the learned and pure man is alone and strange—there are only found individuals in each generation.

The answer is that the existence of all these created beings is for two reasons; one, to serve that (unique) individual, for if all people were learned and philosophizing, the world would be lost and man destroyed from it in a short while, for man is greatly lacking and in need of many things and it would be necessary for him to learn harvesting and sowing, threshing and grinding and cooking and making tools for all this in order to obtain food, and so he would need to learn spinning and weaving in order to weave something to wear, and construction to build for himself a shelter, and to make tools for all these, and the life of Methusaleh [*who lived 969 years*; Genesis 5.26–27] would not suffice to learn all the crafts that man absolutely needs in order to survive. And if so, when will he learn wisdom and understand knowledge? Therefore, all these (other people) are found in order to perform these labors which the world needs, and the learned man exists for himself, and thus is the world built and wisdom found; and how lovely is the proverb which says: "Were it not for fools, the world would be destroyed." There is no greater foolishness than this that man weak of soul and of bodily constitution travels from the ends of the second climate to the ends of the sixth, and crosses seas in the days of winter and deserts in the burning heat of summer, and endangers himself to various species of predatory beasts, in order that perhaps he may earn a dollar. And when he collects all that money for which he has given all his soul, he gives it to craftsmen to build for him a solid foundation with lime and stones on virgin earth in order to erect a building that will stand hundreds of years, and he knows for a fact that there does not remain of his life even enough to consume (dwell in) a building of reeds. Is there a greater stupidity than this? So all the pleasures of the world and its delights are stupidity so that the world may be built (may function), and therefore our sages, peace to them, called one who has not learned: *'am ha-ares* [literally, '*people of the earth*']; that is, that he was not created except for the building of the earth, and therefore is he associated with it.

RATIONALISM

Al-Farabi (Abu Nasr Muhammad al-Farabi, 870?–950), of Turkish descent, was born in Transoxania, in present day Uzbekistan, an independent republic in the southern part of what was formerly the Soviet Union. He studied in Khorasan (covering parts of present-day Iran and Afghanistan) and Baghdad. At least part of his studies were under Syriac-speaking Christian philosophers who represented the tradition of the Alexandrian school. After the Muslim conquest of Alexandria, the school had moved first to Antioch and then to Harran (Carrhae). Al-Farabi studied under a teacher of this school, Yuhanna Ibn Haylan, in Baghdad and may have studied in Harran also. When he was seventy-two, al-Farabi migrated to Syria under the patronage of Prince Sayf al-Dawlah in Aleppo. Three years later, the prince conquered Damascus, where al-Farabi lived until his death at age eighty.

Before al-Farabi, ancient Greek and later Hellenistic philosophy did have some influence in the Muslim world. A center for the translation of Greek works into Arabic was established under state sponsorship, and, partly as a result of exposure to Greek and Christian philosophy, various sects of dialectical theologians debated issues of some philosophical interest. They did so, however, in a purely theological context, taking the revealed religion of the Koran as their principle. Before al-Farabi, no one had tried to master these systems and apply them as such to theoretical and practical problems.

The dialectical theologians came to form the center of Islamic orthodoxy. In the 250 years following al-Farabi's death, dialectical theology opposed the study of Greek and Christian philosophy with increasing fervor. Political upheavals, often involving intrigues initiated by these sects of theologians, afflicted the lives of many Islamic philosophers during this period. Al-Farabi, however, seems to have escaped such misfortunes.

Al-Farabi carefully grounds all aspects of his philosophy in his metaphysics—that is, in his theory of the nature of the world and its first and ultimate cause. The dependence of all of philosophy on metaphysics and, in particular, on our knowledge of the existence and nature of God, is reflected in the structure of most of his works. Al-Farabi initially sets out his metaphysical system, arguing that God exists, is unique, is one, and is all-knowing and perfectly wise, great, beautiful, and happy. Al-Farabi then proceeds to introduce his theory of knowledge, his ethics, and finally his political theory. Into this overarching system, whose broad strokes are adapted from Plato, Aristotle, and later Neoplatonic philosophers, he introduces a theory of prophecy and revealed religion.

Avicenna (Abu 'Ali al-Husayn ibn 'Abd Allah ibn Sina, 980–1037), was born in Persia near Bukhara (in present-day Uzbekistan), son of the provincial governor. He spent his life in Persia. Avicenna showed his gifts for study and learning as a child; he had memorized the Koran by the age of ten. He benefited from his father's association with learned men, and his father provided for his education enthusiastically. By the age of eighteen, Avicenna was teaching himself, having outgrown his teachers; by twenty-one, he had a reputation as a physician at the court of the ruling Samanid family. His favor at this court got him, among other things, access to an extensive royal library.

The circumstances so auspicious for the germination of Avicenna's talents ended abruptly with the Samanids' defeat at the hands of the Turkish leader Mahmud of Ghazna. For the rest of his life, Avicenna pursued his work only in the brief periods of calm he could find in an era of great political upheaval and turmoil.

Avicenna wandered to Rayy (near Tehran), where he practiced medicine. Unable to pursue his work in philosophy, he traveled to Hamadan and entered the service of the prince. Here he found enough leisure to begin some of his most famous works, although he had time for writing only after completing his duties as administrator and physician to the court. In addition, court intrigues forced him more than once to suffer imprisonment or to go into hiding. But in hiding and in prison, he wrote; when in the service of the court, he dispatched his duties during the day and met with students at night for general philosophical discussions, music, revelry, and work on his treatises.

When Avicenna was forty-two, the prince died. Refusing to serve under the prince's son, Avicenna went to Isfahan, south of Tehran, after a short period of hiding and imprisonment in Hamadan. (He escaped by disguising himself as a Sufi.) He found great favor at this court, where he finished the writing he started in Hamadan and produced many other treatises. His duties at Isfahan obliged him to accompany his patron into battles. On one such campaign, Avicenna fell ill. Though he acted as his own physician, he died in Hamadan at the age of fifty-seven.

Avicenna is known primarily as an outstanding metaphysician and physician. More than either al-Farabi before him or Averroës after him, Avicenna shows a mystical side in his writings. In some tracts, he interrupts the dry exposition of systematic philosophy for an evocation of blissful union with God. This shows an affinity with Sufism, whose followers disdain worldly pursuits and enter on a harsh asceticism in order to attain such a direct union with God.

For Avicenna, as for al-Farabi, all of philosophy must rest on a metaphysical foundation. But for Avicenna, a practicing physician, the theory of knowledge has great importance, for it defines proper scientific method and, more generally, the proper role of reason in acquiring knowledge. Al-Farabi, following Aristotle, begins his metaphysics by defining God as the First Cause, ultimately responsible for the existence of everything else. Avicenna, in contrast, begins by defining God as the Necessary Being. He analyzes the nature of substance, contrasts necessity with contingency, and then demonstrates the nature of the Necessary Being.

Averroës, or, in Arabic, ibn Rushd (1126–1198), was influential both within Islamic philosophy and in Christian philosophy in the West. He was born in Córdoba, Spain, the grandson (and perhaps also the son) of Córdoba's chief judge, or *qadi*, an important civil and religious authority. Averroës studied theology and law in Spain. At twenty-seven, he traveled to Marrakesh, where he observed the star Canope and became convinced of Aristotle's view that the world is round. Like

Avicenna, he studied medicine and wrote a medical handbook. The sultan of Marrakesh noticed Averroës, was impressed by his intelligence, and supported his research for some fourteen years. The sultan then obtained an appointment for Averroës as *qadi* of Seville, in Spain, a post that Averroës assumed at age forty-three. Just two years later, he returned to Córdoba as *qadi,* eventually, like his father and grandfather, becoming chief *qadi.* At fifty-six, he returned to Marrakesh to become the sultan's physician. He retained that position for thirteen years, finally retiring shortly before he turned seventy.

Averroës' commentaries on Aristotle were extremely influential in Western Europe for centuries. Nevertheless, Averroës' own philosophy is more Neoplatonic than Aristotelian. Aristotle insists that 'being' is said in many senses; Averroës rejects this cornerstone of Aristotelian metaphysics, maintaining instead that 'being' is univocal. Everything, according to Averroës, fits into a unified, coherent, hierarchical structure of levels or degrees—but not different kinds—of being. The "great chain of being" has God at the top, followed by the heavenly bodies, man, animals, and inanimate objects on earth. God not only acts as first mover, being causally responsible for the movements of everything on lower levels, but also is the first intelligence, responsible for the intellectual activity of all other beings.

Averroës tries to harmonize religion and philosophy. In *The Incoherence of the Incoherence* he attacks al-Ghazali's critiques of philosophical arguments and his implicit assertion that reason cannot achieve understanding of religious truth. Averroës argues that there are several paths—the rhetorical, open to anyone; the religious, open to many; and the philosophical, open to a few—to a single, unified truth. Christian philosophers would later attack Averroës for allegedly holding a doctrine of "double truth," according to which religious and philosophical conclusions conflicted but were nevertheless both fully true. Clearly, however, neither al-Ghazali nor Averroës holds such a position. Al-Ghazali argues that religion and philosophy do conflict, but, he concludes, so much the worse for philosophy. Averroës argues that religion and philosophy are harmonious; he wrote a work entitled *On the Harmony between Religion and Philosophy* precisely to establish that point.

Perhaps the most distinctive aspect of Averroës' thought concerns his philosophy of mind. Averroës, like Aristotle, maintains that the intellect, in its main capacity, is passive; it mostly receives sensible forms from outside. The mind abstracts general ideas from the material of sensation and imagination; nothing appears in the mind without also appearing in sense or imagination. Averroës calls this capacity of the mind the *passive intellect.* But the intellect cannot be completely passive, driven by outside forces. We ask ourselves questions and look around for answers; we perform chains of reasoning, mathematical constructions, and other mental acts that are truly active and cannot be understood as effects of sensation or imagination. Averroës, again following Aristotle, therefore posits the *active intellect* as the aspect of mind that directs such mental activity. The active and passive intellects working together constitute the *acquired intellect.* Averroës' striking and original contribution to this theory of mind rests on his assertion that the active intellect is pure form and is therefore a *kind* of intellect rather than an individual entity. The active intellect, to direct our thinking appropriately and correctly, must have access to the full range of the forms without regard to their presence in sense or imagination in an individual human being. It must therefore be able to think anything at all nonabstractively. Only the intellect of God, however, could do this. Averroës thus identifies the active intellect with the mind of God. In thinking, we partially unite with God; the union becomes complete only at death, when our bodies are destroyed and we fuse with the mind of God. We are immortal, Averroës holds, but we do not enjoy a personal afterlife; instead we blend into the mind of God. This union is possible, we know, because we can conjoin with the active intellect in our everyday thinking.

AL-FARABI

from *Principles of the Views of the Citizens of the Best State*

SECTION I / THE FIRST CAUSE

CHAPTER 1 / THE FIRST CAUSE IS ONE AND MIND

§1. The First Existent is the First Cause of the existence of all the other existents. It is free of every kind of deficiency, whereas there must be in everything else some kind of deficiency, either one or more than one; but the First is free of all their deficiencies. Thus its existence is the most excellent and precedes every other existence. No existence can be more excellent than or prior to, its existence. Thus it has the highest kind of excellent existence and the most elevated rank of perfect existence. Therefore its existence and substance cannot be adulterated by non-existence at all. It can in no way have existence potentially, and there is no possibility whatsoever that it should not exist. Therefore it is without beginning, and everlasting in its substance and essence, without being in need of any other thing, which would provide its permanence in order to be eternal; its substance suffices for its permanence and its everlasting existence. No existence at all can be like its existence; nor is there any existence of the same rank of its existence which the First would have and which it does not have already. It is the existent for whose existence there can be no cause through which, or out of which, or for the sake of which, it has come to exist. For it is neither matter nor is it at all sustained by a matter or a substratum; its existence is free of all matter and substratum. Nor does it have form, because form can exist only in matter. If it had form, its essence would be composed of matter and form, and if it were like that, it would be sustained by the two parts of which it would be composed and its existence would have a cause. Likewise its existence has no purpose and no aim, so that it would exist merely to fulfill that aim and that purpose; otherwise that would have been a cause of its existence, so that it would not be the First Cause. Likewise it has not derived its existence from something else prior to it, and even less so from inferior to it.

§2. The First Existent is different in its substance from everything else, and it is impossible for anything else to have the existence it has. For between the First and whatever were to have the same existence as the First, there could be no difference and no distinction at all. Thus there would not be two things but one essence only, because, if there were a difference between the two, that in which they differed would not be the same as that which they shared, and thus that point of difference between the two would be a part of that which sustains the existence of both, and that which they have in common the other part. Thus each of them would be divisible in thought, and each of the two parts of the First would be a cause for the subsistence of its essence; and it would not be the First but there would be another existent prior to it and a cause for its existence—and that is impossible.

If that other existent were the one which contained the thing by which it differed from the (First) and the First only differed from it in not having the thing by which that other existent differs from it, then it would necessarily follow that the thing by which that other existent differed from the First would be the existence which that other (existent) has in particular, whereas the existence of the First would be common to both. Then the existence of that other would be composed of two things, one which it would have in particular and one which it would have in common with the First. Then the existence of that other would not be the existence of the First, the essence of the First rather being simple and indivisible, whereas the essence of that other existent would be divisible. Then the other existent would have two parts by which it would be sustained, and its existence would then have a cause, and it would be inferior to the existence of the First and deficient in comparison with it. It would then not be in the first rank of existence.

Again, if, apart from the First, some other thing like it in species were to exist, the existence of the First would not be perfect: for that which is "perfect" means the thing apart from which no other existent of its species can exist. This applies equally to everything: what is perfect in magnitude is that apart from which no magnitude of this species exists: what is perfect in beauty is that apart from which no beauty of its species exists; equally what is perfect in substance is that apart from which no substance of its species exists. Equally, in the case of every perfect body nothing else can be in the same species, as in the case of the sun, the moon and each one of the other planets. If, then, the First has perfect existence, it is impossible that any other existent should have the same existence. Therefore the First alone has this existence and it is unique in this respect.

§3. Further, the First cannot have a contrary. This will become clear when the meaning of 'contrary' is understood. For a thing and its contrary are different, and it is impossible that the contrary of a thing should ever be identical with that particular thing. Not everything, however, that differs from another thing is its contrary, nor is everything that cannot be that particular thing its contrary, but only that which is, in addition, opposing it, so that each of the two will annihilate and destroy the other when they happen to meet: it is of the nature of such contraries that the absence of B entails the existence of A in all places where B exists (now) and that the existence of B being established where A is established now entails the absence of A from that place. This generally applies to everything which can possibly have a contrary. For if a thing is the contrary of the other in its actions only and not in its other modes, this description will apply only to their actions; if they are contrary to each other in their qualities, this will apply only to their qualities; and if they are contrary to each other in their substances, this description will apply (only) to their substances. Now, if the First were to have a contrary, this would be its relation to its contrary. It would follow, then, that each of them would tend to destroy the other, and that the First could be destroyed by its contrary and in its very substance. But what can be destroyed cannot derive its own subsistence and permanence from its own substance, but also its own substance is not sufficient to bring it into existence. Nor is its own substance sufficient for producing its existence; this would rather be caused by something else. But what may possibly not exist cannot be eternal. And anything whose substance is not sufficient for its permanence or its existence will owe its existence or its permanence to another, different, cause, so it will not be the First. Again, the First would in this way owe its existence to the absence of its contrary, and then the absence of its contrary would be the cause of its existence. The First Existent would then not be the First Cause in the absolute meaning of the term.

Again, it would follow that they both should have some common 'where' to receive them, either a substratum or a genus, or something else different from both of them, so that by their meeting in it it would be possible for each of them to destroy the other. That 'where' would be permanent, and the two would occupy it in turn. And that 'where' would then be prior in existence to each of them.

Now should someone posit as 'contrary' something which does not answer this description, the thing posited would not be a contrary. Rather would it differ from the First in another way. We do not deny, indeed, that the First may have other things different from it, but not a contrary nor something which has the same existence which it has. Thus no existent can be of the same rank of existence as the First, because two contraries are (always) in one and the same rank of existence. Thus the First is unique in its existence, and there is no other existent to share its species. Hence it is one and, in addition, utterly unique by virtue of its rank. And it is one in this respect as well.

§4. Again, the First is not divisible in thought into things which would constitute its substance. For it is impossible that each part of the explanation of the meaning of the First should denote one of the parts by which the First's substance is constituted. If this were the case, the parts which constitute its substance would be causes of its existence, in the same way as the meanings denoted by the parts of the definition of a thing are causes of the existence of the thing defined and in the same way as matter and form are causes of the existence of the thing composed of them. But this is impossible in the case of the First, since it is the First and since its existence has no cause whatsoever.

If it is thus not divisible into these parts, it is still less possible to divide it into quantitative parts or into any other kinds of parts. This necessarily entails also that it has no magnitude and is absolutely incorporeal. Hence it is also one in this respect, because one of the meanings denoted by 'one' is 'the indivisible'. For whatever is indivisible in some respect is one in that respect in which it is indivisible. If it is indivisible in its action, it is one in that respect; if it is indivisible in its quality, it is one according to its quality. But what is indivisible in its substance is one with regard to its substance.

§5. If then the First is indivisible with regard to its substance, the existence it has, by which it is distinguished from all other existents, cannot be any other than that by which it exists in itself. Therefore its distinction from all the others is due to a oneness which is its essence. For one of the meanings of oneness is the particular existence by which each existent is distinguished from all others; on the strength of this meaning of oneness each existent is called 'one' inasmuch as it has its own particular existence. This meaning of the term 'one' goes necessarily with 'existence'. Thus the First is one in this respect as well, and deserves more than any other one the name and the meaning (of 'the one').

§6. Because the First is not in matter and has itself no matter in any way whatsoever, it is in its substance actual intellect; for what prevents the form from being intellect and from actually thinking (intelligizing) is the matter in which a thing exists. And when a thing exists without being in need of matter, that very thing will in its substance be actual intellect; and that is the status of the First. It is, then, actual intellect. The First is also intelligible through its substance; for, again, what prevents a thing from being actually intelligible and being intelligible through its substance is matter. It is intelligible by virtue of its being intellect; for the One whose identity is intellect is intelligible by the One whose identity is intellect. In order to be intelligible the First is in no need of another essence outside itself which would think it but it itself thinks its own essence. As a result of its thinking its own essence, it becomes actually thinking and intellect, and, as a result of its essence thinking (intelligizing) it, it becomes actually intelligized. In the same way, in order to be actual intellect and to be actually thinking, it is in no need of an essence which it would think and which it would acquire from the outside, but is intellect and thinking by thinking its own essence. For the essence which is thought is the essence which thinks, and so it is intellect by virtue of its being intelligized. Thus it is intellect and intelligized and thinking, all this being one essence and one indivisible substance—whereas man, for instance, is intelligible, but what is intelligible in his case is not actually intelligized but potentially intelligible; he becomes subsequently actually intelligized after the intellect has thought him. What is intelligible in the case of man is thus not always the subject which thinks, nor is, in his case, the intellect always the same as the intelligible object, nor is our intellect intelligible because it is intellect. We think, but not because our substance is intellect; we think with an intellect which is not what constitutes our substance; but the First is different; the intellect, the thinker and the intelligible (and intelligized) have in its case one meaning and are one essence and one indivisible substance.

§7. That the First is 'knowing' is to be understood in the same way. For it is, in order to know, in no need of an essence other than its own, through the knowledge of which it would acquire excellence, nor is it, in order to be knowable, in need of another essence which would know it, but its substance suffices for it to be knowing and to be known. Its knowledge of its essence is nothing else than its substance. Thus the fact that it knows and that it is knowable and that it is knowledge refers to one essence and one substance.

§8. The same applies to its being 'wise'. For wisdom consists in thinking the most excellent thing through the most excellent knowledge. By the fact that it intelligizes its essence and through the knowledge of it it knows the most excellent thing. The most excellent knowledge is the permanent knowledge, which cannot cease to exist, of what is permanent and cannot cease to exist. That is its knowledge of its essence. . . .

§11. When any thing whose existence is utterly perfect is thought (intelligized) and known, the result of that process of thinking of the thing which goes on in our minds and conforms to its existence will be in accordance with its existence outside our minds. If its existence is deficient, what we think of it in our minds will be deficient. Thus, in the case of motion, time, infinity, privation and other existents like them the result of our thinking each of them in our minds will be deficient, since they are themselves deficient existents. In the case of number, triangle, square and their like, the result of our thinking them in our minds will be more perfect, because they are themselves more perfect. Hence, since the First has the highest perfection of existence, it follows that what we think of it in our minds ought to have utmost perfection as well. We find, however, that this is not the case. One ought to realize that for the First it is not difficult to apprehend itself, since the First itself is of the utmost perfection. But it is difficult and hard for us to apprehend (perceive) it and to represent it to ourselves because of the weakness of our intellectual faculties, mixed as they are with matter and non-being: we are too weak to think it as it really is. For its overwhelming perfection dazzles us, and that is why we are not strong enough to represent it to ourselves perfectly (completely). Likewise, light is the first and most perfect and most luminous visible, the other visibles become visible through it, and it is the cause of the colours becoming visible. Hence our visual apprehension of any colour which is more perfect and powerful (strong) should have been more perfect. But we see that just the opposite happens. The more perfect and the more powerful a visible is, the weaker is our visual apprehension of it, and not because of its being hidden or deficient—it has, on the contrary, in itself the utmost brightness and luminosity —but because the perfection of its splendour dazzles our sight so that our eyes are bewildered. Thus are our minds in relation to the First Cause, the First Intellect and the First Living. Our thinking it is deficient, not because of any deficiency in the First, and our apprehension of it is difficult for us, not because of its substance being difficult to apprehend, but because our minds are too weak to represent it to ourselves. That is why the intelligibles within our minds are deficient. Our representation of them is of two kinds: one kind of intelligible is in itself impossible for man to represent to himself or to think of by way of perfect representation, because of the weak nature of their existence and the defeats of their essences and substances. The other kind of intelligible could in itself be represented completely and as perfectly as they are, but since our minds are weak and far from the substances of these objects, it is impossible for us to represent them to ourselves completely and with all the perfection of their existence. Each of these two things is at opposite extremes, one being of the utmost perfection, the other of the utmost deficiency. Since we are mixed up with matter and since matter is the cause of our substances being remote from the First Substance, the nearer our substances draw to it, the more exact and the truer will necessarily be our apprehension of it. Because the nearer we draw to separating ourselves from matter, the more complete will be our apprehension of the First Substance. We come nearer to it only by becoming actual [or "actually"] intellect. When we are completely separated from matter, our mental apprehension of the First will be at its most perfect.

§12. The same applies to its greatness, its majesty and its glory. For majesty, greatness and glory exist in a thing in proportion to its perfection, either with regard to its substance or to one of its (special) properties. Whenever this is said of us, it is mostly said on account of the perfection of some "accidental" things (goods) which we possess, such as riches or knowledge or some bodily quality. But since the perfection of the First surpasses every perfection, its greatness, majesty and glory surpass all those (others) which are endowed with greatness and glory; in this case, surpassing greatness and glory are in its substance and not in anything else apart from its substance and its essence. For it is its essence which is possessed of majesty and glory, and it does not make any difference whether anybody else exalts it or does not, praises its greatness or does not, glorifies it or does not.

§13. Beauty and brilliance and splendour mean in the case of every existent that it is in its most excellent state of existence and that it has attained its ultimate perfection. But since the First is in the most excellent state of existence, its beauty surpasses the beauty of every other beautiful existent, and the same applies to its splendour and its brilliance. Further, it has all these in its substance and essence by itself and by thinking (intelligizing) its essence. But we have beauty and splendour and brilliance as a result of accidental qualities (of our souls), and of what our bodies have in them and because of exterior things, but they are not in our substance. The Beautiful and the beauty in the First are nothing but one essence, and the same applies to the other things predicated of it.

§14. Pleasure and delight and enjoyment result and increase only when the most accurate apprehension concerns itself with the most beautiful, the most brilliant and the most splendid objects. Now, since the First is absolutely the most beautiful, the most brilliant and the most splendid, and since its apprehension of its own essence is most accurate in the extreme and its knowledge of its own substance most excellent in the absolute meaning of the term, the pleasure which the First enjoys is a pleasure whose character we do not understand and whose intensity we fail to apprehend, except by analogy and by relating it to the amount of pleasure which we feel, when we have most accurately and most completely apprehended what is most perfect and most splendid on our level, either through sensing it or representing it to ourselves or through becoming aware of it intellectually. For we experience in this state an amount (degree) of pleasure which we assume to surpass every other pleasure in intensity and are filled with a feeling of utmost self-enjoyment as a result of the knowledge which we have attained. But whereas this state in us lasts but a short time and disappears speedily, the First's knowledge and the First's apprehension of what is most excellent and most beautiful and most splendid in its essence is, as compared with our knowledge and our apprehension of what is most beautiful and most splendid on our level, like its pleasure and its delight and its enjoyment of itself as compared with the limited amount of pleasure and delight and self-enjoyment which is attained by us. And since our apprehension and its apprehension have nothing in common nor do the object of our knowledge and the object of its knowledge nor the most beautiful on our level and the most beautiful in its essence—and if they had anything in common, it would be insignificant—then the pleasure which we feel and our delight and our enjoyment of ourselves and the corresponding state of the First have nothing in common. If they had anything in common it would be very insignificant—for how can that which is only a small part and that whose extension is unlimited in time have anything in common, and how can that which is very deficient have anything in common with that which is of utmost perfection?

§15. Since the more something enjoys its own essence and the greater pleasure and happiness it feels about it the more it likes and loves its essence and the greater is the pride it takes in it, it is evident that the relation which exists between the First's necessary love and liking of its essence and its pride in it and our love of ourselves, which arises from our enjoyment of the excellence of our essence, is the same as the relation between the excellence and the perfection of its essence and our excellence and perfection of which we are proud. In its case, subject and object of affection, subject and object of pride, subject and object of love are identical, and that is just the opposite of what exists in our case. What is loved in us is excellence and beauty, but what loves in us is not excellence and beauty, but is another faculty, which is however not what is loved in us. What loves in us, then, is not identical with what is loved in us. But, in the First's case, subject and object of love and affection are identical. It does not make any difference whether anybody likes it or not, loves it or not: it is the first object of love and the first object of affection. . . .

AVICENNA

from *A Treatise on Logic*

From Avicenna's Treatise on Logic: Part One of Danesh-Name Alai. *Translated by Farhang Zabeeh. The Hague: Martinus Nijhoff, 1971.*

PART ONE OF *DANESH-NAME ALAI* (A CONCISE PHILOSOPHICAL ENCYCLOPAEDIA)

The Purpose and Use of Logic

There are two kinds of cognition: One is called intuitive or perceptive or apprehensive (Tasawor in Arabic). For example, if someone says, 'Man', or 'Fairy', or 'Angel', or the like, you will understand, conceive and grasp what he means by the expression. The other kind of cognition is judgment (Tasdiq in Arabic). As for example, when you acknowledge that angels exist or human beings are under surveillance and the like.

Cognition can again be analyzed into two kinds. One is the kind that may be known through Intellect; it is known necessarily by reasoning through itself. For example, there are the intuitive cognitions of the whatness of the soul, and judgments about what is grasped by intuitive cognition, such as, the soul is eternal.

The other kind of cognition is one that is known by intuition. Judgments about these intuitions, however, are made, not by Intellect, or by reason but by the First Principle. For example, it is known that if two things are equal to the same thing then those things are equal to each other. Then there is the kind of cognition known by the senses, such as, the knowledge that the sun is bright. Also, there is the knowledge that is received from authority such as those received from sages and prophets. And the kind that is obtained from the general opinion and those we are brought by it, for example, that it is wrong to lie and injustice ought not to be done. And still other kinds—which may be named later.

Whatever is known by Intellect, whether it is simple intuitive cognition, or judgment about intuitive cognition, or cognitive judgment, should be based on something which is known prior to the thing, (a posteriori).

An example of an intuitive or perceptual cognition is this: If we don't know what 'man' means, and someone tells us that a man is an animal who talks, we first have to know the meaning of 'animal' and 'talking', and we must have intuitive cognition of these things before we can learn something we didn't know before about man.

An example of a judgment acquired by Intellect is this: If we don't know the meaning of 'the world was created,' and someone tells us that the world possesses color, and whatever possesses color is created; then, and only then, can we know what we didn't know before about the world.

Thus, whatever is not known but desired to be known, can be known through what is known before. But it is not the case that whatever is known can be a ground for knowing what is unknown. Because for everything that is unknown there is a proper class of known things that can be used for knowing the unknown.

There is a method by which one can discover the unknown from what is known. It is the science of logic. Through it one may know how to obtain the unknown from the known. This science is also concerned with the different kinds of valid, invalid, and near valid inferences.

The science of logic is the science of scales. Other sciences are practical, they can give direction in life. The salvation of men lies in their purity of soul. This purity of soul is attainable by contemplating the pure form and avoiding this-worldly inclinations. And the way to these two are through science. And no science which cannot be examined by the balance of logic is certain and exact. Thus, without the acquisition of logic, nothing can be truly called science. Therefore, there is no way except learning the science of logic. It is characteristic of the ancient sciences that the student, at the beginning of his study, is unable to see the use or application of the sciences. This is so, because only after a thorough study of the whole body of science will the real value of his endeavor become apparent. Thus I pray that the reader of this book will not grow impatient in reading things which do not appear of use upon first sight. . . .

A Discussion of Essential and Accidental Universals

The universal contains its particulars either (a) essentially or (b) accidentally. The Essential Universal and its Particulars are apprehended if, at least, three conditions are fulfilled:

1. The particular has meaning. Thus, if you know the meaning of 'animal', 'man', 'number', and 'number four', you cannot help knowing the meaning of the expressions, 'man is an animal' and 'four is a number'. But if you add 'exists' or 'is white' to the word 'animal' and 'number', you will not understand the meaning of the resulting expressions "man exists," "number four exists," or "man is not white" or "man is white."
2. The existence of the Essential Universal is prerequisite for the existence of its Particular. For example, there should first be animal in order that animal be man, and first there should be number in order that number be four, and first there should be human being in order that human being be Zid.
3. Nothing gives meaning to a particular, rather its meaning is derived from its essence. For example, nothing makes human being animal, and nothing makes four number, except its essence. For if it were otherwise, if the essence of a thing did not exist, there could be a man which is not animal, and there could be four, but no number; but this is impossible.

To further elaborate what has been said, take the saying "something may make some other thing." Its meaning is this: a thing can not be in its essence another thing, but only could be that other thing by means of something else which is accidental to it. If it is impossible for a thing to be what another thing is, nothing could make it that thing. That thing which makes man, man, makes animal, animal. But it does not make man, animal, since man in itself is animal, and four in itself is number. But this relation does not exist between whiteness and man. Hence, there should be something which makes man, white.

Thus, when every meaning has the above three characteristics it is essential. Whatever does not have all these characteristics is accidental. Accidental qualities are those which can never arise from the essence of a thing, not even by imagination. Therefore, they are unlike kinds of deduction that are made in the case of number thousand which is an even number or in the case of a triangle, the sum total of whose angles is equal to two right angles. An example of an accidental quality is laughter, an attribute of men. This problem will be discussed later on.

And I should have mentioned also that a human being has two characteristics: essential and accidental. His essential characteristic may be exemplified by his ability to speak, because this property is the essence of his soul. An accidental quality of his is laughter, because it is the character of man, on seeing or hearing a strange and unfamiliar thing, (unless hindered by instinct or habit), to perchance laugh. But before there be wonder and laughter there must be a soul for a man, in order that this soul be united with a body and man becomes a man. First, there should be a soul in order that there be a man; not first, there should be laughter in order that there be a soul. Thus, the characteristic which comes first is essential, and whatever does not come from a man is not essential, but accidental. When you say, "Zid is seated," "Zid slept," "Zid is old," and "Zid is young," these characteristics, without doubt, are accidental, no matter what their temporal sequence be. . . .

A Discussion of Premises

There are thirteen kinds of non-derivable premises.

1. *First Principle premises.* They are known by the First Intellect and cannot be doubted. No one

can even remember doubting them in the past. If a person imagines that he came into the world knowing nothing except the meaning of two parts of a First Principle premise and he was asked to doubt the truth of the premise he would not be able to do so. For example, if a person knows by intuition the meaning of 'whole' and 'part' 'greater' and 'lesser', then he cannot help knowing that "the whole is greater than its parts," and that "things which are equal to the same thing are equal to each other."

2. *Perceptual premises.* They are apprehended through the senses, such as, the sun rises and sets, and the moon wanes and waxes.

3. *Experimental premises.* They are not known only by pure reason or only by pure sense, but are known by means of both. Such as, when we discover through the senses that certain things always have the same characteristics and we know by reason that the occurrence of these characteristics did not happen by chance. An example is "knowing that fire burns."

4. *Testimonial premises.* They are accepted by reason because they are testified to by many. We know, although we haven't been there, that Baghdad and Egypt exist. If, however, the report is doubted, it cannot be regarded as testimony. The more testimony we have, the more certain we are.

5. *Premises which contain syllogisms.*

6. *Premises known by custom.* They are the notions which people learn in their early childhood. They are not known by reason but rather are derived from the general constitution of man, i.e., shame, mercy, etc. Or they may be known by induction, or be based on some notion which people generally are unaware of, i.e., the ideas that "it is necessary to be just," that "one ought not to tell a lie," and that "God is omnipotent." These premises may be true like the examples given above. Their truth, although questionable, can be known by reasoning. Some of these premises are false except under certain conditions. For example, it should not be said that God is omnipotent unconditionally for God cannot do what is logically impossible.

7. *Premises derived from the imagination.* These premises are false but have a powerful influence on the psyche, so much so, that it is not easy to cast doubt on them. They are of two kinds: One cannot be proved or disproved by reason. The other kind is one which the imagination regards falsely as a perceptual premise. It is more than perceptual. Thus, it cannot really be given to the imagination, since only what is perceptual can be imagined. No wonder we cannot have an image of our imagination!

8. *Premises known by authority.* These premises are accepted by everyone because they have been uttered by wise men. Yet, they are neither as true as First Principle premises, or as true as Perceptual premises.

9. *Implicative premises.* These premises are the ones which a person deduces from the argument of an opponent and uses against him without considering their truth or falsity.

10. *Dubious premises.* These premises are false, but they may be made to appear self-evident by one's opponent in argument.

11. *Premises which appear to be accepted by custom.* These premises, at first sight, appear to be taken as true by all people. An example is the belief that one ought to help his friend whether he is in the right or the wrong. On first thought, a person may believe that this opinion is the right one under all conditions. But the truth is that the principle is contrary to another universally accepted opinion that no one ought to help the unjust, whether friend or enemy.

12. *Premises raised by our suspicions and fears.* These premises are based on our fears and suspicions which reason tells us are groundless. For example, we know that "x" has a correspondence with our enemy, therefore "x" is our enemy.

13. *Premises raised by emotions.* These premises, though known by reason to be false, are induced by our passions. For example, the effect produced in a person when someone says that what you are now eating will not make you bilious.

The Function of Premises in the Deductive Sciences

First Principle, Perceptual, Experiential, and Testimonial premises are used in syllogistic reasoning. This kind of reasoning gives certainty and truth.

Premises based on authority and custom are used in dialectic. This sort of reasoning has four advantages. (1) One can defeat, in argument, those people who pretend to have knowledge, but who are really ignorant of the premises of their argument. (2) One can demonstrate truth to those who do not understand syllogistic reasoning. (3) It is often the case that students of the minor sciences, like medicine, geometry, and natural science, take on faith the principles of their science. The teacher of metaphysics, the science of sciences, can show these students, by means of dialectic, how the premises of their sciences are derived from metaphysics. (4) One can show what things taken to be true, are false, and what things taken to be false, are true. In so doing, one can alert the student to errors and deficiencies in argument.

However, since the aim of this book is the discovery of truth, there will be no further discussion of dialectic.

Dubious premises and those inspired by the imagination are used in sophistical reasoning. This argument gives no knowledge.

Premises known by authority, and those which appear to be known by custom, and those based on our fears and suspicions, are employed in the science of rhetoric. This science is used both by politicians and theologians.

Premises inspired by emotion are used in poetic reasoning. . . .

A Discussion of the Different Kinds of Scientific Statements

There are four kinds of scientific questions. (1) One is a question about the "existence" or "non-existence" of things. (2) Another is about the "whatness" of things. (3) And another is about the "whichness" or "thatness" of things. (4) Also, there is the question about the "cause" of things. However, there are no questions, in scientific discourse, about "quantity," "quality," "time," or "space."

Question (1) is analyzable into two other questions. (1a) One asks "whether or not x exists." (1b) The other asks, "What is x?"

Question (2) is also divisible into two other questions. (2a) This question asks about the meaning of a term. For example, "What do you mean by the term 'triangle'?" (2b) And this question asks, "What is triangle in its essence?"

Question (2a) is prior to question (I), because before it can be known whether or not a thing exists, it is necessary to know the meaning of that thing. And question (1) is prior to question (2b), because before it can be known what a thing is, it is necessary to know whether or not that thing exists. The answer to question (2) is an interpretation or definition of *Essence*. The answer to question (3), the question about "whichness," is a statement about differentia or particulars.

Question (4), the question about "causation," involves two other questions. One asks (4a), "Why did you say that?"; the other asks (4b), "Why does it exist?"

The answers to questions (1) and (4) involve judgment and reasoning. Answers to questions (2) and (3) involve intuition or perception. . . .

AVICENNA

On the Nature of God

From Avicenna on Theology. *Translated by Arthur J. Aiberry. London: John Murray, 1951.*

That There Is a Necessary Being

Whatever has being must either have a reason for its being, or have no reason for it. If it has a reason, then it is contingent, equally before it comes into being (if we make this mental hypothesis) and when it is in the state of being—for in the case of a thing whose being is contingent the mere fact of its entering upon being does not remove from it the contingent nature of its being. If on the other hand it has no reason for its being in any way whatsoever, then it is necessary in its being. This rule having been confirmed, I shall now proceed to prove that there is in being a being which has no reason for its being.

Such a being is either contingent or necessary. If it is necessary, then the point we sought to prove is established. If on the other hand it is contingent, that which is contingent cannot enter upon being except for some reason which sways the scales in favour of its being and against its not-being. If the reason is also contingent, there is then a chain of contingents linked one to the other, and there is no being at all; for this being which is the subject of our hypothesis cannot enter into being so long as it is not preceded by an infinite succession of beings, which is absurd. Therefore contingent beings end in a Necessary Being.

Of the Unicity of God

It is not possible in any way that the Necessary Being should be two. Demonstration: Let us suppose that there is another necessary being: one must be distinguishable from the other, so that the terms "this" and "that" may be used with reference to them. This distinction must be either essential or accidental. If the distinction between them is accidental, this accidental element cannot but be present in each of them, or in one and not the other. If each of them has an accidental element by which it is distinguished from the other, both of them must be caused; for an accident is what is adjoined to a thing after its essence is realized. If the accidental element is regarded as adhering to its being, and is present in one of the two and not in the other, then the one which has no accidental element is a necessary being and the other is not a necessary being. If, however, the distinction is essential, the element of essentiality is that whereby the essence as such subsists; and if this element of essentiality is different in each and the two are distinguishable by virtue of it, then each of the two must be a compound; and compounds are caused; so that neither of them will be a necessary being. If the element of essentiality belongs to one only, and the other is one in every respect and there is no compounding of any kind in it, then the one which has no element of essentiality is a necessary being, and the other is not a necessary being. Since it is thus established that the Necessary Being cannot be two, but is All Truth, then by virtue of His Essential Reality, in respect of which He is a Truth, He is United and One, and no other shares with Him in that Unity: however the All-Truth attains existence, it is through Himself.

That God is Without Cause

A necessary being has no cause whatsoever. Causes are of four kinds: that from which a thing has being, or the active cause; that on account of which a thing has being, or the final and completive cause; that in which a thing has being, or the material cause; and that through which a thing has being, or the formal cause.

The justification for limiting causes to these four varieties is that the reason for a thing is either internal in its subsistence, or a part of its being, or external to it. If it is internal, then it is either that part in which the thing is, potentially and not actually, that is to say its matter; or it is that part in which the thing becomes actually, that is to say its form. If it is external, then it can only be either that from which the thing has being, that is to say the agent, or that on account of which the thing has being, that is to say its purpose and end.

Since it is established that these are the roots and principles of this matter, let us rest on them and clarify the problems which are constructed upon them.

Demonstration that He has no active cause: This is self-evident: for if He had any reason for being, this would be adventitious and that would be a necessary being. Since it is established that He has no active cause, it follows on this line of reasoning that His Quiddity is not other than His Identity, that is to say, other than His Being; neither will He be a subsistence or an accident. There cannot be two, each of which derives its being from the other; nor can He be a necessary being in one respect, and a contingent being in another respect.

Proof that His Quiddity is not other than His Identity, but rather that His Being is unified in His Reality: If His Being were not the same as His Reality, then His Being would be other than His Reality. Every accident is caused, and every thing caused requires a reason. Now this reason is either external to His Quiddity, or is itself His Quiddity: if it is external, then He is not a necessary being, and is not exempt from an active cause; while if the reason is itself the Quiddity, then the reason must necessarily be itself a complete being in order that the being of another may result from it. Quiddity before being has no being; and if it had being before this, it would not require a second being. The question therefore returns to the problem of being. If the Being of the Quiddity is accidental, whence did this Being supervene and adhere? It is therefore established that the Identity of the Necessary Being is His Quiddity, and that He has no active cause; the necessary nature of His Being is like the quiddity of all other things. From this it is evident that the Necessary Being does not resemble any other thing in any respect whatsoever; for with all other things their being is other than their quiddity.

Proof that He is not an accident: An accident is a being in a locus. The locus is precedent to it, and its being is not possible without the locus. But we have stated that a being which is necessary has no reason for its being.

Proof that there cannot be two necessary beings, each deriving its being from the other: Each of them, in as much as it derives its being from the other, would be subsequent to the other, while at the same time by virtue of supplying being to the other, each would be precedent to the other: but one and the same thing cannot be both precedent and subsequent in relation to its being. Moreover, if we assume for the sake of argument that the other is non-existent: would the first then be a necessary being, or not? If it were a necessary being, it would have no connexion with the other: if it were not a necessary being, it would be a contingent being and would require another necessary being. Since the Necessary Being is One, and does not derive Its being from any one, it follows that He is a Necessary Being in every respect; while anything else derives its being from another.

Proof that He cannot be a Necessary Being in one respect and a contingent being in another respect: Such a being, in as much as it is a contingent being, would be connected in being with something else, and so it has a reason; but in as much as it is a necessary being, it would have no connexions with anything else. In that case it would both have being and not have being; and that is absurd.

Demonstration that He has no material and receptive cause: The receptive cause is the cause for the provision of the place in which a thing is received; that is to say, the place prepared for the reception of being, or the perfection of being. Now the Necessary Being is a perfection in pure actuality, and is not impaired by any deficiency; every perfection belongs to Him, derives from Him, and is preceded by His Essence, while every deficiency, even if it be metaphorical, is negated to Him. All perfection and all beauty are of His Being; indeed, these are the vestiges of the perfection of His Being; how then should He derive perfection from any other? Since it is thus established that He has no receptive cause, it follows that He does not possess anything potentially, and that He has no attribute yet to be awaited; on the contrary, His Perfection has been realized in actuality; and He has no material cause. We say "realized in actuality," using this as a common term of expression, meaning that every perfection belonging to any other is non-existent and yet to be awaited, whereas all perfection belonging to Him has being and is present. His Perfect Essence, preceding all relations, is One. From this it is manifest that His Attributes are not an augmentation of His Essence; for if they were an augmentation of His Essence, the Attributes would be potential with reference to the Essence and the Essence would be the reason for the Attributes. In that case the Attributes would be subsequent to a precedent, so that they would be in one respect active and in another receptive; their being active would be other than the aspect of their being receptive; and in consequence they would possess two mutually exclusive aspects. Now this is impossible in the case of anything whatsoever; when a body is in motion, the motivation is from one quarter and the movement from another.

If it were to be stated that His Attributes are not an augmentation of His Essence, but that they entered into the constitution of the Essence, and that the Essence cannot be conceived of as existing without these Attributes, then the Essence would be compound, and the Oneness would be destroyed. It is also evident, as a result of denying the existence of a receptive cause, that it is impossible for Him to change; for the meaning of change is the passing away of one attribute and the establishment of another; and if He were susceptible to change, He would possess potentially an element of passing-away and an element of establishment; and that is absurd. It is clear from this that He has no opposite and no contrary; for opposites are essences which succeed each other in the occupation of a single locus, there being between them the extreme of contrariety. But He is not receptive to accidents, much less to opposites. And if the term "opposite" is used to denote one who disputes with Him in His Rulership, it is clear too on this count that He has no opposite. It is further clear that it is impossible for Him not to be; for since it is established that His Being is necessary, it follows that it is impossible for Him not to be; because everything which exists potentially cannot exist actually, otherwise it would have two aspects. Anything which is receptive to a thing does not cease to be receptive when reception has actually taken place; if this were not so, it would result in the removal of both being and not-being, and that is untenable. This rule applies to every essence and every unified reality, such as angels and human spirits; they are not susceptible to not-being at all, since they are free from corporeal adjunctions.

Demonstration that He has no formal cause: A formal, corporeal cause only exists and is confirmed when a thing is possessed of matter: the matter has a share in the being of the form, in the same way that the form has a part in the disposition of the matter in being in actuality; such a thing is therefore caused. It is further evident as a result of denying this cause to Him, that He is also to be denied all corporeal attributes, such as time, space, direction, and being in one place to the exclusion of all other; in short, whatever is possible in relation to corporeal things is impossible in relation to Him.

Proof that He has no final cause: The final cause is that on account of which a thing has being; and the First Truth has not being for the sake of anything. Rather does everything exist on account of the perfection of His Essence, being consequent to His Being and derived from His Being. Moreover the final cause, even if it be posterior in respect of being to all other causes, yet it is mentally prior to them all. It is the final cause which makes the active cause become a cause in actuality, that is to say in respect of its being a final cause.

Since it is established that He is exalted above this last kind of cause too, it is clear that there is no cause to His Attributes. It is also evident that He is Pure Benevolence and True Perfection; the meaning of His Self-Sufficiency likewise becomes manifest, namely that he approves of nothing and disapproves of nothing. For if He approved of anything, that thing would come into being and would continue to be; while if He disapproved of anything, that thing would be converted into not-being and would be annulled. The very divergency of these beings proves the nullity of such a proposition; for a thing which is one in every respect cannot approve of a thing and of its opposite. It is also not necessary for Him to observe the rule of greater expediency or of expediency, as certain Qualitarians have idly pretended; for if His acts of expediency were obligatory to Him,

He would not merit gratitude and praise for such acts, since He would merely be fulfilling that which it is His obligation to perform, and He would be to all intents and purposes as one paying a debt; He would therefore deserve nothing at all for such benevolence. In fact His acts proceed on the contrary from Him and for Him, as we shall demonstrate later.

His Attributes as Interpreted According to the Foregoing Principles

Since it is established that God is a Necessary Being, that He is One in every respect, that He is exalted above all causes, and that He has no reason of any kind for His Being; since it is further established that His Attributes do not augment His Essence, and that He is qualified by the Attributes of Praise and Perfection; it follows necessarily that we must state that He is Knowing, Living, Willing, Omnipotent, Speaking, Seeing, Hearing, and Possessed of all the other Loveliest Attributes. It is also necessary to recognize that His Attributes are to be classified as negative, positive, and a compound of the two: since His Attributes are of this order, it follows that their multiplicity does not destroy His Unity or contradict the necessary nature of His Being. Pre-eternity for instance is essentially the negation of not-being in the first place, and the denial of causality and of primality in the second place; similarly the term One means that He is indivisible in every respect, both verbally and actually. When it is stated that He is a Necessary Being, this means that He is a Being without a cause, and that He is the Cause of other than Himself: this is a combination of the negative and the positive. Examples of the positive Attributes are His being Creator, Originator, Shaper, and the entire Attributes of Action. As for the compound of both, this kind is illustrated by His being Willing and Omnipotent, for these Attributes are a compound of Knowledge with the addition of Creativeness.

God's Knowledge

God has knowledge of His Essence: His Knowledge, His Being Known and His Knowing are one and the same thing. He knows other than Himself, and all objects of knowledge. He knows all things by virtue of one knowledge, and in a single manner. His Knowledge does not change according to whether the thing known has being or not-being.

Proof that God has knowledge of His Essence: We have stated that God is One, and that He is exalted above all causes. The meaning of knowledge is the supervention of an idea divested of all corporeal coverings. Since it is established that He is One, and that He is divested of body, and His Attributes also; and as this idea as just described supervenes upon Him; and since whoever has an abstract idea supervening upon him is possessed of knowledge, and it is immaterial whether it is his essence or other than himself; and as further His Essence is not absent from Himself; it follows from all this that He knows Himself.

Proof that He is Knowledge, Knowing and Known: Knowledge is another term for an abstract idea. Since this idea is abstract, it follows that He is Knowledge; since this abstract idea belongs to Him, is present with Him, and is not veiled from Him, it follows that He is Knowing; and since this abstract idea does not supervene save through Him, it follows that He is Known. The terms employed in each case are different; otherwise it might be said that Knowledge, Knowing and Known are, in relation to His Essence, one. Take your own experience as a parallel. If you know yourself, the object of your knowledge is either yourself or something else; if the object of your knowledge is something other than yourself, then you do not know yourself. But if the object of your knowledge is yourself, then both the one knowing and the thing known are your self. If the image of your self is impressed upon your self, then it is your self which is the knowledge. Now if you look back upon yourself reflectively, you will not find any impression of the idea and quiddity of your self in yourself a second time, so as to give rise within you to a sense that your self is more than one. Therefore since it is established that He has intelligence of His Essence, and since His Intelligence is His Essence and does not augment His Essence, it follows that He is Knowing, Knowledge and Known without any multiplicity attaching to Him through these Attributes; and there is no difference between "one who has knowledge" and "one who has intelligence," since both are terms for describing the negation of matter absolutely.

Proof that He has knowledge of other than Himself: Whoever knows himself, if thereafter he does not know other than himself this is due to some impediment. If the impediment is essential, this implies necessarily that he does not know himself either; while if the impediment is of an external nature, that which is external can be removed. Therefore it is possible—nay, necessary—that He should have knowledge of other than Himself, as you shall learn from this chapter.

Proof that He has knowledge of all objects of knowledge: Since it is established that He is a Necessary Being, that He is One, and that the universe is brought into being from Him and has resulted out of His Being; since it is established further that He has knowledge of His Own Essence, His Knowledge of His Essence being what it is, namely that He is the Origin of all realities and of all things that have being; it follows that nothing in heaven or earth is remote from His Knowledge—on the contrary, all that comes into being does so by reason of Him: He is the causer of all reasons, and He knows that of which He is the Reason, the Giver of being and the Originator.

Proof that He knows all things by virtue of one knowledge, in a manner which changes not according to the change in the thing known: It has been established that His Knowledge does not augment His Essence, and that He is the Origin of all things that have being, while being exalted above accident and changes; it therefore follows that He knows things in a manner unchanging. The objects of knowledge are a consequence of His Knowledge; His Knowledge is not a consequence of the things known, that it should change as they change; for His Knowledge of things is the reason for their having being. Hence it is manifest that Knowledge is itself Omnipotence. He knows all contingent things, even as He knows all things that have being, even though we know them not; for the contingent, in relation to us, is a thing whose being is possible and whose not-being is also possible; but in relation to Him one of the two alternatives is actually known. Therefore His Knowledge of genera, species, things with being, contingent things, manifest and secret things—this Knowledge is a single knowledge.

Acts Emanating from God

Since you now know that He is a Necessary Being, that He is One, and that He has no Attribute which augments His Essence (for that would imply a succession of various acts, whereas the Act of God is the vestiges of the Perfection of His Essence); this being so, it follows that His First Act is one. For if there had emanated from Him two acts, the emanation would have been in two different manners, for duality in the act implies duality in the agent. He who acts by virtue of his own essence, if his essence is one only one act emanates from it; whereas if he has a duality of essence, he must be a compound; and we have proved the impossibility of this as regards God. It follows necessarily that the first thing to emanate from God was not a body; for every body is compounded of matter and form, and these require either two causes, or a single cause with two aspects; this being so, it is impossible that these two should have emanated from God, it having been established that there is no compounding in God whatsoever. Since the first thing to emanate from God was not a body, it follows that it was an abstract substance, namely, the First Intelligence. This has been confirmed by the true religion, for the Prophet said, "The first thing God created was Intelligence," and again, "The first thing God created was the Pen." The phrase *Thou shalt not find any change in the Way of God* (Koran xxxiii. 62) refers to the perpetuity of the Creation; the phrase *Thou shalt not find any alteration in the Way of God* (Koran xxxv. 41) refers to the perpetuity of the Command. Certainly, the Universe emanated from Him in due succession of order and media. So when we say that this Act emanated from Him through a reason, and that that reason was of Him also, this implies no imperfection in His Activity; on the contrary, totality emanated from Him, through Him, and unto Him. Therefore all things having being emanated from Him according to a known order and known media: that which came later cannot be earlier, and that which came earlier cannot be later, for it is He Who causes things to be earlier and later. Indeed, the first thing having being that emanated from Him was the noblest; thereafter came a descent from the nobler to the lower, until the lowliest of all was reached. First was Intelligence; then Soul; then the Body of Heaven; then the materials of the four Elements with their forms (for their materials are common to all, only their forms differ). Then there is a mounting up from the lowliest to the noblest; the noblest of all ending at a degree parallel to the degree of the Intelligence. Through this process of origination and returning back, God is said to be the Originator and the Returner.

AVERROËS

from *The Incoherence of the Incoherence*

From Averroes' Tahafut al Tahafut (The Incoherence of the Incoherence). *Translated by Simon van den Bergh. London: Luzac & Co., 1954.*

THE FOURTH DISCUSSION / SHOWING THAT THEY ARE UNABLE TO PROVE THE EXISTENCE OF A CREATOR OF THE WORLD

Ghazali says:

> We say: Mankind is divided into two categories; one, the men of truth who have acknowledged that the world has become and know by necessity that what has become does not become by itself but needs a creator, and the reasonableness of their view lies in their affirmation of a creator; the other, the materialists, believe the world, in the state in which it exists, to be eternal and do not attribute a creator to it, and their doctrine is intelligible, although their proof shows its inanity. But as to the philosophers, they believe the world to be eternal and still attribute a creator to it. This theory is self-contradictory and needs no refutation.

I say:

The theory of the philosophers is, because of the factual evidence, more intelligible than both the other theories together. There are two kinds of agent: (1) the agent to which the object which proceeds from it is only attached during the process of its becoming; once this process is finished, the object is not any more in need of it—for instance, the coming into existence of a house through the builder; (2) the agent from which nothing proceeds but an act which has no other existence than its dependence on it. The distinctive mark of this act is that it is convertible with the existence of its object, i.e. when the act does not exist the object does not exist, and when the act exists the object exists—they are inseparable. This kind of agent is superior to the former and is more truly an agent, for this agent brings its object to being and conserves it, whereas the other agent only brings its objects to being, but requires another agent for its further conservation. The mover is such a superior agent in relation to the moved and to the things whose existence consists only in their movement. The philosophers, believing that movement is the act of a mover and that the existence of the world is only perfected through motion, say that the agent of motion is the agent of the world, and if the agent refrained for only one moment from its action, the world would be annihilated. They use the following syllogism: The world is an act, or a thing whose existence is consequent upon this act. Each act by its existence implies the existence of an agent. Therefore the world has an agent existing by reason of its existence. The man who regards it as necessary that the act which proceeds from the agent of the world should have begun in time says: The world is temporal through an eternal agent. But the man for whom the act of the Eternal is eternal says: The world has come into being from an eternal agent having an eternal act, i.e. an act without beginning or end; which does, however, not mean that the world is eternal by itself, as people who call the world eternal imagine it to be.

Ghazali says, on behalf of the philosophers:

> The philosophers might answer: When we affirm that the world has a creator, we do not understand thereby a voluntary agent who acts after not having acted, as we observe in the various kinds of agents, like tailors, weavers, and builders, but we mean the cause of the world, and we call it the First Principle, understanding by this that there is no cause for its existence, but that it is a cause of the existence of other things; and if we call this principle the Creator, it is in this sense. . . .

I say:

This argument carries a certain conviction, but still it is not true. For the term 'cause' is attributed equivocally to the four causes—agent, form, matter, and end. Therefore if this were the answer of the philosophers, it would be defective. For if they were asked which cause they mean by their statement that the world has a first cause, and if they answered, "That agent whose act is uncreated and everlasting, and whose object is identical with its act," their answer would be true according to their doctrine; for against this conception, in the way we expounded it, there is no objection. But if they answered "The formal cause," the objection would be raised whether they supposed the form of the world to subsist by itself in the world, and if they answered, "We mean a form separate from matter," their statement would be in harmony with their theory; but if they answered, "We mean a form in matter" this would imply that the First Principle was not something incorporeal; and this does not accord with philosophical doctrine. Further, if they said, "It is a cause which acts for an end," this again would agree with the philosophical doctrine. As you see, this statement is capable of many interpretations, and how can it be represented there as an answer of the philosophers?

And as to Ghazali's words:

> We call it the First Principle, understanding by this that there is no cause for its existence, but that it is a cause for the existence of other things.

this again is a defective statement, for this might be said also of the first sphere, or of heaven in its entirety, or generally of any kind of existents which could be supposed to exist without a cause; and between this and the materialistic theory there is no difference.

And as to Ghazali's words:

> It is easy to establish by a strict proof an existent for the existence of which there is no cause.

this again is a defective statement, for the causes must be specified, and it must be shown that each kind has an initial term without cause—that is, that the agents lead upwards to a first agent, the formal causes to a first form, the material causes to a first matter, and the final causes to a first end. And then it must still be shown that these four ultimate causes lead to a first cause. This is not clear from the statement as he expresses it here.

And in the same way the statement in which he brings a proof for the existence of a first cause is defective, i.e. his statement:

> For we say that the world and its existents either have a cause or have not. . . .

For the term 'cause' is used in an equivocal way. And similarly the infinite regress of causes is according to philosophical doctrine in one way impossible, in another way necessary; impossible when this regress is essential and in a straight line and the prior cause is a condition of the existence of the posterior, not impossible when this regress is accidental and circular, when the prior is not a condition for the posterior and when there exists an essential first cause—for instance, the origin of rain from a cloud, the origin of a cloud from vapour, the origin of vapour from rain. And this is according to the philosophers an eternal circular process, which of necessity, however, presupposes a first cause. And similarly the coming into existence of one man from another is an eternal process, for in such cases the existence of the prior is not a condition for the existence of the posterior; indeed, the destruction of some of them is often a necessary condition. . . .

And as to Ghazali's words:

> And if the world existed by itself without cause, then it would be clear what the First Principle is.

he means that the materialists as well as others acknowledge a first cause which has no cause, and their difference of opinion concerns only this principle, for the materialists say that it is the highest sphere and the others that it is a principle beyond the sphere and that the sphere is an effect; but these others are divided into two parties, those who say that the sphere is an act that has a beginning and those who say that it is an eternal act. And having declared that the acknowledgement of a first cause is common to the materialists as well as to others, Ghazali says:

> However, it is not possible that the First Principle should be the heavens, for there are many of these and the proof of unity contradicts this;

meaning that from the order of the universe it is evident that its directing principle is one, just as it appears from the order in an army that its leader is one, namely, the commander of the army. And all this is true.

And as to Ghazali's words:

> Nor can it be said that one single heaven or one single body, the sun or any other body, can be the First Principle; for all these are bodies, and body is composed of matter and form, and the first body cannot be composite.

I say:

The statement that each body is composed of matter and form does not accord with the theory of the philosophers (with the exception of Avicenna) about the heavenly body, unless one uses 'matter' here equivocally. For according to the philosophers everything composed of matter and form has a beginning, like the coming into existence of a house and a cupboard; and the heavens, according to them, have not come into existence in this sense, and so they called them eternal, because their existence is coeternal with the First Principle. For since according to them the cause of corruption is matter, that which is incorruptible could not possess matter, but must be a simple entity. If generation and corruption were not found in sublunary bodies, we should not draw the conclusion that they were composed of matter and form, for the fundamental principle is that body is a single essence not less in its existence than in perception, and if there were no corruption of sublunary bodies, we should judge that they were simple and that matter was body. But the fact that the body of the heavens does not suffer corruption shows that its matter is actual corporeality. And the soul which exists in this body does not exist in it because this body requires, as the bodies of animals do, the soul for its continuance, nor because it is necessary for the existence of this body to be animated, but only because the superior must of necessity exist in the condition of the superior and the animate is superior to the inanimate. According to the philosophers there is no change in the heavenly bodies, for they do not possess a potency in their substance. They therefore need not have matter in the way the generable bodies need this, but they are either, as Themistius affirms, forms, or possess matter in an equivocal sense of the word. And I say that either the matters of the heavenly bodies are identical with their souls, or these matters are essentially alive, not alive through a life bestowed on them.

Ghazali says:

> To this there are two answers. The first is that it can be said: Since it follows from the tenets of your school that the bodies of the world are eternal, it must follow too that they have no cause, and your statement that on a second examination such a conclusion must be rejected will itself be rejected when we discuss God's unity and afterwards the denial of attributes to God.

I say:

Ghazali means that since they cannot prove the unity of the First Principle, and since they cannot prove either that the One cannot be body—for since they cannot deny the attributes, the First Principle must, according to them, be an essence endowed with attributes, and such an essence must be a body or a potency in a body—it follows that the First Principle which has no cause is the celestial bodies. And this conclusion is valid against those who might argue in the way he says the philosophers argue. The philosophers, however, do not argue thus, and do not say that they are unable to prove the unity and incorporeality of the First Principle. But this question will be discussed later.

Ghazali says:

> The second answer, and it is the answer proper to this question, is to say: it is established as a possibility that these existents can have a cause, but perhaps for this cause there is another cause, and so on *ad infinitum*. And you have no right to assert that to admit an infinite series of causes is impossible, for we ask you, 'Do you know this by immediate necessary intuition or through a middle term?' Any claim to intuition is

> excluded, and any method of deductive proof is forbidden to you, since you admit celestial revolutions without an initial term; and if you permit a coming into existence for what is without end, it is not impossible that the series should consist of causal relations and have as a final term an effect which has no further effect, although in the other direction the series does not end in a cause which has no anterior cause, just as the past has a final term, namely the everchanging present, but no first term. If you protest that the past occurrences do not exist together at one moment or at certain moments, and that what does not exist cannot be described as finite or infinite, you are forced to admit this simultaneous existence for human souls in abstraction from their bodies; for they do not perish, according to you, and the number of souls in abstraction from their bodies is infinite, since the series of becoming from sperma to man and from man to sperma is infinite, and every man dies, but his soul remains and is numerically different from the soul of any man who dies before, simultaneously, or afterwards, although all these souls are one in species. Therefore at any moment there is an infinite number of souls in existence. . . .

I say: As to Ghazali's words:

> But perhaps for this cause there is another cause and so on *ad infinitum* . . . and any method of deductive proof is forbidden to you, since you admit celestial revolutions without an initial term:

To this difficulty an answer was given above, when we said that the philosophers do not allow an infinite causal series, because this would lead to an effect without a cause, but assert that there is such a series accidentally from an eternal cause—not, however, in a straight line, nor simultaneously, nor in infinite matters, but only as a circular process.

What he says here about Avicenna, that he regarded an infinite number of souls as possible and that infinity is only impossible in what has a position, is not true and no philosopher has said it; indeed, its impossibility is apparent from their general proof which we mentioned, and no conclusion can be drawn against them from this assumption of an actual infinity of souls. Indeed, those who believed that the souls are of a certain number through the number of bodies and that they are individually immortal profess to avoid this assumption through the doctrine of the transmigration of souls. . . .

Ghazali says on behalf of the philosophers:

> The philosophers might say: The strict proof of the impossibility of an infinite causal series is as follows: each single cause of a series is either possible in itself or necessary; if it is necessary, it needs no cause, and if it is possible, then the whole series needs a cause additional to its essence, a cause standing outside the series.

I say:

The first man to bring into philosophy the proof which Ghazali gives here as a philosophical one, was Avicenna, who regarded this proof as superior to those given by the ancients, since he claimed it to be based on the essence of the existent, whereas the older proofs are based on accidents consequent on the First Principle. This proof Avicenna took from the theologians, who regarded the dichotomy of existence into possible and necessary as self-evident, and assumed that the possible needs an agent and that the world in its totality, as being possible, needs an agent of a necessary existence. This was a theory of the Mu'tazilites before the Ash'arites, and it is excellent, and the only flaw in it is their assumption that the world in its totality is possible, for this is not self-evident. Avicenna wanted to give a general sense to this statement, and he gave to the 'possible' the meaning of 'what has a cause', as Ghazali relates. And even if this designation can be conceded, it does not effect the division which he had in view. For a primary division of existence into what has a cause and what has no cause is by no means self-evident. Further, what has a cause can be divided into what is possible and what is necessary. If we understand by 'possible' the truly possible we arrive at the necessary-possible and not at the necessary which has no cause; and if we understand by 'possible' that which has a cause and is also necessary, there only follows from this that what has a cause has a cause and we may assume that this cause has a cause and so *ad infinitum*. We do not therefore arrive at an existent without cause—for this is the meaning of the expression 'entity of a necessary existence'—unless by the possible which Avicenna assumes as the opposite of what has no cause we understand the truly possible, for in these possibles there cannot exist an infinite series of causes. But if by 'possible' is meant those necessary things which have a cause, it has not yet been proved that their infinite number is impossible, in the way it is evident of the truly possible existents, and it is not yet proved that there is a necessary existent which needs a cause, so that from this assumption one can arrive at a necessary entity existing without a cause. Indeed, one has to prove that what applies to the total causal series of possible entities applies also to the total causal series of necessary existents.

Ghazali says:

> The terms 'possible' and 'necessary' are obscure, unless one understands by 'necessary' that which has no cause for its existence and by 'possible' that which has a cause for its existence. . . .

I say:

The assumption of infinite possible causes implies the assumption of a possible without an agent, but the assumption of infinite necessary entities having causes implies only that what was assumed to have a cause has none, and this argument is true with the restriction that the impossibility of infinite entities which are of a possible nature does not involve the impossibility of infinite necessary entities. If one wanted to give a demonstrative form to the argument used by Avicenna one should say: Possible existents must of necessity have causes which precede them, and if these causes again are possible it follows that they have causes and that there is an infinite regress; and if there is an infinite regress there is no cause, and the possible will exist without a cause, and this is impossible. Therefore the series must end in a necessary cause, and in this case this necessary cause must be necessary through a cause or without a cause, and if through a cause, this cause must have a cause and so on infinitely; and if we have an infinite regress here, it follows that what was assumed to have a cause has no cause, and this is impossible. Therefore the series must end in a cause necessary without a cause, i.e. necessary by itself, and this necessarily is the necessary existent. And when these distinctions are indicated, the proof becomes valid. But if this argument is given in the form in which Avicenna gives it, it is invalid for many reasons, one of which is that the term 'possible' used in it is an equivocal one and that in this argument the primary dichotomy of all existents into what is possible and what is not possible, i.e. this division comprising the existent *qua* existent, is not true.

And as to Ghazali's words in his refutation of the philosophers:

> We say: Each member of a causal series is possible in this sense of 'possible', namely, that it has a cause additional to its essence, but the whole series is not possible in this sense of 'possible'.

I say:

Ghazali means that when the philosophers concede that they understand by 'possible existent' that which has a cause and by 'necessary existent' that which has no cause, it can be said to them: "According to your own principles the existence of an infinite causal series is not impossible, and the series in its totality will be a necessary existent," for according to their own principles the philosophers admit that different judgements apply to the part and to the whole collectively. This statement is erroneous for many reasons, one of which is that the philosophers, as was mentioned before, do not allow an infinite series of essential causes, whether causes and effects of a possible or of a necessary nature, as we have shown. The objection which can be directed against Avicenna is that when you divide existence into possible and necessary and identify the possible existent with that which has a cause and the necessary existent with that which has none, you can no longer prove the impossibility of the existence of an infinite causal series, for from its infinite character it follows that it is to be classed with existents which have no cause and it must therefore be of the nature of the necessary existent, especially as, according to him and his school, eternity can consist of an infinite series of causes each of which is temporal. The fault in Avicenna's argument arises only from his division of the existent into that which has a cause and that which has none. If he had made his division in the way we have done, none of these objections could be directed against him. And Ghazali's statement that the ancients, since they admit an infinite number of circular movements, make the eternal consist of an infinite number of entities, is false. For the term 'eternal', when it is attributed both to this infinite series and to the one eternal being, is used equivocally.

And as to the words of Ghazali:

> If it is objected that this makes the necessary existent consist of possible existents, and this is impossible, we answer: By defining 'necessary' and 'possible' as we have done you have all that is needed, and we do not concede that it is impossible.

I say:

Ghazali means that the philosophers understand by 'necessary' that which has no cause and by 'possible' that which has a cause, and that he, Ghazali, does not regard it as impossible that what has no cause should consist of an infinite number of causes, because, if he conceded that this was impossible, he would be denying the possibility of an infinity of causes, whereas he only wants to show that the philosophers' deduction of a necessary being is a *petitio principii*.

Then Ghazali says:

> To say that it is impossible would be like saying that it is impossible that what is eternal should be made up of what is temporal, for time, according to you philosophers, is eternal, but the individual circular movements are temporal and have initial terms; therefore that which has no initial term consists of entities having initial terms, and it is true of the single units that they have a beginning, but not true of them collectively. In the same way it can be said of each term of the causal series that it has a cause, but not of the series as a whole. And so not everything that is true of single units is true of their collectivity, for it is true of each single unit that it is one and a portion and a part, but not true of their collectivity.

I say:

Ghazali means that it is not impossible that what has no cause should consist of infinite effects in the way the eternal, according to the philosophers, consists of temporal entities, which are infinite in number. For time, according to the philosophers, is eternal, and consists of limited temporal parts, and likewise the movement of heaven is eternal according to the philosophers, and the circular movements of which it consists are infinite. And the answer is that the existence of an eternal consisting of temporal parts, in so far as they are infinite in number, is not a philosophical principle; on the contrary they deny it most strongly, and only the materialists affirm it. For the sum must consist either of a finite number of transitory members or of an infinite number. If the former is the case, it is generally admitted that the members must also be generically transitory. For the latter case there are two theories. The materialists believe that the totality is of a possible nature and that the collectivity must be eternal and without a cause. The philosophers admit this infinity and believe that such genera, because they consist of possible transitory constituents, must necessarily have an external cause, lasting and eternal, from which they acquire their eternity. It is not true either, as Ghazali seems to imply, that the philosophers believe that the impossibility of an infinite series of causes depends on the impossibility that the eternal should consist of an infinity of constituents. They affirm that the eternity of these generically different movements must lead to one single movement, and that the reason why there exist genera which are transitory in their individuals, but eternal as a whole, is that there is an existent, eternal partly and totally, and this is the body of the heavens. The infinite movements are generically infinite only because of the one single continuous eternal movement of the body of the heavens. And only for the mind does the movement of heaven seem composed of many circular movements. And the movement of the body of the heavens acquires its eternity—even if its particular movements are transitory—through a mover which must always move and through a body which also must always be moved and cannot stop in its motion, as happens with things which are moved in the sublunary world.

About genera there are three theories, that of those who say that all genera are transitory, because the individuals in them are finite, and that of those who say that there are genera which are eternal and have no first or last term, because they appear by their nature to have infinite individuals; the latter are divided into two groups: those, namely the philosophers, who say that such genera can only be truly said to be everlasting, because of one and the same necessary cause, without which they would perish on innumerable occasions in infinite time; and those, namely the materialists, who believe that the existence of the individuals of these genera is sufficient to make them eternal. It is important to take note of these three theories, for the whole controversy about the eternity or non-eternity of the world, and whether the world has an agent or not, is based on these fundamental propositions. The theologians and those who believe in a temporal creation of the world are at one extreme, the materialists at the other, while the philosophers hold an intermediate position.

If all this is once established, you will see that the proposition that the man who allows the existence of an infinite series of causes cannot admit a first cause is false, and that on the contrary the opposite is evident, namely, that the man who does not acknowledge infinite causes cannot prove the existence of an eternal first cause, since it is the existence of infinite effects which demands the necessity of an eternal cause from which the infinite causes acquire their existence; for if not, the genera, all of whose individuals are temporal, would be necessarily finite. And in this and no other way can the eternal become the cause of temporal existents, and the existence of infinite temporal existents renders the existence of a single eternal first principle necessary, and there is no God but He. . . .

PART III South Asia

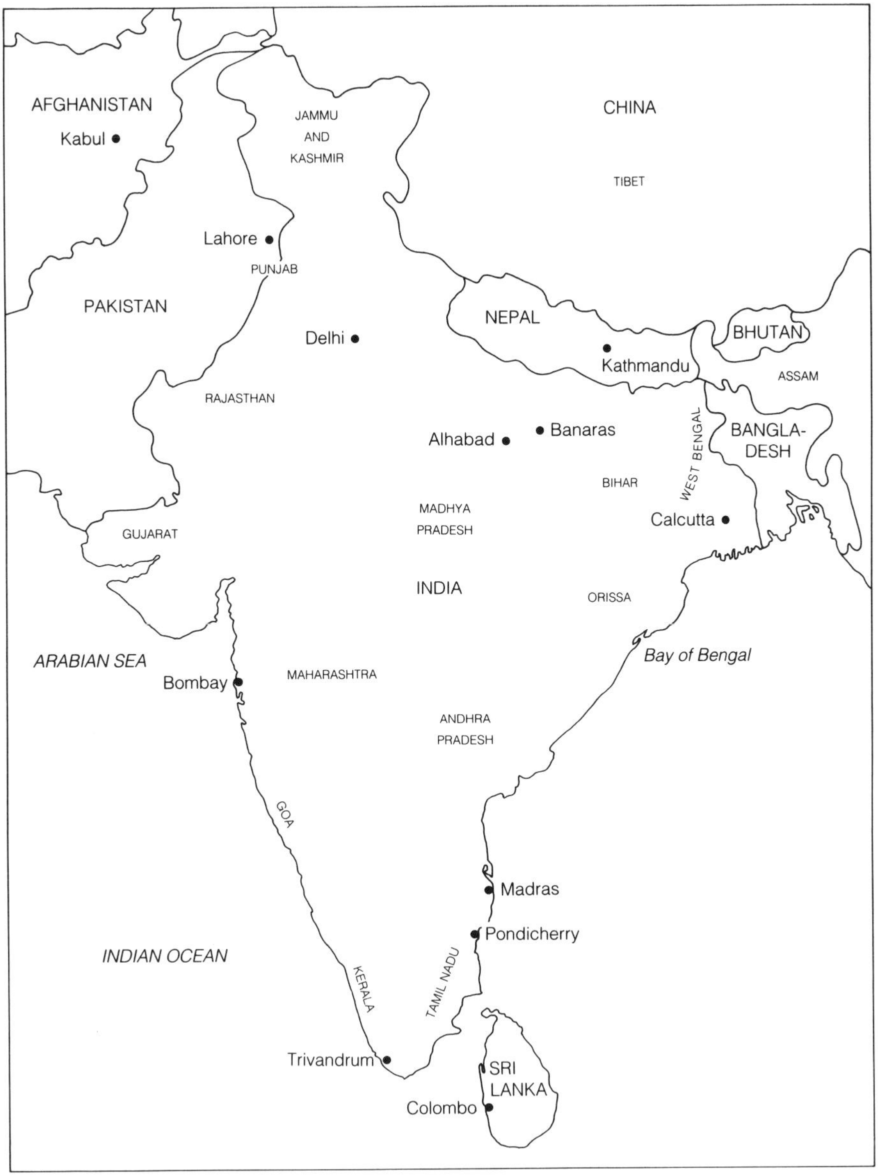

SĀṂKHYA, YOGA, AND THE *BHAGAVAD GĪTĀ*

Arguably as old as any systematic philosophy in South Asia is Sāṃkhya, a term meaning "analysis of nature." This philosophical view holds that reality consists of two irreducible elements: nature (*prakṛti*) and the conscious being (*puruṣa*). Like other early Indian world views, the system is wedded to ideas about a mystical enlightenment, a *summum bonum*, or personal supreme good. By attaining a proper understanding of what is *other* to consciousness—namely, nature—the individual conscious being finds himself and disengages from the world. Thus the individual recovers a blissful aloneness separate from nature or—in an alternative interpretation described in the *Bhagavad Gītā*—achieves an ecstatic transcendence *within* the world.

The germs of Sāṃkhya are first expressed in the Upanishads, which are among the oldest texts in Sanskrit, the intellectual language of ancient and classical India. Hindus regard the Upanishads as sacred and revealed. Sāṃkhya ideas appear in several Upanishads as early as the fifth century B.C.E. Similar ideas are also prominent in the *Mahābhārata*, the "Great Indian Epic," a work of about the same time. The *Bhagavad Gītā*—which is the most famous portion of the Great Epic and probably the most revered of all texts sacred to Hindus—weaves Sāṃkhya themes within a complex theology and teaching of *yoga* (psychological discipline). Through the practice of yoga one would be led to a mystical salvation within the world. Then in the *Yogasūtra* (the basic text of the Yoga system) and the *Sāṃkhya-kārikā* (a book of commentaries on the Sāṃkhya philosophy by the Indian philosopher Īśvarakṛṣṇa), similar mystic themes are elaborated, but the goal is somewhat differently conceived: the *summum bonum* is an absolute rupture separating the conscious being, *puruṣa*, from nature. These two texts belong to the period after 200 C.E., when philosophy became more argument-oriented and systematic.

Thus there are three major varieties of Sāṃkhya developed through the more than two thousand years of philosophic and religious writing in Sanskrit: (1) an atheistic Sāṃkhya championing a goal of total transcendence whose most refined and elaborate expression is the *Verses on Analysis of Nature*, or *Sāṃkhya-kārikā;* (2) a theistic Sāṃkhya found in the *Gītā*, with its goal of personal transformation within the world; and (3) the Yoga philosophy of the *Yogasūtra** and its commentaries. The Yoga system is closer to the views of the *Verses on Analysis of Nature* than to the *Gītā*. But unlike the *Verses on Analysis of Nature*, the Yoga system includes a concept of God. The *Kyogasūtra* and the *Gītā* set forth different concepts of God. In the *Yogasūtra*, God is an archetypal liberated yogin, never sullied by contact with the world; in the *Gītā*, the Supreme Being is conceived along lines not so different

* A *sūtra* is an aphorism (particularly a philosophical aphorism) or a collection of aphorisms.

from the theology of Western religions. Portions of each of the three works are included here.

A theme common to all three of the philosophies is an analysis of nature—including one's personal nature, mind, proclivities, and so on—in terms of three *guṇas,* or "strands." These are *sattva* (light, clarity, intelligence); *rajas* (passion, dynamism); and *tamas* (darkness, inertia, stupidity). Overlapping this division is a hierarchy of manifestations of nature: the body and the senses; the sensational or emotional mind (*manas*); the ego-sense (*ahaṃkāra*); and the rational mind, or intelligence (*buddhi*). In some texts, the individual conscious being—or, alternatively, God—is placed at the top of the order. Apparently, one attains the mystical *summum bonum* by progressively detaching oneself from each manifestation of nature.

from the *Kaṭha Upanishad*

From the Katha Upanishad. *Translated by E. Hume,* The Thirteen Principal Upanishads. *(London: Oxford, 1931.)*

CHAPTER 3

3. Know thou the soul as riding in a chariot,
The body as the chariot.
Know thou the intellect as the chariot-driver,
And the mind as the reins.

4. The senses, they say, are the horses;
The objects of sense, what they range over.
The self combined with senses and mind
Wise men call "the enjoyer."

5. He who has not understanding,
Whose mind is not constantly held firm—
His senses are uncontrolled,
Like the vicious horses of a chariot-driver.

6. He, however, who has understanding,
Whose mind is constantly held firm—
His senses are under control,
Like the good horses of a chariot-driver.

7. He, however, who has not understanding,
Who is unmindful and ever impure,
Reaches not the goal,
But goes on to reincarnation.

8. He, however, who has understanding,
Who is mindful and ever pure,
Reaches the goal
From which he is born no more.

9. He, however, who has the understanding of a chariot-driver,
A man who reins in his mind—
He reaches the end of his journey,
The highest place of Vishnu.

10. Higher than the senses are the objects of sense.
Higher than the objects of sense is the mind;
And higher than the mind is the intellect.
Higher than the intellect is the Great Self.

11. Higher than the Great is the Unmanifest.
Higher than the Unmanifest is the Person.
Higher than the Person there is nothing at all.
That is the goal. That is the highest course.

12. Though He is hidden in all things,
That Soul shines not forth.
But he is seen by subtle seers
With superior, subtle intellect.

13. An intelligent man should suppress his speech and his mind.
The latter he should suppress in the Understanding-Self.
The understanding he should suppress in the Great Self.
That he should suppress in the Tranquil Self.

from the *Bhagavad Gītā* (*Song of God*)

CHAPTER XIII

The Blessed One* said:

1. This body, son of Kuntī,
Is called the Field.
Who knows this, he is called
Field-knower by those who know him.

. . . .

5. The gross elements, the I-faculty,
The consciousness, and the unmanifest,
The senses ten and one,
And the five objects on which the senses
(of perception) play,

6. Desire, loathing, pleasure, pain,
Association, intellect, steadfastness,
This in brief as the Field
Is described with its modifications.

. . . .

12. What is the object of knowledge, that I shall
declare,
Knowing which one attains freedom from
death:
(It is) the beginningless Brahman, ruled
by Me;
Neither existent nor non-existent it is called.

13. It has hands and feet on all sides,
Eyes, heads, and faces on all sides,
Hearing on all sides in the world,
And it remains constantly enveloping all;

14. Having the semblance of the qualities of all
the senses,
(Yet) freed from all the senses,
Unattached, and yet all-maintaining;
Free from the Strands, yet experiencing the
Strands (of matter);

15. Outside of beings, and within them,
Unmoving, and yet moving;
Because of its subtleness it cannot be
comprehended:
Both far away and near it is.

16. Both undivided in beings,
And seemingly divided it remains;
Both as the supporter of beings it is to be
known,
And as (their) consumer and originator.

17. Of lights also it is the light
Beyond darkness, so 'tis declared;
Knowledge, the object of knowledge, and the
goal of knowledge;
(It is) settled in the heart of all.

18. Thus the Field, and also knowledge,
And the object of knowledge have been
declared in brief;
My devotee, understanding this,
Attains unto My estate.

19. Both material nature and the spirit,
Know thou, are equally beginningless;
Both the modifications and the Strands,
Know thou, spring from material nature.

20. In anything that concerns effect, instrument,
or agent,
Material nature is declared the cause;
The spirit, in pleasure-and-pain's
Experiencing is declared the cause.

21. For the spirit, abiding in material nature,
Experiences the Strands born of material
nature;
Attachment to the Strands is the cause of his
Births in good and evil wombs.

* Krishna.—Ed.

22. The onlooker and consenter,
The supporter, experiencer, great Lord,
The supreme soul also is declared to be
The highest spirit, in this body.

23. Whoso thus knows the spirit
And material nature along with its Strands,
Tho he exist in any condition at all,
He is not reborn again.

24. By meditation, in the self see
Some the self by the self;
Others by discipline of reason,
And others by discipline of action.

25. But others, not having this knowledge,
Hearing it from others, revere it;
Even they also, nevertheless, cross over
Death, devoted to the holy revelation which they hear.

26. In so far as is produced any
Creature, stationary or moving,
From union of Field and Field-knower
Know that (is sprung), best of Bharatas.

27. Alike in all beings
Abiding, the supreme Lord,
Not perishing when they perish,
Who sees him, he (truly) sees.

28. For seeing in all the same
Lord established,
He harms not himself (in others) by himself;
Then he goes to the highest goal.

29. Both that by material-nature alone actions
Are performed altogether,
Who sees, and likewise that (his) self
Is not the doer, he (truly) sees.

30. When the various states of beings
He perceives as abiding in One,
And from that alone their expansion,
Then he attains Brahman.*

31. Because he is beginningless and free from the Strands,
This supreme self, imperishable,
Even abiding in the body, son of Kuntī,
Acts not, nor is he stained (by actions).

* The Absolute Spirit—Ed.

32. As because of its subtleness the omnipresent
Ether is not stained (by contact with other elements),
Abiding in every body
The self is not stained likewise.

33. As alone illumines
This whole world the sun,
So the Field-owner the whole Field
Illumines, son of Bharata.

34. Thus between Field and Field-knower
The difference, with the eye of knowledge,
And release from the material nature of beings,
Those who know (these), they go to the highest.

Here ends the Thirteenth Chapter, called Discipline of Distinction of Field and Field-knower.

CHAPTER XIV

The Blessed One said: . . .

5. Goodness, passion, and darkness,
The Strands that spring from material nature,
Bind, O great-armed one,
In the body the immortal embodied (soul).

6. Among these goodness, because it is stainless,
Is illuminating and free from disease;
It binds by attachment to bliss,
And by attachment to knowledge, blameless one.

7. Know that passion is of the nature of desire,
Springing from thirst and attachment;
It, son of Kuntī, binds
The embodied (soul) by attachment to actions.

8. But know that darkness is born of ignorance,
The deluder of all embodied (souls);
By heedlessness, sloth, and sleep
It binds, son of Bharata.

9. Goodness causes attachment to bliss,
Passion to action, son of Bharata,
But darkness, obscuring knowledge,
Causes attachment to heedlessness likewise.

10. Prevailing over passion and darkness,
Goodness comes to be, son of Bharata;
Passion, (prevailing over) goodness and darkness likewise,
And so darkness, (prevailing over) goodness and passion.

11. In all the gates (orifices) in this body
An illumination appears,
Which is knowledge; when that happens, then one shall know
Also that goodness is dominant,

12. Greed, activity, the undertaking
Of actions, unrest, longing,
These are produced when passion
Is dominant, bull of Bharatas.

13. Unillumination, and inactivity,
Heedlessness, and mere delusion,
These are produced when darkness
Is dominant, son of Kuru.

14. But when under dominance of goodness
The body-bearing (soul) goes to dissolution,
Then to the worlds of them that know the highest,
The spotless (worlds), he attains.

15. Going to dissolution in (dominance of) passion,
He is born among those attached to actions;
And so when dissolved in (dominance of) darkness,
He is born in deluded wombs.

16. Of action well done, they say
The fruit is spotless and of the nature of goodness;
But the fruit of passion is pain;
The fruit of darkness is ignorance.

17. From goodness is born knowledge,
From passion greed rather,
Heedlessness and delusion from darkness
Arise, and ignorance.

18. Those that abide in goodness go on high;
The men of passion remain in the middle (states);
Abiding in the scope of the base Strand,
The men of darkness go below.

19. No other agent than the Strands
When the Beholder (soul) perceives,
And knows the higher-than-the-Strands,
He goes unto My estate.

20. Transcending these three Strands,
That spring from the body, the embodied (soul),
From birth, death, old age, and sorrow
Freed, attains deathlessness.

Arjuna said:

21. By what marks, when these three Strands
He has transcended, is he characterized, O Lord?
What is his conduct, and how these
Three Strands does he get beyond?

The Blessed One said:

22. Both illumination and activity
And delusion, son of Pāṇḍu,
He does not loathe when they have arisen,
Nor crave when they have ceased.

23. Sitting as one sitting apart (indifferent),
Who is not perturbed by the Strands,
Thinking 'The Strands operate' only,
Who remains firm and is unshaken,

24. To whom pain and pleasure are alike, abiding in the self,
To whom clods, stones, and gold are all one,
To whom loved and unloved are equal, wise,
To whom blame and praise of himself are equal,

25. Alike to honor and disgrace,
Alike to parties of friend and foe,
Abandoning all undertakings,
He is called the man that has transcended the Strands.

26. And whoso Me with unswerving
Discipline of devotion serves,
He, transcending these Strands,
Is fit for becoming Brahman.

. . . .

Here ends the Fourteenth Chapter, called Discipline of Distinction of the Three Strands.

from the *Yogasūtra*

1.1. Now instruction in yoga.

1.2. Yoga is cessation of the fluctuations of mind and awareness.

1.3. Then the seer (the conscious being) rests in the true self.

1.4. At other times, he identifies with the fluctuations.

1.5. The fluctuations are of five types, and are either detrimental or nondetrimental.

1.6. [The five are] (a) veridical awareness, (b) its opposite (illusion), (c) thought and imagination, (d) sleep, and (e) memory. . . .

1.12. The cessation of the fluctuations is accomplished through practice and disinterestedness.

1.13. Practice is effort to hold fast the cessation.

1.14. Practice is firmly grounded only through proper effort uninterrupted and stretching over a long time.

1.15. Disinterestedness is the intention to control on the part of someone who has no desire either for worldly or revealed objects. . . .

1.33. Calming illumination of the mind is furthered through friendship, compassion, happiness, and indifference to objects whether pleasant or painful, virtuous or full of vice.

1.34. Or, this can be brought about by controlled exhalation and retention of the breath.

1.35. Or, this (calming illumination) is brought about by particular activity centered on an object and arresting mentality.

1.36. Or, it is brought about by activity that is free from sorrow and luminous.

1.37. Or, it is achieved when the mind contemplates an object devoid of allure.

1.38. Another means involves the mind brought to a knowledge of sleep and dreams.

1.39. Or, from meditation as is appropriate. . . .

2.2. Yoga is practiced to achieve mystic trance as well as to attenuate the detrimental fluctuations or afflictions (*kleśa*).

2.3. The afflictions are spiritual ignorance, egoism, passion, hatred, and attachment to life. . . .

2.11. These (detrimental) fluctuations are banished through meditation.

2.12. (Action-inducing) karmic latencies, to be experienced in the current or in future births, are rooted in the afflictions.*

2.13. So long as this root endures its fruit will endure, the (triple) fruit, namely, of birth, life, and apparent enjoyment.

2.14. These three bring joy or suffering according to the merit or lack thereof (in accumulated karmic latencies).

2.15. A person of discriminating judgment sees all as suffering because of the pain in continual change, in tortured states of mind, and in subliminal latencies. Suffering is caused by conflicting fluctuations.

2.16. Future suffering is to be banished.

2.17. That which is to be banished stands caused by a conjunction of the seer (the conscious being) and that to be seen (nature).

2.18. What is to be seen (i.e., nature) is characterized by the (three qualities or strands) of intelligence, activity, and inertia; it includes the gross elements and the sense organs, and has as its raison d'être enjoyments for or liberation of the conscious being. . . .

* The Yogic theory of *karma* supposes that every action creates a subliminal impression (or karmic latency) that impels future action, whether in this or a future lifetime.—Ed.

2.22. Although destroyed (for the liberated) yogin whose purpose is accomplished, nature is not destroyed for others (who are not liberated), because she is common among them.

2.23. The conjunction between the power of phenomena and the power of their lord (the conscious being) is caused by a perception of the two's identity.

2.24. Spiritual ignorance is its reason (i.e., the reason the conjunction endures).

2.25. When spiritual ignorance is no longer, the conjunction is no longer. This is the relinquishment, the "aloneness" (*kaivalya*, i.e., salvation) of the seer (the conscious being).

2.26. Unbroken practice of discriminative discernment is the way to that relinquishment.

2.27. For such a yogin, sevenfold wisdom and insight (*prajñā*) arise as the highest foundation.

2.28. By practice of the "limbs of yoga," impurity is attenuated. Awareness is illuminated up to discriminative discernment.

2.29. (Ethical) restraints, constraints, *āsanas* [yogic postures, stretching exercises] breath control, withdrawal of the senses (and three stages of meditation, viz.), concentration, "meditation," and mystic trance are the eight "limbs of yoga."

2.30. Of these, the restraints are noninjury (*ahiṃsā*), truthfulness, refraining from stealing, celibacy, and lack of avarice.

2.31. These practiced universally, irrespective of station and circumstance of time and place, constitute the "great vow."

2.32. The constraints are purity, contentment, asceticism, self-study, and focusing on God (as the archetypal liberated yogin). . . .

3.1. Concentration is binding the mind down to a single spot.

3.2. Of the three (stages of meditation), meditation proper (*dhyāna*) is a single ideational focus.

3.3. Mystic trance is this carried to the point where there is illumination only of the object as object, empty, as it were, of what it essentially is.

3.4. The three together are called "conscious power" (*saṃyama*).

3.5. Through its mastery comes the light of wisdom and insight (*prajñā*).

3.49. The yogin whose awareness is restricted to the perception of the difference between (the strand of nature called) intelligence (*sattva*) and the conscious being achieves lordship over all states of being and omniscience as well.

3.50. Through disinterest in that achievement arises aloneness (*kaivalya*) in the attenuation of the seeds of defects. . . .

3.55. When the intelligence (strand, i.e., *sattva*) and the conscious being are equal in purity, "aloneness" ensues. . . .

4.15. Since, with regard to one and the same object, mind (*citta*) differs (on different occasions of perception), the two (*citta* and objects) have a distinct mode of being.

4.16. And to exist a thing does not depend on a single mind or awareness (*citta*). When it is not cognized by that mind, what then would it be?

4.17. Something is known or unknown to a particular mind, depending on the coloring conferred.

4.18. The fluctuations of mind are always known to their lord (the conscious being), since the conscious being (*puruṣa*) is unchanging.

4.19. That (the *citta*) is not self-luminous, because it is something to be perceived.

4.20. And there is no possibility of cognizing both (objects and subject) at the same time.

4.21. It would be to assume too much to require one intelligence after another in order that a single mind or awareness be perceived. This would also mean memory's (impossibility because of) confusion.*

* The argument seems to be that the unity of the conscious being accounts for our sense of mental unity, including memory.—Ed.

4.22. Self-awareness occurs when the mind assumes the form of consciousness that (as the nature of the conscious being) is transcendently unchanging.

4.23. A mind (*citta*) that is colored by both the seer and that to be seen is capable of cognizing anything.

4.24. Although the mind is moved by countless subliminal valences, it works by unifying (diversities) for the sake of the other (the conscious being).

4.25. For one who sees the distinction (between nature and the conscious being), the projection of sense of self in nature ceases.

4.26. Then the mind settling into deep discrimination is carried on toward (reflecting) the aloneness (of the conscious being).

4.27. In the gaps (or weaknesses) of discrimination, other ideational presentations (i.e., distractions) may arise by force of (unexhausted) subliminal valences.

4.28. These are banished like the afflictions, in the ways explained. . . .

4.34. Aloneness (*kaivalya,* the *summum bonum*) entails the reversal of the course of the strands or qualities of nature, now empty of meaning and value for the conscious being. Or, it may be understood as the power of consciousness returned and established in its own true self.

ĪŚVARAKṚṢṆA

from the *Verses on Analysis of Nature* (*Sāṃkhya-kārikā*)

From Classical Sāmkhya *by Gerald Larson. (Delhi: Motilal Banarsidass, 1979.)*

I. Because of the torment of the threefold suffering, (there arises) the desire to know the means of counteracting it. If (it is said that) this (desire—i.e., inquiry) is useless because perceptible (means of removal are available), (we say) no, since perceptible means are not final or abiding.

II. The revealed (or scriptural) means of removing the torment are like the perceptible (—i.e., ultimately ineffective), for they are connected with impurity, destruction and excess; a superior method, different from both, is the (discriminative) knowledge of the manifest, the unmanifest and the knowing one (or knower—i.e., *puruṣa*).

III. Primordial nature (*mūlaprakṛti*) is uncreated. The seven—the great one, etc.—are both created and creative. The sixteen are created.* *Puruṣa* is neither created nor creative.†

IV. The attainment of reliable knowledge is based on determining the means of correct knowledge. The accepted means of correct knowledge are three because (these three) comprehend all means of correct knowledge. These three means (are as follows): (a) perception, (b) inference, (c) reliable authority.

V. Perception is the selective ascertainment of particular sense-objects. Inference, which is

* In the hierarchy of the manifestations of nature, a "top" seven are said to be both created and creative, whereas a "bottom" sixteen, including material elements, are said to be only created.—Ed.

† Although the present writer has rendered *mūlaprakṛti* as "primordial nature," generally the term *mūlaprakṛti* or *prakṛti* is left untranslated in this translation. The terms "nature" or "matter" come closest to the notion of *prakṛti,* but no English term effectively captures the significance of the Sanskrit. . . .

of three kinds, depends upon a characteristic mark and that which bears the mark. Reliable authority is trustworthy verbal testimony.

VI. The understanding of things beyond the senses is by means of (or from) inference by analogy. That which is beyond even inference, is established by means of reliable authority.

VII. (Perception may be impossible due to the following):
(a) because something is too far away;
(b) because something is too close;
(c) because of an injured sense-organ;
(d) because of inattention;
(e) because of being exceedingly subtle;
(f) because of intervention (of an object between an organ and the object to be perceived);
(g) because of suppression (i.e., seeing the sun but no planets);
(h) because of intermixture with what is similar.

VIII. The non-perception (of *prakṛti*) is because of its subtlety—not because of its non-existence. Its apprehension is because of (or by means of) its effect. Its effect—the great one (*mahat*), etc.—is different from yet similar to *prakṛti*.

IX. The effect exists (before the operation of cause)
(a) because of the non-productivity of non-being;
(b) because of the need for an (appropriate) material cause;
(c) because of the impossibility of all things coming from all things;
(d) because something can only produce what it is capable of producing;
(e) because of the nature of the cause (or, because the effect is non-different from the cause). . . .

XI. (Both) the manifest and unmanifest are
(a) (characterized by the) three *guṇas* ("constituents" or "strands");
(b) undiscriminated;
(c) objective;
(d) general;
(e) non-conscious;
(f) productive;
the *puruṣa* is the opposite of them, although similar.

XII. The *guṇas,* whose natures are pleasure, pain and indifference, (serve to) manifest, activate and limit. They successively dominate, support, activate, and interact with one another.

XIII. *Sattva* is buoyant and shining;
rajas is stimulating and moving;
tamas is heavy and enveloping.
They function for the sake
of the *puruṣa* like a lamp.

XIV. Lack of discrimination, etc., is established because of (the manifest) having the three *guṇas* and because of the absence (of the *guṇas*) in the opposite of that (i.e., in the *puruṣa*). The unmanifest is likewise established because of the *guṇa*-nature in the cause of the effect (or because the effect has the same qualities as the cause). . . .

XVIII. The plurality of *puruṣas* is established,
(a) because of the diversity of births, deaths, and faculties;
(b) because of actions or functions (that take place) at different times;
(c) and because of differences in the proportions of the three *guṇas* (in different entities).

XIX. And, therefore, because (the *puruṣa*) (is) the opposite (of the unmanifest), it is established that *puruṣa* is
(a) a witness;
(b) possessed of isolation or freedom;
(c) indifferent;
(d) a spectator;
(e) and inactive.

XX. Because of the proximity (or association) of the two—i.e., *prakṛti* and *puruṣa*—the unconscious one appears as if characterized by consciousness. Similarly, the indifferent one appears as if characterized by activity, because of the activities of the three *guṇas.*

XXI. The proximity (or association) of the two, which is like that of a blind man and a lame man, is for the purpose of seeing the *pradhāna** and for the purpose of the isolation of the *puruṣa*. From this (association) creation proceeds.

XXII. From *prakṛti* (emerges) the great one (*mahat*); from that (comes) self-awareness (*ahaṃkāra*); from that (comes) the group of sixteen. Moreover, from five of the sixteen (come) the five gross elements.

XXIII. The *buddhi* ("will" or "intellect") is (characterized by) ascertainment or determination. Virtue, knowledge, non-attachment, and possession of power are its *sāttvika* form. Its *tāmasa* form is the opposite (of these four).

XXIV. Self-awareness (*ahaṃkāra*) is self-conceit (*abhimāna*). From it a twofold creation emerges: the group of eleven and the five subtle elements.

* I.e., *prakṛti*.—Ed.

EARLY BUDDHISM

The Buddha lived in the sixth century B.C.E. in the Ganges valley in what is now Nepal. He was born Siddhārtha Gautama of the Śākya clan. According to the oldest versions of his life, he was a prince. Although he did not inherit his father's throne, he did as a young man lead a life of pleasure and enjoyment in the palace. He was encouraged in this by his father, who, fearing a prophecy that his son would become a religious mendicant, tried to protect him from the sight of anything unpleasant or evil. But one day the young prince journeyed some distance from the royal gardens and pleasure grounds and encountered first a diseased person, then a wrinkled and decrepit old man, and finally a corpse. (Buddhists came to view these conditions as the "three evils.") Inquiring about each in turn and being told that all persons are subject to such infirmities, the prince renounced his life of enjoyments, vowing to search tirelessly for the origin and cause of these evils and the power to root them up. His experience of enlightenment, or awakening (in Sanskrit, the word *buddha* means literally "the awakened one"), did not occur right away, however; he tried out various paths of asceticism before arriving at the Middle Way, a way of life he later proclaimed to his disciples. Finally, after a long ordeal in meditation under a Bodhi tree, he achieved the *summum bonum,* an extinction of evil at its roots. The remainder of his life he spent traveling and preaching, helping others to reach this supreme good, which he called *nirvāṇa.*

The Buddha himself did not write anything. Records of his teachings and sermons were kept by his disciples, and during the reign of the Buddhist emperor Aśoka in the third century B.C.E., an enormous canon of literature sacred to Southern Buddhists was compiled. In the contemporary world, the southern branch of Buddhism, known as Theravāda Buddhism, is prevalent in Sri Lanka, Burma, Thailand, and other parts of Southeast Asia. The northern branch of Buddhism, known as Mahāyāna Buddhism (prevalent in Nepal, Tibet, China, Korea, and Japan) recognizes a distinct literature as sacred, though it does not entirely reject the teachings of the Southern Canon. The distinct Mahāyāna literature was composed centuries after the oldest sections of the Southern Canon. Scholars use the term 'Early Buddhism' to refer to doctrines proclaimed in the Southern Canon, particularly teachings of the *sutta* portion, which consists of sermons ascribed to the Buddha.

Among the most important teachings presented in Early Buddhism are the Four Noble Truths: (1) All is suffering; (2) The root of suffering is desire, attachment, or personal clinging; (3) There is a way to eliminate desire and thereby eliminate suffering, namely *nirvāṇa* experience; (4) The way to this supreme good is the Eightfold Noble Path—right thought, right resolve, right speech, right conduct, right livelihood, right effort, right mindfulness, and right concentration or meditation. Other important doctrines include the causal interdependence of all things, their insubstantiality and phenomenal nature as mere groups of qualities or states of consciousness (*dharma*), and the insubstantiality of the self or soul—there is no soul, according to the Buddha. The Buddha seems to have seen false identification with the body, mind, emotions, and desires as the prime obstacle to spiritual accomplishment. Much thought and elaboration in later years was directed to an analysis of the apparent person as a "bundle" of qualities or states.

But more than any metaphysical teaching, the Buddha of the sermons of the Southern Canon emphasizes the practice of meditation and compassion, thereby inspiring others to lead the noble life. Indeed, anti-intellectualism becomes a prominent theme in much later Buddhist writing, in particular with Nāgārjuna and his Mādhyamika school (see p. 145).

The selections below include a sermon enunciating the Four Noble Truths and a famous anti-metaphysics sermon, *the Majjhima Nikāya*. The sermons are followed by selections from what scholars view as the later portion of the Southern Canon (clearly later than the sermons attributed to the Buddha). The passage from *The Path of Purification* (*Visuddhi-Magga*), written by a revered philosopher of the southern tradition, Buddhaghoṣa (ca. 400 B.C.E.), lists the *dharmas*—phenomenal qualities or states of consciousness—that make up the apparent person. The *Milindapañha* is a question put by the monk Nāgasena to the Greek king Milinda (a satrap presumably established by Alexander in what is now northwest Pakistan) concerning false identification of a soul. The final selection is Buddhaghoṣa's "The Duration of Life." This short passage has recently been made famous by the Argentinian writer Jorgé Luis Borges.

The First Sermon

These two extremes, O monks, are not to be practised by one who has gone forth from the world. What are the two? That conjoined with the passions, low, vulgar, common, ignoble, and useless, and that conjoined with self-torture, painful, ignoble, and useless. Avoiding these two extremes the Tathāgata* has gained the knowledge of the Middle Way, which gives sight and knowledge, and tends to calm, to insight, enlightenment, *nirvāṇa*.

What, O monks, is the Middle Way, which gives sight . . . ? It is the noble Eightfold Path, namely, right views, right intention, right speech, right action, right livelihood, right effort, right mindfulness, right concentration. This, O monks, is the Middle Way. . . .

1. Now this, O monks, is the noble truth of pain: birth is painful, old age is painful, sickness is painful, death is painful, sorrow, lamentation, dejection, and despair are painful. Contact with unpleasant things is painful, not getting what one wishes is painful. In short the five *khaṇḍhas* of grasping are painful.

2. Now this, O monks, is the noble truth of the cause of pain: that craving which leads to rebirth, combined with pleasure and lust, finding pleasure here and there, namely, the craving for passion, the craving for existence, the craving for non-existence.

3. Now this, O monks, is the noble truth of the cessation of pain: the cessation without a remainder of that craving, abandonment, forsaking, release, non-attachment.

4. Now this, O monks, is the noble truth of the way that leads to the cessation of pain: this is the noble Eightfold Path, namely, right views, right intention, right speech, right action, right livelihood, right effort, right mindfulness, right concentration. . . .

As long as in these noble truths my threefold knowledge and insight duly with its twelve divisions was not well purified, even so long, O monks, in the world with its gods, Mārā, Brahmā, with ascetics, *brahmins,* gods, and men, I had not attained the highest complete enlightenment. Thus I knew.

But when in these noble truths my threefold knowledge and insight duly with its twelve divisions was well purified, then, O monks, in the world . . . I had attained the highest complete enlightenment. Thus I knew. Knowledge arose in me; insight arose that the release of my mind is unshakable; this is my last existence; now there is no rebirth.

*A term meaning "one who has thus become." It refers to the Buddha. —Ed.

from the *Majjhima-Nikāya*

From Buddhism in Translations, *translated by Henry Clarke Warren (Cambridge: Harvard University Press, 1896).*

"Māluñkyāputta,* any one who should say, 'I will not lead the religious life under The Blessed One until The Blessed One shall elucidate to me either that the world is eternal, or that the world is not eternal, . . . or that the saint neither exists nor does not exist after death';—that person would die, Māluñkyāputta, before The Tathāgata had ever elucidated this to him.

"It is as if, Māluñkyāputta, a man had been wounded by an arrow thickly smeared with poison, and his friends and companions, his relatives and kinsfolk, were to procure for him a physician or surgeon; and the sick man were to say, 'I will not have this arrow taken out until I have learnt whether the man who wounded me belonged to the warrior caste, or to the Brahman caste, or to the agricultural caste, or to the menial caste.'

"Or again he were to say, 'I will not have this arrow taken out until I have learnt the name of the man who wounded me, and to what clan he belongs.'

"Or again he were to say, 'I will not have this arrow taken out until I have learnt whether the man who wounded me was tall, or short, or of the middle height.'

"Or again he were to say, 'I will not have this arrow taken out until I have learnt whether the man who wounded me was black, or dusky, or of a yellow skin.'

"Or again he were to say, 'I will not have this arrow taken out until I have learnt whether the man who wounded me was from this or that village, or town, or city.'

"Or again he were to say, 'I will not have this arrow taken out until I have learnt whether the bow which wounded me was a cāpa, or a kodaṇḍa.'

"Or again he were to say, 'I will not have this arrow taken out until I have learnt whether the bow-string which wounded me was made from swallow-wort, or bamboo, or sinew, or maruva, or from milk-weed.'

"Or again he were to say, 'I will not have this arrow taken out until I have learnt whether the shaft which wounded me was a kaccha or a ropima.'

"Or again he were to say, 'I will not have this arrow taken out until I have learnt whether the shaft which wounded me was feathered from the wings of a vulture, or of a heron, or of a falcon, or of a peacock, or of a sithilahanu.'

"Or again he were to say, 'I will not have this arrow taken out until I have learnt whether the shaft which wounded me was wound round with the sinews of an ox, or of a buffalo, or of a ruru deer, or of a monkey.'

"Or again he were to say, 'I will not have this arrow taken out until I have learnt whether the arrow which wounded me was an ordinary arrow, or a claw-headed arrow, or a vekaṇḍa, or an iron arrow, or a calf-tooth arrow, or a karavīrapatta.' That man would die, Māluñkyāputta, without ever having learnt this.

"In exactly the same way, Māluñkyāputta, any one who should say, 'I will not lead the religious life under The Blessed One until The Blessed One shall elucidate to me either that the world is eternal, or that the world is not eternal, . . . or that the saint neither exists nor does not exist after death';—that person would die, Māluñkyāputta, before The Tathāgata had ever elucidated this to him.

"The religious life, Māluñkyāputta, does not depend on the dogma that the world is eternal; nor does the religious life, Māluñkyāputta, depend on the dogma that the world is not eternal. Whether the dogma obtain, Māluñkyāputta, that the world is eternal, or that the world is not eternal, there still remain birth, old age, death, sorrow, lamentation, misery, grief, and despair, for the extinction of which in the present life I am prescribing.

"The religious life, Māluñkyāputta, does not depend on the dogma that the world is finite; . . .

* Māluñkyāputta was a disciple of the Buddha.—Ed.

"The religious life, Māluṅkyāputta, does not depend on the dogma that the soul and the body are identical; . . .

"The religious life, Māluṅkyāputta, does not depend on the dogma that the saint exists after death; . . .

"The religious life, Māluṅkyāputta, does not depend on the dogma that the saint both exists and does not exist after death; nor does the religious life, Māluṅkyāputta, depend on the dogma that the saint neither exists nor does not exist after death. Whether the dogma obtain, Māluṅkyāputta, that the saint both exists and does not exist after death, or that the saint neither exists nor does not exist after death, there still remain birth, old age, death, sorrow, lamentation, misery, grief, and despair, for the extinction of which in the present life I am prescribing.

"Accordingly, Māluṅkyāputta, bear always in mind what it is that I have not elucidated, and what it is that I have elucidated. And what, Māluṅkyāputta, have I not elucidated? I have not elucidated, Māluṅkyāputta, that the world is eternal; I have not elucidated that the world is not eternal; I have not elucidated that the world is finite; I have not elucidated that the world is infinite; I have not elucidated that the soul and the body are identical; I have not elucidated that the soul is one thing and the body another; I have not elucidated that the saint exists after death; I have not elucidated that the saint does not exist after death; I have not elucidated that the saint both exists and does not exist after death; I have not elucidated that the saint neither exists nor does not exist after death. And why, Māluṅkyāputta, have I not elucidated this? Because, Māluṅkyāputta, this profits not, nor has to do with the fundamentals of religion, nor tends to aversion, absence of passion, cessation, quiescence, the supernatural faculties, supreme wisdom, and Nirvana; therefore have I not elucidated it.

"And what, Māluṅkyāputta, have I elucidated? Misery, Māluṅkyāputta, have I elucidated; the origin of misery have I elucidated; the cessation of misery have I elucidated; and the path leading to the cessation of misery have I elucidated. And why, Māluṅkyāputta, have I elucidated this? Because, Māluṅkyāputta, this does profit, has to do with the fundamentals of religion, and tends to aversion, absence of passion, cessation, quiescence, knowledge, supreme wisdom, and Nirvana; therefore have I elucidated it. Accordingly, Māluṅkyāputta, bear always in mind what it is that I have not elucidated, and what it is that I have elucidated."

Thus spake The Blessed One; and, delighted, the venerable Māluṅkyāputta applauded the speech of The Blessed One.

BUDDHAGHOṢA

from *The Path of Purification (Visuddhi-Magga)*

From Buddhaghosa's Visuddhi-Magga, The Path of Purification, *Vol. Two. Translated by Bhikku Ñyāṇamol. (Boulder: Shambala, 1976.)*

*[According to Association with the 89 Kinds of Consciousness]**

I. Herein, firstly, those associated with the first sense-sphere, profitable consciousnesses amount to thirty-six, that is to say, the constant ones, which are the twenty-seven given in the texts as such, and the four 'or-whatever-states', and also the five inconstant ones.

Herein, the twenty-seven given as such are these:

(i) contact,

(ii) volition,

(iii) applied-thought,

* I.e., *dharma*.—ED.

(iv) sustained-thought,
(v) happiness (interest),
(vi) energy,
(vii) life,
(viii) concentration,
(ix) faith,
(x) mindfulness,
(xi) conscience,
(xii) shame,
(xiii) non-greed,
(xiv) non-hate,
(xv) non-delusion,
(xvi) tranquillity of the [mental] body,
(xvii) tranquillity of consciousness,
(xviii) lightness of the [mental] body,
(xix) lightness of consciousness,
(xx) malleability of the [mental] body,
(xxi) malleability of consciousness,
(xxii) wieldiness of the [mental] body,
(xxiii) wieldiness of consciousness,
(xxiv) proficiency of the [mental] body,
(xxv) proficiency of consciousness,
(xxvi) rectitude of the [mental] body,
(xxvii) rectitude of consciousness.

The four 'or-whatever-states' are these:

(xxviii) zeal (desire),
(xxix) resolution,
(xxx) attention (bringing to mind),
(xxxi) specific neutrality.

And the five inconstant are these:

(xxxii) compassion,
(xxxiii) gladness,
(xxxiv) abstinence from bodily misconduct,
(xxxv) abstinence from verbal misconduct,
(xxxvi) abstinence from wrong livelihood.

These last arise sometimes [but not always], and when they arise they do not do so together. . . .

[Consciousness-born Materiality]

Also as regards the consciousness-born kinds, the analysis should be understood as thus: (1) consciousness, (2) what is originated by consciousness, (3) what has consciousness as its condition, (4) what is originated by nutriment that has consciousness as its condition, (5) what is originated by temperature that has consciousness as its condition.

Herein, (1) *Consciousness* is the 89 kinds of consciousness.* Among these

Consciousnesses thirty-two,
And twenty-six, and nineteen too,
Are reckoned to give birth to matter,
Postures, also intimation;
Sixteen kinds of consciousness
Are reckoned to give birth to none.

As regards the sense sphere, thirty-two consciousnesses, namely, the eight profitable consciousnesses, the twelve unprofitable, the ten functional, excluding the mind element, and the two direct knowledge consciousnesses as profitable and functional, give rise to materiality, to postures and to intimation. The twenty-six consciousnesses, namely, the ten of the fine-material sphere, and the eight of the immaterial sphere, excluding the resultant [in both cases], the eight supramundane, give rise to materiality, to postures but not to intimation. The nineteen consciousnesses, namely the ten life-continuum consciousnesses in the sense sphere, the five in the fine-material sphere, the three mind elements, and the one resultant mind-consciousness element without root-cause and accompanied by joy, give rise to materiality only, not to postures or to intimation. The sixteen consciousnesses, namely, the two sets of five consciousnesses, the rebirth-linking consciousness of all beings, the death consciousness of those whose cankers are destroyed, and the four immaterial resultant consciousnesses, do not give rise to materiality or to postures or to intimation. And those herein that do give rise to materiality do not do so at the instant of their presence or at the instant of their dissolution, for consciousness is weak then. But it is strong at the instant of arising. Consequently it originates materiality then with the prenascent physical basis as its support.

* I.e., *dharma*.—Ed.

from *Questions to King Milinda (Milindapañha)*

From Buddhism in Translations, *translated by Henry Clarke Warren (Cambridge: Harvard University Press, 1896).*

Then drew near Milinda the king to where the venerable Nāgasena was; and having drawn near, he greeted the venerable Nāgasena; and having passed the compliments of friendship and civility, he sat down respectfully at one side. And the venerable Nāgasena returned the greeting; by which, verily, he won the heart of king Milinda.

And Milinda the king spoke to the venerable Nāgasena as follows:—

"How is your reverence called? Bhante, what is your name?"

"Your majesty, I am called Nāgasena; my fellow-priests, your majesty, address me as Nāgasena: but whether parents give one the name Nāgasena, or Sūrasena, or Vīrasena, or Sīhasena, it is, nevertheless, your majesty, but a way of counting, a term, an appellation, a convenient designation, a mere name, this Nāgasena; for there is no Ego here to be found."

Then said Milinda the king,—

"Listen to me, my lords, ye five hundred Yonakas, and ye eighty thousand priests! Nāgasena here says thus: 'There is no Ego here to be found.' Is it possible, pray, for me to assent to what he says?"

And Milinda the king spoke to the venerable Nāgasena as follows:—

"Bhante Nāgasena, if there is no Ego to be found, who is it then furnishes you priests with the priestly requisites,—robes, food, bedding, and medicine, the reliance of the sick? who is it makes use of the same? Who is it keeps the precepts? who is it applies himself to meditation? who is it realizes the Paths, the Fruits, and Nirvana? . . . When you say, 'My fellow-priests, your majesty, address me as Nāgasena,' what then is this Nāgasena? Pray, bhante, is the hair of the head Nāgasena?"

"Nay, verily, your majesty."

"Is the hair of the body Nāgasena?"

"Nay, verily, your majesty."

"Are nails . . . teeth . . . skin . . . flesh . . . sinews . . . bones . . . marrow of the bones . . . kidneys . . . heart . . . liver . . . pleura . . . spleen . . . lungs . . . intestines . . . mesentery . . . stomach . . . faeces . . . bile . . . phlegm . . . pus . . . blood . . . sweat . . . fat . . . tears . . . lymph . . . saliva . . . snot . . . synovial fluid . . . urine . . . brain of the head Nāgasena?"

"Nay, verily, your majesty."

"Is now, bhante, form Nāgasena?"

"Nay, verily, your majesty."

"Is sensation Nāgasena?"

"Nay, verily, your majesty."

"Is perception Nāgasena?"

"Nay, verily, your majesty."

"Are the predispositions Nāgasena?"

"Nay, verily, your majesty."

"Is consciousness Nāgasena?"

"Nay, verily, your majesty."

"Are, then, bhante, form, sensation, perception, the predispositions, and consciousness unitedly Nāgasena?"

"Nay, verily, your majesty."

"Is it, then, bhante, something besides form, sensation, perception, the predispositions, and consciousness, which is Nāgasena?"

"Nay, verily, your majesty."

"Bhante, although I question you very closely, I fail to discover any Nāgasena. Verily, now, bhante, Nāgasena is a mere empty sound. What Nāgasena is there here? Bhante, you speak a falsehood, a lie: there is no Nāgasena."

Then the venerable Nāgasena spoke to Milinda the king as follows:—

"Your majesty, you are a delicate prince, an exceedingly delicate prince; and if, your majesty, you walk in the middle of the day on hot sandy ground, and you tread on rough grit, gravel, and sand, your feet become sore, your body tired, the mind is oppressed, and the body-consciousness suffers. Pray, did you come afoot, or riding?"

"Bhante, I do not go afoot: I came in a chariot."

"Your majesty, if you came in a chariot, declare to

me the chariot. Pray, your majesty, is the pole the chariot?"

"Nay, verily, bhante."

"Is the axle the chariot?"

"Nay, verily, bhante."

"Are the wheels the chariot?"

"Nay, verily, bhante."

"Is the chariot-body the chariot?"

"Nay, verily, bhante."

"Is the banner-staff the chariot?"

"Nay, verily, bhante."

"Is the yoke the chariot?"

"Nay, verily, bhante."

"Are the reins the chariot?"

"Nay, verily, bhante."

"Is the goading-stick the chariot?"

"Nay, verily, bhante."

"Pray, your majesty, are pole, axle, wheels, chariot-body, banner-staff, yoke, reins, and goad unitedly the chariot?"

"Nay, verily, bhante."

"Is it, then, your majesty, something else besides pole, axle, wheels, chariot-body, banner-staff, yoke, reins, and goad which is the chariot?"

"Nay, verily, bhante."

"Your majesty, although I question you very closely, I fail to discover any chariot. Verily now, your majesty, the word chariot is a mere empty sound. What chariot is there here? Your majesty, you speak a falsehood, a lie: there is no chariot. Your majesty, you are the chief king in all the continent of India; of whom are you afraid that you speak a lie? Listen to me, my lords, ye five hundred Yonakas, and ye eighty thousand priests! Milinda the king here says thus: 'I came in a chariot;' and being requested, 'Your majesty, if you came in a chariot, declare to me the chariot,' he fails to produce any chariot. Is it possible, pray, for me to assent to what he says?"

When he had thus spoken, the five hundred Yonakas applauded the venerable Nāgasena and spoke to Milinda the king as follows:—

"Now, your majesty, answer, if you can."

Then Milinda the king spoke to the venerable Nāgasena as follows:—

"Bhante Nāgasena, I speak no lie: the word 'chariot' is but a way of counting, term, appellation, convenient designation, and name for pole, axle, wheels, chariot-body, and banner-staff."

"Thoroughly well, your majesty, do you understand a chariot. In exactly the same way, your majesty, in respect of me, Nāgasena is but a way of counting, term, appellation, convenient designation, mere name for the hair of my head, hair of my body . . . brain of the head, form, sensation, perception, the predispositions, and consciousness. But in the absolute sense there is no Ego here to be found. And the priestess Vajirā, your majesty, said as follows in the presence of The Blessed One:—

"'Even as the word of "chariot" means
That members join to frame a whole;
So when the Groups appear to view,
We use the phrase, "A living being."'"

"It is wonderful, bhante Nāgasena! It is marvellous, bhante Nāgasena! Brilliant and prompt is the wit of your replies. If The Buddha were alive, he would applaud. Well done, well done, Nāgasena! Brilliant and prompt is the wit of your replies."

BUDDHAGHOṢA

The Duration of Life

From Buddhism in Translations, *translated by Henry Clarke Warren (Cambridge: Harvard University Press, 1896).*

Strictly speaking, the duration of the life of a living being is exceedingly brief, lasting only while a thought lasts. Just as a chariot-wheel in rolling rolls only at one point of the tire, and in resting rests only at one point; in exactly the same way, the life of a living being lasts only for a period of one thought. As soon as that thought has ceased the being is said to have ceased. As it has been said:—

"The being of a past moment of thought has lived, but does not live, nor will it live.

"The being of a future moment of thought will live, but has not lived, nor does it live.

"The being of the present moment of thought does live, but has not lived, nor will it live."

JAINISM

Mahāvīra, the founder of Jainism, lived in the sixth century B.C.E.; he was roughly contemporary with the Buddha. Mahāvīra is also known as the Jina, "the Victor" (over passion). There is some evidence that his followers merged with another group to establish the religion of the Jina. Unlike Sāṃkhya, Yoga, and Hindu schools generally, Jains (or Jainas) and Buddhists disavow all explicit allegiance to Upanishadic traditions and do not practice caste.

Like other Indian philosophies of the early period, however, Jainism proclaims a mystical *summum bonum*. But of all the mystically oriented early Indian views, the Jain is the most renowned for its ethical commitment to the value of life. Jains are vegetarians; moreover, Jain monks have been known to wear masks so that their breathing will not cause injury to insects. Regarding even vegetable life as sentient, some Jain monks have starved themselves to death to prevent injury to others. Noninjury, *ahiṃsā,* an ideal popularized in modern times by Mahatma Gandhi, was propagated in ancient and classical India foremost by Jains. Noninjury was also propagated by Buddhists, whose views on many counts are close to those of the Jains.

Like Buddhist scriptures, the Jain canon is immense. The first selection below, from the *Acaraṅga Sūtra,* concerns *ahiṃsā* and its justification. Here the practice is justified not simply because it is conducive to one's own good or because it is the teaching of Mahāvīra, but because all souls are equally valuable. Thus, if I recognize that injury to me is bad for me, I conclude that injury to others is similarly bad for them. Their souls are as valuable as my own. Therefore, I must refrain from committing injury to others at all times.

Noninjury is a universally prescribed moral dictum. But in the details of ethical precepts, monks and nuns on the one hand and laypersons on the other have duties that differ. Not only asceticism but also prescribed "reflections"—e.g., on the impermanence of things, human helplessness, and the difficulty of enlightenment —mark the lives of nuns and monks. Householders desist from dishonest business practices, lying, illicit sexual relations, and so on, but do not aspire for "liberation" in this lifetime. As with Buddhist and other early Indian enlightenment theories, rebirth is presupposed. Jains believe that only the enlightened are liberated, i.e., not reborn.

In metaphysics, later Jain thinkers became especially famous for propagating two engaging metaphilosophical positions, *non-absolutism* and *maybe-ism*. The two may be seen as an extension of the noninjury ethic into the area of philosophic polemics. Late Jains declare that no metaphysical claim should be taken as absolutely true. Every view represents only one perspective among many. Further, every view should be regarded as right *maybe* (or 'in some respects'). There is at least a grain of truth in every position, and the modality of the 'maybe' directs the intelligence to find and appreciate what is correct in what an opponent is saying.

The second selection, from Vādi Devasūri (ca. 1150), introduces these positions by way of the Jain *doctrine of predication,* called the *Sapta-Bhaṅgī.* The translator and commentator, Dr. Hari Satya Bhattacharya, renders *syāt* (maybe) as "in some respects." This text grounds the doctrine of nonabsolutism in the infinitely many aspects an object exhibits from various points of view.

from the *Acaranga Sūtra*

Reprinted from Ayaro (Acarañga Sūtra), *translated by Muni Mahendra Kumar (New Delhi: Today and Tomorrow's Printers and Publishers, 1981). Copyright © 1981 by Jain Vishva Bharati.*

The True Doctrine: Non-violence

1. I say —

   The *Arhats* (Venerable Ones) of the past, those of the present and the future narrate thus, discourse thus, proclaim thus, and asseverate thus:

   One should not injure, subjugate, enslave, torture or kill any animal, living being, organism or sentient being.

2. This Doctrine of Non-violence (viz. *Ahiṃsā-dharma*) is immaculate, immutable and eternal.

   The Self-realised *Arhats,* having comprehended the world (of living beings), have propounded this (Doctrine).

3. (The *Arhats* have propounded the Doctrine of Non-violence for one and all, equally for)
   those who are intent on practising it and those who are not;
   those who are desirous to practise it and those who are not;
   those who have eschewed violence and those who have not;
   those who are acquisitive and those who are not;
   those who are deeply engrossed in worldly ties and those who are not.

4. This Doctrine of *Ahiṃsā* is Truth. It is truely axiomatic. It is rightly enunciated here (i.e. in the Teachings of the *Arhats*).

5. Having accepted this (Great vow of Non-violence), one should neither vitiate it nor forsake it.

   Comprehending the true spirit of the Doctrine, (one should practise it till one's last breath).

6. He should be dispassionate towards sensual objects.

7. He should refrain from worldly desires. [Annotation] The three main worldly desires are—craving for son, wealth and longevity. A *sādhaka** should not cherish these as well as such other worldly desires.

8. How can one who is bereft of the knowledge of this (Doctrine of *Ahiṃsā*), have the knowledge of other (Doctrines)?

9. This (Doctrine of Non-violence) which is being expounded has been perceived, heard, deliberated upon and thoroughly understood.

10. Those who resort to and remain engrossed in violence suffer (the miseries of) transmigration again and again.

11. O *Sādhaka!* You, who are endeavouring day and night; discern that those who are stupefied are outside the sphere of the Doctrine (of Non-violence). You should, therefore, be alert and always sedulous. . . .

20. Some put forth mutually . . . contradictory doctrines in the field (of philosophy).

    Some of them contend: "The following doctrine has been perceived, heard, reflected upon, thoroughly, comprehended and scrutinized in all directions—upwards, downwards and lateral:

* A person following the Path. —Ed.

'All animals, living beings, organisms and sentient creatures may be injured, governed, enslaved, tortured and killed.'

"Know that there is no sin in committing violence."

21. This (approval of violence) is the doctrine of the ignoble ones.

22. Those who are Noble Ones assert thus: "O Protagonists of the doctrine of violence! Whatever you have perceived, heard, reflected upon, thoroughly comprehended and scrutinized in all directions—upwards, downwards and lateral, is fallacious, and hence, you say, speak, assert and preach: 'All animals, living beings, organisms and sentient creatures may be injured, governed, enslaved, tortured and killed: Know that there is no sin in committing violence.'

23. "We, on the other hand, say, speak, assert and preach: 'All animals, living beings, organisms and sentient creatures should not be injured, governed, enslaved, tortured and killed.' Know that it is non-violence which is (completely) free from sin."

24. This (approval of non-violence) is the doctrine of the Noble ones.

25. First, we shall ask (each philosopher) to enunciate his own doctrine and then put the following question to him: "O philosophers! Is suffering pleasing to you or painful?

26. "(If you say that suffering is pleasing to you, your answer is contradictory to what is self-evident. And if you, on the other hand, say that suffering is painful to you, then) your answer is valid. Then, we want to tell you that just as suffering is painful to you, in the same way it is painful, disquieting and terrifying to all animals, living beings, organisms and sentient beings."

122. Through observation and scrutiny find out for yourself that inquietude is distasteful to, highly terrifying and painful for all animals, all beings, all those throbbing with life and all souls. So do I say. . . .

123. (Being overwhelmed by grief), the creatures are scared from (all) directions and intermediate directions. . . .

124. See! Almost everywhere the passionate man are tormenting (mobile-beings).

125. (Each of the) mobile-beings has its own body to inhabit.

126. See! Every (ascetic who has ceased from causing violence to these beings), leads a life of self-discipline.

127. (And discern from them) those psuedo-monks who, despite professing, "We are mendicants," (act like householders i.e. cause violence to the mobile-beings).

131. Some monk either indulges himself in action causing violence to the mobile-beings through various kinds of weapons, makes others to cause violence to the mobile-beings, or approves of others causing violence to the mobile-beings.

132. Such an act of violence proves baneful for him, such an act of violence deprives him of enlightenment.

133. He (true ascetic), comprehending it (i.e. consequences of an act of violence), becomes vigilant over the practice of self-discipline.

134. Hearing from the Bhagavān Mahāvīra Himself or from the monks, one comes to know:—It (i.e. causing violence to the mobile-beings), in fact, is the knot of bondage,
it, in fact, is the delusion,
it, in fact, is the death,
it, in fact, is the hell.

137. I say —Just as consciousness of a man born without any sense-organs (i.e. one who is blind, deaf, dumb, crippled, etc. from birth) is not manifest, the consciousness of the mobile-beings is also not manifest. (Nevertheless) such a man (the one born organless) (experiences pain) when struck or cut with a weapon (so also do the mobile beings).

138. (On simultaneously) cutting and severing with weapons, (all the following thirty-two anatomical features of a man, he suffers excruciating pain though he would not be able to express it): Foot, ankle, leg, knee, thigh, waist, belly, stomach, flank, back, bosom, heart, breast, shoulder, arm, hand, finger, nail, neck, chin, lip, tooth, tongue, palate, throat, temple, ear, nose, eye, brow, forehead and head. (So is the case with the mobile-being).

139. Man (experiences pain) when forced into unconsciousness or when he is deprived of life. (So do the mobile-beings).

143. Having discerned this, a sage should neither use any weapon causing violence to the mobile-being, nor cause others to use it nor approve of others using it.

144. He who discerns (i.e. comprehends and forswears) the actions that cause violence to the mobile-beings, can be regarded as a (true) ascetic (for a true ascetic is he) who has discerningly forsworn actions.

145. (One who practices non-violence) becomes competent to practise abstinence from causing violence to the beings of air-body.

146. It is he who perceives (that violence causes) terror (and that it would be to) his own detriment (becomes competent to practise non-violence).

147. One who knows the inner-self knows the external (world) as well: One who knows the external (world) knows the inner-self as well. . . .

148. Try to realise the significance of this 'equality'. . . .

171. Those (who do not rejoice in the practice of the ethical code), while indulging in violence, preach (to others) the ethical code.

174. One who is rich in the enlightenment (i.e. one who practices non-violence) should not indulge in any sinful action (i.e. causing violence and self-indulgence) through his conscience (guided) by the intellect fully illuminated with Truth. . . .

VĀDI DEVASŪRI

from *The Ornament Illuminating the Means and Principles of Knowledge (Pramāna-naya-tattvālokālaṅkāraḥ)*

From Vādi Devasūri's Pramāna-naya-tattvālokālaṅkāraḥ. *Translated by Hari Satya Bhattacharya. (Bombay: Jain Sahitya Vikas Mandal, 1967.)*

SŪTRA: In all cases a Word in expressing its Object follows the Law of Sevenfold predication by its affirmation and negation.

COMMENTARY: According to the principle of the Jaina philosophy, a Thing is not confined to one aspect only but has many aspects (*anekānta*). Thus in some sense, it is existent; in some sense, again, it is non-existent. Similarly, viewed from one standpoint, a thing is eternal, but viewed from another, it is impermanent. As a matter of fact seven such aspects may be found out in a thing from seven viewpoints. Now, Word is but a counterpart of the thing and like those in the Thing, a Word also has seven aspects, so far as its manners of expressing it are concerned.

SŪTRA: The law of Sevenfold Predication consists in using seven sorts of expression, regarding one and the same thing with reference to its particular aspects, one by one, without any inconsistency, by means of affirmation and negation, made either separately or together, all these seven expressions being marked with 'in some respects' (*syāt*).

COMMENTARY: This is a description of the celebrated doctrine of the Sapta-Bhaṅgī or the Law of Sevenfold Predication. Analysing the description given above, we can thus find out the nature and conditions of the Sapta-Bhaṅgī.

1. The Seven Predications are to be made regarding one and the same Thing, e.g., Jīva or Animal. The Words, 'one and the same thing' prevent the predications being 'a hundred-fold' (i.e., many-fold) one, things in the world being so many, hundreds and hundreds, in number.
2. The Seven Predications are to be made not only with regard to one and the same thing but with reference to 'one' only of its various attributes, e.g., Existence. Seven propositions, indicating seven different attributes of a Thing, do not constitute the Sapta Bhaṅga. Attributes, as aspects of a thing, are infinite in number. If one of such attributes or aspects be taken into consideration, we shall see that Seven Predications or Statements can be made with reference to it. It is thus that a predication is said to be seven-fold and not Infinite-fold. Of course, if it is contended that the attributes or aspects of a thing are infinite in number and that with reference to each one of these attributes and aspects, seven predications can be made and that consequently, Predication may be Infinitely-seven-fold, well, the Jaina Philosophers have no objection to that position.
3. Each of these Predications must be based on principles of 'affirmation' and 'negation'.
4. That Seven Predications must be made in such a way that none of them be inconsistent with the facts of Perception, etc.
5. Each of these statements must be marked with the expression, 'in some respects'. . . .

. . . That which was non-existent comes into existence; that which is existent vanishes into non-existence; the Substratum persists; well, these are the three peculiar characteristics of the phenomena of Origination, etc., well-known to all. Then again the three phenomena, although different from each other in some respects are not absolutely so. They are all connected with each other. There is no Origination without Decay and Persistence; there is no Decay without Origination and Persistence; and there is no Persistence without Origination and Decay. The facts of Origination, Persistence and Decay are thus dependent on each other and inhere in the Thing. Why then can a Thing not have a triple nature? The following poetic lines are also interesting in this connection:

"When the pitcher on her head was destroyed, the daughter was sorry; the son was glad; and the king was indifferent." In the same light the truth is to be understood that a Thing has a triple nature; one of its forms is destroyed; another is generated; the Substratum underlying both the forms persists. Thus it is that a Thing is both permanent and impermanent and as such many-sided.

Similarly it may be shown that a Thing is many-sided inasmuch as it is both existent and non-existent. One may of course contend: Well, that is a Contradiction; how can one and the same thing, e.g., a pitcher, be both existent and non-existent? Existence and Non-existence repudiate each other; otherwise, they would have been identical phenomena; hence if a fact is existent, how can it be non-existent? And if it is non-existent, how can it be existent? The Jaina philosophers point out that the contention is unsound. The objection might have force, if it were held that a Thing is existent in those very respects in which it is non-existent and that it is non-existent in those very respects in which it is existent. A Thing may be said to be existent with respect to its (1) own Form, e.g., that of a pitcher, (2) own Substance, e.g., gold, (3) own Place, e.g., a city and (4) own Time, e.g., spring-season. There would be no inconsistency or contradiction, if it is said that the Thing, e.g., the pitcher does not exist (1) as a cloth, (2) as made up of Threads, (3) as a thing made in a village and (4) as a thing of the summer-season. . . .

A thing which is a Mode, e.g., a pitcher or a cloth has thus an aspect of Existence and an aspect of Non-existence or negation. It is not rightly conceived or described, if it is said to be simply Existent. From the view-point of its own Substance, a thing is certainly Existent; but so far as the Substance of other things is concerned, it has also an element of Non-existence or negation in itself; the result is that a thing which is thus a negation of things other than itself has no chance of identifying itself with these other things.

It is clear that a thing has many aspects (*anekānta*) viz., the Existent and the Non-existent. In the same manner, an intelligent man should understand the manifold character of similar other aspects of a thing, should see, that is, how a thing is, for example, different from another thing (in some respects) as also not different from it (in some respects). . . .

. . . The Ārhatas or the thinkers of the Jaina School hold that all things, e.g., the Soul etc., are Anekānta in nature, i.e., that all reals have various aspects. Hence they are prepared to admit every well-reasoned truth. It is redundant accordingly to argue or urge the matter of such truths as that the Soul exists etc., before the Jainas, the truths being well-known to them.

NĀGĀRJUNA AND MĀDHYAMIKA BUDDHISM

Early in the history of Buddhism, a split occurred among its followers concerning the goal of the practices taught by the Buddha. According to the schools that came to be associated with the Southern Canon, the ideal is to become an *arhat* (saint), who loses all individual personality in *nirvāṇa,* a universal, impersonal, unconceptualizable bliss and awareness that somehow underlies appearance. According to Northern, or Mahāyāna, Buddhism, in contrast, the truest aim is to become a *bodhisattva,* who, unlike the *arhat,* turns back from the final bliss and extinction of personality in *nirvāṇa* to help every conscious being attain it.

From the perspective of a Mahāyānist, the Southern Canon presents, by and large, a course of spiritual discipline and a goal that are not the best and the highest, because they are personally oriented. Mahāyānists, instead, focus their efforts on acquiring the six moral, intellectual, and spiritual perfections (*pāramitā*) possessed by the Buddha, which enable them to promote the welfare of all. Mahāyānists do not deny many of the doctrines of the Southern Canon but interpret them as only a part of the story: as the Buddha's means of aiding people unable to appreciate higher spiritual truths.

At the time of the split over the *arhat* and *bodhisattva* conceptions, there was also much dispute about how to understand the aggregate of qualities or states of consciousness (*dharma*) that the Buddha had taught make up an apparent person. Some early Buddhist thinkers believed that the components of the false appearance of the self could be identified and analyzed. As we saw earlier in the Buddhaghoṣa reading, these thinkers attempt to provide comprehensive lists of these components and their groupings, sometimes with considerable sophistication. But the philosopher Nāgārjuna (ca. 1000 C.E.), a Mahāyānist, believes these efforts lead away from the practical message of the Buddha and his opposition to metaphysics. To Nāgārjuna, this practical end is something to which thought and mind have no direct access. Motivated by this belief, he identifies paradoxes, contradictions, and impossibilities in the positions of the quarreling schools of Buddhist interpretation.

Nāgārjuna's identification of impossibilities is also part of a strategy that he claims the Buddha uses: by seeing the absurdities that arise in viewing anything as having an independent existence, one realizes that everything is *niḥsvabhāva,* "without a reality of its own." Applying this to oneself, one comes to see the truth of the Buddha's teaching of *anātman,* "no-self." This realization is viewed as a step toward the *summum bonum* of enlightenment and perfection.

But his soteriological motivation notwithstanding, Nāgārjuna achieves greatness as a philosopher simply through the difficulty of the questions he raises—not only for Buddhist theorists but also for others. In particular, Nāgārjuna mounts an onslaught on the Nyāya notion of a justifier, or source of knowledge. He identifies the metaepistemological problem of an infinite regress concerning justification. If, for example, it is my sense experience that justifies my belief that I am now typing on a computer keyboard, what justifies my belief that my sense experience plays this role? Any answer seems to invite a further question, ad infinitum. This debate continues in the Nyāya section (p. 174) and in the selection by B. K. Matilal (p. 222).

Nāgārjuna identifies other paradoxes and conceptual problems as well, and his followers, known as Mādhyamikas, become greatly adept in finding difficulties in the positions of others. They see the ability to knock down others' views as a manifestation of *prajñā* (wisdom or insight), the most important of the "perfections" that are the mark of a *bodhisattva.* But there is also a division among Nāgārjuna's followers: his Mādhyamika school split into the Prasaṅgikas, for whom refutation and the development of insight are all-important, and the Svatantrikas, who develop a more positive philosophical stance and defend definite positions. The first selection here is Nāgārjuna's *Averting the Arguments,* in which his opponents may be presumed to be principally Nyāya realists and advocates of a commonsense view of knowledge. The second selection is from Candrakīrti's *Reasoning into Reality.* Candrakīrti, a Prasaṅgika who lived in the seventh century, is one of the most famous of Nāgārjuna's disciples.

NĀGĀRJUNA

from *Averting the Arguments*

Emptiness: A Study in Religious Meaning *(New York: Abingdon Press, 1967), pp. 222–227; A Translation of* Vigrahavyāvartanī: *AVERTING THE ARGUMENTS. Reprinted with permission of Frederick J. Streng.*

PART I / THE ARGUMENTS OF THE OPPONENTS

1. If self-existence (*svabhāva*) does not exist anywhere in any existing thing,
   Your statement, [itself] being without self-existence, is not able to discard self-existence.
2. But if that statement has [its own] self-existence, then your initial proposition is refuted;
   There is a [logical] inconsistency in this, and you ought to explain the grounds of the difference [between the principle of validity in your statement and others].
3. Should your opinion be that [your statement] is like "Do not make a sound," this is not possible;
   For in this case by a [present] sound there will be a [future] prevention of that [sound].
4. If [your statement] were that: "This is a denial of a denial," that is not true;
   Thus your thesis, as to a defining mark—not mine—is in error.
5. If you deny existing things while being seen by direct perception,
   Then that direct perception, by which things are seen, also does not exist.
6. By [denying] direct perception inference is denied, as also Scripture and analogy.
   [As well as] the points to be proved by inference and Scripture and those points to be proved by a similar instance.
7. The people who know the modes of the *dharmas* know [there is] a good self-existence of good *dharmas*.
   As to the others, the application is the same.
8. There is a self-existence of liberation in those [*dharmas*] mentioned as liberative modes of *dharmas*.
   Likewise, there is that which is non-liberative, etc.
9. And, if there would be no self-existence of *dharmas*, then that would be "non-self-existence";
   In that case the name would not exist, for certainly there is nothing without substance [to which it refers].
10. If [one asserts:] That which is self-existent exists, but the self-existence of the *dharmas* does not exist,
    One should give the explanation concerning that of which there is self-existence without *dharmas*.
11. As there must be a denial of something that exists, as [in the statement:] "There is not a pot in the house,"
    That denial of yours which is seen must be a denial of self-existence that exists.
12. Or if that self-existence does not exist, what do you deny by that statement?

Certainly, the denial of what does not exist is proved without a word!

13. Just as children erroneously apprehend that there is "non-water" in a mirage,
So you would erroneously apprehend a non-existing thing as deniable.

14. If this is so, then there is the apprehension, "what is apprehended" and the one who apprehends,
Also the denial, "what is denied" and the one who denies—six all together.

15. However, if the apprehension, "what is apprehended" and the one who apprehends do not exist,
Then is it not true that denial, "what is denied," and the one who denies do not exist?

16. If denial, "what is denied," and the one who denies do not exist,
Then all existing things as well as the self-existence of them are proved [since you have eliminated their denial].

17. Because of non-self-existence there is no proof of any grounds [of knowledge]; whence are your grounds?
There is no proof of a "point" possible for you if it has no grounds.

18. If the proof of your denial of a self-existent thing is not a result of grounds of knowledge,
Then my affirmation of the existence of a self-existent thing is proved without grounds.

19. Or if you maintain: "The real existence of grounds is such that it is a non-self-existent thing (*asvabhāva*)"—this is not justified;
Because no thing whatever in the world exists lacking its own nature (*niḥsvabhāva*).

20. When it is said: The denial precedes "what is denied," this is not justified.
[Denial] is not justified either later or simultaneously. Therefore self-existence is real.

PART II / NĀGĀRJUNA'S REPLIES TO THE ARGUMENTS OF THE OPPONENTS*

21. If my thesis does not bear on the totality of causes and conditions, or on them separately,
Is not emptiness proved because of the fact that there is no self-existence in existing things?

22. The "being dependent nature" of existing things: that is called "emptiness."
That which has a nature of "being dependent" —of that there is a non-self-existent nature.

23. Just as a magically formed phantom could deny a phantom created by its own magic,
Just so would be that negation.

24. This statement [regarding emptiness] is not "that which is self-existent"; therefore, there is no refutation of my assertion.
There is no inconsistency and [thus] the grounds for the difference need not be explained.

25. [Regarding] "Do not make a sound"—this example introduced by you is not pertinent,
Since there is a negation of sound by sound. That is not like [my denial of self-existence].

26. For, if there is prevention of that which lacks self-existence by that which lacks self-existence,
Then that which lacks self-existence would cease, and self-existence would be proved.

27. Or, as a phantom could destroy the erroneous apprehension concerning a phantom woman that:
"There is a woman," just so this is true in our case.

* The replies take up in turn the preceding arguments of the opponents.—Ed.

28. Or else the grounds [of proof] are that which is to be proved; certainly sound does not exist as real.
For we do not speak without accepting, for practical purposes, the work-a-day world.

29. If I would make any proposition whatever, then by that I would have a logical error;
But I do not make a proposition; therefore I am not in error.

30. If there is something, while being seen by means of the objects of direct perceptions, etc.,
[It is] affirmed or denied. That [denial] of mine is a non-apprehension of non-things.

31. And if, for you, there is a source [of knowledge] of each and every object of proof,
Then tell how, in turn, for you there is proof of those sources.

32. If by other sources [of knowledge] there would be the proof of a source—that would be an "infinite regress";
In that case neither a beginning, middle, nor an end is proved.

33. Or if there is proof of those [objects] without sources, your argument is refuted.
There is a [logical] inconsistency in this, and you ought to explain the cause of the difference [between the principles of validity in your statement and others].

34. That reconciliation of difficulty is not [realized in the claim:] "Fire illumines itself."
Certainly it is not like the non-manifest appearance of a pot in the dark.

35. And if, according to your statement, fire illumines its own self,
Then is this not like a fire which would illumine its own self and something else?

36. If, according to your statement, fire would illumine both its "own self" and an "other self,"
Then also darkness, like fire, would darken itself and an "other self."

37. Darkness does not exist in the glow of a fire; and where the glow remains in an "other individual self,"
How could it produce light? Indeed light is the death of darkness.

38. [If you say:] "Fire illumines when it is being produced," this statement is not true;
For, when being produced, fire certainly does not touch darkness.

39. Now if that glow can destroy the darkness again and again without touching it,
Then that [glow] which is located here would destroy the darkness in "every corner" of the world.

40. If your sources [of knowledge] are proved by their own strength, then, for you, the sources are proved without respect to "that which is to be proved";
Then you have a proof of a source, [but] no sources are proved without relation to something else.

41. If, according to you, the sources [of knowledge] are proved without being related to the objects of "that which is to be proved,"
Then these sources will not prove anything.

42. Or if [you say]: What error is there in thinking, "The relationship of these [sources of knowledge to their objects] is [already] proved"?
[The answer is:] This would be the proving of what is proved. Indeed "that which is not proved" is not related to something else.

43. Or if the sources [of knowledge] in every case are proved in relation to "what is to be proved,"
Then "what is to be proved" is proved without relation to the sources.

44. And if "what is to be proved" is proved without relation to the sources [of knowledge],
What [purpose] is the proof of the sources for you—since that for the purpose of which those [sources] exist is already proved!

45. Or if, for you, the sources [of knowledge] are proved in relation to "what is to be proved,"
Then, for you, there exists an interchange between the sources and "what is to be proved."

46. Or if, for you, there are the sources [of knowledge] being proved when there is proof of "what is to be proved," and if "what is to be proved" exists when
The source is proved, then, for you, the proof of them both does not exist.

47. If those things which are to be proved are proved by those sources [of knowledge], and those things which are proved
By "what is to be proved," how will they prove [anything]?

48. And if those sources [of knowledge] are proved by what is to be proved, and those things which are proved
By the sources, how will they prove [anything]?

49. If a son is produced by a father, and if that [father] is produced by that very son [when he is born],
Then tell me, in this case, who produces whom?

50. You tell me! Which of the two becomes the father, and which the son—
Since they both carry characteristics of "father" and "son"? In that case there is doubt.

51. The proof of the sources [of knowledge] is not [established] by itself, not by each other, or not by other sources;
It does not exist by that which is to be proved and not from nothing at all.

52. If those who know the modes of the *dharmas* say that there is good self-existence of good *dharmas,*
That [self-existence] must be stated in contradistinction to something else.

53. If a good self-existence were produced in relation to [something else],
Then that self-existence of the good *dharmas* is an "other existence." How, then, does [self-existence] exist?

54. Or if there is that self-existence of good *dharmas,* while not being related to something else,
There would be no state of a spiritual way of life.

55. There would be neither vice nor virtue, and worldly practical activities would not be possible;
Self-existent things would be eternal because that without a cause would be eternal.

56. Regarding [your view of] bad, "liberative," and undefined [*dharmas*], there is an error;
Therefore, all composite products exist as non-composite elements.

57. He who would impute a really existing name to a really existing thing
Could be refuted by you; but we do not assert a name.

58. And that [assertion]: "The name is unreal"—would that relate to a real or a non-real thing?
If it were a real thing, or if it were a non-real thing—in both cases your entire proposition is refuted.

59. The emptiness of all existing things has been demonstrated previously;
Therefore, this attack is against that which is not my thesis.

60. Or if [it is said]: "Self-existence exists, but that [self-existence] of *dharmas* does not exist"—
That is questionable; but that which was said [by me] is not questionable.

61. If the denial concerns something real, then is not emptiness proved?
Then you would deny the non-self-existence of things.

62. Or if you deny emptiness, and there is no emptiness,
Then is not your assertion: "The denial concerns something real" refuted?

63. Since anything being denied does not exist, I do not deny anything;
Therefore, [the statement]: "You deny"—which was made by you—is a false accusation.

64. Regarding what was said concerning what does not exist: "The statement of denial is proved without a word,"
In that case the statement expresses: "[That object] does not exist"; [the words] do not destroy that [object].

65. Regarding the great censure formerly made by you through the instance of the mirage—
Now hear the ascertainment whereby that instance is logically possible.

66. If that apprehension [of the mirage] is "something which is self-existent," it would not have originated presupposing [other things];
But that apprehension which exists presupposing [other things]—is that not emptiness?

67. If that apprehension is "something which is self-existent," with what could the apprehension be negated?
This understanding [applies] in the remaining [five factors: "what is apprehended," the one who apprehends, the denial, "what is denied," and the one who denies]; therefore that is an invalid censure.

68. By this [argument] the absence of a cause [for denying self-existence] is refuted—on the basis of the similarity [with the foregoing]:
Namely, that which was already said regarding the exclusion of the instance of the mirage.

69. That which is the cause for the three times is refuted from what is similar to that [given] before;
Negation of cause for the three times affirms emptiness.

70. All things prevail for him for whom emptiness prevails;
Nothing whatever prevails for him for whom emptiness prevails.

CANDRAKĪRTI

from *Reasoning into Reality*

From Candrakirti's Reasoning into Reality. *Translated by Christian Lindtner,* Masters of Wisdom. *(Oakland: Dharma Publishing, 1987.)*

The Selflessness of Phenomena

6.8. Nothing can arise from itself, yet how [can it arise] from another? It does not [arise] from both [itself and another], nor could it be without a cause? There is no point to a thing arising from itself. Moreover, it is wrong for that which is already produced to be produced yet again.

6.9. If you conceive that that which is already produced gives rise to further production, then this does not admit of production of the shoots and the rest. Seeds would produce [shoots] in profusion till the end of existence. How would all these [shoots] disintegrate these [seeds]?

6.10. For you [Sāṃkhya philosophers] the distinctions of the sprout's shape, colour, taste, capacity, and development would not be distinct from the seed's creative cause. If after the removal of its former self, that thing, it becomes a different entity, how could it be that thing at such a time?

6.11. If for you the seed and sprout are not different then, like the seed, the so-called 'sprout' would not be apprehended either. Or again, because they are the same, the [seed] would be apprehended when the sprout is. This you cannot assert.

6.12. Because the effect is seen only if the cause is destroyed, not even by conventional criteria are they the same. Therefore, to impute that "things arise from a self" is incorrect, both in reality and conventionally.

6.13. If self-production were to be asserted then product, producer, object and agent alike would be identical. As they are not identical, do not assert self-production because of the objectional consequences extensively explained [in Nāgārjuna's work].

6.14. If something were to arise in dependence on something else, well then thick darkness would arise even from flames. And moreover, everything would be produced from everything. Why? Because all non-producers are equally different [from the result].

6.15. Qualm: Because [something] has been able to carry through an action, [its] product can be stated with certainty. That which is able to produce [an effect] is a cause, even though it is different [from the effect]. They belong to the one continuum (*saṃtāna*), [the effect] was produced from a producer and so it is not the case that a rice sprout is [produced] from barley [seed] and so on.

6.16. [Mādhyamika:] Just as barley, gesar and kinshuka flowers, and so on, are not judged to be producers of rice sprouts [since] they lack the ability [to produce them], do not belong to a common continuum, and are qualitatively dissimilar. Similarly, a rice seed is no [exception] because it is quite different [from a sprout].

6.17. Seed and sprout do not exist simultaneously, and if they were not different how could the seed *become* different? Therefore, you will not prove production of a sprout from a seed. Instead relinquish the position that "there is production from another."

6.18. Qualm: Just as [the movements of] the two beams of a balance, when level, [i.e.] with one higher and the other lower, are seen to be simultaneous, so too the production of a product and ceasation of the producer [are simultaneous].

[Mādhyamika:] [The balance beams may] be simultaneous, but [producers and their products] do not exist at the same time.

6.19. You assert that during production, [the product] does not exist because the production phase [is operating] and that during cessation [a product] exists though the cessation phase [is operating]. How then could these instances be equivalent to a balance? Such production has no agent and therefore is not a viable process (*bhava*).

6.20. If the visual consciousness [1] [arose] simultaneously with its producers—the eye, and so forth—and with its associated discriminations, and so forth, or if [2] it was different from [these], then what need would there be for it to come into existence? [Yet] the faults in saying "[production] does not exist at all" have already been explained.

6.21. If a producer is a cause producing another, then the product is counted as an existent, or a non-existent, both, or neither. If [the product] exists, then what need is there of a producer? Then, what has the [producer] done if [the product] is non-existent? What was done if it is both or if it was neither?

6.22. [Qualm:] We maintain that worldly consensus is a valid instrument* within the domain of its own viewpoint. Therefore, of

* I.e., source of knowledge.—Ed.

what use are your reasoned explanations in this [context]? Worldly consensus also understands that something different arises from another, and thus that there is production from another. What need of logic here?

The System of Two Realities

6.23. [Mādhyamika:] All things are seen with accurate or deceptive perception; anything can be taken to have a dual nature. Any object of a correct perception is reality while deceptive perceptions are declared to be conventional reality.

6.24. Further, we assert that deceptive perceptions have two modes: one having a clear sense-faculty [the other] a defective sense-faculty. We assert that knowledge from defective sense-faculties is wrong compared with knowledge derived from good sense faculties.

6.25. From a conventional standpoint anything which is apprehended through the six undamaged sense-faculties is—for the world—reality. Everything else is deemed to be wrong from a conventional standpoint.

6.26. The non-Buddhist philosophers who are much affected by the sleep of ignorance, impute a self. Their imputations are illusions, mirages and the like, since even from a worldly perspective these do not exist.

6.27. As with eyes, the observations of a victim of opthalmia does not contravert the knowledge of one without opthalmia. Likewise, the intellect that forsakes uncontaminated knowledge does not contravert the uncontaminated intellect.

6.28. Delusion is conventional because its nature is to cover. Whatever appears conventionally is as if an artificial truth, and the Sage has called this a "conventional reality." The things that are artificialities are conventionalities.

6.29–30. Delusive entities [such as] hair-lines, and so on, are projected due to opthalmia. One should know the reality seen by anyone with pure sight to be accurate reality, for, if worldly [cognition] was the measure of validity, then worldly [cognition] would perceive reality. What need then for others, the saints? What use of a saintly path? Validity for fools, though, is not correct.

6.31. Because every worldly aspect is invalid, [the saints'] perspective of reality is not contraverted by the worldly perspective. If worldly matters could be repudiated by worldly consensus, then the worldly is impugned.

6.32. [Although] the commoner only impregnates the sperm, he declares: "I have created this child," but to those who understand "This is just like planting a tree," there is no production from another, [even] for the worldly.

6.33. So, the sprout is not [intrinsically] different from the seed, and thus the seed is not destroyed when there is a sprout. Hence, because they do not exist as one thing, do not say there exists a seed when there is a sprout.

6.34. If [things] depended on their defining properties, then by denying those [properties in the vision of emptiness one] would destroy things, and emptiness would then become a cause for destroying things. But this is not correct and therefore things do not [intrinsically] exist.

6.35. If one analyses things in detail, other than their essential reality, they are unlocatable. Therefore, do not make a detailed analysis in terms of worldly interpersonal truth.

6.36. From the perspective of reality, production from self or other is incorrect by any standard of reason. For this reason it is also incorrect conventionally. Therefore, how could your [view of] production be [correct]?

6.37–38. Empty things such as reflections, and so on, which depend on a nexus [of causes] are well established by consensus. And just as an empty reflection, and so on, can give rise to a knowledge of its features, similarly, though all things are empty, they can be entirely produced within pure emptiness. And because neither of the two realities is intrinsically existent, they are not permanent and nor are they nothingness.

6.39. Because there is no intrinsic cessation, [one should] know that it is possible—even without [positing] a source consciousness—for an action that has long since ceased to give rise to a genuine effect.

6.40. The fool generates attachment for sensual objects that are seen in a dream or on awakening. Similarly, an action has ceased and had no intrinsic existence, yet the action still has an effect.

6.41. With regard to the shape of the hair lines that are seen by the ophthalmic, though the [seen] objects are as equally non-existent [as the horns of a rabbit, and so on] still the ophthalmic sees these [hairs] and not the shapes of [these] other [fictitious] objects. Similarly, one should know that the ripening of an action is not arbitrary.

6.42. Thus, it can be seen that negative actions maturate in unwholesome [effects] while wholesome [effects] mature from virtuous actions. One who cognises the non[-intrinsic] existence of what is wholesome and unwholesome will become liberated. Still, [because the specific relationships between actions and their results cannot be comprehended by ordinary people, the Buddha] placed limits on thinking about [specific] actions and results.

6.43. The [Buddha's] teachings that "a source consciousness exists," "a personality exists," and "the psycho-physical organism exists as only this" are meant [as a pedagogical tool] for those who cannot comprehend the most profound subject [i.e. emptiness].

6.44. Although the buddhas are free from the view of individuality they still teach [and use the concepts of an] 'I' and 'mine'. Similarly, though things have no intrinsic existence, [the buddhas] have taught that they do exist, as a topic for interpretation.

BUDDHIST IDEALISM AND LOGIC

Despite the efforts of the Mādhyamikas (particularly of the Prasaṅgika branch) to ban speculation among Buddhists and to encourage skepticism toward intellectualization in general, Buddhist philosophic speculation did not cease. Mahāyāna scriptures seemed to propose a cosmological understanding of enlightenment: everything, in essence, is the 'Buddha mind'. And systematic philosophers known as Yogācārins—or Buddhist idealists—try to explain all phenomena on idealist premises.

Early Yogācārins view the *nirvāṇa* experience as the original state of nature and propound a doctrine of *vijñaptimātra* (mind alone). According to this doctrine, immediate awareness is in essence nothing but the illumination of the *nirvāṇa* type of meditation, with an affective or emotional side free of desire and full of compassion as exemplified in the life of the Buddha. The problem, then, is to explain, not this original state, but deviation from it. To this end, the early Yogācārins posit a beginningless *ālayavijñāna* (storehouse consciousness) consisting of numberless subliminal urges and memory impressions that deform awareness yet account for our ordinary experience.

The early Buddhist idealists also present various arguments shoring up phenomenalist theory. We see this in the tract by Dignāga (ca. 450) excerpted below. His objections to atomism and realism are based on the way things appear. Only the stream of awareness can be said to exist; the view that objects are external to consciousness is wrong.

The later Yogācārin and Buddhist logician Dharmakīrti (ca. 600) takes a somewhat different approach, most evident in his treatment of perceptual illusion. To Dignāga, error results from conceptual interpretation, but experience in itself is always reliable. According to Dharmakīrti, in contrast, sense presentations are not to be trusted in some circumstances—for example, seeing white objects as yellow when one is sick with hepatitis. Such perceptual illusion would not be misinterpretation but would be due to a malfunction in the causal process. Dharmakīrti, like Dignāga, is concerned chiefly with issues of epistemology and logic, but he incorporates all his theorizing within an understanding of what an object is. Causality is central to what the object is; that is, causal ability to produce an effect is the mark of the real. (The horn of a hare, for example, is unreal because it has no effects in the world.) Dharmakīrti pushes Buddhist and all Indian philosophy forward by finding causal relations underlying both true perceptions and valid inferences about the world.

Then, true to his idealist upbringing, Dharmakīrti argues that the causal understanding holds only so long as we are conditioned by desire, untransformed and unadept in the Buddhist Way. The teaching of the Buddha, preserved in scripture, tells us so; moreover, when we look closely with disinterested intellect, as Nāgārjuna advocates, we see paradoxes in any naïve causal view of the world.

Dharmakīrti's brilliance lies in his ability to maintain a dual perspective, at once proposing a view of causal interaction that accounts for the everyday world (conditioned by our desires) and the possibility of a transcendent perspective.

The selections that follow are taken from the *Suraṅgama Sūtra*, an early Mahāyāna scripture; from Dignāga's *The Investigation of the Object of Awareness* (*Ālambanaparīkṣā*), including a commentary by his disciple Vinītadeva (ca. 750); and from Dharmakīrti's *The Pith of Right Thinking* (*Nyāyabindu*), including a commentary by Dharmottara (ca. 770).

from *The Surangama Sūtra*

From Dwight Goddard (ed.), A Buddhist Bible. *Translated by Bhikshu Wai-Tao and Dwight Goddard. Copyright © 1938 by Beacon Press.*

CHAPTER ONE / THE MANY MANIFESTATIONS OF THE WONDERFUL ESSENCE-MIND, AND OF THE PERFECT PRINCIPLE OF THE THREE EXCELLENCIES WITHIN THE ALL-INCLUSIVE UNITY OF THE WOMB OF TATHĀGATA.

(False Mind vs True Mind.)

When Ānanda came into the presence of the Lord Buddha, he bowed down to the ground in great humility, blaming himself that he had not yet fully developed the potentialities of Enlightenment, because from the beginning of his previous lives, he had too much devoted himself to study and learning. He earnestly pleaded with the Lord Buddha and with all the other Tathāgatas from the ten quarters of the Universe, to support him in attaining perfect Enlightenment, that is, to support him in his practice of the Three Excellencies of Dhyāna, Samādhi and Samāpatti,* by some most fundamental and expedient means.

At the same time, all of the Bodhisattvas-Mahāsattva, as numerous as the sands of the river Ganges, together with all the Arhats, Pratyeka-Buddhas, from all the ten quarters, with one accord and with gladness of heart, prepared to listen to the instruction to be given to Ānanda by the Lord Buddha. With one accord they paid homage to the Lord and then resuming their seats, waited in perfect quietness and patience to receive the sacred teaching.

* These are three types of mystic trance.—Ed.

Then the Lord Buddha spoke to Ānanda, saying:—Ānanda, you and I are from the same ancestral blood and we have always cherished a fraternal affection for each other. Let me ask you a few questions and you answer me spontaneously and freely. When you first began to be interested in Buddhism what was it that impressed you in our Buddhist way of life and most influenced you to forsake all worldly pleasures and enabled you to cut asunder your youthful sexual cravings?

Ānanda replied:—Oh, my Lord! The first thing that impressed me were the thirty-two marks of excellency in my Lord's personality. They appeared to me so fine, as tender and brilliant, and transparent as a crystal.

From that time I have constantly thought about them and have been more and more convinced that these marks of excellence would be impossible for anyone who was not free from all sexual passion and desire. And why? Because when anyone becomes inflamed by sexual passion, his mind becomes disturbed and confused, he loses self-control and becomes reckless and crude. Besides, in sexual intercourse, the blood becomes inflamed and impure and adulterated with impure secretions. Naturally from such a source, there can never originate an aureole of such transcendently pure and golden brightness as I have seen emanating from the person of my Lord. It was because of this that I admired my Lord and it was this that influenced me to become one of thy true followers.

The Lord Buddha then said:—Very good, Ānanda! All of you in this Great Dharma Assembly ought to know and appreciate that the reason why sentient beings by their previous lives since beginningless time have formed a succession of deaths and rebirths, life after life, is because they have never realized the true Essence of Mind and its self-purifying brightness. On the contrary they have been absorbed all the time busying themselves with their deluding and transient thoughts which are nothing but falsity and vanity. Hence they have prepared for themselves the conditions for this ever returning cycle of deaths and rebirths. . . .

Ānanda then addressed the Lord Buddha, saying:—Noble Lord! Some time ago when my Lord was discussing the intrinsic Dharma with the four great Bodhisattva-Mahāsattvas, . . . I overheard my Lord to say, that the essence of the discerning, perceiving, conscious mind existed neither inside nor outside, nor between, in fact, that it had no location of existence. Since my Lord has interpreted this in his teachings just now, I have ceased to grasp any arbitrary conception as to the location of mind, but if this is true, and it is something intangible, in what sense can it be thought of as "my mind."

The Lord Buddha replied:—Ānanda, as to what you have just said that the essence of the discerning, perceptive, conscious mind has no definite location anywhere, the meaning is clear; it is neither in this world, in the vast open spaces, neither in water, nor on land, neither flying with wings, nor walking, nor is it anywhere. But when you say that your mind no longer grasps any arbitrary conception of the existence of the phenomena of mind, what do you mean by it? Do you mean that the phenomena have no true existence, or that they have no tangible existence? If you mean that they have no true existence, that would mean that they are like hair on a tortoise, or like horns on a rabbit. But so long as you retain this notion of not grasping, you cannot mean perfect non-existence. But what do you mean? Of course if your mind is perfectly blank, it must mean, as far as you are concerned, absolute non-existence, but if you are still cherishing some arbitrary conception of phenomena, you must mean some kind of existence. How is it then, that so long as the notion of not-grasping of anything, as for instance, the notion of "my mind," that you mean its non-existence? Therefore, Ānanda, you ought to see that what you have just said concerning the non-existence of anything just because you no longer cherish a conception of it within your mind, and that would mean the non-existence of a discerning, perceptive, conscious mind, would be quite absurd, would it not?

Thereupon, Ānanda rose from his place in the midst of the assembly, adjusted his ceremonial scarf, knelt upon his right knee, placed the palms of his hands together, and respectfully addressed the Lord Buddha, saying:—

My Noble Lord! I have the honor of being thy youngest relative and thou hast always treated me with affectionate kindness. Although I am now only one of your many converts, thou dost still continue to show thy affection for me. But in spite of all I have gained mentally, I have not become liberated from contaminations and attachments and consequently I could not overcome the magic spell at the home of a harlot. My mind became confused and I was at the point of drowning in its defilement. I can see now that it was wholly due to my ignorance as to the right realization of what is true and essential Mind. I pray thee, Oh my Lord, to have pity and mercy upon me and show me the right Path to the spiritual graces of the Samāpatti so that I may attain to self-mastery and become emancipated from the lure of evil myself, and be able to free all heretics from the bonds of their false ideas and craft.

When Ānanda had finished his plea, he bowed humbly before the Lord Buddha, with hands and forehead touching the ground, and the whole audience, awed into intense excitement, waited with earnest and reverential hearts for the response of the Blessed One.

Suddenly in the Meditation Hall, filled with its awed and expectant throng, there appeared a most marvelous sight that transcended everything that had ever been seen before. The Hall was filled with a radiant splendor that emanated from the moon-life face of the Blessed One, like hundreds of thousands of sunbeams scintillating everywhere, and wherever the rays reached immediately there were seen celestial Buddha-lands. Moreover, the person of the Lord Buddha was vibrant with the six transcendental motions simultaneously manifesting and embracing all the Buddha-lands of the ten quarters of all the universes, as numerous as the finest particles of dust in the sunlight. And this all-embracing, blessed and transcendent glory united all these unnumerable Buddha-lands into one single whole, and all the great Bodhisattvas of all these innumerable Buddha-lands were seen to be each in his own place with hands raised and pressed together expectantly waiting for the words of the Blessed One.

Then the Lord Buddha addressed the assembly, saying:—Ānanda, from beginningless time, from life to life, all sentient beings have had their disturbing illusions that have been manifested in their natural development each under the conditioning power of his own individual karma, such as the seed-pod of the okra which when opening always drops three seeds in each group. The reason why all devoted disciples do not at once attain to supreme enlightenment is because they do not realize two primary principles and because of it some attain only to Arhatship, or to Pratyekaship, and some to even lower attainments, to the state of devas and heretics, and some to Mārā kings and their dependents. The reason for these great differences is because, not knowing these two basic principles, they become confused in mind and fall into wrong practices. It is as if they were trying to cook fine delicacies by boiling stones or sand, which of course they could never do if they tried for countless kalpas.

What are these two fundamental principles, Ānanda? The First Fundamental Principle is the primary cause of the succession of deaths and rebirths from beginningless time. (It is the Principle of Ignorance, the outgoing principle of individuation, manifestation, transformation, succession and discrimination.) From the working out of this Principle there has resulted the various differentiation of minds of all sentient beings, and all the time they have been taking these limited and perturbed and contaminated minds to be their true and natural Essence of Mind.

The Second Fundamental Principle is the primary cause of the pure unity of Enlightenment and Nirvāṇa that has existed from beginningless time. (It is the Principle of integrating compassion, the in-drawing, unifying principle of purity, harmony, likeness, rhythm, permanency and peace.) By the in-drawing of this Principle within the brightness of your own nature, its unifying spirit can be discovered and developed and realized under all varieties of conditions. The reason why this unifying spirit is so quickly lost amongst the conditions is because you so quickly forget the brightness and purity of your own essential nature, and amid the activities of the day, you cease to realize its existence. That is why, Ānanda, you and all sentient beings have fallen through ignorance into misfortune and into different realms of existence. . . .

Thereupon the Blessed Lord laid his hand affectionately upon the head of Ānanda and proceeded to explain the true and Essence nature of Mind, desiring to awaken in them a consciousness of that which transcended phenomena. He explained to them how necessary it was to keep the mind free from all discriminating thoughts of self and not-self if they were to correctly understand it.

He continued:—Ānanda and all my Disciples! I have always taught you that all phenomena and their developments are simply manifestations of mind. All causes and effects, from great universes to the fine dust only seen in the sunlight come into apparent existence only by means of the discriminating mind. If we examine the origin of anything in all the universe, we find that it is but a manifestation of some primal essence. Even the tiny leaves of herbs, knots of thread, everything, if we examine them carefully we find that there is some essence in its originality. Even open space is not nothingness. How can it be then that the wonderful, pure, tranquil and enlightened Mind, which is the source of all conceptions of manifested phenomena, should have no essence of itself. . . .

DIGNĀGA

from *The Investigation of the Object of Awareness (Alambanaparīkṣā)* With Extracts from Vinītadeva's Commentary

From Dignāga's Ālambanaparīkṣā. Translated by N. Aiyaswami Sastri. (Madras: Adyar, 1942)

A Treatise on the Examination of the Object [Cause] of Consciousness

1. Though atoms serve as causes of the consciousness (*vijñapti*) of the sense-organs, they are not its actual objects like the sense-organs; because the consciousness does not represent the image of the atoms.

[As regards the nature of] the object, [declares the author,] consciousness grasps only the form of its own; because it arises in that form. Though the atoms are causes of consciousness, they do not possess the form reflected in consciousness just like the sense-organs.[1] Therefore they cannot become its actual objects (*ālambana*).

Though aggregates of atoms are alike the image of consciousness, [they cannot become its actual objects;] because

2a. The consciousness does not arise from what is represented in it.

What object produces the consciousness endowed with the image of the object, is properly said to be the actual object[2] (*ālambana*) of the consciousness. . . .

2b. Because they do not exist in substance just like the double moon.

The double moon is perceived [by a man] on account of defects of his sense-organs. But [this perception is not produced by the double moon, as] there exists no object like the double moon. Similarly the aggregates of atoms do not exist in substance and cannot act as causes of consciousness. Hence they are not its actual objects.

2c–d. Thus both the external things are unfit to be real objects of consciousness.

The external things, atoms and their aggregates, cannot serve as the actual objects of consciousness, as both of them are defective in one or other respect.[3]

3a–b. Some hold that the combined form of atoms is the cause of consciousness. . . .

3c–d. The atomic form does not become the object of consciousness just like the attributes such as solidity, etc.

Just as the attributes, solidity and others, though existent in atoms, are not perceived by the visual consciousness, so also the atomic form.

4a–b. In that case, the [different] perceptions of a pot, cup, etc. will be identical.

Though the atoms of a pot are greater in number and that of a cup [less], there exists no distinction whatever amongst the atoms.

4c. If [the opponent says that] the perception differs in accordance with differences in the forms of the pot and others; . . .

[1] Though [the organ] is the cause [that produces consciousness], it is not capable of being the object itself; because the consciousness which is born of this [organ] does not grasp the proper nature of the organ.

[2] When consciousness occurs according to the form of the object and this object produces consciousness, this object (*artha*) is capable of being the perceivable object (*ālambana*).

[3] That is, (1) when, for the thesis of atoms, though there is causality, there is no form, and (2) when, for the thesis of aggregate, though there is form, there is no causality.

4d–5a. But it never exists in the atoms which exist in substance, because the atoms are absolutely identical in their dimensions.

Though the atoms are different in substance, there exists absolutely no distinction in their atomic size.

5b. Therefore the differentiation goes along with things substantially non-existent. . . .
5c–d. For, if you remove one by one the atoms [of the pot, etc.] the perception illuminating the image of the pot, etc. will immediately vanish away. . . .

. . . It is, therefore, rationally deduced that the objects of different sensual cognitions do not exist externally.

6a–c. It is the object (*artha*) which exists internally in knowledge itself as a knowable aspect and which appears to us as if it exists externally.

Though the external things are denied, what exists internally in knowledge itself [*i.e.* its knowable aspect] and appears to us as though it is existent externally, serves as a condition of the actual object (*ālambanapratyaya*) [to consciousness[4]].

6c–d. Because consciousness is the essence [of the external object] and that [object essence of which is consciousness] acts as the condition [to consciousness].

The internal consciousness appears as [manifold external] object (*artha*) and also arises from that [objective aspect of its own]. Thus the internal consciousness is endowed with two parts (*i.e.* image and cause) and therefore what exists internally in the consciousness (*i.e.* the objective aspect) is the object-condition (*ālambanapratyaya*) to the consciousness.

If only the objective appearance of consciousness is experienced, [it will be a part of the consciousness and appearing simultaneously with it]. How can a part of consciousness and appearing simultaneously be a condition to the consciousness[5] [itself]?

7a. [Though the external object] is only a part [of the internal consciousness,] it is a condition [to the consciousness], because it is invariably associated with the consciousness.

[The objective aspect of consciousness,] though arising simultaneously with it, becomes condition to [the consciousness] which is produced by other [conditions]. . . .

Or,[6]

7b. It becomes condition also in succession by transmitting the force.[7]

It is also possible successively that the objective appearance of consciousness, in order to give rise to a result homogeneous with itself, makes the force seated in the [store-house] consciousness, and it is not contradictory [to the reasoning].

[The opponent says:] If only the self of consciousness constitutes the object-condition, how should we explain [the saying that] the visual consciousness arises depending upon the eye and [form[8]]?

[The author replies:]

7c–d. What is the sense-organ is [nothing but] the force itself [in consciousness] by virtue of its acting

---

[4] For example, for the eye-diseased person, appearances of hairs, flies, etc., appear in the perception with the forms of hairs, flies, etc., [real]. Likewise, since the knowable aspect is capable of being characteristic of the object (*artha*), one calls it the conditional cause of the perceivable object (*ālambana*).

[5] [The opponent says:] In all cases, one comprehends that what is perceivable internally existent (*i.e.*, subjectively) in the consciousness, *be thus the appearance itself* (= what appears). But, he will say, if this perceivable object appears as an appearance designed by the character of what is perceivable, this perceivable object will be *what appears at the same time as a part of this* [appearance]. *How could* [such an appearance] *be conditional cause* [of the object perceivable by the consciousness]?

If it was possible, this would be "oneself made by oneself," or the knowable aspect would produce the knowable aspect; horns of the right and left of the ox would themselves produce one by the other; this would be a formidable error.

[6] Having thus explained that the existence of the object and the existence of that which perceives the object exist at the same time, the author, now, explains that the existence of the object and the existence of that which perceives the object arise also successively.

[7] When the knowable aspect disposes the dominant force, it objectivizes itself into a proper being which produces successively [consciousness]; for, while destroying itself, this knowable aspect deposits at this moment its dominant force on the *Ālayavijñāna* [storehouse consciousness].

[8] It is so because, the eye acting simultaneously with the force which had already appeared, had produced [visual] consciousness. But if the interior form had not appeared previously to the eye, how could it produce the visual consciousness in acting simultaneously with the interior form?

simultaneously [with the object] as an auxiliary cause [for raising up of consciousness]. . . .

8a. That force is not contradictory to the consciousness.[9]

8b–d. Thus[10] the objective aspect [of consciousness] and the force [called sense-organ] go mutually conditioned from immemorial time.

Depending upon the force called eye and the interior form arises the consciousness which appears as though it is the external object, but it arises undifferentiated from the perceivable object. These two act mutually conditioned without beginning in time. Sometime when the force [called *vāsanā*] gets matured, consciousness is transformed into a form of object and sometime the force arises from [the consciousness] endowed with the form of object. The consciousness and force, both may be said to be either different from or identical with one another as one may like. Thus the interior object [which is not different from consciousness] is endowed with two factors [image and cause], and therefore it is logically concluded that consciousness [alone] is transformed into [external] object.

[9] The opponent says: The dominant force depends on the possessor of that force; for, without basis the dominant force is not capable to exist. The possessor of the force is one of the organs; now this [organ] itself has been constituted by the elements.

The author answers: If one considers *the representation* of consciousness, [the conception] of one basis for the dominant force *is not contradictory.* This being admitted, if one basis is necessary, the consciousness itself is capable of being this basis; for, in the consciousness, there is a proper being which knows the object and [at the same time] a proper being which knows itself.

[10] [The opponent asks:] Then what is thus the cause of the dominant force of the organ?

The author replies: Just as consciousness arises from the dominant force of the organ, so this dominant force of the organ arises equally from the previous consciousness which causes the activity of the organ, and this previous consciousness arises from the dominant force of the organ still more anterior. Thus, etc.

DHARMAKĪRTI

from *The Pith of Right Thinking (Nyāyabindu)* With a Commentary by Dharmottara

From Buddhist Logic, *vol. II, by F. T. Stcherbatsky. (New York: Dover, 1962.)*

CHAPTER I / PERCEPTION*

§1. *Subject Matter and Purpose of this Work*

1. All successful human action is preceded by knowledge. Therefore this (knowledge will be here) investigated.

. . . Wishing to show that this treatise deserves to be written, the author points to the importance of its subject matter. Because (says he) all successful human action is preceded by knowledge, therefore this (phenomenon) must be investigated, and with this aim the present treatise is undertaken. Such is the meaning of the (prefatory) sentence. . . .

. . . Indeed, when reasonable men presume that a thing may be of some use to them, they (immediately) set to work; whereas when they suspect that it is of no use, they give it up. Therefore the author of a scientific work is especially expected to make at the beginning a statement about the connection (between his aim

* For purposes of clarity, we have translated certain terms that the translator left in the original Sanskrit, and in some instances we have altered the translations of key terms to make them consistent with other readings in this book.—Ed.

and the subject matter). For it is all very well for writers of romance to make false statements in order to amuse, but we cannot imagine what would be the aim of a scientific author if he went (the length of) misstating his subject-matter. Neither (do we see that this actually) occurs. Therefore it is natural to expect inquisitiveness concerning such (works). If it were not stated, the student might possibly think that the subject matter served no purpose at all as, e.g., an enquiry about the teeth of a crow; or that (the aim) was irrealizable as, e.g., the instruction to adorn oneself with the demon Takṣaka's crest jewel which releases from fever; or that its aim was undesirable, like the instruction about the ritual to be followed at the (re-)marriage ceremony of one's own mother; or that the aim could possibly be attained in an easier way than through this book; or again that it was altogether useless. If any such presentiment of uselessness arises, reasonable men will not apply themselves to the study of the book. By stating the subject matter etc. some useful purpose is (always) suggested, and this checks the suspicion of uselessness. Reasonable men are thus incited to take action. Thus it is clear that the connection (between the subject matter and the purpose) is stated in order that the book may be credited with efficiency, since such consideration incites human activity.

§2. *Knowledge Defined*

Knowledge is cognition not contradicted (by experience). In common life we likewise say that (a man) has spoken truth when he makes us reach the object he has first pointed out. Similarly (we can also say) that knowledge is right when it makes us reach an object it did point to. But by "making us reach an object" nothing else is meant than the fact of turning (our attention) straight to the object. Indeed knowledge does not create an object and does not offer it to us, but in turning (our attention) straight to the object is makes us reach it. Again "to turn a man straight to the object" is nothing else than to point it out as an aim of a (possible) purposive action. Indeed, (one should not imagine) that knowledge has the power forcibly to incite a man (against his will). . . .

(Turning now to the different modes of cognition we see that) when an object has been apprehended by direct experience it has been converted into an object of (possible) purposive action through sense-perception. Because (we say) that sense-perception has pointed out an object, when the function of that knowledge which consists in making us feel its presence in our ken is followed by a construction (of its image). Therefore (we say) that an object has been pointed out by sense-perception, when it is cognized as something directly perceived. Inference (or indirect cognition, differs) in that it points out the mark of the object, and by thus (indirectly) making sure (its existence) submits it as an object of possible purposive action. Thus it is that sense-perception points out a definite object (i.e., an object localized in time and space), which appears before us directly, and inference likewise points out a definite object by way of the mark it is connected with. . . . But an object pointed out in some different way, not according to the above mentioned two (methods of knowledge), is either absolutely unreal as, e.g., water seen as a vision in a desert—it does not exist, it cannot be reached—or it is uncertain as to whether it exists or not as, e.g., every problematic object. . . .

(Sentient beings) strive for desired ends. They want that knowledge which leads them to the attainment of objects fitted for successful action. The knowledge that is investigated by the theory (of cognition) is just the knowledge they want. Therefore knowledge is cognition which points to reality, (a reality which) is capable of satisfying purposive action. And that object alone which has been pointed out by such knowledge can be "reached". . . .

(The prefatory sentence) mentions knowledge which "precedes" successful human action, i.e., which is the cause of it. The cause exists previously to the result, therefore it is said that knowledge precedes (action). If the word "cause" had been used (instead of "precedes") we might have understood that knowledge is the immediate cause producing successful human action. But by using the word "precedes" its mere antecedence (is elicited). . . .

Success is the (actual) attaining or avoiding of the object. When success is achieved by causes, it is called production. But when it is achieved by knowledge it is called behaviour. It consists in avoiding the avoidable and attaining the attainable. Behaviour consisting in such activity is called successful action. . . .

§3. *Varieties of Knowledge*

In order to reject misconception regarding the number of its varieties, it is said,—

2. Knowledge is twofold. . . .
3. Direct and indirect (perceptive and inferential).

The word for direct knowledge (or perception) means knowledge dependent upon the senses. . . .

The word "and" (connecting direct and indirect knowledge) coordinates perception and inference as having equal force. Just as perception is a source of knowledge, because being always connected with some (real) object it leads to successful purposive action, just the same is the case of inference. It likewise is a source of knowledge always connected with some (real) object, in as much as it leads to the attainment of an object circumscribed by its mark.

§4. *Perception Defined*

4. Direct knowledge means here neither construction (judgment) nor illusion. . . .

Direct knowledge is here taken as subject and the characteristics of non-constructive and non-illusive (cognition) are predicated. . . . The term "direct knowledge" (or perception) is familiar to everybody from its application (to that variety of direct cognition) which makes the object present to our sense-faculties and which is invariably connected with them.

This (perception) is referred to, and the characteristics of being neither a construction nor an illusion are predicated. Not to be a construction means to be foreign to construction, not to have the nature of an arrangement (or judgment). "Not an illusion" means not contradicted by that (underlying) essence of reality which possesses efficiency. . . .

. . . (There are some who maintain that) the vision of a moving tree (by an observer travelling by ship) and similar perceptions are right perceptions, because (there is in this case an underlying reality which) is not a construction. Indeed a man acting upon such a perception reaches something which is a tree, hence (it is supposed) that experience supports his perception. It would thus be consistent knowledge and so far would be direct, as not being a (mere) construction. In order to guard against this view the characteristic of "not being an illusion" has been inserted. It is an illusion. It is not a (right) perception. Neither is it an inference. . . . We maintain therefore that the vision of a moving tree is error. If it is error, how are we to explain that a tree is nevertheless reached (when acting upon such erroneous perception)? The tree is not (really) reached upon it, since a tree changing its position in space is the definite image (corresponding to the visual sensation), and a tree fixed on one place is actually reached. . . .

What kind of "construction" is here alluded to?

5. Construction (or judgment) implies a distinct cognition of a mental reflex which is capable of coalescing with a verbal designation.

A "verbal designation" is a word of speech through which something is denoted. . . . When the denoted fact and the word denoting it have entered into one act of cognition, then the word and the object have "coalesced". . . .

A distinct cognition of such a denoted reflex is thus mentioned which is *capable* of coalescing with a word. We may have, indeed, a distinct cognition in which the mental reflex has coalesced with its designation by speech as, e.g., the constructed (cognition) "jar" with a man to whom this word is familiar. It contains such a mental reflex which is accompanied by the word "jar."

But we may also have (mental constructions) which, although not accompanied by corresponding words, are capable of being so accompanied as, e.g., the mental constructions of a baby not knowing the import of words. If constructions referring to mental reflexes accompanied by words were (alone) here mentioned, the constructions of those who do not speak would not have been included. But since it is said "*capable* of coalescing," they also are included. Although the mental constructions of a new born babe are not accompanied by words, they certainly are suitable for such a connection. Those that are connected are also suitable. Thus by inserting the word "capable" both (the primitive and developed constructions) are included. . . .

. . . An object apprehended (by acquaintance) can produce in the mind only something limited (to the actually present) as, e.g., a patch of colour producing a visual impression can only produce a mental reflex limited to that very patch. But constructed knowledge is not produced only by the object (actually apprehended) and therefore it is not a (narrowly) restricted mental reflex. . . . A cognition which unites former experiences with later ones has not its object present to it, because the former experience is not present. Not having its object present it does not depend upon it. An independent cognition is not a reflex (narrowly) restricted (to one momentary sensation), because the (assembled) factors which would (exactly) correspond (to the synthetic image) are absent. Such (a synthetic image) is capable of coalescing with a word. Sense-knowledge is (strictly) dependent upon its object, since it is receptive only in regard to what is (really) present before it. And since the (real) object is a cause confining the reflex (to itself), (the corresponding cognition) refers to a (strictly) limited reflex, (to something unique) which therefore is not capable of coalescing with a word. . . .

6. Cognition exempt from such (construction), when it is not affected by an illusion produced by colour-blindness, rapid motion, travelling on board a ship, sickness or other causes, is perceptive knowledge.

Cognition which is free from constructiveness, i.e., contains (an element that is not) an arrangement (or judgment), if it is (at the same time) not illusive, is perceptive knowledge. . . . Thus it is shown that both these characteristics combined with one another determine the essence of right perception.

Colour-blindness is an eye-disease. This is a cause of illusion located in the organ of sense. Rapid movement (calls forth an illusion) as, e.g., when we rapidly swing a firebrand, (we have the illusion of a fiery circle). If we swing the firebrand slowly, we do not have it. Therefore the swinging is qualified by the word "rapid." This is a cause of delusion which is located in the object of perception. Travelling by ship (produces illusion as, e.g.), when the ship is moving, a person standing (on the deck) has the illusion of moving trees on the shore. The word "travelling" points to this circumstance. Here illusion depends on the place where one is situated. Disease is . . . an internal cause of illusion. But each of these causes, whether they be located in the organ or in the object, whether external or internal, invariably affect the organ of sense, because when the organ of sense is normal there can be no illusive sensation. All these causes . . . are but an exemplification of the possible causes. The words "and other causes" are added in order to include such organic diseases as the disturbance of vision by jaundice, such objective causes as a rapid movement to and fro. When, e.g., the firebrand is seen rapidly moving to and fro, we have the illusion of a fiery-coloured stick. Such external causes as riding on an elephant and such internal ones as the effect of strong blows on vulnerable parts of the body are also included. Cognition when it is free from illusion called forth by these causes is perceptive knowledge.

MĪMĀṂSĀ (EXEGESIS)

Competing with the Buddhists in many aspects of religion and culture were conservative Brahmins, the priests and intellectuals of Hinduism—or, more precisely, of Brahminism, the high-brow religion concerned with interpreting sacred texts and defending the caste system. What we call today Hinduism had and has little unity; the worship of popular gods and goddesses was socially far removed from the efforts of the high-caste priests to explain and interpret sacred texts. These priests did not view the lower castes as fit to read their scriptures. (In recent times, there have been revolutions within Hindu sects, but many still practice caste, at least in marriage.)

Proponents of the classical school *Mīmāṃsā* (a term meaning "exegesis") were most concerned with the proper interpretation of the texts they viewed as revealed, namely the Veda and its various appendages. The Veda is a collection of ancient hymns and poems (ca. 1200–900 B.C.E.) in an archaic Sanskrit. The Exegetes looked at the Vedic literature with an eye to questions of *dharma*, "right practice." The Exegetes understood *dharma* chiefly as the performance of certain rituals, as opposed to the term's meaning in the *Gītā*, for instance, where it is used more broadly as "right way of life."

Exegetes often debated Buddhists in the courts of kings and wealthy patrons and tried to refute their arguments. Thus they were moved to take up the philosophical topics addressed in rival schools, and some of them worked out theories of their own on a wide range of issues. This expansion of interests occurred over several centuries, paralleling the development of Buddhist philosophy and of other less conservative Hindu schools.

The Mīmāṃsā root text is the *Mīmāṃsā-sūtra* (ca. 100 C.E.), which sets forth the broad lines of an approach to the Vedic revelation. This text itself does not contain much critical inquiry, although it does feature interesting reflection on questions of sentence meaning. But some of the *Mīmāṃsā-sūtra* commentaries not only refine semantics and philosophy of language but also address many of the issues that concern philosophers: the self and self-awareness, reality of the external world, justification and canons of debate and argument, rebirth and the possibility of liberation and enlightenment.

The Exegetes are realists; that is, they maintin that the objects of consciousness exist independently of consciousness. The passage below is excerpted from the *Ślokavārttika*, a commentary on the *Mīmāṃsā-sūtra* by a seventh-century philosopher named Kumārila, perhaps the greatest of the Exegetes. Here, as he often does, Kumārila directs his argument against Buddhist positions. His aim is to refute both the phenomenalism of the Buddhist idealists and the skepticism or nihilism of the Mādhyamika followers of Nāgārjuna.

KUMĀRILA

from *the Ślokavārttika (Notes on the Verses)*

From Kumāṅla's Ślokavārttika, *translated by Ganganatha Jha. (Calcutta: Bibliotheca India, 1908.)*

1–3. Authoritativeness and Non-authoritativeness,—Virtue and Vice and the effects thereof,—the assumptions of the objects of Injunctions, Eulogistic passages, Mantras, and Names,—in short, the very existence of the various Chapters (of the Sutra) based upon the various proofs,—the differentiation of the Question from the Reply, by means of distinctions in the style of expression,—the relation between actions and their results in this world, as well as beyond this world, &c.,—all these would be groundless (unreasonable), if Ideas (or cognitions) were devoid of (corresponding) objects (in the External World).

4. Therefore those who wish (to know) Duty, should examine the question of the existence or non-existence of (external) objects, by means of proofs accepted (as such) by people,—for the sake of the (accomplishment of) Actions.

5. [A Buddhist:] "Even if only the 'Idea' (or sensation) is accepted (to be a real entity), all this (that is ordinarily known as the 'External World') may be explained as '*Samvriti* Reality'*; and as such it is useless for you to persist in holding the reality of the (external) object." . . .

8–9. Thus then the words "Samvriti" and "Mithyā" (false) being synonymous [as the Buddhists suppose] the assumption (of "Samvriti Reality") is only meant to hood-wink ordinary men, just like the word "Vaktrāsava" (mouth-wine) as used with reference to the saliva. . . . And so is also their theory of the *assumed* reality (of external objects); because there can be no assumption of the indivisible (consciousness which alone is real, for the Buddhist) in the void (*i.e.*, the external world, whose existence is denied by the Buddhist).

10. Therefore it must be admitted that that which does not exist, does not exist; and that which really exists is real, while all else is unreal; and therefore there can be no assumption of two kinds of reality.

11. There is a theory current (among the Buddhists) that the experiences (of Heaven, &c.), are similar to the experiences of a dream; and it is for the refutation of this theory that we seek to prove the *reality* of external objects.

12–13. It cannot be for the mere pleasures of a dream that people engage in the performance of Duty. Dream coming to a man spontaneously, during sleep, the learned would only lie down quietly, instead of performing sacrifices, &c., when desirous of obtaining real results. For these reasons, we must try our best, by arguments, to establish (the truth of) the conception of external objects (as realities).

14–16. (Among the Buddhists) the Yogacāras hold that 'Ideas' are without corresponding realities (in the external world); and those that hold the Mādhyamika doctrine deny the reality of the Idea also. In both of these theories however the denial of the external object is common. . . .

* I.e., empirical reality.—Ed.

17–18. The denial of the external object is of two kinds: one is based upon an examination of the object itself, and another is based upon reasoning. Of these, that which is based upon a consideration of the object may be laid aside for the present; that which is based upon reasoning, and as such is the root (of the theory), is what is here examined.

18–19. Here too the denial has been introduced in two ways: at first through Inference, and then, after an examination of the applicability of Sense-perception, through its inapplicability (to external objects). . . .

20–22. *Objection:* "(1). It has been declared that 'Sense-perception' is only that which is produced by a contact (of the sense) with the particular object; but there is no relation between the objects and the Sense-organ, in reality; while, as for an *assumed* contact, this is present in a dream also; therefore it is not possible to have any such differentiation (in reality) as that into (cognitions) *produced by such contact,* and (those) *not so produced.* (2) And again, it has been said that falsity is only of two kinds, and not more; but here it is added that all (cognition) is false; why then should there be any such specification?"

23. "The cognition of a pole is false, because it is a *cognition*; because whatever is a cognition has always been found to be false,—*f.i.* the cognitions in a dream." . . .

24–25. . . . And further, because of the acceptance (by the Buddhists) of the reality of the idea of the cognition itself, what is here denied is only the reality of the external objects of perception." . . .

34. It is only the denial of an object, comprehended by means of a faulty cognition, that can be correct. If there be a denial of every conception, then your own theory too cannot be established. . . .

36. If the cognition, of the Subject and Predicate, as belonging to the speaker and the hearer, were without corresponding realities, then both of them would stand self-contradicted.

37. Nor would any differentiation be possible, between the Subject and the Predicate. For these reasons the declaration of your conclusion cannot be right.

38. "But we do not admit of any such entity, as the *Character of having no real corresponding object;* therefore it is not right to raise any questions as to the absence or otherwise of such entities."

39. If the cognition is not a real entity, then in what way do you wish to explain it to us? Or, how do you yourself comprehend it?

39–40. If it be urged that "we assume its existence and then seek to prove it,"—then (we reply), how can there be an assumption of something that does not exist? And even if it is assumed, it comes (by the mere fact of this assumption) to be an entity. . . .

CĀRVĀKA SKEPTICISM

In classical India, not all thinkers took their philosophic orientations from religious or mystical traditions. The most striking opposition to religious notions comes from a school known as *Cārvāka,* also called *Lokāyata,* a term meaning "those attached to the ways of the world." Cārvāka philosophers are materialists; that is, they believe that physical matter is the only reality and that we can know only what we perceive through our senses. According to the Cārvākas, we cannot assert the validity of any inferences we make about what we perceive. Because they reject inference, the Cārvākas are commonly referred to as skeptics.

By arguing that inferential reasoning cannot establish anything, the Cārvākas attack ideas of an immortal soul, rebirth, God, a mystical enlightenment or liberation, and other notions. That is to say, by showing that inference is unreliable, whatever the topic, these skeptics would strip away all excesses of belief beyond the simple facts of pleasure, pain, and the body. The body exists in an inexplicable material world.

Opponents retort that the Cārvāka attack is self-defeating, for it utilizes the very processes of thinking that it aims to show invalid. The Cārvāka response is that the burden of proof is on the other side.

In the following selection, the attack presupposes familiarity with an argument form that had become standard in philosophical debates in the classical age. A paradigm case:

(0) There is fire on yonder hill. (The conclusion to be proved. How? Because:)

(1) There is smoke rising from it.

(2) Wherever there's smoke, there's fire.

(3) This smoke-possessing-hill is an example of the "wherever" of the universal proposition (2).
(Therefore:)

(4) There is fire on yonder hill.

Here, 'fire' is an example of a *major term,* 'smoke' a *middle term.* The universal proposition (2) expresses an *invariable connection.*

Most Cārvāka texts have been lost, but references to their arguments occur in many of their opponents' works. (The *Tattvoplavasiṃha* by Jayarāśi, ca. 650, is in fact the only complete Cārvāka text extant.) The selection that follows is taken from a late (ca. 1500) Sanskrit compendium of philosophic views compiled by a person named Mādhava, who was not himself a Cārvāka.

from Mādhava's *Compendium of Philosophy*

Reprinted from The Sarva-Darsana-Samgraha, *translated by E. B. Cowell and A. E. Gough (London: Kegan Paul, Trench, Trubner, 1914).*

The efforts of Cārvāka are indeed hard to be eradicated, for the majority of living beings hold by the current refrain—

While life is yours, live joyously;
None can escape Death's searching eye:
When once this frame of ours they burn,
How shall it e'er again return?

The mass of men, in accordance with the Śāstras of policy and enjoyment, considering wealth and desire the only ends of man and denying the existence of any object belonging to a future world, are found to follow only the doctrine of Cārvāka. Hence another name for that school is Lokāyata,—a name well accordant with the thing signified.

In this school the four elements, earth, & c., are the original principles; from these alone, when transformed into the body, intelligence is produced, just as the inebriating power is developed from the mixing of certain ingredients; and when these are destroyed, intelligence at once perishes also. They quote the *sruti* [Vedic text] for this [*Brhadaranyaka Upanishad* ii.iv.12]: "Springing forth from these elements, itself solid knowledge, it is destroyed when they are destroyed,–after death no intelligence remains." Therefore the soul is only the body distinguished by the attribute of intelligence, since there is no evidence for any self distinct from the body, as such cannot be proved, since this school holds that perception is the only source of knowledge and does not allow inference, &c.

The only end of man is enjoyment produced by sensual pleasures. Nor may you say that such cannot be called the end of man as they are always mixed with some kind of pain, because it is our wisdom to enjoy the pure pleasure as far as we can, and to avoid the pain which inevitably accompanies it; just as the man who desires fish takes the fish with their scales and bones, and having taken as many as he wants, desists; or just as the man who desires rice, takes the rice, straw and all, and having taken as much as he wants, desists. It is not therefore for us, through a fear of pain, to reject the pleasure which our nature instinctively recognises as congenial. Men do not refrain from sowing rice, because forsooth there are wild animals to devour it; nor do they refuse to set the cooking-pots on the fire, because forsooth there are beggars to pester us for a share of the contents. If any one were so timid as to forsake a visible pleasure, he would indeed be foolish like a beast, as has been said by the poet—

The pleasure which arises to men from contact with
    sensible objects,
Is to be relinquished as accompanied by pain,—such is
    the reasoning of fools;
The berries of paddy, rich with the finest white grains,
What man, seeking his true interest, would fling away
    because covered with husk and dust?

If you object that, if there be no such thing as happiness in a future world, then how should men of experienced wisdom engage in the *Agnihotra*[1] and other sacrifices, which can only be performed with great expenditure of money and bodily fatigue, your objection cannot be accepted as any proof to the contrary, since the *Agnihotra,* &c., are only useful as means of livelihood, for the Veda is tainted by the three faults of untruth, self-contradiction, and tautology; then again the impostors who call themselves Vaidic [or Vedic] pandits are mutually destructive, as the authority of the *jñana-khaṇḍa* (section on knowledge) is overthrown by those who

[1] Sacrificial offering to fire.

maintain that of the *karma-khaṇḍa* (section on action), while those who maintain the authority of the *jñana-khaṇḍa* reject that of the *karma-khaṇḍa*; and lastly, the three Vedas themselves are only the incoherent rhapsodies of knaves, and to this effect runs the popular saying—

The *Agnihotra*, the three Vedas, the ascetic's three staves, and smearing oneself with ashes,—
Brhaspati says these are but means of livelihood for those who have no manliness nor sense.

Hence it follows that there is no other hell than mundane pain produced by purely mundane causes, as thorns, &c.; the only Supreme is the earthly monarch whose existence is proved by all the world's eyesight; and the only liberation is the dissolution of the body. By holding the doctrine that the soul is identical with the body, such phrases as "I am thin," "I am black," &c., are at once intelligible, as the attributes of thinness, &c., and self-consciousness will reside in the same subject (the body); and the use of the phrase "my body" is metaphorical like "the head of Rahu" [Rahu being really *all head*].

All this has been thus summed up—
In this school there are four elements, earth, water, fire, and air;
And from these four elements alone is intelligence produced,—
Just like the intoxicating power from *kinva*,[2] &c., mixed together;
Since in "I am fat," "I am lean," these attributes abide in the same subject,
And since fatness, &c., reside only in the body, it alone is the soul and no other,
And such phrases as "my body" are only significant metaphorically.

"Be it so," says the opponent; "your wish would be gained if inference, &c., had no force of proof; but then they have this force; else, if they had not, then how, on perceiving smoke, should the thoughts of the intelligent immediately proceed to fire; or why, on hearing another say, 'There are fruits on the bank of the river,' do those who desire fruit proceed at once to the shore?"

[2] An intoxicating herb.

All this, however, is only the inflation of the world of fancy.

Those who maintain the authority of inference accept the sign or middle term as the cause of knowledge, which middle term must be found in the minor and be itself invariably connected with the major. Now this invariable connection must be a relation destitute of any condition accepted or disputed; and this connection does not possess its power of causing inference by virtue of its existence, as the eye, &c., are the cause of perception, but by virtue of its being known. What then is the means of this connection's being known?

We will first show that it is not perception. Now perception is held to be of two kinds, external and internal [i.e., as produced by the external senses, or by the inner sense, mind]. The former is not the required means; for although it is possible that the actual contact of the senses and the object will produce the knowledge of the particular object thus brought in contact, yet as there can never be such contact in the case of the past or the future, the universal proposition which was to embrace the invariable connection of the middle and major terms in every case becomes impossible to be known. Nor may you maintain that this knowledge of the universal proposition has the general class as its object, because, if so, there might arise a doubt as to the existence of the invariable connection in this particular case [as, for instance, in this particular smoke as implying fire].

Nor is internal perception the means, since you cannot establish that the mind has any power to act independently towards an external object, since all allow that it is dependent on the external senses, as has been said by one of the logicians, "The eye, &c., have their objects as described; but mind externally is dependent on the others."

Nor can inference be the means of the knowledge of the universal proposition, since in the case of this inference we should also require another inference to establish it, and so on, and hence would arise the fallacy of an *ad infinitum* retrogression.

Nor can testimony be the means thereof, since we may either allege in reply . . . that this is included in the topic of inference; or else we may hold that this fresh proof of testimony is unable to leap over the old barrier that stopped the progress of inference, since it depends itself on the recognition of a sign in the form of the language used in the child's presence by the old man; and, moreover, there is no . . . reason for our believing on another's word that smoke and fire are invariably connected. . . .

And again, if testimony were to be accepted as the only means of the knowledge of the universal proposition, then in the case of a man to whom the fact of the invariable connection between the middle and major terms had not been pointed out by another person, there could be no inference of one thing [as fire] on seeing another thing [as smoke]; hence, on your own showing, the whole topic of inference for oneself would have to end in mere idle words.

Then again, comparison, &c., must be utterly rejected as the means of the knowledge of the universal proposition, since it is impossible that they can produce the knowledge of the unconditioned connection [i.e., the universal proposition], because their end is to produce the knowledge of quite another connection, viz., the relation of a name to something so named.

Again, this same absence of a condition, which has been given as the definition of an invariable connection [i.e., a universal proposition], can itself never be known; since it is impossible to establish that all conditions must be objects of perception; and therefore, although the absence of perceptible things may be itself perceptible, the absence of non-perceptible things must be itself non-perceptible; and thus, since we must here too have recourse to inference, &c., we cannot leap over the obstacle which has already been planted to bar them. Again, we must accept as the definition of the condition, "it is that which is reciprocal or equipollent in extension with the major term though not constantly accompanying the middle." These three distinguishing clauses, "not constantly accompanying the middle term," "constantly accompanying the major term," and "being constantly accompanied by it" [i.e., reciprocal], are needed in the full definition to stop respectively three such fallacious conditions, in the argument to prove the non-eternity of sound, as "being produced," "the nature of a jar," and "the not causing audition"; wherefore the definition holds. . . .

But since the knowledge of the condition must here precede the knowledge of the condition's absence, it is only when there is the knowledge of the condition, that the knowledge of the universality of the proposition is possible, i.e., a knowledge in the form of such a connection between the middle term and major term as is distinguished by the absence of any such condition; and, on the other hand, the knowledge of the condition depends upon the knowledge of the invariable connection. Thus we fasten on our opponents as with adamantine glue the thunderbolt-like fallacy of reasoning in a circle. Hence by the impossibility of knowing the universality of a proposition it becomes impossible to establish inference, &c.

The step which the mind takes from the knowledge of smoke, &c., to the knowledge of fire, &c., can be accounted for by its being based on a former perception or by its being an error; and that in some cases this step is justified by the result is accidental just like the coincidence of effects observed in the employment of gems, charms, drugs, &c.

From this it follows that fate, &c., do not exist, since these can only be proved by inference. But an opponent will say, if you thus do not allow *adṛṣṭa*,[3] the various phenomena of the world become destitute of any cause. But we cannot accept this objection as valid, since these phenomena can all be produced spontaneously from the inherent nature of things. Thus it has been said—

The fire is hot, the water cold, refreshing cool the
breeze of morn;
By whom came this variety? from their own nature was
it born. . . .
There is no heaven, no final liberation, nor any soul in
another world,
Nor do the actions of the four castes, orders, &c., produce any real effect.
The *Agnihotra*, the three Vedas, the ascetic's three
staves, and smearing oneself with ashes,
Were made by Nature as the livelihood of those destitute of knowledge and manliness.
If a beast slain in the *Jyotiṣṭoma* rite[4] will itself go to
heaven,
Why then does not the sacrificer forthwith offer his
own father?

[3] The unseen force.

[4] A Vedic sacrifice.

If the *Śrāddha*[5] produces gratification to beings who are dead,
Then here, too, in the case of travellers when they start, it is needless to give provisions for the journey.
If beings in heaven are gratified by our offering the *Śrāddha* here,
Then why not give the food down below to those who are standing on the housetop?
While life remains let a man live happily, let him feed on ghee even though he runs in debt;
When once the body becomes ashes, how can it ever return again?
If he who departs from the body goes to another world,
How is it that he comes not back again, restless for love of his kindred?

[5] Oblations to the dead.

Hence it is only as a means of livelihood that *brāhmins* have established here
All these ceremonies for the dead—there is no other fruit anywhere.
The three authors of the Vedas were buffoons, knaves, and demons.
All the well-known formulas of the pandits . . .
And all the obscene rites for the queen . . . ,
These were invented by buffoons, and so all the various kinds of presents to the priests,
While the eating of flesh was similarly commanded by night-prowling demons.

Hence in kindness to the mass of living beings must we fly for refuge to the doctrine of Cārvāka. Such is the pleasant consummation.

NYĀYA-VAIŚEṢIKA EPISTEMIC LOGIC AND ONTOLOGY

Two long-running schools with a realist attitude toward the objects of experience are the Vaiśeṣika (particularism) and the *Nyāya* (logic). For centuries, Indian philosophers considered the two distinct, and each could claim its own self-defining literature. But with Udayana, who lived around 1000 C.E., the schools merge, and proponents afterwards are called simply Naiyāyikas, i.e., adherents of Nyāya. Udayana was not the first Naiyāyika to rely on positions hammered out in the Vaiśeṣika literature, but he was the first to treat the two systems as a unity.

In pre-Udayana works, Vaiśeṣika tends to focus more on the question "What is there?" The Nyāya, in contrast, is more concerned with the questions "How do we know what we know?" and "What are the right methods of inquiry and debate?" Vaiśeṣika philosophers try to work out a system of categories (*padārtha,* literally, "types of things to which words refer") into which we can classify everything that we talk about on the basis of experience. Nyāya philosophers reflect less on what we know than on how we know it, and the earliest Nyāya work, the *Nyāya-sūtra,* is concerned mainly with the means of right cognition: perception, inference, analogical acquisition of vocabulary, and reliable testimony.

After Udayana, the philosophers of the combined school are willing to address almost any topic. The main thrust of their work, however, remains logic and the nature of cognition and knowledge. These late classical thinkers, dating from 1000 to 1700 and even later, evolve abstruse, technical views and methods of analysis that anticipate much in modern mathematical logic and the philosophy of language. Little of this New Logic, or Navya-Nyāya, has been translated into modern languages or thoroughly studied.

To the question "What is there?" the early Vaiśeṣikas answer that most generally there are three types of things that exist:

1. Substances, such as a pot or a cloth
2. Qualities, such as shapes and colors
3. Actions, such as moving up

There are also other categories, which allow us to make meaningful sentences:

4. Inherence, e.g., the relationship between substances and qualities. (In the case of a blue pot, inherence is the relationship between the pot and the color blue.)
5. Universality, such as potness and cowness
6. Individualizer, which differentiates ultimate particulars, such as atoms
7. Absence, such as of an elephant in this room (a category that is not made explicit in the *Vaiśeṣika-sūtra* but that is defended in all later Vaiśeṣika texts).

The first selection below, from the *Vaiśeṣika-sūtra* (ca. 150 C.E.), are concerned mainly with explaining and elaborating these.

The selections from the *Nyāya-sūtra* (ca. 200) and a commentary (*bhāṣya*) by Vātsyāyana (ca. 400) present characterizations of the four means of knowledge: perception, inference, analogical acquisition of vocabulary, and reliable testimony. They also address the issue of whether a whole ever exists over and above the parts of which it is composed. This issue is hotly disputed with the Buddhists. Naiyāyikas affirm that there is such a real whole, whereas certain Buddhists vehemently disagree. The whole/part discussion is followed by a response to Nāgārjuna. Nāgārjuna claims that analyzing the concept of the means of knowledge leads to a vicious infinite regress: How are the means of knowledge known? Gautama, the author of the *sūtras*, and Vātsyāyana try to disarm the objection by drawing an analogy to a scale. A scale is a means of knowledge when the weight of a piece of gold, for example, is in question. But the same scale would be the object of knowledge, what is to be known—and the piece of gold the means of knowledge—when the question is calibration. (This response is elaborated by B. K. Matilal, p. 222.)

Naiyāyikas are theists, and the next selection, from a work by Udayana, presents arguments for the existence of God. The final selection is taken from Gaṅgeśa's classic, *The Jewel of Thought about Reality* (*Tattvacintāmani*) (ca. 1350). Gaṅgeśa, who is commonly credited with founding the New Logic, addresses the problem of how an *inference-grounding pervasion* is known. The idea is that if something *x* is to be inferred from something else *y*, then *x* must be *pervaded* by *y*. But how are pervasions themselves known? Gaṅgeśa theory may be regarded as an attempt to justify induction, a topic that has received much attention in Western philosophy.

The theory of the means of knowledge (*pramāṇa*) is the Nyāya school's outstanding philosophical contribution. But the breadth of Nyāya-Vaiśeṣika philosophy is also striking—this is an entire system and world view evolving over centuries, not just a theory of knowledge.

from the *Vaiśeṣika Sūtra*

From The Vaiśeṣika Sūtras of Kaṇāda, *translated by Nandalal Sinha. The Sacred Books of the Hindus, Vol. VI (Allahabad: Panini office, 1923).*

BOOK I

CHAPTER 1*

1. Now, therefore, we shall explain *dharma* (righteousness).
2. *Dharma* (is) that from which (results) the accomplishment of exaltation and of the supreme good.
3. The authoritativeness of the Veda (arises from its) being the Word of God.
4. The Supreme Good (results) from the knowledge, produced by a particular *dharma,* of the essence of the [categories] substance, attribute, action, genus, species, and combination [inherence] by means of their resemblances and differences.
5. Earth, water, fire, air, ether, time, space, self (or soul), and mind (are) the only substances.
6. Attributes are color, taste, smell, and touch, numbers, measures, separateness, conjunction and disjunction, priority and posteriority, understandings, pleasure and pain, desire and aversion, and volitions.
7. Throwing upwards, throwing downwards, contraction, expansion, and motion are actions.
8. The resemblance of substance, attribute, and action lies in this that they are existent and non-eternal, have substance as their combinative cause, are effect as well as cause, and are both genus and species.
9. The resemblance of substance and attribute is the characteristic of being the originators of their class concepts.
10. Substances originate another substance, and attributes another attribute.
15. It possesses action and attribute, it is a combinative cause—such (is) the mark of substance.
16. Inhering in substance, not possessing attribute, not an independent cause in conjunctions and disjunctions,—such is the mark of attribute.
17. Residing in one substance only, not possessing attribute, an independent cause of conjunctions and disjunctions—such is the mark of action.
20. Action is the common cause of conjunction, disjunction, and impetus.
21. Action is not the cause of substances.
22. (Action is not the cause of substance) because of its cessation.

BOOK I

CHAPTER 2

1. Non-existence of effect (follows) from the non-existence of cause.
2. But non-existence of cause (does) not (follow) from the non-existence of the effect.
3. The notions, genus and species, are relative to the understanding.
4. Existence, being the cause of assimilation only, is only a genus.
5. Substantiality, and attribute-ness and action-ness are both genera and species.

* For purposes of clarity, we have translated certain terms that the translator left in the original Sanskrit, and in some instances we have altered the translations of key terms to make them consistent with other readings in this book.—Ed.

6. (The statement of genus and species has been made) with the exception of the final species.
7. Existence is that to which are due the belief and usage, namely "(it is) existent," in respect of substance, attribute, and action.

BOOK II

CHAPTER 1

1. Earth possesses color, taste, smell, and touch.
2. Waters possess color, taste, and touch, and are fluid and viscid.
3. Fire possesses color and touch.
4. Air possesses touch.
5. These (characteristics) are not in ether.*
27. By the method of elimination (sound) is the mark of ether.
29. The unity (of ether is explained) by (the explanation of the unity of) existence.
30. (Ether is one), because there is no difference in sound which is its mark, and because there exists no other distinguishing mark.
31. And individuality also belongs to ether, since individuality follows unity.

BOOK II

CHAPTER 2

2. Smell is established in earth.
4. Hotness (is the characteristic) of fire.
5. Coldness (is the characteristic) of water.
6. "Posteriority" in respect of that which is posterior, "simultaneous," "slow," "quick,"—such (cognitions) are the marks of time.
8. The unity (of time is explained), by (the explanation of the unity of) existence.

*Ether is considered the medium of sound, as water is the medium of taste and earth particles the medium of smell.—Ed.

9. The name time is applicable to a cause, inasmuch as it does not exist in eternal substances and exists in non-eternal substances.
10. That which gives rise to such (cognition and usage) as "This (is remote, etc.) from this,"—(the same is) the mark of space.
11. The substantiality and eternality (of space are) explained by (the explanation of the substantiality and eternality of) air.
12. The unity (of space is explained) by (the explanation of the unity of) existence.

BOOK III

CHAPTER 1

1. The objects of the senses are universally known.
2. The universal experience of the objects of the senses is the mark of (the existence of an) object different from the senses and their [phenomenal] objects.
4. (The body or the senses cannot be the seat of perception), because there is no consciousness in the causes [i.e., the component parts, of the body].
19. And activity and inactivity, observed in one's own self, are the marks of (the existence of) other selves.

BOOK III

CHAPTER 2

1. The appearance and non-appearance of knowledge, on contact of the self with the senses and the objects are the marks (of the existence) of the mind.
3. From the non-simultaneity of volitions, and from the non-simultaneity of cognitions, (it follows that there is only) one (mind) (in each organism).
4. The ascending life-breath, the descending life-breath, the closing of the eye-lids, the opening

of the eye-lids, life, the movement of the mind, and the affections of the other senses, and also pleasure, pain, desire, aversion, and volition are marks (of the existence) of the self.

6. [Objection:] There is no visible mark (of the existence of the self), because there being contact (of the senses with the body of Yajñadatta) perception does not arise (that this self is Yajñadatta).
7. And from a commonly-observed mark (there is) no (inference of anything in) particular.
8. Therefore (the self is) proved by revelation.
9. [Answer:] (The proof of the existence of the self is not solely) from revelation, because of the non-application of the word "I" (to other designates or objects).
10. If (there are) such sensuous observations (or perceptions) as "I am Devadatta," "I am Yajñadatta," (then there is no need of inference).
11. As in the case of other percepts, so, if the self, which is grasped by perception, is also accompanied with, or comes at the top of, marks (from which it can be inferred), then, by means of confirmation, the intuition becomes fastened to one and only one object.
14. Because the intuition "I" exists in one's own self, and because it does not exist otherwhere, therefore the intuition has the individual self as the object of perception.
18. (The self is) not proved (only) by revelation, since, (as ether is proved by sound, so) (the self is) proved in particular by the innate as well as the sensible cognition in the form of "I," accompanied by the invariable divergence (of such cognition from all other things), as is the case with sound.

BOOK IV

CHAPTER 1

1. The eternal is that which is existent and uncaused.
2. The effect is the mark (of the existence) of the ultimate atom.
5. (It is) an error (to suppose that the ultimate atom is not eternal).
21. Space, time, and also ether are inactive, because of their difference from that which possesses activity.
23. (The relation) of the inactive [i.e., attribute and action] (to substance), is combination [inherence], (which is) independent of actions.

BOOK VII

CHAPTER 1

2. The color, taste, smell, and touch of earth, water, fire, and air, are also non-eternal, on account of the non-eternality of their substrata.
22. Ether, in consequence of its vast expansion, is infinitely large. So also is the self.
23. In consequence of non-existence of universal expansion, mind is atomic or infinitely small.
24. By attributes, space is explained (to be all-pervading).
25. Time (is the name given) to (a specific, or a universal) cause. (Hence, in either case it is all-pervading.)

BOOK VII

CHAPTER 2

9. Conjunction is produced by action of any one of two things, is produced by action of both, and is produced by conjunction, also.
10. By this disjunction is explained.
21. The prior and the posterior (are produced by two objects) lying in the same direction, existing at the same time, and being near and remote.
22. (Temporal priority and temporal posteriority are said, by suggestion, to arise respectively)

from priority of the cause and from posteriority of the effect.

26. That is combination [inherence] by virtue of which (arises the intuition) in the form of "This is here," with regard to [subject and attribute].

BOOK VIII

CHAPTER 1

2. Among substances, the self, the mind and others are not objects of perception.
4. Substance is the cause of the production of cognition, where attributes and actions are in contact (with the senses).
6. (Cognition which is produced) in respect of substance, attributes and action, (is) dependent upon genus and species.

BOOK VIII

CHAPTER 2

5. By reason of (its) predominance, and of possession of smell, earth is the material cause of the olfactory sense.
6. In like manner, water, fire and air (are the material causes of the sense-organs of taste, color and touch), inasmuch as there is no difference in the taste, color and touch (which they respectively possess, from what they respectively apprehend).

BOOK IX

CHAPTER 1

1. In consequence of the non-application of action and attribute (to it), (an effect is) non-existent prior (to its production).
3. (The existent is) a different object (from the non-existent), inasmuch as action and attribute cannot be predicated of the non-existent.
5. And that which is a different non-existent from these, is (absolutely) non-existent.
9. That which has not been produced, does not exist;—this is a [tautological] proposition.
11. Perceptual cognition of the self (results) from a particular conjunction of the self and the mind in the self.

BOOK IX

CHAPTER 2

6. Reminiscence (results) from a particular conjunction between the soul and the mind and also from impression or latency.
10. False knowledge (arises) from imperfection of the senses and from imperfection of impression.
11. That (i.e., *avidyā*) is imperfect knowledge.
12. (Cognition) free from imperfection, is (called) *vidyā* or scientific knowledge.
13. Cognition of advanced sages, as also vision of the Perfected Ones, (results) from *dharma* or merits.

from the *Nyāya-sūtra* With a Commentary by Vātsyāyana

From the Nyāya-sutra. *Translated by Mrinalkanti Gangopadhyay. (Calcutta: Indian Studies, 1982.)*

Sūtra 4: Perception is the knowledge resulting from sense-object contact [and which is] 'not due to words', 'invariably related' [to the object] and is 'of a definite character'. (i.1.4)

Bhāṣya: The knowledge which results from the contact of the sense with the object is called perception. (Objection) But, then, it is not so. (It results when) the self (*ātman*) comes in contact with the mind (*manas*), the mind with the sense and the sense with the object. (Answer) It (the *sūtra*) does not specify the cause as "it alone is the cause of perception." It rather states the special cause [of perception]. That which is the special cause of perceptual knowledge is stated here, but it does not exclude the cause common to the inferential and other forms of knowledge.

(Objection) But, then, the contact of the mind with the sense should be stated. (Answer) This (the contact of the mind with the sense) does not differ in the different cases of perceptual knowledge and as such, being alike (*i.e.* being a common cause like the contact of self with mind), is not mentioned.

There are as many 'naming words' as there are objects. (Every object has a word standing for it.) By these (*i.e.* words) the objects are properly known. Usage depends on the proper knowledge of the object. Now, this knowledge of object resulting from sense-object contact assumes the form: "It is colour" (*rūpa*) or "It is taste" (*rasa*). The words like *rūpa* and *rasa* are names of objects. Pieces of knowledge are referred to by these, e.g., one knows that it is colour or one knows that it is taste. (Such pieces of knowledge) being referred to by words naming these, there is the apprehension of considering them as but due to words. Therefore, [*i.e.* to remove such an apprehension] (Gautama) says, not due to words.

Knowledge on the part of those unaware of the relation between the word and its corresponding object (*e.g.* of the infant and the dumb) is not referred to by the words naming the objects. Even if the relation between the word and the corresponding object is known, there is the knowledge that this word is the name of this object (*i.e.* even for those who are aware of the relation between a word and its corresponding object, the knowledge of the object is not due to the word naming it). When that object is known, the knowledge does not differ from the afore-mentioned knowledge of the object (*i.e.* of the infant and the dumb). This knowledge of the object is but similar to that. But this knowledge of the object has no other word to name it, being conveyed by which (word) it can be subject to usage, because there is no usage with what is not properly known. . . . Therefore, the knowledge of the object resulting from sense-object contact is not due to word.

During the summer the flickering rays of the sun intermingled with the heat radiating from the surface of the earth come in contact with the eyes of a person at a distance. Due to this sense-object contact, there arises, in the rays of the sun, the knowledge*: this is water. Even such a knowledge may be taken for valid perceptual knowledge. Hence (Gautama) says, 'invariably connected with the object'. An erroneous perception is the perception of an object as something which it is not. A right perception is the perception of an object as it actually is.

Perceiving with eyes an object at a distance, a person cannot decide whether it is smoke or dust. But such an 'indecisive knowledge' resulting from sense-object contact may be taken for perceptual knowledge. Hence (Gautama) says, 'of a definite character'. It cannot, however, be claimed that this indecisive knowledge is due only to the contact of self with mind (*i.e.* is not due to the contact of the sense with the object). Indecisive knowledge (like this) arises only after one

* The Sanskrit term is *jñāna,* which here, and elsewhere below, would be better translated "cognition," since according to English usage, there can be no false *knowledge*—Ed.

sees the object with the eyes. Just as the object perceived by the senses is eventually perceived by the mind, so also an object is indecisively apprehended by the mind after being indecisively apprehended by the senses. Doubt is only the 'vacillating knowledge' with a drive for the perception of some unique character which is apprehended by mind after being apprehended by the sense, and not the previous one (*i.e.* not the indecisive knowledge which is apprehended by the mind alone after the termination of the function of the senses). In all cases of perception the knower has the definite knowledge of an object through the sense, for persons with impaired sense-organs cannot have any 'after-knowledge' (cognising the first, *i.e.* the knowledge due to sense-object contact).

[Objection] A separate definition of perception needs to be given (to cover the perceptions of) the self etc. and pleasure etc., because it (the perception of self or pleasure) is not due to sense-object contact. [Answer] Though mind is a sense, it is mentioned separately from the other senses because of its different nature. The other senses are 'made of the elements' and have fixed objects. These become senses by virtue of their possessing (the respective) qualities. Mind, on the other hand, is not made of elements, has no fixed object (lit., having everything for its object) and it does not become a sense by virtue of its possessing the quality. As we shall later explain, in spite of the sense-object contact, its (*i.e.* of mind) connection or absence of connection is the cause why a number of perceptions do not simultaneously occur. Since mind also is a sense, no separate definition (for such perception) is called for. This is to be learnt from what is discussed in 'the other system'. The viewpoint of others, when not refuted, becomes one's own. . . . Here ends the explanation of perception.

Sūtra 5: Next [is discussed] inference, which is preceded by it [*i.e.* by perception], and is of three kinds, namely, *pūrvavat* (*i.e.* having the antecedent as the probans), *śeṣavat* (*i.e.* having the consequent as the probans) and *sāmanyatodṛṣṭa* (*i.e.* where the *vyāpti** is ascertained by general observation). (i.1.5)

Bhāṣya: By the expression 'preceded by it' is meant 'the perception of the (invariable) relation between the probans and the probandum' as well as 'the perception of the probans'. By the perception of the invariably related probans and the probandum is meant the recollection of the probans. Through this recollection and the perception of the probans is inferred the object which at that time 'is not directly cognised'.

Now, *pūrvavat*: When the effect is inferred from its cause, e.g. from the rising cloud (it is inferred that) it will rain. *Śeṣavat*: When the cause is inferred from its effect. On perceiving the water of the river as different from what it was before, (and further perceiving) the fullness of the river and the swiftness of the current, it is inferred that there was rain. *Sāmānyatodṛṣṭa*: the perception of an object at some place which was previously seen somewhere else is due to its movement; so also that of the sun. Therefore (it is inferred that), though imperceptible, the sun has movement.

Alternatively. *Pūrvavat*: when an object not perceived at the moment is inferred through the perception of one of the two objects as they were previously perceived. As for example, fire from smoke. [Two objects were previously (*pūrva*) perceived as being invariably related. An object similar to one of these is now perceived. From this is inferred an object similar to the other, though the object thus inferred is not perceived now.]

Śeṣavat means . . . residual. It is the definite knowledge resting on the residual after the elimination of (certain) possible objects and because of the irrelevance in the cases of (still) other objects. As for example, by characterising sound as existent and non-eternal, which are the common characteristics of substance, quality and action, it is differentiated from universal, particularity and inherence. When doubt arises whether it (sound) is a substance, quality or action, (we eliminate as follows). It is not substance, because it has only a single substance (as the inherent cause) and it is not action, because it is the cause of a subsequent sound. Then it is what is the residual and sound is proved to be a quality.

Sāmānyatodṛṣṭa: When the relation between the probans and the probandum being imperceptible, the probandum is known from a probans having the same nature with any other object. As for example, self from desire etc. Desire etc. are qualities. Qualities reside in substances. Therefore, that which is the substratum of these (*i.e.* desire etc.) is the self. . . .

Perception has for its object things present. Inference has for its object things both present and absent. Why? Because of its capacity for knowing objects

* Pervasion.—Ed.

belonging to the three times (*i.e.* past, present and future). By inference one knows objects belonging to the three times. We infer: it will be, it is, and it was. By 'absent' here is meant the past and the future (objects).

Next is *upamāna*.*

Sūtra 6: Comparison is the instrument of the valid knowledge of an object derived through its similarity with another well-known object. (i.1.6.)

Bhāṣya: Comparison is 'definite knowledge' of the 'object sought to be definitely known' through its similarity with an object already wellknown. (Example) "The *gavaya* (a wild cow without the dew-lap) is like the cow." (Objection) What is the function here of comparison as an instrument of valid knowledge? When one perceives its similarity with the cow, one knows the object by perception itself. [Answer] As Gautama says, the function of comparison is to impart knowledge of the relation of the name [with the corresponding object]. When the proposition conveying the comparison "the *gavaya* is like the cow" is employed, a person perceiving through sense-object contact an object having similarity with the cow learns 'the relation between the naming word and the object denoted' in the following way: this object is denoted by the word *gavaya*. After the propositions conveying a comparison "the *mudgaparṇī* (a kind of herb) is like the *mudga*" and "the *māṣaparṇī* (another kind of herb) is like the *māṣa*" are employed, a person acquires the knowledge of the relation between the naming word and the object denoted and he collects the herbs for preparing medicines. Thus, many other things are to be known as the objects of comparison in everyday life.

Next is verbal testimony.

Sụtra 7: Verbal testimony is the communication from a 'trustworthy person'. (i.1.7)

Bhāṣya: A trustworthy person is the speaker who has the direct knowledge of an object and is motivated by the desire of communicating the object as directly known by him. . . . This definition (of a trustworthy person) is equally applicable to the seer, noble and barbarian (*mleccha*—person without Vedic practices). Thus the practice of everybody is carried on.

* This term is rendered as "comparison" in this version. A more precise translation is "analogical acquisition of vocabulary."—ED.

In this way, the activities of god, man and animal are maintained with the help of these instruments of valid knowledge and not otherwise. . . .

Sūtra 33: (Objection) There is doubt about the existence of the whole (*i.e.* the whole standing over and above the parts), because it (*i.e.* the whole) is 'not yet proved'. (ii.1.33)

Bhāṣya: (Objection) . . . It is yet to be proved that an entity (viz. the whole) distinct (from the parts themselves) is produced by the causes (*i.e.* the constituent parts). That is, this has not yet been logically demonstrated. Thus, there is the knowledge of two contradictory assertions (viz. "the whole exists" and "the whole does not exist") and from this knowledge of the contradictory assertions there results the doubt about the (existence of the) whole.

Sūtra 34: (Answer) If the existence of the whole is denied, then there can be no knowledge of anything. (ii.1.34)

Bhāṣya: (Answer) If the whole does not exist, everything will remain unknown. What is meant here by everything? Substance, quality, activity, universal, particularity and inherence. But how (are we to understand that without admitting the whole everything remains unknown)? The (mere) assemblage of the atoms cannot be the object of visual sense, because the atoms are imperceptible. (In your view) there is no other entity in the form of the whole, which can be the object of the visual sense. But these substance etc. are apprehended as the object of the visual sense. Therefore, they cannot be apprehended without having any real basis. But (substance etc.) are perceived in the form: "this jar is black; is one; is big; is conjoined; is vibrating; is existing and is made of earth." And (also in the form) "the quality etc. exist." Therefore, from the perception of everything we observe that there is a distinct entity (known as the whole).

Sūtra 35: (Answer continued) Also from being gripped and pulled (is proved the existence of the whole as distinct from the aggregate of parts or atoms). (ii.1.35)

Bhāṣya: (Answer) The whole is an entity distinct (from the aggregate of atoms, because things like the tree can be gripped and pulled).

(Vātsyāyana raises a possible objection against this argument and refutes it. The objection is:) The cause of being gripped and pulled is the collectivity (of the atoms). Collectivity implies a distinct quality coexisting with conjunction and produced by viscosity and fluidity. (E.g., the quality produced) in the unbaked jar due to the conjunction of water and in the baked jar due to the conjunction of fire. Had (the peculiarity of being gripped and pulled) been due to the whole, then it would have been possible even in the case of a handful of dust etc. (Further, in your view) in the cases of grass, pebble and wood, lumped together with lac, there would have been no (possibility of being gripped and pulled) because in this case no distinct entity is produced. Now, what question are you going to put to those who deny the existence of the whole and, in defence of perception, admit the aggregate itself to be the object of perception?

(Answer) The question to be asked is: what exactly is the object of knowledge when it (*i.e.* the knowledge) takes the form "this is *one single* substance?" Does this knowledge of one single substance reveal one object or a multiplicity of objects? (If it is assumed that) it reveals one single substance, then the whole will be proved from the admission of a distinct entity (as the object of that perceptual knowledge).

(If it is assumed that) it reveals a multiplicity of objects, then the knowledge of one single substance cannot belong to such a multiplicity of objects. The self-contradictory knowledge, viz. "this is a single substance" in respect of a multiplicity of objects is never observed.

Sūtra 36: (Objection) (In spite of there being nothing called the whole) we have the perception of the (aggregate of atoms) like (the perception of) the army or the forest. (Answer) This is not possible, because atoms are (intrinsically) imperceptible. (ii.1.36)

Bhāṣya: (Objection) Just as in the case of the army-units (viz. the elephant-riders, cavalry, charioteers and infantry) and in the case of the forest-units (viz. the groups of trees constituting the forest), where the perception of individual differences is not possible due to distance, we have knowledge in the form: "this is one" (viz. "this is *an* army" and "this is *a* forest"). Similarly, when the atoms are collected together and the individual difference of each is not perceived, we have the apprehension in the form: "this is a single object."

(Answer) The individual differences of the army-units and forest-units are not perceived from a distance because of the presence of some special cause; nevertheless the individual differences of these are perceived (in the absence of the specific cause preventing their perception). For example, in the case of the forest, though the differences among the species are perceptible, these are not perceived as *palāśa* or *khadira** from a distance. Similarly, (in the case of the individual trees) though the movements (of leaves and branches) are perceptible, yet these are not perceived from a distance. Thus, there is 'the wrong perception that this is one' only in objects (intrinsically) perceptible when their individual differences are not perceived (due to some specific cause, viz. distance). But there can be no such wrong perception in the case of the atoms as: "this is one." Because the atoms are intrinsically imperceptible, (though the objector wrongly claims) that the individual differences of these are unperceived simply because of the presence of some specific cause.

The question being examined is: Is the aggregate of the atoms the real object of the 'knowledge of oneness in a thing' or is it not so? (The objector may claim) that the army-units and the forest-units are nothing but aggregates of atoms. (Our answer is) that it is illogical to cite as an instance a phenomenon under investigation, 'because it is yet to be proved'. (The objector may claim), it is an observed fact. (We answer) No; because its object is to be critically established. Even though you consider that because of the non-awareness of individual differences, the army-units and forest-units are found to be apprehended as single units and that the observed fact cannot be denied—still the case is not so, because its (*i.e.* of the knowledge) object is to be critically established. The nature of the object of what is observed is being examined. (That is, the real implication of) 'the knowledge of oneness in a thing' is being examined. The mere knowledge (of oneness in an object) cannot prove either of the alternatives, namely, that the object of that knowledge is an independent entity or that it is an aggregate of atoms.

* These are particular kinds of trees.—Ed.

Again, because of the multiplicity of the atoms and moreover because of the absence of the knowledge of individual differences, their apprehension as one single entity is the knowledge of something as something else, like the knowledge of a person in a pillar. (Objection) So what? (Answer) Since the knowledge of something as something else (*i.e.* erroneous or secondary knowledge) presupposes a primary knowledge (*i.e.* the knowledge of something as it is = valid knowledge), it (*i.e.* the erroneous knowledge of something as something else) proves the existence of the primary knowledge. In the case of the knowledge of a person in a pillar, which is the primary knowledge? The knowledge of the person as the person; only when there is such a primary knowledge, there can be (the secondary or erroneous) knowledge of a person in a pillar from the apprehension of the similarity (of the pillar) with a person. Similarly, the (secondary or erroneous) knowledge of oneness in a multiplicity of objects (*i.e.* in the atoms) is possible from the apprehension of oneness only when there is the primary knowledge (of oneness). But this primary knowledge is not possible (in the Buddhist view), because of the absurdity of the non-awareness of everything. Therefore, this perception of non-difference in the form "this is one," is actually a perception of a single object (*i.e.* of the whole). . . .

Critical Examination of the Instruments of Knowledge in General

The terms *pramāṇa* and *prameya** may coexist (*i.e.* may be inter-changeable) in the same object, if there is adequate ground for using the terms (inter-changeably). And the grounds for using the terms are (as follows): *pramāṇa* is that which produces knowledge and *prameya* is that which becomes the object of knowledge. In the event of an object of knowledge becoming instrumental in producing the knowledge of something else, the same object is termed both a *pramāṇa* and a *prameya*. To convey this implication is said the following—

Sūtra 16: Just as the 'measuring instrument' (which usually has the status of a *pramāṇa*) can be a *prameya* as well (*i.e.* when its own accuracy is subject to investigation). (ii.1.16)

Bhāṣya: The measuring instrument is a *pramāṇa* when it gives the knowledge of correct weight. The objects of knowledge, in this case, are gold etc. which have weight. If however the accuracy of another measuring instrument is determined by gold etc., then for the knowledge of the other measuring instrument, gold etc. are *pramāṇa*-s. And the other measuring instrument is a *prameya*. Similarly are to be understood all the categories enumerated (in *Nyāya-sūtra* i.1.1.). Thus the self is mentioned in the list of *prameya*-s, because of its being the object of knowledge. It is (also) considered *pramātṛ* (knower), because of its independent role in producing knowledge. Knowledge (*buddhi*) is considered to be a *pramāṇa* when it leads to another knowledge, it is a *prameya* when it is itself the object of another knowledge, it is *pramiti* (right knowledge) when it is neither of the two (*i.e.* neither a *pramāṇa* nor a *prameya*). In this way, the assemblage of different epithets in the same category is to be understood.

Sūtra 19: . . . these (*ie.* perception etc.) are apprehended in the same way as the light of a lamp. (ii. 1.19)

Bhāṣya: As for example, the light of the lamp, which is an auxiliary cause of perception, is itself an instrument of knowledge in the perception of the visible objects and it is apprehended over again by another instrument of valid perceptual knowledge, viz. its contact with the eyes. (The lamp) is inferred to be a cause of visual perception, because the presence and absence of the lamp are followed by the presence and absence of visual perception. Further, (the lamp) is known to be (the cause of visual perception) also from verbal testimony. (As it is advised) "the lamp is to be taken up in darkness." In this way, perception etc. are apprehended by perception etc. as is observed in actual cases. . . .

* "Means of knowledge" and "object of knowledge," respectively.—Ed.

UDAYANA

Proofs of the Existence of God

From Udayana's Nyàyakusumañjalī. Translated by José Pereira, Hindu Theology, A Reader. *New York: Doubleday, 1976.)*

I. The Seven Ways

From (1) effects, (2) atomic combinations, (3) the suspension and other states of the world, (4) the existence of human skills, (5) the existence of authoritative knowledge, (6) the existence of Revelation and (7) the numerical combination of atoms —from all these we can prove the existence of the all-knowing, imperishable God.

1. *Argument from effects*
   Things like the earth must have a cause.
   Because they are effects.
   Like a pot.
   By having a cause I mean active production by someone possessed of the intent to produce, and a direct knowledge concerning the matter from which the production is to be.
2. *Argument from atomic combinations*
   [The world, it must be remembered, is a combination of atoms, in different degrees of complexity.] Combination is an action, and hence an action occurring at the beginning of creation that brings about the bonding of two atoms, thus originating a dyad. Such a combination is always consequent on the activity of a conscious agent.
   Because it is action.
   As, for instance, the action of our bodies.
3. *Argument from the suspension of the world*
   The world is supported by an active being which impedes it from falling.
   Because it has the character of something suspended.
   Like a twig held in the air by a bird.
   By "*suspension*" I mean the absence of falling in things that possess weight. When I say "the suspension and *other states* of the world," I mean destruction. For the world is destructible by an active being; because its nature is destructible; like that of a torn cloth.
4. *Argument from the existence of human skills* . . . or the arts of life.
   Traditional arts, like weaving, need to be launched by an independent person.
   Because of their character as human usages.
   Like modern writing and such other usages.
5. *Argument from the existence of authoritative knowledge.* Authoritative knowledge, that is, knowledge through authoritative norms.
   The knowledge produced by the Veda is due to positive qualities in the cause of that knowledge.
   Because of its character as normative knowledge.
   As in a norm such as experience.
6. *Arguments from the existence of Revelation.* Revelation, that is to say, the Veda.
   a. The Veda is personally originant.
   Because of its capacity to instruct [instruction being conveyed through one person dialoguing with another].
   Like the Veda of medicine [which all accept to have been humanly, or personally, produced].
   b. Again, the Veda is personally originant.
   Because it is composed of sentences.
   Like the *Mahābhārata* [epic of the Great Indian War].
   c. And the Veda's sentences are personally originant.
   Because they are sentences.
   Like our own sentences.
7. *Argument from numerical augmentation*
   [Physical objects, which have measure, are produced from combinations of atoms, beginning with the dyads. But atoms themselves have no measure. How then do dyads? For the following reasons:]

a. A dyad's measure is produced by *number.*

Because, though not produced through the aggregation of measures, it still remains a *produced* measure.

As, for instance [of pot sections of equal size], the measure of a pot composed of three sections is greater than that of a pot composed of two such sections [the former's greater size thus being due to number alone].

b. An atomic measure does not produce measure.

Because its measure is eternal [and hence incapable of the temporal change that all production entails]; or because its measure is infinitesimal.

In this way, at the beginning of creation, the dual number—the reason for the dyad's measure—needs to be implanted in atoms. [According to the tenets of our combined Logicist-Atomist system, things exist singly, or monadically, and can be combined only by a faculty that reduces these monads to unity and order—the Methodizing Mind]. The combination cannot have been produced at that [primordial] time by the Methodizing Mind of beings like ourselves [then nonexistent]. Hence there exists such a Mind coeval with that time, that is to say, God's.

Finally, by the words "the all-knowing, imperishable God," I mean that the quality of imperishableness belongs to Him essentially [and is inconceivable apart]. It is certain then that an everlasting knowledge embracing all things exists.

II. Five Objections to the Argument from Effects

"There are five fallacies in your inferent sign, 'effectness.'

a. Causality is qualified by corporeity. [A cause always has a body; the body is thus the qualifier and the cause the qualified.] To negate the qualifier is to negate the qualified. [You deny that God is corporeal: so you must deny that He is a cause.]

b. And there is the counter-syllogism [that serves to neutralize your argument]:

There is no production by a cause [in the case of things like the earth].

Because the invariable concomitance between 'production by a cause' and 'production by a body' is there lacking.

c. 'The cause is always corporeal'—here is a concomitance that counters yours [that 'effects always have causes'].

d. From a concomitance unfolded by the perception of things as they are, we infer that a cause is corporeal [for experience shows us that causes always have bodies]. In your argument, however, the inherence of the inferent sign 'effectness' in the subject 'the earth,' does not serve to prove the inferendum ["God"] as qualified by incorporeity. There is, besides, a contradiction between qualifier [incorporeity] and qualified [the cause, always perceived as corporeal].

e. We can also introduce into your argument a vitiating contingency [a contingency which invalidates the concomitance, basic to your whole argument, between your inferent sign 'effectness' and your inferendum 'cause.' It is as if you were to assume the concomitance between fire and smoke, and argue that 'The mountain is smoky, because it has fire.' But the concomitance is vitiated by the contingency of wet fuel, and I could contend that 'The mountain is smoky, because it has wet fuel']. Here this vitiating contingency is 'being produced by a body' [and the argument could be presented thus: 'Things like the earth must have a cause, because they are produced by a body']. But then your concomitance between effect and causality [the causality of an incorporeal being] would be inconclusive."

III. Reply to Objections

Our argument is not invalidated, because of the efficacity of its inferent sign; and it is not contraposed, because of the feebleness of the disproofs. But whether demonstrative or not, our reasoning is free of contradiction, and its inconclusiveness is baselessly alleged.

a. The negation of corporeity, the qualifier, in God, the subject qualified, does not imply negation of causality. Without knowledge about the subject, there cannot be knowledge about what the subject lacks. [God, the subject, is as you say not known: so it cannot be known whether He has a body.] Greater cogency has that effectness which both demonstrates the existence of the qualified subject and generates a knowledge of it, since it is a reason we are all constrained to recognize. Our argument is also not overridden by your syllogism "God is not a cause, because He has no body."

b. "Things like the earth have no cause, because they are not produced by a body." This is not a valid contraposition to our argument because, for the purposes of a countersyllogism, the qualification "body" has no probative relevance. [It is as if you argued: "The mountain is fiery, because it has golden-colored smoke." Smoke and fire are concomitant; the color qualifying the smoke is immaterial.] So qualified, your concomitant [between no production by cause and no production by body] is inconclusive; so your disproof is feeble.

c. As for your third objection, the effect-cause concomitance has the greater cogency, because of the inherence of the inferent sign "effectness" in the subject "earth," and because of the presence of reasons precluding all instances to the contrary [as there are no effects ever devoid of causes]. To this your own postulated concomitance "the cause is always corporeal" is too feeble to be a contrapositive.

d. As for your fourth objection [contradiction], the inherence of the inferent sign "effectness" in the subject "earth" either entails the incorporeity of the cause, in which case there cannot be contradiction, as the correlation between causality and incorporeity has been recognized; or it does not, in which case there can be no contradiction either, as there is no subject to which the contradiction can be predicated.

e. As for your fifth objection, since our argument has reasons preclusive of contrary instances, there cannot be any inconclusiveness in the shape of ignorance occasioned by their absence. Neither is there the inconclusiveness of concomitance [between cause and effect]. The vitiating contingency "being produced by a body," unable as it is to preclude contrary instances [such as God] can be disregarded.

IV. Harmony Between Faith and Reason

"If God is a cause, He must be corporeal. Thus we are confronted with adversative reasoning and the absence of supportive proof."

To this I say: the flawed reasoning of some thinkers has only the semblance of logic, and so is no refutation at all. But the supportive reasoning from the absence of effects [resulting from absence of causes] is our own position's enhancement.

The adversative arguments, supposing God as unproved, are devoid of a subject [to which they can predicate corporeity, in which the main force of their reasoning lies]. Hence they have only the semblance of logic. On the other hand "There is no effect without a cause"—such a reasoning is an enhancement: in other words, efficacious.

Our view is supported by Sacred Tradition too:

> I am the source of all: all things evolve from Me.
> The wise know this, and filled with emotion worship Me.*

[And as the sage Manu says:]

> A man who determines the sages' teachings on the Law through a logic not discordant with Revelation and the sacred sciences, only he, no other, knows that Law.†

These words evince the greater cogency of Sacred Tradition when reinforced by logic.

* *Gītā* 8.10.

† *Mānava Dharma Śāstra* 12.106.

GAṄGEŚA

from *The Jewel of Thought about Reality (Tattvacintāmaṇi)*

From Gaṅgeśa's Tattvacintāmaṇi, *edited by N. S. Ramanuja Tatacharya, Volume II, Part I, anumāna-khaṇḍa (Tirupati: Sanskrit Vidyapeetha, 1973), pp. 192–201.*

Context: Gaṅgeśa has argued that indirect proof, which is said to be one way to grasp an inference-grounding pervasion (e.g., between smoke and fire), is itself grounded in a grasping of a pervasion. The translation begins with an imaginary opponent expressing an objection to this view. Later, a historical opponent of Nyāya, the Vedāntin Śrīharṣa (see the Vedānta section), is quoted and refuted by Gaṅgeśa.

Objection: Since indirect proof is itself grounded in the grasping of a pervasion, there would be an infinite regress (on your view).

Gaṅgeśa: No. Indirect proof is appropriately pursued only so long as there is doubt. Where there would be pragmatic contradiction (i.e., speech or other behavior contradicting the negation of the thesis to be established)—and indeed no doubt occurring—one can grasp the pervasion without resorting to indirect proof.

As an example, consider the particular doubt (against the indirect proof I earlier said demolishes doubt about concomitance of smoke with fire). If smoke is not produced from a set of causes excluding fire, then (in conformity with the doubt about the concomitance) *smoke*—if it were not produced from a causal complex including fire—*would not be produced* (a conclusion in contradiction, presumably, with the doubter's belief that smoke is produced). Now the doubt (against this indirect proof): Could the smoke come to be from something that is not fire? Or could it arise, just in some instances, without fire? Or could it come to be simply by chance (*ahetuka*, without a cause)?

Were a person P, who has ascertained thoroughgoing positive correlations (*x* wherever *y*) and negative correlations (wherever no *y*, no *x*), to doubt that an effect might arise without a cause then—to take up the example of smoke and fire—why should P regularly, as he does, resort to fire for smoke (in the case, say, of a desire to get rid of mosquitoes)? (Similarly), to food to allay hunger, and to speech to communicate to another person?

For (there would be a presupposition to P's doubt, namely) that without the one the other is possible. Therefore, just the resorting to this and that (i.e., the causes of the desired effects) blocks and terminates (*pratibandhaka*) such a doubt.

When there is doubt, there is no regular pattern of behavior (with respect to using *x* to bring about *y*). When there is (such) a regular pattern, doubt does not occur.

Thus it has been said (by Udayana): "That is doubted concerning which as doubted there occurs no contradiction with the doubter's action."

For it is not possible at once to resort regularly to fire and the like for smoke and the like and to doubt that fire causes it (it would be meaningless behavior). This is how we should understand (Udayana's) saying.

Thus we may reject the argument that contradiction—understood as natural opposition (*virodha*), governing precisely which *x* cannot occur along with precisely which *y* (as horsehood and cowhood in the same individual)—cannot block a vicious infinite regress. It is the doubter's own behavior that proves the lie to the doubt, i.e., that blocks it (*pratibandhaka*).

Therefore, the view Śrīharṣa expresses with the following may be rejected:

> "If there is contradiction, then there is doubt. If none, there is doubt all the more.
>
> Contradiction includes doubt within its borders; how

then can indirect proof be the border (or end) of doubt)?"

For (cognition of contradiction) does not depend on (the occurrence of) doubt. Rather, behavior blocks doubt with whomever.

There is the further difficulty on this (Śrīharṣa's) view that even with experience of (doubt-resolving) particulars (such as of hands and feet with respect to a doubt whether an object in the distance is a post or a person) there would never be cessation of doubt.

Moreover, the indirect proof such as was cited above does not come into play without wide experience of correlation between the terms of the (inference-grounding) pervasion (of the presence of smoke by the presence of fire). . . .

VEDĀNTA

Vedānta is a school of philosophy with distinct branches. The term *vedānta* was originally an epithet for the Upanishads, which are among the oldest texts in Sanskrit, dating to 900 B.C.E. The term later came to designate the philosophical schools that expressly embrace Upanishadic views.

The teaching of the Upanishads centers on questions of theological metaphysics: What is the ultimate reality, what is its nature and relation to the world, and how can it be known? The ultimate reality is called *Brahman,* and all Vedānta is Brahman-centered philosophy.

Brahman—the Absolute by all counts—is thought of by some proponents as God and by others as an impersonal Ground of Being. In all cases, the notion of knowledge or realization of Brahman, i.e., *brahma-vidyā,* is prominent. However, the term does not have the same meaning for Advaita Vedāntins and theists. Advaitins, or Non-Dualists (*advaita* = non-dualism), hold that the self (*ātman*) is in reality nothing other than Brahman and that in the mystical knowledge of Brahman one knows only the One, the Sole True Existent, whose nature is perfect being, consciousness, and bliss. Vedāntin theists, in contrast, hold that the individual and God are meaningfully distinct. Thus they are called Dualists. According to the Dualists, the individual cannot know the Absolute in precisely the fashion that God knows God, for an individual knower is not identical with his or her Creator and Ground.

The history of Vedānta, then, has two tracts, both of which are presented in the selections below. Advaita Vedāntins stress meditation and study of the Upanishads to attain the mystical *summum bonum,* whereas Vedāntic theists stress love and devotion to God.

The selections begin with a hymn from the *Ṛg Veda,* commonly called the Hymn of Creation, in which speculation typical of the Upanishads can be discerned. This is a very old text, possibly dating as far back as 1000 B.C.E. and prior to all but perhaps the very oldest passages of the Upanishads. It is thus a precursor of Upanishadic Brahman-philosophy. Next we have selections from the *Bṛihadāraṇyaka, Chāndogya,* and *Muṇḍaka* Upanishads, which are source texts for both the Advaita and theistic Vedāntin schools. The *Chāndogya* passage is a favorite of Advaitins, but it is especially important for Indian theistic views of creation: God cannot create ex nihilo but emits or manifests the world out of God's own "stuff." Śaṅkara (ca. 700), whose writing follows, is the leading Advaita Vedāntin. The selection is from his commentary on an early systematization of Vedāntic philosophy known as the *Brahma-sūtra;* the commentary is the definitive text for classical Advaita. There Śaṅkara argues that the appearances of our world are a fundamental illusion—only Brahman is real.

In the later classical period, a dialectical Advaita Vedānta also emerges. Advaitin skeptics offer Nāgārjuna-like arguments against the realism of Nyāya. The selection below from Śrīharṣa (ca. 1150) is an example. Śrīharṣa is intent on showing the incoherence of the Naiyāyika concept of difference, an incoherence he apparently believes is necessitated by Brahman as the one and omnipresent reality. By thinking of things—e.g., a pot and a cloth—as fundamentally distinct as opposed to appearances or manifestations of the Nondual One, we are led into paradox.

In later classical times, the Vedāntic theistic notion of *bhakti*, love and devotion to God, effloresces, along with correlate conceptions such as the idea that the world is God's play (*līlā*). As we see in the selection from Rūpa Gosvāmī (ca. 1500), Vedāntic theists conceive of the supreme personal good as an act of spiritual lovemaking.

Vedānta stretches beyond the classical age through the resilience not only of the classical philosophies but of folk traditions centered on a *guru*, a spiritual teacher with disciples. Indeed, all the Indian world views propounding a goal of mystic self-transformation grew up within traditions marked by the prominence of a guru. Within Hinduism, each guru fashions his or her own heritage from the wealth of spiritual literature preserved through the ages. Thus such moderns as Swami Vivekananda (1863–1902) and Sri Aurobindo (1872–1950) are so-called folk Vedāntins. They have no strict allegiance to a school of classical philosophy, although they draw on the Upanishads and other works influenced by Vedāntic conceptions. Vivekananda and Aurobindo are sometimes also referred to as neo-Vedāntins. Both learned Sanskrit, but both write in English.

In the selections below, Vivekananda defends Vedānta as the plastic philosophy of Hinduism, and Aurobindo articulates a conception of Brahman he sees as suited for modern times—a Brahman-centered philosophy that is attuned to science yet provides a deep explanation of which science, he argues, is incapable. In the writings of both these folk Vedāntins, mystical strains of the Upanishads can be heard. Vivekananda is the great popularizer of Vedānta to the West; the passages selected are addresses to the Parliament of World Religions in Chicago in 1893. Aurobindo is the premier Indian philosopher of the twentieth century. Although, like Vivekananda, Aurobindo was a yogin and spiritual teacher as well as a nonacademic, he presents a philosophy that is far more systematic than Vivekananda's and shows more Western influence. (Aurobindo has been counted an early twentieth-century British philosopher; he attended Cambridge University and other schools in England for fourteen years.) Among professional academics in India in the modern period, there are many other neo-Vedāntins, Advaitins in particular. Some are first-class philosophers and present much more professional argumentation than either Vivekananda or Aurobindo. Aurobindo's world view is most notable chiefly for its originality; Vivekananda's speeches for the depths of the Hindu culture they plumb.

from the *Ṛg Veda*

Hymns from the Ṛg Veda. *Translated by A. A. Macdonell. (London: Oxford University Press, 1922.)*

HYMN OF CREATION

1. Non-being then existed not nor being:
   There was no air, nor sky that is beyond it.
   What was concealed? Wherein? In whose
   protection?
   And was there deep unfathomable water?
2. Death then existed not nor life immortal;
   Of neither night nor day was any token.
   By its inherent force the One breathed
   windless:
   No other thing than that beyond existed.
3. Darkness there was at first by darkness hidden;
   Without distinctive marks, this all was water.
   That which, becoming, by the void was
   covered,
   That One by force of heat came into being.
4. Desire entered the One in the beginning:
   It was the earliest seed, of thought the product.
   The sages searching in their hearts with
   wisdom,
   Found out the bond of being in non-being.
5. Their ray extended light across the darkness:
   But was the One above or was it under?
   Creative force was there, and fertile power:
   Below was energy, above was impulse.
6. Who knows for certain? Who shall here
   declare it?
   Whence was it born, and whence came this
   creation?
   The gods were born after this world's creation:
   Then who can know from whence it has
   arisen?
7. None knoweth whence creation has arisen;
   And whether he has or has not produced it:
   He who surveys it in the highest heaven,
   He only knows, or haply he may know not.

---

from the *Bṛhadāraṇyaka Upanishad*

From The Thirteen Principal Upanishads, *translated by E. Hume (London: Oxford, 1931).*

CHAPTER 4 / THE THEORETICAL UNKNOWABILITY OF THE IMMANENT BRAHMAN*

* "Brahma," in this translation. Translation is altered to "Brahman" throughout all selections from the Upanishads.—ED.

1. Then Ushasta Cākrāyaṇa questioned him. "Yājñavalkya," said he, "explain to me him who is the Brahman present and not beyond our ken, him who is the Soul in all things."

"He is your soul (*ātman*), which is in all things."

"Which one, O Yājñavalkya, is in all things?"

"He who breathes in with your breathing in (*prāṇa*) is the Soul of yours, which is in all things. He who breathes out with your breathing out (*apāna*) is the Soul of yours, which is in all things. He who breathes about with your breathing about (*vyāna*) is the Soul of yours, which is in all things. He who breathes up with your breathing up (*udāna*) is the Soul of yours, which is in all things. He is your soul, which is in all things."

2. Ushasta Cākrāyaṇa said: "This has been explained to me just as one might say, 'This is a cow. This is a horse.' Explain to me him who is just the Brahman present and not beyond our ken, him who is the Soul in all things."

"He is your soul, which is in all things."

"Which one, O Yājñavalkya, is in all things?"

"You could not see the seer of seeing.
You could not hear the hearer of hearing.
You could not think the thinker of thinking.
You could not understand the understander of understanding. He is your soul, which is in all things. Aught else than Him [or, than this] is wretched."

Thereupon Ushasta Cākrāyaṇa held his peace.

CHAPTER 5 / THE PRACTICAL WAY OF KNOWING BRAHMAN — BY RENUNCIATION

Now Kahola Kaushītakeya questioned him. "Yājñavalkya," said he, "explain to me him who is just the Brahman present and not beyond our ken, him who is the Soul in all things."

"He is your soul, which is in all things."

"Which one, O Yājñavalkya, is in all things?"

"He who passes beyond hunger and thirst, beyond sorrow and delusion, beyond old age and death—Brahmins* who know such a Soul overcome desire for sons, desire for wealth, desire for worlds, and live the life of mendicants. For desire for sons is desire for wealth, and desire for wealth is desire for worlds, for both these are merely desires. Therefore let a Brahmin become disgusted with learning and desire to live as a child. When he has become disgusted both with the state of childhood and with learning, then he becomes an ascetic (*muni*). When he has become disgusted both with the non-ascetic state and with the ascetic state, then he becomes a Brahmin."

"By what means would he become a Brahmin?"

"By that means by which he does become such a one. Aught else than this Soul (*Ātman*) is wretched."

Thereupon Kahola Kaushītakeya held his peace.

* "Brahmans," in this translation. Translation altered to "Brahmin" throughout all selections from the Upanishads.—Ed.

CHAPTER 6 / THE REGRESSUS TO BRAHMAN, THE ULTIMATE WORLD-GROUND

Then Gārgī Vācaknavī questioned him. "Yājñavalkya," said she, "since all this world is woven, warp and woof, on water, on what, pray, is the water woven, warp and woof?"

"On wind, O Gārgī."

"On what then, pray, is the wind woven, warp and woof?"

"On the atmosphere-worlds, O Gārgī."

"On what then, pray, are the atmosphere-worlds woven, warp and woof?"

"On the worlds of the Gandharvas*, O Gārgī."

"On what then, pray, are the worlds of the Gandharvas woven, warp and woof?"

"On the worlds of the sun, O Gārgī."

"On what then, pray, are the worlds of the sun woven, warp and woof?"

"On the worlds of the moon, O Gārgī."

"On what then, pray, are the worlds of the moon woven, warp and woof?"

"On the worlds of the stars, O Gārgī."

"On what then, pray, are the worlds of the stars woven, warp and woof?"

"On the worlds of the gods, O Gārgī."

"On what then, pray, are the worlds of the gods woven, warp and woof?"

"On the worlds of Indra, O Gārgī."

"On what then, pray, are the worlds of Indra woven, warp and woof?"

"On the worlds of Prajāpati, O Gārgī."

* Heavenly musicians.—Ed.

"On what then, pray, are the worlds of Prajāpati woven, warp and woof?"

"On the worlds of Brahman, O Gārgī."

"On what then, pray, are the worlds of Brahman woven, warp and woof?"

Yājñavalkya said: "Gārgī, do not question too much, lest your head fall off. In truth, you are questioning too much about a divinity about which further questions cannot be asked. Gārgī, do not over-question."

Thereupon Gārgī Vācaknavī held her peace.

CHAPTER 7 / WIND, THE STRING HOLDING THE WORLD TOGETHER; THE IMMORTAL IMMANENT SOUL, THE INNER CONTROLLER

1. Then Uddālaka Āruṇi questioned him. "Yājñavalkya," said he, "we were dwelling among the Madras in the house of Patañcala Kāpya, studying the sacrifice. He had a wife possessed by a spirit (*gandharva*). We asked him: 'Who are you?' He said: 'I am Kabandha Ātharvaṇa.' He said to Patañcala Kāpya and to us students of the sacrifice: 'Do you know, O Kāpya, that thread by which this world and the other world and all things are tied together?' Patañcala Kāpya said: 'I do not know it, sir.' He said to Patañcala Kāpya and to us students of the sacrifice: 'Pray do you know, O Kāpya, that Inner Controller who from within controls this world and the other world and all things?' Patañcala Kāpya said: 'I do not know him, sir.' He said to Patañcala Kāpya and to us students of the sacrifice: 'Verily, Kāpya, he who knows that thread and the so-called Inner Controller knows Brahman, he knows the worlds, he knows the gods, he knows the Vedas, he knows created things, he knows the Soul, he knows everything.' Thus he [i.e. the spirit] explained it to them. And I know it. If you, O Yājñavalkya, drive away the Brahma-cows without knowing that thread and the Inner Controller, your head will fall off."

   "Verily, I know that thread and the Inner Controller, O Gautama."

   "Anyone might say "I know, I know." Do you tell what you know."
2. He [i.e. Yājñavalkya] said: "Wind, verily, O Gautama, is that thread. By wind, verily, O Gautama, as by a thread, this world and the other world and all things are tied together. Therefore, verily, O Gautama, they say of a deceased person, 'His limbs become unstrung,' for by wind, O Gautama, as by a thread, they are strung together."

   "Quite so, O Yājñavalkya. Declare the Inner Controller."
3. "He who, dwelling in the earth, yet is other than the earth, whom the earth does not know, whose body the earth is, who controls the earth from within—He is your Soul, the Inner Controller, the Immortal.
4. He who, dwelling in the waters, yet is other than the waters, whom the waters do not know, whose body the waters are, who controls the waters from within—He is your Soul, the Inner Controller, the Immortal.
5. He who, dwelling in the fire, yet is other than the fire, whom the fire does not know, whose body the fire is, who controls the fire from within—He is your Soul, the Inner Controller, the Immortal.
6. He who, dwelling in the atmosphere, yet is other than the atmosphere, whom the atmosphere does not know, whose body the atmosphere is, who controls the atmosphere from within—He is your Soul, the Inner Controller, the Immortal.
7. He who, dwelling in the wind, yet is other than the wind, whom the wind does not know, whose body the wind is, who controls the wind from within—He is your Soul, the Inner Controller, the Immortal.
8. He who, dwelling in the sky, yet is other than the sky, whom the sky does not know, whose body the sky is, who controls the sky from within—He is your Soul, the Inner Controller, the Immortal.
9. He who, dwelling in the sun, yet is other than the sun, whom the sun does not know, whose body the sun is, who controls the sun from

within—He is your Soul, the Inner Controller, the Immortal.

10. He who, dwelling in the quarters of heaven, yet is other than the quarters of heaven, whom the quarters of heaven do not know, whose body the quarters of heaven are, who controls the quarters of heaven from within—He is your Soul, the Inner Controller, the Immortal.
11. He who, dwelling in the moon and stars, yet is other than the moon and stars, whom the moon and stars do not know, whose body the moon and stars are, who controls the moon and stars from within—He is your Soul, the Inner Controller, the Immortal.
12. He who, dwelling in space, yet is other than space, whom space does not know, whose body space is, who controls space from within—He is your Soul, the Inner Controller, the Immortal.
13. He who, dwelling in the darkness, yet is other than the darkness, whom the darkness does not know, whose body the darkness is, who controls the darkness from within—He is your Soul, the Inner Controller, the Immortal.
14. He who, dwelling in the light, yet is other than the light, whom the light does not know, whose body the light is, who controls the light from within—He is your Soul, the Inner Controller, the Immortal.

    —Thus far with reference to the divinities. Now with reference to material existence (*adhi-bhūta*).—

15. He who, dwelling in all things, yet is other than all things, whom all things do not know, whose body all things are, who controls all things from within—He is your Soul, the Inner Controller, the Immortal.

    —Thus far with reference to material existence. Now with reference to the self.—

16. He who, dwelling in breath, yet is other than breath, whom the breath does not know, whose body the breath is, who controls the breath from within—He is your Soul, the Inner Controller, the Immortal.
17. He who, dwelling in speech, yet is other than speech, whom the speech does not know, whose body the speech is, who controls the speech from within—He is your Soul, the Inner Controller, the Immortal.
18. He who, dwelling in the eye, yet is other than the eye, whom the eye does not know, whose body the eye is, who controls the eye from within—He is your Soul, the Inner Controller, the Immortal.
19. He who, dwelling in the ear, yet is other than the ear, whom the ear does not know, whose body the ear is, who controls the ear from within—He is your Soul, the Inner Controller, the Immortal.
20. He who, dwelling in the mind, yet is other than the mind, whom the mind does not know, whose body the mind is, who controls the mind from within—He is your Soul, the Inner Controller, the Immortal.
21. He who, dwelling in the skin, yet is other than the skin, whom the skin does not know, whose body the skin is, who controls the skin from within—He is your Soul, the Inner Controller, the Immortal.
22. He who, dwelling in the understanding, yet is other than the understanding, whom the understanding does not know, whose body the understanding is, who controls the understanding from within—He is your Soul, the Inner Controller, the Immortal.
23. He who, dwelling in the semen, yet is other than the semen, whom the semen does not know, whose body the semen is, who controls the semen from within—He is your Soul, the Inner Controller, the Immortal.

    He is the unseen Seer, the unheard Hearer, the unthought Thinker, the ununderstood Understander. Other than He there is no seer. Other than He there is no hearer. Other than He there is no thinker. Other than He there is no understander. He is your Soul, the Inner Controller, the Immortal."

Thereupon Uddālaka Āruṇi held his peace.

from the *Chāndogya Upanishad*

From The Thirteen Principal Upanishads, *translated by E. Hume (London: Oxford, 1931).*

CHAPTER 6 / THE INSTRUCTION OF ŚVETAKETU BY UDDĀLAKA CONCERNING THE KEY TO ALL KNOWLEDGE

1. *Om*! Now, there was Śvetaketu Āruṇeya. To him his father said: "Live the life of a student of sacred knowledge. Verily, my dear, from our family there is no one unlearned [in the Vedas], a Brahmin by connection, as it were."
2. He then, having become a pupil at the age of twelve, having studied all the Vedas, returned at the age of twenty-four, conceited, thinking himself learned, proud.
3. Then his father said to him: "Śvetaketu, my dear, since now you are conceited, think yourself learned, and are proud, did you also ask for that teaching whereby what has not been heard of becomes heard of, what has not been thought of becomes thought of, what has not been understood becomes understood?"
4. "How, pray, sir, is that teaching?"
   "Just as, my dear, by one piece of clay everything made of clay may be known—the modification is merely a verbal distinction, a name; the reality is just 'clay'—
5. Just as, my dear, by one copper ornament everything made of copper may be known—the modification is merely a verbal distinction, a name; the reality is just 'copper'—
6. Just as, my dear, by one nail-scissors everything made of iron may be known—the modification is merely a verbal distinction, a name; the reality is just 'iron'—so, my dear, is that teaching."
7. "Verily, those honored men did not know this; for, if they had known it, why would they not have told me? But do you, sir, tell me it."
   "So be it, my dear," said he.

CHAPTER 6.2

1. "In the beginning, my dear, this world was just Being (*sat*), one only, without a second. To be sure, some people say: 'In the beginning this world was just Non-being (*a-sat*), one only, without a second; from that Non-being Being was produced.'
2. But verily, my dear, whence could this be?" said he. "How from Non-being could Being be produced? On the contrary, my dear, in the beginning this world was just Being, one only, without a second. . . ."

from the *Muṇḍaka Upanishad*

From The Thirteen Principal Upanishads, *translated by E. Hume (London: Oxford, 1931).*

CHAPTER 2.2

The All-Inclusive Brahman

1. Manifest, [yet] hidden; called "Moving-in-secret";
The great abode! Therein is placed that
Which moves and breathes and winks.
What that is, know as Being (*sad*) and Non-being (*a-sad*),
As the object of desire, higher than understanding,
As what is the best of creatures!

2. That which is flaming, which is subtler than the subtle,
On which the worlds are set, and their inhabitants—
That is the imperishable Brahman.
It is life (*prāṇa*), and It is speech and mind.
That is the real. It is immortal.
It is [a mark] to be penetrated. Penetrate It, my friend!

A Target to Be Penetrated by Meditation on "Om"

3. Taking as a bow the great weapon of the Upanishad,
One should put upon it an arrow sharpened by meditation.
Stretching it with a thought directed to the essence of That,
Penetrate that Imperishable as the mark, my friend.

4. The mystic syllable *Om* (*praṇava*) is the bow.
The arrow is the soul (*ātman*).
Brahma is said to be the mark (*lakṣya*).
By the undistracted man is It to be penetrated.
One should come to be in It, as the arrow [in the mark].

The Immortal Soul, the One Warp of the World and of the Individual

5. He on whom the sky, the earth, and the atmosphere
Are woven, and the mind, together with all the life-breaths (*prāṇa*),
Him alone know as the one Soul (Ātman).
Other words dismiss. He is the bridge to immortality.

The Great Soul to Be Found in the Heart

6. Where the channels are brought together
Like the spokes in the hub of a wheel—
Therein he moves about,
Becoming manifold.

Om!—Thus meditate upon the Soul (Ātman). Success to you in crossing to the farther shore beyond darkness!

7. He who is all-knowing, all-wise,
Whose is this greatness on the earth—
He is in the divine Brahman city
And in the heaven established! The Soul (Ātman)!
Consisting of mind, leader of the life-breaths and of the body,
He is established on food, controlling the heart.
By this knowledge the wise perceive
The blissful Immortal that gleams forth.

Deliverance Gained through Vision of Him

8. The knot of the heart is loosened,
All doubts are cut off,
And one's deeds (*karman*) cease
When He is seen—both the higher and the lower.

The Self-Luminous Light of the World

9. In the highest golden sheath
Is Brahman without stain, without parts.
Brilliant is It, the light of lights—
That which knowers of the Soul (Ātman) do know!

10. The sun shines not there, nor the moon and stars;
These lightnings shine not, much less this [earthy] fire!
After Him, as He shines, doth everything shine.
This whole world is illumined with His light.

The Omnipresent Brahman

11. Brahman, indeed, is this immortal Brahman before,
Brahman behind, to right and to left.
Stretched forth below and above,
Brahman, indeed, is this whole world, this widest extent.

ŚAṄKARA

from *Brahmasūtra Commentary*

The Vedanta Sūtras of Bādarāyaṇa. Translated by George Thibant. (Sacred Books of the East, 1890.)

CHAPTER 1.1

It is a matter not requiring any proof that the object and the subject[1] whose respective spheres are the notion of the 'Thou' (the Non-Ego[2]) and the 'Ego', and which are opposed to each other as much as darkness and light are, cannot be identified. All the less can their respective attributes be identified. Hence it follows that it is wrong to superimpose[3] upon the subject—whose Self is intelligence, and which has for its sphere the notion of the Ego—the object whose sphere is the notion of the Non-Ego, and the attributes of the object, and vice versa to superimpose the subject and the attributes of the subject on the object. In spite of this it is on the part of man a natural[4] procedure—which has its cause in wrong knowledge—not to distinguish the two entities (object and subject) and their respective attributes, although they are absolutely distinct, but to superimpose upon each the characteristic nature and the attributes of the other, and thus, coupling

[1] The subject is the universal Self whose nature is intelligence; the object comprises whatever is of a non-intelligent nature, viz. bodies with their sense-organs, internal organs, and the objects of the senses, i.e. the external material world.

[2] The object is said to have for its sphere the notion of the 'thou' (yushmat), not the notion of the 'this' or 'that' (idam), in order better to mark its absolute opposition to the subject or Ego. Language allows of the co-ordination of the pronouns of the first and the third person ('It is I,' 'I am he who, ' &c.;) but not of the co-ordination of the pronouns of the first and second person.

[3] Adhyâsa, literally 'superimposition' in the sense of (mistaken) ascription or imputation, to something, of an essential nature or attributes not belonging to it. See later on.

[4] Natural, i.e. original, beginningless; for the modes of speech and action which characterise transmigratory existence have existed, with the latter, from all eternity.

the Real and the Unreal[5], to make use of expressions such as "That am I," "That is mine."[6] But what have we to understand by the term 'superimposition'?—The apparent presentation, in the form of remembrance, to consciousness of something previously observed, in some other things.[7]

Some indeed define the term 'superimposition' as the superimposition of the attributes of one thing on another thing. Others, again, define superimposition as the error founded on the non-apprehension of the difference of that which is superimposed from that on which it is superimposed. Others, again, define it as the fictitious assumption of attributes contrary to the nature of that thing on which something else is superimposed. But all these definitions agree in so far as they represent superimposition as the apparent presentation of the attributes of one thing in another thing. And therewith agrees also the popular view which is exemplified by expressions such as the following: "Mother-of-pearl appears like silver," "The moon although one only appears as if she were double." But how is it possible that on the interior self which itself is not an object there should be superimposed objects and their attributes? For every one superimposes an object only on such other objects as are placed before him (i.e. in contact with his sense-organs), and you have said before that the interior Self which is entirely disconnected from the idea of the Thou (the Non-Ego) is never an object. It is not, we reply, non-object in the absolute sense. For it is the object of the notion of the Ego,[8] and the interior Self is well known to exist on account of its immediate (intuitive) presentation. Nor is it an exceptionless rule that objects can be superimposed only on such other objects as are before us, i.e. in contact with our sense-organs; for non-discerning men superimpose on the ether, which is not the object of sensuous perception, dark-blue colour.

Hence it follows that the assumption of the Non-Self being superimposed on the interior Self is not unreasonable.

This superimposition thus defined, learned men consider to be Nescience (avidyā) and the ascertainment of the true nature of that which is (the Self) by means of the discrimination of that (which is superimposed on the Self), they call knowledge (vidyâ). There being such knowledge (neither the Self nor the Non-Self) are affected in the least by any blemish or (good) quality produced by their mutual superimposition. The mutual superimposition of the Self and the Non-Self, which is termed Nescience, is the presupposition on which there base all the practical distinctions—those made in ordinary life as well as those laid down by the Veda—between means of knowledge, objects of knowledge (and knowing persons), and all scriptural texts, whether they are concerned with injunctions and prohibitions (of meritorious and non-meritorious actions), or with final release—But how can the means of right knowledge such as perception, inference, &c., and scriptural texts have for their object that which is dependent on Nescience?[9]—Because, we reply, the means of right knowledge cannot operate unless there be a knowing personality, and because the existence of the latter depends on the erroneous notion that the body, the senses, and so on, are identical with, or belong to, the Self of the knowing person. For without the employment of the senses, perception and the other means of right knowledge cannot operate. And without a basis (i.e. the body) the senses cannot act. Nor does anybody act by means of a body on which the nature of the Self is not superimposed. Nor can, in the absence of all that[10], the Self which, in its own nature is free from all contact, become a knowing agent. And if there is no knowing agent, the means of right knowledge

[5] I.e. the intelligent Self which is the only reality and the non-real objects, viz. body and so on, which are the product of wrong knowledge.

[6] 'The body, &c. is my Self;' 'sickness, death, children, wealth, &c., belong to my Self.'

[7] Literally "in some other place." . . .

[8] The pratyagâtman ("interior self") is in reality non-object, for it is svayamprakâsa, self-luminous, i.e. the subjective factor in all cognition. But it becomes the object of the idea of the Ego in so far as it is limited, conditioned by its adjuncts which are the product of Nescience, viz. the internal organ, the senses and the subtle and gross bodies, i.e. in so far as it is jîva, individual or personal soul. . . .

[9] It being of course the function of the means of right knowledge to determine Truth and Reality.

[10] I.e. in the absence of the mutual superimposition of the Self and the Non-Self and their attributes.

cannot operate (as said above). Hence perception and the other means of right knowledge, and the Vedic texts have for their object that which is dependent on Nescience. (That human cognitional activity has for its presupposition the superimposition described above), follows also from the non-difference in that respect of men from animals. Animals, when sounds or other sensible qualities affect their sense of hearing or other senses, recede or advance according as the idea derived from the sensation is a comforting or disquieting one. A cow, for instance, when she sees a man approaching with a raised stick in his hand, thinks that he wants to beat her, and therefore moves away; while she walks up to a man who advances with some fresh grass in his hand. Thus men also—who possess a higher intelligence—run away when they see strong fierce-looking fellows drawing near with shouts and brandishing swords; while they confidently approach persons of contrary appearance and behaviour. We thus see that men and animals follow the same course of procedure with reference to the means and objects of knowledge. Now it is well known that the procedure of animals bases on the non-distinction (of Self and Non-Self); we therefore conclude that, as they present the same appearances, men also—although distinguished by superior intelligence—proceed with regard to perception and so on, in the same way as animals do; as long, that is to say, as the mutual superimposition of Self and Non-Self lasts. With reference again to that kind of activity which is founded on the Veda (sacrifices and the like), it is true indeed that the reflecting man who is qualified to enter on it, does so not without knowing that the Self has a relation to another world; yet that qualification does not depend on the knowledge, derivable from the Vedanta-texts, of the true nature of the Self as free from all wants, raised above the distinctions of the Brahmaṇa and Kshattriya-classes and so on, transcending transmigratory existence. For such knowledge is useless and even contradictory to the claim (on the part of sacrificers, &c. to perform certain actions and enjoy their fruits). And before such knowledge of the Self has arisen, the Vedic texts continue in their operation, to have for their object that which is dependent on Nescience. For such texts as the following, "A Brahmaṇa is to sacrifice," are operative only on the supposition that on the Self are superimposed particular conditions such as caste, stage of life, age, outward circumstances, and so on. That by superimposition we have to understand the notion of something in some other thing we have already explained. (The superimposition of the Non-Self will be understood more definitely from the following examples.) Extra-personal attributes are superimposed on the Self, if a man considers himself sound and entire, or the contrary, as long as his wife, children, and so on are sound and entire or not. Attributes of the body are superimposed on the Self, if a man thinks of himself (his Self) as stout, lean, fair, as standing, walking, or jumping. Attributes of the sense-organs, if he thinks "I am mute, or deaf, or one-eyed, or blind." Attributes of the internal organ when he considers himself subject to desire, intention, doubt, determination, and so on. Thus the producer of the notion of the Ego (i.e. the internal organ) is superimposed on the interior Self, which, in reality, is the witness of all the modifications of the internal organ, and vice versa the interior Self, which is the witness of everything, is superimposed on the internal organ, the senses, and so on. In this way there goes on this natural beginningless—and endless-superimposition, which appears in the form of wrong conception, is the cause of individual souls appearing as agents and enjoyers (of the results of their actions), and is observed by every one.

With a view to freeing one's self from that wrong notion which is the cause of all evil and attaining thereby the knowledge of the absolute unity of the Self the study of the Vedanta-texts is begun.

ŚRĪHARṢA

Critique of Difference

From Hindu Theology, A Reader *(New York: Doubleday, 1976).*

Here is another point which deserves scrutiny. The invalidation of the "Identity" Scripture* which you announce—an invalidation that grasps the difference between things, like pots and cloths, through norms, such as experience—in what sort of meaning does it express itself? Does it signify (a) the difference deriving from a thing's *essence,* (b) the *mutual exclusion* of things, (c) *difference in attributes,* or (d) some other factor?

It cannot be (a) the difference deriving from a thing's *essence.* In such a case the essence of the pot and of the cloth will lie in what distinguishes the one from the other—something impossible to conceive unless the one object *implies* the other. For difference is difference *from* something: otherwise to say that "essence is difference" is to make the two terms synonymous. If experience apprehends the essence of a cloth through concepts like "the cloth is different from the pot," then even the pot will be included in the cloth's essence. The difference-grasping experience will really have fathomed the essential identity of pot and cloth, and you will have arrived at a conclusion quite the reverse of what you intended.

"The experience you describe is expressed in terms of non-difference. Perhaps you might consider describing it in terms of difference as well! If pot and cloth were not different, experience would express itself in terms of 'pot' and 'cloth,' and not as 'the cloth is different from the pot.'"

Such a rejoinder could be countenanced if, while upholding absolute non-difference, we were to repudiate the difference rendered extant through Ignorance. Hence a knowledge imperceptive of non-difference is impercipient of difference too. It is then valid only for non-difference, not for difference [its contradictory], for then it would wreck its own foundation.

"Well then, the essence of cloth is unqualified difference. When we add the qualification 'from the pot,' the essence becomes explicated by means of the pot, which is different from it."

This theory is also implausible. A difference devoid of a correlative is beyond the reach of normative knowledge: such a knowledge only operates in instances of correlative-connected difference. What kind of logic is this that the essence of a cloth, intrinsically related to something else, only becomes distinct from it after it has been explicated by it? What is intrinsically blue does not become so only subsequent to its explication by yellow.

If you maintain that difference is the essence of the cloth in so far as it is explicated by its correlative the pot, what, in your opinion, does the correlative character of the pot to this cloth consist in: in its essence, or in some attribute?

If we take the first alternative, then the pot's essence will lie only in its being the cloth's correlative, and the cloth will be included in the pot's essence. To what can all this conclude but to non-difference?

"Well then, supposing unqualified correlativeness to be the pot's essence, the qualification 'to the pot' will be something superadded."

This cannot be maintained either. Normative knowledge has nothing to do with correlatives that correlate with nothing. As for the qualification "to the pot," we shall have to ask ourselves whether it is the pot's essence or attribute, and the same logical flaws will apply.

The second alternative will also not hold. Correlation to the cloth is the pot's attribute, and hence

* The "Identity" Scripture to which Śrīharṣa refers is "Thou Art That" (i.e., Brahman or God) from the Chāndogya Upanishad, 6.8.6.—Ed.

included in its nature; thus pot and cloth will be non-different. And if the cloth becomes the pot's attribute, then, by parity of reasoning, the pot will also become the attribute of the cloth. No other relation is possible to the pot, the correlative of the cloth—and the cloth is itself explicated by its own correlative, the pot: we thus land ourselves in a vicious circle. No norm of knowledge exists which has for its object a pot-intrinsic-to-a-cloth or a cloth-intrinsic-to-a-pot.

Besides, if the attribute and its subject are not connected, the attribute would have unrestricted scope [and anything could have any attribute whatsoever]. If they are connected, each connection will need another, and so on, without limit, and we shall have an infinite regress. If [to avoid this] we postulate an immediate and essential connection, either at the beginning of the regress or later, that essential connection would be present in the very essence of the subject of the connection, and would thus entail non-difference. This argument applies no matter what attributes one postulates. Therefore experience, the norm you employ to establish difference deriving from the essence, really becomes the norm guaranteeing non-difference.

[Śrīharṣa then proceeds, in great detail, to reduce the remaining three alternatives to absurdity by showing them to be mostly variations of the fallacies of circularity and infinite regress.]

RŪPA GOSVĀMĪ

The Mystical Theology of Passion

From Hindu Theology, A Reader *(New York: Doubleday, 1976).*

1. Manifested gloriously among the dwellers of Vraja land is Passion-Souled Devotion, upon which follows the Passion-Sequent.
2. I shall first explain the Passion-Souled variety to ensure a clear comprehension of the Passion-Sequent.

I. Passion-Souled Devotion

3. Passion is a spontaneous and total engrossment in one's chosen deity. Absorbing devotion is here affirmed to be Passion-Souled.
4. This devotion is of two kinds, erotic and associatory.
5. In the seventh canto of the *Bhāgavata,* the sage Nārada tells king Yudhiṣthira: "Many have fixed their minds on the Supreme Lord, through devotion, expressed as passion, hate, fear, affection, have freed themselves of sin and have reached liberation—
6. The cowherdesses through passion, king Kaṁsa through fear, the Cedi princes through hate, the Yādava tribesmen through companionship, you, king Yudhiṣthira, through affection, and I myself through devotion."
7. I have left out fear and hate as being contrary to the agreeable nature of devotion. As affection connotes [passionless] friendship, I have classed it under Injunctional Devotion.
8. Also, when love is only a means to an end, it does not help realize Passion-Souled Devotion. Nārada's words "and I myself through devotion" clearly evince a devotion of an Injunctional kind.
9. If God's enemies and friends are said to have the identical goal, then the Brahman and Kṛṣṇa are one, comparably with a ray and the sun.
10. Viṣṇu's enemies are generally dissolved into the Brahman. Some arrive at a semblance of similarity with him, but subside into the qualityless Brahman bliss.
11. As the *Brahmāṇḍa Purāṇa* says: "Beyond darkness are the worlds of the blessed. There live

the blessed, and the fiends that Viṣṇu killed, immersed in the Brahman-bliss."

12. Sprayed with the nectar of His lotus feet, God's dear devotees, the very embodiments of love, go worshiping Him with intense attachment.
13. In the tenth canto of the *Bhāgavata* the goddesses of Revelation, hymning Kṛṣṇa, exclaim: "The Brahman—Whom the sages worship through firm control of their hidden breaths, their minds and their senses—Your enemies attain through recollection, and Your women through intentiveness on Your pleasure-giving arms lovely like the body of the serpent king. We are alike and share their feelings, absorbing the nectar of Your lotus feet."
14. *Erotic Passion-Souled Devotion.* Next is Passion-Souled Devotion of the erotic kind. Erotic-Souled passion—functioning solely for Kṛṣṇa's delight—is what reduces the appetite for pleasure to a subsistent state.
15. It is among the goddesses of Vraja* that this type of devotion is perpetually refulgent. Their singular love has acquired an unwonted sweetness. Inciting as it does amorous play, the wise call it Eros.
16. As the *Tantra* says: "It is only the love of the cowherds' beautiful wives that has come to be celebrated as passion."
17. So Uddhava and others dear to God have come to envy that love.
18. It is thought that [the hunchback woman] Kubjā's amorous urges are very like the Passion described above.
19. *Associatory Passion-Souled Devotion.* Next is Associatory Passion-Souled Devotion. Associatory Devotion is the belief of oneself as linked with Kṛṣṇa in a relationship like the parental, a relation which the Yādava cowherds, by implication, share. [In their relations with Kṛṣṇa,] the knowledge of His divine sovereignty is absent and Passion predominates.
20. The two types of Passion-Souled Devotion, having pure love as their essence and implanted in Kṛṣṇa's eternal associates, are not discussed here in detail.

II. Passion-Sequent Devotion

21. Passion-Souled Devotion being twofold, Passion-Sequent Devotion is twofold too, and admitted to have two forms—the Erotic-Sequent and the Associatory-Sequent.
22. *Eligibles for Passion-Sequent Devotion.* As for the eligibles of these two types—those burning to experience the emotions of people like the dwellers of Vraja, undeviating in their Passion-Souled love, are eligible for Passion-Sequent Devotion.
23. The rise of this burning desire is discernible when the mind is intent only on hearing of the sweetness of the emotions [and of all else to do with Kṛṣṇa and His associates], and where neither sacred science nor reasoning has any place.
24. The sacred sciences and reasoning are right for those eligible for Injunctional Devotion—until the emotions described manifest themselves.
25. The followers of Passion-Sequent Devotion should live only in Vraja, thinking always of their beloved Kṛṣṇa and of those dear to Him, listening to talk about Him being their only delight.
26. One eager to experience those emotions—as a beginner or as a perfect master—must serve God in accordance with the practice of Vraja's eternal inhabitants.
27. The practices of Injunctional Devotion described above—as listening to recitals of Kṛṣṇa's delights, the celebration of His praises—are also useful here, as the wise should know.
28. *Erotic-Sequent Devotion.* Next is Erotic-Sequent Devotion, an appetite for pleasure patterned on that of Passion-Souled Devotion.
29. It is of two kinds—avidity for the joys of divine sex and of divine amorous feelings.

* A heaven of devotees of Kṛṣṇa; originally, the land of Kṛṣṇa's childhood—Ed.

30. Avidity for the joys of divine sex has lascivious play in mind; avidity for divine amorous feelings is a craze for sweet emotional experience.
31. Those who contemplate the sweetness of His august image, who listen to recitals of His playful exploits and who crave to experience the emotions of the Vraja women—they are the ones eligible for the two kinds of Passion-Sequent Devotion. Men also qualify, as one hears from the *Padma Purāṇa* accounts.
32. In the following one, for instance: "Once all the great ṛṣis [rishis] living in the Daṇḍaka forest saw Viṣṇu incarnate as Rāma and yearned to enjoy His beautiful body.
33. Becoming women, they were all born in Gokula, where they espoused Viṣṇu with passion, becoming thereby saved from the ocean of transmigration."
34. Anyone, desirous of divine sex-play, who serves the Beloved in accordance with the way of Injunctional Devotion only, will become one of Kṛṣṇa's queens in Dvārakā city.
35. As the great *Kūrma Purāṇa* says: "Through ascetic practices the fire-god's sons acquired both womanliness and a husband in Vāsudeva's Son Kṛṣṇa—the increate, the all-pervading, the source of the universe."
36. *Associatory Sequent Devotion*. Next is Associatory Sequent Devotion. It consists, as the wise say, in assuming or imagining oneself in the role of Kṛṣṇa's parent or friend.
37. Aspirants drawn to such emotions as parental tenderness should practice a devotion replicating the feelings of Nanda, the Vraja chieftain [Kṛṣṇa's foster father] and Suvala [Kṛṣṇa's friend].
38. The sacred books tell us of an old carpenter who lived in Hastināpura. On Nārada's advice he worshiped the image of Nanda's Son, with the feelings of a father for his son, and so succeeded in having Kṛṣṇa become his Son in fact.
39. The *Hymn to Nārāyaṇa's Theophanies* says: "Those who always think of Viṣṇu as Husband, Son, Companion, Brother, Father and Friend with alacrity—reverence to them!"
40. Passion-Sequent Devotion is the one which aims only to attain the compassion of Kṛṣṇa and His devotees. Some [like Vallabha] call it the Way of Fullness.

VIVEKANANDA

Addresses at the Parliament of Religions

From Selections from Swami Vivekananda *(Calcutta: Advaita Ashram, 1944).*

Response to Welcome

At the World's Parliament of Religions, Chicago, 11th September 1893

Sisters and Brothers of America,

It fills my heart with joy unspeakable to rise in response to the warm and cordial welcome which you have given us. I thank you in the name of the most ancient order of monks in the world; I thank you in the name of the mother of religions; and I thank you in the name of the millions and millions of Hindu people of all classes and sects.

My thanks, also, to some of the speakers on this platform who, referring to the delegates from the Orient, have told you that these men from far-off nations may well claim the honour of bearing to different lands the idea of toleration. I am proud to belong to a religion which has taught the world both tolerance and universal acceptance. We believe not only in universal toleration, but we accept all religions as true. I am proud to belong to a nation which has sheltered the persecuted and the refugees of all religions and all nations of the earth. I am proud to tell you that we have gathered in our bosom the purest remnant of the Israelites who came to Southern India and took refuge with us in the very year in which their holy temple was shattered to pieces by Roman tyranny. I am proud to belong to the religion which has sheltered and is still fostering the remnant of the grand Zoroastrian nation. I will quote to you, brethren, a few lines from a hymn which I remember to have repeated from my earliest boyhood, which is every day repeated by millions of human beings: "*As the different streams having their sources in different places all mingle their water in the sea, so, O Lord, the different paths which men take through different tendencies, various though they appear, crooked or straight, all lead to Thee.*"

The present convention, which is one of the most august assemblies ever held, is in itself a vindication, a declaration to the world of the wonderful doctrine preached in the Gita: "*Whosoever comes to Me, through whatsoever form, I reach him; all men are struggling through paths which in the end lead to Me.*" Sectarianism, bigotry, and its horrible descendant, fanaticism, have long possessed this beautiful earth. They have filled the earth with violence, drenched it often and often with human blood, destroyed civilisation, and sent whole nations to despair. Had it not been for these horrible demons, human society would be far more advanced than it is now. But their time is come; and I fervently hope that the bell that tolled this morning in honour of this convention may be the death-knell of all fanaticism, of all persecutions with the sword or with the pen, and of all uncharitable feelings between persons wending their way to the same goal.

Why We Disagree

15th September 1893

I will tell you a little story. You have heard the eloquent speaker who has just finished say, "Let us cease from abusing each other," and he was very sorry that there should be always so much variance.

But I think I should tell you a story which would illustrate the cause of this variance. A frog lived in a well. It had lived there for a long time. It was born there and brought up there, and yet was a little, small frog. Of course the evolutionists were not there then to tell us whether the frog lost its eyes or not, but, for our story's sake, we must take it for granted that it had its eyes, and that it every day cleansed the water of all the worms and bacilli that lived in it with an energy that would do credit to our modern bacteriologists. In this way it went on and became a little sleek and fat. Well, one day another frog that lived in the sea came and fell into the well.

"Where are you from?"

"I am from the sea."

"The sea! How big is that? Is it as big as my well?" and he took a leap from one side of the well to the other.

"My friend," said the frog of the sea, "how do you compare the sea with your little well?"

Then the frog took another leap and asked, "Is your sea so big?"

"What nonsense you speak, to compare the sea with your well!"

"Well, then," said the frog of the well, "nothing can be bigger than my well; there can be nothing bigger than this; this fellow is a liar, so turn him out."

That has been the difficulty all the while.

I am a Hindu. I am sitting in my own little well and thinking that the whole world is my little well. The Christian sits in his little well and thinks the whole world is his well. The Mohammedan sits in his little well and thinks that is the whole world. I have to thank you of America for the great attempt you are making to break down the barriers of this little world of ours, and hope that, in the future, the Lord will help you to accomplish your purpose.

Paper on Hinduism

Read at the Parliament on 19th September 1893

Three religions now stand in the world which have come down to us from time prehistoric—Hinduism, Zoroastrianism and Judaism. They have all received tremendous shocks and all of them prove by their survival their internal strength. But while Judaism failed to absorb Christianity and was driven out of its place of birth by its all-conquering daughter, and a handful of Parsees is all that remains to tell the tale of their grand religion, sect after sect arose in India and seemed to shake the religion of the Vedas to its very foundations, but like the waters of the seashore in a tremendous earthquake it receded only for a while, only to return in an all-absorbing flood, a thousand times more vigorous, and when the tumult of the rush was over, these sects were all sucked in, absorbed and assimilated into the immense body of the mother faith.

From the high spiritual flights of the Vedanta philosophy, of which the latest discoveries of science seem like echoes, to the low ideas of idolatry with its multifarious mythology, the agnosticism of the Buddhists and the atheism of the Jains, each and all have a place in the Hindu's religion.

Where then, the question arises, where is the common centre to which all these widely diverging radii converge? Where is the common basis upon which all these seemingly hopeless contradictions rest? And this is the question I shall attempt to answer.

The Hindus have received their religion through revelation, the Vedas. They hold that the Vedas are without beginning and without end. It may sound ludicrous to this audience, how a book can be without beginning or end. But by the Vedas no books are meant. They mean the accumulated treasury of spiritual laws discovered by different persons in different times. Just as the law of gravitation existed before its discovery, and would exist if all humanity forgot it, so is it with the laws that govern the spiritual world. The moral, ethical, and spiritual relations between soul and soul and between individual spirits and the Father of all spirits, were there before their discovery, and would remain even if we forgot them.

The discoverers of these laws are called Rishis, and we honour them as perfected beings. I am glad to tell this audience that some of the very greatest of them were women.

Here it may be said that these laws as laws may be without end, but they must have had a beginning. The Vedas teach us that creation is without beginning or end. Science is said to have proved that the sum total of cosmic energy is always the same. Then, if there was a time when nothing existed, where was all this manifested energy? Some say it was in a potential form in God. In that case God is sometimes potential and sometimes kinetic, which would make Him mutable. Everything mutable is a compound, and everything compound must undergo that change which is called destruction. So God would die, which is absurd. Therefore there never was a time when there was no creation.

If I may be allowed to use a simile, creation and creator are two lines, without beginning and without end, running parallel to each other. God is the ever-active providence, by whose power systems after systems are being evolved out of chaos, made to run for a time and again destroyed. This is what the Brahmin boy repeats every day: "*The sun and the moon, the Lord created like the suns and moons of previous cycles.*" And this agrees with modern science.

Here I stand and if I shut my eyes, and try to conceive my existence, "I," "I," "I," what is the idea before me? The idea of a body. Am I, then, nothing but a combination of material substances? The Vedas declare "No." I am a spirit living in a body. I am not the body. The body will die, but I shall not die. Here am I in this body; it will fall, but I shall go on living. I had also a past. The soul was not created, for creation means a combination which means a certain future dissolution. If then the soul was created, it must die. Some are born happy, enjoy perfect health, with beautiful body, mental vigour, and all wants supplied. Others are born miserable, some are without hands or feet, others again are idiots, and only drag on a wretched existence. Why, if they are all created, why does a just and merciful God create one happy and another unhappy, why is He so partial? Nor would it mend matters in the least to hold that those who are miserable in this life will be happy in a future one. Why should a man be miserable even here in the reign of a just and merciful God?

In the second place, the idea of a creator God does not explain the anomaly, but simply expresses the cruel fiat of an all-powerful being. There must have been causes, then, before his birth, to make a man miserable or happy and those were his past actions.

Are not all the tendencies of the mind and the body accounted for by inherited aptitude? Here are two parallel lines of existence—one of the mind, the other of matter. If matter and its transformations answer for all that we have, there is no necessity for supposing the existence of a soul. But it cannot be proved that thought has been evolved out of matter; and if a philosophical monism is inevitable, spiritual monism is certainly logical and no less desirable than a materialistic monism; but neither of these is necessary here.

We cannot deny that bodies acquire certain tendencies from heredity, but those tendencies only mean the physical configuration through which a peculiar mind alone can act in a peculiar way. There are other tendencies peculiar to a soul caused by his past action. And a soul with a certain tendency would by the laws of affinity take birth in a body which is the fittest instrument for the display of that tendency. This is in accord with science, for science wants to explain everything by habit, and habit is got through repetitions. So repetitions are necessary to explain the natural habits of a new-born soul. And since they were not obtained in this present life, they must have come down from past lives.

There is another suggestion. Taking all these for granted, how is it that I do not remember anything of my past life? This can be easily explained. I am now speaking English. It is not my mother tongue, in fact no words of my mother tongue are now present in my consciousness, but let me try to bring them up, and they rush in. That shows that consciousness is only the surface of the mental ocean, and within its depths are stored up all our experiences. Try and struggle, they would come up and you would be conscious even of your past life.

This is direct and demonstrative evidence. Verification is the perfect proof of a theory, and here is the challenge thrown to the world by the Rishis. We have discovered the secret by which the very depths of the ocean of memory can be stirred up—try it and you would get a complete reminiscence of your past life.

So then the Hindu believes that he is spirit. Him the sword cannot pierce—him the fire cannot burn —him the water cannot melt—him the air cannot dry. The Hindu believes that every soul is a circle whose circumference is nowhere, but whose centre is located in the body, and that death means the change of this centre from body to body. Nor is the soul bound by the conditions of matter. In its very essence, it is free, unbounded, holy, pure, and perfect. But somehow or other it finds itself tied down to matter, and thinks of itself as matter.

Why should the free, perfect, and pure being be thus under the thraldom of matter, is the next question. How can the perfect soul be deluded into the belief that it is imperfect? We have been told that that Hindus shirk the question and say that no such question can be there. Some thinkers want to answer it by positing one or more quasi-perfect beings, and use big scientific names to fill up the gap. But naming is not explaining. The question remains the same. How can the perfect become the quasi-perfect; how can the pure, the absolute, change even a microscopic particle of its nature? But the Hindu is sincere. He does not want to take shelter under sophistry. He is brave enough to face the question in a manly fashion; and his answer is: "I do not know. I do not know how the perfect being, the soul, came to think of itself as imperfect, as joined to and conditioned by matter." But the fact is a fact for all that. It is a fact in everybody's consciousness that one thinks of oneself as the body. The Hindu does not attempt to explain why one thinks one is the body. The answer that it is the will of God is no explanation. This is nothing more than what the Hindu says, "I do not know."

Well, then, the human soul is eternal and immortal, perfect and infinite, and death means only a change of centre from one body to another. The present is determined by our past actions, and the future by the present. The soul will go on evolving up or reverting back from birth to birth and death to death. But here is another question: Is man a tiny boat in a tempest, raised one moment on the foamy crest of a billow and dashed down into a yawning chasm the next, rolling to and fro at the mercy of good and bad actions—a powerless, helpless wreck in an ever-raging, ever-rushing, uncompromising current of cause and effect; a little moth placed under the wheel of causation which rolls on crushing everything in its way and waits not for the widow's tears or the orphan's cry? The heart sinks at the idea, yet this is the law of Nature. Is there no hope? Is there no escape?—was the cry that went up from the bottom of the heart of despair. It reached the throne of mercy, and words of hope and consolation came down and inspired a Vedic sage, and he stood up before the world and in trumpet voice proclaimed the glad tidings: "Hear, ye children of immortal bliss! even ye that reside in higher spheres! I have found the Ancient One, who is beyond all darkness, all delusion: knowing Him alone you shall be saved from death over again." "Children of immortal bliss"—what a sweet, what a hopeful name! Allow me to call you, brethren, by that sweet name—heirs of immortal bliss—yea, the Hindu refuses to call you sinners. Ye are the Children of God, the sharers of immortal bliss, holy and perfect beings. Ye divinities on earth—sinners! It is a sin to call a man so; it is a standing libel on human nature. Come up, O lions, and shake off the delusion that you are sheep; you are souls immortal, spirits free, blest and eternal; ye are not matter, ye are not bodies; matter is your servant, not you the servant of matter.

Thus it is that the Vedas proclaim not a dreadful combination of unforgiving laws, not an endless prison of cause and effect, but that at the head of all these laws, in and through every particle of matter and force, stands one, "By whose command the wind blows, the fire burns, the clouds rain, and death stalks upon the earth."

And what is His nature?

He is everywhere, the pure and formless One, the Almighty and the All-merciful. "Thou art our father, Thou art our mother, Thou art our beloved friend, Thou art the source of all strength; give us strength. Thou art He that beareth the burdens of the universe; help me bear the little burden of this life." Thus sang the Rishis of the Veda. And how to worship Him? Through love. "He is to be worshiped as the one beloved, dearer than everything in this and the next life."

This is the doctrine of love declared in the Vedas, and let us see how it is fully developed and taught by Krishna, whom the Hindus believe to have been God incarnate on earth.

He taught that a man ought to live in this world like a lotus leaf, which grows in water but is never moistened by water; so a man ought to live in the world—his heart to God and his hands to work.

It is good to love God for hope of reward in this or the next world, but it is better to love God for love's sake, and the prayer goes: "Lord, I do not want wealth, nor children, nor learning. If it be Thy will, I shall go from birth to birth, but grant me this that I may love Thee without the hope of reward—love unselfishly for love's sake." One of the disciples of Krishna, the then Emperor of India, was driven from his kingdom by his enemies and had to take shelter with his queen, in a forest in the Himalayas, and there one day the queen asked him how it was that he, the most virtuous of men, should suffer so much misery. Yudhishthira answered: "Behold, my queen, the Himalayas, how grand and beautiful they are; I love them. They do not give me anything, but my nature is to love the grand, the beautiful, therefore I love them. Similarly, I love the Lord. He is the source of all beauty, of all sublimity. He is the only object to be loved; my nature is to love Him, and therefore I love. I do not pray for anything; I do not ask for anything. Let him place me wherever He likes. I must love Him for love's sake. I cannot trade in love."

The Vedas teach that the soul is divine, only held in the bondage of matter; perfection will be reached when this bond will burst, and the word they use for it is therefore Mukti—freedom, freedom from the bonds of imperfection, freedom from death and misery.

And this bondage can only fall off through the mercy of God, and this mercy comes on the pure. So purity is the condition of His mercy. How does that mercy act? He reveals Himself to the pure heart; the pure and the stainless see God, yea even in this life. Then and then only all the crookedness of the heart is made straight; then all doubt ceases. He is no more the freak of a terrible law of causation. This is the very centre, the very vital conception of Hinduism. The Hindu does not want to live upon words and theories. If there are existences beyond the ordinary sensuous existence, he wants to come face to face with them. If there is a soul in him which is not matter, if there is an all-merciful universal Soul, he will go to Him direct. He must see Him and that alone can destroy all doubts. So the best proof a Hindu sage gives about the soul, about God, is—"I have seen the soul; I have seen God." And that is the only condition of perfection. The Hindu religion does not consist in struggles and attempts to believe a certain doctrine or dogma, but in realising—not in believing, but in being and becoming.

Thus the whole object of their system is by constant struggle to become perfect, to become divine, to reach God and see God, and this reaching God, seeing God, becoming perfect even as the Father in Heaven is perfect, constitutes the religion of the Hindus.

And what becomes of a man when he attains perfection? He lives a life of bliss infinite. He enjoys infinite and perfect bliss, having obtained the only thing in which man ought to have pleasure, namely God, and enjoys the bliss with God.

So far all the Hindus are agreed. This is the common religion of all the sects of India; but then perfection is absolute, and the absolute cannot be two or three. It cannot have any qualities. It cannot be an individual. And so when a soul becomes perfect and absolute, it must become one with Brahman, and it would only realise the Lord as the perfection, the reality, of its own nature and existence, the existence absolute, knowledge absolute, and bliss absolute. We have often and often read this called the losing of individuality and becoming a stock or a stone.

"He jests at scars that never felt a wound."

I tell you it is nothing of the kind. If it is happiness to enjoy the consciousness of this small body, it must be greater happiness to enjoy the consciousness of two bodies, the measure of happiness increasing with the consciousness of an increasing number of bodies, the aim, the ultimate of happiness being reached when it would become a universal consciousness.

Therefore, to gain this infinite universal individuality, this miserable little prison-individuality must go. Then alone can death cease when I am one with life, then alone can misery cease when I am one with happiness itself, then alone can all errors cease when I am one with knowledge itself; and this is the necessary scientific conclusion. Science has proved to me that physical individuality is a delusion, that really my body is one little continuously changing body in an unbroken ocean of matter, and Advaita (unity) is the necessary conclusion with my other counterpart, Soul.

Science is nothing but the finding of unity. As soon as science would reach perfect unity, it would stop from further progress, because it would reach the goal. Thus chemistry could not progress farther when it would discover one element out of which all others could be made. Physics would stop when it would be able to fulfil its services in discovering one energy of which all the others are but manifestations, and the science of religion become perfect when it would discover Him who is the one life in a universe of death. Him who is the constant basis of an ever-changing world, One who is the only Soul of which all souls are but delusive manifestations. Thus is it, through multiplicity and duality, the ultimate unity is reached. Religion can go no farther. This is the goal of all science.

All science is bound to come to this conclusion in the long run. Manifestation, and not creation, is the word of science today, and the Hindu is only glad that what he has been cherishing in his bosom for ages is going to be taught in more forcible language, and with further light from the latest conclusions of science.

Descend we now from the aspirations of philosophy to the religion of the ignorant. At the very outset, I may tell you that there is no *polytheism* in India. In every temple, if one stands by and listens, one will find the worshippers applying all the attributes of God, including omnipresence, to the images. It is not polytheism, nor would the name henotheism explain the situation. "The rose called by any other name would smell as sweet." Names are not explanations.

I remember, as a boy, hearing a Christian missionary preach to a crowd in India. Among other sweet things he was telling them was, that if he gave a blow to their idol with his stick, what could it do? One of his hearers sharply answered, "If I abuse your God, what can He do?" "You would be punished," said the preacher, "when you die." "So my idol will punish you when you die," retorted the Hindu.

The tree is known by its fruits. When I have seen amongst them that are called idolaters, men, the like of whom in morality and spirituality and love, I have never seen anywhere, I stop and ask myself, "Can sin beget holiness?"

Superstition is a great enemy of man, but bigotry is worse. Why does a Christian go to church? Why is the cross holy? Why is the face turned toward the sky in prayer? Why are there so many images in the Catholic Church? Why are there so many images in the minds of Protestants when they pray? My brethren, we can no more think about anything without a mental image than we can live without breathing. By the law of association the material image calls up the mental idea and vice versa. This is why the Hindu uses an external symbol when he worships. He will tell you, it helps to keep his mind fixed on the Being to whom he prays. He knows as well as you do that the image is not God, is not omnipresent. After all how much does omnipresence mean to almost the whole world? It stands merely as a word, a symbol. Has God superficial area? If not, when we repeat that word "omnipresent," we think of the extended sky or of space, that is all.

As we find that somehow or other, by the laws of our mental constitution, we have to associate our ideas of infinity with the image of the blue sky, or of the sea, so we naturally connect our idea of holiness with the image of a church, a mosque, or a cross. The Hindus have associated the ideas of holiness, purity, truth, omnipresence, and such other ideas with different images and forms. But with this difference that while some people devote their whole lives to their idol of a church and never rise higher because with them religion means an intellectual assent to certain doctrines and doing good to their fellows, the whole religion of the Hindu is centred in realisation. Man is to become divine by realising the divine. Idols or temples or churches or books are only the supports, the helps, of his spiritual childhood: but on and on he must progress.

He must not stop anywhere. "*External worship, material worship*," say the scriptures, "*is the lowest stage; struggling to rise high, mental prayer is the next stage, but the highest stage is when the Lord has been realised.*" Mark, the same earnest man who is kneeling before the idol tells you: "*Him the sun cannot express, nor the moon, nor the stars, the lightning cannot express Him, nor what we speak of as fire; through Him they shine.*" But he does not abuse anyone's idol or call its worship sin. He recognises in it a necessary stage of life. "*The child is father of the man.*" Would it be right for an old man to say that childhood is a sin or youth a sin?

If a man can realise his divine nature with the help of an image, would it be right to call that a sin? Nor, even when he has passed that stage, should he call it an error. To the Hindu, man is not travelling from error to truth, but from truth to truth, from lower to higher truth. To him all the religions, from the lowest fetishism to the highest absolutism, mean so many attempts of the human soul to grasp and realise the Infinite, each determined by the conditions of its birth and association, and each of these marks a stage of progress; and every soul is a young eagle soaring higher and higher, gathering more and more strength till it reaches the Glorious Sun.

Unity in variety is the plan of nature, and the Hindu has recognised it. Every other religion lays down certain fixed dogmas, and tries to force society to adopt them. It places before society only one coat which must fit Jack and John and Henry, all alike. If it does not fit John or Henry, he must go without a coat to cover his body. The Hindus have discovered that the absolute can only be realised, or thought of, or stated, through the relative, and the images, crosses, and crescents are simply so many symbols —so many pegs to hang the spiritual ideas on. It is not that this help is necessary for every one, but those that do not need it have no right to say that it is wrong. Nor is it compulsory in Hinduism.

One thing I must tell you. Idolatry in India does not mean anything horrible. It is not the mother of harlots. On the other hand, it is the attempt of undeveloped minds to grasp high spiritual truths. The Hindus have their faults, they sometimes have their exceptions; but mark this, they are always for punishing their own bodies, and never for cutting the throats of their neighbours. If the Hindu fanatic burns himself on the pyre, he never lights the fire of Inquisition. And even this cannot be laid at the door of his religion any more than the burning of witches can be laid at the door of Christianity.

To the Hindus, then, the whole world of religions is only a travelling, a coming up, of different men and women, through various conditions and circumstances, to the same goal. Every religion is only evolving a God out of the material man, and the same God is the inspirer of all of them. Why, then, are there so many contradictions? They are only apparent, says the Hindu. The contradictions come from the same truth adapting itself to the varying circumstances of different natures.

It is the same light coming through glasses of different colours. And these little variations are necessary for purposes of adaptation. But in the heart of everything the same truth reigns. The Lord has declared to the Hindu in His incarnation as Krishna: "*I am in every religion as the thread through a string of pearls. Wherever thou seest extraordinary holiness and extraordinary power raising and purifying humanity, know thou that I am there.*" And what has been the result? I challenge the world to find, throughout the whole system of Sanskrit philosophy, any such expression as that the Hindu alone will be saved and not others. Says Vyasa, "*We find perfect men even beyond the pale of our caste and creed.*" One thing more. How, then, can the Hindu, whose whole fabric of thought centres in God, believe in Buddhism which is agnostic, or in Jainism which is atheistic?

The Buddhists or the Jains do not depend upon God; but the whole force of their religion is directed to the great central truth in every religion, to evolve a God out of man. They have not seen the Father, but they have seen the Son. And he that hath seen the Son hath seen the Father also.

This, brethren, is a short sketch of the religious ideas of the Hindus. The Hindu may have failed to carry out all his plans, but if there is ever to be a universal religion, it must be one which will have no location in place or time; which will be infinite, like the God it will preach, and whose sun will shine upon the followers of Krishna and of Christ, on saints and sinners alike; which will not be Brahminic or Buddhistic, Christian or Mohammedan, but the sum total of all these and still have infinite space for development; which in its catholicity will embrace in its infinite arms, and find a place for, every human being, from the lowest grovelling savage not far removed from the brute, to the highest man towering by the virtues of his head and heart almost above humanity, making society stand in awe of him and doubt his human nature. It will be a religion which will have no place for persecution or intolerance in its polity, which will recognise divinity in every man and woman, and whose whole scope, whose whole force, will be centred in aiding humanity to realise its own true, divine nature.

Offer such a religion and all the nations will follow you. Asoka's council was a council of the Buddhist faith. Akbar's, though more to the purpose, was only a parlour-meeting. It was reserved for America to proclaim to all quarters of the globe that the Lord is in every religion.

May He who is the Brahman of the Hindus, the Ahura-Mazda of the Zoroastrians, the Buddha of the Buddhists, the Jehovah of the Jews, the Father in Heaven of the Christians, give strength to you to carry out your noble idea! The star arose in the East; it travelled steadily towards the West, sometimes dimmed and sometimes effulgent, till it made a circuit of the world, and now it is again rising on the very horizon of the East, the borders of the Sanpo, a thousandfold more effulgent than it ever was before.

Hail, Columbia, motherland of liberty! It has been given to thee, who never dipped her hand in her neighbour's blood, who never found out that the shortest way of becoming rich was by robbing one's neighbours, it has been given to thee to march at the vanguard of civilisation with the flag of harmony.

AUROBINDO

from *The Life Divine*

BOOK TWO

CHAPTER I / INDETERMINATES AND COSMIC DETERMINATIONS

. . . Actually to our Science this infinite or indeterminate Existence reveals itself as an Energy, known not by itself but by its works, which throws up in its motion waves of energism and in them a multitude of infinitesimals; these, grouping themselves to form larger infinitesimals, become a basis for all the creations of the Energy, even those farthest away from the material basis, for the emergence of a world of organised Matter, for the emergence of Life, for the emergence of Consciousness, for all the still unexplained activities of evolutionary Nature. On the original process are erected a multitude of processes which we can observe, follow, can take advantage of many of them, utilise; but they are none of them, fundamentally, explicable. We know now that different groupings and a varying number of electric infinitesimals can produce or serve as the constituent occasion—miscalled the cause, for here there seems to be only a necessary antecedent condition,—for the appearance of larger atomic infinitesimals of different natures, qualities, powers; but we fail to discover how these different dispositions can come to constitute these different atoms,—how the differentiae in the constituent occasion or cause necessitate the differentiae in the constituted outcome or result. We know also that certain combinations of certain invisible atomic infinitesimals produce or occasion new and visible determinations quite different in nature, quality and power from the constituent infinitesimals; but we fail to discover, for instance, how a fixed formula for the combination of oxygen and hydrogen comes to determine the appearance of water which is evidently something more than a combination of gases, a new creation, a new form of substance, a material manifestation of a quite new character. We see that a seed develops into a tree, we follow the line of the process of production and we utilise it; but we do not discover how a tree can grow out of a seed, how the life and form of the tree come to be implied in the substance or energy of the seed or, if that be rather the fact, how the seed can develop into a tree. We know that genes and chromosomes are the cause of hereditary transmissions, not only of physical but of psychological variations; but we do not discover how psychological characteristics can be contained and transmitted in this inconscient material vehicle. We do not see or know, but it is expounded to us as a cogent account of Nature-process, that a play of electrons, of atoms and their resultant molecules, of cells, glands, chemical secretions and physiological processes manages by their activity on the nerves and brain of a Shakespeare or a Plato to produce or could be perhaps the dynamic occasion for the production of a *Hamlet* or a *Symposium* or a *Republic*; but we fail to discover or appreciate how such material movements could have composed or necessitated the composition of these highest points of thought and literature: the divergence here of the determinants and the determination becomes so wide that we are no longer able to follow the process, much less understand or utilise. These formulae of Science may be pragmatically correct and infallible, they may govern the practical how of Nature's processes, but they do not disclose the intrinsic how or why; rather they have the air of the formulae of a cosmic Magician, precise, irresistible, automatically successful each in its field, but their rationale is fundamentally unintelligible. . . .

It is only when we follow the yogic process of quieting the mind itself that a profounder result of our self-observation becomes possible. For first we discover that mind is a subtle substance, a general determinate—or generic indeterminate—which mental energy when it operates throws into forms or particular determinations of itself, thoughts, concepts, percepts, mental sentiments, activities of will and reactions of feeling, but which, when the energy is quiescent, can live either in an inert torpor or in an immobile silence and peace of self-existence. Next we see that the determinations of our mind do not all proceed from itself; for waves and currents of mental energy enter into it from outside: these take form in it or appear already formed from some universal Mind or from other minds and are accepted by us as our own thinking. We can perceive also an occult or subliminal mind in ourselves from which thoughts and perceptions and will-impulses and mental feelings arise; we can perceive too higher planes of consciousness from which a superior mind energy works through us or upon us. Finally we discover that that which observes all this is a mental being supporting the mind substance and mind energy; without this presence, their upholder and source of sanctions, they could not exist or operate. This mental being or Purusha first appears as a silent witness and, if that were all, we would have to accept the determinations of mind as a phenomenal activity imposed upon the being by Nature, by Prakriti, or else as a creation presented to it by Prakriti, a world of thought which Nature constructs and offers to the observing Purusha. But afterwards we find that the Purusha, the mental being, can depart from its posture of a silent or accepting Witness; it can become the source of reactions, accept, reject, even rule and regulate, become the giver of the command, the knower. A knowledge also arises that this mind-substance manifests the mental being, is its own expressive substance and the mental energy is its own consciousness-force, so that it is reasonable to conclude that all mind determinations arise from the being of the Purusha. But this conclusion is complicated by the fact that from another viewpoint our personal mind seems to be little more than a formation of universal Mind, an engine for the reception, modification, propagation of cosmic thought-waves, idea-currents, will-suggestions, waves of feeling, sense-suggestions, form-suggestions. It has no doubt its own already realised expression, predispositions, propensities, personal temperament and nature; what comes from the universal can only find a place there if it is accepted and assimilated into the self-expression of the individual mental being, the personal Prakriti of the Purusha. But still, in view of these complexities, the question remains entire whether all this evolution and action is a phenomenal creation by some universal Energy presented to the mental being or an activity imposed by Mind-Energy on the Purusha's indeterminate, perhaps indeterminable existence, or whether the whole is something predetermined by some dynamic truth of Self within and only manifested on the mind surface. To know that we would have to touch or to enter into a cosmic state of being and consciousness to which the totality of things and their integral principle would be better manifest than to our limited mind experience. . . .

Our fundamental cognition of the Absolute, our substantial spiritual experience of it is the intuition or the direct experience of an infinite and eternal Existence, an infinite and eternal Consciousness, an infinite and eternal Delight of Existence. In overmental and mental cognition it is possible to make discrete and even to separate this original unity into three self-existent aspects: for we can experience a pure causeless eternal Bliss so intense that we are that alone; existence, consciousness seem to be swallowed up in it, no longer ostensibly in presence; a similar experience of pure and absolute consciousness and a similar exclusive identity with it is possible, and there can be too a like identifying experience of pure and absolute existence. But to a supermind cognition these three are always an inseparable Trinity, even though one can stand in front of the others and manifest its own spiritual determinates; for each has its primal aspects or its inherent self-formations, but all of these together are original to the triune Absolute. Love, Joy and Beauty are the fundamental determinates of the Divine Delight of Existence, and we can see at once that these are of the very stuff and nature of that Delight: they are not alien impositions on the being of the Absolute or creations supported by it but outside it; they are truths of its being, native to its consciousness, powers of its force of existence. So too is it with the fundamental determinates of the absolute consciousness,—knowledge and will; they are truths and powers of the original Consciousness-Force and are inherent in its very nature. This authenticity becomes still more evident when we regard the fundamental spiritual determinates of the absolute Existence; they are its triune powers, necessary first postulates for all its self-creation or manifestation,—Self, the Divine, the Conscious Being; Atman, Ishwara,* Purusha.

If we pursue the process of self-manifestation farther, we shall see that each of these aspects or powers reposes in its first action on a triad or trinity; for Knowledge inevitably takes its stand in a trinity of the Knower, the Known and Knowledge; Love finds itself in a trinity of the Lover, the Beloved and Love; Will is self-fulfilled in a trinity of the Lord of the Will, the object of the Will and the executive Force; Joy has its original and utter gladness in a trinity of the Enjoyer, the Enjoyed and the Delight that unites them; Self as inevitably appears and founds its manifestation in a trinity of Self as subject, Self as object and self-awareness holding together Self as subject-object. These and other primal powers and aspects assume their status among the fundamental spiritual self-determinations of the Infinite; all others are determinates of the fundamental spiritual determinates, significant relations, significant powers, significant forms of being, consciousness, force, delight,—energies, conditions, ways, lines of the truth-process of the Consciousness-Force of the Eternal, imperatives, possibilities, actualities of its manifestation. All this deploying of powers and possibilities and their inherent consequences is held together by supermind cognition in an intimate oneness; it keeps them founded consciously on the original Truth and maintained in the harmony of the truths they manifest and are in their nature. There is here no imposition of imaginations, no arbitrary creation, neither is there any division, fragmentation, irreconcilable contrariety or disparateness. But in Mind of Ignorance these phenomena appear; for there a limited consciousness sees and deals with everything as if all were separate objects of cognition or separate existences and it seeks so to know, possess and enjoy them and gets mastery over them or suffers their mastery: but, behind its ignorance, what the soul in it is seeking for is the Reality, the Truth, the Consciousness, the Power, the Delight by which they exist; the mind has to learn to awaken to this true seeking and true knowledge veiled within itself, to the Reality from which all things hold their truth, to the Consciousness of which all consciousnesses are entities, to the Power from which all get what force of being they have within them, to the Delight of which all delights are partial figures. This limitation of consciousness and this awakening to the integrality of consciousness are also a process of self-manifestation, are a self-determination of the Spirit; even when contrary to the Truth in their appearances, the things of the limited consciousness have in their deeper sense and reality a divine significance; they too bring out a truth or a possibility of the Infinite. Of some such nature, as far as it can be expressed in mental formulas, would be the supramental cognition of things which sees the one Truth everywhere and would so arrange its account to us of our existence, its report of the secret of creation and the significance of the universe.

At the same time indeterminability is also a necessary element in our conception of the Absolute and in our spiritual experience: this is the other side of the supramental regard on being and on things. The Absolute is not limitable or definable by any one determination or by any sum of determinations; on the other side, it is not bound down to an indeterminable vacancy of pure existence. On the contrary, it is the source of all determinations: its indeterminability is the natural, the necessary condition both of its infinity of being and its infinity of power of being; it can be infinitely all things because it is no thing in particular and exceeds any definable totality. It is this essential indeterminability of the Absolute that translates itself into our consciousness through the fundamental negating positives of our spiritual experience, the immobile immutable Self, the Nirguna Brahman, the Eternal without qualities, the pure featureless One Existence, the Impersonal, the Silence void of activities, the Non-being, the Ineffable and the Unknowable. On the other side it is the essence and source of all determinations, and this dynamic essentiality manifests to us through the fundamental affirming positives in which the Absolute equally meets us; for it is the Self that becomes all things, the Saguna Brahman, the Eternal with infinite qualities, the One who is the Many, the infinite Person who is the source and foundation of all persons and personalities, the Lord of

* I.e., God.—Ed.

creation, the Word, the Master of all works and action; it is that which being known all is known: these affirmatives correspond to those negatives. For it is not possible in a supramental cognition to split asunder the two sides of the One Existence,—even to speak of them as sides is excessive, for they are in each other, their co-existence or one-existence is eternal and their powers sustaining each other found the self-manifestation of the Infinite. . . .

CHAPTER XXIV / THE EVOLUTION OF THE SPIRITUAL MAN

> Even as men come to Me, so I accept them. It is my path that men follow from all sides. . . . Whatever form the worshippper chooses to worship with faith, I set in him firm faith in it, and with that faith he puts his yearning into his adoration and gets his desire dispensed by Me. But limited is that fruit. Those whose sacrifice is to the gods, to elemental spirits, reach the gods, reach the elemental spirits, but those whose sacrifice is to Me, to Me they come.
>
> *Gita.*

> In these there is not the Wonder and the Might; the truths occult exist not for the mind of the ignorant.
>
> *Rig Veda.*

> As a seer working out the occult truths and their discoveries of knowledge, he brought into being the seven Craftsmen of heaven and in the light of day they spoke and wrought the things of their wisdom.
>
> *Rig Veda.*

> Seer-wisdoms, secret words that speak their meaning to the seer.
>
> *Rig Veda.*

> None knows the birth of these; they know each other's way of begetting: but the Wise perceives these hidden mysteries, even that which the great Goddess, the many-hued Mother, bears as her teat of knowledge.
>
> *Rig Veda.*

> Made certain of the meaning of the highest spiritual knowledge, purified in their being.
>
> *Mundaka Upanishad.*

> He strives by these means and has the knowledge: in him this spirit enters into its supreme status. . . . Satisfied in knowledge, having built up their spiritual being, the Wise, in union with the spiritual self, reach the Omnipresent everywhere and enter into the All.
>
> *Mundaka Upanishad.*

In the earliest stages of evolutionary Nature we are met by the dumb secrecy of her inconscience; there is no revelation of any significance or purpose in her works, no hint of any other principles of being than that first formulation which is her immediate preoccupation and seems to be for ever her only business: for in her primal works Matter alone appears, the sole dumb and stark cosmic reality. A Witness of creation, if there had been one conscious but uninstructed, would only have seen appearing out of a vast abyss of an apparent non-existence an Energy busy with the creation of Matter, a material world and material objects, organising the infinity of the Inconscient into the scheme of a boundless universe or a system of countless universes that stretched around him into Space without any certain end or limit, a tireless creation of nebulae and star-clusters and suns and planets, existing only for itself, without a sense in it, empty of cause or purpose. It might have seemed to him a stupendous machinery without a use, a mighty meaningless movement, an aeonic spectacle without a witness, a cosmic edifice without an inhabitant; for he would have seen no sign of an indwelling Spirit, no being for whose delight it was made. A creation of this kind could only be the outcome of an inconscient Energy or an illusion-cinema, a shadow-play or puppet-play of forms reflected on a superconscient indifferent Absolute. He would have seen no evidence of a soul and no hint of Mind or Life in this immeasurable and interminable display of Matter. It would not have seemed to him possible or imaginable that there could at all be in this desert universe for ever inanimate and insensible an outbreak of teeming life, a first vibration of something occult and incalculable, alive and conscious, a secret spiritual entity feeling its way towards the surface.

But after some aeons, looking out once more on that vain panorama, he might have detected in one small corner at least of the universe this phenomenon, a corner where Matter had been prepared, its operations sufficiently fixed, organised, made stable, adapted as a scene of a new development,—the phenomenon of a living Matter, a Life in things that had emerged and become visible: but still the Witness would have understood nothing, for evolutionary Nature still veils her secret. He would have seen a Nature concerned only with establishing this outburst of Life, this new creation, but Life living for itself with no significance in it,—a wanton and abundant creatrix busy scattering the seed of her new power and establishing a multitude of its forms in a beautiful and luxurious profusion or, later, multiplying endlessly genus and species for the pure pleasure of creation: a small touch of lively colour and movement would have been flung into the immense cosmic desert and nothing more. The Witness could not have imagined that a thinking mind would appear in this minute island of life, that a consciousness could awake in the Inconscient, a new and greater subtler vibration come to the surface and betray more clearly the existence of the submerged Spirit. It would have seemed to him at first that Life had somehow become aware of itself and that was all; for this scanty new-born mind seemed to be only a servant of life, a contrivance to help life to live, a machinery for its maintenance, for attack and defence, for certain needs and vital satisfactions, for the liberation of life-instinct and life-impulse. It could not have seemed possible to him that in this little life, so inconspicuous amid the immensities, in one species out of this petty multitude, a mental being would emerge, a Mind serving Life still but also making Life and Matter its servants, using them for the fulfilment of its own ideas, will, wishes,—a mental being who would create all manner of utensils, tools, instruments out of Matter for all kinds of utilities, erect out of it cities, houses, temples, theatres, laboratories, factories, chisel from it statues and carve cave-cathedrals, invent architecture, sculpture, painting, poetry and a hundred crafts and arts, discover the mathematics and physics of the universe and the hidden secret of its structure, live for the sake of Mind and its interests, for thought and knowledge, develop into the thinker, the philosopher and scientist and, as a supreme defiance to the reign of Matter, awake in himself to the hidden Godhead, become the hunter after the invisible, the mystic and the spiritual seeker.

But if after several ages or cycles the Witness had looked again and seen this miracle in full process, even then perhaps, obscured by his original experience of the sole reality of Matter in the universe, he would still not have understood; it would still seem impossible to him that the hidden Spirit could wholly emerge, complete in its consciousness, and dwell upon the earth as the self-knower and world-knower, Nature's ruler and possessor. "Impossible!" he might say, "all that has happened is nothing much, a little bubbling of sensitive grey stuff of brain, a queer freak in a bit of inanimate Matter moving about on a small dot in the Universe." On the contrary, a new Witness intervening at the end of the story, informed of the past developments but unobsessed by the deception of the beginning, might cry out, "Ah, then, this was the intended miracle, the last of many,—the Spirit that was submerged in the Inconscience has broken out from it and now inhabits, unveiled, the form of things which, veiled, it had created as its dwelling-place and the scene of its emergence." But in fact a more conscious Witness might have discovered the clue at an early period of the unfolding, even in each step of its process; for at each stage Nature's mute secrecy, though still there, diminishes; a hint is given of the next step, a more overtly significant preparation is visible. Already, in what seems to be inconscient in Life, the signs of sensation coming towards the surface are visible; in moving and breathing Life the emergence of sensitive Mind is apparent and the preparation of thinking Mind is not entirely hidden, while in thinking Mind, when it develops, there appear at an early stage the rudimentary strivings and afterwards the more developed seekings of a spiritual consciousness. As plant-life contains in itself the obscure possibility of the conscious animal, as the animal-mind is astir with the movements of feeling and perception and the rudiments of conception that are the first ground for man the thinker, so man the mental being is sublimated by the endeavour of the evolutionary Energy to develop out of him the spiritual man, the fully conscious being, man exceeding his first material self and discoverer of his true self and highest nature. . . .

MODERN ACADEMIC PHILOSOPHY

Philosophy has continued to be expressed in Sanskrit in the modern period. In particular, the New Logic school has thrived in recent centuries, and original work has been written in Sanskrit as late as the twentieth century, although the last great Naiyāyika, Gadādhara, lived in the seventeenth. But Sanskrit is no longer the intellectual language of India. India has a university system like that of the West, with English predominant. The British were colonial rulers of India during the late eighteenth, nineteenth, and the first half of the twentieth centuries, and their legacy is nowhere more pronounced than in education. Although in primary and secondary schools, various regional vernaculars—Hindi, Bengali, Gujarati, Tamil, Malayalam, Telegu, others—are usually the media of instruction, the Indian university system is modeled on the British, and most courses are taught in English. Brahmin priests and others study Sanskrit, and all over India traditional pundits have kept Sanskrit traditions alive. Still, the old traditions are on the decline and have been since 1832, when the British declared that government funds would no longer support Sanskrit schools.

The classical philosophies have, however, found new life in the universities among academics who are, for the most part, intellectual historians. But classical Indian philosophy is also increasingly becoming a resource for philosophers whose interests are not mainly historical. No doubt it will be at least another hundred years before the inclusion of classical Indian thought in the standard graduate curriculum in philosophy in universities worldwide is as routine as the inclusion of ancient Greek philosophy now. (Every philosophy student knows something about Plato and Aristotle; the same cannot be said yet for Nāgārjuna or the *Nyāya-sūtra*.) Nevertheless, the trend to globalism is well-established, and the classical Indian schools are becoming markedly better known.

The leaders in this process of assimilation are professional philosophers who use classical debates to advance or teach philosophy outside the context of tradition. The selections below, an essay by J. N. Mohanty on consciousness and a tract by B. K. Matilal on knowledge and skepticism, illustrate how Nyāya, Mīmāṃsā, and other traditional schools can be put in the service of ongoing philosophical inquiry.

To help us understand the concept of consciousness, Mohanty presents two classical views about how we know what we know. He shows that the criticism advanced by the modern philosopher Gilbert Ryle against one of these views not only fails to discredit that view but also is used, in the classical discussion, by *advocates* of that same view against their opponents. Through such discussion, Mohanty at once deepens our appreciation of a classical debate and uses that debate to deepen our understanding of a topic of epistemology and metaphysics.

B. K. Matilal elaborates the metaepistemological debate between classical Naiyāyikas and skeptics—especially Nāgārjuna—who reject the Naiyāyika doctrine of *pramāṇa*, reliable means of knowledge. Matilal's tract is thoroughly comparative; he ranges through recent epistemology and the positions of early modern Europeans, ancient Greeks, and classical Indians as his argument demands. He reveals the general parameters of philosophic skepticism, the threat of paradoxicality, live options, and skepticism's appeal. He takes the skepticism of Nāgārjuna very seriously. But the thrust of his piece is to defend the classical Naiyāyika response expressed by Vātsyāyana and Uddyotakara, the authors of the two oldest commentaries on the *Nyāya-sūtra*. Matilal argues that this response is on target. Whether it absolutely defeats the skeptic he is less sure, however, and he closes with some insights into the various motives of skeptics and with interesting cross-cultural analogies.

J. N. MOHANTY

Gilbert Ryle's Criticisms of the Concept of Consciousness

From The Visva Bharat: Journel of Philosophy, *III, 1966–67.*

1. In Chapter VI sec. (2) of his *The Concept of Mind* (London, 1949) Gilbert Ryle criticises a concept of consciousness which in my opinion is one of the most important of all the different concepts of consciousness to be found in the different schools of philosophy. This is the concept of consciousness as self-intimating, self-revealing, self-luminous etc. By making this supposedly distinguishing feature of consciousness his main target for criticism, Ryle has done the service of drawing attention to the right point, even if by way of criticism. For Western philosophy as yet had only one clear formulation of a positive distinguishing feature of consciousness: this is what Brentano and Husserl called 'intentionality'. The self-luminousness theory however, implicit though in much of traditional Western philosophy, has never come to the forefront except perhaps in Kant's notion of the 'I think' which according to Kant must necessarily be able to accompany all our representations and in Samuel Alexander's notion of 'enjoyment' as distinguished from 'contemplation'. In Indian philosophy, on the other hand, the schools of Mimamsa and Vedanta have made the notion of self-luminousness (*svayamprakāśatva*) of consciousness the cornerstone of their epistemology and metaphysics. Considering the eight pages of Ryle's arguments from the point of view of this Indian tradition, his arguments appear to me to be a curious mixture of insight and misunderstanding to both of which this paper seeks to draw attention.

2. To start with, Ryle's emphasis on the analogy of light seems to hold good also of the Indian discussions of this theme. Just as light reveals other objects while revealing itself, so does consciousness reveal itself while revealing objects other than itself. If another lamp were required for the revelation of light, that would surely lead to an infinite regress. So also, it is argued, if consciousness were not self-luminous but needed something else in order to be revealed, that something else would need other revealing agencies and thus an infinite number of revealing agencies would have to be postulated. As in the case of light, so also in the case of consciousness, the infinite regress can be stopped by admitting some one member as self-luminous, as needing no revealing agency other than itself.

While the analogy of light is so commonplace, it is far from the truth to assert with Ryle that the myth of consciousness is "a piece of para-optics."[1] The Indian philosophers were well aware that while speaking of self-luminousness they were not doing anything more than making use of a highly appropriate analogy. "Consciousness," says Ryle, "was imported to play in the mental world the part played by light in the mechanical world."[2] This division of labour gives a false impression of the real nature of the point at stake. The analogy fails in the long run, for light itself in order to be revealed requires the self-luminousness of consciousness. The self-luminousness of consciousness is admitted not merely to explain the way we apprehend the episodes enacted in the second theatre called mind, but also to explain how anything at all could be known. The distinction between the physical world and the mental world is not essential to this notion of

[1] *The Concept of Mind,* p. 159.

[2] *Ibid.,* p. 159.

consciousness. Ryle's statement of the notion of self-luminousness owes its inaccuracies to one reason amongst others that he introduces and considers in the context of a two-world theory which however is not an essential background for the notion. I am not of course denying that many of those who uphold the self-luminousness theory have also upheld the two-world theory.

3. I will now present the self-luminousness theory in the context of Indian philosophical tradition and within such limits as in my opinion are necessary for my present purpose. Then I will consider the criticisms of Ryle. This will help in clarifying the points I propose to make against Ryle.

The traditional Indian philosophers asked a question which may be formulated as: "How do I know that I know something?" Supposing I know that S is p, the object of my knowledge is the fact that S is p. But how do I know that I know that S is p? There are two groups of answers to this question. There are some, the Naiyāyika, who hold that if K_1 is the knowledge of an object O, K_1 is known only by becoming the object of another knowledge K_2. K_2 however need not be known, but can be known if so desired and if circumstances permit. When however it is known, it becomes the object of K_3. This amounts to saying that neither K_1 nor K_2 nor any other knowledge is known by itself. If K_1 is the primary knowledge (seeing, hearing etc.), K_2, K_3 etc. are introspections. A knowledge is the knowledge of its own object and not of any other object. K_1, by hypothesis, is knowledge of O. Hence, argues the Naiyāyika, only O, and not K_1 itself, is known by K_1. K_1 therefore is not self-intimating. No knowledge can be so for the same reason.

To the above argument of the Naiyāyika, those who defend the self-luminousness theory reply as follows. To suppose that K_1 can be known only by K_2 and K_2 by K_3 would lead to an infinite regress. My awareness of my knowledge would then depend upon the completion of an infinite series. An infinite number of knowledges has to be postulated. In that case, I would never come to know that I know. We must therefore suppose that the series must somewhere have an end. Wherever we agree to close the series, the last member must be known without being the object of another knowledge, i.e., it must be self-luminous. If such a self-luminous knowledge has at all to be admitted, why not say that K_1 itself is so?

4. Under such circumstances we cannot but wonder as to the real target of one of Ryle's major arguments. In this argument, Ryle insists on the endless regress which the theory he is attacking involves, i.e. on the "infinite numbers of onion-skins of consciousness" that the theory under consideration has to postulate. But what precisely is the theory against which this criticism holds good? Not the self-luminousness theory, for this theory has just the special advantage that it dispenses with the supposed endless regress. And I have in the above paragraph drawn attention to the fact that the Indian defenders of the self-luminous theory attack the Naiyāyika with the same weapon with which Ryle seeks to deal his last death-blow at the self-luminousness theory.

To decide what precisely is the theory against which Ryle's last argument holds good, let us see how he proves the infinite regress. In his example, K_1 is an inferential knowledge of O. K_2 is the apprehension of K_1, i.e. of the inferring. K_2 to be known must require K_3 and so on *ad infinitum*. The theory which Ryle here criticises differs from the Naiyāyika's theory in two respects, and these differences place the theory mid-way between the Naiyāyika's and the Vedantist's theories. Like the Naiyāyika, the theory criticised by Ryle holds that K_1 is known by K_2 and K_2 by K_3. But unlike the Naiyāyika, the theory that is being criticised by Ryle takes the higher order knowings in a non-dispositional sense. Whereas all that the Naiyāyika claims is that K_2 can be, if so desired and if circumstances permit, known by K_3, this theory holds that K_2 is necessarily made the object of K_3. Further, this theory differs from the Naiyāyika's in the further point that whereas for the Naiyāyika K_1, K_2, K_3 are succeeding cognitions, for this theory they are simultaneously imbedded in any and every mental state. For the Indian self-luminousness theory, on the other hand, K_1 is actually known (in a non-dispositional sense) but not by K_2 but by itself. K_2, K_3, etc. are uncalled for.

Thus we find that the infinite regress does not vitiate the Indian formulation of the self-luminousness theory, for the very point about the Indian theory is the assertion that K_1 is known without being the object of another knowledge, K_2.

It is also interesting to see that the Naiyāyika by making the higher order knowings from K_2 onwards merely possible cognitions has a good argument by which he could avoid the charge of infinite regress. For the Naiyāyika will argue that K_1 alone is required for O to be known, and that K_1 is invariably followed by K_2 while K_2 need not be known unless there is a special desire for it to be known, that when it is known it becomes the object of K_3 and that the same is true of K_3. There is therefore no infinite regress.

The Vedantist of course would try to show that an unknown knowledge is a self-contradiction and that if K_2 is unknown there cannot be any desire on one's part to know it.

It is rather Ryle's version of the self-luminousness theory (which is the Naiyāyika's theory with the differences that the higher order knowings are not taken to be merely possible and that K_1, K_2, K_3, etc. are taken not to be successive but to be simultaneous) that lies flagrantly open to the charge Ryle urges against it. The self-luminousness theory as formulated by the Indian philosophers however escapes Ryle's death-blow.

Ryle himself is not totally unaware of this truth. For he sees[3] that the self-luminousness theory does not imply that there are two acts of knowing either as synchronous performances or as somehow indissolubly welded together. If this be so, one fails to understand why he ascribes to that theory the view that there is, for example, an apprehension of inferring over and above the inferring of which it is the apprehension.

6. Another argument which Ryle advances against the self-luminousness theory is admitted by him to be merely persuasive. Nevertheless, I will try to find out a reply. The question is, how do we, as ordinary men, vindicate our assertions of fact. Ryle argues that we never appeal in our vindications to 'immediate awareness' or to any 'direct deliverance of consciousness'. We would rather support our statements of fact by saying that we see, hear, smell or taste so and so. Asked if one really knows something, one never replies, Ryle argues, "Oh yes, certainly I do, for I am conscious of doing so."

I imagine the following conversation:

Mr. A.—"Look here, there is a bird's nest in the tree!"
Mr. B.—"How do you know that?"
Mr. A.—"Well, I see it."

Mr. B unless he has been made sophisticated by study of philosophy would not normally ask "How do you know that you are seeing?" But even an unsophisticated person may ask other questions: "Are you sure you are really seeing one?" "Are you sure you are really seeing a bird's nest, or are you seeing something else up there?" "Are you sure you are seeing one or are you imagining one?" etc.

The second group of questions is of course answered, and the answer vindicated, without appealing to the self-luminousness of consciousness. Further, Mr. A need not—now I am answering Ryle—vindicate his assertion of the fact that there is a bird's nest up there by appealing to any direct deliverance of consciousness. He says, and need say even on the self-luminousness theory, that he sees one. But the sophisticated question "How do you know that you know?" has to be answered, if we are to avoid an infinite regress, by admitting at some point of the answer that something is known without being an object of another knowledge. The self-luminousness theory says that my knowing that I am seeing is not another act synchronous with seeing or indissolubly welded with it (Ryle, to be fair, sees this), but that my knowing O and my knowing that I am knowing O are one and the same act. The Vedantist is well aware that when the self-luminous consciousness is said to be 'known' by itself, this word 'known' is used in a pickwickian sense and not in the same sense in which one says of a proposition that it is known. That which makes possible all knowledge cannot itself be an object of knowledge: this was also the point Kant wanted to make out against the rationalist psychology of his time.

7. Of all Ryle's arguments, it remains to consider the one appealing to facts like self-delusion. Although the self-luminousness theory does not claim to provide, as has been pointed out, an answer to the question "Are you really seeing one or are you imagining you are seeing one?" yet—it may be argued—does not the very possibility of this question cut at the roots of the theory? For, how, if consciousness be self-intimating, can I be at all deceived about my mental states? How can I at all entertain a

[3] *Ibid.*, pp. 159–9 [*sic*]

doubt about the mental state I am experiencing? How can I ask myself "Am I really seeing or am I imagining I am seeing?"? "If consciousness was what it is described as being," writes Ryle,[4] "it would be logically impossible for such failures and mistakes in recognition to take place."

Replying, let me at once say what I have said before, namely that self-luminousness is not a property of mental states (admitting, provisionally though, the two-world theory) just as it is not a property of non-mental objects. It is the property of awareness, be it the awareness of a physical object or of a mental state, be it awareness of the object seen or of my seeing of it. Awareness itself is not a mental state.

If mental states and non-mental objects are so far on a par, cases of mistaking one physical object for another (e.g., a rope for a snake) and cases of mistaking one mental state for another (e.g. an imagining for a seeing) have equal relevance for the issue at stake. But none of these two groups of cases disproves the self-luminousness theory, for this theory accounts not for the truth of any knowledge but for the fact that I am not only aware of the object known but at the same time am aware of my own awareness, or using Samuel Alexander's phraseology, for the fact that I 'enjoy' my own awareness without making the latter the object of another awareness. False awareness is also an 'awareness of . . .' and this awareness is as much 'enjoyed' as correct apprehension is. Only, the theory would add, nothing—neither physical nor mental—can be known unless this self-luminous awareness were there, that is to say, if consciousness were not self-luminous.

For the same reason, unconscious mental states (to which Freud has drawn attention) present as little difficulty as unknown physical objects.

I should add at the end that the purpose of this paper is not to maintain that the self-luminousness theory as stated here is philosophically invulnerable. My purpose has been to show that Ryle's criticisms do not succeed in exploding this notion.

[4] *Ibid.*, p. 162.

B. K. MATILAL

from *Perception: An Essay on Classical Indian Theories of Knowledge*

SCEPTICISM

> The unexamined life is not worth living
>
> SOCRATES

2.1. *The Paradoxicality of Scepticism*

Uncompromising empiricism leads to scepticism. One can stop short of the sceptical route by making some sort of a compromise. But compromises need not always be degrading or scandalous. The question arises, on the other hand, whether scepticism itself is a coherent position. Would not the sceptic himself run into some dilemma of his own? It may be claimed that even the "uncompromising" sceptic eventually makes a compromise of a sort. I shall pursue this question here, after presenting the arguments of the Indian sceptics, viz. those who reject altogether the *pramāṇa** doctrine along with its emphasis upon the empirical foundation of knowledge, while tentatively accepting the empiricist stance of their opponents.

A philosopher has to learn to live with the sceptic, for they are both in the same profession, so to

* Reliable means of knowledge.—Ed.

speak. A sceptic is not an intruder in the "Temple of Truth," he shares the same concern for truth with the philosopher, and is reluctant to accept anything less. A sceptic is first and foremost an "inquirer," and in this regard, all philosophers participate in inquiries and play the role, at least provisionally, of a sceptic to varying degrees. Both persist in seeking and probing, but a sceptic is distinguished by his persistence or concern, which is (the philosopher rightly points out) out of proportion, and hence, "impractical." Thus Kumārila says about the hyper-sceptic: "If somebody imagines (the existence of) even some unknown counter-argument, he, doubting his own self, would be destroyed in all practical behaviour."[1] But this rebuke which the sceptic receives from his opponent—the rebuke of being impractical, holding an impossible position and leading to an impossible situation—seldom matters to the sceptic, for I think (as will be shown below) he can argue his way out. Thus the frequent jokes and insults that are normally heaped upon the sceptic are wide of the mark. For instance, Udayana points out that if the sceptic does not *believe* what he does not *see,* then he should not believe that his wife is alive when he is out in the street and hence should mourn for her death. Against such attacks the sceptic can justifiably claim that his point has been seriously and severely misunderstood. Or if, as Russell has said, radical scepticism is untenable and impractical, for "from blank doubt, no argument can begin," the Indian sceptic might reply: (i) that he does not see a great virtue in practicality when one is seriously embarking upon a theoretical dispute; and (ii) that he is again being misunderstood for he does not doubt simply for the sake of doubting, nor does he seek nothing beyond uncertainty ('blank doubt'); he simply refuses to prejudge the issue and to believe beforehand that there is "the rock or clay" (the indubitable ground for certainty) to be reached once we have "cast aside the loose earth."[2]

[1] This is quoted by Ratnakīrti (p. 38) from Kumārila's lost work *Bṛhaṭṭīkā*. See also Udayana's comment under *Nyāyakusumāñjali* Ch. 3, verse 6.

[2] Thus Descartes' well-known expression: "My design was only to provide myself with good ground for assurance, and to reject the quicksand and mud in order to find the rock or clay." *Discourse on Method,* Pt. II.

The sceptic claims that his sceptical position is what is demanded by consistency for he sees that the *pro*-arguments and the *contra*-arguments for any thesis are equally balanced. If it is shown however that scepticism itself involves some inconsistency, or that it is an incoherent position to hold, then it would be a serious objection indeed and should be answered adequately. Nāgārjuna's scepticism about all existents (*bhāva*), or about all philosophical positions was actually accused of paradoxicality and therefore inconsistency. This critique presented by the *pramāṇa* theorists such as Nyāya can be given in the form of a dilemma: if all things lack existence or all theses lack certainty (in Nāgārjuna's language, lack *svabhāva* or 'essence' or 'own-being'), then this particular thesis (and it is also a 'thing') must not lack essence. For if it does, there is no reason for us to believe it and Nāgārjuna should refrain from asserting it. And if it does not, there is at least one counter-example to falsify Nāgārjuna's thesis. Objections of this sort were formulated in the *Nyāya-sūtra* and in Vātsyāyana's commentary.

We can use the notion of utterance and meaning to formulate the same problem. If the sceptic's position is that all utterances are devoid of (i.e. empty (*śūnya*) of) meaning, then this itself cannot be an utterance. For if it is, it falsifies itself. We can think of 'meaning' here as something that is not necessarily separable from thinking or intending. This is at least the non-technical sense of 'meaning'. For we cannot *mean* something by utterances unless we have thoughts that we intend our utterances to mean. Both Nāgārjuna and his opponents use such schematic terms as *bhāva* and *sva-bhāva* which are general enough to allow such interpretations. Their argument presupposes that a statement or an utterance is to be included in the domain of *bhāva*. For it is stated as follows: "If all *bhāvas* are empty of their *svabhāva,* then your utterance (*vacana* or saying) that all *bhāvas* are empty must also be empty of its *sva-bhāva* for it is also a *bhāva*."[3]

Whether the above formulation expresses a genuine paradox or not, it did have the consquence of showing that pure scepticism (or the Mādhyamika scepticism) cannot be consistently maintained.

[3] Nāgārjuna, Vv, verse I, p. 277. [Above, p. 147.]

Nāgārjuna's reply is to be found in the *Vigrahavyāvartanī*. He says: "I have no proposition, no thesis to defend (which may lack any essence). If I had any thesis, I would have been guilty of the faults you ascribe to me. But I do not, hence I have no fault."[4]

This reply of Nāgārjuna is amazingly simple. But can he get away with this? The purport is that "no (philosophic) thesis has *svabhāva,* i.e. 'essence' "—is itself not a thesis. It is not an assertion. It may be an utterance but only an *empty* utterance. To put it another way: "No statement is certain, or has *svabhāva,* or is meaningful" should not be regarded as a statement, so that we cannot raise such questions whether or not it is itself certain, has *svabhāva,* or is meaningful. I think this reply should be satisfactory, for at least it is not inconsistent on the face of it. For it is quite possible that every thesis lacks essence or *svabhāva,* and this will remain so even if there is nobody (not even a Nāgārjuna) who asserts it as a thesis. If anyone asserted it, he would falsify it; but if nobody did, there is no falsification. We can imagine a possible world where all assertions made are empty but there is nobody to make the crucial assertion that all assertions are empty. A. N. Prior once followed J. Buridan in resolving the paradox with "no statement is true" in more or less the same way: "But if God were to annihilate all negative propositions, there would in fact be no negative propositions, even if this were not being asserted by any proposition at all."[5] The air of paradoxicality in the sceptical position, then, can be resolved only at the expense of disallowing the sceptic to assert his own position. For it is possible for a sceptic to believe that all beliefs have dubious value, including the said belief in question! One can raise many questions here against Nāgārjuna. Is not his way of wriggling out of paradoxicality incomplete without a Buridan-like assumption that there is a higher power which decrees what is or is not in the world? I think Nāgārjuna would rephrase the point differently: "It just so *happens* that everything is empty (lacks *svabhāva*), but it must remain *unsaid,* for to assert (say) it is to falsify it."

[4] Ibid., verse 29 p. 285. [Above, p. 149.]

[5] A. N. Prior, *Papers in Logic and Ethics,* ed. Geach & Kenny (London: Duckworth, 1976), p. 144.

Dismissing the air of paradoxicality in the above manner, Nāgārjuna proceeded to formulate some serious criticisms of his rivals, the *pramāṇa* theorists, the Naiyāyikas in particular. What he called in question was the very concept of *pramāṇa,* our standards of proof, our evidence for knowledge. He did not use what is generally called argument from illusion, nor did he appeal to the fallibility of our cognitive process. He did not argue on the basis of the fact that we do misperceive on many occasions, or that we make false judgements more often than not. Instead he developed a very strong and devastating critique of the whole epistemological enterprise itself and therefore his arguments have a lasting philosophic value.

2.2 Nāgārjuna's Critique of Knowledge and Pramāṇas

If we claim that we have means of knowing (*pramāṇa*) the way the world is, or if we believe that we have such means available to us, it stands to reason to ask further: how do we *know* those means of knowing? For, obviously, we have to know or recognize that those are the means we have; otherwise, it would be like having in our pocket some money, the presence of which we are unaware and which therefore would be useless for all practical purposes. A means is not a means unless it does something and hence if we have the means, we have to make them effective. To make them effective, we have to *know* that they are there. Nāgārjuna therefore raises the legitimate question: how, or through what means, do we know that they are there? By raising such a question, Nāgārjuna is not simply urging a fault of circularity against his opponents. For there will be other serious logical difficulties in store for the Naiyāyika or the *pramāṇa* theorist.

In the above argument, the *pramāṇa* theorist seems to have conceded already that the means of knowing can also be, or can be turned into, the object of knowing. (A *pramāṇa* is also a *prameya,* i.e. is among the knowables. If this is so, then we need further *pramāṇas* to "measure" them.) If our means is turned into an end, then to achieve that end we need further means. If our standards for determining others are themselves to be determined by another set of standards and then a further set is needed for the second set of standards, we may regress into infinity and our search for the final standard may never come to an end. In the words of Nāgārjuna: 'If the proof of the *pramāṇas* were by means of other *pramāṇas*, then there would be an "infinite regress" (*anavasthā*). There would be no proof of the first, nor of the middle, nor of the last."[6] In Sanskrit dialectics this fault is called *anavasthā*, literally "lack of a firm grounding." This situation as the sceptic envisions it would partly be comparable to the never-ending search for the rock-bottom certainty. In Cartesian epistemology for instance, a similar sort of scepticism is presupposed and the epistemologist tries to come forward with either the *cogito*, or the sense-impression, or the self-evident sense-data, as his final court of appeal.

There may be objections against my use of the term 'scepticism' in connection with Nāgārjuna. One could say that Nāgārjuna was a Buddhist and not a sceptic. It may also be said that if a sceptic is simply one whom Descartes characterized as a person who doubts only "that he may doubt and seeks nothing beyond uncertainty itself," then he would try to cast doubt upon as many fundamental beliefs of the *pramāṇa* theorists as possible and certainly Nāgārjuna has not followed this method. In my defence I would point out that I do not have such a narrow definition of scepticism in my mind (as should be clear from the introductory comments). By calling Nāgārjuna a sceptic, or rather by using his arguments to delineate the position of my sceptical opponent of the *pramāna* theorists, I have only proposed a probable extension of the application of the term 'scepticism'. Here as well as elsewhere, I would urge my readers not to dispute too much over mere labels but to pay attention to the formulation of a position (in the Indian context) and the arguments adduced in favour of it. Sometimes descriptive labels are put on theories in order to familiarize them to readers and hence they need not always be too strictly interpreted.

It is worth noting that my extended use of the notion of scepticism can be discussed in the context of A. J. Ayer's characterization of 'philosophical scepticism': ". . . his [the sceptic's] charge against our standards of proof is *not that they work badly;* he does not suggest that there are others which work better. The ground on which he attacks them is that they are *logically defective,* or if not defective, at any rate logically questionable."[7]

Such a general characterization would undoubtedly be applicable to Nāgārjuna, Jayarāśi, and Śrīharṣa, although I understand that even in Ayer's discussion the sceptic becomes more specific in raising some questions. He raises questions about such things as whether, or how, we are justified in making assertions about physical objects on the basis of our sense-experience, or in assuming and talking about other minds on the basis of their bodily behaviour, or in regarding our memories as giving us knowledge of the past. Nāgārjuna, however, raises more fundamental questions about the consistency of the *pramāṇa* doctrine as a whole: he asks whether or not our so-called standards of proof form a coherent system, whether our fundamental assumptions are endowed with at least psychological certainty. It is his contention that in the long run the concept of the standard of proof would be found to be self-refuting or self-stultifying.

However, the charge of infinite regress against the *pramāṇa* theory is not a formidable objection for there are obviously several alternative ways of answering it. Nāgārjuna anticipated and countered most of them. Some of his counter-arguments will be examined here so that one may appreciate the position of the sceptic in so far as he offers formidable objections to the *pramāṇa* theory.

The purported answers of the *pramāṇa* theorists may fall into two general categories. First it may be claimed that there are some, if not all, means of knowing which do not require any further means for knowing them, for they are what may be called self-evident or self-supporting (*svataḥ prasiddhiḥ*). Second, the authoritativeness of the means of knowing may be derivative in a way that need not lead to any infinite regress. The *locus classicus* of this argument is *Vigrahavyāvartanī*, verse 51. I shall, however rearrange the alternatives as follows:

[6] Nāgārjuna, Vv., verse 32, p. 286. [Above, p. 149.]

[7] A. J. Ayer, *The Problem of Knowledge* (London: 1956), p. 40.

A. Neither knowledge nor means of knowing derive their authority (or validity) from anything else. They have (intrinsic and natural) authority and validity.

A proof is used to prove something else but it itself does not require a further proof. A piece of evidence is evidence for something else but is itself self-evident. This can obviously have two ramifications:

i. Each piece of knowledge is self-validating, each means of knowing is self-supporting, each piece of evidence is self-evident.

ii. A subset of knowledge-pieces or a subset of *pramāṇas* are self-supporting and self-evident and upon these we base others of their kind.

In either case the analogy would be fire or light which reveals itself besides revealing others. (Nāgārjuna confounds the argument based upon fire-analogy as we will see later.) The first view is upheld by the Mīmāṃsakas (including the Vedāntins) as well as the Buddhist *pramāṇa* theorists. The second view may be attributed to the epistemologists in the Cartesian or the Humean tradition who want to reach rock-bottom certainty, casting aside the loose earth and sand. Nāgārjuna's criticism is applicable to both of them with equal force. For in either case we have introduced a clear-cut dichotomy. The *pramāṇas* belong to a privileged class, the set of the self-evident, self-supporting items, while the other items, viz. *prameyas,** are not so. Nāgārjuna questions this dichotomy as well as the validity of the principle lying behind it.

The question is why certain items, the so-called self-evident or the self-supporting 'means', should be sacrosanct, i.e. should enjoy the privilege of being independent of any requirement for further support. A dichotomy proposed by a philosopher should be based upon some dichotomizing principle and the philosopher concerned should be prepared to spell out the latter. In other words he should not only say what the difference is but also, and more importantly, account for the same. This is exactly what Nāgārjuna demands: "*Viśeṣa-hetuś ca vaktavyaḥ.*" (And the reason for such differentiation should be stated).[8]

What exactly is being asked here? The *pramāṇa* theorist has to account for the fact that why out of all items in the world certain items do not stand in need of being established or revealed to us by a 'means', while others necessarily do. What accounts for this difference in character? To say that it is the nature of one kind of things to reveal and that of the other to be revealed will not serve the purpose, for that will be hardly more helpful than saying, as we have already said, that one group comprises the 'means' of knowledge (*pramāṇas*) while the other group comprises the 'objects' of knowledge (*prameyas*). For in philosophy appeal to the nature of things is almost as good (or as bad) as an appeal to the caprices of Nature or Providence.

The second difficulty, Nāgārjuna points out, is that the *pramāṇa* theorist by introducing this dichotomy contradicts his original thesis—the very thesis that started the debate (*vihīyate vādaḥ*). The *pramāṇa* theorist started with the fundamental thesis that everything is established, or made known by, some *pramāṇa* or other. In fact the very well-known and much-debated Nyāya thesis is that to be an object of knowledge (*prameya*) is a feature shared by all things whatsoever. Now it is being suggested that there are certain things, self-supporting *pramāṇas* themselves or self-evident pieces of knowledge, which do not require a further *pramāṇa* or a further support. If to answer this difficulty it is urged that these self-supporting 'means' of knowing are not absolutely independent but simply require nothing beyond themselves to be proven valid or sound, then Nāgārjuna could go back to his first criticism: how to account for the alleged difference or discrimination between *pramāṇas* and *prameyas*?

The question Nāgārjuna raises is fundamental to scepticism in the Indian tradition. The early Nyāya method is essentially a programme that presupposes an initial doubt (*saṃśaya*), and through the employment of *pramāṇa*, moves on to reach a certitude (*nirṇaya*) at the end of the inquiry. (This is not exactly Descartes' project of pure inquiry which is carried on with the fictional *malin genie* who devotes all his efforts to deceive us.) According to Nyāya, if a state of dubiety is to be entertained with regard to the truth of any proposition (thesis) before certitude is reached through the application of *pramāṇas*, means of knowledge or evidence, then a similar state of doubt could *ipso facto* be entertained

* Objects to be known.—*Ed.*

[8] Nāgārjuna, Vv, verse 33, p. 286. [Above, p. 149.]

with regard to those very means of knowledge or evidence before certitude regarding their effectiveness or efficacy can be reached. This is presupposed by the Nyāya programme for arriving at certitude. . . . If the 'means' or evidence for knowledge is not subjected to this procedure, then Nyāya is simply arguing for a preferential or privileged treatment for a set of items, the *pramāṇas*, which is unwarranted. By admitting the universal possibility of doubt Nyāya is committed by the same token, according to Nāgārjuna, to the possibility of universal doubt.

The Naiyāyika cannot say that he has chosen the means of knowing as requiring no further evidence and hence immune from doubt because of our subjective feeling about their certitude or indubitability. For one thing, this subjective feeling may not be universal. The Nyāya programme is to establish objective evidence for all things whatsoever and hence the same requirement must be met for the means of knowing as well. It is true that the self-evidence or self-validity of knowledge, or its means, is not accepted by the Nyāya school. But in so far as the Nyāya method is partially accepted by philosophers who argue for the 'self-evidence' thesis, Nāgārjuna's criticism would be relevant. In his sceptical refutation of the *pramāṇas* , a Nagarjunite obviously moves here from the universal possibility of doubt to the possibility of universal doubt, though this passage from one to the other may not be logically warranted. . . .

I have already indicated that Nāgārjuna's critique of knowledge would be relevant even if we transpose it to the Cartesian programme for the foundation of knowledge. Descartes himself paved the way for the super-critic by introducing the fiction of the *malin genie*. His own programme was to reach a set of irresistible and indubitable propositions on which to lay the foundation of other kinds of knowledge. This was quite in line with the general task of any philosopher, whether of East or West: to cast doubt on everything in order to reach certainty, to destroy apparent platitudes in order to gain genuine certitudes. Or as Ryle once suggested, the task is comparable to "the destruction-tests by which engineers discover the strength of materials."[9] We all know that the destructive side of the Cartesian programme proved more convincing and successful than its positive side. To be sure, Descartes' search for truth was also a search for knowledge as well as a search for certainty. An obvious criticism was that he set his standards too high to make it attainable by his programme. But this criticism does not apply to the Nyāya method, for there the standard for certainty is not set too high. Without doubt it is made to depend upon standard means of knowing and evidence. Once the standard means of knowing are recognized, very little remains to frustrate the programme. If the initial doubt is removed through standard procedures, we have obtained a piece of knowledge. Hence Nāgārjuna's strategy was to find an internal inconsistency in the very presupposition of the programme. If everything is to be considered certified (certain) when and only when the means of knowing certifies them, why should the means of knowing not be certified in a similar way?

Where Descartes would reach his set of irresistible and indubitable propositions, the *cogito* or the idea of a benevolent creator for the successful completion of his programme, a Nagarjunite could very well say: "Why are the indubitables indubitable, while the others are not?" It is well known that Descartes involved himself into a circularity for he used the criterion of self-evidence in order to prove the existence of God and then used God to validate the criterion of self-evidence. A Nāgārjunite would have loved to expose this circularity for his sceptical claim is that either all propositions should be subjected to doubt to ensure their final and objective certitude, or none should be so subjected. If we select some, that would be unwarranted preferential treatment. The moment our programme sets objective certitude of propositions as its goal we forfeit the claim to demand objective indubitability of our self-evident, subjectively irresistible propositions such as envisioned in the *cogito* or the benevolent creator.

The epistemologist may give up the claim of self-evidence or the non-derivative nature of the authority pertaining to the means of knowledge or knowledge itself. He may choose the second alternative and say:

B. A piece of knowledge or a means of knowing derives its authority and validity from something

[9] G. Ryle, *Philosophical Arguments* (Oxford, 1945), p. 6.

other than itself (*paratah*). This can lead to the following possible positions:[10]

(i) A piece of knowledge derives its authority from another piece of knowledge. One instance of perception is proven by another instance of perception or by an inference. One instance of inference is proven by an instance of perception or by another inference. A piece of verbal knowledge is proven by an instance of perception or an inference and so on. Nāgārjuna notes all these cases in *Vṛtti* (verse 51).

(ii) A piece of knowledge is validated by its 'object', which is part of the independently existent real. It assumes that there is a knowledge-independent world and that there are independently existing entities, the nature of which is known when we have knowledge. The 'real' object validates knowledge as well as its means.

(iii) Our 'means' of knowledge and our 'objects' of knowledge are mutually dependent. They validate each other. (Notice that this answer tries to bypass the question of the existence of a knowledge-independent world.)

A third alternative *C* is also formulated by Nāgārjuna, which says that the validation of the means of knowledge is *a-kasmāt* 'unaccountable', neither intrinsic nor derivative. This however could be included in alternative *A* (the non-derivativeness of the *pramāṇas*).

Alternative *B*(i) is summarily rejected on pain of the *regressus ad infinitum*. But this may not be as absurd as it is made to appear under the sceptic's scrutiny. This may be a very pragmatic solution of the age-old problem. To prove *A* we may need *B* and to prove *B* we may need *C*, but it is then possible that we do not need to prove *C* also. The reason for not requiring to prove *C* may not be the claim that *C* is self-evident, but that the question regarding *C*'s validity has not arisen. Such contingency may stop the regress, but that is not the crux of the argument. The main point is: must we necessarily validate *C* before we use it as a means to prove *B*?

There is the dubiety principle which we must accept: If *C* proves *B*, and *C* is doubtful, then *B* is also doubtful. There is also the invalidation principle. If *C* is the only way to prove *B*, and *C* is invalidated, then *B* is invalidated. But we may not require a validation principle along the same line: If *C* proves *B*, and *C* is validated, then and then only *B* is validated. For this would be too strong. We can simply say: If *C* proves *B*, then *B* is validated. The issue here is connected with two broader questions about the concept of knowledge. First, if I know that *p*, must I know that I know that *p*? Second, if I know that *p*, must I always feel certain or will there simply be an absence of doubt? As we shall see later, the Naiyāyika argued that from the fact that somebody knows that *p*, it does not necessarily follow that he knows that he knows that *p*. For example, on entering this room someone may know, on the basis of perception, that there are four chairs in this room without by the same token knowing that he knows that there are four chairs there. His knowledge-episode proves here that there are four chairs there, and hence the proposition that there are four chairs there is validated. But it would be too odd to claim that his knowledge-episode must also and always be validated by another knowledge-episode. (For he may not always know that he knows!) . . . the regress to infinity can be stopped, and is actually stopped, despite Nāgārjuna's insinuation.

Alternative *B*(ii) can indeed be upheld. For a knowledge-independent world can indeed validate our knowledge and its means, provided they are *in accord* with that knowledge-independent world as it really is. But the sceptic is quick to point out that the existence of that very knowledge-independent world is what is in question here. An epistemologist can say of a cognitive situation that it yields knowledge only when it is in accord with his experience. For we cannot know about a cognitive situation that it is in accord with the world as it really is without encompassing that knowledge-independent world within the act of cognition. We thereby run into circularity. We posit the world (the *prameya*) to validate knowledge and then validate the world by the criteria of that knowledge itself. It is like Descartes' attempt to prove God through self-evidence and then use God to validate the criterion of self-evidence.

Alternative *B*(iii) is rejected by Nāgārjuna because of the fault of mutual dependence, which is

[10] Nāgārjuna, Vv, verses 45–7, pp. 288–9. [Above, p. 150.]

no doubt a kind of circularity. But why the position is asserted at all by explicitly courting the mutual dependence? Is there any sense in which it seems plausible? The answer is yes. I think the model of mutual dependence is not necessarily a faulty model. For when two sides are equally weak and uncertain, mutual dependence in the form of mutual reinforcement of certainty may be regarded as a virtue rather than a vice. If two propositions are mutually dependent upon each other, while both lack certitude, is there any comparative gain? It may be argued that both may be allowed to stand until either is proven wrong or right. There may be greater collective plausibility to both of them, although there is no strong argument in favour of either.

Besides, the mutuality of the means of knowing and the object of knowledge may point up another direction. If the object depends upon the means and the means upon the object, then both may be said to be knowledge-dependent. This position will then have a consequence that will be welcome to the Buddhist phenomenalists and other idealists. If we locate the object in what appears in experience, and identify knowledge with what makes it appear the way it does, we court some sort of mutuality between knowledge and its object, which may point up their essential non-difference. In any case, such a position cannot be treated lightly or rejected on frivolous grounds. . . .

2.3 *Nyāya Defence of Knowledge and* Pramāṇas

Analogy is often a powerful argument in fundamental matters. The analogy of knowledge or its means with the light of a lamp adds just that much credence to the *pramāṇa* theory as to make the epistemologist's programme both plausible and possible. The position is an extended version of the 'self-evidence' thesis discussed above. Knowledge or means of knowledge establishes both itself and its object, for it is like the light of a lamp which reveals both itself and others. Nāgārjuna criticizes it as follows:

> It may be said—my 'means' of knowing establishes both itself and the other. As it has been said: Fire (i.e. light) reveals itself in the same way as it does others. The 'means' likewise establishes itself and the others . . . in reply we say: 'This analogy is improper. Fire does not reveal itself. For unlike the pot, fire is not seen to be unrevealed in darkness.' . . . If it were the case that just as the pot is first unrevealed by fire while it lies in darkness and afterwards being revealed by fire (light) it is perceived, similarly fire being unrevealed by fire first lies in darkness and afterwards it is revealed by fire itself, then it would happen that fire reveals itself. But this is not so.[11]

Nāgārjuna's source for this light analogy is not known to us, but an argument based on it is recorded in a similar vein in *Nyāyasūtra* 2.1.19. In reply to an objection raised in *Nyāyasūtra* 2.1.18 that if a 'means' is not revealed by another 'means' it remains for ever unrevealed or unestablished, it says: "It (the *pramāṇa*) is established like the lamplight."[12] If this cryptic comment means that a piece of knowledge as well as its means establishes both itself and its object just as the lamplight reveals both itself and other objects, then Nāgārjuna's criticism becomes relevant. (Vātsyāyana, however, proposes a different interpretation of the *sūtra* as we shall see below.)

Nāgārjuna rejects the light analogy by arguing mainly that it is improper to claim that "light reveals itself" is a true proposition. For, he claims, it is more proper to say that light does not reveal itself. Hence the analogy does not work. But I think Nāgārjuna does not completely succeed in this rejection. For what does he mean when he claims that light does not reveal itself? Is it, according to him, meaningless to say that light reveals itself? Further, if light does not reveal itself, does it simply mean that it is revealed by something else? Or is it revealed at all? Probably Nāgārjuna would have claimed that it does not make any sense to say that light is revealed. For the expression "light is revealed" may presuppose a prior existence of light before its revelation. We may concede the point that "light reveals objects" is truly an awkward formulation. The expression may simply mean that there is revelation of objects. It may be that we are in fact

[11] Ibid., verses 34–9, pp. 286–7. (cf. above, p. 149.]

[12] Akṣapāda Gotama, *Nyāyasūtra*, 2.1.19. [cf. above, p. 184.]

asserting here the existence of some state of affairs or the happening of an event.

It is a stylistic device in language (as well as in thought connected with it) to separate agent, action, and object-patient, although we may be reporting a single happening or event. For example, when we report a battle we may say, "They fought a battle." "Light reveals object" may simply be a stylistic way of saying "There is revelation of objects." Thus "Light reveals itself" may be a stylistic variant for saying "There is light." But now we can push this point further to upset Nāgārjuna's own strategy. The expression "There is light" may be only a variant way of saying "There is revelation of objects." For it is impossible to separate clearly the existence of light and revelation of objects. If this is so, Nāgārjuna has raised a vacuous question to confuse the issue. For you cannot have your cake and eat it. Nāgārjuna intends to reject the statement "The means of knowledge reveals or establishes itself" as meaningless because the analogical statement "Light reveals itself" is meaningless to Nāgārjuna as it stands. If instead of saying "Light reveals itself" we are simply warranted to say "There is light here and now," we can, instead of saying "The means of knowing reveals itself," say *mutatis mutandis* "There is or has been a means of knowing" or "A means of knowledge has occurred or taken place." Or, better still, we can say that there is revelation or establishment of objects whenever there happens to be a means of knowledge, just as we say that there is revelation of objects whenever there is light. If the matter is resolved in this way, then the proposed fault of infinite regress or circularity cannot arise. For we cannot raise such questions as "What does reveal the object?" or "What does reveal the means?" For, it may be argued, it is not necessary for some agent to reveal the object whenever such revelation takes place. The agent–action–patient distinction may be an arbitrary linguistic device and not an ontologically significant one. The same applies to the means. Talk of a means may be a stylistic device only, and need not be taken to be ontologically significant.

The light analogy in *Nyāyasūtra* 2.1.19 presents, however, an exegetical problem. For, if it is cited to support the self-revealing character of knowledge or its means, that would not be in accord with the prevailing standard view of the Nyāya school. The standard Nyāya view is that a cognitive event called knowledge or knowing is neither self-revealing nor self-validating, but is revealed (known) by another episode of knowing and validated also by something besides itself. The first theory is technically called *parataḥ prakāśa* and the second *parataḥ pramāṇya*. As I have already noted, according to the view of *parataḥ prakāśa*, from the fact that someone knows that *p* it does not necessarily follow that he knows that he knows that *p*. A means of knowing, in Nyāya view, cannot be likewise self-validated; it is to be validated, if necessary, by another means. Vātsyāyana, therefore, interpreted the light analogy of the *sūtra* in a way compatible with the standard Nyāya view.[13]

Vātsyāyana explains that the light (of the lamp) becomes a 'means' when it is an aid to an act of perception of a visible object, but the same lamplight becomes itself an 'object' of another perception caused by its contact with the sense of sight. In this way, the light plays the role of a 'means' when it helps us to see an 'object', and that of an 'object' when it is itself seen by the sense of sight. The 'means' and 'object' of knowledge are therefore not two distinct types of entities forming two ontological categories. The same entity (the same thing or the same substance) may play different roles—that of an 'instrument' or a 'means' as in "I see the table by the light," and of an 'object' as in "I see the light by the sense of sight." Ontologically, the same light doubles as a 'means' and as an 'object', depending upon different linguistic descriptions. The grammatical case-inflection expresses the particular role that our particular thought-construction has assigned to the thing in a given context. This is what Vātsyāyana means when he claims that different *kārakas** are not denotative of different things, but of potentialities (*śakti*) for different role-playing in the construction, and therefore the same thing or substance may appear in different roles indicated by the use of different case-inflections as in the following sentence constructions:

1. The tree stands there. (Nominative or agent)
2. He cuts the tree. (Accusative or patient)

[13] See Vātsyāyana under *Nyāyasūtra*, 2.1.19. [Above, p. 184.]

* Grammatical case endings.—Ed.

3. He shows the moon by the tree. (Instrumental)
4. He sprinkles water in the tree. (Dative)
5. Leaves fall from the tree. (Ablative)
6. Birds live in the tree. (Locative)

Once we have thus understood the difference in the roles played by the same ontological entity, i.e. a particular tree, it becomes easy for us to understand, so argues Vātsyāyana, that the difference between 'means' of knowledge and 'objects' of knowledge is the assigning of different roles to the entities in a given knowledge-situation. Certainly to be a 'means' signifies nothing but playing the role of an 'instrument' in the generation of knowledge, and to be an 'object' means to fill in the role of an accusative case in a knowledge-situation. Notice that Vātsyāyana's argument partly answers one of the Nāgārjunian criticisms: *viśeṣahetuś ca vaktavyaḥ*, "the distinction (between 'means' and 'objects' of knowing) must be accounted for." As this is not an ontological-type distinction, we need not go any further than what has already been said to account for it.

Nāgārjuna asks for the formulation of the criterion for some ontological or typological distinction, that between the *pramāṇas* and the *prameyas*, the 'means' and the 'object'. Vātsyāyana, I think rightly, resolves the issue by pointing out that the so-called distinction is only a distinction in role-playing, or, to be exact, a distinction in grammatical features. To ask why the same tree is the 'object' (accusative) in (2) above and a 'means' (instrument) in (3) above is to conflate an ontological issue with that of grammatical categories. Under one description the tree has becomes the 'object' and under another it becomes a 'means'. In this connection one may be reminded of the correct warning of G. E. M. Anscombe about the prevalent confusion regarding the nature of grammatical concepts: "Grammatical understanding and grammatical concepts, even the most familiar ones like sentence, verb, noun, are not so straightforward and down-to-earth a matter of plain physical realities as I believe people sometimes suppose."[14] Here Vātsyāyana explains the underlying grammatical structure to answer a puzzle posed by Nāgārjuna.

The charge of infinite regress is tackled by Vātsyāyana in an ingenious way. He argues that it is perfectly natural for a 'means' to be revealed or established by another 'means' just as the lamplight reveals the table while it is itself revealed by our sense of sight. This process need not regress to infinity. For it is not essential for every entity to be *known* or revealed to us first before it can play the role of a 'means'. We see with our eyes, the sense of sight, but we do not see the sense itself. We can infer that the sense of sight exists in us from the fact that we can see, but the fact of seeing does not depend upon our prior knowledge of the sense of sight. In order to use the money in my pocket, I would have to know that I have money there; but in order to use my ear-organ, my faculty of hearing, to hear a noise, I do not have to know first that this is my faculty of hearing. A prior knowledge of the 'means' is not always necessary before that means can be used for the generation of a piece of knowledge. This also does not imply that such a means is a self-evident one.

Nyāyasūtra 2.1.16 uses another analogy (besides the light analogy) to answer the Nāgārjunian sceptic. It is the analogy of the weighing-scale (cf. *tulā*).[15] Vātsyāyana says: "The scale is the measuring instrument for the knowledge of the weight measure, the heavy substance such as a lump of gold is what is measured, the 'object' of knowledge. When by such a lump of gold another scale is examined, then in ascertaining the second scale the lump of gold is the 'instrument' (*pramāṇa*) and the scale the object measured (*prameya*)."

Uddyotakara explains the light example of the *sūtra* in a slightly different way. He does not think that the example is intended to show that some or all pieces of knowledge or their means are self-evident or self-validating. It only shows, according to him, that the rigid distinction between what is a 'means' of knowledge and what counts as an 'object' of knowledge collapses, without necessarily implying thereby that the same item which acts as a means, or a piece of evidence, for something else is also evidence for itself. The opponent, i.e. the sceptic, insists that there are, according to the *pramāṇa* theory, two separate domains—one is the domain of

[14] G.E.M. Anscombe, *Collected Papers* vol. II (Oxford, 1981), p. 8.

[15] See Vātsyāyana under *Nyāyasūtra*, 2.1.16. [Above, p. 184.]

the means or evidence, the other, of the objects. A member of the first domain establishes, or is evidence for, some member of the second domain, and hence there would be a need for a third or a fourth domain (and so on *ad infinitum*) to contain items that would be evidence for members of the second (or the third) domain. Uddyotakara argues that the example of the lamp is used to point out that the rigid distinction between the first domain and the second domain collapses (for the same item can sometimes be a means and sometimes an object) and there is therefore no need to regress to infinity.[16]

Uddyotakara cites an interesting case to illustrate his position in regard to the problem of self-validation of the means of knowledge. He says that when someone wishes to test the water of a lake, for example, he takes a sample, viz. one bucket of water, and puts it to test. Having tested the sample, he proves the water of the lake to be pure (or impure as the case may be). Here the sample of water is the evidence for the purity of the lake water and what establishes the purity of the sample of water also establishes the purity of the lake water. People say that the sample of water is the means for knowing the purity of the lake water, although it is part of the same water in reality. Just as we do not say in this case that the evidence is also evidence for itself, we need not say similarly that a means of knowledge is also a means for itself.[17]

Uddyotakara's position is that something *a* can be taken to be evidence for something else, say *b*, and if and only if we search for *a*'s evidence might we obtain another item, *c*, as evidence for *a*; but in practice, for every bit of evidence, we do not always need to search for further evidence. For practical life (*vyavahāra*) goes on well as long as we are satisfied with the evidence that is available.

It is maintained that a thing can be a measuring instrument to measure a lump of gold, for example, but what gives the measure of that lump of gold, can itself be tested by another measuring device. What measures the lump of gold is what we call a 'measuring instrument' (a *pramāṇa*) in so far as the lump of gold and such other things are concerned; but other devices are also available when we need to measure our 'measuring instrument', and in that context we should call it a 'measurable object' rather than a means of measuring.

It may be argued that if our calling something a means of knowing or an instrument of measuring is in this way made dependent upon its direct connection with the act of knowing or measuring, then indeed we would not call something a 'means' when in fact it does not aid any measuring act or a knowing act. A measuring-stick will not be called a measuring-stick unless we measure something with it. Uddyotakara points out that our practice of calling something a means for knowledge, or for measurement, does not obey this ruling. For example, we do call somebody a cook (*pācaka*) even when he is walking along the street and is not cooking, e.g. "There goes our cook." Our practice or verbal usage is not simply arbitrary or unreasonable, for it is based upon the notion of *powers* or potentialities. The person we call 'cook' does not lose his 'power' or potency to cook just after one cooking. The power (*śakti*) existed in him even before the present act of cooking and will continue to be there, under normal circumstances, long after the present act of cooking. Hence when we see him walking along the street we say, "There goes our cook." This paradigm is applicable to our use of the term *pramāṇa* or *prameya*, 'means of knowing' and 'objects of knowing'. We can call something to be a 'means' even when it is not acting as an instrument in generating knowledge. Uddyotakara says, "He who does not understand the use of *pramāṇa* and *prameya* with reference to the three time-stages (past, present, and future) contradicts even such ordinary uses as "Fetch the cook.'"[18]

The ontic status of 'power' or potentiality is, however, a highly controversial topic. Uddyotakara does not go into it here. He simply states that our use of words may be justified on the basis of this assumed presence of power or potentiality (to cook, for example) even when such power is not manifest. In other words, he argues for two different states of the same power—a manifest state when the power is actualized in action and an unmanifest state when the

[16] Uddyotakara (B), pp. 193 f.

[17] Uddyotakara (B), under 2.1.19, p. 199.

[18] Ibid., p. 188 (under 2.1.11).

presence of such power is only assumed but not visible in the form of action. It is pointed out that even an ordinary object like a table or pot could be said to have an 'unmanifest' state when it lies in darkness invisible to anyone and a 'manifest' state when it is visible in light. It is not clear from Uddyotakara whether he would accept causal power or potentiality as forming a distinct reality locatable in the thing itself. It is the Mīmāṃsaka who accepts 'power' or potentiality to be a distinct category (*padārtha*) on a par with things and qualities. The prevailing Nyāya view, despite Uddyotakara's point here, is that causal power does not form a separate category, and it was Udayana who elaborately refuted the Mīmāṃsaka view about causal power.[19]

The Nāgārjunian sceptic may argue that there are no means of knowledge such as perception and inference, for they do not establish objects in any of the three time stages, past, present, or future. In reply, Uddyotakara claims that the sceptic contradicts his own statement (*sva-vacana-vyāghāta*). For the negation in the implicit premise ("that which can never establish any object is not a means") cannot, by the same token, negate. Such a statement cannot be a means for establishing the said negation (non-existence) of the means, without itself being a means in the first place. Uddyotakara says that the case is like that of one who wishes to burn others by lighting his own finger. For either he would be able to burn others by burning, in the process, his own finger, or he would not be able to burn anything if he does not first burn his own finger.[20]

I have already pointed out that Nāgārjuna would allow such a situation. He would let his finger be burned with all readiness (destroy his own proposition, *nāsti kācana pratijñā me*) if that allows him to burn all others. This, however, may be an impossible feat, for if I first burn my own finger, I cannot use it as a means for burning others, for that would be using a non-existent (already destroyed) means. However, Nāgārjuna can remain silent without formulating his own statement, for if all other propositions do not in any case exist, a statement is not needed to refute them!

[19]Udayana, *Nyāyakusumāñjali*, ch. I, verse 10, pp. 107–25.

[20]Uddyotakara (B), under 2.1.12, p. 189.

2.4 Is Radical Scepticism Feasible?

The upshot is that a radical scepticism of this kind is not, or does not seem to be, a statable position. For if it is statable, it becomes incoherent or paradoxical. In other words such a position could be coherent only at the risk of being unstatable! It seems to me that both radical scepticism and Nāgārjunian Buddhism would welcome this situation, for here we may find the significance of the doctrine of silence in Mādhyamika. (The same point may also explain the ironical comment of Aristotle, though not the irony of it, regarding Cratylus who only wiggled his finger, instead of teaching anything.) Is it the only way to make radical scepticism a coherent position? If it is, then the teacher-philosopher is forced to remain mute and so lose any chance of success in communicating his doctrine. But there is another way. The sceptic may claim, as Śrīharṣa explicitly did, that he enters into a debate simply to refute others and it is not his responsibility to state his position, much less to defend it. . . . Assuming the standards of argument and proof of his opponent as only provisionally correct or acceptable, he would be inclined to show that the opponent's position is wrong, and there ends his philosophic discourse. In other words, his philosophic activity consists in *refutation* only, not in *assertion*.

The obvious difficulty here would be that the sceptic would have to answer the following challenge: How can he logically not *assert* anything while he refutes something? Is refutation of a proposition possible without any (implicit) assertion? According to the standard notion of logic, refutation cannot be successful without negating something, i.e. some proposition, and negation of some proposition *p* is equivalent to assertion of *not-p*. If we follow this line of argument then it is difficult to see how the sceptic can simply refute without asserting or stating anything. In other words, it is impossible to maintain the position of 'non-assertion' or 'non-statement', even though the sceptic enters into debate only for the sake of refutation. I think the radical sceptic has an easy answer to this problem. He may say that his refutation should not, and need not, be equated with the negation as it is understood in standard logic (where to negate *p* means to assert *not-p*). His refutation is a strong refutation of a possibility. . . . but without any implication for the contrary or contradictory possibilities. This notion of refutation is more or less prominent in our question-and-answer activity. It is a non-committal act of refutation or what I once called the commitmentless denial of the Mādhyamikas.

What emerges here is that the problem of negation or the ambiguity of negative statement is philosophically very central. Negation, as Richard Routley has commented (in private correspondence) "is a fundamental, but ill-understood, ill-explained, and much-disputed notion across a wide philosophical spectrum." The sceptic may or may not find his position paradoxical, but what we should not do is to attack or threaten the sceptic with the two very sharp horns of a dilemma, or a paradox which has been generated in the first place by our own standard classical logical definition of negation. The standard classical theory of negation in a two-valued system does capture, we must admit, a very pervasive sense of negation. But it is also a fact that some important uses of negation are left out in the account that we get from standard logic. The sceptic's use of negation, perhaps, can be better understood as an act of refutation, an illocutionary act where one negates some illocutionary force rather than a proposition.

I wish to refer here to J.R. Searle's distinction between a propositional negation and an illocutionary negation to explain the sceptic's point.[21] This is, I think, quite suitable to explain . . . the Nāgārjuna-type negation. . . . If we construe assertion as an illocutionary act and the proposition is represented by *p*, then we can write, "I assert that *p*." By illocutionary negation, we can then write for the sceptic's utterance, "I do not assert that *p*." . . . Here the sceptic does not make another assertion such as '*not-p*', for illocutionary negation usually negates the act or the illocutionary force. A propositional negation would leave the illocutionary force unchanged, for the result would be another proposition, a negative one, similarly asserted as the affirmative one.

The sceptic's attitude of non-assertion is therefore a possible one, and this does not force him into a contradiction. He can very well say, "I do not say that it is *p*. Nor do I say that it is *not-p*," just as I can say, "I do not promise to come, nor do I promise not to come." I think the Buddhist dilemma or tetralemma could be better explained in the context of such illocutionary acts. Consider also the following. Suppose *p* stands for the proposition that everything is empty or that all assertions are false. A Nāgārjunian sceptic has the perfect right to say, "I do not assert that *p*, nor do I assert that *not-p*." This does not seem to lead him to any position even when the sceptic participates in the debate only for the sake of refutation.

The sceptic in the . . . Nāgārjuna tradition is more in line with the Greek sophist or the Pyrrhonist (as described by Sextus Empiricus) than with the Cartesian sceptic. But, nevertheless, the critique of knowledge and evidence that the Indian sceptic has generated can hardly be ignored by an epistemologist in any tradition. In classical India, as I have already indicated, the generally accepted style of philosophizing was the formulation of a *pramāṇa* theory as the basis for a defence of some metaphysical system or other. The Nāgārjunian critique was that this style of philosophizing is at best a distortion and at worst an illusion. For it assumes more than what is warranted by pure experience. The force of such arguments was to persuade us to recognize our philosophic activity, our *pramāṇa* doctrine, for what it is, a fabrication, a convenient myth-making or make-believe, the inherent value of which lies only in making day-to-day life work smoothly and rendering inter-subjective communication successful. In short, the sceptic says that the *pramāṇa* theorist either begs the question (while talking about 'evidence' or 'ways' or 'means' of knowing, such as perception and inference) by using a very questionable criterion to establish the standard for what should count as true, or he regresses to infinity to find out another criterion for this criterion and so on. I have already summed up how the *pramāṇa* theorists in general, and Nyāya in particular, would answer this challenge.

The sceptic's argumentation, through constant practice, is supposed to lead one to an *insight* into the nature of what is ultimately real (*prajñā*). This transition from radical scepticism to some sort of

[21] J. R. Searle, *Speech Acts* (Cambridge, 1969), pp. 32–3.

mysticism (where the truth is supposed to dawn upon the person if he can rid himself of all false or unwarranted beliefs) is very pronounced in the Indian tradition, and it seems to be somewhat marginal in the Western tradition. Śrīharṣa claims that his Brahman does not need to be established through any means, for the eternal truth will illuminate and show itself as soon as the fabricated walls of misconceptions and false beliefs are destroyed, and dialectics only help to destroy them. Jayarāśi, however, does not say anything about how the truth will come to light. For him all philosophic questions remain open, and in practical life he recommends common sense and normal behaviour. He says that those who understand the ultimate purpose recommend that we follow ordinary worldly behaviour (*laukika mārga*), for "with regard to ordinary behaviour the wise resembles the fool or the child."[22] Sextus' own commendation is not very far from it: "We live in accordance with the normal rules of life, undogmatically, seeing that we cannot remain wholly inactive."[23]

Even the 'sudden illumination' theory of the Indian sceptic-mystic is matched by another comment of Sextus. He compares the sceptic with Apelles, court-painter of Alexander the Great. Once Apelles was painting a horse and wanted to paint the horse's foam. Being unsuccessful several times, in despair he flung a sponge at the picture and, lo and behold, the foam was automatically painted by the throwing of the sponge. Sceptics get their *ataraxia* in this way all of a sudden. A Buddhist Zen master would have loved this analogy.

[22] Jayarāśi, p. 1.

[23] Sextus, p. 23.

PART IV East Asia

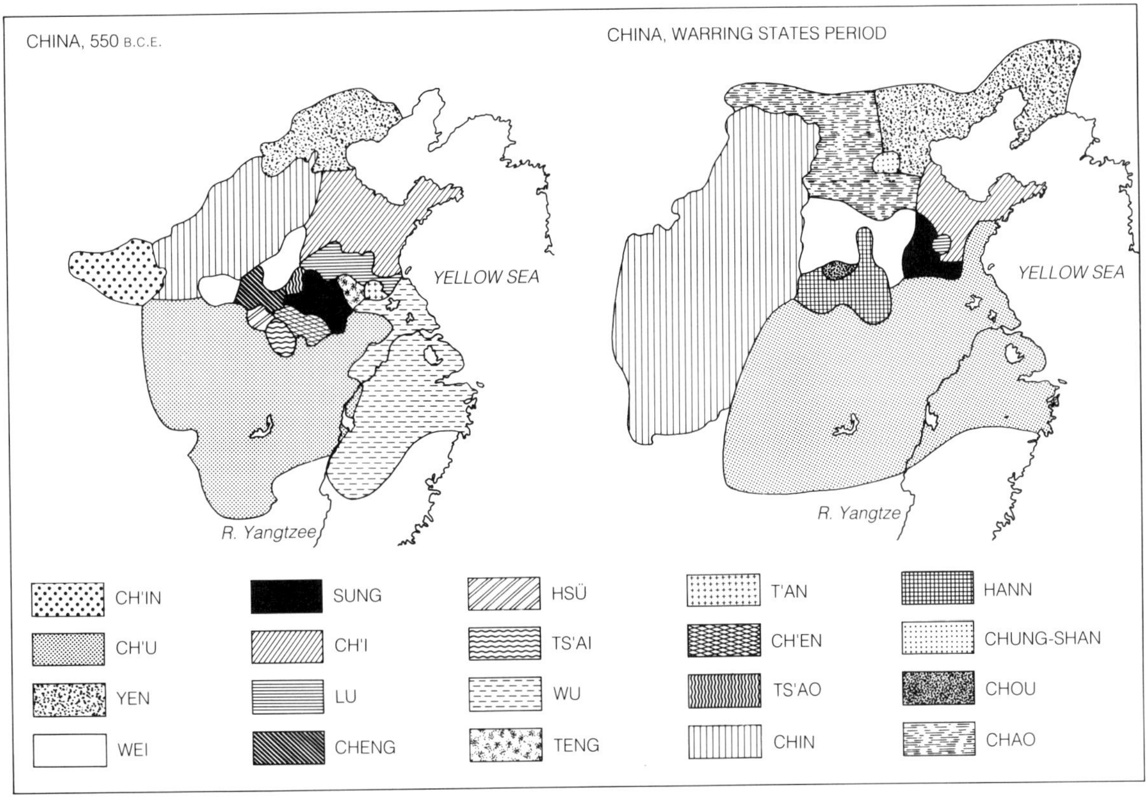

CONFUCIANISM

K'ung Fu-Tzu (Grand Master K'ung) or, as he became known in the West, Confucius (551–479 B.C.E.), has been called the most influential and revered person in the history of China. Born in the small state of Lu to a noble but poor family, he was completely self-educated. (His father had died when Confucius was three.) During his twenties, he became a granary keeper and a supervisor of flocks. Confucius then began teaching. His interest in politics led him to travel to the neighboring state, Ch'i (in the Pinyin transliteration, Qi), where he served as a government consultant for several years during his thirties. These were times of great political and intellectual upheaval; eventually, his life in danger, Confucius left Ch'i.

Returning to Lu, he refused entreaties to support various politicians. He became the first professional teacher in Chinese history, traveling at one point to see Lao Tzu in Chou (Zhou). In his fifties Confucius became a magistrate and then minister of justice in Chou, where he met great success. He recovered land from Ch'i through negotiations and conquered three important and rival cities. At age fifty-six, however, he fell out of favor and spent the next thirteen years traveling and teaching. Finding the rulers of other states uninterested in his ideas, he returned to Lu at sixty-eight and taught there until his death eight years later. He is reputed to have had over three thousand students.

The Analects is a collection of the sayings of Confucius himself; *The Great Learning* and *The Doctrine of the Mean,* many scholars think, are works by his pupils—by his grandson, Tzu Ssu, according to tradition—although some place their composition two or three centuries later. These three works, together with *The Book of Mencius,* were grouped together by a later thinker, Chu Hsi, as the Four Books, which formed the basis of Chinese civil service examinations for about six centuries.

Confucian doctrine is sometimes summarized as *ethical humanism*. Confucius is certainly a humanist, and his works are primarily ethical. Like Aristotle, Confucius centers his ethics on the concept of virtue. He transforms the traditional notion of a superior person, literally, "child of a ruler," into the notion of a morally upright person, one of superior character. The idea that human excellence is a function of character rather than birth, upbringing, social position, or even achievement was, and remains, revolutionary. Confucius uses the term *jen* (humanity) as a term for virtue in general. The virtuous person, according to Confucius, is benevolent, kind, generous, and above all, balanced, observing the Mean in all things. Again like Aristotle, Confucius thinks of virtue as a mean between extremes; the properly generous person, for example, gives appropriately, neither too much nor too little, to the right people in the right circumstances.

Confucius's view of virtue crucially involves propriety, the observance of proper rites, ceremonies, and principles. The word he uses is *li*, which originally referred to religious sacrifice. It has come to mean ceremony, rite, ritual, decorum, propriety, principle, and proper form or custom. Almost all translators, therefore, render it differently in different contexts. Most often, Confucius uses *li* to refer to traditional social rules and practices. Philosophically, all three aspects of *li* are important. They are traditional: they are mandated by custom and connect us with the past. They are social: they concern relations between people in society and constitute a significant part of the social order. Finally, they are rules or practices: they govern how people with certain characteristics should behave in certain situations. Many features of propriety, according to Confucius, arise from particular social relations—the relation of parent and child, for example. Some, however, seem universal. Confucius articulates a version of the Golden Rule, which he calls a rule of reciprocity: "What you do not want done to yourself, do not do to others."

Mencius (372?–289? B.C.E.), originally, Meng Tzu, was perhaps the greatest ancient disciple of Confucius. Born in what is now Shantung province, he lived during the turbulent Warring States period. He studied under a student of a student of Tzu Ssu, Confucius's grandson. He became a professional teacher and for about forty years traveled throughout China offering advice to various nobles and officials. In his fifties he served as an official in Ch'i.

Mencius abides by the chief doctrines of Confucius, but he develops Confucianism in a number of original and important ways. First, Mencius argues that human nature is originally and essentially good. He observes that anyone seeing a baby fall into a well would rush to help without thinking. This shows that human nature is itself altruistic. Specifically, Mencius holds that four kinds of virtue are inherent in human nature: humanity (*jen*), righteousness or justice (*yi*), decency, and knowledge. We innately feel compassion, which is the beginning of humanity; shame and dislike, the beginnings of righteousness or justice; modesty, the beginnng of decency; and approval and disapproval, the beginnings of knowledge. The relation of these virtues to innate feeling leads Mencius to place great emphasis on conscience and moral intuition.

Second, Mencius treats humanity as a virtue that good people can attain rather than as an unattainable ideal. Confucius speaks of only the sages of antiquity as having true humanity. Mencius, in contrast, maintains that we are all born with a disposition to humanity. We must preserve and cultivate this intuition, to be sure, but our innate moral intuition gives us the ability to achieve humanity in the fullest sense.

Third, Mencius stresses the concept of righteousness or justice (*yi*). This concept plays some role in Confucius's thought, but it is the foundation of Mo Tzu's utilitarianism (see p. 279). Mencius tries to synthesize these approaches by treating humanity and justice as independent, fundamental notions. Confucius talks about the obligations of rulers, the characteristics of good rulers, and other political topics, but he has no conception of rights. Mencius, however, treats justice as the primary political virtue and understands it, not in terms of good consequences, as Mo Tzu does, but in terms of respect for the rights of others. Mencius does not develop a theory of rights; in his view, rights arise from tradition and custom, not from an abstract set of rules or a code of laws. Humanity and justice are linked: in W.A.C.H. Dobson's words, "a man is *jen* when he is what he should be, and *yi* when he does what he should do."*

* W.A.C.H. Dobson, *Mencius* (London: Oxford University Press, 1963), 132.

Mencius attacks Mo Tzu's utilitarianism and his attendant doctrine of universal love. For Confucius, moral obligations stem from specific human relations, such as that of parent to child. Mencius argues that Moism places too little value on these relations. Suppose, for instance, that two people are drowning, that you can save only one, and that one of the two is your own child. What should you do? Moism implies that it makes no ethical difference which you save. Any simple utilitarian theory like Mo Tzu's directs us to maximize the amount of good in the community. From the perspective of such a theory, it makes no difference who has what amount of good. So, it makes no difference whether your own child lives or dies, provided that another is saved in its place.

In Mencius's view, this result is absurd. Of course you should save your own child; your relation as parent and child gives you special obligations to each other that go beyond obligations we all have to one another as human beings. Mencius's objection thus goes beyond the specifics of Moism to the impartiality inherent in many forms of moral theory, such as utilitarianism. Even if not all obligations stem from particular social relations, Mencius argues, some surely do. If so, then purely universal and impartial ethical theories can at most tell part of the story.

Hsün Tzu (also known as Xunzi; 310?–212? B.C.E.) was born in Chao (Zhao), one of the states that gave the Warring States period its name. His was a time of intense regional conflict. Hsün Tzu was an extremely talented student, leaving home at fifteen to study at Chi Hsia (Jixia) academy, the intellectual center of ancient China. There he had the opportunity to present his ideas to the prime minister of Ch'i, one of the most powerful officials in the country. Like Confucius and Mencius, however, Hsün Tzu found that the government paid little heed to philosophers.

The combined armies of several states invaded Ch'i in 284 B.C.E., routing the army and scattering the scholars at Chi Hsia. Hsün Tzu fled to Ch'i, which in turn suffered a series of devastating military defeats; he returned to Ch'u around 275. While in Ch'u, however, Hsün Tzu became acquainted with the works of Mo Tzu and his followers. It is unclear what Hsün Tzu himself wrote, but on his return to Ch'i, he was recognized as the "most eminent elder scholar," even though he was only in his mid thirties. He returned to the Chi Hsia Academy and attracted students, such as Han Fei and Li Ssi, who would become famous in their own right.

In his late forties, Hsün Tzu spent several years at the court of Ch'in (Qin), the most powerful of the warring states. Though he was able to have audiences with various Ch'in leaders, including the king, Hsün Tzu found his advice unheeded. He received no offer of a government post for putting his ideas into practice. But his experiences there did more than produce frustration; they led him to reconsider his entire philosophy. Hsün Tzu recognized that Ch'in, a wealthy but intellectually unsophisticated state that manifested none of the traditional Confucian virtues, nevertheless seemed both successful and well-ordered. It had attracted a series of exceptionally brilliant ministers by operating as a meritocracy, granting advancement without regard to social class to those who demonstrated skill and achieved success.

Ch'in, during Hsün Tzu's stay, carried on a war of expansion, winning victory after victory. Finally, in 260 B.C.E., it attacked his native Chao. Hsün Tzu decided to return to help resist the assault. Initially, matters appeared very grave for Chao: its entire army surrendered, and all but a few were buried alive; the Ch'in forces laid siege to the Chao capital; the Chao king proved ineffectual. Hsün Tzu advised other Chao leaders on defense, writing several works on warfare in the process. By ignoring and sometimes disobeying the king, with the city near starvation, they managed a remarkable turnaround, defeating Ch'in in 257.

Hsün Tzu, a contemporary of Aristotle, adopts a naturalistic approach to philosophy. His ethical theory directly opposes that of Mencius. Confucius declares that all people are by nature alike but differ by training. Mencius amplifies this doctrine, claiming that everyone is by nature good. Hsün Tzu argues, in contrast, that people are originally evil. Human nature, he insists, is entirely bad; everything good is acquired by education, training, or socialization. By nature, we are selfish, combative, envious, lecherous, and hostile.

It is important to distinguish our natural dispositions from our natural capacities. Prior to training or education, we are disposed to evil. We nevertheless have the capacity for good. We can nurture and develop that capacity, becoming good in spite of our natures. But this requires effort. Hsün Tzu thus opposes not only Mencius but also Taoism. For Lao Tzu, things, including people, naturally tend toward the good. This implies an ethics of noninterference; we should let things follow their natural courses. For Hsün Tzu, in contrast, people naturally tend toward evil. This implies an ethic of active interference. People must be restrained from doing evil and taught to overcome their natural tendencies and become good.

This need for restraint, according to Hsün Tzu, justifies the existence of government. People can become good only with the help of rules of proper conduct and government to make them obey the rules. Eventually, the good person obeys the rules willingly, not from fear of being punished. But people can reach that state only through the training the rules provide. Like Confucius, then, Hsün Tzu stresses the importance of *li* (propriety), the observance of social rules. Confucius, however, thinks of propriety as an individual virtue, an attitude or state of mind of respect for rules and traditions. Hsün Tzu thinks of propriety much more as an external virtue akin to obedience.

CONFUCIUS

from *The Analects*

The following passages were revised and emended by Daniel Bonevac from The Four Books, *edited and translated by James Legge, originally published in* The Chinese Classics, *Volume I (Oxford: Clarendon, 1893).*

1:1. The Master said, "Isn't it pleasant to learn with constant perseverance and application? Isn't it delightful to have friends coming from distant quarters? Isn't he a man of complete virtue who doesn't get angry that others don't recognize him?"

1:2. Yu said, "Few filial and fraternal people like to offend their superiors, and nobody who doesn't like to offend superiors likes to stir up rebellion. The superior man attends to the root of things. From the root grows the Way (*tao*). Filial piety and fraternal submission are the root of benevolence (*jen*)."

1:4. Tseng said, "I daily examine myself on three points: whether, with others, I may have been unfaithful; whether, with friends, I may have been untrustworthy; whether I may have failed to master and practice the instructions of my teacher."

1:6. The Master said, "A youth at home should be filial; abroad, respectful to elders. He should be earnest and truthful. He should overflow with love to all and cultivate the friendship of the good. When he has time and opportunity after doing these things, he should study."

1:7. Tzu-Hsia said, "If a man turns from love of beauty to sincere love of virtue; if he can serve his parents with all his strength; if he can serve his prince with his life; if his words to his friends are sincere; although men say he has not learned, I will certainly say that he has."

1:8. The Master said, "A scholar who is not serious will not be venerated, and his learning will not be solid. Hold faithfulness and sincerity as first principles. Have no friends not equal to yourself. When you have faults, do not fear to abandon them."

1:11. The Master said, "When a man's father is alive, look at the bent of his will. When his father is dead, look at his conduct. If for three years he does not swerve from the way of his father, he may be called filial."

1:12. Yu said, "In practicing propriety, a natural ease is best. This is the excellence of the ancient kings, and in things small and great we follow them. Yet it is not to be observed in all cases. Anyone who knows and manifests such ease must regulate it by propriety."

1:14. The Master said, "A superior man doesn't seek gratification or comfort. He is earnest in what he does; he is careful in speech. He associates with men of principle to rectify himself. Such a person truly loves to learn."

1:15. Tzu-kung said, "What do you say about the poor man who doesn't flatter and the rich man who isn't arrogant?" The Master replied: "They will do, but they are not equal to someone who is poor and yet cheerful, or rich and yet loves propriety." . . .

1:16. The Master said, "I will not grieve at others' not knowing me; I will grieve at my not knowing them."

2:1. The Master said, "He who governs virtuously is like the North Star; it keeps its place, and all the stars revolve around it."

2:2. The Master said, "In the *Book of Poetry** are three hundred pieces, but the design of them all may be embraced in one sentence: 'Have no depraved thoughts.'"

2:3. The Master said, "If the people are led by laws and restrained by punishments, they will try to avoid them without any sense of shame. If they are led by virtue and restrained by propriety, they will have a sense of shame and become good."

2:4. The Master said, "At fifteen, I had my mind bent on learning. At thirty, I stood firm. At forty, I had no doubts. At fifty, I knew the decrees of Heaven. At sixty, my ear obeyed truth. At seventy, I could follow what my heart desired without transgressing what was right."

2:5. Meng I asked what filial piety was. The Master said, "Not being disobedient." As Fan Ch'ih was driving him, the Master said, "Mang-sun asked me what filial piety was, and I answered, 'Not being disobedient.'" Fan Ch'ih said, "What did you mean?" The Master replied, "Parents, when alive, should be served according to propriety. When dead, they should be buried according to propriety and sacrificed to according to propriety."

2:10. The Master said, "See what a man does. Mark his motives. Examine his habits. How can a man conceal his character? How can a man conceal his character?"

2:12. The Master said, "The superior man is no tool."

2:13. Tzu-kung asked what constituted the superior man. The Master said, "He acts before he speaks, and then speaks as he acts."

2:14. The Master said, "The superior man is open-minded and not partisan. The mean man is partisan and not open-minded."

2:15. The Master said, "Learning without thought is labor lost; thought without learning is perilous."

2:16. The Master said, "The study of strange doctrines is injurious indeed!"

2:17. The Master said, "Yu, shall I teach you what knowledge is? When you know something, to maintain that you know it; when you don't know something, to admit that you don't know it—this is knowledge."

2:19. The duke Ai asked, "What should be done to secure the people's compliance?" Confucius replied, "Advance the upright and set aside the crooked, and the people will comply. Advance the crooked and set aside the upright, and the people won't comply."

2:20. Chi K'ang asked how to make the people revere their ruler, be faithful to him, and train themselves to be virtuous. The Master said, "If he presides over them solemnly, they'll revere him. If he is filial and kind to all, they'll be faithful to him. If he advances the good and teaches the incompetent, they'll eagerly seek to be virtuous."

2:24. The Master said, "For a man to sacrifice to someone else's ancestor is flattery. To see what is right and not do it is cowardice."

4:2. The Master said, "Those without virtue cannot abide long in a condition of poverty and hardship, or in a condition of enjoyment. The virtuous are at ease with virtue (*jen*); the wise desire virtue."

* *The Book of Poetry*, also called *The Book of Odes*, is a Confucian classic. It contains 305 poems and songs—some religious, some popular—from the early Chou dynasty (1111–249 B.C.E.). It and *The Book of History* are the earliest existing texts of Chinese literature. According to tradition, Confucius edited these works, finding inspiration in them for his own ethical ideas.—ED.

4:3. The Master said, "Only the truly virtuous (*jen*) know what to love or hate in others."

4:4. The Master said, "One whose mind is set on virtue (*jen*) will not practice wickedness."

4:5. The Master said, "Wealth and honor are what men desire. If they can't be obtained in the proper way, they shouldn't be held. Poverty and meanness are what men dislike. If they can't be avoided in the proper way, they shouldn't be avoided. If a superior man abandons virtue (*jen*), how can he deserve that name? The superior man doesn't, even for the space of a single meal, act contrary to virtue. In moments of haste, he clings to it. In seasons of danger he clings to it."

4:6. The Master said, "I haven't seen anyone who loved virtue (*jen*) or hated what wasn't virtuous. He who loved virtue would esteem nothing above it. He who hated what isn't virtuous would practice virtue so that only the virtuous would get near him. Is anyone able for one day to devote his strength to virtue? I haven't seen anyone whose strength would be insufficient. If there's such a case, I haven't seen it."

4:7. The Master said, "The faults of men reveal their character. By observing a man's faults, you may know him to be virtuous."

4:10. The Master said, "The superior man in the world is not for anything or against anything; he follows what is right."

4:11. The Master said, "The superior man thinks of virtue; the small man thinks of comfort. The superior man thinks of the law; the small man thinks of favors."

4:12. The Master said, "He who acts with a constant view to his own advantage will be murmured against."

4:14. The Master said, "I'm not concerned that I have no place; I'm concerned to fit myself for one. I'm not concerned that I'm not known; I seek to be worthy to be known."

4:15. The Master said, "Shen, my doctrine is one thread." Tseng replied, "Yes." The Master went out, and the other disciples asked, "What do his words mean?" Tsang said, "Our Master's doctrine is to be true to the principles of our nature and to exercise them benevolently toward others—this and nothing more."

4:16. The Master said, "The mind of the superior man is conversant with righteousness; the mind of the inferior man is conversant with gain."

4:17. The Master said, "When we see men of worth, we should think of equaling them; when we see men of a contrary character, we should turn inward and examine ourselves."

4:18. The Master said, "In serving his parents, a son may remonstrate with them, but gently; when he sees that they are not inclined to listen, he still reveres them, but maintains his purpose. Should they punish him, he doesn't complain."

4:19. The Master said, "While his parents are alive, a son may not travel far. If he does, he must have a fixed itinerary."

4:22. The Master said, "The ancients did not speak readily, for they feared that their actions would not come up to their words."

4:23. The Master said, "The cautious seldom err."

4:24. The Master said, "The superior man wishes to be slow in speech but earnest in conduct."

4:25. The Master said, "Virtue is not left to stand alone. Whoever practices it will have neighbors."

5:10. The Master said, "I haven't seen a firm and unbending man." Someone replied, "There's Shan Ch'ang." "Ch'ang" said the Master, "is under the influence of his passions; how can he be pronounced firm and unbending?"

5:11. Tzu-kung said, "What I don't want others to do to me, I also want not to do to others." The Master said, "Tz'u, you have not attained to that."

5:12. Tzu-kung said, "We may hear the Master on letters and culture. But we may not hear him on human nature and the way of Heaven."*

6:18. The Master said, "Those who know the way aren't equal to those who love it, and those who love it aren't equal to those who delight in it."

6:20. Fan Ch'ih asked what constituted wisdom. The Master said, "To give oneself earnestly to duties due to men, and to respect spiritual beings but keep aloof from them, may be called wisdom." He asked about perfect virtue (*jen*). The man of virtue thinks first of difficulties, and only then of success. This may be called perfect virtue."

6:23. The Master said, "A cornered vessel without corners? A strange cornered vessel! A strange cornered vessel!"

6:24. Tsai Wo asked, "A benevolent man, told 'There is a man in the well,' will go in after him, I suppose." Confucius said, "Why should he? A superior man may be made to go to the well, but not to go down into it. One may impose upon him, but not make a fool of him."

6:25. The Master said, "The superior man studies all learning extensively and restrains himself by propriety. So, he doesn't swerve from the Way."

6:27. The Master said, "Perfect is the virtue that accords with the Constant Mean! For a long time, its practice has been rare among the people."

6:28. Tzu-kung said, "What would you say of a man who confers benefits on the people extensively and assists everyone? May he be called perfectly virtuous (*jen*)?" The Master said, "Why only virtuous? Must he not have the qualities of a sage? Even Yao and Shun weren't like this.* A man of perfect virtue (*jen*), wishing to establish himself, establishes others; wishing to enlarge himself, enlarges others. To be able to judge others by what is right in ourselves is the art of virtue (*jen*)."

7:27. The Master said, "Maybe some act without knowing why. I don't. Hearing much, selecting what is good, and following it, seeing much and remembering it, are the second style of knowledge."

7:36. The Master said, "The superior man is satisfied and composed; the mean man is always distressed."

7:37. The Master was mild but dignified; majestic but not harsh; respectful but at ease.

8:2. The Master said, "Respectfulness without propriety becomes laborious bustle. Caution without propriety becomes timidity. Boldness without propriety becomes insubordination; straightforwardness without propriety becomes rudeness. Officials who perform their duties well arouse the people to virtue. If they don't neglect their friends, they save the people from meanness."

8:8. The Master said, "The mind is stimulated by poetry. Character is established by propriety. Music applies the finish."

8:13. The Master said, "Have sincere faith and love learning. Be willing to die to pursue the Way. Don't enter a tottering state or dwell in a disorganized one. When the kingdom is governed according to the Way, show yourself; otherwise hide. When the Way prevails in a country, be ashamed of poverty and meanness. Otherwise, be ashamed of wealth and honor."

* The distinction here is between nature and nurture. Confucius would speak to his students about culture, i.e., about aspects of their character developed through nurture, which they could affect. But he refused to speak of human nature itself.—ED.

* Confucius, Mencius, and other Chinese philosophers refer to Yao, Shun, and Duke Chou as ideal rulers and sages. Yao and Shun were legendary successive rulers of the third millennium B.C.E. Duke Chou helped to establish the Chou dynasty in 1111 B.C.E.—ED.

9:4. The Master was entirely free of four things: foregone conclusions, arbitrariness, obstinacy, and egotism.

11:11. Chi Lu asked about serving the spirits. The Master said, "If you can't serve men, how can you serve spirits?" Chi Lu added, "I venture to ask about death." Confucius answered, "If you don't know about life, how can you know about death?"

12:1. Yen Yüan asked about perfect virtue (*jen*). The Master said, "To subdue oneself and return to propriety is virtue. If a man can subdue himself and return to propriety for one day, all under heaven will ascribe virtue to him. Is the practice of virtue from oneself alone, or does it depend on others?" Yen Yüan said, "I want to ask about these steps." The Master replied, "Don't look at what is contrary to propriety; don't listen to what is contrary to propriety; don't speak what is contrary to propriety; don't make a move that is contrary to propriety." Yen Yüan then said, "I'm not intelligent or energetic, but I'll do my best to practice this."

12:2. Chung-kung asked about perfect virtue (*jen*). The Master said, "When you travel, act as if you were receiving a great guest. Employ the people as if you were assisting at a great sacrifice. Don't do to others what you wouldn't want done to yourself. Then no one in the country or your family will complain about you." Chung-kung said, "I'm not intelligent or energetic, but I'll do my best to practice this."

12:9. Duke Ai asked Yu Zo, "Suppose the year is one of scarcity and the government faces a deficit. What is to be done?" Yu Zo replied, "Why not demand from the people a tenth of their income?" "With two tenths there isn't enough," said the Duke. "How could I get by with one tenth?" Yu Zo answered, "If the people have plenty, their ruler won't be needy alone. If the people are needy, their ruler can't enjoy plenty alone."

12:17. Chi K'ang asked Confucius about government. He replied, "To govern (*cheng*) means to rectify (*cheng*). If you lead correctly, who will dare to be incorrect?"*

12:22. Fan Ch'ih asked about benevolence (*jen*). The Master said, "It is to love everyone." He asked about knowledge. The Master said, "It is to know everyone." . . .

13:3. Tzu-lu said, "The ruler of Wei is waiting for you to help him govern. What should be done first?" The Master replied, "Rectify names." "Really?" said Tzu-lu. "You're wide of the mark. Why rectify names?" The Master said, "How uncultivated you are, Yu! A superior man shows a cautious reserve about what he doesn't know." . . .

13:6. The Master said, "If a ruler acts correctly, he can govern without issuing orders. If he acts incorrectly, his orders won't be followed."

13:9. When the Master went to Wei, Zan Yu drove his carriage. The Master observed, "The people are numerous here." Yu said, "Since they are numerous, what more should a leader do for them?" "Enrich them," was the reply. "When they've been enriched, what more should a leader do?" The Master said, "Teach them."

13:11. The Master said, " 'If good men were to govern for a hundred years, they could transform the violently bad and dispense with capital punishment.' True indeed."

13:13. The Master said, "If a minister makes his own conduct correct, what difficulty will he have in governing? If he can't rectify himself, how can he rectify others?"

13:16. The duke of Sheh asked about government. The Master said, "Good government makes happy those who are near and attracts those who are far away."

13:17. Tzu-hsia, governor of Chü-fu, asked about government. The Master said, "Don't try to

*'Govern' and 'rectify' are both *cheng;* moreover, the character for 'govern' contains the radical for 'right' or 'rectify'.—ED.

do things quickly; don't look at small advantages. Trying to do things quickly keeps them from being done thoroughly. Looking at small advantages prevents one from accomplishing great things."

13:18. The duke of Sheh told Confucius, "Some of us are upright. If our father had stolen a sheep, we'd bear witness to it." Confucius said, "In my country the upright are different. The father conceals the misconduct of the son, and the son conceals the misconduct of the father. Uprightness is to be found in this."

13:19. Fan Ch'ih asked about perfect virtue (*jen*). The Master said, "It is to be solemn at rest, attentive in business, and sincere with others. Even if you live among barbarians, you may not abandon it."

14:25. The Master said, "In ancient times, men learned to improve themselves. Now they learn to win approval from others."

14:30. The Master said, "The way of the superior man is threefold, but I am not equal to it. Virtuous (*jen*), he is free from anxieties; wise, he is free from perplexities; bold, he is free from fear." Tsze-kung said, "Master, that's you."

14:36. Someone said, "What do you say about the principle of repaying injury with kindness?" The Master said, "How then will you repay kindness? Repay injury with justice and kindness with kindness."

15:2. The Master said, "Tz'u, I suppose you think I'm one who learns many things and remembers them?" Tzu-kung replied, "Yes—but perhaps it's not true?" "No," was the answer, "I seek one thread."

15:17. The Master said, "The superior man takes righteousness (*yi*) to be essential. He practices it according to propriety. He brings it forth in humility. He completes it with sincerity. This is indeed a superior man."

15:18. The Master said, "The superior man is distressed at his lack of ability. He is not distressed at his lack of recognition."

15:19. The Master said, "The superior man dislikes the thought of his name being forgotten after his death."

15:20. The Master said, "What the superior man seeks is in himself. What the inferior man seeks is in others."

15:23. Tzu-kung asked, "Is there one word to serve as a rule for practice throughout life?" Confucius said, "It is *reciprocity.* What you don't want done to yourself, don't do to others."

15:28. The Master said, "The value of the Way depends on man; the value of man doesn't depend on the Way."

15:38. The Master said, "In teaching there should be no class distinctions."

15:39. The Master said, "Those whose paths diverge can't lay plans for one another."

15:40. The Master said, "In language all that matters is conveying meaning."

16:10. Confucius said, "The superior man thoughtfully considers nine things: With his eyes, he wants to see clearly. With his ears, he wants to hear distinctly. In countenance, he wants to be warm. In demeanor, he wants to be respectful. In speech, he wants to be sincere. In business, he wants to be careful. When in doubt, he wants to ask others. When angry, he thinks of difficulties that might result. When he sees opportunity for gain, he thinks of righteousness (*yi*)."

17:2. The Master said, "By nature, men are alike. By practice, they grow apart."

17:6. Tzu-chang asked Confucius about perfect virtue (*jen*). Confucius said, "To be able to practice five things everywhere under heaven constitutes perfect virtue." He begged to know what they were, and was told, "Seriousness, generosity, sincerity, diligence, and kindness. If you're serious, you won't be treated with disrespect. If you're generous, you'll win all hearts. If you're sincere, you'll be trusted. If you're diligent, you'll accomplish much. If you're kind, you'll enjoy the service of others."

17:8. The Master said, "Yu, have you heard the six things accompanied by six confusions?" Yu replied, "I haven't." "Sit down and I'll tell you. The love of benevolence without the love of learning leads to an ignorant simplicity. The love of knowledge without the love of learning leads to dissipation of mind. The love of sincerity without the love of learning leads to recklessness. The love of straightforwardness without the love of learning leads to rudeness. The love of boldness without the love of learning leads to insubordination. The love of strength of character without the love of learning leads to extravagance."

20:3. The Master said, "Without recognizing the ordinances of heaven, it's impossible to be a superior man. Without acquaintance with propriety, it's impossible to establish one's character. Without knowing the force of words, it's impossible to know men."

The Great Learning

The following passages were revised and emended by Daniel Bonevac from The Sacred Books of China: The Texts of Confucianism, Part IV, *translated by James Legge; Volume XXVIII of* The Sacred Books of the East, *edited by Max Müller (Oxford: Clarendon, 1885).*

1. What the Great Learning teaches is to illustrate illustrious virtue, to love the people, and to rest in the highest excellence.
2. Knowing where to rest, one can determine what to pursue; having determined that, one can attain peace of mind. A tranquil repose will follow that peace, and in that repose will be careful deliberation, followed by the attainment of the desired end.
3. Things have their roots and their branches; affairs have their ends and their beginnings. To know what is first and what is last will lead toward what the Great Learning teaches.
4. The ancients who wanted to illustrate illustrious virtue throughout the kingdom first well-ordered their states. Wanting to well-order their states, they first regulated their families. Wanting to regulate their families, they first cultivated themselves. Wanting to cultivate themselves, they first rectified their hearts. Wanting to rectify their hearts, they first sought to be sincere in their thoughts. Wanting to be sincere in their thoughts, they first extended their knowledge to the utmost. One extends knowledge by investigating things.
5. Things being investigated, their knowledge became complete. Their knowledge being complete, their thoughts were sincere. Their thoughts being sincere, their hearts were then rectified. Their hearts being rectified, they themselves were cultivated. They themselves being cultivated, their families were regulated. The families being regulated, their states were well-ordered. Their states being well-ordered, the whole kingdom was made tranquil and happy.
6. From the Son of Heaven [that is, the Emperor] to the multitude, all considered self-cultivation to be the root of everything else.
7. When the root is neglected, what springs from it cannot be well-ordered. Never has that of great importance been slightly cared for while that of slight importance was greatly cared for.

MENCIUS

from *The Book of Mencius*

Reprinted from The Works of Mencius, *edited and translated by James Legge. From* The Chinese Classics, *Volume II (Oxford: Clarendon, 1895).*

2A6. Mencius said, "All men have a mind which cannot bear to see the sufferings of others.

"The ancient kings had this commiserating mind, and they, as a matter of course, had likewise a commiserating government. When with a commiserating mind was practised a commiserating government, to rule the kingdom was as easy a matter as to make anything go round in the palm.

"When I say that all men have a mind which cannot bear to see the sufferings of others, my meaning may be illustrated thus:—even now-a-days, if men suddenly see a child about to fall into a well, they will without exception experience a feeling of alarm and distress. They will feel so, not as a ground on which they may gain the favour of the child's parents, nor as a ground on which they may seek the praise of their neighbours and friends, nor from a dislike to the reputation of having been unmoved by such a thing.

"From this case we may perceive that the feeling of commiseration is essential to man, that the feeling of shame and dislike is essential to man, that the feeling of modesty and complaisance is essential to man, and that the feeling of approving and disapproving is essential to man.

"The feeling of commiseration is the principle of benevolence. The feeling of shame and dislike is the principle of righteousness. The feeling of modesty and complaisance is the principle of propriety. The feeling of approving and disapproving is the principle of knowledge.

"Men have these four principles just as they have their four limbs. When men, having these four principles, yet say of themselves that they cannot develop them, they play the thief with themselves, and he who says of his prince that he cannot develop them plays the thief with his prince.

"Since all men have these four principles in themselves, let them know to give them all their development and completion, and the issue will be like that of fire which has begun to burn, or that of a spring which has begun to find vent. Let them have their complete development, and they will suffice to love and protect all within the four seas. Let them be denied that development, and they will not suffice for a man to serve his parents with."

2A7. Mencius said, "Is the arrow-maker less benevolent than the maker of armour of defence? And yet the arrow-maker's only fear is lest men should not be hurt, and the armour-maker's only fear is lest men should be hurt. So it is with the priest and the coffin-maker. The choice of profession, therefore, is a thing in which great caution is required.

"Confucius said, 'It is virtuous manners which constitute the excellence of a neighbourhood. If a man, in selecting a residence, does not fix on one where such prevail, how can he be wise?' Now benevolence is the most honourable dignity conferred by Heaven, and the quiet home in which man should dwell. Since no one can hinder us from being so, if yet we are not benevolent;—this is being not wise.

"From the want of benevolence and the want of wisdom will ensue the entire absence of propriety and righteousness;—he who is in such a case must be the servant of other men. To be the servant of men and yet ashamed of such servitude, is like a bow-maker's being ashamed to make bows, or an arrow-maker's being ashamed to make arrows.

"If he be ashamed of his case, his best course is to practise benevolence.

"The man who would be benevolent is like the archer. The archer adjusts himself and then shoots. If he misses, he does not murmur against those who surpass himself. He simply turns round and seeks the cause of his failure in himself."

4A11. Mencius said, "The path of duty lies in what is near, and men seek for it in what is remote. The work of duty lies in what is easy, and men seek for it in what is difficult. If each man would love his parents and show the due respect to his elders, the whole land would enjoy tranquillity."

4B8. Mencius said, "Men must be decided on what they will NOT do, and then they are able to act with vigour in what they ought to do."

4B11. Mencius said, "The great man does not think beforehand of his words that they may be sincere, nor of his actions that they may be resolute:—he simply speaks and does what is right."

4B12. Mencius said, "The great man is he who does not lose his child's-heart."

4B19. Mencius said, "That whereby man differs from the lower animals is but small. The mass of people cast it away, while superior men preserve it.

"Shun clearly understood the multitude of things, and closely observed the relations of humanity. He walked along the path of benevolence and righteousness; he did not need to pursue benevolence and righteousness."

4B28. Mencius said, "That whereby the superior man is distinguished from other men is that he preserves in his heart;—namely, benevolence and propriety.

"The benevolent man loves others. The man of propriety shows respect to others.

"He who loves others is constantly loved by them. He who respects others is constantly respected by them.

"Here is a man, who treats me in a perverse and unreasonable manner. The superior man in such a case will turn round upon himself—'I must have been wanting in benevolence; I must have been wanting in propriety;—how should this have happened to me?'

"He examines himself, and is specially benevolent. He turns round upon himself, and is specially observant of propriety. The perversity and unreasonableness of the other, however, are still the same. The superior man will again turn around on himself—'I must have been failing to do my utmost.'

"He turns round upon himself, and proceeds to do his utmost, but still the perversity and unreasonableness of the other are repeated. On this the superior man says, 'This is a man utterly lost indeed! Since he conducts himself so, what is there to choose between him and a brute? Why should I go to contend with a brute?'

"Thus it is that the superior man has a lifelong anxiety and not one morning's calamity. As to what is a matter of anxiety to him, that indeed he has.—He says, 'Shun was a man, and I also am a man. But Shun became an example to all the kingdom, and his conduct was worthy to be handed down to after ages, while I am nothing better than a villager.' This indeed is the proper matter of anxiety to him. And in what way is he anxious about it? Just that he may be like Shun:—then only will he stop. As to what the superior man would feel to be a calamity, there is no such thing. He does nothing which is not according to propriety. If there should befall him one morning's calamity, the superior man does not account it a calamity."

4B32. The officer Ch'u said to Mencius, "Master, the king sent persons to spy out whether you were really different from other men." Mencius said, "How should I be different from other men? Yao and Shun were just the same as other men."

6A1. The philosopher Kao said, "Man's nature is like the *ch'i*-willow, and righteousness is like a cup or a bowl. The fashioning benevolence and righteousness out of man's nature is like the making cups and bowls from the *ch'i*-willow."

Mencius replied, "Can you, leaving untouched the nature of the willow, make with it cups and bowls? You must do violence and injury to the willow, before you can make cups and bowls with it. If you must do violence and injury to the willow in order to make cups and bowls with it, on your principles you must in the same way do violence and injury to humanity in order to fashion from it benevolence and righteousness! Your words, alas! would certainly lead all men on to reckon benevolence and righteousness to be calamities."

6A2. The philosopher Kao said, "Man's nature is like water whirling round in a corner. Open a passage for it to the east, and it will flow to the east; open a passage for it to the west, and it will flow to the west. Man's nature is indifferent to good and evil, just as the water is indifferent to the east and west."

Mencius replied, "Water indeed will flow indiferently to the east or west, but will it flow indifferently up or down? The tendency of man's nature to good is like the tendency of water to flow downwards. There are none but have this tendency to good, just as all water flows downwards.

"Now by striking water and causing it to leap up, you may make it go over your forehead, and by damming and leading it, you may force it up a hill;—but are such movements according to the nature of water? It is the force applied which causes them. When men are made to do what is not good, their nature is dealt with in this way."

6A8. Mencius said, "The trees of the Niu mountain were once beautiful. Being situated, however, in the borders of a large State, they were hewn down with axes and bills;—and could they retain their beauty? Still through the activity of the vegetative life day and night, and the nourishing influence of the rain and dew, they were not without buds and sprouts springing forth, but then came the cattle and goats and browsed upon them. To these things is owing the bare and stripped appearance of the mountain, and when people now see it, they think it was never finely wooded. But is this the nature of the mountain?

"And so also of what properly belongs to man;—shall it be said that the mind of any man was without benevolence and righteousness? The way in which a man loses his proper goodness of mind is like the way in which the trees are denuded by axes and bills. Hewn down day after day, can it—the mind—retain its beauty? But there is a development of its life day and night, and in the calm air of the morning, just between night and day, the mind feels in a degree those desires and aversions which are proper to humanity, but the feeling is not strong, and it is fettered and destroyed by what takes place during the day. This fettering taking place again and again, the restorative influence of the night is not sufficient to preserve the proper goodness of the mind; and when this proves insufficient for that purpose, the nature becomes not much different from that of the irrational animals, and when people now see it, they think that it never had those powers which I assert. But does this condition represent the feelings proper to humanity?

"Therefore, if it receive its proper nourishment, there is nothing which will not grow. If it lose its proper nourishment, there is nothing which will not decay away.

"Confucius said, 'Hold it fast, and it remains with you. Let it go, and you lose it. Its outgoing and incoming cannot be defined as to time or place.' It is the mind of which this is said."

6A11. Mencius said, "Benevolence is man's mind, and righteousness is man's path.

"How lamentable is it to neglect the path and not pursue it, to lose this mind and not know to seek it again!

"When men's fowls and dogs are lost, they know to seek for them again, but they lose their mind, and do not know to seek for it.

"The great end of learning is nothing else but to seek for the lost mind."

6A15. The disciple Kung-tu said, "All are equally men, but some are great men, and some are little men;—how is this?" Mencius replied, "Those who follow that part of themselves which is great are great men; those who follow that part which is little are little men."

Kung-tu pursued, "All are equally men, but some follow that part of themselves which is great, and some follow that part which is little;—how is this?" Mencius answered, "The senses of hearing and seeing do not think, and are obscured by external things. When one thing comes into contact with another, as a matter of course it leads it away. To the mind belongs the office of thinking. By thinking, it gets the right view of things; by neglecting to think, it fails to do this. These—the senses and the mind—are what Heaven has given to us. Let a man first stand fast in the supremacy of the nobler part of his constitution, and the inferior part will not be able to take it from him. It is simply this which makes the great man."

7A15. Mencius said, "The ability possessed by men without having been acquired by learning is intuitive ability, and the knowledge possessed by them without the exercise of thought is their intuitive knowledge.

"Children carried in the arms all know to love their parents, and when they are grown a little, they all know to love their elder brothers.

"Filial affection, for parents, is the working of benevolence. Respect for elders is the working of righteousness. There is no other reason for those feelings;—they belong to all under heaven."

7A17. Mencius said, "Let a man not do what his own sense of righteousness tells him not to do, and let him not desire what his sense of righteousness tells him not to desire;—to act thus is all he has to do."

7A20. Mencius said, "The superior man has three things in which he delights, and to be ruler over the kingdom is not one of them.

"That his father and mother are both alive, and that the condition of his brothers affords no cause of anxiety;—this is one delight.

"That, when looking up, he has no occasion for shame before Heaven, and, below, he has no occasion to blush before men;—this is a second delight.

'That he can get from the whole kingdom the most talented individuals, and teach and nourish them;—this is the third delight.

"The superior man has three things in which he delights, and to be ruler over the kingdom is not one of them."

7A26. Mencius said, "The principle of the philosopher Yang was—'Each one for himself.' Though he might have benefitted the whole kingdom by plucking out a single hair, he would not have done it.

"The philosopher Mo loves all equally. If by rubbing smooth his whole body from the crown to the heel, he could have benefited the kingdom, he would have done it.

"Tsze-mo holds a medium between these. By holding that medium, he is nearer the right. But by holding it without leaving room for the exigency of circumstances, it becomes like their holding their one point.

"The reason why I hate that holding to one point is the injury it does to the way of right principle. It takes up one point and disregards a hundred others."

7B35. Mencius said, "To nourish the mind there is nothing better than to make the desires few. Here is a man whose desires are few;—in some things he may not be able to keep his heart, but they will be few."

HSÜN TZU

from the *Hsün Tzu*

Reprinted from The Works of Hsüntze, *translated by Homer H. Dubs (London: Arthur Probsthain, 1928).* That the Nature Is Evil *reprinted from* The Works of Mencius, *edited and translated by James Legge. From* The Chinese Classics, *Volume II (Oxford: Clarendon, 1895).*

AN ENCOURAGEMENT TO STUDY

The superior man says: Study should never stop. Green dye is taken from blue, but it is nearer the colour of nature than is blue. Ice comes from water, but is colder than water. If wood is straight, it conforms to the plumb-line; steam it and bend it, and it can be used for a wheel, but its curvature must be in accord with the compass. Although it were dried in the sun it would not again become straight—the bending made it that way. For wood must undergo the use of the plumb-line to be straight; iron must be ground on the whetstone to be sharp; the superior man must make his learning broad and daily examine himself in order to have his knowledge exact and his actions without blemish.

In the beginning, the ancient Kings founded their rule on benevolence (*Jen*) and Justice (*Yi*); the rules of proper conduct (*Li*) controlled their ingoings and outgoings, their entire path. If a person lifts his fur neck wrapper, bends his fingers, rubs it with his hand, the hairs which follow his action are innumerable. To try to act according to the *Odes* and *History* without making the rules of proper conduct (*Li*) your pattern, is like sounding a river with the fingers or using a spear to pound millet or using an awl in eating from a pot—it will not succeed. For if a person exalts the rules of proper conduct (*Li*), although he may not be renowned, he will be a learned man of principle. If he does not exalt the rules of proper conduct (*Li*), although he should investigate and discuss, he would be a useless scholar. If a person asks something evil, do not tell him; if he wants to tell something that is evil, do not ask; if he speaks about what is evil, do not listen; if he wishes to quarrel, do not discuss with him. If a student comes in the right way (*Tao*), then only should he be given instruction. If he does not come in the right way (*Tao*), avoid him. For one must first reverence the rules of proper conduct (*Li*), and then only can he speak of the means of obtaining virtue (*Tao*); his speech must accord with the rules of proper conduct (*Li*), and then only can he speak of the principles of virtue (*Tao*); his demeanour must conform to the rules of proper conduct (*Li*), and then only can he speak of attaining to virtue (*Tao*). For talking about what one is not able to talk is heedless talking; not talking about what one is able to talk is secretiveness; talking without observing the listener's countenance is blindness. The superior man is not heedless, nor secretive, nor blind; he is careful to adapt his speech to his audience. The ode says:—

They are neither discourteous nor are they negligent,
Hence the Son of Heaven has gifts for them—

this expresses my meaning.

To miss once in a hundred shots is sufficient to prevent a person from being classed as an expert shot; to fail to go the last half step in a thousand *lî** is enough to prevent a person from being classed as an expert driver; to fail to understand the niceties of human relationships and to fail to concentrate on benevolence (*Jen*) and justice (*Yi*) is sufficient to prevent a person from being classed as an eminent scholar. Scholarship is to know things thoroughly and to unify them; to be unified in learning and unified in teaching. The goodness of the man on the street is little, his lack of goodness is great; as for

*A measure of distance; not to be confused with *li* (propriety).—ED.

example, Chieh, Chou, and the robber Chih.* Scholarship must be complete and exhaustive.

The superior man knows that his knowledge is not complete or perspicuous, insufficient to be classed as fine; so he recites the Classics sentence by sentence in order to make them a part of himself, he seeks to search into them in order to understand them; he puts himself into the places of the writers in order to understand their viewpoint; he expels any wrong from his nature in order to grasp and mature his knowledge: he makes his eye unwilling to see what is not right; he makes his ears unwilling to hear what is not right; he makes his mouth unwilling to speak what is not right; he makes his heart unwilling to think what is not right; until he obtains what he most desires—the five colours his eyes love, the five sounds his ears love; the five tastes his mouth loves, the empire which rejoices his heart. For this reason, he cannot be overturned by force; mobs of common people cannot change him; the country cannot move him. His life will be according to this, and his death will be according to it. This is what is meant by firmly grasping virtue. When he has firmly grasped virtue, he will be able to fix his mind without distraction; when he has fixed his mind, he will be able to respond to the situation. When he can fix his mind and can respond to the situation, he can be classed as a perfect man. Heaven exhibits its brilliance; Earth exhibits its vastness; the superior man values his own completeness.

SELF-CULTIVATION

. . . Though the road (*Tao*) be short, if a person does not travel on it, he will never get there; though a matter be small, if he does not do it, it will never be accomplished; if a man takes many days of leisure, he will not show much progress. He who loves to follow the Way and carries it out is a scholar. He who has a firm purpose and treads the Way is a superior man. He who is inexhaustibly wise and illustrious in virtue is the sage.

A man who is without a rule for action is bewildered; if he has a rule, but does not understand it, he is timid; if he relies upon the rule and knows of what kind it is, then only is he calm.

The rules of proper conduct (*Li*) is that whereby a person's character is corrected; a teacher is that whereby the rules of proper conduct (*Li*) are corrected. Without rules for proper conduct (*Li*) how can I correct myself? Without a teacher how can I know what particular action is according to the rules of proper conduct? If a person is to live according to the rules of proper conduct (*Li*), then his emotions must be naturally those that go with the rules of proper conduct (*Li*); if he is to speak like his teacher, then his knowledge must be equal to that of his teacher. When a person's emotions are naturally in accordance with the rules of proper conduct (*Li*), and his knowledge is equal to that of his teacher, then he is a sage. For to go contrary to the rules for proper action (*Li*) is the same as to be without a rule for action; to go contrary to one's teacher is the same as to be without a teacher. Not to hold as right the ways of one's teacher and to prefer one's own ways, is like a blind man distinguishing colours or a deaf man distinguishing sounds; there is no way of getting rid of confusion and error. Hence the student follows the rules of proper conduct (*Li*) and the ways of his teacher. But the teacher considers himself to be the correct measure of all things and honours that which nature has implanted within him. The ode says:

He has not learned, he did not know,
But he followed the laws of God—

this expresses what I mean.

Upright, honest, obedient, and reverent to elders —such a one can be said to be a good young man. Add to that a love of study, respectfulness, brilliancy, and not feeling himself superior to his equals—such a one can become a superior man. Weak, stupid, afraid to work, without humility or a sense of shame, but fond of eating and drinking—such a one can be called a bad young man. Add to that the qualities of being dissolute, overbearing, disobedient, dangerous, injurious, and disrespectful—such a one can be called an unfortunate young man, who, when led into wrong, may suffer capital punishment. . . .

* Chieh and Chou were emperors regarded as tyrants. Chih was a rebel.—ED.

FROM *AGAINST PHYSIOGNOMY*

. . . Wherein is it that man is truly man? Because he makes distinctions. When he is hungry he desires to eat; when he is cold he desires to be warm; when he is tired he desires to rest; he likes what is helpful and dislikes what is injurious—man is born with these ways of acting; he does not have to wait to get them. In these matters Yü* and Chieh were alike. However, man is not truly man more particularly in that he has two feet and no feathers, but rather in that he makes distinctions. Now the yellow-haired ape also has two feet and no feathers; but in contrast the superior man sips his soup and carves his slices of meat. Hence man is not truly man more particularly in that he has two feet and no feathers, but in that he makes distinctions. The birds and beasts have fathers and sons, but not the affection between father and son; they are female and male, but they do not have the proper separation between males and females.

Hence the path (*Tao*) of human life cannot be without its distinctions; no distinction is greater than social divisions; no social division is greater than the rules for proper conduct (*Li*); the rules for proper conduct are not greater than the Sage-Kings. . . .

Why cannot the Sage be cheated? The Sage measures things by himself. Hence by present men he measures ancient men; by the events of his day he measures their events; by his classifications he measures their classifications; by his doctrines he measures their merit; by the right Way of life (*Tao*) he can completely comprehend things; the ancient times and the present are alike. If the classification is not violated, although it is old, the principle remains the same. Hence to consider wrong doctrines (*Tao*) and not be misled, to look at a heterogeneous lot of things and not be confused, can be done by this way of measuring. . . .

. . . The longer things have been handed down, the more in outline they are; the more recent they are, the more detailed they are. When in outline they merely mention the big things; when detailed, they mention the small things. The stupid man hears the outline, but does not know the details; or else he hears the small things and does not know the big things. This is destroying rules of conduct by preserving them too long, losing ceremonials by collecting them too long.

* Yü, founder of the Hsia dynasty, ruled from 2183–2175 B.C.E. Like Yao, Shun, and Duke Chou, Yü was legendary as an ideal ruler and sage. He was known for his great practical achievements in flood control as well as for his great moral character. —ED.

THAT THE NATURE IS EVIL

The nature of man is evil; the good which it shows is factitious. There belongs to it, even at his birth, the love of gain, and as actions are in accordance with this, contentions and robberies grow up, and self-denial and yielding to others are not to be found; there belong to it envy and dislike, and as actions are in accordance with these, violence and injuries spring up, and self-devotedness and faith are not to be found; there belong to it the desires of the ears and the eyes, leading to the love of sounds and beauty, and as the actions are in accordance with these, lewdness and disorder spring up, and righteousness and propriety, with their various orderly displays, are not to be found. It thus appears, that to follow man's nature and yield obedience to its feelings will assuredly conduct to contentions and robberies, to the violation of the duties belonging to every one's lot, and the confounding of all distinctions, till the issue will be in a state of savagism; and that there must be the influence of teachers and laws, and the guidance of propriety and righteousness, from which will spring self-denial, yielding to others, and an observance of the well-ordered regulations of conduct, till the issue will be a state of good government.—From all this it is plain that the nature of man is evil; the good which it shows is factitious.

To illustrate.—A crooked stick must be submitted to the pressing-frame to soften and bend it, and then it becomes straight; a blunt knife must be submitted to the grindstone and whetstone, and then it becomes sharp; so, the nature of man, being evil, must be submitted to teachers and laws, and then it becomes correct; it must be submitted to propriety and righteousness, and then it comes under government. If men were without teachers and laws, their condition would be one of deflection and insecurity, entirely incorrect; if they were without propriety and righteousness, their condition would be one of rebellious disorder, rejecting all government. The sage kings of antiquity, understanding that the nature of man was thus evil, in a state of hazardous deflection, and incorrect, rebellious and disorderly, and refusing to be governed, set up the principles of righteousness and propriety, and framed laws and regulations to straighten and ornament the feelings of that nature and correct them, to tame and change those same feelings and guide them, so that they might all go forth in the way of moral government and in agreement with reason. Now, the man who is transformed by teachers and laws, gathers on himself the ornament of learning, and proceeds in the path of propriety and righteousness is a superior man; and he who gives the reins to his nature and its feelings, indulges its resentments, and walks contrary to propriety and righteousness is a mean man. Looking at the subject in this way, we see clearly that the nature of man is evil; the good which it shows is factitious.

Mencius said, "Man has only to learn, and his nature appears to be good;" but I reply,—It is not so. To say so shows that he had not attained to the knowledge of man's nature, nor examined into the difference between what is natural in man and what is factitious. The natural is what the constitution spontaneously moves to:—it needs not to be learned, it needs not to be followed hard after; propriety and righteousness are what the sages have given birth to:—it is by learning that men become capable of them, it is by hard practice that they achieve them. That which is in man, not needing to be learned and striven after, is what I call natural; that in man which is attained to by learning, and achieved by hard striving, is what I call factitious. This is the distinction between those two. By the nature of man, the eyes are capable of seeing, and the ears are capable of hearing. But the power of seeing is inseparable from the eyes, and the power of hearing is inseparable from the ears;—it is plain that the faculties of seeing and hearing do not need to be learned. Mencius says, "The nature of man is good, but all lose and ruin their nature, and therefore it becomes bad;" but I say that this representation is erroneous. Man being born with his nature, when he thereafter departs from its simple constituent elements, he must lose it. From this consideration we may see clearly that man's nature is evil. What might be called the nature's being good, would be if there were no departing from its simplicity to beautify it, no departing from its elementary dispositions to sharpen it. Suppose that those simple elements no more needed beautifying, and the mind's thoughts no more needed to be turned to good, than the power of vision which is inseparable from the eyes, and the power of hearing which is inseparable from the ears, need to be learned, then we might say that the nature is good, just as we say that the eyes see and the ears hear. It is the nature of man, when hungry, to desire to be filled; when cold, to desire to be warmed; when tired, to desire rest:—these are the feelings and nature of man. But now, a man is hungry, and in the presence of an elder he does not dare to eat before him:—he is yielding to that elder; he is tired with labour, and he does not dare to ask for rest:—he is working for some one. A son's yielding to his father and a younger brother to his elder, a son's labouring for his father and a younger brother for his elder:—these two instances of conduct are contrary to the nature and against the feelings; but they are according to the course laid down for a filial son, and to the refined distinction of propriety and righteousness. It appears that if there were an accordance with the feelings and the nature, there would be no self-denial and yielding to others. Self-denial and yielding to others are contrary to the feelings and the nature. In this way we come to see how clear it is that the nature of man is evil; the good which it shows is factitious.

An inquirer will ask, "If man's nature be evil, whence do propriety and righteousness arise?" I reply:—All propriety and righteousness are the artificial production of the sages, and are not to be considered as growing out of the nature of man. It is just as when a potter makes a vessel from the clay;—the vessel is the product of the workman's art, and is not to be considered as growing out of his nature. Or it is as when another workman cuts and hews a vessel out of wood;—it is the product of his art, and is not to be considered as growing out of his nature. The sages pondered long in thought and gave themselves to practice, and so they succeeded in producing propriety and righteousness, and setting up laws and regulations. Thus it is that propriety and righteousness, laws and regulations, are the artificial product of the sages, and are not to be considered as growing properly from the nature of man.

If we speak of the fondness of the eyes for beauty, or of the mouth for pleasant flavours, or of the mind for gain, or of the bones and skin for the enjoyment of ease;—all these grow out of the natural feelings of man. The object is presented and the desire is felt; there needs no effort to produce it. But when the object is presented, and the affection does not move till after hard effort, I say that this effect is factitious. Those cases prove the difference between what is produced by nature and what is produced by art.

Thus the sages transformed their nature, and commenced their artificial work. Having commenced this work with their nature, they produced propriety and righteousness. When propriety and righteousness were produced, they proceeded to frame laws and regulations. It appears, therefore, that propriety and righteousness, laws and regulations, are given birth to by the sages. Wherein they agree with all other men and do not differ from them, is their nature; wherein they differ from and exceed other men, is this artificial work.

Now to love gain and desire to get;—this is the natural feeling of men. Suppose the case that there is an amount of property or money to be divided among brothers, and let this natural feeling to love gain and to desire to get come into play;—why, then the brothers will be opposing, and snatching from, one another. But where the changing influence of propriety and righteousness, with their refined distinctions, has taken effect, a man will give up to any other man. Thus it is that if they act in accordance with their natural feelings, brothers will quarrel together; and if they have come under the transforming influence of propriety and righteousness, men will give up to the other men, to say nothing of brothers. Again, the fact that men wish to do what is good, is because their nature is bad. The thin wishes to be thick; the ugly wish to be beautiful; the narrow wishes to be wide; the poor wish to be rich; the mean wish to be noble:—when anything is not possessed in one's self, he seeks for it outside himself. But the rich do not wish for wealth; the noble do not wish for position:—when anything is possessed by one's self, he does not need to go beyond himself for it. When we look at things in this way, we perceive that the fact of men's wishing to do what is good is because their nature is evil. It is the case indeed, that man's nature is without propriety and benevolence:—he therefore studies them with vigorous effort and seeks to have them. It is the case that by nature he does not know propriety and righteousness:—he therefore thinks and reflects and seeks to know them. Speaking of man, therefore, as he is by birth simply, he is without propriety and righteousness, without the knowledge of propriety and righteousness. Without propriety and righteousness, man must be all confusion and disorder; without the knowledge of propriety and righteousness, there must ensue all the manifestations of disorder. Man, as he is born, therefore, has in him nothing but the elements of disorder, passive and active. It is plain from this view of the subject that the nature of man is evil; the good which it shows is factitious.

When Mencius says that "Man's nature is good," I affirm that it is not so. In ancient times and now, throughout the kingdom, what is meant by good is a condition of correctness, regulation, and happy government; and what is meant by evil, is a condition of deflection, insecurity, and refusing to be under government:—in this lies the distinction between being good and being evil. And now, if man's nature be really so correct, regulated, and happily governed in itself, where would be the use for sage kings? Where would be the use for propriety and righteousness? Although there were the sage kings, propriety, and righteousness, what could they add to the nature so correct, regulated, and happily ruled in itself? But it is not so; the nature of man is bad. It was on this account, that anciently the sage kings, understanding that man's nature was bad, in a state of deflection and insecurity, instead of being correct; in a state of rebellious disorder, instead of one of happy rule, set up therefore the majesty of princes and governors to awe it; and set forth propriety and righteousness to change it; and framed laws and statutes of correctness to rule it; and devised severe punishments to restrain it: so that its outgoings might be under the dominion of rule, and in accordance with what is good. This is the true account of the governance of the sage kings, and the transforming power of propriety and righteousness. Let us suppose a state of things in which there shall be no majesty of rulers and governors, no influences of propriety and righteousness, no rule of laws and statutes, no restraints of punishment:—what would be the relations of men with one another, all under heaven? The strong would be injuring the weak, and spoiling them; the many would be tyrannizing over the few, and hooting them; a universal disorder and mutual destruction would speedily ensue. When we look at the subject in this way, we see clearly that the nature of man is evil; the good which it shows is factitious. . . .

An inquirer may say again, "Propriety and righteousness, though seen in an accumulation of factitious deeds, do yet belong to the nature of man; and thus it was that the sages were able to produce them." I reply:—It is not so. A potter takes a piece of clay, and produces an earthen dish from it; but are that dish and clay the nature of the potter? A carpenter plies his tools upon a piece of wood, and produces a vessel; but are that vessel and wood the nature of the carpenter? So it is with the sages and propriety and righteousness; they produced them, just as the potter works with the clay. It is plain that there is no reason for saying that propriety and righteousness, and the accumulation of their factitious actions, belong to the proper nature of man. Speaking of the nature of man, it is the same in all,—the same in Yao and Shun and in Chieh and the robber Chih, the same in the superior man and in the mean man. If you say that propriety and righteousness, with the factitious actions accumulated from them, are the nature of man, on what ground do you proceed to ennoble Yao and Yü, to ennoble generally the superior man? The ground on which we ennoble Yao, Yü, and the superior man, is their ability to change the nature, and to produce factitious conduct. That factitious conduct being produced, out of it there are brought propriety and righteousness. The sages stand indeed in the same relation to propriety and righteousness, and the factitious conduct resulting from them, as the potter does to his clay: —we have a product in either case. This representation makes it clear that propriety and righteousness, with their factitious results, do not properly belong to the nature of man. On the other hand, that which we consider mean in Chieh, the robber Chih, and the mean man generally, is that they follow their nature, act in accordance with its feelings, and indulge its resentments, till all its outgoings are a greed of gain, contentions, and rapine.—It is plain that the nature of man is bad, the good which it shows is factitious. . . .

What is the meaning of the saying, that "Any traveller on the road may become like Yü?" I answer:— All that made Yü what he was, was his practice of benevolence, righteousness, and his observance of laws and rectitude. But benevolence, righteousness, laws, and rectitude are all capable of being known and being practised. Moreover, any traveller on the road has the capacity of knowing these, and the ability to practise them:—it is plain that he may become like Yü. If you say that benevolence, righteousness, laws, and rectitude are not capable of being known and practised, then Yü himself could not have known, could not have practised them. If you will have it that any traveller on the road is really without the capacity of knowing these things, and the ability to practise them, then, in his home, it will not be competent for him to know the righteousness that should rule between father and son, and, abroad, it will not be competent for him to know the rectitude that should rule between sovereign and minister. But it is not so. There is no one who travels along the road, but may know both that righteousness and that rectitude:—it is plain that the capacity to know and the ability to practise belong to every traveller on the way. Let him, therefore, with his capacity of knowing and ability to practise, take his ground on the knowableness and practicableness of benevolence and righteousness;—and it is clear that he may become like Yü. Yea, let any traveller on the way addict himself to the art of learning with all his heart and the entire bent of his will, thinking, searching, and closely examining;—let him do this day after day, through a long space of time, accumulating what is good, and he will penetrate as far as a spiritual Intelligence, he will become a ternion with Heaven and Earth. It follows that the characters of the sages were what any man may reach by accumulation.

It may be said:—"To be sage may thus be reached by accumulation;—why is it that all men cannot accumulate to this extent?" I reply:—They may do so, but they cannot be made to do so. The mean man might become a superior man, but he is not willing to be a superior man. The superior man might become a mean man, but he is not willing to be a mean man. . . .

There is a knowledge characteristic of the sage; a knowledge characteristic of the scholar and superior man; a knowledge characteristic of the mean man; and a knowledge characteristic of the mere servant. In much speech to show his cultivation and maintain consistency, and though he may discuss for a whole day the reasons of a subject, to have a unity pervading the ten thousand changes of discourse:—this is the knowledge of the sage. To speak seldom, and in a brief and sparing manner, and to be orderly in his reasoning, as if its parts were connected with a string:—this is the knowledge of the scholar and superior man. Flattering words and disorderly conduct, with undertakings often followed by regrets:—these mark the knowledge of the mean man. Hasty, officious, smart, and swift, but without consistency; versatile, able, of extensive capabilities, but without use; decisive in discourse, rapid, exact, but the subject unimportant; regardless of right and wrong, taking no account of crooked and straight, to get the victory over others the guiding object:—this is the knowledge of the mere servant.

There is bravery of the highest order; bravery of the middle order; bravery of the lowest order. Boldly to take up his position in the place of the universally acknowledged Mean; boldly to carry into practice his views of the doctrines of the ancient kings; in a high situation, not to defer to a bad sovereign, and in a low situation not to follow the current of a bad people; to consider that there is no poverty where there is virtue, and no wealth or honour where virtue is not; when appreciated by the world, to desire to share in all men's joys and sorrows; when unknown by the world, to stand up grandly alone between heaven and earth, and have no fears:—this is the bravery of the highest order. To be reverently observant of propriety, and sober-minded; to attach importance to adherence to fidelity, and set little store by material wealth; to have the boldness to push forward men of worth and exalt them, to hold back undeserving men, and get them deposed:—this is the bravery of the middle order. To be devoid of self-respect and set a great value on wealth; to feel complacent in calamity, and always have plenty to say for himself; saving himself in any way, without regard to right and wrong; whatever be the real state of a case, making it his object to get the victory over others:—this is the bravery of the lowest order.

The *fan-zao* and the *chü-shu* were the best bows of antiquity; but without their regulators, they could not adjust themselves. The *tsung* of duke Hwan, the *chueh* of T'âi-kung, the *lu* of king Wan, the *hu* of prince Chwang, the *kan-tsiang, mo-ye, chü-chüeh* and *p'i-lü* of Ho-lü—these were the best swords of antiquity; but without the grindstone and whetstone they would not have been sharp; without the strength of the arms that wielded them they would not have cut anything.

The *hwa-liu,* the *li-ch'i,* the *hsien-li,* and the *lü-r*—these were the best horses of antiquity; but there were still necessary for them the restraints in front of bit and bridle, the stimulants behind of whip and cane, and the skillful driving of a Tsao-fu, and then they could accomplish a thousand *lî* in one day.

So it is with man:—granted to him an excellent capacity of nature and the faculty of intellect, he must still seek for good teachers under whom to place himself, and make choice of friends with whom he may be intimate. Having got good masters and placed himself under them, what he will hear will be the doctrines of Yao, Shun, Yü, and T'ang; having got good friends and become intimate with them, what he will see will be deeds of self-consecration, fidelity, reverence, and complaisance:—he will go on from day to day to benevolence and righteousness, without being conscious of it: a natural following of them will make him do so. On the other hand, if he lives with bad men, what he will hear will be the language of deceit, calumny, imposture, and hypocrisy; what he will see will be conduct of filthiness, insolence, lewdness, corruptness, and greed:—he will be going on from day to day to punishment and disgrace, without being conscious of it; a natural following of them will make him do so.

The Record says, "If you do not know your son, look at his friends; if you do not know your prince, look at his confidants." All is the influence of association! All is the influence of association!

ON THE RULES OF PROPER CONDUCT (*LI*)

Whence do the rules of proper conduct (*Li*) arise? Man by birth has desire. When desire is not satisfied, then he cannot be without a seeking for satisfaction. When this seeking for satisfaction is without measure or of limits, then there cannot but be contention. When there is contention, there will be disorder; when there is disorder, then there will be poverty. The former Kings hated this confusion hence they established the rules of proper conduct (*Li*) and justice (*Yi*) in order to set limits to this confusion, to educate, and nourish men's desires, to give opportunity for this seeking for satisfaction, in order that desire should never be extinguished by things, nor should things be used up by desire; that these two should support each other and should continue to exist. This is whence the rules of proper conduct (*Li*) arise.

Thus the rules of proper conduct (*Li*) are to educate and nourish. . . . When the superior man has gotten its education and nourishment, he also esteems its distinctions.

What are meant by its distinctions? There are the classes of the noble and the base; there are the inequalities of the senior and the younger; there is what is appropriate to those who are poor and those who are rich, to those who are unimportant and those who are important. . . .

. . . the rules of proper conduct (*Li*) are the utmost of human morality (*Tao*). Moreover those who do not follow the rules of proper conduct (*Li*) neither are satisfied with it, are people without a direction in life; they who follow the rules of proper conduct (*Li*) and are satisfied with it are gentlemen who have a direction to their life. To be able to meditate deeply in the rules of proper conduct (*Li*) is to be able to reflect; to be able to keep from deviating from the rules of proper conduct (*Li*) is to have the power to be firm. He who is able to think deeply and to be firm and adds to that a love of *Li*, is a Sage. For as heaven is the utmost in height, the earth is the utmost in depth, the boundless is the utmost in breadth, so the Sage is the utmost in morality (*Tao*). Hence the student who resolutely studies *Li* becomes a Sage; without especially studying it, he is a person without direction. . . .

THE REMOVAL OF PREJUDICES

Everything that men suffer is from being prejudiced by one false thing: and so the great principles are hidden from them. Good government consists in returning to the principles of the Classics; other doubtful principles lead into error. In the world there are not two Ways (*Tao*); the Sages had not two minds. . . .

What brings prejudice? Desire can bring prejudice; that can bring prejudice; the beginning can bring prejudice; the end can bring prejudice; distance can bring prejudice; nearness can bring prejudice; the profound can bring prejudice; the superficial can bring prejudice; the ancient can bring prejudice; the present can bring prejudice. Everything that is unorthodox cannot help from bringing prejudice—this is the universal affliction of the mind. . . .

The Sage knows the afflictions which befall the mind and sees the calamities which come from being prejudiced and hindered from knowing the truth. Hence he considers neither desire nor hate, neither beginning nor end, neither nearness nor distance, neither the universal nor the superficial, neither the ancient nor the present. He is equally able to dispose of all things, and keeps the balances level. For this reason all the sects are not able to prejudice him, nor do they confuse his perception of the organizing principles of life.

What can be considered to be the weight used in the balances? It is the Way (*Tao*). Hence one's mind dare not be ignorant of the right (*Tao*). If one's mind is ignorant of the right (*Tao*) then it cannot will to do the right (*Tao*), and can only will to act contrary to the right (*Tao*). What man desires to obtain license to do what he does not will, and to prohibit what he wills? If he selects men according to a mind which does not will to do right (*Tao*), then he will necessarily be like vicious (un-*Tao*) men, and not be like virtuous (*Tao*) men. If he discusses virtuous (*Tao*) men with vicious (un-*Tao*) men according to a mind which is unwilling to do right (*Tao*)—this is the origin of disorder. Then how is he to know the right (*Tao*)? When a man's mind knows the right (*Tao*), then only can he will to do the right (*Tao*). When he can will to do the right (*Tao*), then only can he do the right (*Tao*) and abstain from doing the wrong (not-*Tao*). If he picks men according to a mind which is willing to do the right (*Tao*), then he will be like virtuous (*Tao*) men and unlike vicious (un-*Tao*) men. To discuss the wicked (not-*Tao*) with virtuous (*Tao*) men according to a mind willing to do the right (*Tao*) is the important thing in good government. What harm is there in not knowing virtuous men? The important thing in good government is knowing virtuous (*Tao*) men.

How can a person know the right (*Tao*)? By the mind. How does the mind know? By emptiness, unity or concentration, and unperturbedness. The mind never ceases to store away impressions, yet there is that which may be called emptiness. The mind has always a multiplicity, yet there is that which may be called a unity. The mind is always in motion, yet there is that which may be called quiescence or unperturbedness.

A man from birth has the capacity to know things; this capacity to know things has its collected data; these collected data are what are meant by stored away impressions. Moreover he has that which may be called emptiness. That which does not allow what is already stored away to injure that which is about to be received is called the mind's emptiness. The mind from birth has the capacity for knowledge; this knowledge contains distinctions; these distinctions consist of at the same time perceiving more than one thing. To perceive more than one thing at the same time is plurality. Yet the mind has that which may be called a unity. That which does not allow that impression to harm this impression is called the mind's unity. When the mind sleeps, it dreams; when it takes its ease, it indulges in reverie; when it is used, it reflects. Hence the mind is always in motion. Yet it has that which may be called unperturbedness. That which does not permit dreams to disturb one's knowledge is called the mind's unperturbedness.

If a person is seeking for the right way of life (*Tao*), but does not know it, he should make his mind empty, unified, and unperturbed, and act in that way. Cause him who is seeking for the Way (*Tao*) to make his mind empty, and then he can receive it; cause him who is serving the right (*Tao*) to make his mind unified, and when his mind is unified, he can do the right in its entirety; cause him who desires the right (*Tao*) to make his mind unperturbed; when his mind is unperturbed, he can arrive at the truth. He who perceives the right (*Tao*) and gets at the truth of it, he who perceives the right (*Tao*) and does it, can be said to embody the right (*Tao*). He who makes his mind empty, unified, and unperturbed can be said to follow right principle and to be illustrious in virtue. There is nothing visible which does not disclose its qualities to him; there is nothing that he sees which he cannot discuss; in discussing he never errs. He sits in his chamber and sees the world; he lives in the present and discusses the ancient and the distant. He looks through all things and sees their nature; he investigates good and bad government and arrives at their laws. He understands the whole of Heaven and Earth, and regulates all things; he governs according to the great principle and the universe is rectified. He is very great—who knows his limits? He is very splendid—who knows his virtue? His character is very intricate—who knows its form? He is brilliant, equal with the sun and moon; his greatness fills the whole world. This is what is meant by being a truly great man.

The mind is the ruler of the body and the master of the spirit. It gives commands and all parts of the body obey. It itself makes prohibitions; it itself gives commands; it itself makes decisions; it itself makes choices; it itself causes action; it itself stops action. The mouth can exert itself forcibly and make the silent speak; the body can exert itself forcibly and make the bent straight; the mind cannot exert itself forcibly and change one perception; if it does this, then it would be in error and must resign its lordship. Hence I say: The mind must bear what it chooses. It cannot prevent the results of its action appearing of themselves. The mind's objects are confused and extensive; its essence is a unity. . . .

The Sage gives reign to his desires and satisfies his passions, nevertheless he is controlled by principle; so why need he be forced or repressed or anxious? For the acting out of the right Way (*Tao*) by the benevolent (*Jen*) man is without effort; the performance of the right Way (*Tao*) by the Sage is without forcing himself. The thoughts of the benevolent (*Jen*) man reverence the thoughts of the Sage. To rejoice at this is the way (*Tao*) of the man of a controlled mind. . . .

TAOISM

Lao Tzu (sixth century B.C.E.) founded Taoism. We know little about his life. A native of Ch'u, he apparently served as curator of the archive in the capital of Chou (Zhou). Legend has it that he was conceived by a shooting star and born sixty-two years later. According to tradition, Confucius visited him to ask about ceremonies, and Lao Tzu composed the *Tao-te Ching*, the *Classic of the Way and Its Virtue*, upon his retirement. Many scholars believe, however, that the book was compiled over perhaps two centuries by a variety of people. The book's title, literally "Way-virtue-classic," has been translated variously as *The Way of Life, The Book of Tao, The Book of the Way*, and *The Way and Its Power.*

Taoism opposes Confucianism in many respects. Confucius emphasizes traditional social rules, activity, and government; Lao Tzu stresses nonconformity, tranquillity, and individual transcendence. Confucius uses the term *Tao* (the Way) to refer to moral truth or proper moral conduct; Lao Tzu uses it to refer to the One, which underlies everything but admits no description. Lao Tzu speaks of it as natural and eternal, but also as changing and spontaneous. Throughout the *Tao-te Ching*, however, he makes it clear that language is inadequate to describe the One. At most, language can suggest or evoke it.

The One also has moral force. It is the foundation for ethics applied to affairs of government as well as to individual action. The One, as embodied in a particular thing, is that thing's *te*—its power, force, character, or virtue. It is not only an active principle guiding the thing, but a principle for what the thing ought to do and to be. The excellence of a thing thus stems from its *Tao*.

This twofold character of *te*—power and virtue or, in different terminology, guiding and regulating principle—leads to the distinctive ethical principles of Taoism. Lao Tzu advocates inaction. He recommends weakness, simplicity, and tranquillity. It often seems as if he recommends passivity and laziness. But the inaction Lao Tzu advocates is one of letting nature take its course, of letting the guiding principles of things guide them without interference. The coincidence of guiding and regulating principles in *te* means that things naturally tend to their own state of excellence. Interference with this natural process prevents them from attaining excellence and is therefore bad. The individual should adopt a policy of noninterference.

Similarly, because we cannot describe the One, we should not seek enlightenment through language. Language, reason, reflection, and other forms of intellectual activity lead us away from the ultimate truth, from the recognition of the world's unity. Taoism is therefore an anti-intellectual doctrine. Ordinarily, we think in order to understand; we reflect to try to uncover answers to questions that arise in experience or that reason poses to us. In Lao Tzu's view, however, thinking leads us away from understanding. We understand most clearly when we set reason, language, and thinking aside. This aspect of Taoism had significant influence on some forms of Buddhism, in particular, on Zen.

Chuang Tzu (fourth century B.C.E.) gives Taoism a mystical turn. The One, for Chuang Tzu, is a universal process of spontaneous, perpetual change. Wisdom consists in seeking unity with the One. To do this, one needs to abandon thoughts of self and adapt oneself to the never-ceasing flow of Nature. Chuang Tzu thus agrees with Lao Tzu in recommending a policy of passive noninterference. But the two philosophers differ in some ways. Chuang Tzu stresses the importance of self-development, since transformation is the essence of Nature. This process is very different from Confucian education, however; it involves blending with Nature rather than combating it. Also, Chuang Tzu is even fonder of paradox than Lao Tzu, suggesting that true understanding requires overcoming the distinctions and divisions inherent in intellectual activity. Hsün Tzu emphasizes the significance of rules and distinctions; Chuang Tzu emphasizes the need for seeing beyond them. As Chu Hsi summarizes the difference between Lao Tzu and Chuang Tzu: "Lao Tzu still wanted to do something, but Chuang Tzu did not want to do anything at all."

Yang Chu (440–360 B.C.E?) reportedly announced that he would not pluck a single hair from his head, even to save the entire world. He sometimes seems to be arguing for an extreme form of egoism. The Yang Chu chapter of the *Lieh Tzu*—which almost certainly is not the work of either Yang Chu or Lieh Tzu—presents a completely negative version of Taoism. The perspective of the chapter is profoundly pessimistic. Death is inevitable and a great equalizer. It makes no ultimate difference whether any of us live morally. Therefore, Yang Chu concludes, we should seek pleasure and look out for our own welfare, for there are no deeper ends to pursue.

LAO TZU

from *Tao-te Ching*

From The Tao Te Ching: A New Translation with Commentary, *by Ellen M. Chen (New York: Paragon House, 1989). Copyright © 1989 by Paragon House.*

CHAPTER 1

1. Tao that can be spoken of,
Is not the Everlasting Tao.
Name that can be named,
Is not the Everlasting name.

2a.* Nameless, the origin of heaven and earth;
Named, the mother of ten thousand things.
Alternate,
2b. Non-being, to name the origin
of heaven and earth;
Being, to name the mother of ten thousand things.

3a. Therefore, always without desire,
In order to observe the hidden mystery;
Always with desire,
In order to observe the manifestations.
Alternate,
3b. Therefore, by the Everlasting Non-Being,
We desire to observe its hidden mystery;
By the Everlasting Being,
We desire to observe the manifestations.

4. These two issue from the same origin,
Though named differently.
Both are called the dark.
Dark and even darker,
The door to all hidden mysteries.

* Verses 2a and 2b (also 3a and 3b) are different readings of the same ambiguous passage.—Ed.

CHAPTER 2

1. When all under heaven know beauty as beauty,
There is then ugliness;
When all know the good good,
There is then the not good.

2. Therefore being and non-being give rise to each other,
The difficult and easy complement each other,
The long and short shape each other,
The high and low lean on each other,
Voices and instruments harmonize with one another,
The front and rear follow upon each other.

3. Therefore the sage manages affairs without action,
Carries out teaching without speech.
Ten thousand things arise and he does not initiate them,
They come to be and he claims no possession of them,
He works without holding on,
Accomplishes without claiming merit.
Because he does not claim merit
His merit does not go away.

CHAPTER 3

1. Do not honor the worthy,
So that the people will not contend with one another.
Do not value hard-to-get goods,
So that the people will not turn robbers.
Do not show objects of desire,
So that the people's minds are not disturbed.

2. Therefore, when the sage rules:
He empties the minds of his people,
Fills their bellies,
Weakens their wills,
And strengthens their bones.
Always he keeps his people in no-knowledge and no-desire,
Such that he who knows dares not act.
3. Act by no-action,
Then, nothing is not in order.

CHAPTER 4

1. Tao is a whirling emptiness,
Yet in use is inexhaustible.
Fathomless,
It seems to be the ancestor of ten thousand beings.
2. It blunts the sharp,
Unties the entangled,
Harmonizes the bright,
Mixes the dust.
Dark,
It seems perhaps to exist.

CHAPTER 5

1. Heaven and earth are not humane (*jen*),
They treat the ten thousand beings as straw dogs.
The sage is not humane (*jen*),
He treats the hundred families as straw dogs.
2. Between heaven and earth,
How like a bellows it is!
Empty and yet inexhaustible,
Moving and yet it pours out ever more.
3. By many words one's reckoning is exhausted.
It is better to abide by the center.

CHAPTER 8

1. A person with superior goodness is like water,
Water is good in benefiting all beings,
Without contending with any.
Situated in places shunned by many others,
Thereby it is near Tao.
2. (Such a person's) dwelling is the good earth,
(His/her) mind is the good deep water,
(His/her) associates are good kind people (*jen*),
(His/her) speech shows good trust,
(His/her) governing is the good order,
(His/her) projects are carried out by good talents,
(His/her) activities are good in timing.
3. Because he does not contend with any,
He commits no wrong.

CHAPTER 10

1. In bringing your spiritual (*ying*) and bodily souls to embrace the One,
Can you never depart from it?
2. In concentrating your breath to attain softness,
Can you be like an infant?
3. In cleansing your mirror of the dark,
Can you make it spotless?
4. In opening and closing heaven's gate,
Can you be the female?
5. In being enlightened and comprehending all,
Can you do it without knowledge?
6. In loving the people and governing the state,
Can you practice non-action?
7. To give birth, to nurture.
To give birth yet not to claim possession,
To act yet not to hold on to,
To grow yet not to lord over,
This is called the dark virtue.

CHAPTER 11

1. Thirty spokes share one hub to make a wheel.
Through its non-being,
There is the use of the carriage.

Mold clay into a vessel.
Through its non-being,
There is the use of the vessel.

Cut out doors and windows to make a house.

Through its non-being,
There is the use of the house.

2. Therefore in the being of a thing,
There lies the benefit.
In the non-being of a thing,
There lies its use.

CHAPTER 12

1. The five colors blind a person's eyes;
The five musical notes deafen a person's ears;
The five flavors ruin a person's taste buds.

2. Horse-racing, hunting and chasing,
Drive a person's mind to madness.

3. Hard-to-get goods,
Hinder a person's actions.

4. Therefore the sage is for the belly, not for the eyes.
Therefore he leaves this and chooses that.

CHAPTER 14

1. What is looked at but not seen,
Is named the extremely dim.
What is listened to but not heard,
Is named the extremely faint.
What is grabbed but not caught,
Is named the extremely small.
These three cannot be comprehended,
Thus they blend into one.

2. As to the one, its coming up is not light,
Its going down is not darkness.
Unceasing, unnameable,
Again it reverts to nothing.
Therefore it is called the formless form,
The image of nothing.
Therefore it is said to be illusive and evasive.

3. Come toward it one does not see its head,
Follow behind it one does not see its rear.
Holding on to the Tao of old,
So as to steer in the world of now.
To be able to know the beginning of old,
It is to know the thread of Tao.

CHAPTER 15

1. Those in the past who were good at practicing Tao,
Were subtle, mysterious, dark, penetrating,
Deep and unrecognizable.
Because they were unrecognizable,
I am forced to describe their appearance.

2. Careful, like crossing a river in winter,
Hesitating, like fearing neighbors on four sides,
Reverent, like being guests,
Dissolving, like ice beginning to melt,
Thick, like uncarved wood,
Open, like a valley,
Chaotic, like murky water.

3. What can stop the murkiness?
Quieting down, gradually it clarifies.
What can keep still for long?
Moving, gradually it stirs into life.

4. Those who keep this Tao,
Do not want to be filled to the full.
Because they are not full,
They can renew themselves before being worn out.

CHAPTER 16

1. Reach the pole of emptiness,
Abide in genuine quietude.
Ten thousand beings flourish together,
I am to contemplate their return.

2. Now things grow profusely,
Each again returns to its root.
To return to the root is to attain quietude,
It is called to recover life.
To recover life is to attain the Everlasting,
To know the Everlasting is to be illumined.

3. Not knowing the Everlasting,
One commits evils wantonly.
Knowing the Everlasting one becomes all containing.
To be all containing is to be public.
To be public is to be kingly.
To be kingly is to be like heaven.
To be like heaven is to be like Tao.

To be like Tao is to last long.
This is to lose the body without becoming exhausted.

CHAPTER 17

1. The best government, the people know it is just there.
   The next best, they love and praise it.
   The next, they fear it.
   The next, they revile against it.
2. When you don't trust [the people] enough,
   Then they are untrustworthy.
   Quiet, why value words?
3. Work is accomplished, things are done.
   People all say that I am natural.

CHAPTER 18

1. On the decline of the great Tao,
   There are humanity (*jen*) and righteousness (*i*).
2. When intelligence and knowledge appear,
   There is great artificiality.
3. When the six relations are not in harmony,
   There are filial piety and parental love.
4. When a nation is in darkness and disorder,
   There are loyal ministers.

CHAPTER 19

1. Eliminate sagacity, discard knowledge,
   People will be profited a hundredfold.
2. Elminate humanity (*jen*), discard righteousness (*i*),
   People will again practice filial piety and parental love.
3. Abolish artistry, discard profit-seeking,
   Robbers and thieves shall disappear.
4. These three pairs adorn what is deficient.
   Therefore, let there be the advice:
   Look to the undyed silk, hold on to the uncarved wood (*p'u*),
   Reduce your sense of self and lessen your desires.

CHAPTER 20

1. Eliminate learning so as to have no worries
   Yes and no, how far apart are they?
   Good and evil, how far apart are they?
2. What the sages (*jen*) fear,
   I must not not fear.
   I am the wilderness before the dawn.
3. The multitude are busy and active,
   Like partaking of the sacrificial feast,
   Like ascending the platform in spring;
   I alone am bland,
   As if I have not yet emerged into form.
   Like an infant who has not yet smiled,
   Lost, like one who has nowhere to return.
4. The multitudes all have too much;
   I alone am deficient.
   My mind is that of a fool,
   Nebulous.
5. Worldly people are luminous;
   I alone am dark.
   Worldly people are clear-sighted;
   I alone am dull,
   I am calm like the sea,
   Like the high winds I never stop.
6. The multitudes all have their use;
   I alone am untamable like lowly material.
   I alone am different from others.
   For I treasure feeding on the Mother.

CHAPTER 21

1. The features of the vast Te,
   Follows entirely from Tao.
2. Tao as a thing,
   Is entirely illusive and evasive.
   Evasive and illusive,
   In it there is image.
   Illusive and evasive,
   In it there is thinghood.
   Dark and dim,
   In it there is life seed.
   Its life seed being very genuine,
   In it there is growth power.

3. As it is today, so it was in the days of old,
   Its name goes not away,
   So that we may survey the origins of the many.
   How do I know that the origins of the many
   are such?
   Because of this.

CHAPTER 22

1. Bent, thus preserved whole,
   Unjustly accused, thus exonerated,
   Hollow, thus filled (*ying*),
   Battered thus renewed,
   Scanty, thus receiving (*te*),
   Much, thus perplexed.
2. Therefore the sage embraces the One (*pao i*).
   He becomes the model of the world.
   Not self-seeing, hence he is enlightened.
   Not self-justifying, hence he is outstanding.
   Not showing off his deeds, hence he is
   meritorious.
   Not boasting of himself, hence he leads.
   Because he is not contentious,
   Hence no one under heaven can contend with
   him.
3. What the ancients say: "Bent, thus preserved
   whole,"
   Are these empty words?
   Be preserved whole and return.

CHAPTER 23

1. Nature speaks little.
   Hence a squall lasts not a whole morning,
   A rainstorm continues not a whole day.
   What causes these?
   Heaven and earth.
   Even [the actions of] heaven and earth do not
   last long,
   How much less [the works] of humans?
2. Therefore one who follows Tao identifies with
   Tao,
   One who follows *te* (nature) identifies with *te*
   (nature).
   One who follows *shih* (loss) identifies with
   shih.
   One who identifies with Tao is glad to be with
   Tao.
   One who identifies with *te* is glad to be
   with *te*.
   One who identifies with *shih* is glad to be
   with *shih*.
3. When you don't trust (the people) enough,
   Then they are untrustworthy.

CHAPTER 24

1. One who tiptoes cannot stand.
   One who straddles cannot walk.
   One who sees himself is not enlightened.
   One who justifies himself is not outstanding.
   One who shows off his deeds is not
   meritorious.
   One who boasts of himself does not lead.
2. These to a Taoist are called:
   Excess nature (*yü te*) and superfluous actions,
   Avoided even by things.
   Therefore the Taoist does not indulge in them.

CHAPTER 25

1. There was something nebulous existing,
   Born before heaven and earth.
   Silent, empty,
   Standing alone, altering not,
   Moving cyclically without becoming exhausted,
   Which may be called the mother of all under
   heaven.
2. I know not its name,
   I give its alias, Tao.
   If forced to picture it,
   I say it is "great."
   To say it is "great" is to say it is "moving away,"
   To say it is "moving away" is to say it is "far
   away,"
   To say it is "far away" is to say it is "returning."
3. Therefore Tao is great,
   Heaven is great,

Earth is great,
The king is also great.
In the realm there are four greats,
And the king is one of them.

4. Humans follow earth,
Earth follows heaven,
Heaven follows Tao,
Tao follows self-becoming.

CHAPTER 32

1. Tao everlasting
is the nameless uncarved wood.
Though small,
Nothing under heaven can subjugate it.
If kings and barons can abide by it,
All creatures will arrive as guests to a banquet.

2. Heaven and earth unite,
To send down the sweet rain.
Without being commanded by the people,
If falls evenly by itself.

3. At the beginning of institution names come to be.
Once there are names,
One must know when to stop.
One who knows when to stop does not become exhausted.

4. Tao in the world is like
Valley streams flowing into rivers and seas.

CHAPTER 33

1. One who knows others is knowledgeable;
One who knows the self is enlightened.

2. One who overcomes others has physical might;
One who overcomes the self is strong.

3. One who knows contentment is rich;
One who acts strongly has will power.

4. One who does not lose where one belongs lasts long;
One who dies without perishing has longevity.

CHAPTER 37

1. Tao everlasting does not act,
And yet nothing is not done.
If kings and barons can abide by it,
The ten thousand things will transform by themselves.

2. If in transforming desire is aroused,
I shall suppress it by the nameless uncarved wood.
With the nameless uncarved wood,
There shall be no desire.

3. Without desire there is thus quietude.
The world shall be self-ordered.

CHAPTER 38

1. A person of high *te* is not *te,*
Therefore such a person has *te*;
A person of low *te* does not lose *te,*
Therefore such a person has no *te.*

2. A person of high *te* does not act,
For such a person has no cause for action;
A person of low *te* acts,
For such a person has cause for action.

3. A person of high *jen* (humanity) acts,
Yet such a person has no cause for action;
A person of high *i* (righteousness) acts,
For such a person has cause for action.

4. A person of high *li* (propriety) acts,
Yet finding no response,
Proceeds to bare the arms and throw a rope.

5. Therefore when Tao is lost, then there is *te.*
When *te* is lost, then there is *jen* (humanity).
When *jen* is lost, then there is *i* (righteousness).
When *i* is lost, then there is *li* (propriety).

6. As to *li,* it is the thin edge of loyalty and faithfullness,
And the beginning of disorder;
As to foreknowledge, it is the flowering of Tao,
And the beginning of stupidity.

7. Thus a great person, abiding in the thick,
Does not dwell in the thin;

Abiding in the kernel,
Does not dwell in the flower.
Therefore such a person leaves that and takes
this.

CHAPTER 47

1. Without stepping out the door,
Know the world.
Without looking out the window,
See the Tao of Heaven.
The farther one comes out,
The less one knows.

2. Therefore the sage knows without
travelling,
Names things without seeing them,
Accomplishes without work.

CHAPTER 48

1. To pursue learning one increases daily.
To pursue Tao one decreases daily.
To decrease and again to decrease,
Until one arrives at not doing.
Not doing and yet nothing is not done.

2. Always take the empire when there are no
businesses.
If there are businesses,
It is not worthwhile to take the empire.

CHAPTER 49

1. The sage has no set mind,
He takes the mind of the people as his mind.

2. The good I am good to them,
The not good I am also good to them.
This is the goodness of nature (*te*).
The trustworthy I trust them,
The not trustworthy I also trust them.
This is the trust of nature (*te*).

3. The sage in the world,
Mixes the minds of all.
The people lift up their eyes and ears,
The sage treats them all like children.

CHAPTER 51

1. Tao gives birth,
Te rears,
Things shape,
Circumstances complete.

2. Therefore the ten thousand things,
None do not respect Tao and treasure *te*.
Tao is respected,
Te is treasured,
Not by decree,
But by spontaneity.

3. Therefore Tao gives birth,
Te keeps, grows, nurtures, matures, ripens,
covers and buries.

4. To give birth without possession,
To act without holding on to,
To grow without lording over,
This is called the dark *te*.

CHAPTER 56

1. One who knows does not speak,
One who speaks does not know.

2. Stop the apertures,
Close the door;
Blunt the sharp,
Untie the entangled;
Harmonize the bright,
Make identical the dust.
This is called the mystical identity.

3. Therefore with this person you cannot get
intimate,
Cannot get distant,
Cannot benefit,
Cannot harm,
Cannot exalt
Cannot humiliate.
Therefore such person is the exalted of the
world.

CHAPTER 57

1. Govern a state by the normal;
Conduct warfare as the abnormal;
Take the empire when there is no business.

2. How do I know such should be the case? By the following:
In an empire with many prohibitions,
People are often poor;
When people have many sharp weapons,
The state is in great darkness;
When persons abound in ingenuity,
Abnormal objects multiply;
When laws are abundantly promulgated,
There are many thieves and brigands.

3. Therefore the sage says:
I do not act,
Hence the people transform by themselves;
I love tranquillity,
Hence the people are normal by themselves;
I have no business,
Hence the people grow rich by themselves;
I have no desire,
Hence the people are like the uncarved wood by themselves.

CHAPTER 58

1. When the government is dull,
Its people are wholesome;
When the government is efficient,
Its people are deficient.

2. Calamities are what blessings depend on,
In blessings are latent calamities.
Who knows where is the turning point?

3. Because there is no longer the normal,
The normal reverts and appears as the strange,
The good reverts and appears as the uncanny.
Rulers have lost their way,
For a long stretch of days.

4. Therefore the sage is square but not cutting,
Sharp but not injurious,
Straight but not overreaching,
Bright but not dazzling.

CHAPTER 63

1. Do when there is nothing to do,
Manage affairs when there are none to manage,
Know by not knowing.
Regard the great as small, the much as little.
Repay injury with *te*.

2. Plan the difficult while it is easy.
Accomplish the great when it is small.
Difficult affairs of the world,
Must be done while they are easy.
Great affairs of the world,
Must be done while they are small.
The sage never does anything great,
Therefore he can accomplish the great.

3. He who makes promises lightly seldom keeps his words.
He who takes much to be easy finds much to be difficult.
Therefore even the sage takes things to be difficult,
So that in the end they are not difficult.

CHAPTER 67

1. All under heaven say that my Tao is great,
That it seems useless.
Because it is great,
Therefore it seems useless.
If it were useful,
It would have long been small.

2. I have three treasures,
To hold and to keep:
The first is motherly love,
The second is frugality,
The third is daring not be at the world's front.

3. With motherly love one can be courageous,
With frugality one can be wide reaching,
Daring not be at the world's front,
One can grow to a full vessel.

4. Now to discard motherly love, yet to be courageous,
To discard frugality, yet to be wide reaching,

To discard staying behind, yet to be at the front,
One dies!

5. One with motherly love is victorious in battle,
Invulnerable in defense.
When Heaven wills to save a people,
It guards them with motherly love.

CHAPTER 71

1. From knowing to not knowing,
This is superior.
From not knowing to knowing,
This is sickness.
It is by being sick of sickness,
That one is not sick.

2. The sage is not sick.
Because he is sick of sickness,
Therefore he is not sick.

CHAPTER 72

1. When the people fear no power,
Then great power has indeed arrived.
Do not disturb them in their dwellings,
Do not weary them in their living.
It is because you do not weary them,
That they are not wearied of you.

2. Therefore the sage knows himself,
But does not see himself.
He loves himself,
But does not exalt himself.
Therefore he leaves that and takes this.

CHAPTER 73

1. One who is courageous out of daring is killed.
One who is courageous out of not daring lives.
Of these two, this is beneficial while that is harmful.
What heaven hates, who knows the reason?
Therefore even the sage takes it to be difficult.

2. The way of heaven:
Without contending, it is yet good at winning,
Without speaking, it is yet good in responding,
Without being beckoned, it yet comes of its own accord,
Unhurried, it is yet good at planning.
The net of heaven is vast,
Widely spaced, yet missing nothing.

CHAPTER 81

1. Truthful words are not beautiful,
Beautiful words are not truthful.
The good does not distinguish,
One who distinguishes is not good.
One who knows does not accumulate knowledge,
One who accumulates knowledge does not know.

2. The sage does not hoard.
Having worked for his fellow beings,
The more he possesses.
Having donated himself to his fellow beings,
The more abundant he becomes.

3. The way of heaven,
It benefits, but does not harm.
The way of the sage,
He works, but does not contend.

CHUANG TZU

from the *Chuang Tzu*

From Chung Tzu, Taoist Philosopher and Chinese Mystic, *translated by Herbert A Giles. London: Allen and Unwin, 1926.*

CHAPTER II / THE IDENTITY OF CONTRARIES

"Great knowledge [said Tzu Ch'i of Nan-kuo] embraces the whole: small knowledge, a part only. Great speech is universal: small speech is particular.

"For whether the mind is locked in sleep or whether in waking hours the body is released, we are subject to daily mental perturbations,—indecision, want of penetration, concealment, fretting fear, and trembling terror. Now like a javelin the mind flies forth, the arbiter of right and wrong. Now like a solemn covenanter it remains firm, the guardian of rights secured. Then, as under autumn and winter's blight, comes gradual decay, a passing away, like the flow of water, never to return. Finally, the block when all is choked up like an old drain—the failing mind which shall not see light again.

"Joy and anger, sorrow and happiness, caution and remorse, come upon us by turns, with ever-changing mood. They come like music from hollowness, like mushrooms from damp. Daily and nightly they alternate within us, but we cannot tell whence they spring. Can we then hope in a moment to lay our finger upon their very Cause?

"But for these emotions *I* should not be. But for me, *they* would have no scope. So far we can go; but we do not know what it is that brings them into play. 'Twould seem to be a *soul*; but the clue to its existence is wanting. That such a Power operates, is credible enough, though we cannot see its form. Perhaps it has functions without form.

"Take the human body with all its manifold divisions. Which part of it does a man love best? Does he not cherish all equally, or has he a preference? Do not all equally serve him? And do these servitors then govern themselves, or are they subdivided into rulers and subjects? Surely there is some soul which sways them all.

"But whether or not we ascertain what are the functions of this soul, it matters but little to the soul itself. For coming into existence with this mortal coil of mine, with the exhaustion of this mortal coil its mandate will also be exhausted. To be harassed by the wear and tear of life, and to pass rapidly through it without possibility of arresting one's course,—is not this pitiful indeed? To labour without ceasing, and then, without living to enjoy the fruit, worn out, to depart, suddenly, one knows not whither,—is not that a just cause for grief?

"What advantage is there in what men call not dying? The body decomposes, and the mind goes with it. This is our real cause for sorrow. Can the world be so dull as not to see this? Or is it I alone who am dull, and others not so?

"If we are to be guided by the criteria of our own minds, who shall be without a guide? . . .

"Speech is not mere breath. It is differentiated by meaning. Take away that, and you cannot say whether it is speech or not. Can you even distinguish it from the chirping of young birds?

"But how can TAO be so obscured that we speak of it as true and false? And how can speech be so obscured that it admits the idea of contraries? How can TAO go away and yet not remain? How can speech exist and yet be impossible?

"TAO is obscured by our want of grasp. Speech is obscured by the gloss of this world. Hence the affirmatives and negatives of the Confucian and Mihist schools, each denying what the other affirmed and affirming what the other denied. But he who would reconcile affirmative with negative and negative with affirmative, must do so by the light of nature.

"There is nothing which is not objective: there is nothing which is not subjective. But it is impossible to start from the objective. Only from subjective knowledge is it possible to proceed to objective knowledge. Hence it has been said, 'The objective emanates from the subjective; the subjective is consequent upon the objective. This is the *Alternation Theory*.' Nevertheless, when one is born, the other dies. When one is possible, the other is impossible. When one is affirmative the other is negative. Which being the case, the true sage rejects all distinctions of this and that. He takes his refuge in God, and places himself in subjective relation with all things.

"And inasmuch as the subjective is also objective, and the objective also subjective, and as the contraries under each are indistinguishably blended, does it not become impossible for us to say whether subjective and objective really exist at all?

"When subjective and objective are both without their correlates, that is the very axis of Tao. And when that axis passes through the centre at which all Infinities converge, positive and negative alike blend into an infinite One. Hence it has been said that there is nothing like the light of nature.

"To take a finger in illustration of a finger not being a finger is not so good as to take something which is not a finger. To take a horse in illustration of a horse not being a horse is not so good as to take something which is not a horse.

"So with the universe and all that in it is. These things are but fingers and horses in this sense. The possible is possible: the impossible is impossible. Tao operates, and given results follow. Things receive names and are what they are. They achieve this by their natural affinity for what they are and their natural antagonism to what they are not. For all things have their own particular constitutions and potentialities. Nothing can exist without these.

"Therefore it is that, viewed from the standpoint of Tao, a beam and a pillar are identical. So are ugliness and beauty, greatness, wickedness, perverseness, and strangeness. Separation is the same as construction: construction is the same as destruction. Nothing is subject either to construction or to destruction, for these conditions are brought together into One.

"Only the truly intelligent understand this principle of the identity of all things. They do not view things as apprehended by themselves, subjectively; but transfer themselves into the position of the things viewed. And viewing them thus they are able to comprehend them, nay, to master them;—and he who can master them is near. So it is that to place oneself in subjective relation with externals, without consciousness of their objectivity,—this is Tao. But to wear out one's intellect in an obstinate adherence to the individuality of things, not recognizing the fact that all things are One,—this is called *Three in the Morning*."

"What is *Three in the Morning*?" asked Tzu Yu.

"A keeper of monkeys," replied Tzu-Ch'i, "said with regard to their rations of chestnuts that each monkey was to have three in the morning and four at night. But at this the monkeys were very angry, so the keeper said they might have four in the morning and three at night, with which arrangement they were all well pleased. The actual number of the chestnuts remained the same, but there was an adaptation to the likes and dislikes of those concerned. Such is the principle of putting oneself into subjective relation with externals.

"Wherefore the true Sage, while regarding contraries as identical, adapts himself to the laws of Heaven. This is called following two courses at once. . . .

"Therefore what the true Sage aims at is the light which comes out of darkness. He does not view things as apprehended by himself, subjectively, but transfers himself into the position of the things viewed. This is called using the light.

"There remains, however, Speech. Is that to be enrolled under either category of contraries, or not? Whether it is so enrolled or not, it will in any case belong to one or the other, and thus be as though it had an objective existence. At any rate, I should like to hear some speech which belongs to neither category. . . .

. . . "The universe and I came into being together; and I, and everything therein, are One.

"If then all things are One, what room is there for Speech? On the other hand, since I can utter these words, how can Speech not exist?

"If it does exist, we have One and Speech = two; and two and one = three. From which point onwards even the best mathematicians will fail to reach: how much more then will ordinary people fail?

"Hence, if from nothing you can proceed to something, and subsequently reach three, it follows that it would be still more easy if you were to start from something. To avoid such progression, you must put yourself into subjective relation with the external.

"Before conditions existed, TAO was. Before definitions existed, Speech was. Subjectively, we are conscious of certain delimitations which are—

Right	and	Left
Relationship	and	Obligation
Division	and	Discrimination
Emulation	and	Contention

These are called the *Eight Predicables*. For the true Sage, beyond the limits of an external world, they exist, but are not recognized. By the true Sage, within the limits of an external world, they are recognized, but are not assigned. And so, with regard to the wisdom of the ancients, as embodied in the canon of *Spring and Autumn,* the true Sage assigns, but does not justify by argument. And thus, classifying he does not classify; arguing, he does not argue."

"How can that be?" asked Tzu Yu.

"The true Sage," answered Tzu Ch'i, "keeps his knowledge within him, while men in general set forth theirs in argument, in order to convince each other. And therefore it is said that in argument he does not manifest himself.

"'Perfect TAO does not declare itself. Nor does perfect argument express itself in words. Nor does perfect charity show itself in act. Nor is perfect honesty absolutely incorruptible. Nor is perfect courage absolutely unyielding.

"For the TAO which shines forth is not TAO. Speech which argues falls short of its aim. Charity which has fixed points loses its scope. Honesty which is absolute is wanting in credit. Courage which is absolute misses its object. These five are, as it were, round, with a strong bias towards squareness. Therefore that knowledge which stops at what it does not know, is the highest knowledge.

"Who knows the argument which can be argued without words?—the TAO which does not declare itself as TAO? He who knows this may be said to be of GOD. To be able to pour in without making full, and pour out without making empty, in ignorance of the power by which such results are accomplished, —this is accounted *Light*."

Of old, the Emperor Yao said to Shun, "I would smite the Tsungs, and the Kueis, and the Hsü-aos. Ever since I have been on the throne I have had this desire. What do you think?"

"These three States," replied Shun, "are paltry out-of-the-way places. Why can you not shake off this desire? Once upon a time, ten suns came out together, and all things were illuminated thereby. How much more then should virtue excel suns?"

Yeh Ch'üeh asked Wang I, saying, "Do you know for certain that all things are subjectively the same?"

"How can I know?" answered Wang I. "Do you know what you do not know?"

"How can I know?" replied Yeh Ch'üeh. "But can then nothing be known?"

"How can I know?" said Wang I. "Nevertheless, I will try to tell you. How can it be known that what I call knowing is not really not knowing and that what I call not knowing is not really knowing? Now I would ask you this. If a man sleeps in a damp place, he gets lumbago and dies. But how about an eel? And living up in a tree is precarious and trying to the nerves:—but how about monkeys? Of the man, the eel, and the monkey, whose habitat is the right one, absolutely? Human beings feed on flesh, deer on grass, centipedes on snakes' brains, owls and crows on mice. Of these four, whose is the right taste, absolutely? Monkey mates with monkey, the buck with the doe; eels consort with fishes, while men admire Mao Ch'iang and Li Chi, at the sight of whom fishes plunge deep down in the water, birds soar high in the air, and deer hurry away. Yet who shall say which is the correct standard of beauty? In my opinion, the standard of human virtue, and of positive and negative, is so obscured that it is impossible to actually know it as such."

"If you then," asked Yeh Ch'üeh, "do not know what is bad for you, is the Perfect Man equally without this knowledge?"

"The Perfect Man," answered Wang I, "is a spiritual being. Were the ocean itself scorched up, he would not feel hot. Were the Milky Way frozen hard, he would not feel cold. Were the mountains to be riven with thunder, and the great deep to be thrown up by storm, he would not tremble. In such case, he would mount upon the clouds of heaven, and driving the sun and the moon before him, would pass beyond the limits of this external world, where death and life have no more victory over man;—how much less what is bad for him?"

Chü Ch'iao addressed Chang Wu Tzu as follows: "I heard Confucius say, 'The true sage pays no heed to mundane affairs. He neither seeks gain nor avoids injury. He asks nothing at the hands of man. He adheres, without questioning, to TAO. Without speaking, he can speak; and he can speak and yet say nothing. And so he roams beyond the limits of this dusty world. These,' added Confucius, 'are wild words.' Now to me they are the skilful embodiment of TAO. What, Sir, is your opinion?"

"Points upon which the Yellow Emperor doubted," replied Chang Wu Tzu, "how should Confucius know? You are going too fast. You see your egg, and expect to hear it crow. You look at your cross-bow, and expect to have broiled pigeon before you. I will say a few words to you at random, and do you listen at random.

"How does the Sage seat himself by the sun and moon, and hold the universe in his grasp? He blends everything into one harmonious whole, rejecting the confusion of this and that. Rank and precedence, which the vulgar prize, the Sage stolidly ignores. The revolutions of ten thousand years leave his Unity unscathed. The universe itself may pass away, but he will flourish still.

"How do I know that love of life is not a delusion after all? How do I know but that he who dreads to die is not as a child who has lost the way and cannot find his home?

"The Lady Li Chi was the daughter of Ai Feng. When the Duke of Chin first got her, she wept until the bosom of her dress was drenched with tears. But when she came to the royal residence, and lived with the Duke, and ate rich food, she repented of having wept. How then do I know but that the dead repent of having previously clung to life?

"Those who dream of the banquet, wake to lamentation and sorrow. Those who dream of lamentation and sorrow wake to join the hunt. While they dream, they do not know that they dream. Some will even interpret the very dream they are dreaming; and only when they awake do they know it was a dream.

"By and by comes the Great Awakening, and then we find out that this life is really a great dream. Fools think they are awake now, and flatter themselves they know if they are really princes or peasants. Confucius and you are both dreams; and I who say you are dreams,—I am but a dream myself. This is a paradox. Tomorrow a sage may arise to explain it; but that tomorrow will not be until ten thousand generations have gone by.

"Granting that you and I argue. If you beat me, and not I you, are you necessarily right and I wrong? Or if I beat you and not you me, am I necessarily right and you wrong? Or are we both partly right and partly wrong? Or are we both wholly right and wholly wrong? You and I cannot know this, and consequently the world will be in ignorance of the truth.

"Who shall I employ as arbiter between us? If I employ some one who takes your view, he will side with you. How can such a one arbitrate between us? If I employ some one who takes my view, he will side with me. How can such a one arbitrate between us? And if I employ some one who either differs from, or agrees with, both of us, he will be equally unable to decide between us. Since then you, and I, and man, cannot decide, must we not depend upon Another? Such dependence is as though it were not dependence. We are embraced in the obliterating unity of God. There is perfect adaptation to whatever may eventuate; and so we complete our allotted span.

"But what is it to be embraced in the obliterating unity of God? It is this. With reference to positive and negative, to that which is so and that which is not so,—if the positive is really positive, it must necessarily be different from its negative: there is no room for argument. And if that which is so really is so, it must necessarily be different from that which is not so: there is no room for argument.

"Take no heed of time, nor of right and wrong. But passing into the realm of the Infinite, take your final rest therein."

The Penumbra said to the Umbra,* "At one moment you move: at another you are at rest. At one moment you sit down: at another you get up. Why

* *Umbra* is shadow; *penumbra* refers to the edge of a shadow.—ED.

this instability of purpose?" "I depend," replied the Umbra, "upon something which causes me to do as I do; and that something depends in turn upon something else which causes it to do as it does. My dependence is like that of a snake's scales or of a cicada's wings. How can I tell why I do one thing, or why I do not do another?"

Once upon a time, I, Chuang Tzu, dreamt I was a butterfly, fluttering hither and thither, to all intents and purposes a butterfly. I was conscious only of following my fancies as a butterfly, and was unconscious of my individuality as a man. Suddenly, I awaked, and there I lay, myself again. Now I do not know whether I was then a man dreaming I was a butterfly, or whether I am now a butterfly, dreaming I am a man. . . .

The Yang Chu Chapter

Yang Chu said, "One hundred years is the limit of a long life. Not one in a thousand ever attains it. Suppose there is one such person. Infancy and feeble old age take almost half of this time. Rest during sleep at night and what is wasted during waking hours in the daytime take almost half of that. Pain and sickness, sorrow and suffering, death [of relatives], and worry and fear take almost half of the rest. In the ten and some years that is left, I reckon, there is not one moment in which we can be happily at ease without worry.

"This being the case, what is life for? What pleasure is there? For beauty and abundance, that is all. For music and sex, that is all. But the desire for beauty and abundance cannot always be satisfied, and music and sex cannot always be enjoyed. Besides, we are prohibited by punishment and exhorted by rewards, pushed by fame and checked by law. We busily strive for the empty praise which is only temporary, and seek extra glory that would come after death. Being alone ourselves, we pay great care to what our ears hear and what our eyes see, and are much concerned with what is right or wrong for our bodies and minds. Thus we lose the great happiness of the present and cannot give ourselves free rein for a single moment. What is the difference between that and many chains and double prisons?

"Men of great antiquity knew that life meant to be temporarily present and death meant to be temporarily away. Therefore they acted as they pleased and did not turn away from what they naturally desired. They would not give up what could amuse their own persons at the time. Therefore they were not exhorted by fame. They roamed as their nature directed and would not be at odds with anything. They did not care for a name after death and therefore punishment never touched them. They took no heed of fame, being ahead or being behind, or the span of life."

Yang Chu said, "The myriad creatures are different in life but the same in death. In life they may be worthy or stupid, honorable or humble. This is where they differ. In death they all stink, rot, disintegrate, and disappear. This is where they are the same. However, being worthy, stupid, honorable, or humble is beyond their power, and to stink, rot, disintegrate, and disappear is also beyond their power. Thus life, death, worthiness, stupidity, honor, and humble station are not of their own making. All creatures are equal in these, [that is, they all return to nature]. The one who lives for ten years dies. The one who lives for a hundred years also dies. The man of virtue and the sage both die; the wicked and the stupid also die. In life they were (sage-emperors) Yao and Shun; in death they were rotten bones. In life they were (wicked kings) Chieh and Chou, in death they were rotten bones. Thus they all became rotten bones just the same. Who knows their difference? Let us hasten to enjoy our present life. Why bother about what comes after death?". . .

Yang Chu said, "Po-ch'eng Tzu-kao refused to pluck one hair to benefit things. He gave up his kingdom and became a hermit farmer. Great Yü refused to benefit himself [but instead devoted his energies to diverting floods to rivers and the sea], and his body was half paralyzed. Men of antiquity did not prefer to sacrifice one single hair to benefit the world. Nor did they choose to have the world support them. If everyone refrains from sacrificing even a single hair and if everyone refrains from benefiting the world, the world will be in order."

OTHER SCHOOLS

Ancient China witnessed a great burst of philosophy in what has become known as the Hundred Schools period. Confucianism and Taoism were only two of the approaches that philosophers adopted and tried to develop. Many of the other schools quickly faded. Two, however, exerted lasting influence.

Mo Tzu (470?–391? B.C.E.), a rival of Confucius, founded a school of philosophy known as Moism. Very little is known about his life. Born in either Sung or Lu, he became the chief officer of Sung. For a time he traveled, serving as consultant to various feudal lords and public officials. He found government officials no more willing to listen, however, than Confucius or Mencius did, and founded a school to train people for public service. He had around three hundred followers. Until about 200 B.C.E. Moism and Confucianism were the two most important philosophical theories in China.

Moism presents an interesting ethical theory. It opposes Confucianism in almost every respect. Confucius stresses the importance of rituals, ceremonies, and public respect; Mo Tzu finds these wasteful. Confucius emphasizes tradition and continuity with the past; Mo Tzu formulates a principle for evaluating actions that is thoroughly oriented toward the future. Confucius bases his theory of virtue on the concept of humanity (*jen*); Mo Tzu founds his on righteousness or justice (*yi*), which he links directly to the will of Heaven. In this sense, Mo Tzu opposes Confucian humanism.

More fundamentally, Mo Tzu and Confucius have very different approaches to the moral life in general. Confucius argues that the good life is valuable in itself. In effect, he argues that virtue is its own reward. Mo Tzu, however, advocates the good life because of its good consequences. Moism is strikingly similar to modern *utilitarianism*, the doctrine that actions, or kinds of actions, are good to the extent that they maximize the good. Mo Tzu believes that virtue brings many benefits to the person who has it and to the society at large. He evaluates actions by examining their effects.

Mo Tzu's utilitarianism leads to another important difference from Confucius. Confucius holds that moral obligation arises from specific and contingent human relations—of parent and child, for example, or sibling and sibling—whereas Mo Tzu believes that our obligation to maximize good arises directly from the will of Heaven. Thus, Confucianism implies that our obligations to others depend on who we are, who they are, and how they relate to us. Mo Tzu's doctrine, in contrast, implies that our obligations are universal. In keeping with Confucius's principle of reciprocity and strongly foreshadowing Immanuel Kant's categorical imperative, Mo Tzu contends that the universal is good and the particular is bad. Immoral action involves making an exception for ourselves or our friends. Morality demands that we treat everyone with equal respect—indeed, in Mo Tzu's view, with equal love—regardless of our relation to them. According to Moism, we should love everyone as we love ourselves. Only this attitude can lead to universal peace and harmony.

Wang Ch'ung (27–100? C.E.) developed a form of naturalism that thoroughly opposes the Confucian naturalism of Hsün Tzu. Wang, an orphan, read books at a bookstore, studied at the national university, returned to his hometown to teach, and became widely known as a genius. He advanced skeptical arguments, chiefly against the Confucians. In his time, Confucianism was the dominant philosophical doctrine and had been for at least a century. It was gradually becoming a religion, and some of its followers were calling Confucius a god. The religion, moreover, was accumulating a heavy load of superstition. Wang Ch'ung argues, against the reigning orthodoxy, that nature is spontaneous. Heaven takes no action, and natural events have no religious meaning. On a deeper level, Wang argues that natural events are not directed at any particular goal; we can explain them only by understanding their causes. He contends that hypotheses should be tested against the evidence by reason, and, against Mencius and Hsün Tzu, that humans are not entirely good or evil by nature, but have both good and evil dispositions.

MO TZU

from *Universal Love*

Reprinted from The Works of Mencius, *edited and translated by James Legge. From* The Chinese Classics, *Volume II (Oxford: Clarendon, 1895).*

CHAPTER 1

It is the business of the sages to effect the good government of the world. They must know, therefore, whence disorder and confusion arise, for without this knowledge their object cannot be effected. We may compare them to a physician who undertakes to cure men's diseases:—he must ascertain whence a disease has arisen, and then he can assail it with effect, while, without such knowledge, his endeavors will be in vain. Why should we except the case of those who have to regulate disorder from this rule? They must know whence it has arisen, and then they can regulate it.

It is the business of the sages to effect the good government of the world. They must examine therefore into the cause of disorder; and when they do so they will find that it arises from the want of mutual love. When a minister and a son are not filial to their sovereign and their father, this is what is called disorder. A son loves himself, and does not love his father;—he therefore wrongs his father, and seeks his own advantage: a younger brother loves himself and does not love his elder brother;—he therefore wrongs his elder brother, and seeks his own advantage: a minister loves himself, and does not love his sovereign;—he therefore wrongs his sovereign, and seeks his own advantage:—all these are cases of what is called disorder. Though it be the father who is not kind to his son, or the elder brother who is not kind to his younger brother, or the sovereign who is not gracious to his minister:—the case comes equally under the general name of disorder. The father loves himself, and does not love his son:—he therefore wrongs his son, and seeks his own advantage: the elder brother loves himself, and does not love his younger brother;—he therefore wrongs his younger brother, and seeks his own advantage: the sovereign loves himself, and does not love his minister;—he therefore wrongs his minister, and seeks his own advantage. How do these things come to pass? They all arise from the want of mutual love. Take the case of any thief or robber:—it is just the same with him. The thief loves his own house, and does not love his neighbour's house:—he therefore steals from his neighbour's house to benefit his own: the robber loves his own person, and does not love his neighbour;—he therefore does violence to his neighbour to benefit himself. How is this? It all arises from the want of mutual love. Come to the case of great officers throwing each other's Families into confusion, and of princes attacking one another's States:—it is just the same with them. The great officer loves his own Family, and does not love his neighbour's;—he therefore throws the neighbour's Family into disorder to benefit his own: the prince loves his own State, and does not love his neighbour's:—he therefore attacks his neighbour's State to benefit his own. All disorder in the kingdom has the same explanation. When we examine into the cause of it, it is found to be the want of mutual love.

Suppose that universal, mutual love prevailed throughout the kingdom;—if men loved others as they love themselves, disliking to exhibit what was unfilial. . . . And moreover would there be those who were unkind? Looking on their sons, younger brothers, and ministers as themselves, and disliking to exhibit what was unkind . . . the want of filial duty would disappear. And would there be thieves and robbers? When every man regarded his neighbour's house as his own, who would be found to steal? When every one regarded his neighbour's person as his own, who would be found to rob? Thieves and robbers would disappear. And would there be great officers throwing one another's Families into confusion, and princes attacking one another's States? When officers regarded the Families of others as their own, what one would make confusion? When princes regarded other States as their own, what one would begin an attack? Great officers throwing one another's Families into confusion, and princes attacking one another's States, would disappear.

If, indeed, universal, mutual love prevailed throughout the kingdom; one State not attacking another, and one Family not throwing another into confusion; thieves and robbers nowhere existing; rulers and ministers, fathers and sons, all being filial and kind:—in such a condition the nation would be well governed. On this account, how many sages, whose business it is to effect the good government of the kingdom, do but prohibit hatred and advise to love? On this account it is affirmed that universal mutual love throughout the country will lead to its happy order, and that mutual hatred leads to confusion. This was what our master, the philosopher Mo, meant, when he said, "We must above all inculcate the love of others."

CHAPTER II

Our Master, the philosopher Mo, said, "That which benevolent men consider to be incumbent on them as their business, is to stimulate and promote all that will be advantageous to the nation, and to take away all that is injurious to it. This is what they consider to be their business."

And what are the things advantageous to the nation, and the things injurious to it? Our master said, "The mutual attacks of State on State; the mutual usurpations of Family on Family; the mutual robberies of man on man; the want of kindness on the part of the ruler and of loyalty on the part of the minister; the want of tenderness and filial duty between father and son and of harmony between brothers:—these, and such as these, are the things injurious to the kingdom."

And from what do we find, on examination, that these injurious things are produced? Is it not from the want of mutual love?

Our Master said, "Yes, they are produced by the want of mutual love. Here is a prince who only knows to love his own State, and does not love his neighbour's;—he therefore does not shrink from raising all the power of his State to attack his neighbour. Here is the chief of a Family who only knows to love it, and does not love his neighbour's;—he therefore does not shrink from raising all his powers to seize on that other Family. Here is a man who only knows to love his own person, and does not love his neighbour's;—he therefore does not shrink from using all his resources to rob his neighbour. Thus it happens, that the princes, not loving one another, have their battle-fields; and the chiefs of Families, not loving one another, have their mutual usurpations; and men, not loving one another, have their mutual robberies; and rulers and ministers, not loving one another, become unkind and disloyal; and fathers and sons, not loving one another, lose their affection and filial duty; and brothers, not loving one another, contract irreconcilable enmities. Yea, men in general not loving one another, the strong make prey of the weak; the rich do despite to the poor; the noble are insolent to the mean; and the deceitful impose upon the stupid. All the miseries, usurpations, enmities, and hatreds in the world, when traced to their origin, will be found to arise from the want of mutual love. On this account, the benevolent condemn it."

They may condemn it; but how shall they change it?

Our Master said, "They may change it by the law of universal mutual love and by the interchange of mutual benefits."

How will this law of universal mutual love and the interchange of mutual benefits accomplish this?

Our Master said, "It would lead to the regarding another's kingdom as one's own: another's family as one's own: another's person as one's own. That being the case, the princes, loving one another, would have no battle-fields; the chiefs of families, loving one another, would attempt no usurpations; men, loving one another, would commit no robberies; rulers and ministers, loving one another, would be gracious and loyal; fathers and sons, loving one another, would be kind and filial; brothers, loving one another, would be harmonious and easily reconciled. Yea, men in general loving one another, the strong would not make prey of the weak; the many would not plunder the few; the rich would not insult the poor; the noble would not be insolent to the mean; and the deceitful would not impose upon the simple. The way in which all the miseries, usurpations, enmities, and hatreds in the world, may be made not to arise, is universal mutual love. On this account, the benevolent value and praise it."

Yes; but the scholars of the kingdom and superior men say, "True; if there were this universal love, it would be good. It is, however, the most difficult thing in the world."

Our Master said, "This is because the scholars and superior men simply do not understand the advantageousness of the law, and to conduct their reasonings upon that. Take the case of assaulting a city, or of a battle-field, or of the sacrificing one's life for the sake of fame:—this is felt by the people everywhere to be a difficult thing. Yet, if the ruler be pleased with it, both officers and people are able to do it:—how much more might they attain to universal mutual love, and the interchange of mutual benefits, which is different from this! When a man loves others, they respond to and love him; when a man benefits others, they respond to and benefit him; when a man injures others, they respond to and injure him; when a man hates others, they respond to and hate him:—what difficulty is there in the matter? It is only that rulers will not carry on the government on this principle, and so officers do not carry it out in their practice. . . ."

CHAPTER III

Our Master, the philosopher Mo, said, "The business of benevolent men requires that they should strive to stimulate and promote what is advantageous to the kingdom, and to take away what is injurious to it."

Speaking, now, of the present time, what are to be accounted the most injurious things to the kingdom? They are such as the attacking of small States by great ones; the inroads on small Families by great ones; the plunder of the weak by the strong; the oppression of the few by the many; the scheming of the crafty against the simple; the insolence of the noble to the mean. To the same class belong the ungraciousness of rulers, and the disloyalty of ministers; the unkindness of fathers, and the want of filial duty on the part of sons. Yea, there is to be added to these the conduct of the mean men, who employ their edged weapons and poisoned stuff, water and fire, to rob and injure one another.

Pushing on the inquiry now, let us ask whence all these injurious things arise. Is it from loving others and advantaging others? It must be answered "No"; and it must likewise be said, "They arise clearly from hating others and doing violence to others." If it be further asked whether those who hate and do violence to others hold the principle of loving all, or that of making distinctions, it must be replied, "They make distinctions." So then, it is this principle of making distinctions between man and man, which gives rise to all that is most injurious in the kingdom. On this account we conclude that that principle is wrong.

Our Master said, "He who condemns others must have whereby to change them." To condemn men, and have no means of changing them, is like saving them from fire by plunging them in water. A man's language in such a case must be improper. On this account our Master said, "There is the principle of loving all, to take the place of that which makes distinctions." If, now, we ask, "And how is it that universal love can change the consequences of that other principle which makes distinctions?" the answer is, "If princes were as much for the States of others as for their own, what one among them would raise the forces of his State to attack that of another?—he is for that other as much as for himself. If they were for the capitals of others as much as for their own, what one would raise the forces of his capital to attack that of another?—he is for that as much as for his own. If chiefs regarded the families of others as their own, what one would lead the power of his Family to throw that of another into confusion?—he is for that other as much as for himself. If, now, States did not attack, nor holders of capitals smite, one another, and if Families were guilty of no mutual aggressions, would this be injurious to the kingdom, or its benefit?" It must be replied, "This would be advantageous to the kingdom." Pushing on the inquiry, now, let us ask whence all these benefits arise. Is it from hating others and doing violence to others? It must be answered, "No"; and it must likewise be said, "They arise clearly from loving others and doing good to others." If it be further asked whether those who love others and do good to others hold the principle of making distinctions between man and man, or that of loving all, it must be replied, "They love all." So then it is this principle of universal mutual love which really gives rise to all that is most beneficial to the nation. On this account we conclude that that principle is right.

Our Master said, a little while ago, "The business of benevolent men requires that they should strive to stimulate and promote what is advantageous to the kingdom, and to take away what is injurious to it." We have now traced the subject up, and found that it is the principle of universal love which produces all that is most beneficial to the kingdom, and the principle of making distinctions which produces all that is injurious to it. On this account what our Master said, "The principle of making distinctions between man and man is wrong, and the principle of universal love is right," turns out to be correct as the sides of a square.

If, now, we just desire to promote the benefit of the kingdom, and select for that purpose the principle of universal love, then the acute ears and piercing eyes of people will hear and see for one another; and the strong limbs of people will move and be ruled for one another; and men of principle will instruct one another. It will come about that the old, who have neither wife nor children, will get supporters who will enable them to complete their years; and the young and weak, who have no parents, will yet find helpers that shall bring them up. On the contrary, if this principle of universal love is held not to be correct, what benefits will arise from such a view? . . .

. . . How is that the scholars throughout the kingdom condemn this universal love, whenever they hear of it? Plain as the case is, the words of those who condemn the principle of universal love do not cease. They say, "It is not advantageous to the entire devotion to parents which is required:—it is injurious to filial piety." Our Master said, "Let us bring this objection to the test:—A filial son, having the happiness of his parents at heart, considers how it is to be secured. Now, does he, so considering, wish men to love and benefit his parents? or does he wish them to hate and injure his parents?" On this view of the question, it must be evident that he wishes men to love and benefit his parents. And what must he himself first do in order to gain this object? If I first address myself to love and benefit men's parents, will they for that return love and benefit to my parents? or if I first address myself to hate men's parents, will they for that return love and benefit to my parents? It is clear that I must first address myself to love and benefit men's parents, and they will return to me love and benefit to my parents. The conclusion is that a filial son has no alternative.—He must address himself in the first place to love and do good to the parents of others. If it be supposed that this is an accidental course, to be followed on emergency by a filial son, and not sufficient to be regarded as a general rule, let us bring it to the test of what we find in the Books of the ancient kings.—It is said in the Ta Ya,

Every word finds its answer;
Every action its recompense

He threw me a peach;
I returned him a plum.

These words show that he who loves others will be loved, and that he who hates others will be hated. How is it that the scholars throughout the kingdom condemn the principle of universal love, when they hear it? . . .

. . . And now, as to universal mutual love, it is an advantageous thing and easily practiced,—beyond all calculation. The only reason why it is not practised is, in my opinion, because superiors do not take pleasure in it. If superiors were to take pleasure in it, stimulating men to it by rewards and praise, and awing them from opposition to it by punishments and fines, they would, in my opinion, move to it,—the practice of universal mutual love, and the interchange of mutual benefits,—as fire rises upwards, and as water flows downwards:—nothing would be able to check them. This universal love was the way of the sage kings; it is the principle to secure peace for kings, dukes, and great men; it is the means to secure plenty of food and clothes for the myriads of the people. The best course for the superior man is to well understand the principle of universal love, and to exert himself to practise it. It requires the sovereign to be gracious, and the minister to be loyal; the father to be kind, and the son to be filial; the elder brother to be friendly, and the younger to be obedient. Therefore the superior man,—with whom the chief desire is to see gracious sovereigns and loyal ministers; kind fathers and filial sons; friendly elder brothers and obedient younger ones,—ought to insist on the indispensableness of the practice of universal love. It was the way of the sage kings; it would be the most advantageous thing for the myriads of the people.

WANG CH'UNG

from *Balanced Inquiries*

From Lun-Heng: Philosophical Essays of Wang Ch'ung, vol. I, translated by Alfred Fonke. New York: Paragon Book Gallery, 1907.

ON ORIGINAL NATURE

Natural feelings and natural disposition are the basis of human activity, and the source from which morals and music spring. Morals impede, and music checks the excesses of original nature. The natural disposition may be humble, modest, and yielding. The moral laws are enforced with a view to generalizing such praiseworthy qualities. The natural feelings may be good or bad, cheerful or angry, mournful or merry. Music is made in order to make every one behave respectfully. What morals and music aim at are the natural feelings and natural disposition.

The ancient literati and scholars who have written essays have all touched upon this question, but could not give a satisfactory answer. The philosopher Shih Tse of the Chou time held that human nature is partly good and partly bad, that, if the good nature in man be cultivated and regulated, his goodness increases, and if his bad nature be, his badness develops. Thus in the human heart there would be two conflicting principles, and good and evil depend on cultivation. Accordingly, Shih Tse composed a chapter on cultivation. . . .

Mencius wrote a chapter on the goodness of nature, contending that all men are originally good, and that the bad ones are corrupted by the world. Men, he says, are created by heaven and earth; they are all provided with a good nature, but when they grow up and come into contact with the world, they run wild, and are perverted, and their wickedness increases daily. According to Mencius' opinion, man, when young, would be invariably good. . . .

Chou's wickedness dated from his childhood, and Shi-Wo's rebellion could be foretold from the new-born's whine. As a new-born child has not yet had any intercourse with the world, who could have brought about his perversion?

Tan Chu was born in Yao's palace, and Shang Chün in Shun's hall. Under the reign of these two sovereigns, the people house by house were worthy of being entrusted with fief. Those with whom the two might have mixed, were most excellent, and the persons forming the suit of the two emperors, were all most virtuous. Nevertheless, Tan Chu was haughty, and Shang Chün brutal. Both lacked imperial decorum to such a degree, that they were set up as a warning to coming generations. . . .

. . . What Mencius says about original nature is not true.

Yet something may have contributed to the idea of the goodness of nature. A man may be benevolent or just, it is the wonderful proficiency of his nature, as in his locomotion and movements he shows his extraordinary natural ability. But his colour, whether white or black, and his stature, whether long or short, remain unchanged until old age and final death. Such is his heavenly nature.

Everybody knows that water, earth, and other substances differ in their natures, but people are not aware that good and evil are due to different natural dispositions. A one year old baby is not inclined to violent robbery. After it has grown up, its greed may gradually develop, and lead to ferocity and aggressiveness. . . .

In opposition to Mencius, Sun Ching [Hsün Tzu] wrote a chapter on the wickedness of nature, supposing human nature to be wicked, and its goodness to be fictitious. Wickedness of nature means to say that men, when they are born, have all a bad nature, and fictitiousness that, after they have grown up, they are forcibly induced to do good. According to this view of Sun Ching, among men, even as children, there are no good ones.

Chi as a boy amused himself with planting trees. When Confucius could walk, he played with sacrificial vessels. When a stone is produced, it is hard, when a fragrant flower comes forth, it smells. All things imbued with a good fluid develop accordingly with their growth. He who amused himself with tree planting became the minister of T'ang, and the boy who played with sacrificial vessels, the sage of Chou. Things with a fragrant or stony nature show their hardness and fragrance. Sun Ching's opinion is, therefore, incompatible with truth, yet his belief in the wickedness of nature is not quite without foundation:

A one year old baby has no yielding disposition. Seeing something to eat, it cries, and wants to eat it, and beholding a nice thing, it weeps, and wants to play with it. After it has grown up, its propensities are checked, and its wishes cut down, and it is compelled to do good. . . .

As a matter of fact, human natural disposition is sometimes good, and sometimes bad, just as human faculties can be of a high or of a low order. High ones cannot be low, nor low ones high. To say that human nature is neither good nor bad would be the same as to maintain that human faculties are neither high nor low. The original disposition which Heaven gives to men, and the destiny which it sends down, are essentially alike. By destiny men are honoured or despised, by nature good or bad. If one disputes the existence of goodness and badness in human nature, he might as well call in question that destiny makes men great or miserable. . . .

SPONTANEITY

By the fusion of the fluids of Heaven and Earth all things of the world are produced spontaneously, just as by the mixture of the fluids of husband and wife children are born spontaneously. Among the things thus produced, creatures with blood in their veins are sensitive of hunger and cold. Seeing that grain can be eaten, they use it as food, and discovering that silk and hemp can be worn, they take it as raiment. Some people are of opinion that Heaven produces grain for the purpose of feeding mankind, and silk and hemp to cloth them. That would be tantamount to making Heaven the farmer of man or his mulberry girl, it would not be in accordance with spontaneity, therefore this opinion is very questionable and unacceptable.

Reasoning on Taoist principles we find that Heaven emits its fluid everywhere. Among the many things of this world grain dispels hunger, and silk and hemp protect from cold. For that reason man eats grain, and wears silk and hemp. That Heaven does not produce grain, silk, and hemp purposely, in order to feed and cloth mankind, follows from the fact that by calamitous changes it does not intend to reprove man. Things are produced spontaneously, and man wears and eats them; the fluid changes spontaneously, and man is frightened by it, for the usual theory is disheartening. Where would be spontaneity, if the heavenly signs were intentional, and where inaction?

Why must we assume that Heaven acts spontaneously? Because it has neither mouth nor eyes. Activity is connected with the mouth and the eyes: the mouth wishes to eat, and the eyes to see. These desires within manifest themselves without. That the mouth and the eyes are craving for something, which is considered an advantage, is due to those desires. Now, provided that the mouth and the eye do not affect things, there is nothing which they might long for, why should there be activity then?

How do we know that Heaven possesses neither mouth nor eyes? From Earth. The body of the Earth is formed of earth, and earth has neither mouth nor eyes. Heaven and Earth are like husband and wife. Since the body of the Earth is not provided with a mouth or eyes, we know that Heaven has no mouth or eyes neither. Supposing that Heaven has a body, then it must be like that of the Earth, and should it be air only, this air would be like clouds and fog. How can a cloudy or nebular substance have a mouth or an eye?

Some one might argue that every movement is originally inaction. There is desire provoking the movement, and, as soon as there is motion, there is action. The movements of Heaven are similar to those of man, how could they be inactive? I reply that, when Heaven moves, it emits its fluid. Its body moves, the fluid comes forth, and things are produced. When man moves his fluid, his body moves, his fluid then comes forth, and a child is produced. Man emitting his fluid does not intend to beget a child, yet the fluid being emitted, the child is born of itself. When Heaven is moving, it does not desire to produce things thereby, but things are produced of their own accord. That is spontaneity. Letting out its fluid it does not desire to create things, but things are created of themselves. That is inaction. . . .

The Taoist school argues on spontaneity, but it does not know how to substantiate its cause by evidence. Therefore their theory of spontaneity has not yet found credence. However, in spite of spontaneity there may be activity for a while in support of it. Ploughing, tilling, weeding, and sowing in Spring are human actions. But as soon as the grain has entered the soil, it begins growing by day and night. Man can do nothing for it, or if he does, he spoils the thing.

A man of Sung was sorry that his sprouts were not high enough, therefore he pulled them out, but, on the following day, they were dry, and died. He who wishes to do what is spontaneous, is on a par with this man of Sung.

The following question may be raised:—"Man is born from Heaven and Earth. Since Heaven and Earth are inactive, man who has received the fluid of Heaven, ought to be inactive likewise, wherefore does he act nevertheless?"

For the following reason. A man with the highest, purest, and fullest virtue has been endowed with a large quantity of the heavenly fluid, therefore he can follow the example of Heaven, and be spontaneous and inactive like it. He who has received but a small quota of the fluid, does not live in accordance with righteousness and virtue, and does not resemble Heaven and Earth. . . .

. . . The more people's virtue declined, the more faith began to fail them. In their guile and treachery they broke treaties, and were deaf to admonitions. Treaties and admonitions being of no avail, they reproached one another, and if no change was brought about by these reproaches, they took up arms, and fought, till one was exterminated. Consequently reprimands point to a state of decay and disorder. Therefore it appears very dubious that Heaven should make reprimands.

Those who believe in reprimands, refer to human ways as a proof. Among men a sovereign reprimands his minister, and high Heaven reprimands the sovereign. It does so by means of calamitous events, they say. However, among men it also happens that the minister remonstrates with his sovereign. When Heaven reprimands an emperor by visiting him with calamities, and the latter wishes at that time to remonstrate with high Heaven, how can he do it? If they say that Heaven's virtue is so perfect, that man cannot remonstrate with it, then Heaven possessed of such virtue, ought likewise to keep quiet, and ought not to reprimand. When the sovereign of Wan Shih did wrong, the latter did not say a word, but at table he did not eat, which showed his perfection. An excellent man can remain silent, and august Heaven with his sublime virtue should reprimand? Heaven does not act, therefore it does not speak. The disasters, which so frequently occur, are the work of the spontaneous fluid.

Heaven and Earth cannot act, nor do they possess any knowledge. When there is a cold in the stomach, it aches. This is not caused by man, but the spontaneous working of the fluid. The space between Heaven and Earth is like that between the back and the stomach.

If Heaven is regarded as the author of every calamity, are all abnormities, great and small, complicated and simple, caused by Heaven also? A cow may give birth to a horse, and on a cherry-tree a plum may grow. Does, according to the theory under discussion, the spirit of Heaven enter the belly of the cow to create the horse, or stick a plum upon a cherry-tree?

Lao said, "The Master said," "Having no official employment, I acquired many arts," and he said, "When I was young, my condition was low, and therefore I acquired my ability in many things, but they were mean matters." What is low in people, such as ability and skilfulness, is not practised by the great ones. How could Heaven, which is so majestic and sublime, choose to bring about catastrophes with a view to reprimanding people?

Moreover, auspicious and inauspicious events are like the flushed colour appearing on the face. Man cannot produce it, the colour comes out of itself. Heaven and Earth are like the human body, the transformation of their fluid, like the flushed colour. How can Heaven and Earth cause the sudden change of their fluid, since man cannot produce the flushed colour? The change of the fluid is spontaneous, it appears of itself, as the colour comes out of itself. The soothsayers rely on this, when they foretell the future. . . .

THE REAL NATURE OF KNOWLEDGE

. . . At present all things knowable may be grasped by reflection, but all things unknowable remain incomprehensible without research or inquiry. Neither ancient nor modern history affords any instances of men knowing spontaneously without study or being enlightened without inquiry. For things knowable merely require earnest thought, then even big subjects are not difficult of apprehension, whereas things unknowable, how small soever, do not become easy through mental efforts or research. Consequently great *savants* are not apt to bring about anything without study or to know anything in default of inquiry. . . .

When a man of great natural intelligence and remarkable parts is confined to his own thoughts and has no experience, neither beholding signs and omens nor observing the working of various sorts of beings, he may imagine that after many generations a horse will give birth to an ox, and an ox to a donkey, or that from a peach-tree plums may grow, or cherries from a plum-tree. Could a Sage know this?

If a subject assassinated his sovereign, or a son killed his father and if, on the other side, somebody were as kind-hearted as Yen Yuan, as dutiful a son as Tsêng Tse, as brave as Mêng Pên and Hsia Yü and as critical as Tse Kung and Tse Wo, would a Sage be apt to find this out?

Confucius says that [some other dynasty may follow the Chou, but though it should be at the distance of a hundred ages, its affairs may be known], and elsewhere he remarks, ["A youth is to be regarded with respect. How do we know that his future will not be equal to our present?"] In regard of abrogations and innovations he believes that they may be known, but he asks how the future of a youth could be known. The future of a youth is hard to be pre-ordained, whereas abrogations and innovations are easy to detect.

However, all this is very far away, and nothing that may be heard or investigated.

Let us suppose that somebody standing at that east side of a wall raises his voice, and that a Sage hears him from the west side, would he know whether he was of a dark or a pale complexion, whether he was tall or short, and which was his native place, his surname, his designation, and his origin? When a ditch is dug out and filled with water, affectionate care is bestowed on human skeletons excavated. Provided that the face and the hair of such a skeleton be deformed and partially destroyed, and the flesh decomposed and gone, would a Sage, upon inquiry, be apt to tell whether the deceased was a peasant or a merchant, young or old, or eventually the crime he had committed and for which he had to suffer death? Not that a Sage is devoid of knowledge, but this cannot be known through his knowledge. Something unknowable by knowledge may only be learned by inquiry. Being thus unable to know, Sages and Worthies equally fail.

An opponent might retort with the following story:—When Chan Ho was sitting in his room with a pupil in attendance upon him, a cow was heard lowing outside the gate. The pupil said, "This is a black cow, but it has white hoofs." Chan Ho concurred saying, "Yes, it is a black cow, but with white hoofs," and he sent somebody to look at it. In fact, it was a black cow with its hoofs wrapped in some stuff. Chan Ho being merely a Worthy, was still in a position to distinguish the sound of the cow and to know its colour; should a Sage with his superior insight not be qualified to know this?

I beg leave to put a counter-question:—If Chan Ho knew the cow to be black and to have white hoofs, did he also know to whom it belonged, and for what purpose its hoofs had been made white? With this manner of devices one barely finds out one point, but cannot exhaust the whole truth. People thus may learn one thing, but being questioned and cross-examined, they show that they do not possess the entire knowledge, for only what has been seen with the eyes and asked with the mouth, may be perfectly known. . . .

Things that may be known Worthies and Sages equally know, and things that may not be known, Sages do not comprehend either. I prove it thus:—

Suppose that a Sage by mental abstraction foresees a rainfall, then his nature excells in one thing, but if his understanding does not reach to the remotest principles with all their details, it is not worth speaking of. What we speak of is the gift of prescience, and an intelligent mind, completely understanding the natures of all creatures, and fully apprehending thousands of important methods. If somebody is familiar with one thing, but not with the second, or if he knows the left and ignores the right, he is one-sided and imperfect, crippled in mind and not accomplished, and not what we call a Sage. Should he pass for a Sage it would be evident that a Sage has no superiority, and men like Chan Ho would be Sages, as Confucius and his equals are considered Sages. Then Sages would not distinguish themselves from Worthies, or Worthies come short of Sages.

If Worthies and Sages both possess many abilities, wherefore are Sages held in higher respect than Worthies? If they are both dependent on their schemes and devices, why do not Worthies come up to the standard of Sages? As a matter of fact, neither Worthies nor Sages are apt to know the nature of things, and want their ears and eyes, in order to ascertain their real character. Ears and eyes being thus indispensable, things that may be known are determined by reflexion, and things that may not be known are explained after inquiry. If things under Heaven or worldly affairs may be found out by reflexion, even the stupid can open their minds, if, however, they are unintelligible, even Sages with the highest intelligence cannot make anything out of them.

Confucius said ["I have been the whole day without eating, and the whole night without sleeping—occupied with thinking. It was of no use. The better plan is to learn."] Those things under Heaven which are incomprehensible are like knots that cannot be undone. By instruction one learns how to untie them, and there are no knots but can be undone. In case they cannot be untied, even instruction does not bring about this result. Not that instruction does not qualify to undo knots, but it may be impossible to untie them, and the method of undoing them is of no use.

The Sage knowing things, things must be knowable, if, however, things are unknowable, neither the Sage can understand them. Not that a Sage could not know them, but things may prove incomprehensible, and the knowing faculty cannot be used. Therefore things hard to grasp may be attained by learning, whereas unknowable things cannot be comprehended, neither by inquiry, nor by study.

CHINESE BUDDHISM

Buddhism has been extremely influential in Chinese philosophy and religious thought. Mahāyāna Buddhism, the source of all Chinese Buddhist thought, was developing important strands in India and western China. One of the most important strands of Chinese Buddhism is the Consciousness-Only school, descending from Indian Buddhist idealism. Hsüan-tsang (596–664) entered a Buddhist monastery at thirteen; at twenty-two, he began traveling to monasteries throughout China to study various doctrines, even leaving China against imperial order to study in India for sixteen years. At forty-nine, he returned to China with 657 Buddhist works previously unavailable there. The emperor, despite Hsüan-tsang's disobedience, gave him a grand welcome and supported him and a large group of assistants. The emperor commissioned from them the largest translation project in Chinese history. When Hsüan-tsang died at age sixty-eight, the emperor cancelled all his meetings for three days to mourn.

Most of the texts Hsüan-tsang and his assistants translated were of the Yogācāra school, or Buddhist idealism. Dharmapala (439–507) wrote commentaries on the early Indian Yogācārin Vasabandhu that exerted great influence on Hsüan-tsang's *Treatise on the Establishment of the Doctrine of Consciousness-Only,* which, together with the notes of his student K'uei-chi, articulate a Chinese version of Buddhist idealism.

Hsüan-tsang devotes himself, primarily, to developing an idealistic philosophy of mind. He analyzes the mind into eight consciousnesses: the five senses, a sense-center consciousness that coordinates the senses and forms concepts, a thought-center consciousness that wills and reasons, and storehouse consciousness. All eight are in constant flux. The storehouse consciousness receives sensations and thoughts from other consciousnesses and emits "manifestations," that is, memories, associations, and other thoughts. The thought-center consciousness interacts with storehouse consciousness, using its materials for purposes of intellectual deliberation. The sense-center consciousness combines the five senses into a coherent picture of the external world. All these interactions occur simultaneously, according to laws of cause and effect.

Objects are constructions from these eight forms of consciousness. Some *dharmas*—for example, qualities and phenomenal representations—are purely illusory or imaginary and do not exist. Some depend on other *dharmas* and so exist only temporarily. Some, finally, have their own independent natures and truly exist. Their "perfect reality" is the ultimate reality revealed in *nirvāṇa* experience.

Fa-tsang (643–712) developed Hua-yen philosophy, perhaps the most advanced of all Chinese Buddhist schools. He was born in Sogdiana, a region in central Asia now on the border of China and republics of the former Soviet Union. He studied early texts of Hua-yen philosophy, especially the *Hua-yen ching (Flowery Splendor*

Scripture) and became a monk at twenty-eight. Fa-tsang's writings gained him the enthusiastic support of Empress Wu, who reigned from 684 to 705. At least twice, he gave lectures at her request. The first was so impressive that, in her words, "even the earth shook."

Hua-yen philosophy bears many similarities to some Western forms of idealism. According to Fa-tsang, the universe is the Realm of Dharmas, which comprises four smaller realms: (1) the Realm of Facts, specific and changing, which constitutes the world of appearance; (2) the Realm of Principle, static, formless, outside of space, pure emptiness; (3) the Realm of Principle and Facts, brought together in harmony; and (4) the Realm of All Facts, connected and ultimately identified. The harmony of principle and fact and the ultimate identification of all facts are based on the thesis that all things interrelate and reflect one another. Each *dharma* can be defined only in terms of its relations to all other *dharmas*. It follows that each *dharma* reflects all other *dharmas*; indeed, it can be identified only in terms of them. The world is thus a perfect harmony of *dharmas*, each of which has a character that is in some sense empty; its nature is to be found only in its relations to other *dharmas*.

Zen Buddhism, unike other, earlier forms of Chinese Buddhism, is a distinctly Chinese invention. The Japanese word *zen* derives from the Chinese *ch'an*, which, in turn, derives from the Sanskrit *dhyana* (meditation). In China, however, the Indian idea of meditation yielded to a Taoist notion of concentration and enlightenment. The northern Chinese school of Zen stressed gradual enlightenment based on a process of eliminating error and establishing mental quietude. The southern school, which developed later but eventually won out over its northern competitor, stressed sudden enlightenment. On this conception, the mind is a unity that is simple, in the sense that it is absolutely indivisible. The Buddha is everywhere; anything can bring about its realization. The Zen practitioner seeks a state of mind in which reality becomes transparent and crystalline.

The Buddha-nature, according to both schools, is *nirvāṇa*, which resides in everyone; everyone has the ability to become a Buddha. The northern school distinguishes true mind from false mind and seeks gradual enlightenment through the elimination of false mind. The southern school, however, treats the mind as an inseparable unity, all functions of which reflect true reality, or Suchness (*tathata*).

The southern Zen doctrine of unity and inseparability seems to imply that all distinctions are unfounded and need to be transcended. Isn't Zen itself therefore unfounded? Perhaps, if we take the propositions advanced by Zen as describing the world. But Zen theses are means for reaching an end—*satori* (enlightenment) —rather than literal descriptions of reality. Their point is not to give us descriptive or even normative knowledge but to lead us to undergo certain kinds of experiences.

Of course, there are many ways of undergoing the right kinds of experiences. They need not involve language; if they do, the language need not "make sense" in traditional terms. Zen training methods include meditation, *koans* ("riddles" meant to develop insight), and various arts. Sometimes, Zen masters use more extreme methods to clarify the mind. I-Hsüan (d. 867) founded the Lin-chi school. Called *Rinzai* in Japanese, it is the most radical of the ninth-century Zen schools, which stresses the "lightning" method of shouting and beating to prepare the mind for enlightenment.

HSÜAN-TSANG

from *The Treatise on the Establishment of the Doctrine of Consciousness-Only*

1. The Nonexistence of the Self

1. Because the ideas of the self (*atman*) and dharmas are [constructions produced by causes and therefore] false,
Their characters of all kinds arise.
These characters are [constructions] based on the transformations of consciousness,
Which are of three kinds.

2a. They are the consciousness (the eighth or storehouse consciousness) whose fruits (retribution) ripen at later times,
The consciousness (the seventh or thought-center consciousness) that deliberates, and the consciousness (the sense-center consciousness and the five sense consciousness) that discriminates spheres of objects.

The Treatise says:

Both the world and sacred doctrines declare that the self and dharmas are merely constructions based on false ideas and have no reality of their own. . . . On what basis are [the self and dharmas] produced? Their characters are all constructions based on the evolution and transformation of consciousness. . . .

How do we know that there is really no sphere of objects but only inner consciousness which produces what seem to be the external spheres of objects? Because neither the real self nor the real dharma is possible.

Why is the real self impossible? Theories of the self held by the various schools may be reduced to three kinds. The first holds that the substance of the self is eternal, universal, and as extensive as empty space. It acts anywhere and as a consequence enjoys happiness or suffers sorrow. The second holds that although the substance of the self is eternal, its extension is indeterminate, because it expands or contracts according to the size of the body. The third holds that the substance of the self is eternal and infinitesimal like an atom, lying deeply and moving around within the body and thus acts.

The first theory is contrary to reason. Why? If it is held that the self is eternal, universal, and as extensive as empty space, it should not enjoy happiness or suffer sorrow along with the body. Furthermore, being eternal and universal, it should be motionless. How can it act along with the body? Again, is the self so conceived the same or different among all sentient beings? If it is the same, when one being acts, receives the fruits of action, or achieves salvation, all beings should do the same. But this would of course be a great mistake. If it is different, then the selves of all sentient beings would universally penetrate one another and their substance would be mixed, and since the field of abode of all selves is the same, the acts of one being or the fruits of action received by him should be the act or fruits of all beings. If it is said that action and fruits belong to each being separately and there would not be the mistake just described, such a contention is also contrary to reason, because action, fruits, and body are identified with all selves and it is unreasonable for them to belong to one self but not to another. When one is saved, all should be saved, for the Dharma (truth) practiced and realized would be identical with all selves.

The second theory is also contrary to reason. Why? If in substance the self always remains in the same state, it should not expand or contract along with the body. If it expands or contracts like wind in a bag or a pipe, it is not always remaining in the same state. Furthermore, if the self follows the body, it would be divisible. How can it be held that the substance of the self is one? What this school says is like child's play.

The last theory is also contrary to reason. Why? Since the self is infinitesimal like an atom, how can it cause the whole big body [that extends throughout the world of form] to move? If it is said that although it is small it goes through the body like a whirling wheel of fire so that the whole body seems to move, then the self so conceived is neither one nor eternal, for what comes and goes is neither eternal nor one.

Furthermore, there are three additional theories of the self. The first holds that the self is identical with the aggregates (namely, matter, sensation, thought, disposition, and consciousness). The second holds that it is separated from the aggregates. And the third holds that it is neither identical with nor separated from the aggregates. The first theory is contrary to reason, for the self would be like the aggregates and is therefore neither eternal nor one. Furthermore, the internal matters (the five senses) are surely not the real self, for they are physically obstructed (or restricted) like external matters. The mind and mental qualities are not the real self either, for they are not always continuous and depend on various causes to be produced. Other conditioned things and matters are also not the real self, for like empty space they are without intelligence.

The second theory is also contrary to reason, for the self would then be like empty space, which neither acts nor receives fruits of action.

The last theory is also contrary to reason. This theory allows that the self is based on the aggregates but is neither identical with nor separated from them. The self would then be like a vase [which depends on clay] and has no reality of its own. Also, since it is impossible to say whether it is produced from causes or not produced from causes, it is also impossible to say whether it is a self or not. Therefore the real self conceived in the theory cannot be established.

Again, does the substance of the real self conceived by the various schools think or not? If it does, it would not be eternal, because it does not think all the time. If it does not, it would be like empty space, which neither acts nor receives fruits of action. Therefore on the basis of reason, the self conceived by the theory cannot be established.

Again, does this substance of the real self conceived by the various schools perform any function or not? If it does, it would be like hands and feet and would not be eternal. If it does not, it would be like [illusory] horns of a hare and not the real self. Therefore in either case, the self conceived by them cannot be established.

Again, is the substance of the real self conceived by the various schools an object of the view of the self or not? If it is not, how do advocates of the theory know that there is really a self? If it is, then there should be a view of the self that does not involve any perversion, for that would be knowledge of what really is. In that case, how is it that the perfectly true doctrines believed in by those holding the theory of the self all denounce the view of the self and praise the view of the non-self? [Advocates of the theory themselves] declare that the view of the non-self will lead to Nirvāṇa while clinging to the view of the self will lead to sinking in the sea of life and death (transmigration). Does an erroneous view ever lead to Nirvāṇa and a correct view, on the contrary, lead to transmigration?

Again, the various views of the self [actually] do not take the real self as an object, because it has objects [which are not itself] like the mind takes others [such as external matters] as objects. The object of the view of the self is certainly not the real self, because it [the view] is an object like other dharmas. Therefore the view of the self does not take the real self as an object. Only because the various aggregates are transformed and manifested by inner consciousness, all kinds of imagination and conjecture result in accordance with one's own erroneous opinions. . . .

3. The First Transformation of Consciousness

From what is said above it is clear that the self and dharmas separated from consciousness conceived by the heterodoxical and other schools are all unreal. . . . From this we ought to know that there is really no external sphere of objects. There is only inner consciousness which produces what seems to be the external sphere. . . .

6. Consciousness-Only

. . . Therefore everything produced from causes, everything not produced from causes, and everything seemingly real or unreal, are all inseparable from consciousness. The word "only" is intended to deny that there are real things separated from consciousness, but not to deny that there are mental qualities, dharmas, and so forth inseparable from consciousness. The word "transform" means that the various inner consciousnesses transform and manifest the characters which seem to be the external spheres of the self and dharmas. This process of transformation and change is called discrimination because it is its own nature to make erroneous discriminations [that things are real]. It refers to the mind and mental qualities in the Three Worlds. These, what it holds to be spheres of objects, are called objects of discrimination, that is, the self and dharmas which it erroneously holds to be real. Because of this discrimination, which evolves characters which seem to be the external spheres of the false self and dharmas, what is discriminated as the real self and dharmas are all absolutely nonexistent. This theory has been extensively refuted by the doctrines [of our teachers] already cited.

Therefore everything is consciousness only, because erroneous discrimination in itself is admitted as a fact. Since "only" does not deny the existence of dharmas not separated from consciousness, therefore true Emptiness [mental qualities] and so forth have the nature of being. In this way we steer far away from the two extremes of holding that dharmas are real [although they have no nature of their own] or holding that dharmas are unreal [although they do function as causes and effects], establish the principle of Consciousness-Only, and hold correctly to the Middle Path.

7. Nine Objections to the Consciousness-Only Doctrine and Their Answers

(1) *Objection:* On the basis of what doctrines is the principle of Consciousness-Only established?

Answer: Have we not already explained? However, the explanations are not sufficient. One's own principle cannot be established by demolishing those of others. One should definitely present his own doctrine in order to establish it.

The true scriptures declare that "in the Three Worlds there is nothing but mind," that objects are but manifestations of consciousness-only, that all dharmas are not separated from the mind, that sentient beings become pure or impure in accordance with the mind, that bodhisattvas (saints of the Mahāyāna) who perfected the Four Wisdoms will, following their awakening, penetrate the truth of consciousness-only and the absence of spheres of objects.

The Four Wisdoms are: first, the wisdom that contradictory consciousnesses are but characters. This means that the same thing perceived by ghosts, human beings, and deities appear differently to them in accordance with their past deeds. If there is really an external sphere, how can this be possible? Second, the wisdom that consciousness takes non-being as its object. This means that the past, the future, images in dreams, and things imagined have no real, objective basis. They are possible because they are manifestations of consciousness. If these objective bases are nonexistent, the rest is also nonexistent. The third is the wisdom that naturally there should be no perversion of truth. This means that if the intelligence of ordinary people is able to perceive the real spheres of objects, they should naturally achieve freedom from perversion and should be able to achieve emancipation without any effort. [Since they are not emancipated, it shows that the objective spheres they perceive are not real at all.] The fourth is the wisdom changing with three wisdoms:

a) Changing with the wisdom of the one who is free and at ease. This means that he who has realized the freedom and the ease of mind can change and transform earth [into gold] and so forth without fail according to his desires. If there was really an external sphere, how can these transformations be possible?

b) Changing with the wisdom of the one who meditates and sees clearly. This means that when one who has achieved supreme calmness and has practiced the meditation on the Law meditates on one sphere of objects, its various characters appear in front of him. If the sphere is real, why does it change according to his mind?

c) Changing with the wisdom of no discrimination. This means that as the non-discriminating wisdom which realizes truth arises, all spheres of objects and their characters will cease to appear. If there are real spheres of objects, why should they do so? The bodhisattva who achieves the Four Wisdoms will definitely understand and penetrate the principle of consciousness-only. . . .

FA-TSANG

from *Treatise on the Golden Lion*

1. Clarifying the fact that things arise through causation

It means that gold has no nature of its own. As a result of the conditioning of the skillful craftsman, the character of the lion consequently arises. This arising is purely due to causes. Therefore it is called arising through causation.

2. Distinguishing matter and Emptiness

It means that the character of the lion is unreal; there is only real gold. The lion is not existent, but the substance of the gold is not nonexistent. Therefore they are [separately] called matter and Emptiness. Furthermore, Emptiness has no character of its own; it shows itself by means of matter. This does not obstruct its illusory existence. Therefore they are [separately] called matter and Emptiness.

3. Simply stating the Three Natures

The lion exists because of our feelings. This is called [the nature] arising from vast imagination. The lion seems to exist. This is called [the nature of] dependence on others (gold and craftsman) [for production]. The nature of the gold does not change. This is therefore called [the nature of] Perfect Reality.

4. Showing the nonexistence of characters

It means that as the gold takes in the lion in its totality, apart from the gold there is no character of the lion to be found. Therefore it is called the nonexistence of characters.

5. Explaining non-coming-into-existence

It means that at the moment when we see the lion come into existence, it is only gold that comes into existence. There is nothing apart from the gold. Although the lion comes into existence and goes out of existence, the substance of the gold at bottom neither increases nor decreases. Therefore we say that [dharmas] do not come into existence [nor go out of existence].

6. *Discussing the Five Doctrines*

(1) Although the lion is a dharma produced through causation, and comes into and goes out of existence every moment, there is really no character of the lion to be found. This is called the Small Vehicle (Hīnayāna) Doctrine of Ordinary Disciples [that is, the Hīnayāna schools].

(2) These dharmas produced through causation are each without self-nature. It is absolutely Emptiness. This is called the Initial Doctrine of the Great Vehicle (Mahāyāna) [that is, the Three-Treatise and Conscious-Only Schools].

(3) Although there is absolutely only Emptiness, this does not prevent the illusory dharmas from being clearly what they are. The two characters of coming into existence through causation and dependent existence coexist. This is called the Final Doctrine of the Great Vehicle [that is, the T'ien-t'ai School].

(4) These two characters eliminate each other and both perish, and [consequently] neither [the products of] our feelings nor false existence remain. Neither of them has any more power, and both Emptiness and existence perish. Names and descriptions will be completely discarded and the mind will be at rest and have no more attachment. This is called the Great Vehicle's Doctrine of Sudden Enlightenment [that is, the Zen School].

(5) When the feelings have been eliminated and true substance revealed, all becomes an undifferentiated mass. Great function then arises in abundance, and whenever it does, there is surely Perfect Reality. All phenomena are in great profusion, and are interfused but not mixed (losing their own identity). The all is the one, for both are similar in being nonexistent in nature. And the one is the all, for [the relation between] cause and effect is perfectly clear. As the power [of the one] and the function [of the many] embraces each other, their expansion and contraction are free and at ease. This is called the Rounded (inclusive) Doctrine of the One [all-inclusive] Vehicle. [The Hua-yen School.] . . .

FA-TSANG

from *Hundred Gates to the Sea of Ideas of the Flowery Splendor Scripture*

2. *Harmonious Combination and Spontaneity*

The sea of the nature of things has no shore, and because of that, its characteristics have become many and extensive. Coming-into-existence through causation is unfathomable; thus its many gates are universally prevalent and open. [All things] turn on and on in ten thousand different ways, but the form of expansion and contraction accords with wisdom. Harmoniously combined as one, the conditions of their opening and closing follow the mind. As [the mind is as clear as] shining and does not give rise to incipient [and disturbing] activity, although there are varieties and differences, it is always in harmony with them. And since function does not pervert substance, although [things] are of one flavor, they are always free and without obstacle. We shall now, from the point of view of substance and tendency, briefly discuss ten different principles.

(1) Appreciating principle and fact

For example, the dust has the characters of roundness and smallness. This is fact. Its nature is empty and nonexistent. This is principle. Because facts have no substance, they merge together in accordance with principle. And because the dust has no substance, it universally penetrates everything. For all facts are no different from principle and they are completely manifested in the dust. Therefore the scripture says, "The wide world is the same as the narrow world, and the narrow world is the same as the wide world."

(2) Discerning matter and Emptiness

For example, dust is formed through causation; this is matter. Matter has no substance; this is Emptiness. If Emptiness is spoken of apart from matter, it would mean that there is no false matter in the realm of worldly truth, and that because of false matter there is the True Emptiness in the realm of absolute truth. If matter is spoken of apart from Emptiness, it would mean that there is no True Emptiness in the realm of absolute truth, and that because of True Emptiness there is false matter in the realm of worldly truth. Now, it is only necessary to understand that True Emptiness means that matter is false and has no substance. Emptiness is not so called because there is no matter. The scripture says, "Matter is empty not because it has been destroyed, but because it is of itself empty."

(3) Penetrating the big and the small

For example, dust has the character of roundness; this is smallness. Mount Sumeru is high and wide; this is bigness. But this dust and that mountain, though one is big and the other small, contain each other, turn on and on in accordance with the mind, and neither come into nor go out of existence. For example, when one sees a mountain as high and wide, it is his own mind that manifests it as large; there is no largeness distinct from it. When one sees the dust as round and small, it is also his own mind that manifests it as small; there is no smallness distinct from it. Thus when we see this dust, it is entirely the dust manifested by the mind which sees the mountains as high and wide. Therefore the large is contained right in the small. The scripture says, "The number of Hard Iron Enclosing Mountains is infinite. All of them can be placed at the tip of a hair. In order to understand the largest and the smallest phenomena the bodhisattva therefore begins his resolution [to seek perfect wisdom]."

(4) Taking in both the far and the near

It means that this dust is near and the world of the ten cardinal directions is far away. But as the dust has no substance, it fully penetrates all the ten cardinal directions. In other words, the ten directions are all those of the dust. Therefore the far is always near. However, although the ten directions are far away, they are merely those of the nature of dust. Even though they go beyond a world which cannot be described, they still do not go outside the nature of dust. Why? Because the extension of dust has no substance. It is similar to space and cannot be transcended. Therefore all the ten cardinal directions are but manifestations of the nature of dust. Furthermore, although one leaves this dust and goes to the ten directions, one still sees this dust. Why? Because the dust has no substance, and facts [of which dust is an instance] are clearly manifested in accordance with principle. Therefore when the nature of the dust universally pervades everything, the dust as a fact is also manifested at the same time. This means that in one particle of dust everything is manifested and both the near and the far are clearly before our eyes. As the ten directions enter into one particle of dust, they are always near although they are far, and as the dust universally pervades all the ten directions, it is always far although it is near. Both the dust and the ten directions, and both the far and the near, are clearly identical without any difference. Think of it.

(5) Understanding the pure and the mixed

It means that inasmuch as the dust does not come into existence, all dharmas do not come into existence. This is purity. Nevertheless, in the idea itself that the dust does not come into existence, both principle and fact are fully contained. It is both Emptiness and matter, and both perfect wisdom and Nirvāṇa. This is a case of what is mixed. Principle never obstructs fact, for what is pure is always mixed. Fact always fulfills principle, for the mixed is always pure. Because both principle and fact are free and at ease, they do not obstruct each other.

(6) Comprehending the instant and the infinitely long period

For example, when the dust is perceived, it is a manifestation of the mind for an instant. This manifestation of the mind for an instant is entirely the same as hundreds and thousands of infinitely long periods. Why? Because all these periods are originally formed from an instant. Since they establish each other, both lack substance or nature. Because an instant has no substance, it penetrates the infinitely long periods, and because these periods have no substance, they are fully contained in a single instant. Since both the instant and the long periods have no substance, the characters of length and shortness are naturally harmonized. All worlds, whether far or near, the Buddhas, living beings, and all things in the three ages (past, present, and future) are manifested in one instant. Why? Because all things and dharmas are manifested in accordance with the mind. As there is no obstruction to the instant [of thought], all dharmas are consequently harmonized. Therefore in an instant [of thought] all facts and things in the three ages are clearly seen. The scripture says, "Any instant is the same as hundreds and thousands of infinitely long periods, and hundreds and thousands of infinitely long periods are the same as a single instant."

(7) Discriminating the one and the many

For example, the dust's own character is one. It is because its own oneness is quiescent and calm that it can universally respond to become many. If its own oneness is perturbed, it will lose its universal correspondence [to others] and the many [to which it universally responds] cannot be formed. The same is true of the two, the three, and so forth.

Furthermore, the one and the many established each other. Only when the one is completely the many can it be called the one, and only when the many is completely the one can it be called the many. There is not a separate one outside the many, for we clearly know that it is one within [coincides with] the many. There are not the many outside of the one, for we clearly know they are the many within the one. The reason is that they are not many [separately] and yet they can be many [coinciding with] the one, and that it is not [independently] the one and yet it can be one [coinciding with] the many. Only when we understand that [dharmas] have no nature [of their own] can we have the wisdom about the one and the many. The scripture says, "It is like calculation. From one gradually to ten down to infinity, all comes from the basic number. When viewed with wisdom, there is no difference."

(8) Appreciating the unrestricted and the restricted

It means that the dust has the character of smallness; that is restriction. But the very character has no substance; this is non-restriction. Now, an infinite number of lands and seas are always manifested in the dust. This means the unrestricted is always restricted. But one particle of dust universally pervades all lands and seas. This means the restricted is always unrestricted. Furthermore, the small need not be destroyed to contain the large, which means that the mysterious particle of dust extensively contains the lands [and seas] of the Buddha. The large need not be destroyed in order to dwell in the small, which means that the mysterious lands and seas of the Buddha are always manifested in the dust. This is the non-obstruction between the unrestricted and the restricted.

(9) Understanding expansion and contraction

It means that the dust has no nature [of its own]. When substance comes to the fore and completely permeates the ten cardinal directions, that is expansion. The ten directions have no substance and are entirely manifested in the dust through causation—that is contraction. The scripture says, "One land of the Buddha fills the ten directions, and the ten directions enter into the one [land] without residue." When contracted, all things are manifested in one particle of dust. When expanded, one particle of dust will universally permeate everything. Expanding is the same as ever contracting, for a particle of dust involves everything. Contracting is the same as ever expanding, for everything involves the one particle of dust. This is what is meant by saying that expansion and contraction are free and at ease.

(10) Grasping perfect harmony

It means that as the character of the dust has already ceased to be, deluded consciousness also perishes. Because fact has no substance, it follows principle and becomes perfectly harmonized with it. Because substance involves facts, therefore principle follows fact and is in complete accord with it. Thus they always exist but are at the same time ever empty, for Emptiness does not destroy existence. They are always empty but at the same time ever existent, for existence does not obstruct Emptiness. The Emptiness that does not obstruct existence can harmonize all phenomena, and the existence that does not destroy Emptiness can complete everything. Therefore all phenomena clearly exist before us and one does not obstruct the other.

From the above principles, the tendency of harmonious combination becomes unrestricted because it has no nature, and all phenomena which exist spontaneously can be combined because they rise through causation. As the one and the many totally involve each other, we look at one particle of dust and [everything] suddenly becomes manifest. As the "this" takes in the "other," we look at a tiny hair and all things appear together. The reason is that, when the mind understands, all dharmas can be free and at ease, and because the principle is clear, great wisdom can be achieved. Among seekers after wisdom, who will examine its source? People talking about it seldom investigate its mystery to the limit. What can match the function of spontaneity?

The Recorded Conversations of Zen Master I-Hsüan

1. The Prefect, Policy Advisor Wang, and other officials requested the Master to lecture. The Master ascended the hall and said, "Today it is only because I, a humble monk, reluctantly accommodate human feelings that I sit on this chair. If one is restricted to one's heritage in expounding the fundamental understanding [of salvation], one really cannot say anything and would have nothing to stand on. However, because of the honorable general advisor's strong request today, how can the fundamental doctrines be concealed? Are there any talented men or fighting generals to hurl their banners and unfold their strategy right now? Show it to the group!"

A monk asked, "What is the basic idea of the Law preached by the Buddha?" Thereupon the Master shouted at him. The monk paid reverence. The Master said, "The Master and the monk can argue all right."

Question: "Master, whose tune are you singing? Whose tradition are you perpetuating?"

The Master said, "When I was a disciple of Huang-po, I asked him three times and I was beaten three times."

As the monk hesitated about what to say, the Master shouted at him and then beat him, saying, "Don't nail a stick into empty space."

2. The Master ascended the hall and said, "Over a lump of reddish flesh there sits a pure man who transcends and is no longer attached to any class of Buddhas or sentient beings. He comes in and out of your sense organs all the time. If you are not yet clear about it, look, look!"

At that point a monk came forward and asked, "What is a pure man who does not belong to any class of Buddhas or sentient beings?" The Master came right down from his chair and, taking hold of the monk, exclaimed, "Speak! Speak!" As the monk deliberated what to say, the Master let him go, saying, "What dried human excrement-removing stick is the pure man who does not belong to any class of Buddhas or sentient beings!" Thereupon he returned to his room.

3. The Master ascended the hall. A monk asked, "What is the basic idea of the Law preached by the Buddha?" The Master lifted up his swatter. The monk shouted, and the Master beat him.

[The monk asked again], "What is the basic idea of the Law preached by the Buddha?" The Master again lifted up his swatter. The monk shouted, and the Master shouted also. As the monk hesitated about what to say, the Master beat him.

Thereupon the Master said, "Listen, men. Those who pursue after the Law will not escape from death. I was in my late Master Huang-po's place for twenty years. Three times I asked him about the basic idea of the Law preached by the Buddha and three times he bestowed upon me the staff. I felt I was struck only by a dried stalk. Now I wish to have a real beating. Who can do it to me?"

One monk came out of the group and said, "I can do it."

The Master picked up the staff to give him. As he was about to take it over, the Master beat him.

4. The Master ascended the hall and said, "A man stands on top of a cliff, with no possibility of rising any further. Another man stands at the crossroad, neither facing nor backing anything. Who is in the front and who is in the back? Don't be like Vimalakīrti (who was famous for his purity), and don't be like Great Gentleman Fu (who benefited others). Take care of yourselves."

5. The Master told the congregation: "Seekers of the Way. In Buddhism no effort is necessary. All one has to do is to do nothing, except to move his bowels, urinate, put on his clothing, eat his meals, and lie down if he is tired. The stupid will laugh at him, but the wise one will understand. An ancient person said, 'One who makes effort externally is surely a fool.'"

6. *Question*: "What is meant by the mind's not being different at different times?"

The Master answered, "As you deliberated to ask the question, your mind has already become different. Therefore the nature and character of dharmas have become differentiated. Seekers of the Way, do not make any mistake. All mundane and supramundane dharmas have no nature of their own. Nor have they the nature to be produced [by causes]. They have only the name Emptiness, but even the name is empty. Why do you take this useless name as real? You are greatly mistaken! . . . If you seek after the Buddha, you will be taken over by the devil of the Buddha, and if you seek after the patriarch, you will be taken over by the devil of the patriarch. If you seek after anything, you will always suffer. It is better not to do anything. Some unworthy priests tell their disciples that the Buddha is the ultimate, and that he went through three infinitely long periods, fulfilled his practice, and then achieved Buddhahood. Seekers of the Way, if you say that the Buddha is the ultimate, why did he die lying down sidewise in the forest in Kuśinagara after having lived for eighty years? Where is he now? . . . Those who truly seek after the Law will have no use for the Buddha. They will have no use for the bodhisattvas or arhats. And they will have no use for any excellence in the Three Worlds (of desires, matter, and pure spirit). They will be distinctly free and not bound by material things. Heaven and earth may turn upside down but I shall have no more uncertainty. The Buddhas of the ten cardinal directions may appear before me and I shall not feel happy for a single moment. The three paths (of fire, blood, and swords) to hell may suddenly appear, but I shall not be afraid for a single moment. Why? Because I know that all dharmas are devoid of characters. They exist when there is transformation [in the mind] and cease to exist when there is no transformation. The Three Worlds are but the mind, and all dharmas are consciousness only. Therefore [they are all] dreams, illusions, and flowers in the air. What is the use of grasping and seizing them? . . .

"Seekers of the Way, if you want to achieve the understanding according to the Law, don't be deceived by others and turn to [your thoughts] internally or [objects] externally. Kill anything that you happen on. Kill the Buddha if you happen to meet him. Kill a patriarch or an arhat if you happen to meet him. Kill your parents or relatives if you happen to meet them. Only then can you be free, not bound by material things, and absolutely free and at ease. . . . I have no trick to give people. I merely cure disease and set people free. . . . My views are few. I merely put on clothing and eat meals as usual, and pass my time without doing anything. You people coming from the various directions have all made up your minds to seek the Buddha, seek the Law, seek emancipation, and seek to leave the Three Worlds. Crazy people! If you want to leave the Three Worlds, where can you go? 'Buddha' and 'patriarchs' are terms of praise and also bondage. Do you want to know where the Three Worlds are? They are right in your mind which is now listening to the Law."

7. Ma-ku came to participate in a session. As he arranged his seating cushion, he asked, "Which face of the twelve-face Kuan-yin faces the proper direction?"

The Master got down from the rope chair. With one hand he took away Ma-ku's cushion and with the other he held Ma-ku, saying, "Which direction does the twelve-face Kuan-yin face?"

Ma-ku turned around and was about to sit in the rope chair. The Master picked up the staff and beat him. Ma-ku having grasped the staff, the two dragged each other into the room.

8. The Master asked a monk: "Sometimes a shout is like the sacred sword of the Diamond King. Sometimes a shout is like a golden-haired lion squatting on the ground. Sometimes a shout is like a rod or a piece of grass [used to attract fish]. And sometimes a shout is like one which does not function as a shout at all. How do you know which one to use?"

As the monk was deliberating what to say, the Master shouted.

9. When the Master was among Huang-po's congregation, his conduct was very pure. The senior monk said with a sigh, "Although he is young, he is different from the rest!" He then asked, "Sir, how long have you been here?"

The Master said, "Three years."

The senior monk said, "Have you ever gone to the head monk (Huang-po) and asked him questions?"

The Master said, "I have not. I wouldn't know what to ask."

The senior monk said, "Why don't you go and ask the head monk what the basic idea of the Law preached by the Buddha clearly is?"

The Master went and asked the question. But before he finished, Huang-po beat him. When he came back, the senior monk asked him how the conversation went. The Master said, "Before I finished my question, he already had beaten me. I don't understand." The senior monk told him to go and ask again.

The Master did and Huang-po beat him again. In this way he asked three times and got beaten three times. . . . Huang-po said, "If you go to Ta-yü's place, he will tell you why."

The Master went to Ta-yü, who asked him, "Where have you come from?"

The Master said, "I am from Huang-po's place."

Ta-yü said, "What did Huang-po have to say?"

The Master said, "I asked three times about the basic idea of the Law preached by the Buddha and I was beaten three times. I don't know if I was mistaken."

Ta-yü said, "Old kindly Huang-po has been so earnest with you and you still came here to ask if you were mistaken!"

As soon as the Master heard this, he understood and said, "After all, there is not much in Huang-po's Buddhism."

NEO-CONFUCIANISM

Medieval Chinese philosophy enjoyed a burst of renewal, thanks to the revival of Confucianism. Chu Hsi (Zhu Xi: 1130–1200) was the most influential neo-Confucian and probably the most influential Chinese philosopher of any school during the past two millennia. Born in Fukien (Fujian) he studied under his father, who was head of several departments in the government. Invaders from the north imposed humiliating peace terms on Fukien, the acceptance of which Chu Hsi strongly opposed. He left the capital, becoming a keeper of records. He spent most of his life as a temple guardian, spending his ample free time studying and writing.

Chu Hsi declined many official posts but did accept appointment as a prefect at age forty-nine. Three years later, he was demoted for criticizing his fellow officials as incompetent. At age fifty-eight, he again accepted a post, this time as vice minister of the department of the army, but was demoted shortly thereafter. During the next few years, Chu Hsi held several positions, all very briefly, and evidently made many enemies; at sixty-six, he was accused of ten crimes and removed from all his posts. Some even demanded his execution. Despite his almost constant conflicts with others, his writings had gained him considerable fame. When he died four years later, nearly a thousand people attended his funeral.

Chu Hsi's relation to Confucius is in many ways like that of Thomas Aquinas to Aristotle in the West. Chu Hsi synthesized various elements of Confucianism, bringing the theory to a very high state of development. He standardized *The Analects, The Great Learning, The Doctrine of the Mean,* and *The Book of Mencius* as the Four Books, the classics at the heart of Confucianism which served as the basis of civil service examinations in China for almost six hundred years.

The most important aspects of Chu Hsi's thought are metaphysical and epistemological, though he developed interesting views on ethics and political philosophy that go substantially beyond earlier Confucian doctrines. Chu Hsi's chief concept is that of the Great Ultimate, which in some ways is similar to the One in Taoism. It is one, eternal, and in everything. Taoism treats the One, in a particular thing, as both its power and its virtue—as both guiding and regulating principle. Chu Hsi separates these two. Embodied in a thing, the Great Ultimate involves both principle (*li*) and material force (*ch'i*). Principle is incorporeal, eternal, and unchanging; it constitutes the essence of things. It is purely good. Material force is corporeal, transitory, and changeable. It constitutes the substance of things, acts as an agent of change, and may be either good or evil.

Each of us, according to Chu Hsi, has a moral or spiritual mind that is pure principle and drives us toward the good. But we also have desires and physical dispositions and capacities that mix principle with material force. Desires and physical dispositions are not necessarily bad; they may be either good or evil.

Their presence in human nature, however—in what he calls the natural mind—makes evil possible. And indulging them is the greatest moral danger. Ethical training aims to strengthen the moral mind, helping it to win out over desire and physical disposition.

Chu Hsi asserts, moreover, that our minds are unified with the mind of the universe, in the sense that the principle in each of us is exactly the principle in the universe as a whole. This makes knowledge, including moral knowledge, possible. And it guarantees that the directives our moral mind gives are correct; its directives are the directives of the universe.

Chu Hsi's thought dominated Chinese philosophy for more than three centuries, until Wang Yang-Ming (1472–1529) developed a philosophy called *dynamic idealism* which, in turn, dominated Chinese thought for a century and a half. His views influenced Japanese thought extensively and remain influential in East Asian philosophy.

The China of the late Ming dynasty into which Wang was born was turbulent and decadent. Semi-nomadic tribes raided the country from the north. Rulers were generally incompetent and oppressive. Taxes were high; political favoritism and corruption were common; large numbers of people survived only through crime or other underground economic activity. Freedom of thought and speech were under increasing attack.

The young Wang was so studious and philosophical that he spent his wedding night engrossed in conversation with a Taoist priest. At twenty, he began studying Chu Hsi's philosophy. Wang was so inspired by Chu Hsi's stress on the investigation of things that he and a friend once sat in front of bamboo for seven days to investigate its principles. Wang turned to the study of military affairs and Taoism but returned to Confucianism after finding these alternatives unsatisfying. He began teaching at twenty-eight, attracting some disciples and attacking the then-popular, highly artificial practices of recitation and flowery composition. This got him into serious trouble; at age thirty-four, he was hauled before the emperor, beaten forty times, and banished to what is now Kueichow (Guizhou). Living in isolation and great hardship, he developed many of his most original doctrines. Later he said they were "achieved from a hundred deaths and a thousand sufferings." By the age of forty-two, he was an official at Nanking (Nanjing) and a famous and influential scholar. Despite notable successes, his critique of Chu Hsi earned him more and more enemies, and he was forced into retirement at forty-nine. He continued writing until his death eight years later.

Wang's philosophy is a form of idealism, and his ethical theory is a version of intuitionism. He argues that nothing is external to the mind. In particular, principle and mind are one; the principles of things are to be found within the mind, not in anything external to it. Reacting strongly against the rationalism of Chu Hsi in moral theory, Wang argues that we have innate intuitive knowledge of the good. Nevertheless, Wang accepts many of Chu Hsi's premises. He agrees that we have a moral mind, which contains innately the moral truth, and that the human mind in general tends to stray from the path because it also contains passions. Whereas Chu Hsi holds that we must depend on strength and rational inquiry to combat the passions, Wang, in contrast, contends that we must simply recover what our minds innately share.

What ethical conceptions do our minds innately share? The highest good, Wang answers. Ethical living consists in fostering and extending our in-born knowledge of the good. Since mind is principle, Wang's project so far sounds rationalistic. But he believes that a person of humanity is in some sense united with everything; that person, recognizing the unity, loves everything. Here Wang's thought shows the influence of Taoism and Buddhism; only the small, in his view, make distinctions. A mind united with everything is humane and is the "clear character" mentioned in *The Great Learning*.

Desires can becloud this naturally clear character. The point of moral education is clarifying the mind in the sense of removing the obscurity desire introduces. Thus, for Wang, the key to a good life is in the mind already. He agrees with Mencius that the mind is originally good: "Intuitive knowledge of good is characteristic of all men." We must seek to extend our knowledge, not because we do not know right from wrong—we have at birth a conscience that immediately recognizes them—but because we must rectify our minds, removing the clouds and smudges stemming from desire.

Wang Fu-chih (1619–1692) attacked neo-Confucianism from a strikingly modern perspective. The son of a scholar, he got his civil service degree at twenty-three. Shortly afterward, he raised and led a militia trying to save the Ming dynasty from the invading Manchus. At thirty-three, having been defeated, he retired and devoted himself to writing. Only in the nineteenth and twentieth centuries has his work been recognized and appreciated. He is now regarded as the initiator of Chinese philosophy's modern era.

Wang Fu-chih attacks both Chu Hsi's rationalism and Wang Yang-Ming's idealism. Both take principle (*li*) as prior to and independent of material force (*ch'i*). Indeed, Chu Hsi's philosophy proved vulnerable to Wang Yang-Ming's idealistic attack for precisely this reason. But Wang Fu-chih rejects the priority of principle that earlier neo-Confucians assume. For him, principle depends on material force. We should think of principle, he maintains, not as an abstract law or set of laws but as the concrete order of the world—the arrangement of material objects. The Great Ultimate, the Principle of Nature or Heaven, and other abstractions of earlier neo-Confucian thought Wang likewise reduces to the concrete and material. "The world," Wang Fu-chih insists, "consists only of concrete things."

Wang Fu-chih plays on the similar sound of two distinct Chinese words, written with distinct characters. *Ch'i* appears as "material force," in the sense of the earlier neo-Confucians. It is akin to matter and substance in Western philosophy, but with the dynamic character of force or energy as well. *Ch'i* also appears as "concrete things," tangible objects. Concrete things have both principle and material force. Principle, however, has no independent status. There are only concrete entities. They have the principles they do because of the arrangements of their material parts.

Wang Fu-chih's materialism leads him to reject the ethical outlooks of both Chu Hsi and Wang Yang-Ming. They saw desire as clouding the otherwise clear mirror of the mind. That clarity, however, relies on principle: the moral mind is the assemblage of principles that constitute the Nature. Consequently, Wang Fu-chih rejects the image of the mind as mirror. He also rejects the idea that right action consists in putting principle before desire. His materialism might suggest that he has no place for ethics at all, but, he argues instead, the Way, like principle in general, depends on material force. Moral principle does not stand opposed to desire; it depends on and is found in desire. Wang Fu-chih takes from Taoism the idea that things naturally tend toward improvement, and that—to put the point in neo-Confucian language—principle is inherently good. This injects the realm of values into his materialistic system. Unlike the Taoists, however, Wang Fu-chih does not deduce an ethics of noninterference. People must make choices and, in making them, should strive for the Mean.

CHU HSI

from *The Philosophy of Human Nature*

From Chu Hsi, The Philosophy of Human Nature, *translated by Percy Bruce. London: Probsthain and Co., 1922.*

THE NATURE

Moral Law [*Tao*] is the Nature, and the Nature is Moral Law. It is true, these two are one and the same thing; but we need to understand why the term Nature is used, and why the term Moral Law is used.

"The Nature is Law [*li,* principle]." Subjectively it is the Nature, objectively it is Law.

The principle of life is termed the Nature.

The Nature consists of innumerable principles produced by Heaven.

The Nature consists of substantive principles; Love [*jen*, humanity], Righteousness [*i*, justice], Reverence [*li*, propriety] and Wisdom are all included in it. . . .

After reading some essays by Yün and others on the Nature, the Philosopher said: In discussing the Nature it is important first of all to know what kind of entity the Nature is. (Pi Ta's record adds the words: The Nature as a matter of fact is formless; it consists of principles implanted in man's mind.) Ch'eng Tzu put it well when he said, "The Nature is Law." Now if we regard it as Law, then surely it is without form or similitude. It is nothing but this single principle. In man Love, Righteousness, Reverence, and Wisdom are the Nature, but what form or shape have they? They are principles only. It is because of such principles that men's manifold deeds are done. It is because of them that we are capable of solicitude, that we can be ashamed of wrongdoing, that we can be courteous, and can distinguish between right and wrong. Take as an illustration the nature of drugs, some have cooling and some heating properties. But in the drug itself you cannot see the shape of these properties: it is only by the result which follows upon taking the drug that you know what its property is; and this constitutes its nature. It is so with Love, Righteousness, Reverence, and Wisdom. According to Mencius these four principles have their root in the Mind. When, for example, he speaks of a solicitous mind, he attributes feeling to the Mind.

The Philosopher said further: Shao Yao Fu said, "The Nature is the concrete expression of Moral Order [*Tao*], and the Mind is the enceinte [enclosure] of the Nature." This is well said, for Moral Order in itself is without concrete expression; it finds it in the Nature. But if there were no Mind where could the Nature be? There must be Mind to receive the Nature and carry it into operation; for the principles contained in the Nature are Love, Righteousness, Reverence, and Wisdom, and they are real principles. We of the Confucian cult regard the Nature as real. Buddhists regard it as unreal. To define the Nature as the Mind, as is done so frequently in these days, is incorrect. It is essential first to understand our terms and then proceed to definition. (Pi Ta's record adds: If we point to that which possesses consciousness as the Nature, we are speaking of what is really the Mind.) For example, there is the Nature as implanted by the Decree of Heaven, and there is the physical element. If we regard the Nature, as it is implanted by the Decree of Heaven, as having its origin in the Mind, where will you place the Physical Nature? When, for example, it is said, "The natural mind is unstable, the spiritual mind is but a spark," the word 'mind' is used in both cases, but we do not say that the 'spiritual mind' is Mind, while 'the natural mind' is not Mind. . . .

The Nature of man is universally good. Even Chieh and Chou, who exhausted the possibilities of violence and went to the utmost extreme of wickedness, still knew that their actions were evil. But, *though my Nature is good,* when I would act in accordance with it I fail, and find that it has been made captive by human desire.

The Master asked the question: How does the Nature come to be "the concrete expression of Moral Order?"

Ch'un replied: Moral Order is a principle inherent in the Nature.

The Master said: The term Moral Order is used in a universal sense, the term Nature is used in the individual sense. How do we know that Moral Order exists in the external world? Simply by our experience of it here. (Ti-Lu reads: By seeking it in our own persons.) Wherever the Nature is, there is Moral Order. The Moral Order is Law as we find it in the external world; the Nature is Law as we find it in ourselves. But the laws which we find in the external world are all comprehended in this Law which is in myself. The Nature is the framework of the Moral Order.

Chi Sui, following the teaching of his school, said: You cannot speak of the Nature as being good in the moral sense, for ultimate goodness has no opposite, whereas the moment you say that a thing is good you are contrasting it with evil, and when you speak of it as being good or evil you are speaking of what is not the original Nature. The original Nature is from above, so honourable as to be above comparison. Good as the correlative of evil is from beneath. The moment you say it is good you contrast it with evil, and then you are speaking of what is not the original Nature. When Mencius said, "The Nature is good," he was not speaking of moral goodness, but simply using the language of admiration, as if to say, "What an excellent thing the Nature is!" just as Buddha exclaimed "Excellent!" with reference to "the Path." (This is the theory of Wen Ting.)

In criticizing this statement I said: The original Nature, it is true, is the all-comprehensive perfect goodness apart from any comparison with evil. This is what is imparted to me by Heaven. But the practice of it rests with man, and then it is that you have evil in addition to good. Conduct in accord with this original Nature is good. Conduct out of accord with it is evil. How can it be said that the good is not the original Nature? It is in man's conduct that the distinction arises, but the good conduct is the outcome of the original Nature. If, as Wen Ting says, there is both an absolute and a relative goodness, then there are two natures. Now the Nature which is received from Heaven, and the Nature from which good conduct proceeds, are essentially one; but the moment the good appears, there immediately appears with it the not-good, so that necessarily you speak of good and evil in contrast. It is not that there is an antecedent evil waiting for the goodness to appear with which it is to be contrasted, but that by wrong actions we fall into evil. . . .

. . . Hence the saying of Confucius, referring to the Nature: "It passes on just like this"; and that of Ch'eng Tzu: "It is one with the Moral Order." This principle, both now and from all eternity, never ceases for a single moment day or night; therefore it is said, "It cannot cease."

Again, referring to the saying of Shao Tzu, "The Nature is the concrete expression of Moral Order," the Philosopher said: Though Moral Order is present everywhere, how are we to find it? The answer is: simply by turning and looking within. It is wholly found within our Nature. From the fact that we ourselves possess the principles of Love, Righteousness, Reverence, and Wisdom, we infer that others possess them also; that, indeed, of the thousands and tens of thousands of human beings, and of all things in the universe, there are none without these principles. Extend our investigations as far as we will, we will find that there is nothing which does not possess them. Shao Tzu states it well when he defines the Nature as the concrete expression of Moral Order. . . .

THE NATURE IN MAN AND OTHER CREATURES

Question. Do the Five Agents [Metal, Wood, Water, Fire, and Earth] receive the Supreme Ultimate equally?

Answer. Yes, equally.

Question. Does man embody all the Five Agents, while other creatures receive only one?

Answer. Other creatures also possess all the Five Agents, but receive them partially.

Question. What is your opinion of the statement that the Nature consists of Love [*jen*], Righteousness, Reverence, and Wisdom?

Answer. It corresponds to the saying "Their realization is the Nature." But preceding this are the stages represented by the statements "The alternation of the negative and positive modes" and "The law of their succession is goodness." When the Moral Law of the negative and positive modes alone existed, and before ever the stage of the creation of man and other beings was reached, these four principles were already present. Even the lower orders of life, such as reptiles, all possess them, but partially and not in their perfection, on account of the limitations caused by the grossness of the Ether [*ch'i*, material force].

It is true that in the life of men and other creatures the Nature with which they are endowed differs from the very beginning in the degree of its perfection. But even within the differing degrees of perfection there is the further variation in respect of clearness and translucence. . . .

. . . The approximation to uniformity of the etherial element is exemplified in our sense of heat and cold and of hunger and repletion, in the love of life and shrinking from death, and in the instinctive seeking for what will benefit and shunning what will be prejudicial: all this is common to man with other creatures. The diversity of Law is seen in the existence among ants and bees of the relation between sovereign and minister, in which there is manifested no more than a gleam of Righteousness; or in the existence among wolves and tigers of the relation between parent and child, in which there is manifested no more than a gleam of Love; while of the other principles you can discern nothing. It is just like a mirror, in the centre of which there are one or two spots of light and the rest is all black. Of phenomena in general, it may be said that if the endowment is great in one direction, it is at the expense of some corresponding defect in another direction, as when tender-hearted men are lacking in the judicial faculty, while men in whom the judicial faculty is prominent tend to be tyrannical; for the more Love is developed the more is Righteousness obscured, and the more Righteousness is developed the more Love is obscured. . . .

Question. Men and other creatures are all endowed with the Law of the Universe as their Nature, and all receive the Ether of the Universe for their Form. Granting that the differences in men are due to differing degrees in the translucence and fulness of the Ether, I am not sure whether in the case of other creatures the differences between them are because they are imperfectly endowed with Law, or whether these also are due to the opacity and cloudiness of the Ether.

Answer. It is simply that the Ether received being limited, the immaterial principle received is also correspondingly limited. For example, the physical constitution of dogs and horses being as it is, their functions are correspondingly limited in their range.

Question. Seeing that every individual creature possesses the Supreme Ultimate in its entire substance, does it not follow that Law is universally complete?

Answer. You may call it complete or you may call it partial. As Law it cannot be other than complete, but from the point of view of the material element it is necessarily partial. . . .

CAPACITY

. . . The Nature is the law of the Mind. The Feelings are the activities of the Mind, Capacity is the power of the Feelings to act in a certain way. Feeling and Capacity are in fact nearly alike. But the Feelings are called forth by contact with object, their roads and paths are crooked and curved; Capacity is their power to be so. Bear in mind that the web of consciousness with its innumerable threads proceeds wholly from the Mind. . . .

The law of the Mind is the Supreme Ultimate, its activity and repose are the Two Modes [*yin* and *yang*].

Mind alone is absolute. . . .

Question. Mind is consciousness and the Nature is Law. How do the Mind and Law come to be united as one?

Answer. You must not think of their being made to unite. They start united.

Question. How do they start united?

Answer. Law apart from Mind would have nothing in which to inhere.

Mind is the pure and refined portion of the Ether.

Expounding the word "mind" the Philosopher said: One word will cover it, namely, Life. "The highest attribute of Heaven and Earth is the production of life." It is by receiving the Ether of Heaven and Earth that man lives; therefore the Mind must love, for Love is life. . . .

Mind and Law are one. Law is not a separate entity side by side with Mind, but inherent in Mind. Mind cannot be confined: it issues forth as phenomena present themselves.

At this the Philosopher smiled and said: Saying this makes one smile. It is just like a library with all the books removed and a lamp lighted: on all sides and in every corner it will be flooded with brilliant light just as it is here at this spot. To-day, however, few people are able to look at the matter in this way.

Question. Mind as a distinct entity possesses all laws in their completeness, so that the good manifested undoubtedly proceeds from the Mind. But what about the evil manifested, which consists entirely of the selfishness of the material endowment and creaturely desire? Does this also proceed from the Mind?

Answer. It is not indeed the original substance of the Mind, but it also proceeds from the Mind.

Question. Is this what is called the "natural mind"?

Answer. Yes.

Tzŭ Shêng, following on the above, asked: Does the "natural mind" include both good and evil?

Answer. Yes, both are included.

Question. Is there any connexion between bodily movements and the Mind?

Answer. How can it be otherwise? It is the Mind which causes bodily movements.

Question. Before there are any stirrings of pleasure, anger, sorrow, or joy, the body exercises its functions; for example, the eye sees and the ear hears. Is this before or after the activity of the Mind?

Answer. That, as yet, there are no stirrings of pleasure, anger, sorrow, or joy, is one thing; but sight, hearing, and locomotion also imply the presence of Mind. If the Mind is ignorant of the bodily movements, then it is not present and has not noticed them, in which case to say "before activity" is not applicable. "Before activity" does not mean that the Mind is steeped in unconsciousness. It is spoken of the Mind as continually awake, and not as though it were asleep, as your way of expressing it would suggest. . . .

The Mind that is perfected is like a clear mirror which is free from blemishes. If you look into a mirror with patches which do not reflect, the effect will be that your own person appears blotchy. In the present day the conduct of many is marred by a number of follies and blemishes because their vision of themselves is imperfect. The Mind is essentially formless spirit; all laws are complete within it, and all phenomena come within the sphere of its knowledge. In these days people are for the most part perverted by their physical nature, and beclouded by creaturely desire. Thus their minds are darkened and they are unable to perfect knowledge. This is why the saints and sages placed such emphasis on the exhaustive investigation of principles. . . .

Man lives by the union of the Nature with the Ether. But given this union we find, when we analyse it, that the Nature pertains to Law and is formless, while the Ether pertains to form and is material. The former as pertaining to Law and formless is altruistic and invariably good; the latter as pertaining to form and material is selfish and potentially evil. The manifestations of the former, since it is altruistic and good, are all the workings of Divine Law; the manifestations of the latter, since it is selfish and potentially evil, are all the actions of human desire. Hence the distinction between the "natural mind" and the "spiritual mind" in Shun's admonition to Yü. For this distinction is a root distinction, and not to be explained as excess or shortcoming in the action of the Ether, with subsequent lapse into human desire. But the statement does not go beyond the term "natural mind," and implies, surely, that it is not necessarily wholly evil. It does not go beyond the term "unstable," and equally implies that it is not necessarily foredoomed to become criminal. But seeing that it pertains not to Law but to form, its lapse into evil and even crime is not difficult. This is the reason for its "instability," and herein it differs from the "spiritual mind," which is infallibly good and never evil, is stable and never falls to one side or the other, has its standard, and can be relied upon. In regard to these two, therefore, we must use the utmost discrimination and singleness, and so make the altruistic and invariably good the perpetual master of our entire personality and of all our conduct, while the selfish and potentially evil must be allowed no place in our lives. Then, in everything we do and say, there will be no need to choose between excess and shortcoming: it will spontaneously and unfailingly accord with the Mean. (Whenever you begin your examination of anything you should first consider and decide upon its goodness or otherwise, and then proceed to consider whether it accords with the Mean or not. By "discrimination and singleness" you examine its goodness or otherwise; then by "sincerely holding fast the Mean" there is neither excess nor shortcoming, and the Mean is attained to naturally. You do not seek the Mean by means of discrimination and singleness.) . . .

It is not necessary to go out of one's way to get rid of the natural mind; it needs only that the spiritual mind shall rule. That is, if the natural mind is to be rendered powerless to play the robber, it must be by the spiritual mind. But this is exceedingly difficult to secure, so sudden and rapid are the movements of human desire. . . .

The intellectual powers of the Mind, when they manifest themselves on the plane of ethical principle, constitute the "spiritual mind"; when they manifest themselves in the region of desire, they constitute the "natural mind." . . .

The mind-substance is originally in repose, and yet it cannot but have movement. Its operation is originally good, and yet it is possible for it to lapse into the not-good. Now its movement and lapse into evil cannot be called the original character of the mind-substance, and yet it cannot be termed otherwise than Mind. It is only because it has been beguiled by external things that it becomes evil. . . .

. . . For the incoming and preserved mind is the true mind, and the outgoing and lost mind is also the true mind, but has become lost through the seductions of its environment. . . .

. . . The mind preserved is the spiritual mind, the mind lost is the natural mind. But the Mind is one: it is not that really there are these two minds, each a separate entity without any connexion the one with the other, but only that different terms are used to distinguish between preserving and losing. It is true that when it is lost it is not the original state of the mind; but neither must you say that there is another mind which is both preserved and lost, outgoing and incoming, waiting to return to its source, and that we are to seek to exchange it for still a different mind which has no distinction between preserved and lost, outgoing and incoming. There is only this one Mind. The failure to preserve it is in itself to lose it, not to lose it is to preserve it. There is not the smallest conceivable middle ground. The student, therefore, must be earnest in holding fast and preserving the mind. . . .

The expressions "holding fast" and "letting go," "preserving" and "losing," represent the instability of the natural mind, but the spiritual mind which is "but a spark" is no other than this same mind. . . .

. . . The Mind is the agent by which man rules his body. It is one and not divided. It is subject and not object. It controls the external world and is not its slave. Therefore, with the Mind we contemplate external objects, and so discover the principles of the universe. . . .

"To preserve the Mind" means "to maintain inward correctness by seriousness, and to regulate outward conduct by righteousness" as in what has already been said in explanation of the expressions, "discrimination and singleness," and "holding fast and preserving the Mind." Therefore by perfecting the Mind we can understand our Nature and know Heaven, because, the substance of the Mind being unclouded, we are able to search into this Law as the Self-Existent. . . .

To sum up: The teaching of the sages is, that with the Mind we exhaustively investigate principles, and by following these principles we determine our attitude to external things, just as the body uses the arm, and the arm the hand. . . .

THE MIND, THE NATURE, AND THE FEELINGS

The Nature corresponds to the Supreme Ultimate. The Mind corresponds to the Two Modes [*yin* and *yang*]. The Supreme Ultimate is inherent in the Two Modes and is inseparable from them, but the Supreme Ultimate is the Supreme Ultimate, and the

Two Modes are the Two Modes. So it is with the Nature and Mind. As is expressed in the saying: "One and yet two, two and yet one." . . .

Although the Nature is formless it consists of concrete principles. Although the Mind is a distinct entity, it is formless and therefore can contain innumerable principles. . . .

The Nature consists of the concrete principles contained in the Mind. The Mind is the seat of the assemblage of those principles.

The Nature is Law. The Mind is the receptacle which holds and stores the principles of the Nature, the agent which distributes and sets them in operation.

To the Mind the Nature stands in the relation of substance. The Mind holds the Nature within it like the stuffing of cakes, for the simple reason that it is in virtue of its possession of the Nature that it possesses these principles.

When you have succeeded in describing a thing, and when you have succeeded in naming it, you may claim clearly to understand it. The Mind and the Nature are also very difficult to define.

Answer. A definition which I have already given is: The Nature is the law of the Mind; the Feelings are the Nature in action; and the Mind is the ruler of the Nature and Feelings.

The Nature is undefinable. We are able to assert that the Nature is good because we observe the goodness of the Four Terminals. From these we infer the goodness of the Nature, just as we know the purity of the stream from the purity of its source. The Four Terminals are feelings, while the Nature consists of principles. The issues are Feelings, the source is the Nature. It is the same principle as when you infer the presence of an object from the shadow it casts. . . .

Question. In your comment on "perfecting the Mind" and "understanding the Nature," you, sir, say: "The Mind is without substance: the Nature is its substance." How is it so?

Answer. The Mind is a hollow receptacle: the Nature constitutes its inward content. The principles of the Nature are contained in the Mind, and when activity is put forth that which is put forth pertains to the Nature. It is not that there is a perceptible object inside called the Nature; it is simply the inherent rightness of Law which constitutes the Nature. A man ought to act in a certain way: this is what constitutes his Nature. As to the passage in Mencius beginning with the words: "The feeling of solicitude is the terminal of Love"; these four sentences refer to the Nature, to the Feelings, and to Mind, which it would be well to consider in conjunction with Hêng Ch'ü's dictum: "The Mind unites the Nature and the Feelings." . . .

What we call Moral Law is not something out of the ordinary which has to be sought. It is what we commonly speak of as moral principle, and not some other Tao which needs suddenly to be discovered and seized by me, and so recognized as Moral Law. It is no more than the ordinary principles of everyday life, by which we know that this is right and that is wrong. The recognition of right in everything is Moral Law. In the present day the Buddhists talk of a Tao which is to be apprehended suddenly. But Tao is not a thing which can be felt and handled.

The Moral Law is the Law followed by all in the past and in the present. The kindness of the father, the filial obedience of the son, the benevolence of the sovereign, and the loyalty of the minister, are one principle common to all people. Virtue is the reception of this Law in one's own person; just as, when the sovereign cannot but be benevolent and the minister loyal, it is because they have received this Moral Law within themselves, and therefore manifest this disposition. Yao cultivated it and attained to the virtue of Yao. Shun cultivated it and attained to the virtue of Shun. From before heaven and earth, from the incarnation of the Imperial Hsi, in all there has been but this one Moral Law; from the ages of the past right up till now there has been no other. Only in each generation there appears one who stands out as leader; but he is leader because he has received this truth into his own personality. It is not that Yao had one Moral Law, and Shun another, while King Wên and the Duke Chow, with Confucius, each had theirs. Lao Tzŭ said, "When Tao is lost people follow after Virtue," which shows that he did not understand either of these terms. To distinguish them as two separate entities is to make Tao an empty abstraction. Our Confucian school teaches that they are simply one entity; it is as common to all the ages, and not from the point of view of the individual man, that it is termed Tao. Virtue is this Tao received in its entirety by the individual personality. Lao Tzŭ says, "When Tao is lost, people follow after Virtue, when Virtue is lost people follow after Love, when Love is lost people follow after Righteousness." But if we separate Tao from Love and Righteousness we have no ethical principal at all. In that case how can it be Tao? . . .

Is it maintained that Tao is lofty and distant, inscrutable and mysterious, and beyond the possibility of human study? Then I answer that Tao derives its very name from the fact that it is the principle of right conduct in everyday life for all men, that it is like a road which should be travelled upon by the countless myriads of people within the four seas and nine continents. It is not what the Taoist and Buddhist describe as Tao, empty, formless, still, non-existent, and having no connexion with men. Is it maintained that Tao is far removed from us, so vast as to be out of touch with our needs, and that we are not called upon to study it? Then I say that Tao, present as it is in all the world in the relation between sovereign and minister and between father and son, in down-sitting and uprising and in activity and rest, has everywhere its unchangeable clear law, which cannot fail for a single instant. . . .

WANG YANG-MING

from *Instructions for Practical Life*

From The Philosophy of Wang Yang-Ming, *translated by Frederick Goodrich Henke (Carbondale, Ill.: Open Court Publishing Company, 1916).*

Wang's Interpretation of a "Thing"

I said, "Yesterday when I heard your teaching I clearly realized that the task is as you describe it: having heard your words today, I am still less in doubt. Last night I came to the conclusion that the word 'thing' of 'investigating things' is to be identified with the word 'affair'. Both have reference to the mind."

The Teacher said: "Yes. The controlling power of the body is the mind. The mind originates the idea, and the nature of the idea is knowledge. Wherever the idea is, we have a thing. For instance, when the idea rests on serving one's parents, then serving one's parents is a 'thing'; when it is on serving one's prince, then serving one's prince is a 'thing'; when it is occupied with being benevolent to the people and kind to creatures, then benevolence to the people and kindness to creatures are 'things'; when it is occupied with seeing, hearing, speaking, moving, then each of these becomes a 'thing.' I say there are no principles but those of the mind, and nothing exists apart from the mind. The Doctrine of the Mean says: 'Without sincerity there would be nothing.' The Great Learning makes clear that the illustrating of illustrious virtue consists merely in making one's purpose sincere, and that this latter has reference to investigating things."

The Teacher spoke again saying: "The 'examine' of 'examining into the nature of things', just as the 'rectify' of 'the great man can rectify the mind of the prince', of Mencius, has reference to the fact that the mind is not right. Its object is to reinstate the original rightness. But the idea conveyed is that one must cast out the wrong in order to complete the right, and that there should be no time or place in which one does not harbor heaven-given principles. This includes a most thorough investigation of heaven-given principles. Heaven-given principles are illustrious virtue; they include the manifesting of illustrious virtue."

Innate Knowledge

Again he said: "Knowledge is native to the mind; the mind naturally is able to know. When it perceives the parents it naturally knows what filial piety is; when it perceives the elder brother it naturally knows what respectfulness is; when it sees a child fall into a well it naturally knows what commiseration is. This is intuitive knowledge of good, and is not attained through external investigation. If the thing manifested emanates from the intuitive faculty, it is the more free from the obscuration of selfish purpose. This is what is meant by saying that the mind is filled with commiseration, and that love cannot be exhausted. However, the ordinary man is subject to the obscuration of private aims, so that it is necessary to develop the intuitive faculty to the utmost through investigation of things in order to overcome selfishness and reinstate the rule of natural law. Then the intuitive faculty of the mind will not be subject to obscuration, but having been satiated will function normally. Thus we have a condition in which there is an extension of knowledge. Knowledge having been extended to the utmost, the purpose is sincere."

Propriety in Its Relation to Principles

I made inquiry of the Teacher saying, "Though I ponder deeply I am unable to understand the use of 'extensive study of all learning' in the task of keeping one's self under the restraint of the rules of propriety. Will you kindly explain it somewhat?"

The Teacher said: "The word 'propriety' carries with it the connotation of the word 'principles'. When principles become manifest in action, they can be seen and are then called propriety. When propriety is abstruse and cannot be seen, it is called principles. Nevertheless, they are one thing. In order to keep one's self under the restraint of the rules of propriety it is merely necessary to have a mind completely under the influence of natural law (heaven-given principles). If a person desires to have his mind completely dominated by natural law, he must use effort at the point where principles are manifested. For instance, if they are to be manifested in the matter of serving one's parents, one should learn to harbor these principles in the serving of one's parents. If they are to be manifested in the matter of serving one's prince, one should learn to harbor them in the service of one's prince. If they are to be manifested in the changing fortunes of life, whether of wealth and position, or of poverty and lowliness, one should learn to harbor them whether in wealth and position, or in poverty and lowliness. If they are to be manifested when one meets sorrow and difficulty, or is living among barbarous tribes, one should learn to harbor them in sorrow and difficulty, or when one is among barbarous tribes. Whether working or resting, speaking or silent, under no conditions should it be different. No matter where they are manifested, one should forthwith learn to harbor them. This is what is meant by studying them extensively in all learning, and includes the keeping of one's self under the restraint of the rules of propriety. 'Extensive study of all learning' thus implies devotion to the best (discrimination). 'To keep one's self under the restraint of the rules of propriety' implies devoting one's self to a single purpose (undividedness)."

The Mind is a Unity

I made inquiry saying: "An upright (righteous) mind is master of the body, while a selfish mind is always subject to the decrees (of the body). Using your instruction regarding discrimination and undividedness, this saying appears to be mistaken."

The Teacher said: "The mind is one. In case it has not been corrupted by the passions of men, it is called an upright mind. If corrupted by human aims and passions, it is called a selfish mind. When a selfish mind is rectified it is an upright mind; and when an upright mind loses its rightness it becomes a selfish mind. Originally there were not two minds. The philosopher Ch'eng said, 'A selfish mind is due to selfish desire; an upright mind is natural law (is true to nature).' Even though his discourse separates them, his thought comprehends the situation correctly. Now, you say that if the upright mind is master and the selfish mind is subject to decrees, there are two minds, and that heaven-given principles and selfishness can not co-exist. How can natural law be master, while selfishness follows and is subject to decrees?" . . .

The Mind My Be Compared to a Mirror

Yueh-jen said: "The mind may be compared to a mirror. The mind of the sage is like a bright mirror, the mind of the ordinary man like a dull mirror. The saying of more recent natural philosophy may be compared to using it as a mirror to reflect things. If effort is expended in causing the mirror to reflect while the glass is still dull, how can one succeed? The natural philosophy of the Teacher is like a polished and brightened mirror. When after having been polished the mirror is bright, the power of reflecting has not been lost."

He asked regarding the general plan and the details (fineness and coarseness) of the doctrine. The Teacher said: "The doctrine has neither general plan nor detailed structure. What men consider the general plan and the details may be made clear in examining a house. When one first enters it, one sees only the general plan. After a while one sees the supports and walls. Later still such things as the ornamental duckweed upon the supports become apparent. But all this is only a part of the same house." . . .

The Discussions of Truth Vary Because Truth is Inexhaustible

He made inquiry saying: "Though there is but this one doctrine, yet the doctrinal discussions of the ancients were frequently not alike. Are not some things more essential than others in seeking the path?"

The Teacher said: "Truth (the path) has no form; it cannot be grasped or felt. To seek it in a bigoted and obstinate way in literary style or expression only, is far from correct. It may be compared to men discussing heaven. As a matter of fact, when have they ever seen heaven? They say that sun, moon, wind, and thunder are heaven. They cannot say that men, things, grass, and trees are not heaven, while the doctrine is heaven. When the individual once comprehends, what is there that is not truth? People for the most part think that their little corner of experience determines the limits of truth, and in consequence there is no uniformity in their discussions. If they realized that they need to seek within in order to understand the nature of the mind, there would be neither time nor place that would not be pregnant with truth. Since from ancient times to the very present it is without beginning and without end, in what way would there be any likenesses or differences in truth? The mind is itself truth and truth is heaven. He who knows the mind thereby knows both truth and heaven."

Again he said: "Sirs, if you would truly comprehend truth, you must recognize it from your own minds. It is of no avail to seek it in external things." . . .

WANG YANG-MING

from *Record of Discourses*

From The Philosophy of Wang Yang-Ming, *translated by Frederick Goodrich Henke (Carbondale, Ill.: Open Court Publishing Company, 1916).*

Intuitive Knowledge of Good is Characteristic of All Men

The Teacher said: "The sages, also, have first devoted themselves to study, and thus know the truth. The common people, also, have knowledge of it from birth."

Some one asked, "How can that be?"

He replied: "Intuitive knowledge of good is characteristic of all men. The sage, however, guards and protects it so that nothing obscures it. His contending and anxiety do not cease, and he is indefatigable and energetic in his efforts to guard his intuitive knowledge of the good. This also involves learning. However, his native ability is greater, so that it is said of him that he is born with knowledge of the five duties and practices them with ease. There is nobody who does not in the period from his infancy to his boyhood develop this intuition of good, but it is often obscured. Nevertheless, this original knowledge of good is naturally hard to obliterate. Study and self-control should follow the lead of intuitive knowledge. Only when the capacity for learning is great does the saying apply, 'Some know them from study and practice them from a desire of advantage or gain.'" . . .

Wang Shows that Flowers Are Not External to the Mind

The Teacher was taking recreation at Nanchen. One of his friends pointed to the flowers and trees on a cliff and said: "You say that there is nothing under heaven external to the mind. What relation to my mind have these flowers and trees on the high mountains, which blossom and drop of themselves?"

The Teacher said: "When you cease regarding these flowers, they become quiet with your mind. When you see them, their colors at once become clear. From this you can know that these flowers are not external to your mind."

He further said: "Perception has no structure upon which it depends: it uses the color of all things as its structure. The ear has no structure upon which it depends: it uses the sounds of things as its structure. The nose has no structure: it uses the odors of things as its structure. The mouth has no structure: it uses the taste of things as its structure. The mind has no structure: it uses the right and wrong influences of heaven, earth and things as structure." . . .

Intuitive Knowledge May Be Compared to the Sun, and Desire to the Clouds

He (Chu) made inquiry saying, "Intuitive knowledge should be compared to the sun and desire to clouds. Though the clouds may obscure the sun, they nevertheless have their origin in the condensation of the vapors of heaven. Does not desire also originate from a fusion of the thoughts of the mind?"

The Teacher said: "The seven passions—joy, anger, sorrow, fear, love, hatred, and desire—all have their origin from combinations within the mind. But you should understand intuitive knowledge clearly. It may be compared to the light of the sun. One cannot point out its location. Even when a little chink has been penetrated by the brightness of the sun, the light of the sun is located there. Although the fog of the clouds may come from all four sides, color and form can be distinguished. This, also, implies that at that point the light of the sun has not been destroyed. One cannot, for the simple reason that the clouds may obscure the sun, order heaven to desist from forming clouds. If the seven passions follow their natural courses, they all are functions of the intuitive faculty. They cannot be distinguished as good and evil. However, nothing should be added to them. When something has been added to the seven passions, desire results, and this obscures intuitive knowledge. Still, at the time that something is superimposed, the intuitive faculty is conscious thereof; and since it knows, it should repress it, and return to its original state. If at this point one is able to investigate carefully, the task is easily and thoroughly understood." . . .

from *Reply to Ku Tung-Ch'iao*

From The Philosophy of Wang Yang-Ming, *translated by Frederick Goodrich Henke (Carbondale, Ill.: Open Court Publishing Company, 1916).*

The Principles of Things Are Not External to the Mind

The principles of things are not to be found external to the mind. To seek the principles of things outside the mind results in there being no principles of things. If I neglect the principles of things, but seek to attain the original nature of my mind, what things are there then in my mind? The mind in its original character is nature (disposition), and nature is principles. Since the mind has the experience of being filial, there is a principle of filial piety. If the mind lacks filial piety, there is no principle of filial piety. Since the mind has the experience of being loyal to the prince, there is a principle of loyalty. Without a mind that is loyal to the prince there can be no principle of loyalty. Are these principles external to the mind? Hui-an said: "He who devotes himself to study should devote himself to a study of the mind and of principles." Though the mind in one aspect controls merely the body, it really exercises control over all the principles under the heavens. Though these principles are distributed in ten thousand affairs, they do not exceed the mind of any man. Because one (the philosopher Chu) separates them and another (Wang) unites them, it is inevitable that students should enter into the mistake of making them (mind and principles) separate things. The later scholar's misfortune of merely seeking to attain to the nature of his mind, while losing the principles of things, arises out of his ignorance that mind is the embodiment of principles. He who seeks the principles of things outside the mind will inevitably become confused and unintelligent. The philosopher Kao spoke of the external character of righteousness, and for that reason Mencius said that he did not know what righteousness is. The mind is a unit. The feeling of commiseration of the entire mind is called benevolence (the highest virtue). If one refers to the mind's getting what rightfully belongs to it, one speaks of righteousness. When one refers to its order, one speaks of principles. One should not seek either for the highest virtue or for righteousness outside the mind. Is the search for principles an exception to this? To seek for principles in external things implies separating knowledge and practice. The instruction of the sages, that knowledge and practice are united, implies seeking for principles within the mind. What doubt can you, my disciple, have regarding this? . . .

Wang Points Out One of Chu's Mistakes

Your letter says: "I have heard you say to students that the investigation of the principles of all things with which we come into contact also means finding one's amusement in things and thereby ruining one's aims. You take the philosopher Chu's sayings, such as disliking disorder and controlling it, and preserving and nourishing the source, and exhibit them to students, explaining that they are principles of his old age. May not this also be wrong?"

The saying of the philosopher Chu regarding investigation of things is to be found in the expression, "We must investigate the principles of all things with which we come into contact." This means that in all affairs and things the individual should seek for fundamental principles, and should use his mind in seeking these principles in affairs and things. Thereby mind and principles are separated. This seeking for fundamental principles in things and affairs is exemplified in seeking the principle of filial piety in one's parents. If a man seeks the principle of filial piety in the parents, is it, then, really in his own mind or is it in the person of his parents? If it is in the person of the parents, is it true that after the parents are dead the mind in consequence lacks the principle of filial piety? If one sees a child fall into a well, there must be commiseration. Is this principle of commiseration present in the child or is it to be found in the intuitive faculty of the mind? Whether the individual is unable to follow the child and rescue it from the well, or seizes it with his hand and thus rescues it, this principle is involved. Is it, then, in the person of the child, or is it rather in the intuitive faculty of the mind? What holds here is true with reference to the principles of all affairs and all things. Thus you may know the mistake of severing mind and principles—a severing which is in accordance with the philosopher Kao's sayings that righteousness is external. This mistake Mencius fully exposed. You are familiar with the matter of devoting one's self to external things and thereby losing sight of the internal, as well as that of studying extensively but with meagre results. In what sense is this true? Would it seem improper to say that it implies finding amusement in things and thereby ruining one's aims? What I say about extending knowledge to the utmost through investigation of things means extending and developing my intuitive knowledge of good to the utmost on all affairs and things. The intuitive faculty and its knowledge of good are heaven-given principles. If I extend and develop the heaven-given principles of my intuitive faculty on affairs and things, then all affairs and things partake of heaven-given principles. That extending the intuitive faculty of the mind to the utmost is extending knowledge to the utmost, and that the condition in which all things and affairs partake of these principles is to be identified with the investigation of things, means that mind and principles are one. . . .

Mind is Principles

Mind, I say, is just what is meant by principles. He who studies should study the mind and he who seeks should seek the mind. Mencius said: "The end of learning is nothing else but to seek for the lost mind." This is not the same as when later generations consider fondness of antiquity to consist in extensively remembering and reciting the phrases of the ancients. Moreover, with unremitting effort they seek for renown, gain, and advancement in that which is external. I have previously thoroughly discussed the matter of extensive study and careful inquiry. As regards cherishing old knowledge and yet continually acquiring new knowledge, the philosopher Chu also held that the cherishing of the old referred to honoring one's virtuous nature. Is it possible to search for this virtuous nature outside the mind? Only if this continual acquiring of new knowledge proceeds from the cherishing of the old, can one cherish the old and acquire the new. In this way you can also verify that knowledge and practice are not two things.

As regards the saying of Mencius, "In learning extensively and discussing minutely what is learned, the object is to go back and set forth in brief what is essential," if, as he said, their value lies in opening the way to go back and set forth in brief what is essential, for what reason does he advocate them? Shun in loving to question others and to study their words used only the mean in governing his people, and extended his devotion to the essence of his mind in complete loyalty to the path. A mind loyal to the path of duty is what is meant by the intuitive faculty. When has the learning of the superior man absented itself from the affairs of life and discarded discussions? However, he who devotes himself to the affairs of life and to discussions should know that the unification of knowledge and practice involves developing the intuitive knowledge of his mind. He should not be like the world, which considers vain speaking and hearing as learning, and which, by separating knowledge and practice, is able to discuss an order of first and last in this. . . .

The Mind of the Sage Described

The mind of the sage considers heaven, earth, and all things as one substance. He makes no distinctions between the people of the Empire. Whosoever has blood and life is his brother and child. There is no one whom he does not wish to see perfectly at peace, and whom he does not wish to nourish. This is in accordance with his idea that all things are one substance. The mind of everybody is at first not different from that of the sage. If there is any selfishness in it, which divides it through the obscuration of passion and covetousness, then that which is great is considered small and that which is clear and open as unintelligible and closed. Whoever has this mind gets to the place where he views his father or son or elder and younger brothers as enemies. The sage, distressed because of this, uses the occasion to extend his virtuous attitude, which considers heaven, earth, and all things as one substance, by instructing the people and causing them to subdue their selfishness, remove the obscuration, and revert to the original nature of their minds. . . .

WANG FU-CHIH

from *The Surviving Works of Wang Fu-Chih*

1. *The World of Concrete Things*

The world consists only of concrete things. The Way (*Tao*) is the Way of concrete things, but concrete things may not be called concrete things of the Way. People generally are capable of saying that without its Way there cannot be the concrete thing. However, if there is the concrete thing, there need be no worry about there not being its Way. A sage knows what a superior man does not know, but an ordinary man or woman can do what a sage cannot do. A person may be ignorant of the Way of a thing, and the concrete thing therefore cannot be completed. But not being completed does not mean that there is no concrete thing. Few people are capable of saying that without a concrete thing there cannot be its Way, but it is certainly true.

In the period of wilderness and chaos, there was no Way to bow and yield a throne. At the time of Yao and Shun, there was no Way to pity the suffering people and punish the sinful rulers. During the Han (206 B.C.–A.D. 220) and T'ang (618–907) dynasties there were no Ways as we have today, and there will be many in future years which we do not have now. Before bows and arrows existed, there was no Way of archery. Before chariots and horses existed, there was no Way to drive them. Before sacrificing oxen and wine, presents of jade and silk, or bells, chimes, flutes, and strings existed, there were no Ways of ceremonies and music. Thus there is no Way of the father before there is a son, there is no Way of the elder brother before there is a younger brother, and there are many potential Ways which are not existent. Therefore without a concrete thing, there cannot be its Way. This is indeed a true statement. Only people have not understood it.

Sages of antiquity could manage concrete things but could not manage the Way. What is meant by the Way is the management of concrete things. When the Way is fulfilled, we call it virtue. When the concrete thing is completed, we call it operation. When concrete things function extensively, we call it transformation and penetration. When its effect becomes prominent, we call it achievement. . . .

By "what exists before physical form" [and is therefore without it] does not mean there is no physical form. There is already physical form. As there is physical form, there is that which exists before it. Even if we span past and present, go through all the myriad transformations, and investigate Heaven, Earth, man, and things to the utmost, we will not find any thing existing before physical form [and is without it]. Therefore it is said, "It is only the sage who can put his physical form into full use." He puts into full use what is within a physical form, not what is above it. Quickness of apprehension and intelligence are matters of the ear and the eye, insight and wisdom those of the mind and thought, humanity that of men, righteousness that of events, equilibrium and harmony those of ceremonies and music, great impartiality and perfect correctness those of reward and punishment, advantage and utility those of water, fire, metal, and wood, welfare that of grains, fruits, silk, and hemp, and correct virtue that of the relationship between ruler and minister and between father and son. If one discarded these and sought for that which existed before concrete things, even if he spanned past and present, went through all the myriad transformations, and investigated Heaven, Earth, man, and things to the utmost, he would not be able to give it a name. How much less could he find its reality! Lao Tzu was blind to this and said that the Way existed in vacuity. But vacuity is the vacuity of concrete things. The Buddha was blind to this and said that the Way existed in silence. But silence is the silence of concrete things. One may keep on uttering such extravagant words to no end, but one can never escape from concrete things. Thus if one plays up some name that is separated from concrete things as though he were a divine being, whom could he deceive?

2. *Substance and Function*

All functions in the world are those of existing things. From their functions I know they possess substance. Why should we entertain any doubt? Function exists to become effect, and substance exists to become nature and feelings. Both substance and function exist, and each depends on the other to be concrete. Therefore all that fills the universe demonstrates the principle of mutual dependence. Therefore it is said, "Sincerity (realness) is the beginning and end of things. Without sincerity there will be nothing."

What is the test for this? We believe in what exists but doubt what does not exist. I live from the time I was born to the time I die. As there were ancestors before, so there will be descendants later. From observing the transformations throughout heaven and earth, we see the productive process. Is any of these facts doubtful? . . . Hold on to the concrete things and its Way will be preserved. Cast aside the concrete things and its Way will be destroyed. . . . Therefore those who are expert in speaking of the Way arrive at substance from function but those who are not expert in speaking of the Way erroneously set up substance and dismiss function in order to conform to it.

The state preceding man's birth when his nature is tranquil is beyond their knowledge. Sometimes when they happen to exercise their intelligence abnormally, they paint a picture out of the void, and perforce call it substance. Their intelligence gives them what they are looking for, surveys all things and gets an echo of them, and is therefore able to dismiss all functions completely. From this point on, they can indulge in their perverse doctrines. But how much better it is to seek in the realm where [the process of Change] is acted on and immediately penetrates all things, daily observe its transformations and gradually discover their origin? Therefore if we get hold of descendants and ask for their ancestors, their genealogical lines will not be confused. But how can one correctly imagine the names of descendants when he passes by the ancestral temples and graves?

3. *Being and Non-Being*

Those who talk about non-being do so because they are roused by speakers of being and want to demolish it, and on the basis of what the speakers call being, they say that being does not exist. Is there really anything in the world that can be called non-being? To say that a tortoise has no hair is to talk about a dog [for example, which has hair] and not a tortoise. To say that a rabbit has no horn is to talk about a deer and not a rabbit. A speaker must have a basis before his theory can be established. Suppose a speaker wants to establish non-being in front of him as the basis. Even if he extensively searches for it throughout the universe and throughout history, there will be no end.

There will really be non-being only when there is nothing which can be described as non-being. Since non-being is so-called, it follows that it is merely a denial of being. Because the eye cannot see a thing or the ear cannot hear it, people hastily say that it does not exist. They are obscured because they follow their inferior faculties (eye and ear). Good and evil can be seen and heard but that which produces good and evil cannot be seen or heard.

Therefore people hastily say that there is neither good nor evil.

Those who speak of non-self do so from the point of view of the self. If there were no self, who is going to deny the self? It is obvious that to speak of non-self is to utter extravagant and evasive words.

4. *Principle and Material Force*

Principle depends on material force. When material force is strong, principle prevails. When Heaven accumulates strong and powerful material force, there will be order, and transformations will be refined and daily renewed. This is why on the day of religious fasting an emperor presents an ox [to Heaven] so that the material force will fill the universe and sincerity will penetrate everything. All products in the world are results of refined and beautiful material force. Man takes the best of it to nourish his life, but it is all from Heaven. Material force naturally becomes strong. Sincerity naturally becomes solidified. And principle naturally becomes self-sufficient. If we investigate into the source of these phenomena, we shall find that it is the refined and beautiful transformation of Heaven and Earth.

At bottom principle is not a finished product that can be grasped. It is invisible. The details and order of material force is principle that is visible. Therefore the first time there is any principle is when it is seen in material force. After principles have thus been found, they of course appear to become tendencies. We see principle only in the necessary aspects of tendencies.

Let us investigate principle as we come into contact with things but never set up principle to restrict things. What I dislike about the heterodoxical schools is not that they cannot do anything with principle, but that because they clearly have scarcely understood principle they set it up as a generalization for the whole world. . . . The heterodoxical schools say, "None of the myriad transformations can go beyond our basis." The basis is clearly what they have scarcely understood. But inasmuch as they say it is their basis, can it produce all the myriad transformations? If it cannot produce these transformations, then it is they who cannot go beyond their basis and not the myriad transformations. . . . They (natural phenomena) all follow principle to accomplish their work. It is permissible to say that their principle is identical with the order of their basis. But if they say that all that work is the construction and operation of their basis, who will believe them unless one is the most boastful talker in the world?

5. *Unceasing Growth and Man's Nature and Destiny*

The fact that the things of the world, whether rivers or mountains, plants or animals, those with or without intelligence, and those yielding blossoms or bearing fruits, provide beneficial support for all things is the result of the natural influence of the moving power of material force. It fills the universe. And as it completely provides for the flourish and transformation of all things, it is all the more spatially unrestricted. As it is not spatially restricted, it operates in time and proceeds with time. From morning to evening, from spring to summer, and from the present tracing back to the past, there is no time at which it does not operate, and there is no time at which it does not produce. Consequently, as one sprout bursts forth it becomes a tree with a thousand big branches, and as one egg evolves, it progressively becomes a fish capable of swallowing a ship. . . .

By nature is meant the principle of growth. As one daily grows, one daily achieves completion. Thus by the Mandate of Heaven is not meant that Heaven gives the decree (*ming*, mandate) only at the moment of one's birth. . . . In the production of things by Heaven, the process of transformation never ceases. It is not that at the moment of birth there is no decree. How do we know that there is a decree? Without it, humanity, righteousness, propriety, and wisdom would be without any foundation. Similarly, when one grows from infancy to youth, from youth to maturity, and from maturity to old age, it is not that there are no [continual] decrees. How do we know that there are such decrees? For without further decrees, then as the years pass by, one's nature would be forgotten. A change in physical form is a change leading to excellence. A change through material force, however, is a change leading to growth. The evolution of the two material forces (yin and yang or passive and active cosmic forces) and the substance of the Five Agents (Water, Fire, Wood, Metal, and Earth) are first used to become an embryo and later for growth and support. In either case, there is no difference in the acquisition of the vital essence and the utilization of things, for they all come from the excellence of production by Heaven and Earth. The physical form gets its support every day, every day the material force enjoys its flourish, and principle attains completion every day. These things are received as one is born, but as one continues to live for a day, one keeps receiving them for a day. What one receives has a source. Is this not Heaven? Thus Heaven gives decrees to man every day and man receives decrees from Heaven every day. Therefore we say that by nature is meant the principle of growth. As one daily grows, one daily achieves completion. . . .

Since the mandate is never exhausted and is not constant, therefore nature repeatedly changes and is perpetually different. At the same time, as principle is fundamentally correct and is without any inherent defect, therefore it can return to its own principle without difficulty. What is not completed can be completed, and what has been completed can be changed. Does nature mean that once one has received a physical form, there cannot be any alteration? Therefore in nourishing his nature, the superior man acts naturally as if nothing happens, but that does not mean that he lets things take their own course. Instead, he acts so as to make the best choices and remain firm in holding to the Mean, and dares not go wild or make careless mistakes.

6. *The Principle of Nature and Human Desires*

Although rules of propriety are purely detailed expressions of the Principle of Nature, they must be embodied in human desires to be seen. Principle is a latent principle for activities, but its function will become prominent if it varies and conforms to them. It is precisely for this reason that there can never be a Heaven distinct from man or a principle distinct from desires. It is only with the Buddhists that principle and desires can be separated. . . . Take fondness for wealth and for sex. Heaven, working unseen, has provided all creatures with it, and with it man puts the great virtue of Heaven and Earth into operation. They all regard wealth and sex as preserved resources. Therefore the *Book of Changes* says, "The great characteristic of Heaven and Earth is to produce. The most precious thing for the sage is [the highest] position. To keep his position depends on humanity. How to collect a large population depends on wealth." Thus in sound, color, flavor, and fragrance we can broadly see the open desires of all creatures, and at the same time they also constitute the impartial principle for all of them. Let us be broad and greatly impartial, respond to things as they come, look at them, and listen to them, and follow this way in words and action without seeking anything outside. And let us be unlike Lao Tzu, who said that the five colors blind one's eyes and the five tones deafen one's ears, or the Buddha, who despised them as dust and hated them as robbers. . . . If we do not understand the Principle of Nature from human desires that go with it, then although there may be a principle that can be a basis, nevertheless, it will not have anything to do with the correct activities of our seeing, hearing, speech, and action. They thereupon cut off the universal operation of human life, and wipe it out completely. Aside from one meal a day, they would have nothing to do with material wealth and aside from one sleep under a tree, they would have nothing to do with sex. They exterminate the great character of Heaven and Earth and ruin the great treasure of the sage. They destroy institutions and eliminate culture. Their selfishness is ablaze while principles of humanity are destroyed. It is like the fire of thunder or a dragon. The more one tries to overcome it, the more it goes on. Mencius continued the teaching of Confucius which is that wherever human desires are found, the Principle of Nature is found. . . .

JAPANESE BUDDHISM

The Kyoto school of philosophy consists of a group of Japanese philosophers who elucidate and defend a Buddhist philosophical outlook. Kitaro Nishida (1870–1945), born in a small village near Kanazawa, Japan, established the Kyoto School. He attended Tokyo University and became a high school teacher. Later he became a professor at Kanazawa Junior College. At age forty-one he published *An Inquiry into the Good* which tried to reconcile Zen Buddhism with Western philosophical practice. This earned him an appointment at Kyoto University, where he taught for eighteen years. At fifty-nine he retired, but he continued writing until his death at age seventy-five.

Nishida's works are difficult, partly because he blends Eastern and Western themes and terminologies. For that very reason, however, they are also exciting. Nishida was impressed by Western logic and precision but wanted to preserve something he found at the basis of Asian culture, which he called "seeing the form of the formless and hearing the sound of the soundless."* Influenced by Zen Buddhism, he sought to explain the nature of reality and of the good that Zen enlightenment provides—but in precise, rational terms.

The southern Zen school holds that the mind is a unity, simple in the sense that it is absolutely indivisible. The Buddha is everywhere; anything can bring about its realization. The Zen practitioner seeks a state of mind in which reality becomes transparent and crystalline. Nishida developed from this idea his conception of pure experience. As he describes his method, "I wanted to explain all things on the basis of pure experience as the sole reality."† Nishida begins with experience and tries to construct from it the individual self, the will, and, ultimately, the good. Pure experience is the source of all knowledge. It is prior to the distinction between the knower and the known; it is active, creative, dynamic, and unified. To attain knowledge of pure experience, Nishida recommends that we "discard all artificial assumptions, doubt whatever can be doubted, and proceed directly on the basis of direct and indubitable knowledge."‡ This knowledge alone is knowledge of pure experience.

Daisetz Teitaro Suzuki (1870–1966) was born near Kanazawa, Japan. A schoolmate of Nishida, he came to the Chicago World's Fair when he was twenty-three to teach Westerners about Zen Buddhism. He returned to Japan and became professor at Otani University in Kyoto, where he kept in close contact with Nishida and other members of the Kyoto school of philosophy. Sometimes criticized as a

* *From the Actor to the Seer* (1927), in *Nishida Kitaro Zenshu,* Volume 4 (Tokyo: Iwanami, 1978), 6.

† Preface to *An Inquiry into the Good,* trans. Masao Abe and Christopher Ives (New Haven, Conn.: Yale University Press, 1990).

‡ *An Inquiry into the Good,* 38.

popularizer, Suzuki published many works in English translations, spreading Zen throughout the Western world. He founded a journal, *The Eastern Buddhist,* committed to publishing Zen writings.

Suzuki's version of Zen, called the Rinzai sect, stems from the southern Chinese school and, specifically, from I-Hsüan's radical Lin-chi movement. Like that "lightning method" movement, it is in many ways anti-intellectual. According to Suzuki, all distinctions are illusions. Studying the scriptures of Buddhism and other philosophical texts is, in itself, pointless. Thinking can only take us away from the truth. There is no difference between the real and the unreal, between the holy and the secular, or between the logical and the illogical.

This might seem to lead to paradoxes. The Zen doctrine seems to imply that all doctrines are unfounded and need to be transcended. But Zen does not thereby refute itself. Zen theses are means for reaching an end—*satori* (enlightenment)—rather than literal descriptions of reality. Their point is to lead us to undergo certain kinds of experiences.

Keiji Nishitani, born in 1900, graduated from Kyoto University and was later appointed to the faculty there. A student of Nishida and of the German philosopher Martin Heidegger, he held the chair of philosophy at Kyoto for twenty-one years. Nishitani argues that neither Eastern nor Western thought has devised an adequate answer to *nihilism*, the thesis that there is no ultimate meaning to life. With all life ending in death, with personal survival dubious, and with religions such as Christianity unable to explain the cruel objectivity of scientific law, Nishitani finds nihilism intellectually compelling. But it is not, he maintains, existentially tenable. One must, he argues, invent meaning for oneself. Zen accomplishes this, allowing us to recognize the bottomless emptiness of life as the key to its meaning.

KITARO NISHIDA

from *An Inquiry into the Good*

From Kitaro Nishida, An Inquiry into the Good, *translated by Masao Abe and Christopher Ives (New Haven: Yale University Press, 1990.)*

CHAPTER 12 / NATURE

Although there is only one reality, it appears in various forms in accordance with differing views of it. Nature conceived of as an objective reality totally independent of our subjectivity is an abstract concept, not true reality. The noumenal aspect of nature is the fact of direct experience in which subject and object have not yet separated. For example, what we regard as true grass and trees are grass and trees with living color and forms—they are intuitive facts. Only when we separate the subjective activity from the concrete reality can we think of the grass and trees as purely objective nature. By taking this way of thinking to the extreme, we arrive of the idea of nature in the strictest sense as construed by scientists. This idea is the most abstract and most removed from the true state of reality.

What people usually refer to as *nature* is what remains after the subjective aspect, the unifying activity, is removed from concrete reality. For this reason, there is no self in nature. Nature is simply moved from without according to the law of necessity, and it cannot function spontaneously from within. The linkage and union of natural phenomena is not an internal unity as in mental phenomena, but an accidental linkage in time and space. The laws of nature, attained through the law of induction, are simply assumptions that because two types of phenomena arise in an unchanging succession, one is the cause of the other. No matter how far the natural sciences develop, we obtain no deeper explanation than this one, which becomes ever more detailed and encompassing.

The present tendency of science is to strive to become as objective as possible. As a result, psychological phenomena are explained physiologically, physiological phenomena chemically, chemical phenomena physically, and physical phenomena mechanically. What is the nature of the purely mechanical perspective at the foundation of this type of explanation? Pure water is a reality we cannot even begin to experience, but assuming for the sake of argument that we can experience it to some extent, it must be something that comes forth in our consciousness as a phenomenon of consciousness. Yet all things that appear as facts of consciousness are subjective and cannot be deemed purely objective matter. Moreover, pure matter has no positive qualities that we can grasp; it possesses only purely quantitative characteristics such as spatial and temporal movement. Like a mathematical concept, it is nothing more than a completely abstract concept.

Matter is thought of as something that fills space and can be directly perceived, but the extension of things of which we can think concretely is simply a conscious phenomenon of touch and sight. Even though things may seem large in our sensation of them, they do not necessarily consist of a large amount of matter. Because the amount of physical matter is determined in physics by the amount of energy present,—that is, it is inferred from functional relationships between physical things—it is never an intuitive fact.

Moreover, if we think of nature in the purely material terms discussed above, then there are no distinctions between animals, plants, and life in general, and there is nothing except the activity of a mechanical energy that is everywhere the same. In this approach, natural phenomena lose all of their special characteristics and significance; human beings are no different from clods of dirt.

The real nature that we actually experience is never an abstract concept as described above; nor is it merely an activity of a uniform mechanical energy. Animals are animals, plants are plants, and metals are metals; each is a concrete fact with its own special characteristics and significance. The things that we designate as mountains, rivers, grasses, trees, insects, fish, birds, and beasts all have their own respective individuality. We can explain them from a variety of standpoints and in a variety of ways, but nature in the sense of directly given, intuitive facts cannot be altered in the least.

We usually take purely mechanical nature to be the truly objective reality and concrete nature in direct experience to be a subjective phenomenon, but these ideas are inferred from the assumption that all phenomena of consciousness are subjective phenomena of the self. And as I have said, we can in no way posit a reality apart from the phenomena of consciousness. If we say that something is subjective because it is related to phenomena of consciousness, then purely mechanical nature is subjective as well, for we cannot think of such things as time, space, and motion apart from our phenomena of consciousness. They are only relatively—not absolutely—objective.

Nature as a truly concrete reality does not come into being without having a unifying activity. Nature therefore possesses a kind of self, too. The various forms, variations, and motions a plant or animal expresses are not mere unions or mechanical movements of insignificant matter; because each has an inseparable relationship to the whole, each should be regarded as a developmental expression of one unifying self. For example, the paws, legs, nose, mouth, and other parts of an animal all have a close relation to the goal of survival, and we cannot understand their significance if we consider them apart from this fact. In explaining the phenomena of plants and animals, we must posit the unifying power of nature. Biologists explain all the phenomena of living things in terms of life instincts. This unifying activity is found not only in living things, but is present to some extent even in inorganic crystals, and all minerals have a particular crystalline form. The self of nature, that is, its unifying activity, becomes clearer as we move from inorganic crystals to organisms like plants and animals (with the true self first appearing in spirit).

From the standpoint of the strictly mechanical explanation of present-day science, the teleological development of organisms must be explained in terms of the laws of physics and chemistry. This development comes to be viewed as a mere accidental outcome. Because this view largely disregards facts, scientists try to explain this development through the assumption of a potential power. They say that eggs or seeds possess a potential power that gives rise to the respective organisms. This potential power corresponds to the unifying power of nature we have been discussing.

Even if in our explanation of nature we allow for the activity of such a unifying power apart from mechanical energy, the two need not clash but can complement each other to achieve a complete explanation of nature. Let us take, for example, a bronze statue. The bronze, the statue's raw material, obeys physical and chemical laws yet we cannot view the statue as a mere lump of bronze, for it is a work of art that expresses our ideals. It appeared by means of the unifying power of our ideals. The unifying activity of the ideals and the physical and chemical laws that control the raw material belong to different spheres, and in no way do they clash with each other.

Only when there is a unifying self does nature have a goal, take on significance, and become a truly living nature. The unifying power that is the life of such nature is not an abstract concept artifically created by our thought but a fact that appears in our intuition. When we see our favorite flower or pet animal, we immediately grasp a certain unifying reality in the whole. This reality is the thing's self, its fundamental nature or noumenon. Artists are people who most excel in this kind of intuition. They discern at a glance the truth of a thing and grasp its unifying reality. What they then express is not a superficial fact but an unchanging noumenal reality hidden deep within things.

Goethe devoted himself to the study of living things* and pioneered the present-day theory of evolution. According to his theory, there is behind natural phenomena an "original" phenomenon (*Urphänomen*), which is intuited by poets. Further, the various plants and animals in our world are variations of the original plant and original animal, and present-day plants and animals all reflect a fixed, unchanging pattern. Based on this theory, Goethe argues that all living things have evolved.

But what sort of thing is the unifying self behind nature? Because we think of natural phenomena as purely objective phenomena unrelated to our subjectivity, the unifying power of nature is thought to be unknowable. In true reality, however, subjectivity and objectivity are not separate, and actual nature is not a purely objective, abstract concept but a concrete fact of consciousness that includes both subject and object. Accordingly, the unifying self behind nature is not some unknowable entity totally unrelated to our consciousness but actually none other than the unifying activity of consciousness. Our understanding of the significance and *telos* of nature is thus made possible by virtue of the subjective unification of the self's ideals, feeling, and volition. For example, our ability to understand the fundamental significance of various organs and behaviors of animals comes from our intuiting it directly through our feeling and will—if we did not have feeling and will we could not even begin to understand it. As our ideals, feeling, and volition gain greater depth and width, we become increasingly able to understand the true significance of nature. Our subjective unity and the objective unifying power of nature are originally identical. If we view this objectively, it is the unifying power of nature, and if we view it subjectively, it is the unity of self's knowledge, feeling, and volition.

Some people believe that material force is completely unrelated to our subjective unity. Although it may be the most insignificant unity, even this force does not exist apart from subjective unity. Our belief that there is a force in matter that performs various functions comes from viewing the self's volitional activity objectively.

People usually think that the inference of nature's significance through the self's ideals, feeling, or volition is simply an analogical inference and hence not a firm truth. But their view originates in thinking of subjectivity and objectivity independently and regarding mind and nature as two different types of reality. From the perspective of pure experience, we view them as identical.

CHAPTER 13 / SPIRIT

At a glance, nature appears to be a purely objective reality independent of spirit,* but actually, it is not separate from subjectivity. Seen in terms of their subjective aspect, that is, the unifying activity, so-called natural phenomena are all phenomena of consciousness. For example, here is a stone; if we assume that it has come into being through the power of a certain unknowable reality independent of our subjectivity, then it becomes nature. If we directly view the stone as a fact of direct experience, however, it is not an objectively independent reality but a union of our senses of sight, touch, and so forth; it is a phenomenon of consciousness, established by the unity of our consciousness. When we return to the base of direct experience and view so-called natural phenomena, we grasp them as phenomena of consciousness that are established by subjective unity. This viewpoint generates the idealist statement that the world is our ideas.

Some people believe that when we see the same stone, each of us has the same idea of it. Actually, though, our ideas differ according to our character and experiences. Concrete reality is therefore entirely subjective and individual, and so-called objective reality disappears, for it is simply an abstract concept that we all share.

What then is that which we usually call spirit in opposition to nature? What kind of thing is a sub-

* Goethe pursued research in botany (*Die Metamorphose der Pflanzen*, 1790). His scientific bent also led him to produce a work on optics (*Zur Farbenlehre*, 1810).

* The Japanese term *seishin*, rendered here as "spirit," is roughly equivalent to the German term *Geist* and therefore might also be rendered "mind" or "psyche." Due to the religious connotations of *seishin* found later in this work, we have translated it as "spirit."

jective phenomenon of consciousness? So-called mental phenomena are simply the unifying or active aspect of reality considered abstractly. In reality as it truly exists there are no distinctions between subjectivity and objectivity or spirit and matter, and in the establishment of reality, a unifying activity is necessary. This unifying activity is not apart from reality, though when we view it abstractly and think of it as something standing in opposition to unified objects, it is seen as a mental phenomenon. For example, we might have a sensation here and now, but it is not independent of all other things—it is established in opposition to something else, that is, in comparison with and distinguished from another. The activity of comparison and distinction—the unifying activity—is what we call spirit. As this activity develops, the distinction between spirit and matter becomes increasingly clear. In childhood, our spirit is natural, and the activity of subjectivity is therefore weak. As we mature, the unifying activity flourishes, and we attain to an awareness of our spirit as distinguished from objective nature.

For this reason, people usually consider spirit an independent reality distinguished from objective nature. Yet, just as purely objective nature apart from the subjective unity of spirit is an abstract concept, a purely subjective spirit apart from objective nature is an abstract concept as well. There is something that is unified and an activity that does the unifying. Even though we might assume that there is an essence of spirit that senses the activity of things in the world, there is a thing that functions and a mind that senses it. Spirit that does not function, like things that do not function, is unknowable.

But for what reason is the unifying activity of reality distinguished from its content (that which can be unified), and why does it emerge as if it were an independent reality? The answer undoubtedly lies in the contradictions and conflicts of the various unities in reality. There are various systems—various unities—in reality; when these systematic unities conflict with and contradict each other, they appear clearly in consciousness. Where there are conflicts and contradictions there is spirit, and where there is spirit there are conflicts and contradictions. In the case of volitional action, for example, when there are no conflicts between motives, there is no consciousness, and this approaches so-called objective nature. As the conflict between motives becomes more distinct, one can become clearly conscious of the will and aware of one's mind.*

From where do the conflicts and contradictions of a system arise? They arise from the character of reality itself. As I said before, while reality is infinite conflict, it is also infinite unity. Conflict is an indispensable aspect of unity, for it is through conflict that we advance to an even greater unity. Our spirit, the unifying activity of reality, is conscious of itself not when that unity is functioning, but when there is conflict.

When we have matured in an art, that is when we have attained to the unity of reality, we are unconscious and do not know our own unity. As we try to advance to even greater depths, conflicts arise with that which has already been attained, and in this encounter we become conscious again, for consciousness is always born of such conflicts. The fact that conflicts necessarily accompany spirit should be seen in light of the fact that spirit is accompanied by ideals. Ideals signify contradiction and conflict with actuality. (Since our spirit appears through conflict, there is always suffering in spirit, and the claim of pessimists that our world is characterized by suffering contains an element of truth.)

If we see our spirit as the unifying activity of reality, we must say that there is a unity to all things in reality, that there is spirit in it. On what basis do we separate living and non-living things and distinguish that which has spirit from that which does not? Strictly speaking, we can say that there is spirit throughout reality; and as I said before, there is a unifying self in nature as well, a unifying power identical to our spirit. If a tree, for example, as a phenomenon of consciousness were to appear here, we would ordinarily think of it as an objective reality established by natural powers, but if we see it as constituting a system of phenomena of consciousness, then it is established by the unifying activity of consciousness. In so-called non-living things, the unifying self has not yet appeared in actuality as a

* The Japanese term here used for "mind" *kokoro,* which can also be rendered "heart"—it includes nuances of both "mind" and "heart."

fact of direct experience. The tree itself is not aware of the unifying activity of the self; the unifying self is found in another thing's consciousness, not in the tree itself. The tree is merely a thing unified from outside, not something unified internally, and for this reason it is not yet an independent, self-fulfilled reality. In the contrasting case of animals, an internal unity or self is expressing itself in actuality, and we can view all of the various phenomena of animals (such as their form and behavior) as expressions of this internal unity. All of reality is established through unity, and in spirit the unity emerges as a clear fact. It is only in spirit that reality becomes a perfect reality, an independent, self-fulfilled reality.

In things without spirit, the unity is given from without, and hence it is not an internal unity of the self. The unity hence changes in accordance with the viewer. For instance, we might think that there is a single reality called a tree, but in the eyes of a chemist, the tree is an organic compound, a combination of chemical elements. We might therefore say that there is in fact no separate reality called a tree. But we cannot view the spirit of animals in this way. Although we can regard the physical body of an animal, like a plant, as a compound, spirit cannot be changed in accordance with the viewer; no matter what interpretation we offer, it truly expresses an unmoving unity.

Modern evolutionary theory contends that evolution proceeds from inorganic matter to plants, then to animals, and finally to human beings. This theory indicates that reality gradually expresses its hidden essence as actuality. It is only in the development of spirit that the fundamental character of the establishment of reality appears. As Leibniz said, evolution is involution.

Our self, as the unifier of spirit, is the fundamental unifying activity of reality. According to one school of psychology, the self is simply a union of ideas and feelings apart from which there is no self. This view neglects the side of unity and entails consideration of the self from the side of analytical distinctions only. If we look at all things analytically, we cannot find a unifying activity. But we cannot allow the analytical way of viewing things to make us disregard this activity. Things are established by a unity, and ideas and feelings are made into concrete reality through the power of a unifying self. This unifying power called the self is an expression of the unifying power of reality; it is an eternal unchanging power. Our self is therefore felt to be always creative, free, and infinitely active.

As I said before, though we may reflect inwardly and sense a kind of feeling that is somehow the self, this self is not the true self, for it cannot act. Only when the unity of reality functions inwardly do we feel that we control reality according to our own ideals and that the self is engaging in free activity. Because the unifying activity of reality is infinite, we feel our self to be infinite and to envelop the universe.

From the standpoint of pure experience, the unifying activity of reality of which I speak might be thought of as simply an abstract idea rather than as a fact of direct experience. The facts of our direct experience, however, are not ideas or feelings but the activity of the will, and the unifying activity is an indispensable element of direct experience.

Until now I have considered spirit in opposition to nature—henceforth I want to think a bit about the relation between spirit and nature. Our spirit is usually considered to be the unifying function of reality and to be a special reality vis-à-vis nature. But in actuality, there is no unifying activity apart from that which is unified and no subjective spirit apart from objective nature. To say that we know a thing simply means that the self unites with it. When one sees a flower, the self has become the flower. To investigate a flower and elucidate its basic nature means to discard all of the self's subjective conjectures and thereby unite with the basic nature of the flower. Similarly, reason is not a subjective fancy, for it is not only something common to all people but also the fundamental principle by which objective reality is established. Indisputable truth is gained by constantly discarding our subjective self and becoming objective. To say that our knowledge becomes more profound means that we unite ourselves with objective nature.

This holds not only for knowledge but also for the will. If we are purely subjective, we can do nothing. The will is able to realize itself only by according with objective nature. To move water is to accord with its nature, to control people is to accord with their nature, and to control oneself is to accord with one's own nature. Our wills are effective to the degree that they become objective. Thousands of years after their deaths, Sākyamuni and Christ still have the power to move people only because their spirit was truly objective. Those without a self—those who have extinguished the self—are the greatest.

We usually distinguish mental phenomena and material phenomena in terms of internal and external, thinking of the former as internal and the latter as external. This view originates in the arbitrary assumption that spirit is within the body. But when seen from the perspective of direct experience, all things are phenomena of consciousness, without distinction between internal and external. That which we speak of as the internal, subjective spirit is a highly superficial and feeble spirit, an individual fancy. In contrast, great, deep spirit is the activity of the universe that is united with the truth of the universe. Such spirit of itself accompanies the activity of the external world, and it does nothing but act. The inspiration of an artist is an example of this.

In closing this chapter, I want to say a word about the joy and suffering of the human mind. When our spirit is in a state of completion, a state of unity, we experience pleasure, and when it is in an incomplete state, a state of disunion, we experience pain. As I said, spirit is the unifying activity of reality, and contradictions and conflicts necessarily accompany this unity. We always experience pain when these contradictions and conflicts occur, and the infinite unifying activity immediately attempts to rid itself of them and to achieve an even greater unity. In this attempt, various desires and ideals arise in us, and when we attain to the greater unity—when we are able to satisfy our desires and ideals—we experience pleasure. Thus, one facet of pleasure necessarily includes pain, and one facet of pain is necessarily accompanied by pleasure. This being the case, the human mind cannot arrive at absolute pleasure, but it can maintain infinite happiness when, by effort, it becomes objective and unites with nature.

Psychologists say that what assists our living is pleasure, and what hinders it is pain. Because life is the development of the basic nature of living things—that is, the maintenance of the unity of the self—this theory is the same as saying that whatever supports unity is pleasure and that whatever hinders it is pain.

Again, spirit is the unifying activity of reality. Because great spirit unites with nature, when we take our small self as our self we experience much pain; when the self becomes larger and unites with objective nature, we experience happiness.

D. T. SUZUKI

from *Zen Buddhism*

From D. T. Suzuki, "Zen Buddhism," Monumenta Nipponica *(1938); reprinted in D. T. Suzuki,* Studies in Zen *(New York: Dell Publishing Company, Inc., 1955.)*

. . . Zen abhors words and concepts, and reasoning based on them. We have been misled from the first rising of consciousness to resort too much to ratiocination for the prehension of Reality. We tend to regard ideas and words as facts in themselves, and this way of thinking has entered deeply into the constitution of our consciousness. We now imagine that when we have ideas and words we have all that can be said of our experience of Reality. This means that we take words for Reality itself and neglect experience to reach what really constitutes our inmost experience.

Zen upholds, as every true religion must, the direct experience of Reality. It aspires to drink from the fountain of life itself instead of merely listening to remarks about it. A Zen follower is not satisfied until he scoops with his own hands the living waters of Reality, which alone, as he knows, will quench his thirst. . . .

. . . we read in the *Lankavatara Sutra:* "The ultimate truth (*Paramartha*) is a state of inner experience by means of Noble Wisdom (*Aryavijna*), and as it is beyond the ken of words and discriminations it cannot be adequately expressed by them. Whatever is thus expressible is the product of conditional causation to the law of birth and death. The ultimate truth transcends the antithesis of self and not-self, and words are the products of antithetical thinking. The ultimate truth is Mind itself, which is free from all forms, inner and outer. No words can therefore describe Mind, no discriminations can reveal it."

Discrimination is a term we frequently come across in Buddhist philosophy. It corresponds to intellection or logical reasoning. According to Buddhism, the antithesis of "A" and "not-A" is at the bottom of our ignorance as to the ultimate truth of existence, and this antithesis is discrimination. To discriminate is to be involved in the whirlpool of birth and death, and as long as we are thus involved, there is no emancipation, no attainment of Nirvana, no realization of Buddhahood.

We may ask: "How is this emancipation possible? And does Zen achieve it?"

When we say that we live, it means that we live in this world of dualities and antitheses. Therefore to be emancipated from this world may mean to go out of it, or to deny it by some means, if possible. To do either of these is to put ourselves out of existence. Emancipation is, then, we can say, self-destruction. Does Buddhism teach self-destruction? This kind of interpretation has often been advanced by those who fail to understand the real teaching of Buddhism.

The fact is that this interpretation is not yet an "emancipated" one, and falls short of the Buddhist logic of non-discrimination. This is where Zen comes in, asserting its own way of being "outside the Scripture" and "independent of the letter." The following *mondo* will illustrate my point:

Sekiso (Shih-shuang) asked Dogo: "After your passing, if somebody asks me about the ultimate truth of Buddhism, what shall I say?"

Dogo made no answer but called out to one of his attendants. The attendant answered: "Yes, master"; and the master said: "Have the pitcher filled with water." So ordering, he remained silent for a while, and then turning to Sekiso said: "What did you ask me about just now?" Sekiso repeated his question. Whereupon the master rose from his seat and walked away.

Sekiso was a good Buddhist student and no doubt understood thoroughly the teaching as far as his intellectual understanding went. What he wanted when he questioned his master concerning the ultimate truth of Buddhism was to grasp it in the Zen way. The master was well aware of the situation. If he had wished to explain the matter for Sekiso along the philosophical line of thought he could, of course, have given citations from the Scriptures, and entered into wordy explanations of them. But he was a Zen master; he knew the uselessness and fruitlessness of such a procedure. So he called to his attendant, who immediately responded. He ordered him to fill the pitcher and the deed was immediately done. He was silent for a while, for he had nothing further to say or to do. The ultimate truth of Buddhism could not go beyond this.

But Dogo was kindhearted, indeed too kindhearted, and asked Sekiso what his question was. Sekiso was, however, not intelligent enough to see into the meaning of the entire transaction which had taken place before his eyes. He stupidly repeated his question which was already answered. Hence the master's departure from the room. In fact, this abrupt departure itself told Sekiso all that he wished to know.

Some may say that this kind of answering leads the questioner nowhere, for he remains ignorant just as much as before, perhaps even worse than before. But does a philosophical or explanatory definition give the questioner any better satisfaction—that is, put him in any better position as to real understanding of the ultimate truth? He may have his conceptual stock of knowledge much augmented, but this augmentation is not the clearing up of his doubt—that is, the confirmation of his faith in Buddhism. Mere amassing of knowledge, mere stocking of time-worn concepts, is really suicidal in so far as real emancipation is concerned. We are too used to so-called explanations, and have come to think that when an explanation of a thing is given there is nothing more to ask about it. But there is no better explanation than actual experience, and actual experience is all that is needed in the attainment of Buddhahood. The object of the Buddhist life is to have it in actual actuality and in full abundance, and this not loaded with explanatory notes. . . .

. . . To cut asunder the bonds of ignorance and discrimination is no easy task; unless it is done with the utmost exertion of the will, it can never be accomplished. To let go the hold of a solitary branch of the tree, called intellect, which outstretches over a precipice, and to allow ourselves to fall into a supposedly bottomless abyss—does this not require a desperate effort on the part of one who attempts to sound the depths of the Mind? When a Zen Buddhist monk was asked as to the depths of the Zen river while he was walking over a bridge, he at once seized the questioner and would have thrown him into the rapids had not his friends hurriedly interceded for him. The monk wanted to see the questioner himself go down to the bottom of Zen and survey its depths according to his own measure. The leaping is to be done by oneself; all the help outsiders can offer is to let the person concerned realize the futility of such help. Zen in this respect is harsh and merciless, at least superficially so.

The monk who was trying to throw the questioner over the bridge was a disciple of Rinzai (Lin-chi), one of the greatest masters in the T'ang history of Zen in China. When this monk, who was still a stranger to Zen, asked the master Rinzai what was the ultimate teaching of Buddhism, the master came down from his seat and, taking hold of the monk, exclaimed: "Speak! Speak!" How could the poor bewildered novice in the study of Zen, thus seized by the throat and violently shaken, speak? He wanted to hear the master "speak" instead of his "speaking" in regard to this question. He never imagined his master to be so "direct", and did not know what to say or do. He stood as if in ecstasy. It was only when he was about to bow before the master, as reminded by his fellow-monks, that a realization came to him as to the meaning of the Scripture and the demand to "speak." Even when an intellectual explanation is given, the understanding is an inner growth and not an external addition. This must be much more the case with the Zen understanding. The basic principle, therefore, underlying the whole fabric of Zen is directed towards the self-maturing of an inner experience. Those who are used to intellectual training or moral persuasion or devotional exercises no doubt find in Zen discipline something extraordinary which goes against their expectations. But this is where Zen is unique in the whole history of religion. Zen has developed along this line ever since the T'ang era when Baso (Ma-tsu) and Sekito (Shih-t'ou) brought out fully the characteristic features of the Zen form of Buddhism. The main idea is to live within the thing itself and thus to understand it. What we generally do in order to understand a thing is to describe it from outside, to talk about it objectively as the philosopher would have it, and to try to carry out this method from every possible point of observation except that of inner assimilation or sympathetic merging. The objective method is intellectual and has its field of useful application. Only let us not forget the fact that there is another method which alone gives the key to an effective and all-satisfying understanding. The latter is the method of Zen. . . .

The strange situation created by Zen is that those who understand it do not understand it, and those who do not understand it understand it—a great paradox, indeed, which runs throughout the history of Zen. . . .

To explain this in a more rational manner I may add that Buddhism teaches that all is well where it is; but as soon as a man steps out to see if he is all right or not, an error is committed which leads to an infinite series of negations and affirmations, and he has to make peace within. To Eckhart every morning is "Good Morning" and every day a blessed day. This is our personal experience. When we are saved, we know what it is. However much we inquire about it, salvation never comes. . . .

The Mind, Nature, Buddha, or Buddha-nature—all these are so many ways of giving expression to the one idea, which is Great Affirmation. Zen purposes to bring it to us.

KEIJI NISHITANI

from *Science and Zen*

I

When modern science excluded teleology from the natural world, it dealt a fatal blow to the whole of the teleological world view, which leads from the "life" of organic beings in the natural world, to the "soul" and "spirit" or "mind" of man, and, finally, to the "divine" or "God." The world was no longer seen as having its ground in what may be called a preestablished harmony of the "internal" and "external." Instead it came to be looked upon as an "external" world possessed of its own laws and existing by itself alone.

Max Planck once remarked, after touching on the universality of the invariables at work in the laws of heat radiation and gravitation, that if there were creatures endowed with intellect on other planets, sooner or later they, too, would inevitably come up against these same invariables. The laws of nature, as natural science has come to understand them in modern times, show this kind of cosmic universality. In that view, everything that exists in the universe under the rule of such natural laws is thought to consist of nothing but matter, devoid of life and devoid of spirit. Further, this view sees matter, in its usual state, as subject to conditions that could never serve as an environment for living beings (for example, in conditions of extremely high or extremely low temperatures). The range of the possibility of existence for living beings is like a single dot surrounded by a vast realm of impossibility: one step out of that range and life would immediately perish. Thus, to this way of thinking, the universe in its usual state constitutes a world of death for living beings.

At the beginning of *Thus Spake Zarathustra,* Nietzsche speaks of a camel going out into the middle of a desert. The progress of modern science has painted the true portrait of the world as a desert uninhabitable by living beings; and since, in this world, all things in their various modes of being are finally reduced to material elements—to the grains of sand in the desert of the physical world—modern science has deprived the universe of its character as a "home." Metaphorically speaking, the world has been reduced to a kind of greenhouse with all the windows smashed, to an egg with a broken shell—the boundary of its life-environment. Planck speaks of this as the utter detachment of modern scientific view of nature from anthropomorphism. But this also means that science has given the world a countenance entirely different from that presupposed by most traditional religions.

In other words, directly beneath the field of man's being-in-the-world, and the field of the very possibility of that being, the field of the impossibility of that being has opened up. The field where man has his being is his teleological dwelling place; it is the place where he has his life with a conscious purpose as a rational being. And yet it is disclosed as a field merely floating for a brief moment within a boundless, endless, and meaningless world governed by mechanical laws (in the broad sense of the term) and devoid of any *telos.* Our human life is established on the base of an abyss of death.

But the destruction of the system of teleology by science does not stop at the nullification and annihilation in their essence of the manifold forms of being and of the manifold functionings of "living" being. The various activities of human consciousness itself come to be regarded in the same way as the pheneomena of the external world; they, too, now become processes governed by mechanical laws of nature (in the broader sense). In this progressive exteriorization, not even the thinking activities of man elude the grasp of the mechanistic view. . . .

The result is that, on the one hand, scientists destroy the teleological image of the world, and with it the characteristic feature of that image as an environment for life. In its stead they present material processes without life and spirit and devoid of *telos* and meaning as the true features of the world. On the other hand, as human beings engaged in scientific research these scientists live their own personal existence within a world that constitutes an environment for life. There is a contradiction here that is difficult to describe. It is a contradiction that, rather than being the fault of individual scientists, is natural to science itself and derives from the nature of the scientific standpoint as such. . . .

II

. . . It now becomes imperative for us to consider all the possible consequences that may be expected to arise necessarily, and in the form of a chain reaction, from the collapse of the teleological world view. In science as well as in philosophy, when it assumes the standpoint of "scientism," all phenomena in the universe are regarded as reducible to mechanical, material processes which are in themselves purposeless and meaningless. And yet the scientists and philosophers themselves who hold this view live as human beings, as if their lives had purpose and meaning and as if they were living outside of the mechanical, material universe they are observing. The problem with which we are now faced, however, does not permit us to rest complacent either with philosophical naïveté, as in the case of the scientist, or with the philosophical sophistication of that naïveté, as in the case of the philosophers of "scientism." Nor can we, as philosophers have heretofore done, stop at the stage of discriminating between the world to be ruled by mechanism and the world to be ruled by teleology, and then either regard the latter as transcending and comprehending the former or try to reorganize the whole system anew into a teleological hierarchy under the absolute nature of God. We must have the courage to admit that the "spiritual" basis of our existence, i.e., the ground from which all the teleological systems in religion and philosophy up to now have emerged and on which they have rested, has once and for all been completely destroyed. Science has descended upon the world of teleology like a sword-bearing angel, or rather a new demon. . . .

It should be clear from what has been said so far that the fact that the teleological world view has been excluded by science can not simply stop there. It implies, as a further consequence, that the entire teleological system in traditional religions and philosophies has been robbed of its cornerstone. What we call life, soul, and spirit, including even God, who had been regarded as the ground of their being, have had their "home" destroyed. As has already been suggested, it is as if the very frame of the greenhouse had been dismantled. The human spirit has been deprived of its hearth. House and hearth have been torn apart.

III

For a thinker who faces science existentially, i.e., who accepts it as a problem for his own existence as such, that the usual state of the universe is explained by science in terms of lifeless materiality means that the universe is a field of existential death for himself and for all mankind. It is a field in which one is obliged, to adopt another Zen term, "to abandon oneself and throw away one's own life," a field of absolute negation. An example may help to illustrate the point. The ancient eschatological myth that the cosmos is doomed one day to burn up in a great cosmic fire found its way into Buddhism as well. In interpreting this myth, however, Buddhists have always taken it on the dimension of religious existence, transforming the idea of the end of the world into an existential problem. Seen from this standpoint, this world as it is—with the sun, the moon, and the numerous stars, with mountains, rivers, trees, and flowers—is, as such, the world ablaze in an all-consuming cosmic conflagration. The end of the world is an actuality here and now; it is a fact and a destiny at work directly underfoot. . . .

IV

The Zen masters, on their level of insight, answered the question in terms of a cosmic conflagration or an awesome cold of the spheres, each in his own way, thus making the universe under those conditions an expression of himself or, rather, a revelation of his own selfhood. . . .

The very sword that kills is brandished here as a sword that gives life. At the very point where everything is negated radically and brought to ultimate extinction, the master points to a path of life. Something "immortal"—or rather, in Buddhist terminology, something that is "unborn and imperishable," something uncreated and undying, beyond the duality of life and death—stands self-exposed. Everything that subsists from the first has its subsistence only in virtue of having been delivered there, preserved there, and saved from dissolution into nothing. But, in order for man to realize the unborn for himself and to give testimony to it, he has to travel the path to it existentially, through the Great Death; he must unburden himself of himself, give up his tiny, egotistic self and deliver it over to his "unborn Self," setting himself free from all things including himself, and thus realizing in the unborn his own great Selfhood. . . .

V

So far we have dealt with the effort of modern science to exclude teleology from both the natural and the spiritual worlds. But there is no denying the fact, as a moment's reflection will suffice to remind us, that terms life *life, consciousness, spirit,* and so forth point to actual phenomena of one sort or another. This fact is every bit as undeniable as the fact of the vast, unbounded "desert" of matter stretching all over the universe. Not even science can deny the existence of the world in which living beings are living, adapting themselves to their environment, or the fact that from the "inside" of certain living beings feeling, emotion, will, and thinking have come to evolve. It is one and the same world in which flowers bloom, birds fly, and men sing, and where even scientists may find themselves singing when spring comes. If, somewhere outside of our earth, there are beings of another sort endowed with intelligence and spirituality, developing their own art, philosophy, and religion, then they too should be taken into account here.

Now this perspective on the world, which has formed a basis for the erection of the teleological world view into a complete system, is born out of the womb of nature, whence it continues to emerge up to the present. Following Theodor Fechner, we may call this teleological perspective on the world the *Tagesansicht* (day-aspect) of the world in contrast to the mechanical perspective which is its *Nachtansicht* (night-aspect). The world seen from a teleological outlook, the world of concrete things like mountains and rivers, animals and trees, with their various "forms" (*eidoi*), can be reduced in a mechanistic world view to material processes which can, in turn, be described in terms of mathematical formulas. But it can never, in all its eidetic variety, be *deduced* from material processes. Even though we may think that whatever appears in its aspect of *eidos* (ontological form) can be assumed to be an idea or representation in our consciousness, and that all functions of consciousness can be further reduced to the activities of brain cells, the fact remains that the brain itself, along with its cells, belongs to the world of eidetic variety. Whatever appears in its aspect of *eidos* always presents itself as a whole. Man's intellect, too, takes its start from this whole as a given. Even though it can then go on endlessly analyzing this whole into component elements, our intellect is incapable of creating the original whole with its *eidos* by starting from the mass of analyzed elements as its given. Even in those instances where human technique may at first sight appear to have created new, artificial things never before present in the natural world (for example, nylon, plastics, etc.) it is nature herself that maintains the role of original creator. The technical procedures of manufacturing only serve to prepare the necessary conditions for her creative powers to function. The same may be said with regard to the effort of scientists today to "create" life, to produce some living being. Everything in its aspect of *eidos*, is a qualitative and therefore nonanalyzable unity; so, too, from the same point of view, any component element of any thing constitutes a similar qualitative unity. The world, when viewed eidetically, proves to be imbued with the character of *eidos* through and through.

As stated above, however, it is on the field of bottomlessness that phenomena in their eidetic variety can ultimately show themselves to be what they in fact truly are, and can manifest themselves in their original and consummate quality of truth and fact. In other words, *it is the field of emptiness (śūnyatā or absolute nothingness—or what may perhaps be called the None in contrast to, and beyond the One—which enables the myriad phenomena to attain their true being and realize their real truth*. . . .

The world that manifests itself on such a field of bottomlessness lies beyond both the mechanistically viewed world and the teleologically viewed world. It is at once neither of them—and both of them. On the one hand, no living being whatsoever, with or without a soul or spirit, is there "reduced" to a material mechanism; on the other, no material thing whatsoever is there regarded as "living," endowed with a "soul." This world is neither the merely "scientific" world nor the merely "mythical" world, neither the world of mere "matter" nor the world of mere "life." In other words, it is neither the world merely in its aspect of death nor the world merely in its aspect of life. Although these conflicting viewpoints—the one of a positive orientation and the other of a negative one—partake respectively of one side of the truth, the truth itself demands a single vision that can grasp both sides simultaneously.

To describe this, Zen Buddhists often use expressions like "A wooden man sings and a stone woman dances," and "Iron trees come to bloom in the spring beyond the kalpas." The wooden man who sings and the stone woman who dances neither belong to the world merely in its aspect of "life" and teleology nor merely in its aspect of "matter" and mechanism. They belong to a world beyond these two world views, to a world where they directly interpenetrate each other and are canceled, elevated, and preserved (*aufgehoben* in the Hegelian sense). Yet that world is the actual world as we see it every day, the world in its truth and reality. The spring of this year with its flowers in full bloom, precisely because it is the spring of this year, manifests itself from beyond the universe, from beyond all kalpas and aeons. Here the cherry trees standing in full bloom in the garden are, as such, the "iron trees" in full bloom. Put another way, the actual world with its red flowers and its green willows is, as such, the world in its eschatological state, the world ablaze with the kalpa fire.

Such a bottomless field should not be thought of as something like mere space, for this "field" is nothing other than the essence of religious existence itself. This existence presents itself in its true essence only in emerging as a bottomless field. The world in which iron trees bloom in the spring beyond the kalpas, i.e., in which the cherrry blossoms in the garden are blooming in the spring of this year—which is the same fact in its ultimate real truth—is the world on the field of bottomlessness, and this is the essence of religious existence. This field of bottomlessness is the solitary one showing itself in the midst of all things, mentioned above. This "solitary one laid bare" is truth (*alētheia*) itself. All things bear testimony to their ultimate facticity and truth through that solitary one. . . .

VI

. . . What is needed is the unification of the two contradictory elements: the scientific view of the universe and the investigation of man himself. What is needed is, so to speak, some means by which the scientific view of the universe can directly become an element in the investigation of man himself and can then, by way of the investigation of man, be brought to the ultimate meaning of its own truth.

With regard to the former task, we have stated in this essay that the mechanically viewed universe, into which every sort of mechanism is finally reduced, including the mechanism of human consciousness, should be accepted existentially as the field of the Great Death of man, as a field in which "to abandon oneself and throw away one's own life." With regard to the latter, we have indicated that the universe as such should be seen on a field of "bottomlessness" (*Ungrund*), even while being "contained in the bottomless basket," and that it is there that every phenomenon in the universe emerges as a true fact, manifesting itself in its at once original and ultimate character of truth and facticity.

From another point of view, what is required here is a standpoint beyond the teleological and the mechanistic view of the world, a standpoint beyond the qualitative image of the world that consists of concrete eidetic variety, and the quantitative image of the world that yields to an indefinite analysis.

Therefore, a new vision must needs open up in us, a vision in which these opposite (even contradictorily opposite) ways of viewing the world (the positive and the negative) interpenetrate each other and become one and the same way of looking at the world, a vision that can see "a wooden man sing and a stone woman dance." And this is precisely the vision that belongs to a religious existence embodying the Great Death and the Great Life. The "mental eye" of that vision belongs to "the solitary one laid bare amidst the myriad phenomena." . . .

GUIDE TO SANSKRIT PRONUNCIATION

This guide is written for native speakers of English within North America. Closely similar sounds are suggested. A more precise pronunciation guide may be found in almost any Sanskrit reader or grammar, for example, William Dwight Whitney, *Sanskrit Grammar* (Cambridge, Mass.: Breitkopf and Hartel, 1889), 10–26.

VOWELS (omitting two that rarely occur)

a	like *u* in *mum*
ā	like *a* in *father*
i	like *y* in *woolly*
ī	like Sanskrit *i*, except voiced longer: like *ee* in *feed*
u	like *oo* in *moon*
ū	same *oo* sound, voiced longer
ṛ	You won't pronounce this correctly; try *rea* in *really* (while turning the tip of the tongue up to touch the palate)
e	like *a* in *maze*
ai	like *i* in *mine*
o	like *o* in *go*
au	like *ow* in *cow*

SEMIVOWELS (best understood as a particular class of consonants)*

y	like *y* in *yonder*
r	like *r* in *ram*
l	like *l* in *luck*
v	like *v* in *clover*

CONSONANTS

Guttural class

k	like *ck* in *sack*
kh	like *k* in *Sanskrit*, except aspirated, that is, pronounced while breathing out, as in *keel*
g	like *g* in *gun*
gh	another aspirate, same principle as with *kh*; *g* pronounced while breathing out
ṅ	like *n* in *trunk*, except more guttural

Palatal class

c	like *ch* in *churn*
ch	another aspirate, same principle
j	like *j* in *joy*
jh	aspirated *j*, like *jay*
ñ	like *n* in *canyon*

Lingual class

ṭ	There is no English equivalent: a *t* sound (as in *tough*) but with the tip of the tongue touching the roof of the mouth
ṭh	aspirated *ṭ*
ḍ	like *d* in *deer*, but "lingualized" as with *ṭ*
ḍh	aspirated *ḍ*
ṇ	lingualized *n* sound

Dental class

t	like *t* in *tough*
th	aspirated *t* (not like *th* in *thumb*)
d	like *d* in *dove*
dh	aspirated *d*
n	like *n* in *now*

Labial class

p	like *p* in *pun*
ph	aspirated *p* as in *pin* (not like *ph* in *philosophy*)
b	like *b* in *buck*
bh	aspirated *b*
m	like *m* in *meal*

Sibilants

ś	like *sh* in *shove*
ṣ	lingualized *sh* sound
s	like *s in sun*

And in a class alone

h	like *h* in *heart*

SPECIAL CHARACTERS AND SOUNDS

ḥ	Visarga: calls for breath following a vowel. For example, *duḥkha* ("pain") is pronounced *du* followed by a breath (very short) and then *kha*
ṃ	This is shorthand for all nasals, the particular type of which is determined by the class of the following consonant. For example, the *ṃ* in *sāṃkhya* ("analysis") is equivalent to *ṅ*, since *kh* belongs to the guttural class. (Do not try to remember this rule; just nasalize.)

* By convention, the names of the consonants add an *a* (Sanskrit *a*) in pronunciation. Thus *y* is pronounced *ya* (like *yu* in *yummy*). Vowels, in contrast, are pronounced exactly as written. Note also each vowel corresponds to only one sound, unlike in English. (With a few exceptions, this is true of consonants as well.)

GUIDE TO ARABIC PRONUNCIATION

This guide is written for native speakers of English within North America. In many cases, similar sounds are only rough approximations; Arabic contains several consonants for which there is no close English equivalent.

VOWELS

a	(in unaccented syllables) like *a* in *about*
a	(in accented syllables) like *a* in *father*
ā	like *a* in *bah!*
e	like *e* in *egg*
ē	more elongated, like *ay* in *bay*
i	like *ee* in *beet*
ī	more elongated, like *ee* in *see*
o	like *o* in *open*
ō	more elongated, like *o* in *so*
u	like *oo* in *room*
ū	more elongated, like *ue* in *sue*

CONSONANTS

’	like *tt* in *button*, or the sound between the syllables of *uh-uh*
‘	like the sound between the *a*'s in *baa*, when imitating the sound of sheep
b	like *b* in *baby*
ch	like *ch* in *church*
d	like *d* in *dog*
dh	like *th* in *there*
f	like *f* in *faint*
gh	like g in *agua*, in some Spanish dialects; like Parisian *r*
h	like *h* in *how*
j	like *j* in *judge*
k	like *k* in *kick*
kh	like *j* and *g* in Spanish *Jorge*
l	like *l* in *like*
m	like *m* in *moon*
n	like *n* in *no*
q	like *k* in *Luke*
r	like *r* in Spanish *pero*
s	like *s* in *so*
sh	like *sh* in *shoe*
t	like *t* in *tot*
th	like *th* in *thick*
w	like *w* in *water*
z	like *z* in *zebra*

GUIDE TO CHINESE PRONUNCIATION

This guide is written for native speakers of English within North America. In many cases, similar sounds are only rough approximations. Also, Chinese dialects differ among each other significantly in pronunciation.

VOWELS

a	like *a* in *far*
ai	like *ai* in *aisle*
ao	like *ou* in *loud*
e	like *e* in *her*
ei	like *ei* in *weight*
i	like *i* in *machine*, except as part of *ing*
ing	like *ing* in *wing*
o	like *o* in *open*
u	like *oo* in *rule*
ü	like *oo* in *rule*, or better, like French *u*

CONSONANTS

ch	like *j* in *jam*
ch'	like *ch* in *change*, said emphatically
f	like *f* in *faint*
h	like *h* in *how*, or, better, like *j* or *g* in Spanish *Jorge*
hs	like *sh* in *whoosh*
j	like *r* in *rare*
k	like *g* in *go*
k'	like *k* in *kill*, said emphatically
l	like *l* in *like*
m	like *m* in *moon*
n	like *n* in *no*
p	like *b* in *baby*
p'	like *p* in *pin*, said emphatically
r	like *r* in *rare*
s	like *s* in *so*
sh	like *sh* in *shoe*
t	like *d* in *doll*
t'	like *t* in *tell*, said emphatically
ts, tz	like *dz* in *adze*
ts', tz'	like *ts* in *tsetse*, said emphatically
w	like *w* in *water*

Thus:

Hsün Tzu	like "shoon dzoo"
Lao Tzu	like "lao dzoo"
Chuang Tzu	like "jwong dzoo"
Seng-chao	like "seng jao"
Hsüan-tsang	like "shwawn dzong"
Fa-tsang	like "faw dzong"
I-hsüan	like "ee shwawn"
Chu Hsi	like "joo shee"
Wang Fu-chih	like "wang foo jee"
jen	like "ren"

Glossary

absolutism. In ethics and epistemology, the view that there are absolute truths—truths that do not vary with the person or society considering them; opposed to *relativism*. In political philosophy, government by an absolute ruler.

active intellect. In Islamic philosophy, the aspect of the mind that grasps universal truths.

Advaita. A branch of Vedānta philosophy that stresses the unity of Brahman, the Absolute, and interprets the world insofar as it appears to be separate from Brahman to be illusion, *māyā*.

ahaṃkāra. Egoism; the principle of individuation according to the *Sāṃkhyakārikā*.

ahiṃsā. Non-injury; a central ethical principle in both Jainism and Buddhism.

ālayavijñāna. Storehouse consciousness; a principal concept in early Yogācāra (q.v.).

anātman. No self, or no soul; an important Buddhist doctrine.

arhat. The saint (in southern Buddhism); one who has achieved enlightenment.

artha. Goal, end, value; material gain.

āsana. Yogic postures.

asceticism. The practice of strict self-denial and renunciation of worldly pleasure.

ātman. Self or soul; the Upaniṣadic term for an individual's true or most basic consciousness.

atomism. A term for the Vaiśeṣika school.

ba. In Egyptian thought, the soul.

bhakti. Love and devotion to God; a key term in theistic Vedānta.

bhāṣya. Commentary.

bliss. Complete happiness; in the Upaniṣads, the unqualified delight of consciousness that constitutes the self.

bodhisattva. According to Mahāyāna Buddhism, an enlightened person who does not dissolve all personality in the bliss of *nirvāṇa*, but who out of compassion turns back to the world to help others.

brahman. The Absolute; the key concept of the Upaniṣads according to a prominent group of commentators.

brahmavidyā. Knowledge of the Absolute (or, of God).

Brahmin (Brahmana, Brahmun, Brahman). The first and highest caste of the four traditional Hindu castes; a priest.

buddha. The awakened one, the Buddha; literally, "to have awakened."

buddhi. Reason or rational mentality; an important term in Sāṃkhya.

Buddhism. A philosophy and religion founded by Gautama Siddhartha, the Buddha; widespread in South and East Asia; urges the elimination of desire as a means of conquering the suffering inherent in life. Theravāda Buddhism is atheistic, stressing the centrality of suffering in existence. Mahāyāna Buddhism treats the Buddha as divine and stresses the Bodhisattva. Vajrayāna Buddhism is overtly mystical.

Cārvāka. A materialist and hedonist school of classical Indian philosophy also known as Lokāyata, "those who follow the way of the world."

categorical imperative. The sole fundamental principle of Immanuel Kant's ethics, which he formulates in five different ways: (1) act so that the maxim of your action might be willed as universal law; (2) act so that the maxim of your action might be willed as a law of nature; (3) treat everyone as an end, not merely as a means; (4) act as a legislator in the kingdom of ends; (5) act in accordance with the principle of autonomy.

ch'i. Material force; denotes matter and energy as opposed to principle (*li*).

citta. Mental energy, mind-stuff, mental awareness; an important term in the *Yogasūtra*.

communitarianism. The view that moral value rests ultimately on the good of the community as a whole, and only secondarily on the good of individuals; opposed to *individualism*.

Confucianism. A philosophy and religion stemming from the teachings of Confucius; common in China, Korea, and Japan; promotes the moral perfection of the individual, centers on the concept of *jen*, and stresses the ethical importance of contingent human relations.

consequentialism. The view that moral value rests ultimately on nothing but the consequences of actions; the opposite of *deontologism*.

decolonization. The process in which colonies cast off the formal control and influence of the nations that colonized them.

deontologism. The view that moral value does not rest ultimately on the consequences of actions alone, but in addition, or instead, on intentions, motives, character traits, and so on; the opposite of *consequentialism*.

dharma. (1) The right way of action; right living; duty; justice; the Divine way; (2) a teaching about right action, etc.; (3) qualities, characteristics.

dharmakāya. The body of splendor, the Buddha body; the physical universe transformed.

dhyāna. Meditation.

dialectical materialism. The view developed by Karl Marx and his followers that reality consists solely of matter, which changes in an intelligible pattern of stages of thesis, antithesis, and synthesis, driven by class struggle.

dialectical theologians. Islamic religious thinkers of the eighth, ninth, and tenth centuries C.E. who used Greek philosophical ideas to debate Islamic theology and interpret the Koran.

dynamic idealism. The philosophy developed by Wang Yang-Ming, which identifies mind and principle (*li*) and also knowledge and action.

Eightfold Path. Buddhism's recommended way of life, consisting of right views, right intent, right speech, right conduct, right means of livelihood, right endeavor, right mindfulness, and right meditation.

emancipation. The attainment of freedom—in Buddhism, freedom from suffering; in the Upaniṣads, freedom from limitation, achieved through experiences of self-illumination; in political philosophy, freedom from oppression.

enlightenment. The state of illumination sought by Mahāyāna Buddhists, yogins, etc., in which desire and suffering have ended.

Enlightenment. A period of European thought, during the seventeenth and especially eighteenth centuries, characterized by an emphasis on reason, scientific method, and individualism.

epistemology. The theory of knowledge, its sources, nature, and limitations.

ethical humanism. Confucius's view that ethical value arises from human nature.

ethics. The pursuit of good judgment concerning action and character.

filial piety. Respect and consideration for family; behaving as a son or daughter; a central virtue in Confucian thought.

Forms. In Plato and later philosophers, abstract objects—properties such as justice, unity, and goodness—in which objects participate and which the mind grasps in attaining knowledge.

Four Ends. In the *Mahabharata* and other Indian writings, the four things desired as ends in themselves: virtue (*dharma*), pleasure (*kama*), wealth (*artha*), and freedom (*moksha*).

Four Noble Truths. The foundation of Buddhism: (1) there is suffering; (2) desire causes it; (3) extinguishing desire extinguishes suffering; and (4) the Middle Way defined by the Eightfold Path extinguishes desire.

Great Ultimate. A fundamental concept of neo-Confucianism, originally found in the *Book of Changes* and developed philosophically by Chou Tun-i (1017–1073 C.E.); identified by Chu Hsi with principle in its totality that is complete both in all things considered together and in each thing considered individually.

guṇa. Quality or fundamental mode of nature, according to Sāṃkhya.

guru. Teacher; spiritual preceptor or guide.

idealism. The view that reality is mind-dependent; opposed to *realism.*

indirect proof. A form of argument that establishes a conclusion by showing that denying it leads to a contradiction.

individualism. The view that moral value rests ultimately on the good of individuals; opposed to *communitarianism.*

induction. Reasoning "from the known to the unknown," in John Stuart Mill's phrase, in which premises support, but do not conclusively establish, the conclusion.

integral yoga. Sri Aurobindo's method of integrating the personality and releasing the spiritual self into, rather than out of, the world through discipline.

Intelligible world. In Platonism and Neoplatonism, the realm of Forms.

intelligibles. In medieval philosophy, forms or properties of objects.

intuitionism. The view that people can apprehend ethical truth immediately and directly.

Iśvara. God; the ever-liberated purusa according to the *Yogasūtra.*

Jainism. A religion founded in the sixth century B.C.E. by Mahāvīra that stresses noninjury (*ahimsa*) along with various practices aimed at a mystical *summum bonum.*

jen. Humanity; one of the central virtues of Confucianism; both a particular virtue (benevolence or altruism), and the basis of virtue in general, involving a proper balance of all the virtues. Etymologically, *jen* means "man in society."

jīvanmukti. Living liberation; a person's knowledge of the Absolute or God, and liberation from all entanglement in the world while alive, according to some schools of Vedānta.

ka. In Egyptian thought, a person's vitality, personality, or vital force.

kaivalya. Aloneness, the supreme state of the individual conscious being according to the *Yogasūtra.*

kama. Sexual desire and enjoyment; enjoyment.

karma. (1) Action; (2) a psychological impetus to action created by action; habit.

karmayoga. The yoga of action and sacrifice taught in the *Gītā.*

kleśa. Obstacle, especially any hindrance to yogic practice.

koan. A paradox used by Zen Buddhists to force the mind away from reliance on reason toward sudden, intuitive enlightenment.

the Koran. The fundamental religious text of Islam, which Muslims accept as revelations from the one God, Allah, to the prophet Muhammad through the angel Gabriel.

Kyoto School. A group of twentieth century Japanese philosophers based in Kyoto, who synthesize Buddhism and Western philosophy.

li. Rule, principle, ceremony, rite, ritual, or form; originally, a religious sacrifice.

līlā. Play, Divine play; a prominent concept in theistic Vedānta understood to capture God's relation to the world.

Lin-chi movement. The most radical of seven varieties of southern Chinese Buddhism, founded in the ninth century C.E. by I-hsüan. Known more popularly by its Japanese name, *Rinzai,* it stresses the "lightning method" of sudden enlightenment.

maat. In Egyptian thought, justice, right, rightness, order, or truth.

Mādhyamika. The school of philosophic Buddhism founded by Nāgārjuna; sometimes called Buddhist Mysticism or Buddhist Absolutism.

Mahāyāna. Northern Buddhism; the "Great Vehicle."

manas. Sense-mind; sense-oriented mentality.

māyā. Cosmic illusion.

maybe-ism. A term for syad-vada; see syāt.

metaethics. The study of the project of ethics, concentrating on the meanings of ethical terms and the form of ethical statements and arguments.

metaphysics. The study of the fundamental nature of reality.

Middle Way. In Buddhism, the way of living defined by the Eightfold Path that extinguishes craving or desire and thereby overcomes suffering.

Mīmāṃsā. Exegesis, the classical school most closely tied to Brāhminism (q.v.).

Moism. The philosophy of Mo Tzu, a form of utilitarianism based on the concept of *yi* (righteousness or justice); advocates the good life because of its good consequences and recommends universal love.

mokṣa. Emancipation; liberation from the cycle of birth, death, and rebirth; the mystical *summum bonum* according to several Indian schools.

monad. A unit or unity; an object that is simple, having no parts.

mukti. Liberation, salvation.

mysticism. The view that it is possible to attain direct and immediate knowledge of God or, more generally, ultimate reality.

naturalism. In ethics, the view that ethical value depends on natural, nonmoral features of things; or, the view that ethical value is determined completely by human nature.

Navya-Nyāya. The "new" school of Nyāya (q.v.) founded by Gaṅgeśa (c. 1325) that revolutionizes Indian logic and epistemology with the development of refined logical tools.

neo-Confucianism. The revival of Confucian thought, beginning in the tenth century C.E. and reaching a high point in the thought of Chu Hsi, which continues to be important in interpreting Confucian doctrine; a view characterized by six major concepts—the Great Ultimate, principle (*li*), material force (*ch'i*), nature, the investigation of things, and humanity (*jen*).

nihsvabhava. Not self-caused; without an intrinsic existence; contingency.

nirvāṇa. In Buddhism, the final permanent and transcendent state beyond suffering, in which desire and individual consciousness are extinguished; terminates a series of reincarnations once a person reaches moral perfection; literally, in Sanskrit, "extinguishing."

Nyāya. Logic; the Realist school prominent throughout the classical period, combined with Vaiśeṣika in the later centuries; focused on issues in epistemology but taking positions on a wide range of philosophic topics (proponents are called "Naiyāyikas").

the One. Tao; in Lao Tzu, that which underlies all things but admits no description.

oppression. The unjust exercise of authority or power.

padārtha. "Category," "type of thing to which words refer"; a central Vaiśeṣika concept.

pāramitā. A personal perfection according to Mahāyāna Buddhism.

particular. An individual object existing in space and time, which has no instances but is instead an instance of various universals.

the perplexed. In al-Farabi and Maimonides, those who find it difficult to reconcile religion and reason.

phenomenalism. The doctrine that what is is what appears; that appearances are the only reality; that there are no extra-subjective or physical things that underlie sensations.

pluralism. The view that ultimate values differ in kind.

prakṛti. Nature; a principal Sāṃkhya concept.

pramāṇa. Source of knowledge, justifier, means to true belief.

prameya. Object of knowledge, what is known by means of the sources of knowledge.

pranayama. Breath control.

Pratyeka-buddha. One who seeks enlightenment for himself alone; an *Arhat* as opposed to a *Bodhisattva*.

prophet. A person who receives revelation from God; identified by al-Farabi with the imam and the ideally ethical person.

propriety. The quality of being proper, appropriate, polite; in Confucian thought, the observance of traditional social rules and correct principles, and, in Hsün Tzu, obedience.

proverb. A brief popular epigram, maxim, or adage; often, a tool of instruction.

prudence. The ability to promote one's own interests, especially through the use of reason and judicious choice.

puruṣa. Individual conscious being, according to both Sāṃkhya and Yoga.

rajas. The *guṇa* (q.v.) of action and desire.

realism. The view that reality is mind-independent; opposed to *idealism*.

reciprocity. Mutual dependence, action, influence, or respect; in Confucius, the principle of the Golden Rule: "What you do not want done to yourself, do not do to others."

relativism. The view that what beliefs are true depends on the person holding them or the society that person inhabits; opposed to *absolutism.*

renunciation. Self-denial, giving up worldly goods and pleasures.

rights. Just entitlements indicating what one may properly claim as due; treated by Mencius as defining justice—respect for the rights of others—and as arising from tradition and custom.

Rinzai. A school of Zen Buddhism known for its use of paradoxes or seemingly nonsensical responses and its emphasis on sudden enlightenment. See also *Lin-chi movement.*

saccidānanda. (Absolute) "Existence-Consciousness-Bliss," a popular Vedāntic characterization of *brahman.*

sādhanā. Mystic disciplines, the practice of yoga.

śakti (shakti). Divine energy; a concept from Tantra.

samādhi. Mystic trance.

Sāṃkhya. Analysis; an early school of Indian philosophy concerned with achieving a supreme personal good through psychological disidentification.

saṃyama. Control through conscious identification.

satori. Enlightenment; the state of sudden, intuitive insight that practitioners of Zen seek.

sattva. The *guṇa* (q.v.) of intelligence.

sincerity. A quality of pure, genuine honesty, an important virtue in Confucianism.

skepticism. An attitude of doubt, in general or directed at specific kinds of knowledge claims; or, the view that knowledge of certain kinds is uncertain, unreliable, unjustifiable, or unattainable.

śramaṇa. An ascetic or yogin.

śūdra (shudra). The fourth caste of the four traditional Hindu castes; a laborer.

summum bonum. The highest good—that for which everything ought to strive.

superior man. In Confucius, the ideal person; originally denoted the son of a ruler, but in Confucius and later thinkers, denotes someone of superior character.

sūtra. Literally thread; a philosophic aphorism.

syāt. Maybe; the modality of all assertions, according to Jain philosophy, in relation to multi-aspected facts or reality.

tamas. The *guṇa* (q.v.) of ignorance and inertia.

Tantra. An Indian philosophic and practical soteriological system (or family of related systems) that uses feminine imagery in its ceremonies and myths, and one that values nature as an expression of *sakti* or the Mother Goddess.

tao. In Confucius, the Way, the path of proper ethical conduct; in Lao Tzu, the indescribable, natural, spontaneous One underlying everything.

Taoism. The philosophy founded by Lao Tzu that teaches simplicity, tranquillity, nonconformity, and "going with the flow" of the tao; or, the religion that has developed from that philosophy.

Tathāgata. An epithet for a Buddha; literally, "one who has thus become."

te. Virtue, character, power, force, capacity for excellence; active principle guiding a thing and defining what it should do and be; *tao* particularized in an individual object.

teleology. A view proposing a highest good, for which everything ought to strive, or a goal toward which everything does strive.

Theistic Vedānta. Any of several schools of classical Vedānta (q.v.) espousing a concept of God (*iśvara*), and usually grounding their outlook in teachings of the *Bhagavadgītā* as well as various Upaniṣads.

Theravāda. "The Doctrine of the (Buddhist) Elders"; an early school of philosophic Buddhism, appearing in the Southern Canon.

universal. A property or relation, such as redness or friendship, that may have multiple instances; opposed to *particular.*

universal love. Having equal regard for all people, regardless of one's relation to them; treating everyone with the respect we give ourselves; a basic principle of Moism.

Upaniṣads. Mystic doctrines composed over several centuries beginning as early as the ninth century B.C.E. The Upaniṣads are the source texts for all classical schools of Vedānta (q.v.).

utilitarianism. The consequentialist view that the fundamental principle of ethics is to maximize the good.

Vaiśeṣika. Atomism; a classical philosophy focusing on ontological issues ("What kinds of things are there?") and defending a realist view of material things as composed of atoms; later combined with Nyāya (q.v.).

vāsanā. Subliminal valency; force of karma.

Veda. The oldest texts of South Asian traditions which came to be viewed by many Hindus as sacred and revealed.

Vedānta. Originally an epithet for the Upaniṣads; in the classical period, any of several schools defending Upaniṣadic views, e.g. Advaita (q.v.) and Theistic Vedānta (q.v.).

vijñaptimātra. Consciousness only; the central doctrine of Early Yogācāra Buddhism.

vyāpti. Invariable concommitance; a factual relation that grounds inference according to Nyāya.

the Way. In Confucius, the path of proper ethical conduct; *tao.*

Word. In Philo, the intelligible world, the realm of Forms, which Philo treats as divine.

yi. Righteousness or justice; the quality of acting as one ought to act; the fundamental concept of Moism and one of the foundations of Mencius's thought.

yoga. Self-discipline.

Yoga. A classical philosophy of a supreme personal good much like Sāṃkhya (q.v.) but proposing various exercises of self-discipline (i.e. *yoga*) as the means thereto.

Yogācāra. Buddhist Idealism conveniently divided into (A) Early and (B) Late or Buddhist Logic: Buddhist Logicians (Dignāga, Dharmakīrti, and their followers) propose a much more advanced epistemology concerning worldly knowledge—and are less concerned with the concept of a storehouse consciousness—than are their Early Yogācāra predecessors.

Zen. A form of Mahāyāna Buddhism stressing meditation and the pursuit of sudden enlightenment (*satori*).

Index